Constitutional Judiciary in a New Democracy

Published in the United States of America by
The University of Michigan Press
Manufactured in the United States of America
♾ Printed on acid-free paper

2003 2002 2001 2000 4 3 2 1

A CIP catalog record for this book is available from the British Library.

Library of Congress Cataloging-in-Publication Data

Sólyom, László, 1942–
Constitutional judiciary in a new democracy : the Hungarian Constitutional Court / László Sólyom and Georg Brunner ; with a foreword by Stephen G. Breyer.
p. cm.
Includes bibliographical references and index.
ISBN 0-472-10965-0 (alk. paper)
1. Constitutional law—Hungary—Cases. 2. Hungary. Alkotmânybârâsâg. 3. Constitutional courts—Hungary. I. Brunner, Georg, 1936– II. Title.
KKF2066.5 1999
347.439′01—dc21 99-047903

Constitutional Judiciary in a New Democracy

The Hungarian Constitutional Court

László Sólyom and Georg Brunner

with a Foreword by Justice Stephen G. Breyer

Ann Arbor

THE UNIVERSITY OF MICHIGAN PRESS

Contents

Foreword: Decisions of the Hungarian Constitutional Court

Stephen G. Breyer

The American Constitution contains both a Bill of Rights and other constitutional guarantees and provides for a judiciary with the legal power to make those rights and guarantees meaningful in practice. While we in this country are accustomed to this kind of legal institution and the significant delegation of power to judges that it implies, many other nations are not—or, at least until recently, have not—been willing to grant such authority to courts. Recently, however, we have seen change in this respect, particularly in Eastern Europe, where many nations, as they seek to create modern democratic political institutions, have begun to develop judicial systems with such power. Such systems, of course, do not spring into being full grown; rather, they develop slowly as they interact with, and in turn affect, the customs, expectations, needs, and demands of the particular nation and culture that has called them into existence. This book, compiled by László Sólyom, President of the Hungarian Constitutional Court, with the contribution of Georg Brunner of the University of Cologne, provides us with an important and interesting account of the ongoing development of one such system—that of Hungary.

The American reader will find this book valuable for several reasons. First, it provides an insight into recent political history, as Hungary and its judges grapple with the legal aftermath of the transition from a communist system—which itself arose after the totalitarian governments of World War II—to a system of private property and political democracy. How, for example, can the new government properly compensate those whom earlier governments seriously injured? How can it compensate them, or their descendants, for loss of property? To what extent must efforts at compensation take account of the expectations of more recent users of that property? The Hungarian Constitutional Court's several decisions concerning "compensation" and that concerning "restitution of Jewish possessions" consider these and related important historical issues.

Second, the book will force the American reader to return to, and ask again, the most basic questions about the judicial protection of fundamental liberties—questions that we rarely ask only because in our own system they long ago received answers that we simply take for granted. The Hungarian Constitutional Court has no such developed interpretive history. Thus, as it asks how it can protect free expression or prevent the retroactive application of criminal punishments, for example, it simultaneously requires the reader to ask those questions anew and compare the Hungarian solutions with our own.

Finally, and perhaps most important, the Hungarian courts face new legal problems that strongly resemble those confronting our courts as well. Thus, the Hungarian Constitutional Court has decided cases involving privacy, abortion, the media, separation of church and state, and environmental protection. This similarity of legal issues is not surprising. Nations are no longer distant one from the other. Economic interdependence is the norm. Advances in science, medicine, communications, technology, and economics spread instantly throughout the world. With the growth of roughly comparable judicial institutions across the world, and with ever-increasing similarity in the fundamental problems they face, there is much to be learned from the judicial solutions adopted by other nations.

This book therefore forms part of a conversation that will increasingly take place among judges, lawyers, and members of the public about how the law can or should respond to the significant public problems of our times. It is a most welcome addition.

Acknowledgments

We would like to acknowledge the sterling work done in the preparation of this book by Mr. Allan F. Tatham, B.A., B.C.L., of Gray's Inn, Barrister. Over the last six years, he has composed the headnotes to the decisions and prepared, as a research tool, the Subject Index based on the Systematic Thesaurus used by the Council of Europe in its *Bulletin on Constitutional Case-Law.* In addition, Mr. Tatham has not only acted as language editor but also ensured consistency in citation throughout the text.

Further, we express our gratitude to Dr. Pál Sonnevend, LL.M., for all his efforts in making sure the English translation remained as true to the original Hungarian as possible.

László Sólyom
Georg Brunner

Introduction to the Decisions of the Constitutional Court of the Republic of Hungary

László Sólyom

I. Introduction

This volume publishes selected decisions of the Constitutional Court of the Republic of Hungary in chronological order so that one may better follow the activities of the Court in this truly significant first phase of its existence. This period is exceptional not only for the immense number of decisions it has handed down but also, as the decisions themselves show, for the fact that the Court had to reach so many fundamental decisions within a short period of time. This chronological presentation also reveals the development of the views of the Constitutional Court with respect to important individual constitutional questions. This structure was also chosen because the individual decisions often address multiple essential questions.

The commentaries that accompany the decisions, on the other hand, are arranged according to individual subject-matter areas and related statements from the various decisions. Because the essay by Prof. Georg Brunner provides a systematic overview of the competences and procedures of the Hungarian Constitutional Court, I have limited my comments in this preface to interrelationships that would otherwise remain unknown to the outside observer and to concrete historical circumstances that may assist the reader in understanding the individual decisions.

For reasons of the space, reproduction of the complete texts of the decisions had to be limited. Where it seemed to be appropriate, only excerpts from the opinions have been included in the book. The essays, as well as the introductory notes to each case, are intended to provide a fuller understanding. Originally, I wanted to restrict references to decisions not included in this volume to only those that might prove useful in gaining a complete picture of the concepts of the Court. In the end, too many cases had to be omitted and of those that remained only a few could be published in full. Thus, another means of balance had to be found. Now the headnotes describe the whole case even if only the most important statements of the Court follow; on the other hand, this essay contains more information about cases that have been important in the constitutional development of Hungary and are available in foreign languages from other sources.[1]

Experience has shown that each year brings six to ten decisions that are decisive for constitutional development in Hungary. The continued tracking of the activity of the Constitutional Court is all the more justified, as sequences of decisions already show, in that through this process reinforcements of or changes in the Court's view regarding individual fundamental rights or methodological questions become more clearly apparent. Such lines of development are to be observed especially with regard to the right to life and human dignity, the right to freedom of expression and property, and, as with the constitutional principles, the right to the rule of law and equal treatment. From the major courses of ideas, independent streams branch out and connect different constitutional rights. For instance, in this volume the right to life and human dignity is represented in decisions involving the death penalty and abortion (23/1990 and 64/1991). From there, the idea of self-determination appears in the field of data protection (15/1991), in the position of parties in civil and criminal procedure (9/1992), and in the right of persons to know their own ancestry (57/1991). From the right to life, branches lead to the right to a healthy environment (28/1994). The right to human dignity and the equality principle are interwoven (23/1990; 35/1994(VI.24)AB).[2] Within the cases on communicative freedoms, decisions regarding free speech are founded on each other in a separate chain of decisions (e.g., incitement to hatred, 30/1992; independence of the public media, 37/1992; and defamation of the government, 36/1994(VI.24.)AB).[3] Another line is formed by the cases on freedom of information (32/1992; checking of the past, or "lustration," 60/1994; archives and state secrets, 34/1994(VI.24)AB).[4] Decisions on freedom of religion connect the communicative freedom with dignity and self-determination (4/1993; 8/1993(II.27)AB;[5] 22/1997(IV.25)AB).[6] The exact meaning of the right to property—in the constitutionally mandated "market economy"—has been clarified by many opinions (the results are represented here by 21/1994 and 64/1993). A separate branch constitutes cases on nationalization and compensation (21/1990; 16/1991; Jewish possessions, 16/1993; church property, 4/1993). The problem of compensation then extends to moral damages for loss of life or freedom (22/1996). Another extension of the property rights complex forms the protection of social insurance claims (43/1995). New sequences of decisions have appeared recently in cases on the right of association (parties, 53/1996(XI.22)AB;[7] commercial and professional chambers, 38/1997(VII.1)AB,[8] 39/1997, 40/1997(VII.1)AB;[9] minors, 21/1996), and cases providing a more decisive protection against the arbitrariness of administrative organs ("silence of the administration," 72/1995(XII.15)AB;[10] judicial review, 39/1997). Examination of the cases from another point of view reveals the interdependence between decisions dealing with the special problems of system change: retroactive criminal legislation (11/1992) and compensation (the *ex nunc* decision, 10/1992; and the compensation cases already mentioned). This field is closely related to the decisions consolidating the new state organization (presidential power, 48/1991; independence of the judiciary, 38/1993(VI.11)AB;[11] autonomy of local governments, 4/1993, 64/1993; parliamentarianism, 48/1991; the relationship to direct democracy, 2/1993(I.22)AB,[12] 52/1997).

One can read the cases not only from the viewpoint of the protection of fundamental rights but as a means of following changes in the policies of the Court on how to maintain a balance between activism and self-restraint and how this has been discussed in terms of determining the scope of the Court's competencies. *Activism* not only means that the Court has obviously extended very broad protections of fundamental rights in the spirit of liberal understanding. The Court has also knowingly accepted hard cases for decision—and in that formative period of constitutional review almost every case might figure as such. Accordingly, the Court has accepted all applications whenever possible. It does not feel itself to be strictly bound by the petition but uses it as a procedural starting point in order to render decisions concerning constitutional provisions as often, and as soon, as possible. The purpose of the Court has been to develop the Constitution into a coherent system. On the other hand, examples of self-restraint can also be found. It has always been clear to the constitutional judges that politicization of the Court is inherent in its abstract competences. By interpreting existing rules on jurisdiction, the preventive review was practically abolished in the legislative process on the first application (16/1991) and the "abstract interpretation of the Constitution"—an advisory opinion with binding force for all—was bound by strict conditions. As in 1996, when minority groups in Parliament began to raise that institution from the apparent dead, the government answered with the abolition of preventive review.[13]

Moreover, the Constitutional Court tried to shift its competences from the abstract control of norms toward providing protection against the infringement of rights in individual cases. In the absence of powers to review the decisions of ordinary courts and administrative agencies, it was only possible to go halfway: to extend the control of the Constitutional Court in accordance with the trends represented in the established practice of those organs. Again, by way of interpretation, the Court introduced the concept of the "living law." Since the decision on ancestry (57/1991), the Constitutional Court has not reviewed the language of the law itself as determining the contents of the norm but rather the meaning and the content that can be attributed to it from the consistent and unitary practice of applying the law. This is the "living law," the review of which leads to a decision on the constitutionality of the application of the law by courts and agencies. The same effect can be achieved by means of another institution, which is not provided for in the Constitutional Court Act either but which the Court understands to be a specific application of abstract review. This is the determination of constitutional requirements for the possible interpretation of the legal norm being reviewed, known by the common name the "constitutional interpretation of the norm."[14] At the same time, this method—maintaining the law with a given constitutional sense—allows a finer, more sophisticated delineation between constitutional and unconstitutional than does the rough method of upholding or striking down the whole law. Moreover, such decisions may at least consider the typical facts of typical cases. As a further step away from purely abstract review, in the "holding part" of the decision the Court determines positive rules, which are therefore binding on all.[15] In all of these decisions, dissenting opinions signal that behind the disputes on the competences of the Court there stand graver problems involving the self-understanding and role of the Court.

Besides developing a coherent Constitution, another ambition of the Court was to join and receive in Hungary the standards of constitutionality common in developed democracies. In this respect, the comparative law experience, so traditional with Hungarian civil law scholars who actually form the majority of judges, has undoubtedly been of significance. Although only the jurisprudence of the European Court of Human Rights is, as a rule, cited, the impact of foreign constitutional courts is easy to detect in many decisions. It is to be noted that the traditional German influence, though nearly overwhelming, has been consciously balanced by the experience of other courts, especially those of Italy (from which, among other concepts, living law was borrowed), Portugal, and Spain. The jurisprudence of the U.S. Supreme Court is also echoed in Hungarian decisions—most obviously in those concerning free speech. I hope these relationships will not remain a one-way street. The Hungarian Constitutional Court has, on the one hand, developed its own solutions to the problems of system change, representing a nonrestorative model that was at the same time founded on legality and continuity (11/1992). On the other hand, however, the Court has tried to apply new rationales to classic problems (such as the death penalty and the abortion question, 23/1990 and 64/1991) and to new ones as well (see environmental protection, 28/1994, or restricting the use of the personal identification number [PIN], 15/1991).

Of course, the development of constitutional law is continuous. The time period documented in this volume can nonetheless be understood as a freestanding phase within a longer period of development, partly because the end of term of the first Court has drawn to a close. The last three justices of those elected in 1990 left the Court on 2 July 1999; the President and other "founding fathers" had already left by the end of November 1998. This period evidences all of the beauties and difficulties of a founding phase in which new institutions must be created out of nothing. The contributions as well as the omissions of the Hungarian Constitutional Court must be viewed in this light.

II. Individual Fundamental Rights

The decisions of the Hungarian Constitutional Court evidence a clear hierarchy of fundamental rights. This hierarchy is not based on positive law.[16] The Constitutional Court has also carefully avoided speaking of a "system of values" for the Constitution. Rather, it has sought to base the ranking of rights on the uniqueness of the affected right. The Hungarian Constitution is value neutral to the extent that after the first free elections in June 1990 all references to ideologies or intellectual trends were removed from the text.

At the pinnacle of the hierarchy are the rights to life and human dignity, whose "inviolability" has become absolute: according to the Constitutional Court, these rights cannot be limited conceptually. After these come the rights to communication: freedom of expression, religion, and conscience. As in Germany, other fundamental rights are to be interpreted restrictively when they conflict with these freedoms. Due to the relatively large number of decisions in the area, the rights to judicial legal protection, appeal, and criminal guarantees also achieved a special importance. The protection of property, on the other hand, was qualified not only through the recognition of the so-called social burdens of property—that is, the possibility of its restriction in the interest of public welfare—but also through the problem of compensation for former nationalization. Of the constitutional principles, the rule of law clause perhaps played a disproportionately large role. Given the specific historical circumstances, when the establishment of the formal rule of law over politics was the greatest order of the day, this principle was practically equated with the principle of legal certainty.

The Right to Life and Human Dignity

The right to human dignity was considered on the one hand as a "subsidiary fundamental right," which includes inter alia the rights to free personal development, self-determination, privacy, and general freedom of action, and which might be relied upon by the Constitutional Court to protect an individual's autonomy when no particular constitutional right was applicable. This function of a "mother right" may be familiar from German and American constitutional practice, from the latter as the wide use of *constitutional privacy* or the "penumbras" of constitutional rights. The Constitutional Court determined the right to human dignity in this sense as early as the third month of its existence (see 8/1990) and then derived from it various rights, for instance, the right to know, ascertain, or discover one's parentage (57/1991); the right to marry or form a domestic partnership without regard to the sex of the partners (14/1995);[17] and a series of guarantees of the parties' self-determination in court proceedings, especially in civil actions (9/1992).[18] The right to self-determination gained significance as a test of the constitutionality of the obligatory membership in public law bodies such as professional chambers (of commerce, medical doctors, and so on) (39/1997).[19]

On the other hand, the right to human dignity is considered in conjunction with the right to life (death penalty decision, 23/1990) and even with the right to legal capacity (abortion decision, 64/1991). In their interactions, these three rights comprise the legal expression of the specific human status.

The Court did not want to justify its decision on the unconstitutionality of the death penalty with what is in the end a practical criminological argument nor with its being "cruel and unusual"; it wanted to remove justification from the practical debate.[20] Admittedly, these efforts led to the recognition of certain general values, as the Constitutional Court was unable to argue here in the positivist way it preferred elsewhere. But these values were established outside of the Constitution. The problem to be resolved dogmatically consisted of the fact that the Constitution prohibited (only) the "arbitrary" withdrawal of the rights to life and dignity. The interpretation of *arbitrary* was thus decisive for the case. The concurring opinions regarding the death penalty considered human life and dignity, on the one hand, not as fundamental rights but as preexisting values assigned to the alleged rights, which were the source of the right. The law was to protect these values and was not to put any other values above them; any deviation from this ordering of values would be "arbitrary." My own reasoning sought to prove that without their reciprocity and unconditional character these rights would lose their specific human relatedness. A limitable right to life, which really only amounts to the state duty to protect life, is available to every form of life (including nonhuman life, even if not to the same degree). On the other hand, human beings are distinguished from all other forms of life and from legal persons by the fact that the latter are entirely controllable through the law while the human being is not. This autonomy and its equality are expressed in the right to human dignity. The indivisibility of this dignity and the right to life makes all human life equal in value, that is to say, equally inviolable. One cannot differentiate between the essential content and the limitable parts of the right to life and dignity. The withdrawal of these rights is conceptually "arbitrary."

It is necessary to illustrate this chain of reasoning in order to understand the abortion decision. Immediately after the publication of the death penalty decision, references were made to the difficulties that would arise due to the unconditionality of the right to life. The interpretation of the indivisibility and absolute character of the right to life and human dignity had already been accepted by the majority of the Court in the abortion decision. The referral of the decision on the legal capacity of the fetus back to Parliament (for a determination of its status) can in no way be categorized as a way out or an escape. The reasoning of the decision enlarged not upon the actual challenged regulation of abortion[21] but much more upon the law to be created; the decision itself completed the logic of the inviolability of the right to life. From there it considered the legal status of the fetus as a preliminary question, to which no compelling answer could be found in the Constitution. If the fetus is a human being in the legal sense, then the unconditional subjective right to life and dignity is available to the fetus just as to every other woman and man. However, when the fetus does not enjoy this legal status, then only the objective duty of the State to protect life relates to the fetus. The protection is no longer absolute, that is, it can be balanced against the right to self-determination of the mother. Through this radical posing of the question, the Constitutional Court wanted to avoid in the abortion decision the usual logical breach, which speaks on the one hand of the fetus's right to life but on the other hand considers its "limitation" to be possible. In the context of the synchronization of the biological, ethical, and legal conceptions of humanity, the Constitutional Court compared recognition of the fetus's status as a legal subject with the freeing of the slaves. This was supported in public opinion due to the fact of the "personification" of the fetus, which followed from the new technical means that revealed its personal characteristics. Nevertheless, the opinion is not a hard-core "pro-life" decision; it does leave open the possibility of development in the direction of the fetus being recognized as human as not contradicting the Constitution. In case Parliament does not determine the legal subjectivity of the fetus, the Court has declared that both polar positions—that is, the full freedom of abortion as well as its total prohibition—are unconstitutional. It further has made it clear that Parliament shall determine the indications for a lawful abortion.

Parliament chose the latter solution and made abortion legal in every "crisis situation" of the mother, that is, in situations causing physical or mental shock or unbearable social difficulties and through this endangering the healthy development of the fetus. Nevertheless, the law did not make claims as to the existence of such a situation reviewable.[22] This act is now before the Constitutional Court for a review of its constitutionality. Apparently, the essential question will no longer be the (legal) status of humans but rather the balancing of interests between the objective protection of life and the mother's right to privacy, especially whether the "crisis" indication is definite enough. In the meantime, the Constitutional Court showed that a satisfactory balance might also be achieved by means of positive measures to promote the birth and raising of children: the Court struck down the cutting off of maternal and child care benefits on this ground (43/1995).

The special significance of personhood underlies not only the death penalty and abortion decisions. The Constitutional Court's concept of freedom of conscience is similarly based on the integrity of one's personality. The problems of attending a state- or church-run school and of financing church schools and the rights of conscientious objectors and doctors opposing abortion have been resolved by considering the integrity of the individual's whole personality (4/1993).[23]

On the State's obligation to protect (all kinds) of life the Constitutional Court built its interpretation of the right to a healthy environment (28/1994). The nonderogation principle is as strong a requirement regarding the objective protection of life as the absolute untouchability of the subjective side of the right to life; both reflect the Court's resolve to secure absolute priority to this right in the constitutional hierarchy of rights.[24]

As indicated in connection with the death penalty decision, the right to human dignity has also been linked to the equality principle. The equal dignity of persons became not only the measure of equal treatment (in all compensation cases for pecuniary and moral [material and immaterial] damages [21/1990, 22/1996] and in the same-sex partnership case [14/1995]), but the basis and limit of the extension of the nondiscrimination principle to nonconstitutional rights.[25]

Data Protection and Freedom of Information

One of the few modern features of the Constitution is that it contains express provisions on data protection and public access to records—Art. 49(1) and Art. 61(1). The Court also played a groundbreaking role in this area in that in 1991 it had already actively and broadly interpreted the right to protection of personal data in the sense of a "right to informational self-determination"—a right that the German Constitutional Court had developed shortly before in the famous census decision. But the Hungarian Court went even further when the unlimited use of the personal identification number was declared unconstitutional (15/1991).[26] This was the time when, due to the change in regimes, the extensive data processing bureaucracy was still in a state of uncertainty and was only able to resist by referring to the allegedly huge expense of converting its data banks. As a result of this decision of the Constitutional Court, the use of a PIN on the personal identity card was abolished and the data contained on the card were reduced to a minimum. Private business also adjusted quickly to its own identification symbols. Later the use of the PIN became widespread again. The tax and social security agencies (notwithstanding the "privatization" of the latter) continued to work with the PIN, which led to application of the number in a much broader sphere. In the meantime, the justification of extensive data gathering and processing by the State shifted from an optimistic scientific-progress ideology to a fight against tax fraud and corruption. In this sense, the austerity package adopted by the government in 1995[27] restored the status quo ante of the 15/1991 Court decision on the PIN. The Constitutional Court annulled the Act. At the end of the "war," instead of the uniform PIN a system of three different identification numbers was introduced for use in the public sphere.

The right of access to and dissemination of information of public interest (Art. 61(1) of the Constitution) has also been extensively interpreted by the Court. The expansion affected the body of public data (as a rule, anyone has access to data processed by state organs and local governments) and reversed the burden of proof with regard to the justification of a refusal to publish data from the citizen to the agency (making public the sessions and records of local governments, 32/1992;[28] annulment of restrictions of public registers[29]).

For the freedom of information, the decision on state secrets and academic freedom (34/1994(VI.24)AB)[30] possesses the same significance as the PIN case had in its time for the protection of personal data. Most importantly, the Constitutional Court annulled *all* norms in force with regard to state and official secrets because they empowered a constitutionally unjustifiably broad circle of authorities, and even groups of persons not exercising public authority, to qualify materials as secret at their full discretion. This not only contradicted the principle of legal certainty but it was not in harmony with the limitation of the freedom of information "necessary in a democratic society" according to the European Convention of Human Rights and its case law.

In this case, the Court also interpreted the right to freedom of research under Art. 70/G(1) of the Constitution as a right belonging to the fundamental rights of communication. It required the state to respect the independence of academic life and to remain neutral in academic and scientific matters while guaranteeing the freedom of research and the distribution of its results. The Court set up a sensible system of balances between the necessary and proportionate restrictions of research (in the present case, archival), controls by law and the scientific community itself, and the protection of personal data and the qualification of public data with regard to the former role of the Communist Party in exercising public authority in Hungary.

The secret functions of the (socialist) State had to be dismantled not only in this regard but also concerning the activities and identification of agents of the secret services of the former totalitarian regimes. This still unsolved moral debt of the transition from socialism to democracy has been handled by the Constitutional Court in terms of the interaction between access to public data and protection of personal data, while the political core of the problem—who has to be checked for his past—was decided by means of the equal treatment clause (60/1994).[31] The Court noticed that even if this delayed act could no longer fulfill the original function of the "lustration," the data on the unconstitutional activities of those formerly exercising public power or participating in political life would count as information of public interest even under "normal" conditions in every democratic state.

The Constitutional Court acted in an extraordinarily radical manner in the field of data protection and freedom of information. Despite this, the Court has never been a "data protection fundamentalist." All its radical decisions were necessary because after socialism there was no understanding and no sensibility in Hungarian society as regards data privacy or "government in sunshine." Indeed, the Court's efforts met strong resistance from a section within the state organs, whether motivated by alleged interests of effectiveness or of politics (as in the case of lustration). Under these circumstances, measures such as banning the uniform PIN also had a symbolic effect.[32] It was not pleasing either that after 1994 the arguments of the government against data protection had changed from the usual "scientific-progress" ideology to invoking rather negative sentiments of the population by emphasizing the need to restrict privacy in order to detect tax fraud and other tricks of "the rich." It may be extraordinary, too, to what extent these rights served as neutral technical means in the constitutional settlement of the highly political questions of the system change. (See, besides the background checking of officials, the new foundation for secrecy qualification and the rulings on freedom of science and access to data.) On the other side, it was on the occasion of the data protection cases that the Court spoke out concerning the role of the party in a one-party state (see the academic freedom case, 34/1994(VI.24) AB; ABH 1994, 177; MK 68/1994.) and remembered that the fact remained so constitutionally decisive that in 1989 a revolutionary change had occurred (60/1994).

Fundamental Rights of Communication

Freedom of Expression

The cornerstone of freedom of expression is the question of when the State may encroach upon that freedom with criminal law means and for the protection of which rights or interests. Considering Europe, Strasbourg jurisprudence shows this well. Also, considering the ever-present sensitive nature of this area, the situation in Hungary is exaggerated and politically colored given the change in regimes. On the one hand, under socialism the criminal act of "incitement against a community," that is, "incitement of the people," was politically misused. Not without good reason, the Constitutional Court stressed the ideological neutrality of the Constitution in its relevant decisions and emphasized that freedom of opinion was subject only to the outer limits of the rights of others. On the other hand, following the change in regimes the public expression of suspicion or hatred against ethnic or political groups remained explosive, and because of the heightened tensions the balancing of tolerance and the securing of freedom of expression against the dangers of incitement required a particularly delicate treatment. Thus, it came about that the press, which in effect embodies the "public," played a far greater (political) role than usual and only very slowly found its way to professional and objective reporting. The real constitutional rights issues and the pure business interests of the broadcasting and publishing industries were hard to separate in the first period; they often disguised their concerns as problems of political freedom.

The Constitutional Court considered the right to freedom of expression to be the "mother right" of all fundamental rights dealing with communication (30/1992) and returned to its characteristics in the decisions on freedom of broadcasting (37/1992) and freedom of religion (4/1993). An increased protection of these rights is guaranteed by the fact that, according to the Constitutional Court, laws that restrict the freedom of expression are to be restrictively interpreted. The Court stressed that the right to freedom of expression protects opinion without considering its value or truthfulness. "It is free communication itself—the individual behavior and the social process—which is guaranteed by the Constitution; the fundamental right to freedom of expression does not relate to its content."

The basis for the interpretation of the freedom of expression was established pursuant to a judicial request in criminal proceedings, which were brought against the publisher of a right-wing newspaper for "disparaging a nation." The relevant penal provision in the Criminal Code was invalidated as unconstitutional (30/1992). The opinion addresses the same problem—the limits of the freedom of expression—in that the provisions of the Criminal Code regarding defamation of a public official and the resultant defamation of his office ("government defamation") were also declared unconstitutional (36/1994(VI.24)AB).[33]

Even in the incitement decision, the Constitutional Court declared that the duty of the State to guarantee the conditions necessary for the creation and maintenance of democratic public opinion follows from Art. 61 of the Constitution. This objective guarantee was developed within the framework of the broadcasting decision, specifying for different types of media (print, electronic, and publicly owned) a graduated system of positive measures that had to offer the relevant legal and organizational guarantees. This is in line with the decision on freedom of religion (4/1993), in which the Court was already speaking in terms of financial means that the State had to relinquish to public bodies for the purpose of their operability and to secure their independence from the State in case these bodies helped in the realization of specific fundamental rights.

In the decisions on freedom of expression, the Constitutional Court did not develop any special formula for setting limits on the guarantee of this fundamental right. Although the incitement decision mentioned the clear and present danger test, this was not sufficient to establish why the penalty for incitement to hatred was constitutional and why, in contrast, the penalty for disparagement was not. In this case, it had much more to do with the fact that in the case at hand there was no indication whether "disparagement" was capable of disturbing the public peace or did in fact disturb the public peace.

The evaluation of the "given historical situation" in this case is truly idealistic (compare the statements on the interplay between the openness of the society and its tolerance threshold). The change in regimes increased the tension in society. On the other hand, it had the effect that "[w]ith the freedom of the press having become a reality no-one speaking out publicly may invoke external compulsion, and with every line penned he gives himself and risks his entire moral credibility. Only through self-cleansing may a political culture and a soundly reflexive public opinion emerge. Thus one who uses scurrilous or derisive language stamps himself as such and in the eyes of the public he will become known as a 'mudslinger'."[34] In this context, the Constitutional Court prefers to use substantial damages for immaterial harm rather than criminal penalties. In keeping with this, the Court has dismissed limitations on nonpecuniary (moral) damages as unconstitutional in many decisions.[35]

The decision on government defamation[36] introduced into Hungarian law the standard that was already firmly established in the decisions of the European Court of Human Rights. In the holdings of the decision, the Constitutional Court determined that "the criminal protection of honor or good reputation of an office or an official is not unconstitutional. However, the sphere of the constitutionally nonpunishable expression protected by the freedom of expression is broader with respect to individuals who exercise public power or who appear publicly as politicians than with respect to other persons." Because after the annulment of the crime of "government defamation" the criminal provisions remaining in force did not differentiate "official honor" but penalized its violation in the same category for all persons, the Constitutional Court determined the criteria for the constitutional use of defamation in the case of official persons. Accordingly, pure value judgments are not punishable. Statements or rumors of defamatory facts are only punishable "if the . . . person knew that his utterance as to its essence is false, or if this person was not aware of the falsity of his claim because he neglected to pay the level of attention expectable according to the rules of his profession and appropriate to the object of the claim, the means of the communication and its intended recipients."

The impact of the test in the American case *New York Times v. Sullivan*—concerning "actual malice," the "reckless disregard" of professional standards of journalism—is obvious, although the Hungarian Court decided upon a criminal statute and—as has been shown—preferred nonpecuniary (moral) damages instead of criminal punishment. The other difference between the Hungarian case on the one hand and the Strasbourg and American First Amendment cases on the other is highlighted by the methodological question of whether an undifferentiated abstract judicial review is appropriate for the solution of complex problems. Exercising abstract norm control, the Constitutional Court could only "rewrite" the Criminal Code by the positive ruling cited previously. Implementation in concrete cases remains the responsibility of the ordinary courts. While the decision provides a sufficient solution for the democratic political freedom of expression *in abstracto,* it leaves the ordinary courts, for example, relatively unprotected from contempt (in that it is unlikely that judges will file suit as private complainants against parties who have injured them). For this reason, the Constitutional Court emphasized in its holdings of the decision that criminal protection of the honor of those who exercise public power is not unconstitutional in all situations (Parliament, for instance, could introduce the crime of contempt of court). On the other side, the abstract holding of the Constitutional Court not only represents a borderline between judicial review and legislation, but despite its activism the Court must leave differentiated consideration of the characteristics of each individual case to the ordinary courts. For the purpose of drawing a sufficiently sophisticated line between constitutionally protected criticism and constitutionally required protection of democratic institutions, it would be better to have a competence of the Constitutional Court that goes beyond abstract judicial review in order to be able to differentiate sufficiently between concrete cases.[37]

The broadcasting decision placed itself among the cases that are to be seen as attempts to find a solution to the ongoing disagreement regarding public broadcasting. Decisions in these cases address, among other issues, the President of the Republic's right of appointment (48/1991). Also of importance is that part of the freedom of religion decision that considers the requirement of a qualified majority for passage of certain acts (4/1993).

The central state radio and television industries (with their local programming) were practically in a monopoly position. Privatization of the frequencies finally commenced in 1997. The question of the impartiality of the national public media was constantly on the agenda in the first years of the new regime. The government claimed that the electronic media were beholden to the opposition; the opposition complained that the government was attempting to gain influence over the media. As a result, the legal status of the media remained undetermined until 1996, and the implementation of the Media Act[38] has been accompanied by many political and legal debates. The Act was also challenged before the Constitutional Court. A Government Resolution of 1974 stated only that the government "supervises" the media. This resolution was challenged by the opposition in the broadcasting decision (37/1992). The Court declared the Resolution to be unconstitutional both on formal grounds and based on its content. It went beyond the petition and found an unconstitutional omission on the part of Parliament in failing to enact a media law in conformity with Art. 61(4) of the Constitution.

In the decision, the Constitutional Court determined the constitutional requirements with respect to public law radio and television ("comprehensive, balanced and accurate reporting") and declared that the State is obliged to guarantee "extensive legally regulated organizational solutions." Because the final structure, and thus the distribution of tasks between the national public broadcasters on the one hand and commercial broadcasters on the other, was not then developed, the Constitutional Court did not want to predetermine the solution. The Court simply referred to the "widespread means" of guarantee according to which the Act should create a socially representative committee to oversee the content balance and fundamental organizational decisions. In response to widespread opinion, the Court had to stress that the political representation of society should not replicate itself in this committee, that is, the representation or the consensus of the parliamentary parties was not suited to such a guarantee. (According to the President of the Republic and the then opposition parties, the consensus of the parliamentary parties was also the condition for the appointment and dismissal of the chairmen of both institutions.) In response to the polarized confrontation between "public media-government" in politics, the Court had to emphasize that public radio and television needed to remain free of the influence of Parliament, parties, and other societal groups. The Constitutional Court ordered Parliament to pass a Media Act by 30 November 1992. Until that time, it conditioned the proceedings on that point in time at which the Government Resolution had been annulled. Because the Media Act was not enacted by the specified deadline, in a later decision the Constitutional Court upheld the validity of the Government Resolution until the entry into force of a new Act. This much-criticized decision[39] was based on the idea that if the Constitutional Court did not uphold the only existing legal reference point (the "supervision" right of the government), the public media would fall victim to competing interests. Following the 1994 elections, the President of the Republic abandoned his former position and, in the absence of a consensus in Parliament, appointed the chairmen of the Hungarian State Radio and Hungarian State Television as well. The Media Act was soon passed. Notwithstanding the ongoing struggle, the principles laid down in the broadcasting decision are reflected in the Media Act and remain the accepted test. At this time, even the composition and functioning of the supervisory board has been challenged before the Constitutional Court because of its alleged lack of neutrality as prescribed in the decision.

Freedom of Religion

At this point in time, several decisions on the freedom of religion have been reached, but the first remains the leading authority in all questions concerning this right (4/1993). This decision reviewed the Act regulating questions of ownership of former church property. Judicial review had to be expanded to all basic questions of the freedom of religion and dealt with the content of the right to freedom of religion and the separation of church and state. (As a side effect of this matter, the Constitutional Court established its primary position on the question of when an Act has to be passed with a two-thirds majority.)[40]

The nature of the freedom of religion. Article 60 is among the few Articles of the Constitution that specify the content of a fundamental right in relative detail. It includes the freedom of conviction and conscience, the freedom of all forms of practice of religion, and the freedom of religious assembly and association. Nonetheless, the Constitutional Court was left with the task of clarifying the content of these provisions, an emphasis that surely arose from the given historical situation. Of course, the Constitutional Court took no sides in the anachronistic *Kulturkampf,* which flared up following the system change (resembling the fights in the age of secularization in the second half of the nineteenth century), but it nonetheless had to show that it would not allow any one-sided interpretations.

For this reason, on the one hand the Constitutional Court had to emphasize that the required neutrality of the State does not amount to a preference for either the negative freedom of religion or religious indifference. On the contrary, positive and negative freedoms of religion have equal status. This needed to be stressed in the face of the Communist legacy, which lived on in the notion that negative freedom of religion or indifference was the rule and positive freedom of religion the exception. Thus, in the first opinion the State's duty to "ensure the possibility of free formation of personal convictions" appears in the holdings as an expansion of its duty of neutrality.

The Court held that conscious conviction (and within this, in the given case, religion) is a formative part of the personality, and thus of human nature,[41] and part of the right to human dignity, so that the guarantee of its freedom ensures free expression and the development of a human being's personality, which itself cannot be limited by law. Thus, given the right to freedom of religion the State has a duty to abstain from interference in its exercise. On the other hand, there is also a close relationship between the right to worship and freedom of speech. Since the manifestation of freedom of speech is the exercise of religion or worship, any laws limiting such freedom had to be interpreted restrictively, as with those in respect of free speech. The State is to protect the freedom of conscience and religion without considering its value or its content (thus the right could only have external limits), and it is from such a position that the State draws its neutrality, as underlined by the separation principle in Art. 60(3) of the Constitution.

The second task of the Court was to make it clear that religion and the church are not the same, neither from the perspective of state law nor from the perspective of the religion in question. The fundamental idea of the second decision on the freedom of religion[42] is accordingly that the rights guaranteed in Art. 60 of the Constitution as a whole are based on the freedom of societal practice of religion without regard to whether the collective practice of religion takes place in a legally regulated framework or without any particular legal or organizational form. This unconditional equality before the law does not preclude the state from making various legal forms available to religious communities in order to make it easier for them to conform to the State's legal order in consideration of their characteristics. Religious communities are free to follow these or other organizational forms of worldly law or to renounce them completely. The "church" of state law is completely independent of the conceptions of "church" in various religions, and the State can shape the church's characteristics according to the State's point of view.[43] Thus, the State can, for example, take into consideration the fact that in the common language *church* means a large community, and the State can require a minimum number of members for this form of organization on the condition that equality before the law remains for the churches, smaller communities, and those that do not want to be known as a "church."

With regard to the separation principle, the Constitutional Court had a double task. On the one hand, it insisted on separation (see the distinction between state- and church-run schools, discussed later); on the other, it pointed out in its holdings that the separation of church and state does not forbid the state from taking into consideration the uniqueness of religion and the church. This means that the Court did not follow the notion that would have transplanted into Hungary the American approach, which considers the church to be a kind of private association. Neither did the Court rely on European comparisons.[44] The Constitutional Court wanted to develop an interpretation of separation that would not exclude cooperation according to historical circumstances. This also gave the Court the opportunity to stress either separation or the cooperation in order to maintain the constitutional balance against changing government concepts that either favor constitutionally suspect, overly close cooperation between the church and state or overstate the State's neutrality and passivity.

From this concept, it follows that the neutral State considers all the ways in which the church, from the perspective of its history and its role in society, distinguishes itself from other social organizations, associations, interest groups, and so on. Accordingly the Constitutional Court reaffirmed that the guarantee of the material foundations for the realization or promotion of a fundamental right—in this case the freedom of religion—can constitutionally justify a distinction in the material support of public (law) bodies. At the same time, however, the decision stressed that the return of certain property to the churches was meant to compensate not for former state's impairment of ownership but for the restriction of the fundamental right of the freedom to exercise religion. The Court declared unconstitutional and annulled all restitution that did not conform to this functional approach.

On the other hand, consideration of historical conditions and the contemporary role of the church cannot lead to a favoring of the traditional large churches. While the Court provided for equal treatment for all religious communities,[45] it could not help but take into account either the sociological fact that the large memberships and distinguished histories of churches in many areas facilitate the exercise of religion for their members or the historical fact that only the property of the historical churches had been nationalized and small churches of more recent origin (which had not lost property) could not be compensated for it. Besides compensation, the Court had to deal with this problem in cases reviewing the Government Decree concerning army chaplains (instituted only for the "historical" churches)[46] and the Lustration Act[47] (checking of clergymen only at the request of the churches).[48]

It is to be noted that even if the Constitutional Court had been required to consider the peculiarities of the churches, in all the cases decided thus far positive discrimination (regarding material contribution by the State for facilitating the exercise of a fundamental right) had been extended beyond the churches to public bodies in comparable situations (such as local governments or schools of ethnic minorities).[49] The same equation of organizations resulted from the intention of the Court to prevent negative discrimination against the churches. So the opinion in the religious freedom case forbade, for instance, any restrictive regulation that would affect only churches, not associations in general, and—as a reaction to the former State Authority for Churches, which under socialism exercised total control over religious life in Hungary—declared unconstitutional any special state agency for church affairs.

The Constitutional Court had to prevent attempts to qualify the separation of church and state. The problem is a live issue for the schools in that the churches can demand the return of their former school buildings. The question was how the freedom of religion could be guaranteed to those who did not want religiously related instruction, especially if there was only one school building in a village. For the sake of clarifying the principle of separation, in Decision 4/1993 the Constitutional Court made a rigorous distinction between the (neutral) "state" school and the (religiously affiliated) "church" school on the basis of differing constitutional requirements. Opposing the trend of those days,[50] the Court insisted on the point that schools could not be neutral and at the same time be true to the spirit of a church. A student could adhere to any worldview, and it would impose a much smaller burden (or no burden at all) upon his or her conscience if the student could attend a neutral school. Thus, for those who do not want to attend a school with specific philosophical perspectives, the State must guarantee the legal possibility of behavior in accordance with their consciences (just as the legal possibility of establishment and maintenance of a church school had to be guaranteed). Further, the State must actually provide them with access to a neutral state school.

After demolishing the legal and administrative limits of socialism on freedom of religion, practical problems seemed to concentrate on the economic conditions of its exercise. After the Schools Act of 1994 was enacted in full accordance with the religious freedom decision, problems and constitutional cases related to school financing did not cease to exist. The Constitutional Court had to repeat many times that the State is not constitutionally obliged to set up and run free schools in accordance with the convictions and wishes of the parents—the neutral state school is a constitutionally sufficient alternative to all schools regarding the freedom of conscience. After dismissing various other claims, the Court recognized in accordance with the first decision that the State had to finance religious schools to the extent that they took over from the State obligatory and free schooling (as guaranteed in Art. 70/F(2) of the Constitution). This right is granted to religious and ethnic minority schools, as the Court considers religious beliefs and ethnic identity so decisive for the integrity of the individual personality that they deserve this positive discrimination (22/1997(IV.25)AB).[51]

Freedom of Conscience

The Court's definition of freedom of conscience also reflects its determination to consider personhood in its individual totality. Accordingly, the core of this freedom is the duty of the State to abstain from threatening, by enforcing destructive choices, the integrity of the personality and to provide for alternative actions that might preserve this integrity at the lowest cost (64/1991). This test was first developed in the abortion case and then was applied to the schooling cases and to problems relating to military service.[52] As regards conscientious objectors, the Court found this definition of conscience sufficiently broad because it was connected to an important interior conviction, irrespective of whether this sprung from religious, moral, or other considerations. The instrumental construction of the freedom of conscience further represents the view of the Court on the neutrality of the State and the Constitution as to the content of beliefs, expressed opinions, and so on. The Court enlarged upon the problem of neutrality in questions of practical morals in the homosexual associations case (21/1996)—but even in that case it carefully avoided any judgment on homosexuality.[53]

Criminal and Procedural Guarantees

Article 57 of the Constitution is where the most important rule-of-law guarantees for matters of criminal and legal recourse are to be found. It contains the rights to judicial legal protection; to impartial, fair, and public trial; and to appeal as well as the presumption of innocence, the right to defense (the right to counsel), and the principle of *nullum crimen* and *nulla poena sine lege*. In keeping with the other fundamental rights, the Constitutional Court interprets these guarantees expansively.

Criminal Law Safeguards

The most important guarantee question was raised by the statutory limitations decision (11/1992), which was also politically important, having a decisive impact on the character of the transition to democracy. As for other criminal law guarantees, the habeas corpus provisions of the Constitution (Art. 55) have played a minor role in the Court; such cases concerned only rules of damages for wrongful arrest. Similarly, the right to defense has been reviewed only with regard to such partial aspects as the independence of the procedural rights of the counsel from the determination of the accused and the honorarium for a defense counsel appointed by the court—again the problem of the economic basis of exercising a right.[54] More significant was the declaration as unconstitutional of any form of collective criminal responsibility.[55] The guarantee of presumption of innocence has been extended to administrative law offenses.[56]

The statutory limitations case interpreted expansively the principle prohibiting retroactivity:[57] it has been extended to each element or precondition of criminal responsibility, including statutory limitations. According to the decision, the constitutionality of a criminal norm is not merely to be measured by the criminal law guarantees specifically named in the Constitution. Neither the principle of guilt (subjective responsibility) nor the prohibition of objective criminal responsibility are spelled out specifically in the Constitution. Nonetheless, it can be implied from the right to human dignity that only the guilty actor can be penalized. Similarly, by applying the principle of the rule of law (Art. 2(1) of the Constitution), other criminal law principles can acquire constitutional significance.

The Constitutional Court did not decide the question of the material or procedural character of statutory limitations, although in other democracies this differentiation proved to be of watershed significance. The German Constitutional Court allowed the extension of the limitation period on the basis of its procedural character, so this distinction became decisive for the different ways of handling the politically motivated crimes of the dictatorship. As a result, however, the Hungarian Court's opinion came closer to the view that they are material. According to the Hungarian Constitutional Court, with the expiration of the limitation period a subjective right of the actor arises according to which he or she can no longer be prosecuted or penalized. The Constitutional Court sees in the limitations period a restriction on the criminal power of the State to sentence, through which the State, with concern for legal certainty, accepts the risk of an unsuccessful criminal prosecution.

Criminal law guarantees are as a rule absolute in the eyes of the Constitutional Court; no other fundamental right or constitutional goal can be balanced against them. The presumption of innocence or the expiration of the limitation period cannot be qualified. "Simply put, historical situations, justice etc. are of no consideration in this matter. Exemptions from the guarantees of the criminal law are only possible with their overt disregard, an outcome precluded by the principle of the rule of law" (11/1992).[58] Later, in its fourth statutory limitations decision (53/1993), the Constitutional Court had to ensure conformity of this position with the fact that, according to the generally recognized principles of public international law, war crimes and crimes against humanity have no statutory limitations. The Constitutional Court attempted to resolve the inconsistency between the absolute interpretation of Art. 57 of the Constitution and Art. 7, according to which the legal order of the Republic of Hungary accepts the generally recognized rules of international law. It did so by considering these mandatory norms to be a parallel legal order with its own system of guarantees (including criminal guarantees), which, according to the Constitution, is valid in Hungary's territory.

Between the first and the fourth statutory limitations decisions, the Constitutional Court was occupied with the same topic. The pressure for justice and "overcoming the past" was so evident among some politically powerful players that they did not want to acknowledge the constitutional boundaries of the applicability of criminal law, especially the retroactive amendment of statutory limitations. Instead of looking for other means, they tried to push through their original idea. The Court set aside a resolution of Parliament that contained a binding interpretation of statutory limitations rules, stating that the statute of limitations had been tolled during a time when the State had not exercised its power to sentence. According to the Court, Parliament cannot issue binding interpretations in the form of a resolution—only Acts have such an effect. On the other hand, the resolution was contrary to the first relevant decision of the Constitutional Court and therefore also unconstitutional on this ground. On the same day, another decision of the Constitutional Court was published[59]—based on the request of the President of the Republic, who did not promulgate the Act—which found an amendment to the Criminal Procedure Code to be unconstitutional. The amendment affected all proceedings commenced between the entry into force of the Act and 31 December 1995 for criminal acts that were punishable by imprisonment for at least five years. In these proceedings, neither the investigation nor the trial could be rejected because of the statutory limitations. The judge had to see the process through to the end, determine whether a criminal act had been committed, and, only after that determination, declare the possible statutory limitations and abandon the proceedings for that reason. Further, the reopening of criminal cases was to be possible regardless of the statutory limitations. According to the decision of the Constitutional Court, this planned regulation violated the rule of law, especially against legal certainty; it represented retroactive criminal lawmaking to the detriment of the accused; and the possibility of reopening the proceeding violates the institution of *res judicata,* which is a component of legal certainty. Criminal proceedings, which necessarily limit the rights of the accused and others, cannot constitutionally be applied to goals that are outside the aim of enforcement of criminal responsibility or penalizing the offender. A criminal case may not be turned into moral theater.

It is to be noted that "delivering justice for the crimes under Socialism" is still possible, using the method indicated by the Constitutional Court.[60] The first sentences were delivered in 1996 condemning members of the communist militia who killed unarmed demonstrators during the 1956 Revolution. Similar cases are pending. Compared with states that lifted the statute of limitations for such cases, as Germany and the Czech Republic did, the practical effects of the criminal *Vergangenheitsbewältigung* (a German term for the settling of accounts with the totalitarian past) in Hungary do not differ essentially from those of these countries, although the decisions of the Constitutional Court were interpreted at first as barring the way to justice.

Procedural Guarantees

Access to justice. According to the decisions of the Constitutional Court, the right to judicial legal protection, that is, the guarantee of recourse to the courts, cannot constitutionally depend on the discretion of the judge or another official. This constitutes the fundamental basis for the decision on protests of illegality (9/1992) because this exceptional appeal was dependent upon the free discretion of the President of the Supreme Court or the Chief Public Prosecutor. Similarly, the Constitutional Court annulled in a series of cases rights of the public prosecutor to act in civil proceedings independently or against the will of the parties.[61]

A major achievement of the Constitutional Court was to *extend the judicial review of administrative acts.* In an early decision, the Court declared the omission of Parliament to implement Art. 50(2) of the Constitution, which declared the judicial reviewability of administrative acts; four months later, the corresponding Act introduced administrative review by the ordinary courts.[62] Three important decisions followed this seminal case. The Constitutional Court secured a broad competence for the ordinary courts to review even discretionary decisions of administrative authorities. According to the Constitutional Court, a law is contrary to the Constitution that, by providing for unlimited discretion of the administrative organ, does not contain any provision enabling the ordinary court to test the lawfulness of the exercise of the discretionary power (39/1997). Recently, the Court held that there was no judicial remedy against decisions on administrative offenses. Although Hungary joined the European Convention of Human Rights with a reservation concerning art. 6(1), according to which Hungary would not be able to provide for the judicial review of decisions on administrative offenses, the Court saw in that no reason not to fulfill Art. 50(2) of the Constitution, which renders judicial review of the decisions of public administration without exception. The relevant law was passed by the end of 1998.[63]

The Constitutional Court also obliged Parliament to provide for "effective legal means" for the case of the silence of administration (72/1995(XII.15)AB).[64] The current remedies merely permitted challenging a decision, which had already been made, to claim damages caused by the delay or request a ruling from a superior authority itself not bound by any time limit. Due to posttransformation changes in the administration, in many instances state administrative organs no longer had "superiors" *stricto sensu* that could issue compelling orders. As a result, the complainant was left without any redress. The unconstitutionality of this situation was seen as an infringement upon legal certainty, predictability of laws, and the conduct of those applying laws, which forms a part thereof. Parliament remedied this situation, though only after some delay.[65]

As to general procedural guarantees, the *right of appeal* arose mostly in matters of labor law, administrative law, and the enforcement of judgments as well as in connection with the civil alternative to national service in the armed forces. The Constitutional Court defined the right of appeal as "the possibility to turn to another organ or to a higher forum within the same organization with regard to a meritorious decision."[66] According to argumentation typical of such applications, the right to appeal in every case means the judicial appeal route. The Constitutional Court, however, included the effectiveness of the given appellate route in its balancing of interests: under certain conditions, a complaint to one's superior can be more helpful than the judicial route, which for considerations of time alone would in effect be pointless.[67]

The Right of Association

Article 63(1) of the Constitution provides for the right of association, which includes the right to establish and join an association. This right covers the founding of political parties as well.[68] The freedom to form unions (and the right to strike) are provided for separately in Art. 70/C. These positive provisions have been interpreted by the Court—like the freedom of religion—as including the *negative* freedom of association as well. Indeed, one of the lasting themes of the right of association is the constitutionality of the legally enforced association. Obligatory membership in the bar association, the commercial and industrial chambers, and the Chamber of Medical Doctors and that of architects were all challenged before the Court. Even the underlying provisions of the Civil Code, regulating among legal persons the "public bodies" of which the chambers are a species, had to be reviewed. In the background, a double trend is to be seen. On the one hand, the freedom of association is symbolic of democracy following an era of strict police control and absorbing all civil initiatives into a semistate organizational network.[69] Making the "free professions" actually free, for example, the canceling of limited numbers for lawyers, represents another side of the process. On the other hand, in the last few years "public bodies" have begun to mushroom. Administrative competences have been vested in associations, covering professions or the whole scale of business activities. Even the activities of hobbyists became organized in such a semistate form, having rule-making and enforcement power over large numbers of citizens.[70] A corporate state organization was argued for in 1996–97 as a new constitution was prepared (but then the drafting stopped) in the Parliament.[71] In the cases presented in this book, claims against obligatory membership, calling for protection of the free market and entrepreneurship, represent one side, while, for instance, excessive rights of the medical chamber to protect the jobs of Hungarian doctors from "foreigners" stand for the other.

The Constitutional Court did not discuss corporate statehood. Instead it enlarged upon the negative freedom of association. Maintaining its initial position that public bodies and membership in them are not founded upon the right of association but established by law,[72] the Court held in the commercial chamber case (38/1997(VII.1)AB)[73] that obligatory membership might restrict the freedom of association, too, at least indirectly, as an infringement upon the right of self-determination, which is an aspect of the right to human dignity. In that way, the Court established the ability to review the necessity and proportionality of obligatory membership.[74] Further, it set constitutional barriers to the unreasonable multiplication of public bodies by reviewing whether they did indeed serve a "public purpose," which would render necessary the transfer of some competences of the state administration. It is not enough that the positive requirements are satisfied; the Court also determines whether the public body does in fact prevent the functioning of another organization founded upon the right of association. In all these cases,[75] the Court was in the lucky position that—within "abstract norm control"—it decided upon truly individual cases. There were separate laws applicable to each chamber, and therefore the criteria could be investigated for each case. To this extent, it was possible to understand the differences between the commercial chamber and the medical chamber cases as regards the public purpose.

Restriction of the right to association came before the Court in another context, as this right of special groups of persons—minors and soldiers—were to be decided upon. The Constitutional Court held that the membership of minors in associations related to homosexuality could be excluded or restricted by law or in court decisions on the basis of the State's duty to protect the child from risks in connection with which the immature child is not able to learn and evaluate either the possibilities or the consequences of choice for his or her own personality, later life, and social adaptation (21/1996). Unlike the chambers' cases, here the Constitutional Court did not have the last word on an individual case. The concrete case was generally known and was before the Supreme Court for decision. The President of that Court asked for an abstract advisory opinion on the relationship between the State's duty to protect the child's development and the child's right of association. Therefore, the Constitutional Court's decision laid down general rules on the restrictability of the right of minors to associate. It gave further direction to the ordinary courts as to which circumstances had to be considered in concrete cases concerning homosexual-oriented associations. This rulemaking is conditioned by the special competence of the Constitutional Court to an "abstract interpretation of a provision of the Constitution" invoked in a case that—similar to presidential power cases—does not allow the Court to decide directly the underlying case. But the Court usually prefers general arguments, which are effective far beyond the question in the given case when through this generality even the supposition of positive or negative bias may be prevented. The Court not only abstained from any moral judgment about homosexuality but emphasized that the State could not expose the child to the risk of immature decisions, none of which is related solely to homosexuality. The same method was used in the church property case.[76]

Another case dealt with the prohibition of the active participation of soldiers during service in organizations created for purposes conflicting with the legally defined tasks of the armed forces. The Court found this restriction to be necessary and proportional; it noted, too, that the individual organizations had to be qualified by the ordinary courts as to whether they fell within the restriction.[77]

In Hungary, the Constitutional Court has no power to decide on the constitutionality of political parties; parties shall be registered by ordinary courts if they satisfy the conditions of the Party Act. Nevertheless, provisions of the Party Act regarding the functions of parties remained for constitutional review. In the first case, the Court on formal grounds could avoid taking a position on the constitutionality of party financing out of the state budget.[78] In the second case, the requirement that a party must cease to exist if it does not put up a candidate for parliamentary election in two successive elections proved to be constitutional and, moreover, to be an element of the notion of a political party that follows directly from the constitutional definition of parties. The argument that a legislator may require proof of the seriousness and backing in society of an organization for it to be legally recognized was formerly used by the Court in dealing with the legal notion of the "church."[79]

The Right to a Healthy Environment

The fundamental rights section of the Constitution was created in 1989 through roundtable negotiations in consideration of the relevant international conventions. But as a rule it does not go beyond these standards, which are internationally agreed upon and thus contain minimal requirements. Only the undisputed rules were incorporated. However, there are two exceptions, in which the Hungarian Constitution incorporates rights that are not common in other constitutions and the content of which is not commonly agreed upon. These are the right to the protection of personal data and freedom of information and the right to a healthy environment. The environmental protection rights are mentioned twice in the Constitution. Article 18 provides in the chapter on "General Provisions," which in the socialist tradition contains the foundations of the constitutional order: "The Republic of Hungary shall recognize and enforce everyone's right to a healthy environment." Article 70/D, which is in the fundamental rights chapter and contains "the right to the highest possible level of physical and mental health," includes among the means of realizing this right "protecting the built and natural environment" (Art. 70/D(2)).

In 1990, the Prime Minister and the Environmental Committee of Parliament had already applied for an abstract interpretation of the constitutional provisions regarding the right to a healthy environment. Following long discussions, the Constitutional Court rejected the application for lack of a specific problem suitable for constitutional interpretation.[80] However, in the decision the Constitutional Court said that the language of the Constitution (the right to a "healthy" environment, and the embedding of relevant state tasks in the middle of the bringing about of the right to health) could not be interpreted as a limitation on the right to a healthy environment.

The content of the environmental right was spelled out in connection with a case in which the constitutionality of the repeal of a prohibition of the use of nature reserves for compensation for nationalization and privatization of the property of cooperatives was to be decided. The Constitutional Court held this option to be unconstitutional and declared the duty of the State to maintain the status quo with respect to protecting nature (28/1994). "The Constitutional Court declares that the right to a healthy environment, as defined in Art. 18 of the Constitution, incorporates *inter alia* the responsibility of the Republic of Hungary to ensure that the State does not reduce the degree of the protection of nature as guaranteed under law, unless this is unavoidable in order to enforce any other fundamental right or constitutional value." This nonderogation rule was constructed by means of the analysis of the specific nature of the right in question. It differs from both subjective rights and state goals. The right to a healthy environment is a fundamental right for which institutional protection outweighs other factors; all duties of the State that in connection with other fundamental rights could be resolved using subjective rights must be accomplished here by using institutional and regulatory guarantees. This also results from the fact that the subject of this right could be "humanity" or "nature," respectively. The duty to maintain the status quo similarly arises from the fact that the protected good, the natural foundations of life, is a so-called scarce resource and damage to nature is usually irreversible.

The Right to Property

The Constitutional Right to Property

The transition of the political system necessarily meant a complete reshaping of the rules of property ownership. Private property and the market economy are preconditions for democracy; the Constitution lists in the Preamble the multiparty system, parliamentary democracy, the social market economy, and the rule of law as the goals of the "transition." The text of the Constitution provides in Art. 9 that the economic system of Hungary is to be a market economy and further that the Republic of Hungary recognizes and encourages the right to enterprise and the freedom of economic competition. Article 13 guarantees an unusually strong protection of property: taking is possible only exceptionally, in the public interest, in cases and in a process regulated by an Act of Parliament and under terms of full, unconditional, and immediate compensation. The Constitutional Court itself noted the parallels between the constitutional declaration of the rule of law and the market economy.[81] Creating a new economic order meant for practical purposes the reallocation of national wealth and the formation of a new class of owners; no wonder the process was accompanied by intense political battles. Little wonder, too, that the relative laws lacked systematic theory, coherence, or theoretical foundations. For introducing a market economy, first of all the privatization of former state (or collective) property[82] was necessary. This presupposed, however, the settling of the debate as to whether or not nationalized property should be returned to its former owners. Privatization was connected with nationwide expectations that the "unjust" expropriations of the 1940s and 1950s would be reviewed and made retroactive or that the earlier owners would be fully compensated. All respective laws were referred to the Constitutional Court. It was left to the Court to clarify all the relevant notions and set up a systematic framework. This had a double effect. Even if Parliament and its politics in the beginning paid little attention to the conceptual constructions of the Court, it came to learn with time that the Court would apply its tests and the free scope for politics would become more and more constitutionally limited. On the other hand, even if the Court stressed that it was only judging the constitutional *realization* of given concepts, it determined the main course of the economic transition. For instance, the first compensation case (21/1990) *opened the way for commercial privatization* (instead of the obligation of the State to return property to the former owners). This was as decisive for the character of the whole transition as was the *concept of legal continuity,* on which not only privatization and compensation for material and moral damages were founded but also the constitutional means of prosecution of politically motivated crimes committed under the former regimes.

As background for the new constitutional order of property, the role and content of the provisions for a "market economy," "free competition," and the "right to enterprise" (Constitution, Art. 9), as well as the frequently claimed "freedom of contract," were to be determined. In the early years, in response to earlier state control of the economy, the market economy was commonly understood to mean total freedom from all state intervention and regulation in the sense of a simplified notion of nineteenth-century liberal capitalism. A flood of applications to the Court considered all state measures—from taxation to rent control—to be unconstitutional.

The Constitutional Court, in response, made it clear that state encroachment on property and the freedom to contract can also exist in a market economy, and it attempted to specify its constitutionally permissible limits. Nonetheless, in the early years the Court shared the idea that encroachment was only necessary for the reform of the economic system and thus only temporarily necessary. According to this approach, the ideal—and attainable—condition of the market economy was one in which there was no more state intervention.[83] Accordingly, the constitutionality of an encroachment was often justified by the fact that in the end it was serving the purpose of building the market economy.[84] In keeping with this reasoning, the Constitutional Court considered the freedom of contract first as a fundamental right.

This stage was also characterized by an excessive protection of property. It is to be noted that, although the right to property is not integrated into the Bill of Rights of the Constitution, the Court recognized it as a true fundamental right from the beginning. This time, applicants and the Court typically used the civil law concept of ownership and identified the constitutionally inviolable essence[85] of ownership with its classic Roman law components: possession, use, and disposability. According to this approach, every restraint on alienation or encumbrance violated the Constitution. The constant practice of the Court has confirmed this argument and has held that only a temporary restriction on the power to dispose of property did not disturb the essential content of ownership.[86]

The jurisprudence of the Constitutional Court changed in 1994 in both respects. The case of permissibility of a restriction on the number of taxis offered the Court an opportunity to deliver an authoritative statement on the constitutional meaning of the market economy and free competition as state goals and of the relationship between these and fundamental rights (21/1994). According to the decision, the Constitution does not provide for any specific substantive model of the market economy. Because the Constitution is neutral with respect to the political economy, neither the degree nor the intensity of state intervention can be inferred from it.[87] Only in borderline cases can the Constitutional Court determine the critical size of the interference. Beyond such cases, however, the "market economy" is irrelevant for the review of constitutionality. The lawmaker's notion of the optimal degree of market influence cannot be replaced by the Constitutional Court's notion. The maintenance and protection of the market economy is an ongoing constitutional task (a "state goal") that is to be realized above all through the assertion and protection of relevant individual fundamental rights—which the Court listed in the opinion. Neither is "the freedom of economic competition" a fundamental right. In contrast, the right to enterprise (Art. 9(2)) is a true fundamental right, which the Constitutional Court considers in many respects to be the same as the right to work and to choose and practice freely one's own profession (Art. 70/B). With regard to the constitutionality of limitations on the fundamental right to work (and on choice of profession and enterprise), the Constitutional Court did not take on the "graduated theory" developed in the practice of the German Federal Constitutional Court. In effect, however, it maintained to the same extent the position that limitations on the practice of a profession are to be judged according to less demanding criteria than the choice of profession, where the necessity and proportionality of the objective restrictions of the choice of profession "are to be scrutinized most strictly." On the one side, this interpretation gave the right to work a new and (from the socialist perspective) different meaning.[88] On the other, it was to underlie the decisions to follow on commercial and professional chambers with obligatory membership. Here the Court stated that obligatory membership in the commercial chamber did not encroach upon either the market economy or the right to enterprise and work (39/1997). In connection with the exercise of their profession by foreign medical doctors in Hungary, the Court emphasized that the right to choose a profession and work demonstrated in the Constitution a human right (not a citizens' right, as in many countries). This is also to be subject to strict scrutiny.[89] The decision thus belongs to cases that, in view of future membership in the European Union, will raise problems of free movement, work, and the protection of national interests.

In line with such changes from 1994 on, the Court no longer considers the freedom of contract as a fundamental right; it is protected on the basis of the right to property and constitutional privacy (the right to freedom of action as derived from the right to human dignity).

The other development was the separation of the civil law notion of property from property as a constitutional right. "Taking of property in the constitutional sense does not necessarily mean the loss of property right in the civil law sense; however, the Constitution does not provide unconditional protection against physical expropriation." As a result, the Constitutional Court forged a different path in ascertaining the limitations on property than that used in other restrictions on fundamental rights.[90] This is because the Constitution itself defines *the guarantee of value as the limit on the guarantee of ownership* to the extent it makes possible expropriation for a public purpose. The question of constitutionality, then, is in which cases the owner must accept an encroachment by the public authority without compensation and in which cases he or she has a claim to compensation for restrictions on property in which the property was not actually taken. The focus of the Court's determination of constitutionality is shifting toward the proportionality of the encroachment. Thus, if the guarantee of value is realized, the Constitutional Court requires no stricter "necessity" than public interest, which the Court will not review except in borderline cases such as those in which invoking the public interest is obviously unfounded (64/1993).

A further step in the separation of civil law ownership and the constitutional right to property was the expansion of the protection of property beyond the civil law protection to include other (material) asset rights. The Constitutional Court founded this broad protection on the function of property. "Property is afforded constitutional protection in its capacity as the traditional means of securing an economic basis for the autonomy of individual action. The constitutional protection must track the changing social role of property so as to fulfill this task. Thus, when the protection of individual autonomy is at stake, the constitutional protection of property extends to rights with an economic value which today perform this former role of ownership, even if they be public law entitlements (for instance social insurance claims)."[91] The functional notion of property played a decisive role later on, as the Court based the protection for social security benefits or entitlements on this definition of property (43/1995).[92] This extended notion of property does not lead automatically to constitutional protection of all entitlements. The Court recognized, for instance, that the law that excluded building technicians from membership in the Chamber of Architects (and through this prevented them from undertaking architectural planning) violated their right to property. This restriction was, however, not disproportionate to the public interest underlying the establishment of the Chamber of Architects as a public body.[93]

These changes in the notion of property had a double effect. On the one hand, they extended the use of Art. 13 of the Constitution, which guarantees the right to property. On the other hand, however, they made the protection relative: socially motivated restrictions imposed on property made constitutionally permissible a far-reaching restriction on the autonomy of the property owner.[94] Examples for such permissible encroachments are state regulations on the option to purchase local government apartments, cited extensively earlier, the return of buildings previously owned by the church (4/1993), and the case allowing restrictions on the acquisition of arable land (primarily by Hungarian corporations and non-Hungarians).[95] The latter case clarified serious constitutional problems as well. In accordance with the case law of the European Court of Human Rights but also—exceptionally—citing some U.S. cases,[96] the Court held that the constitutional right to property does not extend to its acquisition. Accordingly, the measure for the constitutionality of discrimination as regards nonfundamental rights was to be elaborated: discrimination that is arbitrary or has no reasonable cause is unconstitutional. Taking into consideration the fact that arable land is a limited good, the legislature's aim to promote the development of appropriate structures of land, and the establishment of realistic land prices and avoidance of land concentration, the Court held the restricting provisions constitutional "as long as the reasonable causes for restrictions in question hold under objective examination."

The Hierarchy of Forms of Ownership

The Constitutional Court participated in the dismantling of the various privileges enjoyed by state and cooperative property in keeping with "equal rights and equal protection" of public and private property (Art. 9), the principle of equality before the law, and the constitutional task of bringing about a market economy. This occurred almost in competition with the Ministry of Justice, which introduced the relevant draft amendments to the Civil Code in Parliament in rapid succession. But it was left to the Constitutional Court to eliminate the preferences in the Civil Code for state property over the original acquisition of ownership[97] and to annul its privileges in the laws of enforcement and corporations.[98] The special protection enjoyed by state property under criminal law was declared to be unconstitutional.[99] Legal institutions that only made sense in a socialist planned economy or for comprehensive state ownership retained no constitutional protection; their repeal or restriction through law was not found to be unconstitutional.[100] When, however, the special criminal law protection for state property was annulled, the Constitutional Court left open the possibility of positive discrimination according to the function of the property: a higher level of protection, for example, in criminal law would not be unconstitutional as the basis for charitable uses or public use of the property.[101]

The Constitutional Court resisted creating new privileges as well. For instance, through the binding of communal property to its special function, the Court could avoid an extensive—and for political reasons excessive—interpretation of the rights of local governments, including the right to ownership.[102] The Constitutional Court determined that the fundamental rights of local governments were to be realized within the framework of the general laws; the Constitution's repeated recognition of the property of the local governments was directed at the legal status of the local government as property owner, which status was essential to its autonomy. “Ownership as a fundamental right of the local governments is the full expression of this legal status as owner but does not guarantee the property of the local governments any special or greater protection” (4/1993).

Compensation Cases: “Partial Reimbursement of Unjustly Caused Damages in Property” and Compensation for Moral Damages

Privatization and Compensation. All new democracies face the problem of settlement of the ownership of confiscated, nationalized, or otherwise “unjustly taken” property by the former regime. The task is inseparable from the constitutional command to turn state into private ownership. The principal choice is the decision for either reprivatization (to return property to the former owners) or privatization on a commercial basis (to sell state property to those offering more for it and/or able to run or operate it in a market economy). The choice may determine the restorative or future-oriented approach to the system change. Reprivatization restores the ownership structure of forty years ago; it is at least partly also a renovation of the former social structure. Reprivatization is interconnected, but only partly, with the demand for *justice.* This claim, however, is double edged: why should only former owners (and only owners of special kinds of property) be compensated when broader classes of society suffered financial losses (and even more people moral damages) under socialism? The retrospective or prospective nature of the changes these points raise must be reflected in the legal and even constitutional handling of the “transition.” Restoration presupposes a total break with previous law (roughly speaking, the consideration of decades of socialism as nonexistent from the legal point of view, meaning that expropriations have no effect today). On the other hand, the prospective approach may emphasize legal continuity and revolutionary changes at the same time. This makes possible compensation of former owners instead of restitution and at the same time commercial privatization. The choice has further consequences for the transformation of the whole economy into the market system, partly as regards social costs (see the skills of the new owners to operate the property) and partly concerning the financial resources of the country for rendering justice. This aspect of the social benefits of privatization or reprivatization was raised in Hungary by the Constitutional Court. The question of legal continuity was also pointed out and elaborated. Generally, it remained for the Court to develop some theoretically consistent and dogmatic order in these questions while legislation and implementation of the relevant acts were at the mercy of the often irrational changes in everyday politics. The reprivatization dilemma in every state in transition had to be resolved as soon as possible for the sake of having clear property relationships (and keeping investors free from the claims of former owners).

This is why immediately after the first free elections in 1990 the Prime Minister asked the Constitutional Court for an advisory opinion.[103] Not only society but also the ruling coalition was divided on the reprivatization issue.[104] To complicate matters, in Hungary the same objects could have changed ownership many times between 1939 and 1989 due to various laws.[105] Thus, a question arose with respect to returning the property: to which of the earlier owners should the property be returned?

The Prime Minister asked for an opinion of the constitutionality of the compromise within the government: reprivatization of land and commercial privatization of other property with partial compensation for the former owners. The Constitutional Court determined that full restoration of previous ownership in land and partial compensation for all other property losses would contradict the principle of equality before the law (Art. 70/A) and that cooperatives—the land of which had been foreseen, besides state property, as being available for use in compensation—enjoyed the same property protection as all other owners. This meant that their expropriation was only possible under the strict conditions of Art. 13 of the Constitution (21/1990). Only after this Court decision was the conception fundamentally altered to entitle all parties that had suffered damage to receive just partial reimbursement in the form of vouchers that could be used to purchase privatized state property or cooperative land. For this latter option, the law granted a certain circle of persons entitled to reimbursement the option to buy land from the cooperatives at auction. The bill was sent to the Court by opposition parties (the decision is 16/1991). Then the enacted law was referred to the Constitutional Court by the President of the Republic, and finally the promulgated Act was challenged by more than three hundred actions brought before the Court. All later amendments to the Act also had to be reviewed for their constitutionality. Apart from several technical problems, the constitutional problem remained at the heart of the dispute on reprivatization: lobbies could still manage it in such a way that some groups might achieve full compensation of land due to manipulation of the methods of estimating losses and the amount of compensation.

This volume contains only the first two decisions, which were fundamental for the whole system change and naturally for all of the later decisions on compensation (21/1990; 16/1991). With these cases, the Court opened and maintained the way for commercial privatization and delivered a constitutional basis for it through the legal continuity theory. In this sense, the State was considered the legal owner of the once-nationalized assets and had the power to privatize them. As to compensation, the Court enforced the equal protection principle and developed a test for positive discrimination (resembling Dworkin's theory on affirmative action). The subsequent decisions would naturally develop a more elaborate discussion of the problems of compensation, but the core for them was set down or at least mentioned *obiter* in the first cases. For instance, even before the full development of the continuity theory, the Court stated in the second compensation case that the Compensation Act created a new title for the claims of the former owner, which "excluded claiming under old titles." The first decision represents the idea that no one has a subjective right to compensation; the second adds that social costs and burdens originating from the transformation of the property system might be placed upon those who acquire the former state property for free. This will be decisive in later cases on altering the original distribution of state and cooperative property[106] and for justifying the whole compensation scheme on the grounds of distributive justice. Of no less importance was the provision of the Court—faithful to the principle that compensation should not endanger the security of privatization—according to which "as soon as the process [of the transformation of state property into private property] is accomplished, the protection of the new property will be complete."

Another set of decisions contributed to the compensation series, as the Court in 1992 elaborated its theory on the nature of the system change, the role of legal continuity, legal certainty, and the (lack of) effect of unconstitutionality of a law for already closed legal facts and relationships (protest of illegality, *ex nunc* and statute of limitations cases: 9/1992; 10/1992; 11/1992, respectively).

According to the Constitutional Court, nationalizations and expropriations of property that were legal at the time they occurred still had legal effect. The Constitution requires neither the return of the property nor full compensation. Partial compensation—to the extent that it does not violate the principle of equality before the law—is constitutional.

In the course of these decisions, the reasons for the positions changed. At first, the Constitutional Court presumed the constitutional freedom of the state as property owner; later, these formal reasons changed to the characteristics of the transition of the political system. The latter reasons were explained in two ways. On the one hand, the continued validity of earlier acquisitions of property for which the legal basis had now become unconstitutional was recognized; on the other, the Constitutional Court based the constitutionality of partial compensation on distributive justice.

In the beginning, the Constitutional Court presumed that "the right of the State to privatization and reprivatization is theoretically unlimited, and this right derives solely from the freedom of ownership. Therefore, no one has the subjective right to privatization or reprivatization without a relevant state decision or under conditions other than those contained in such a decision. . . . The interpretation of the Constitutional Court concerns legally sound state property." Over time—and parallel with the changes in the concept of compensation—the justifications moved from this abstract-formal argument to calling upon the characteristics of the political transition in Hungary. In the interim, it was clarified that property that was legally nationalized at the time of communism was "legally sound"[107] and the Constitutional Court's theory of continuity was also developed. In the last compensation decision, reviewing the Compensation Act in its entirety,[108] the Constitutional Court stated the consequences explicitly: "No requirement may be deduced from the Constitution according to which the State must return property which, by the standards of the new constitutional state, had been expropriated unconstitutionally by the former regime. In a similar vein, the Constitution does not demand that the State provide full compensation for property damage or loss thus incurred. Finally, nor can that obligation be derived from the Constitution according to which the State is compelled to change retroactively civil or administrative law or the rules of civil procedure, or to provide exemptions from their binding force, in order to enable former owners to recover their property or to receive full compensation." Here the Court reinforced the fact that the Compensation Act does not satisfy claims to ownership of former owners. Compensation does not result from the original legal title. Even if the Court in the meantime recognized that not all cases of compensation were ex gratia and the State might also have legal obligations from some earlier laws, it held that the Compensation Act itself was the source and common legal basis not only for reimbursement claims that are based on a legal duty but also for claims that are based on the Compensation Act without such a prior obligation. The last decision also deals with the problem of justice. "The acquisition of property accompanying the formation of the new system of property rights must be harmonized with the carrying of the burdens of the transition. There is no constitutional justification for the legislature to give preferential treatment by the payment of full compensation to former property owners' claims compared with other victims of the former regime's illegal acts who had also been subjected to economic harm and had suffered moral grievances or, for that matter, compared with society which on the whole had to bear the burdens of the transformation. The legislature acts constitutionally if—as it has done in the Compensation Act—it takes stock of the country's ability to pay, if no group is excluded from the shouldering of the burdens of the transformation, and if the preferentially treated parties are also required to share such burdens proportionately. The Constitutional Court points out that the Compensation Act's imposition of some of the burdens of compensation on those recipients of former state property who had obtained such property for free, including the agricultural co-operatives and local governments, is constitutionally permissible. The less than complete nature of compensation may be regarded as a similar burden. In both cases, as the result of the formation of the new property order, new owners acquire property on the basis of new legal claims and titles."

The compensation cases were also important indicators of how to deal carefully with "unique historical circumstances." In this respect, these decisions were predecessors of the statute of limitations discussion. In other words, the Court needed to disassociate itself as early as 1990 from the view strongly represented in politics that the strict requirements of the rule of law were not to be the measure for acts committed under the dictatorship. However, the Constitutional Court never regarded these situations as comprising exceptions to the Constitution, that is, suspension of the constitutional requirements was never contemplated. The question asked by the Constitutional Court was, "How could the unique and specific historical requirements of the change of system be effected on the basis of legal continuity in a manner which comports with constitutional requirements?"[109] Therefore, the Constitutional Court could not satisfy itself with reliance on historical circumstances. Instead, it sought a concrete justification for the truly unique and exceptional legal solutions in the reform of the regulation of property ownership. The Court especially wanted to clarify the legal nature and basis of the compensation. Therefore, the Court developed more than one standard dogmatic formula to which it returned in subsequent cases. Such are, for instance, the "original burdens" imposed on recipients of free state property, or the *novatio,* a shorthand term indicating that the state may preclude reliance on the old legal titles and reduce the old legal duties to a common denominator and merge them with ex gratia compensation (16/1991).[110]

Compensation for moral damages may be attached to compensation for property damages and to the question of the right to property because any kind of compensation of victims after the system change raises similar questions of morality, justice, and even state finances and further because the Constitutional Court applied the same principles in both types of cases. Once compensation begins, more and more groups in society come to feel that they are no less eligible for compensation than those already satisfied, and governments have to count on new claims when striking the initial balance between justice and the state's financial capacities. In the Hungarian system change, the memory of the 1956 Revolution played a decisive as well as a symbolic role. The beginning of the change was signaled by the revision of the official evaluation of 1956 as a "counterrevolution." The new Republic and the Constitution were proclaimed on the anniversary of the Revolution, 23 October 1989, and the legislation started—fully independent of the later compensations—with rehabilitation of the victims of the suppression of the Revolution: all court sentences were declared null and void by an Act of Parliament, and substantial damages were granted for loss of life and wrongful arrest. Compensation for moral damages was gradually extended to all victims of politically motivated criminal or administrative measures between 1945 and 1989. Finally, the requirement was abandoned according to which the loss of life or liberty had to be suffered in connection with a formal criminal or administrative procedure. Moreover, the period of time covered by such compensation was extended back in time—in harmony with the compensation for property damages—to 1939. The latter has been characteristic of the Hungarian transition: the new regime was to be contrasted not only with communism but also with the prewar authoritarian and the short-lived (1944–45) fascist regimes.

The Constitutional Court accepted that the Compensation Act provided moral damages as a common denominator and a new title for all claims created by the Act that in part might have formerly possessed a legal ground but the enforcement of which was improbable. The equality principle, which was decisive for handling compensation for property losses, became even more important as regards moral damages. The role in these cases of the equal dignity of all human beings gained a new dimension when the Court did not permit the creation of any distinction between loss of life caused by the communist or fascist regimes.[111] Finally, the Court declared constitutionally possible a new allocation of resources for cases in which the number of those entitled for compensation increased in scale. In this way, it showed Parliament how to resolve the contradiction between justice and the ability to finance it (22/1996).

Social Rights

According to a popular misconception, the constitutions of the postcommunist states preserved from the former socialist constitutions a long list of social rights that once represented the superiority of socialism to capitalism. In fact, these rights were no more enlarged upon in these old constitutions than in several Western European constitutions bearing the spirit of the postwar Left, as in Italy or, following the fall of the right-wing dictatorship, Portugal. It is to be remembered, too, that the "social state" has flourished in other countries on the basis of very meager constitutional provisions, such as, for instance, the adjective in German Basic Law declaring the Republic to be a "social" *Rechtsstaat* (Arts. 20, 28). The truth in that belief is that in the socialist regimes the State guaranteed an equally modest level of social security to everybody, unemployment remained hidden because needless workplaces were paid for and maintained. The transition to the market economy uncovered this hidden defect in the former system. Jobs became insecure and unemployment rates—a previously unknown social phenomenon—grew to Western levels of 10 percent or more. The loss of social security was perceived by the population as the gravest negative effect of the system change, and in the second free election many people hoped that the leftist parties would restore the old security.

The Hungarian Constitution speaks in the Preamble of developing a "social market economy." Elsewhere it provides only for the right to work, a free choice of workplace and profession, equal payment for equal work, and payment according to the quality and amount of work done (Art. 70/B). The Constitution further contains a "right" to the best possible physical and mental health. Most importantly, Art. 70/E declares the "citizens of the Republic of Hungary have the right to social security; in the case of old age, sickness, disability, being widowed or orphaned, and in the case of unemployment through no fault of their own, they are entitled to the assistance necessary for their subsistence. The Republic of Hungary shall implement the right to social support through the social security system and the system of social institutions."[112] These provisions have to be cited in full for a correct understanding of the constitutional problems and the position of the Court.

With the right to work there emerged relatively few problems. The Constitutional Court soon turned the treatment of persons with equal dignity into the test of the equality principle (thus, the results-oriented claims to equal payment and other issues failed) and equated the right to work with the right to free enterprise (21/1994). It also stated on the negative side that the right to work secured no subjective right to obtain a given job.[113] More controversial was the interpretation of the right to social security. On no other question was the Court so divided (not even on the presidential power cases). A one-person majority also extended the formal understanding of the rule of law to the "Social State."[114] In turn, these justices held social rights to be a "state goal" against the interpretation of the minority who maintained that they are real subjective rights. The majority succeeded in stating that the State would meet its obligation under Art. 70/E if it organized and operated a social insurance scheme and a system of welfare benefits for those not insured. The means whereby this goal was to be reached was not a constitutional question. Further, it was the opinion of the Court that "social security means neither guaranteed income, nor that the achieved living standard could not deteriorate."[115] Nevertheless, disputes flared up repeatedly in numerous cases on the stability of the value of old-age pensions, in which nearly half of the Court regularly dissented.

The most serious fights concerning social rights occurred in 1995—this time, however, between a unanimous Constitutional Court and the government. That year the government pressed through Parliament an austerity package of laws that, among others, contained serious reductions in social benefits. The government claimed an "economic emergency situation" and therefore paid little attention to the constitutional doubts signaled during the drafting and debate on the bill in Parliament. The Court followed its earlier jurisprudence when it did not allow any exemption from strict constitutionality despite the "extraordinary situation" (as it did not in the compensation and retroactive criminal legislation cases). The series of judgments[116] delivered between July 1995 and the end of the year were in principle favorable to a reform of the whole social security system. For instance, the Court stated, that the legislature did have a constitutional ability to transform welfare benefits due as a citizen's right into a benefit based on the principle of need (43/1995). On the other hand, it struck down several provisions of the austerity package or at least blocked the immediate introduction of some reductions. The government, which did not perceive the judgments from the viewpoint of constitutionality and the constitutional possibilities for reform, felt that the Court was politically blocking its program. The situation resembled that at the peak of the New Deal controversy in the United States. The difference is that there occurred "no switch in time" in the Hungarian Court, and the "nine" were not "saved"—at least in the meaning that the continuity of the jurisprudence of the first Court became endangered.[117]

Unity of the Court was attained in another switch: the Court suspended all discussion on the nature of social rights and separated the question of the constitutional criteria for changing welfare benefits through law from the question of what benefits could be claimed pursuant to the right to social security granted in Art. 70/E. So the decision is not founded on this provision of the Constitution but on the protection of acquired rights and reliance, both understood as parts of an extended protection of the right to property, on the one hand, and on the other on the principle of legal certainty.

The Court utilized its concept of the function of property as the material basis for individual autonomy (64/1993) and combined it with the system of compulsory social insurance, the high contributions to which, in Hungary, amounted to an exclusion of the possibility of other kinds of (privately arranged) security for retirement. According to the Constitutional Court, the mandatory and noncapitalized social insurance scheme burdened the State with a special responsibility for the stability of the system and its benefits. The Court set up a system of criteria against which the speed and other conditions of an essential change in social benefits might be tested. These criteria include the mandatory or voluntary type of insurance, the length of the expectation period of time until the fulfillment of the benefit, the nature of the benefit (whether it is for a short and determined time or for a long period of performance, which bears a greater risk of change), the nature of the financial contribution of the beneficiary, and—last but not least—the public interest justifying the reduction of benefits or even the change in their nature. As to those benefits that are not matched with insurance, the property protection cannot be extended. Here the underlying principle of protection is legal certainty. Its effects, however, cannot be determined with the same generality as can the rather abstract rules and tests for propertylike acquired rights. Therefore, the Court considered more concrete circumstances, too, as in the case of maternity and child allowances, which endanger the balance between the State's obligation to protect life and the right of the mother to self-determination as prescribed in the abortion case (43/1995; 64/1991).

Through these decisions a method became established, and usually applied, according to which an infringement upon the social rights provision of the Constitution could only be sustained if the benefits sank below a minimum level determined by the Constitutional Court. This means that the ordinary test for (subjective) fundamental rights—necessity and proportionality—does not apply. This, in turn, amounts to a silent acceptance by the whole Court of the understanding of social rights as being similar to "state goals," for which, as in the case of the market economy or free competition, only excessive infringements reach the level of constitutional significance. This minimum-level test was not decisive—although it was mentioned[118]—in the leading case on family allowances, but it became decisive in many subsequent ones on withdrawing free medical care in several fields. Other cases—for instance, one raising interest rates for housing loans—were decided on the equality clause. Another, which extended the use of the PIN, was decided on the right to informational self-determination.[119] Although these cases could not be included in this book, they demonstrate that the Constitutional Court did not handle the austerity package of the government and the plans to reform the social security system on an ideological basis and less with any intent to conserve the old socialist paternalistic allocation of benefits. On the contrary, the Court accepted the challenge of hard cases and decided each of them on the most suitable basis, always in line with the principles developed earlier. Moreover, the Court drew upon the jurisprudence of other European constitutional courts and reached similar results.[120]

III. Constitutional Principles: The Rule of Law, Democracy, and Equality before the Law

The Rule of Law

Of all constitutional principles, the rule of law played a special, symbolic role: it represented the essence of the system change, being the watershed between the nondemocratic, nonconstitutional, socialist system and the new constitutional democracy. Therefore the rule of law was the constitutional concept in the frame of which the differences in nature and characteristics of the system change could find their expression.[121] Even the traditional difference between the formal and substantial concepts of the *Rechtsstaat* (the formally legal functioning of state machinery as opposed to the protection of fundamental rights) was revived and had to be reinterpreted. There were two ways in which the system change could be adhered to: on one hand, a rather value-neutral, formalistic approach, emphasizing procedural guarantees, legal continuity, and, above all, legal certainty; and on the other hand substantive justice, allowing exceptions from formal guarantees of rights under exceptional circumstances and emphasizing the total break with previous law. Both conceptions have become embedded in wider concepts of "restoration" or a "prospective" type of transition, interdependently, again, with the particular history of the given countries. Hungary (and especially the Constitutional Court, which elaborated the concept) opted for a more neutral and formalistic understanding of the rule of law. From about 1965 on, state socialism in this country was mild; steps toward a market economy had been taken in the 1980s, and suppression of freedoms was not omnipresent or brutal.[122] Paradoxically, even these facts gave the rule of law a unique importance in Hungary: here—and only here—the contrast with the old regime was absolute. The Court made both the politicians and the population conscious of the secure protection of constitutional rights (and through this, of the difference between permission and right) and aware of one of the most important characteristics of the rule of law: political intentions can only be implemented lawfully and within the framework of the Constitution—not vice versa, as before, when the law was conceived as merely a political tool.

It is important to note that the formalistic understanding of the rule of law in Hungary must not be mistaken for a formal legalism that is independent of the quality of the legal rules to be observed and therefore is possible even in dictatorships. On its own, the constitutional order in itself excludes such an interpretation. The Court, moreover, developed a moral explanation of its position. It introduced the paradoxical phrase "revolution under the rule of law." The Court thinks that if revolutionary changes have been introduced by strictly keeping all constitutional guarantees then the system change may be considered to be of a morally higher value than the previous, similarly revolutionary changes, for by respecting constitutional limitations it cannot repeat the crimes and injustices that revolutions usually understand, on the basis of their ideologies, to be justified and permissible. The Hungarian Court has been balancing legal certainty—which presupposes a positivist approach and avoids the basing of decisions on natural law principles or "the values of the Constitution" in general—and a moral reading of the content of particular rights in hard cases, wherein the relevant values may be determined on a broad theoretical and comparative law basis referred to that particular right. This explains, too, how this "positivist" Court can at the same time be an activist Court.

The conceptual differences in the rule of law manifest themselves naturally in the cases in which unavoidable themes of the system change are decided upon and in which formal guarantees and the demand for justice necessarily conflict: compensation for nationalized or confiscated property and retroactive criminal legislation. Accordingly, the Constitutional Court also discussed the rule of law in the context of system change in a series of decisions on these subjects in 1992 (case nos. 9, 10, and 11). These contributed to the technical concept of the rule of law, as well, insofar as they settled legal certainty as to its "essential element." Other technical aspects of the use of this principle will be discussed later. First, some additional explanations of the concept as it has been applied by the Court may be appropriate.

The Court considered the relationship between the rule of law and the system change from different viewpoints. In the statute of limitations case (11/1992), the Constitutional Court presumed that the change of regimes could not mean anything for the law other than that the entire legal order was to conform (or have its conformity retained) to the new Constitution based on the rule of law. The two key concepts of the Constitutional Court with respect to the change of regimes are legality and the rule of law. Because the transition proceeded on the basis of legality (respecting the legislative rules of the old regime and commenced formally by the old, communist Parliament), the Constitutional Court does not distinguish between preconstitutional and postconstitutional law: regardless of when they came into existence, all legal norms should be in compliance with the currently valid Constitution. The Constitutional Court distinguishes between legality and legitimacy: the legitimacy of previous regimes cannot be meaningfully interpreted with respect to the constitutionality of legal norms. In this sense, the Constitutional Court took a position in the debate as to whether a revolution had occurred in Hungary: it applied the paradoxical phrase "revolution under the rule of law." As a practical result, the Constitutional Court supported the principle of legality and the continuity of law, which, however, did not contradict a clear prejudice for a future-oriented transition of systems in the face of all attempts at restoration. In case special assessment of the laws of the old regime would nonetheless be necessary—notwithstanding the recognition of the continuity of law and legality—the Constitutional Court would decide on the basis of the priority of legal certainty. From the beginning, the Constitutional Court developed the content of the rule of law through legal certainty. The two terms were constantly mentioned together. Later the formula was established in which legal certainty is an essential component of the rule of law.

Another group of decisions relied on the continuity of law and on the protection of already established legal relationships. In the *ex nunc* decision (10/1992), legal certainty and the change of regimes were explicitly related to each other: the unlimited susceptibility to challenge of all legal norms of the past—considering the radical changes to the Constitution—should in the interests of legal certainty be counterbalanced by the rule that established legal relationships should remain unchanged: "The result of unconstitutionality of a legal norm must above all else be reached under considerations of legal certainty."

In a third group of decisions, the Constitutional Court occupied itself with the relationship between formal legal certainty and justice. This basic problem was addressed in the decision on protests of illegality (9/1992) with respect to the possible contradiction between the requirement of fair judicial opinions and *res judicata.* According to the Constitutional Court, material justice can only be realized in the framework of legal institutions and guarantees that serve legal certainty; the Constitution does not guarantee any subjective right "to enforcement of substantive justice." This was repeated in the first statute of limitations decision and expanded by means of the thesis that the unjust result of a legal relationship in and of itself is no argument against legal certainty. The summary stated: "Legal certainty which is based upon objective and formal principles is always to be preferred to partial and subjective justice." It is noteworthy that the Constitutional Court was not satisfied with justifying the compensation legislation by invoking "justice" but required a legal basis for it.

In accordance with these explanations, the Court insisted that, while the exceptional character of the historical situation can be taken into account, it cannot lead to the suspension of requirements of constitutionality: "The constitutional state cannot be realized by non-constitutional means" (11/1992). The Constitutional Court should always ask the question: "How could the unique and specific historical requirements of the change of system be effected on the basis of legal continuity in a manner that complies with constitutional requirements?" This role of legal certainty in the transition was at the basis of decisions that dealt with the political transition, not only in the celebrated cases on compensation and retroactive punishment but on the everyday issues of the change dealing with, for instance, the fate of assets of the "old" Socialist Party or of the "old" unions.[123] The principle of legal certainty even appeared throughout the decisions on the competence of the President of the Republic—albeit not expressly—in that the Constitutional Court specified the limits of presidential authority in order to prevent an organization of the competences through political agreements made in concrete cases ("customary law") on the basis of factual power relationships or of the principle of "to the victor go the spoils" (48/1991). It must be seen, however, that "exceptional circumstances" occur not only in the context of political changes that amount to a revolutionary transition from an authoritarian regime to democracy. These are the rather common arguments of governments and lawmakers who wish to justify political solutions that test the guarantees of constitutions in cases of difficult social problems, not only in "emergency situations"[124] but in times of restrictions on social benefit systems. Even the Hungarian Court faced the argument of an "economic emergency situation" in 1995—and refused to accept it.[125]

The technical handling of the principle of the rule of law has run an opposite course compared with other general clauses of the Constitution such as the "mother right" to human dignity or the principles of a market economy and free competition. First, the Court refused to take this as a sufficient basis for establishing a violation of the Constitution. Rather, it required the encumbrances on other, named, constitutional rights that were all seen as components of the rule of law.[126] Then the rule of law developed rapidly to become on its own a sufficient basis of unconstitutionality. This has been the firm practice of the Court since 1992.[127] Of course, this was made possible by the fact that particular rights, the violation of which had originally been required, were replaced with principles held to be the genuine content of and tests for the rule of law. The two underlying principles were legal certainty and the coherence of the Constitution. Both developed their particular components.

So legal certainty is infringed if the wording of a law is not clear and unambiguous enough (see, e.g., 11/1992). By means of legal certainty, the Court enforced the constitutional practice of promulgation of laws. Numerous decisions annulled legal norms because their promulgation occurred after the date of their entry into force or because too short a time frame was left between their publication and their entry into force.[128] After a series of small-scale cases, this principle was connected with the enlarged protection of property rights: the too hasty abolition of maternal and child benefits contradicted the reliance principle or the protection of acquired rights (43/1995). So legal certainty became the principal test for social security cases. The principle of legal certainty also prevailed in decisions that largely excluded free discretion in connection with the assertion of fundamental rights: these decisions concerned rules of (mainly civil and administrative) procedure.[129]

The other technical pillar of the rule of law, to maintain the principled coherence of the Constitution, had already been stressed as a vocation of the Constitutional Court in the death penalty decision. The expression used in my concurring opinion as a metaphor for this, the "invisible constitution," was scandalous in the eyes of Parliament, which read it as a metaphor for the activism and countermajoritarian aspirations of the Court. The coherence question remained connected with the scope of competences even within the Constitutional Court and reached a climax in the presidential power decisions, where the different positions concerning the interpretation of internal contradictions and the filling of gaps within the Constitution divided the Court. In "normal" cases, however, those not too close to a "political question," the coherence has remained a guiding principle for the jurisprudence of the Court on the rule of law.

Finally, it is to be emphasized that the Constitutional Court's practice regarding procedural guarantees as a whole[130] and the separation of powers is part and parcel of the conception of the Court of the rule of law. As to the separation of powers, the independence of the judiciary, the President, and local governments is dealt with in subsequent chapters. On this subject, the Court also set down the principle of cooperation between the highest constitutional organs, a constitutional requirement that seemed hard to grasp in the fresh state machinery, each organ having been occupied too much with its own interests.[131]

The Principle of Democracy

Although the Preamble of the Constitution lists among the goals of the transition "parliamentary democracy" and Art. 2 declares the Republic of Hungary to be a "democratic state under the rule of law," the Constitutional Court has never dealt directly with the principle of democracy. This principle is not mentioned separately in the Constitution either; it rather forms part of parliamentarianism, or of the rule of law, with which the Court has dealt excessively.[132] Nevertheless, singular aspects of the democracy principle have unavoidably been present in the jurisdiction of the Constitutional Court. For instance, the problem of democratic legitimacy and the countermajoritarian difficulty have lain under all discussions concerning the Court's powers and limits, its "activism," and the problem of filling the gaps or eliminating the contradictions in the Constitution by the Court. It may be characteristic of European constitutional courts that the countermajoritarian difficulty remains rather hidden. The explanation may be that all these courts were established in the course of a transition from an authoritarian to a democratic regime; they were foreseen in the new constitutions as an indispensable guarantee of this new quality of the political system and the state; therefore they possessed a kind of "revolutionary legitimacy" that made them self-conscious. Even activism seems to be necessary for the stabilization of a new order within the shortest possible time.[133] One kind of decision addresses the democratic representation principle relatively openly: when the Court cedes to the democratically elected legislator the definition of the "public interest" or the economic policy necessary to develop the "market economy," reserving the possibility of constitutional review only for extreme cases (64/1993; 21/1994). Admittedly, the Court was moved to self-restraint as regards the determination of the public interest by the example of the European Court of Human Rights.

Of course, institutional problems of democracy emerged before the Court, such as the relationship between representative and direct democracy or the role of political parties. The Court requires for the constitutionality of rules of popular referenda that the quorum for validity and the rules of the result have to be shaped in a way that guarantees that the will of the (simple) majority of the enfranchised citizens prevails. This had to be stated because local governments regularly established rules for local referenda that blocked the effective enforcement of the popular will.[134] Regarding other self-governing bodies, the Court justified obligatory membership in commercial and industrial chambers by the need for a right to elect rule-making bodies if the rules are obligatory and enforceable against all those active in the commerce or industry.[135]

The Act on Popular Initiatives and Referenda[136] stemmed from the time immediately before the new Constitution. Representing the then political situation, it provided for an extraordinarily low quorum (100,000 signatures) for the obligatory declaration of a national referendum. On the other hand, the Act contained only a very short list of subjects exempt from referenda (such as tax laws and the state budget). In 1992, a parliamentary party collected more than 100,000 signatures requesting a referendum on the dissolution of Parliament. The Constitution defines the criteria for the dissolution of Parliament, and referenda are not among them. On the motion of the Constitutional Committee of the Parliament, the Court delivered an abstract interpretation (advisory opinion) of that provision, holding that "in the constitutional order of the Republic of Hungary the primary form of exercising popular sovereignty is by representation. A popular referendum can decide on subjects within the competence of the Parliament only on the basis of the Constitution and constitutional laws. . . . The question to be decided through popular referendum may not be directed at a hidden amendment of the Constitution." The Court declared that the cases of dissolution, as defined in the Constitution, represented all the cases: therefore Parliament cannot be forced to dissolve itself by a referendum, which would be a new ground for dissolution.[137]

In summer 1997, Parliament brought detailed rules on referenda into the Constitution, providing that when at least 200,000 voters petition for a national referendum Parliament is obliged to hold one, using for the question the wording formulated in the petition (Art. 28/C(2), "obligatory referendum"). In contrast, a referendum initiated by the President, the government, one-third of the MPs, or 100,000 voters remains within the discretion of Parliament as to whether one shall be held as well as to the wording of the question (Art. 28/C(4), "discretionary referendum").[138] Parliament and government obviously looked at this amendment as a merely technical measure elevating (slightly amended) provisions of the Referendum Act to the level of the Constitution. So it occurred that, after submitting an initiative of 200,000 voters to the Speaker of the Parliament, and during the verification of the signatures, the government approved by its parliamentary majority its own initiative for a referendum on the same issue.[139] In the end, the Parliamentary Commissioner for Civil Rights requested an interpretation of the new constitutional provision. In Decision 52/1997, the Constitutional Court made it clear that rules on referenda in the Constitution have a different bearing than statutory rules do: the relationship between direct and representative democracy had been restated by the amendment in question. The Court held that the direct exercise of power by the people, as defined in Art. 2(2) of the Constitution, was represented in its entirety by the obligatory referendum: both the initiation (including the determination of the question to be decided) and enforceability (regarding the holding of the referendum and the binding force of its result) were under the control of the people and outside the power of organs of the representative democracy. On the other hand, the Court maintained that, although a mandatory referendum was an exceptional form of exercise of the people's sovereign rights, in exceptional situations (limited by the Constitution and excluding certain issues from referendum) it could prevail over the representative organs. So Parliament was obliged not only to ensure that the referendum was held but also to refrain from any act or omission that could influence or frustrate the realization of such exercise, even to the point of preventing government and other state organs from committing like acts or omissions. Accordingly, the petition of at least 200,000 voters directed at an obligatory referendum enjoys precedence over all kinds of discretionary referenda directly on the basis of the Constitution and from the submission of the signatures to the Speaker of Parliament. The Court mandated a complete revision of statutory provisions on referenda as well and prescribed that constitutional requirements be provided for in the revised or new law. Among them, the most important was access to the Constitutional Court in the form of a constitutional complaint against decisions in the matter of referenda.

The Principle of Equality before the Law

An alleged violation of the equality clause[140] is the complaint that most frequently appears in applications for judicial review from the general population. One can suspect the lasting influence of the socialist ideology of equality but also the circumstance that, for a naïve conception of law, equality is the constitutional principle that is most easily understood. Citizens who feel that they have been disadvantaged consider the better circumstances of another person, that is, the difference, to be "unconstitutional." (One lesson from the *actio popularis* was the applicants' rigid formal understanding of equality.) In contrast, the Constitutional Court made its support known early for a differentiated implementation of the equality clause. It considered positive discrimination to be permissible but on the other hand shifted its standard for evaluating the discrimination from result to methodology. Under the new approach, distribution of entitlements was to be determined with the same circumspection and consideration of individual points of view. In this way, everyone would be treated equally, that is to say, as persons with equal dignity.[141] A detailed test was soon provided for this equal treatment (21/1990). For a distinction to be constitutional, the Court required proof that reprivatization would be more favorable for establishing the market economy than commercial privatization or that the total social effect of the discrimination would be more favorable than the result of equal treatment.[142] Subsequently, though, this complicated thought process was not followed. The requirement remained that equal treatment had to relate to the essential factual elements of the regulatory concept. Otherwise, the standard of review was reduced to proving the "constitutional basis" of the distinction and to the formula of equal dignity.

In 1992, the Constitutional Court stated "that the prohibition of discrimination according to Art. 70/A(1) of the Constitution—in the case of a violation of the right to human dignity—extends to the entire legal order," that is, that this principle extends beyond the text of the Constitution regarding "human and citizens rights" and also includes other rights.[143] The Constitutional Court did not succumb to the pressure of popular opinion; rather, it articulated clearly its earlier practice.[144]

This expansive interpretation of the equality clause, in my opinion, is inherent in the nature of the constitutional mandate. Through the obligation to consider equally the individual points of view of every party, that is, their treatment as persons of equal dignity with respect to every right, the equality clause can play a similar role as, for example, a *substantive due process clause.* The problem led to the review of the constitutionality of restrictions on rights beyond the group of fundamental rights. The Constitutional Court stated that simple rights also enjoy the protection of the Constitution, although the criteria for determining the unconstitutionality of restrictions on such rights are milder than for fundamental rights. The "arbitrary" or "lacking every rational basis" restriction of a nonfundamental right can be unconstitutional. This result emerged as the Court reconciled the different methods used previously to extend constitutional protection to nonfundamental rights: the use of protection of "state goals" and "constitutional values"; the feedback of a subsidiary "violation of human dignity" as a link between declaring discrimination concerning simple rights unconstitutional and the wording of Art. 70/A(1) of the Constitution, which speaks of "human and civil rights"; and finally applying specific criteria for certain violations of rights—such as legal certainty—and within this the requirement of clarity of the text of a law. Arbitrariness is thus incompatible with legal certainty, that is, with the rule of law. Similarly, if the discrimination is arbitrary, that is, if it is unjustified or does not have a reasonable cause, then it violates the right to human dignity because in such cases the affected persons were certainly not treated as persons of equal dignity and their viewpoints were not considered with equal care and fairness. Arbitrariness is thus in conflict with the rule of law, equal treatment, and human dignity even when it does not affect fundamental rights.[145]

IV. The Law of State Organization

The Legal Status of the President of the Republic

Throughout the political upheaval in Central and Eastern Europe, the state president appears to have played a unique role. Distinctions must be drawn, however, between personal and historical circumstances on the one hand and constitutional questions on the other. The question of whether a powerful and popular (directly elected) president was required for stability during the change of regimes was fully discussed during the roundtable process of drafting the Constitution and, in good Hungarian tradition, was decided in the negative. Accordingly, presidential powers that correspond to the parliamentary system were included in the Constitution.[146]

Only one of the decisions on presidential powers has been included in this volume (48/1991). This case deals with the competences of the President of the Republic as commander in chief of the armed forces, his power of appointment, and the relationship between the inviolability of the President and his protection from criminal prosecution. Two further decisions develop the theme of the power of appointment. This shows that the debate over the President's right of refusal was understood above all else in the context of the real political situation of the "media war," which dragged on for years.[147] The question was whether the President of the Republic can refuse to sign the dismissal of the chairmen of Hungarian (public) radio and television as proposed by the Prime Minister, and, if so, under what conditions.

It is telling that even the dissenting opinions in the first decision only reject the majority's interpretation of the power of appointment, although the decision is based on a uniform understanding of the legal status of the President and the importance of the power of command extends far beyond the power of appointment. While the new Armed Forces Act was passed in accordance with the decision of the Constitutional Court and the Constitution was even amended accordingly,[148] the battle over appointments did not die because both affected parties—the President and the Prime Minister—interpreted the Court's decision as justifying their original positions. Because the application to the Court had been for an abstract interpretation of the Constitution—and not, for example, for the decision "on conflicts of competence"—it was not possible, in spite of considerable political pressure, to state whether or not the President had acted unconstitutionally in the particular case. Two subsequent applications by the Prime Minister sought a clearer answer to this specific question. The Constitutional Court had to reject several partial questions in the third application because they were too closely tied to the President's justifications for refusing the dismissals and could not be answered with the generality required for an abstract constitutional interpretation. In the wake of the decisions, the interpretations necessarily became ever more concrete[149] until the Constitutional Court reached the limits of its competences. The results of interpretation are in part only further specifications—and thus restrictions—on the limits of the power to review nominations that had been laid down in the first decision; on the other hand, they can only be explained with reference to the case at hand because they are otherwise obvious conditions.[150] The repeated determination of these "self-evident rules" was the outside limit to which the Constitutional Court could go in applying its interpretation to concrete cases without stepping beyond its bounds.[151]

The truly lasting significance of these decisions lies not in the media debate itself. The predicament in which the Court found itself was that the politicians considered constitutional interpretation—and thus the Constitutional Court—to be simply a tool in their dispute. This, as well as the fact that the Constitutional Court had to decide with general validity more on the broad constitutional questions presented than on the actual dispute, is reflected in the decisions as the clarification of important methodological questions. This is closely related to the fact that throughout the proceedings the President of the Republic repeatedly presented his position on the constitutional status of his office. The decision on the constitutionality of how the President perceived himself and his understanding of the role of the presidency lent the decisions a unique importance in the protection of the constitutional parliamentary system.

The President understands his office to be part of the executive branch, within which the Constitution regulates the distribution of competences in most cases either partially, contradictorily or not at all: "Pending the problem's resolution in a new Constitution, these conflicts of competence should be mitigated through arrangements made between the President and the Prime Minister establishing constitutional customary law." With respect to the administrative machinery reporting to the Prime Minister, the President did not want to exercise any authority of review. "However, when the given organ according to the political agreement relating to this or to the laws passed after the transition is not an administrative organ or if it is not (entirely) subject to the direction of the government"—such as the national public media or the armed forces—an appointment can only be made on the basis of a consensus between the President of the Republic and the Prime Minister.[152] However, this position was not supported by positive constitutional provisions. Rather—as has been seen—it derived from the "gaps" in the Constitution.[153]

The first decision stressed that the President stands outside of the executive and that the above construction could not be derived from the Constitution. The Constitution precisely precludes the legal basis for such a collective exercise of power. The concurring opinions go even farther in that they clarify the concept and constitutional law scope of customary law and establish that "constitutional provisions to be interpreted cannot gain a practically accepted essence through agreement between those exercising power."

Inseparable from the preceding question is whether gaps exist in the Constitution and, if so, whether they can be removed by interpretation and who is authorized to carry out such an interpretation. In contrast to the position of the President—who admonished the Constitutional Court to interpret the Constitution literally[154]—one of the concurring opinions explicitly described the method applied in the decision: the Court understands the Constitution to be a unified and consistent system, and there can be neither contradictions nor gaps between the individual provisions of the Constitution that would thwart the decision of constitutional questions. According to the other concurring opinion, the Court would be denying its fundamental task if, because of such a gap, it gave no answer: "The Court's interpretative power is aimed at ensuring the unity of the constitutional system."

The decision was reached through a systematic listing of all of the competences of the President and the rules that depend on his legal status, that is, it presupposed unity in the Constitution. Several times the decision mentioned that all competences must be consistent "with the constitutional status of the President of the Republic in a parliamentary system." Indeed, it was really concerned with the parliamentary constitutional system.

The Constitutional Court relied exclusively on a systematic interpretation in addressing these fundamental questions, although the minutes of the roundtable negotiations could have provided extensive material for the "weak position" of the President agreed to there. This case represents that in its early years the Constitutional Court refrained in general from historical interpretation, perhaps being too close to the roundtable negotiations, the process that led to the Constitution. Today the Court draws upon legislative history: the case on reviewability of international treaties shows this (4/1997(I.22)AB: ABH 1997, 41; MK 7/1997).

The Independence of the Courts

According to the Constitution, judges are independent and subject only to the law. Judges may not belong to a political party or be politically active. The professional judges are to be appointed by the President of the Republic in a legally prescribed process, and the President of the Supreme Court is elected by Parliament with a two-thirds majority upon the proposal of the President of the Republic. Judges may only be removed from their offices for reasons established by an Act and according to the procedures specified therein. Until the amendment of the Constitution in June 1997, both the old and the new Judicature Acts[155] transferred considerable administrative authority to the Minister of Justice—on the condition that its exercise does not violate the independence of the judiciary.

According to the 1991 version of the Act, the Minister of Justice appoints heads of the courts (presidents and vice presidents of the courts of second instance) and proposes the appointment of judges to the President of the Republic. These and other powers were challenged as provisions that violate judicial independence. The occasion for the applications was the interpretation of provisions on cooperation between various judicial bodies and the Minister of Justice in the appointment process. The minister viewed only a single positive vote just as a positive opinion and as the proposed appointment from that body, even when other candidates had achieved majority support. The decision of the Constitutional Court (38/1993(VI.11)AB)[156] specified the sphere of constitutional interpretation of the appointment rules. The decision stated as a general rule that a counterbalance was constitutionally required to mediate the possible political points of view of those who are authorized by another power to appoint, regardless of whether this counterweight is set up inside or outside of the judiciary. The Court ruled that a majority vote of the relevant bodies of judges represented a sufficient guarantee. This method was applied in a series of cases (concerning the administration of the courts' budget by the ministry or the possibility of awarding honors to judges by the government).[157]

On the one hand, the significance of the decision lies in introducing the method of the determination of the scope of possible "constitutional interpretations of a law," that is, maintaining it in force with a given constitutional meaning instead of declaring it null and void. On the other hand, the Constitutional Court takes a critical look at the contemporary meaning of the separation of powers and provides the substantive criteria for independence of the judicial power. The recent amendment to the Constitution, which created an independent Judicial Council (in its majority consisting of and elected by judges) for the proposal of appointments of judges, is fully in line with the view of the Constitutional Court on the independence of the judiciary.

Protection of the Autonomy of Local Governments

The freely elected Parliament considered its first task to be replacement of the socialist system of "local councils" with autonomous local governments. In the summer of 1990, a constitutional amendment secured the right to local government[158] for the voters of a community (the city, the capital city and its districts, and the counties). The Constitution supplied the local governments with "fundamental rights." To protect this autonomy, the Constitution states further that the local government can call on the Constitutional Court to protect its rights. A local representative body can only be dissolved by Parliament if its activities are unconstitutional; the government can submit a corresponding proposal after it obtains an opinion from the Constitutional Court.[159] The local council under socialism administered the state property allocated to it; the local governments received a considerable portion of former state property as their own. The Constitution guarantees in several places the right to property of the local governments.[160]

According to these constitutional provisions, the role of the Court consists of the protection of the newly established autonomy of the local governments. On the other hand, however, the Constitutional Court provides for review of the legality of community lawmaking.[161] The "hierarchical review"—as developed by the Constitutional Court—raises the question of consistency in all three levels of the hierarchy of norms. It could be, namely, that a municipal ordinance corresponds to an Act but contradicts the Constitution or violates the Act but is substantively constitutional. The Constitutional Court includes all three levels in its review and always considers the substantive constitutionality to be relevant.[162]

The protective function of the Constitutional Court is organized upon acceptance of the notion that independence of the local governments must be protected from the central government. In fact, another situation prevails, at least when one considers the numbers: much more, the citizen must be protected from the local government,[163] and the consistency of the legal system has to be maintained in the face of divergent local lawmaking. Notwithstanding this practical summary, the decisions of the Constitutional Court achieved lasting significance due to the clarification of the constitutional content of local government autonomy.

A typical application[164] presumes the nonlimitability of "the fundamental rights of the local governments." But the Constitutional Court never saw a quasi-federative structure in the autonomy of the local governments. Only the ex post facto review of a municipal ordinance could be viewed as a concealed quasi-federative competence review when it is to be decided whether the local government, which is the representative body, exceeded the limits of its lawmaking competence. As in the case of the initial absolutist claims to protection of property, only over time did the Constitutional Court clarify the limits to the fundamental rights of local government. The two themes were also closely related to each other in that the most disputed fundamental right of local government was its "right to property."

The significance of the decision on the freedom of religion (4/1993) extended to the interpretation of the fundamental rights of the local governments. According to the Court, the "fundamental rights" specified in Art. 44/A of the Constitution are indeed the competences of the representative body that are indispensable for the autonomy of the local government—above all else, vis-à-vis the government—and thus cannot be removed by legislative act. The Constitutional Court acknowledged only the right of local voters to have a local government (Art. 42 of the Constitution) as a "true" fundamental right.

On the basis of the gaps in the legal provisions on conditions for local referenda and empowerment of the local governments to regulate their affairs, very different local regulations developed, the unconstitutionality of which often had to be established. The Constitutional Court considered this situation to be unconstitutional, established the omission of the legislature, and called on it to provide by law the fundamental conditions and guarantees for local referenda.[165]

The most frequently disputed fundamental right is the local governments' right to property. Violations of this right were claimed in two regards: on the one hand, in connection with the acquisition of property, that is, the transfer of state property to the local governments; and on the other hand with respect to restrictions and the burdening of property by subsequent state legislation. The Constitutional Court determined on principle early on that local governments have no right to acquire state property and even less to obtain given assets or any portion of them. Further, contemporaneously with the transfer of property at no charge, the new owners can be burdened with encumbrances resulting from the conversion of the property ownership system (16/1991). It was often disputed whether the encumberance of the property arose before the transfer or only after it. The property transfers occurred in numerous stages and on the basis of various laws, which were not without technical flaws. In the interest of legal certainty, as a rule the Constitutional Court precluded the possibility of subsequent correction of the transfers: possible conceptual errors in the conversion of the property ownership system could only be corrected by observing the constitutionality of the acquired rights. This was affirmed and expanded upon in the local government apartments decision (64/1993).

With sufficient foresight on the part of the legislature, subsequent restrictions on the property already acquired by local governments could have been specified as encumbrances that had occurred before the transfer. For example, the return of certain buildings to the churches appeared only in the official rationale for the bill dealing with the transfer of assets to local governments. Thus, according to the decision on freedom of religion, protection was available to the local governments with respect to the former church buildings (4/1993). In the local government apartments case, on the other hand, the reservation of future regulation of the transfer of rental apartments was sufficient for the constitutionality of a subsequent law establishing the option to purchase the apartments by the tenants (64/1993).

The benefit of these decisions was the new interpretation of the right to property, including social burdens and the distinction between civil law ownership and the fundamental right to property. These matters also provided the occasion for turning the classical function of property to the benefit of the individual as the material foundation of his or her autonomy.

While selecting—and later editing—the cases in this book, I intended to provide a comprehensive picture of both the role of the Constitutional Court in the formation of a constitutional democracy in Hungary and the development of the constitutional doctrine/theory. I also wanted to show that these developments did not constitute a one-way street: a new court not only received the wisdom of its elder brothers but might contribute to the common constitutional culture with its own ideas. For a judge who has been involved in these events, all cases seem important, and, indeed, in that foundational period even the smallest may later become a hard and significant case. During negotiations with the publisher on the number of words to be included here, I came to realize that it will be history that makes the true selection. As this book leaves the press, my term and that of the first Constitutional Court of Hungary will be over. Our work will be done. We will leave matters to the judgment of history and, in the representation of history, to that of the reader.

NOTES

1. The citations for the decisions in this book are from the *Hungarian (Official) Gazette* (*Magyar Közlöny* [MK]) since this source may be the most accessible in the United States. The references are to the number of the issue of the *Hungarian Official Gazette* in which the decision was published. Additionally, the yearly volumes of the official collection of the decisions of the Constitutional Court (*Alkotmánybíróság Határozatai*

[ABH]) have also been referenced. Several decisions can be obtained in English and German in the CODICES data base of the European Commission for Democracy through Law (Venice Commission). Decisions included in this book are cited by number and year (e.g., 8/1990).

2. ABH 1994, 197; MK 68/1994.

3. ABH 1994, 219; MK 68/1994.

4. ABH 1994, 177; MK 68/1994.

5. ABH 1993, 99; MK 22/1993.

6. ABH 1997, 107; MK 35/1997.

7. ABH 1996, 165; MK 102/1996.

8. ABH 1997, 249; MK 58/1997.

9. ABH 1997, 282; MK 58/1997.

10. ABH 1995, 351; MK 109/1995.

11. ABH 1993, 256; MK 75/1993.

12. ABH 1993, 33; MK 6/1993.

13. Ironically, even the law abolishing the preventive review was submitted to preventive review, but the Constitutional Court could not maintain it. This competence was given to the Court by the Constitutional Court Act and not by the Constitution (66/1997(XII.29): ABH 1997, 397; MK 120/1997). Thus, the preventive review on the merits of a bill shared the fate of its Spanish predecessor, which was abolished in 1985. At the present time, the President of the Republic has the constitutionally mandated competence to ask the Constitutional Court for review before promulgation of a law. This competence—in contrast to the preventive review applied for by Members of Parliament (MPs)—was very much alive during the first legislative period. The President brought before the Constitutional Court all significant laws to which the opposition had raised constitutional objections during the debate in Parliament. Between 1990 and 1994, nine such cases were decided by the Court. Following the election of a new government in 1994, the President refrained from this practice. Regardless of debates on the constitutionality of bills, he signed and promulgated all laws (cf. n. 151).

14. This method was first applied in 38/1993(VI.11)AB: ABH 1993, 256; MK 75/1993.

15. See, for instance, 36/1994(VI.24)AB: ABH 1994, 219; MK 68/1994 on government defamation. Cf. note 36 and accompanying text.

16. For example, the Hungarian Constitution contains no permanence clause such as that included in the Basic Law of Germany.

17. The Court has construed a "right to marry" when it declared requesting the permission of his or her commander for the marriage of a member of the armed forces unconstitutional, 22/1992(IV. 10)AB: ABH 1992, 122; MK 38/1992.

18. Cf. note 61 and accompanying text.

19. Cf. note 72 and accompanying text.

20. The reasoning of the Hungarian Constitutional Court has been followed by the Constitutional Court of the Republic of South Africa, which eliminated the death penalty immediately after the system change. (S. V. Makwanyane, 1995(4)BCLR 665). The decision of the Hungarian Court was not received without debate. A favorite argument against the Court contends that it exceeded its competences because elimination of the death penalty was necessarily a matter for Parliament to address. This position lacks a legal basis. During the long process, which was well known to the public, there was no relevant initiative in the

Parliament for such an Act. Following a series of infamous murder cases, reinstatement of the death penalty was regularly called for. Some political parties turned this into a campaign issue in the 1994 election and even on the eve of the 1998 one. According to the receptivity of the people to such slogans and the repeated attempts to organize a referendum on the reintroduction of the death penalty, it would appear that a large majority of the population remains in favor of it. On the other hand, elimination of the death penalty is in accordance with the European Convention on Human Rights and its Sixth Protocol, which Hungary ratified after the Constitutional Court's decision in 1993. The abortion decision and the subsequent legislative process, on the other hand, sparked surprisingly little public interest.

21. The ordinance in force at the time—a decree of the minister of health permitting abortion on quite generous indications—could be repealed on formal grounds: rules that affect fundamental rights must be determined by an Act according to Art. 8(2) of the Constitution. On the other hand, it was necessary to establish that abortion really affected fundamental rights and so required regulation by means of an Act.

22. See Act 79/1992 on the Protection of Unborn Life. The Act also requires obligatory counseling, which need not, however, persuade the woman to forego the abortion. Following entry into force of the Act, the number of abortions declined, but after a while it rose again and superseded all previous numbers.

23. See further 22/1997(IV.25)AB: ABH 1997, 107; MK 35/1997; 46/1994(X.21) AB: ABH 1994, 260, MK 103/1994; and 64/1991.

24. The Court emphasized in the abortion decision that a change in the legal status of human beings is only possible in the extensive meaning; any retreat from the status quo would be considered unconstitutional.

25. 35/1994(VI.24)AB: ABH 1994, 197; MK 68/1994. See also notes 143 and 145 and accompanying text.

26. Even before this decision, the right to protection of personal data had been interpreted as informational self-determination (dissenting opinion of Sólyom, 2/1990(II.8) AB: ABH 1990, 18, (22); MK 16/1990), and subsequently the entry of personal identification numbers in business registers was repealed (11/1990(V.1)AB: ABH 1990, 156, MK 40/1990; 18/1990(VIII.1)AB: ABH 1990, 178, MK 74/1990).

27. Cf. note 116 and accompanying text. The relevant decision was 46/1995 (VI.30)AB: ABH 1995, 219; MK 56/1995. The 1991 decision was determinative for the Data Protection Act 1992, which is structured completely in accordance with the principles laid down in the decision. Only the PIN survived until 1996. The three new identification numbers are the tax number, the social security number, and the old PIN, which remains for the use of courts and public administration authorities.

28. 32/1992(V.29)AB: ABH 1992, 182; MK 54/1992.

29. 15/1995(III.13)AB: ABH 1995, 88; MK 20/1995.

30. ABH 1994, 177; MK 68/1994. The petitioners sought review of a series of government decrees dating from 1969, which regulated research into public archives as well as classified materials formerly the property of the Hungarian Socialist Workers [Communist] Party, which was declared to be the property of the state following the change of system in 1989. The Court extended the review to the Law Decree (of 1987) on State and Official Secrets.

31. The case was a preliminary control of the bill. After passing the Act, new cases reached the Court claiming that the implementation measures rendered checking ineffective. For instance, members of the Lustration Committee had no direct access to the files;

they worked with the data obtained from the (present) secret service. Moreover, the new law that was held by the Court to be necessary in order to control public officials beyond the obligatory control provided in the act has so far not even been drafted.

32. Following the democratic change in Portugal, the new Constitution (1976) prohibited the "nationwide uniform PIN for citizens" (Art. 35(2). In Hungary, a Data Protection Ombudsman was elected by Parliament only in 1994, although the Data Protection Act had provided for this office in 1992.

33. ABH 1994, 219; MK 68/1994.

34. 30/1992(V.26)AB: ABH 1992, 167, 180; MK 53/1992.

35. 34/1992(VI.1)AB: ABH 1992, 192, MK 55/1992; 12/1991(IV.11)AB: ABH 1991, 392, MK 38/1991.

36. 36/1994(VI.24)AB: ABH 1994, 219; MK 68/1994.

37. In *New York Times v. Sullivan* (376 U.S. 254), the concrete political facts of the case—that is to say, the connection to the civil rights movement—were also important. In Strasbourg, the European Court of Human Rights decides on the compatibility of court decisions with the European Convention of Human Rights. According to the minority opinion in the Hungarian case, the ordinary courts could have applied the distinction required by the Constitution even in upholding the challenged rules of the Criminal Code; that is, the activist ruling of the Constitutional Court was unnecessary.

38. Act 1/1996 on Radio and Television Broadcasting.

39. 17/1993(III.19)AB: ABH 1993, 157; MK 31/1993.

40. This question was of major political significance and the subject of many parliamentary debates and cases before the Court. The government between 1990 and 1994 had only a simple majority, so for practical reasons the two-thirds-majority rule gave the opposition a veto right.

41. 4/1993(II.12)AB: ABH 1993, 48, (51 and 65); MK 15/1993.

42. 8/1993(II.27)AB: ABH 1993, 99; MK 22/1993.

43. This was expressed in the first opinion (4/1993; ABH 1993, 53).

44. The Court ignored European models with good reason. In contemporary Europe, seven state churches exist and there are countless types of intermediate models from these to radical separation.

45. 8/1993(II.27)AB: ABH 1993, 99; MK 22/1993.

46. 970/B/1994AB: ABH 1994, 739 (not published in the MK). The decree provides for the free exercise of religion and spiritual care for members of any church and permits the institution of army chaplains on the basis of agreements with the respective churches. According to one voluntary poll, 81 percent of all soldiers belonged to the four "historical" churches (Catholics, 62 percent; Calvinists, 15 percent; Lutherans, 3 percent; Jews, 1 percent). Only 0.2 percent were members of other churches, and about 20 percent gave no answer or did not belong to a church. The Court rejected the application.

47. The portion published here of the Decision on Background Checks for Those in Public Office (60/1994), which reviews the Lustration Act, is limited to the problem of lustration and the relationship between the protection of personal data and freedom of information. The unequal treatment of the clergy compared with other public figures was found to be unconstitutional by the Court along with the failure to specify the purposes for which information might be requested and its use. Although not mentioned in the Act, the problem of collaboration is practically relevant as regards the historical churches, given the number of their believers (cf. note 46) and their social role.

48. Disputes may emerge even among traditional churches. In an early case, practicing Jews complained that under the Labour Code one could not work on Sunday in exchange for a different day off. According to the application, Saturday should also count as a work-free day. They considered it discriminatory that only Christian holidays were recognized by the state as nonworking days. The Constitutional Court rejected the request for a determination of unconstitutionality. The original religious content of the holidays is no longer determinative of the nonworking holidays; rather, folk customs are. This could not be claimed for the Jewish holidays. Further, for practical and traditional reasons Sunday is a nonworking day, even if it is not absolutely work free, as was the case under some Anglo-Saxon laws. Finally the Constitutional Court examined vacation rules and found that they sufficiently enabled one to abstain from work, whether on the grounds of conscience or otherwise (10/1993(II.27)AB: ABH 1993, 105; MK 22/1993).

49. The above justification of positive discrimination is not restricted to material help but extends to benefits of other types. See, for example, the exemption of priests from military service—a privilege they share with Members of Parliament and local governments—in 46/1994(X.21)AB: ABH 1994, 260, (272); MK 103/1994. This method of the Court is exercised in other cases when it is important to avoid even the impression of bias for or against the group in question. In the case on the minimum age for membership of homosexual-oriented associations, the Court emphasized that the reasons the State could not expose a child to the risk of immature decisions were not related solely to homosexuality (21/1996).

50. The idea of merging the two types of schools is also reflected in the concurring opinion of Herczegh, J. to the decision, 4/1993.

51. ABH 1997, 107; MK 35/1997.

52. 4/1993; 22/1997(IV.25)AB: ABH 1997, 107; MK 35/1997 (church schools); 46/1994(X.21)AB: ABH 1994, 260; MK 103/1994 (conscientious objectors). According to the latter case, the obligation to fill out a notification form was constitutionally permissible since it was necessary to verify a person's conscientious conviction. It was, however, an unnecessary, unconstitutional limitation on the freedom of conscience to exclude from the possibility of alternative (civilian) service those who possessed firearms. The mere fact of possessing firearms is not conclusive to firm convictions determining the whole personality.

53. The decision reads: "There is no reason in the present case for the Constitutional Court to confine itself to certain questions of sexual morals instead of the protection of the child's personality development as a whole. What is more, in the present case the Constitutional Court does not even consider the problem of homosexuality to be a question of sexual morals—although it is generally regarded as such in public opinion."

54. 30/1995(V.25)AB: ABH 1995, 155; MK 40/1995.

55. Laws from 1945 onward deprived of their real estate those Hungarian citizens who were once members of certain organizations of ethnic Germans. Similarly, members of the former gendarmerie were deprived of all of their social security claims. The Court declared these laws to be unconstitutional (66/1992(XII.17)AB: ABH 1992, 293; MK 126/1992; and 44/1991(VIII.28)AB: ABH 1991, 370; MK 93/1991). However, the Court distinguished collective criminal responsibility from exclusion of groups of persons from benefits on the ground of unworthiness, as in the case of compensation for moral damages, (9/1995(II.8)AB: ABH 1995, 31, 64; MK 10/1995).

56. 41/1991(VII.3)AB: ABH 1991, 193; MK 74/1991.

57. Article 57(4) of the Constitution states that no one shall be declared guilty and sentenced for an act that was not a criminal offence under Hungarian law at the time it was committed.

58. The absolute nature of the criminal guarantees is based on the fact that they already embody the result of balancing; thus there is no room for further balancing (see 9/1992(I.30)AB: ABH 1992, 59, 70; MU 11/1992). This is in clear contrast to the ways in which other fundamental rights—for example, to property—can be qualified.

59. The two decisions are 41/1993(VI.30)AB: ABH 1993, 292; MK 85/1993; and 42/1993(VI.30)AB: ABH 1993, 300; MK 85/1993.

60. Parliament was not successful in enacting a legally valid law that would make possible the prosecution of politically motivated crimes under international law. The Constitutional Court had to annul the relevant Act twice for technical reasons, and finally it suggested that such prosecutions might be based directly on international law and Art. 7 of the Constitution (36/1996(IX.4)AB: ABH 1996, 117; MK 75/1996).

61. See for instance, 1/1994(I.7)AB: ABH 1994, 29; MK 2/1994; and most recently 20/1997(III.19)AB: ABH 1997, 85; MK 24/1997.

62. 32/1990(XII.22)AB: ABH 1990, 145; MK 130/1990. The relevant Act is 26/1991.

63. ABH 1997, 365; 63/1997(XII.12)AB: MK 111/1997.

64. ABH 1995, 351; MK 109/1995.

65. The relevant law was enacted as Act 14/1997: MK 28/1997. The deadline set by the Court was 31 December 1996.

66. 5/1992(I.30)AB: ABH 1992, 27, 31; MK 11/1992.

67. See, for example, in the law of criminal enforcement. See note 66.

68. Article 63(3) requires a qualified majority for laws concerning business activity and the auditing of parties. The freedom to establish parties and their functions are regulated in Art. 3.

69. Attempts to establish civil associations signaled the beginning of societal changes in the mid-1980s in Hungary. Environmental or cultural associations (as a rule, not permitted) represented the forerunners of the system change. See Sólyom, "Hungary: Citizens' Participation in the Environmental Movement," *Ifda Dossier* 64 (March-April 1988): 23. At the same time, there were experiments to take rights, even those declared in the socialist constitution, seriously. These attempts were followed by the founding of political parties in 1988.

70. Lobbies for hunters and anglers achieved the passage of relevant laws. Now there is a hunters' chamber and obligatory membership in anglers' associations.

71. More parties wanted to change over from the present unicameral system to establish an upper house, where—Hungary being too small—the territorial principle could not have played the main role but would represent professions.

72. This was laid down in the cases that held constitutional the obligatory membership in the bar association and the provisions of the Civil Code on public bodies, 22/1994(IV.16)AB: ABH 1994, 127; MK 40/1994; and 1283/B/1995. The latter is not published in the MK, but it is cited in 38/1997(VII.1)AB: ABH 1997, 249; MK 58/1997.

73. ABH 1997, 249; MK 58/1997.

74. The Court found this obligation constitutional as regards people exercising commercial or industrial activities and, on different grounds, as regards lawyers, doctors, and architects, too.

75. See the commercial chamber, Medical Practitioners' Association, and architects' chamber cases: 38, 39, and 40/1997(VII.1)AB, all published in MK 58/1997 and in ABH 1997, 249, 263 and 282.

76. See note 49 and accompanying text.

77. 46/1994(X.21)AB: ABH 1994, 260, 263; MK 103/1994.

78. This most vulnerable point in democracies is even more aggravated in new democracies with new parties and especially in the postsocialist states, where the successor party of the former socialist/communist party controls considerable resources. Restricting laws were reviewed by the Hungarian Constitutional Court, which—in the spirit of the "lawful revolution"—did not allow any negative discrimination. In these cases, the test was developed that restrictions on the right to property had to be of a limited and defined time. See 1154/B/1990/5AB: ABH 1991, 468; and 24/1992(IV.21)AB: ABH 1992, 128; MK 41/1992.

79. 53/1996(XI.22)AB: ABH 1996, 165; MK 102/1996. Sólyom, P., concurring, writes: "It can be deduced from detailed constitutional rules that prescribe indispensable tasks for parties in the operation of the institutional system, that the parties not only in general have a mediating role between the State and society and their sphere of activity is not simply mainly (but not exclusively) that of representation, but the Constitution explicitly realizes a 'multi-party' system in which parties must be represented in Parliament. . . . Taking these provisions into account, the criterion of parties defined in the Act does follow from the Constitution: from among civil organizations, only those political organizations are 'parties' that make an effort to 'express' the 'will of the people' by being represented in Parliament. The legislature's competence is to decide what counts as evidence of the seriousness of the effort, i.e., the suitability of the party to fulfill its role. The requirement of support for nominating a candidate (as given in the Act) is a criterion that cannot be challenged on constitutional grounds. The Constitutional Court established the constitutionality of a similar requirement of support in its . . . decision on the notion of a church" (8/1993(II.27)AB: ABH 1993, 99; MK 22/1993).

80. The applicant sought the interpretation "in the interest of justifying future environmental law-making" and wanted the know the exact content of the right as well as the resulting governmental obligations. According to the Constitutional Court, such specification is not the task of an abstract constitutional interpretation (996/G/1990AB: ABH 1993, 553).

81. Both are "statements of fact and policy at the same time" (11/1992; 21/1994).

82. Under socialism, "collective or social property" meant the property of the State and of the cooperatives; the latter primarily owned arable land. In the following text, the term *state property* or *state ownership* will be used to mean social property. At the beginning of the transition, more than 90 percent of industrial and trade concerns, as well agricultural property, was under state ownership. Today some 63 percent of the gross domestic product (GDP) is produced by private enterprises.

83. This idea, whose influence is visible in countless decisions, appears expressly in the dissenting opinion by Kilényi, J. in Decision 32/1991(VI.6)AB: ABH 1991, 146, 166; MK 61/1991. According to this dissent, art. 226 of the Civil Code would have had to be repealed as unconstitutional in the long run, with a limitation of two to three years, since such state measures were only necessary during the period of reform but were otherwise irreconcilable with the rule of law and the market economy. Article 226 provides that "a legal norm can change the content of a contract which entered into force before the norm only in exceptional cases."

84. 19/1991(IV.23)AB: ABH 1991, 401, 402; MK 43/1991, per Vörös, J.: "Article 9(2) also protects against the state restrictions on economic competition and the right to engage freely in enterpreneurial activities, to the extent these restrictions do serve to expand the market economy." Similarly, for instance, see ABH 1991, 167, 382, 710.

85. Cf. Hungarian Constitution, Art. 8, according to which the essential contents of any fundamental right may not be limited by law.

86. Moreover, the Court required that the time of limitation be fixed or foreseeable.

87. The Constitutional Court had already made this point in decision 33/1993(V.28)AB: ABH 1993, 247, 249; MK 68/1993, per Lábady, J.

88. The socialist understanding of the right to work was to guarantee a job *for everyone.*

89. It was held to be unconstitutional that the licensing of foreign doctors was at the absolute discretion of the medical chamber. At least the conditions had to be defined by a law. This is connected with the problem of the judicial review of that decision of the chamber: in the absence of such a condition, it would make no practical sense.

90. The right to a healthy environment (Art. 18) is another fundamental right of the Constitution that, due to its special characteristics, enjoys a special status as to how it can be limited. See note 80 and accompanying text.

91. 64/1993(XII. 22)AB: ABH 1993, 373 (380); MK 184/1993.

92. See note 116 and accompanying text.

93. ABH 1997, 282; 40/1997(VII.1)AB: MK 58/1997.

94. The Court considers "social burdens," that is, restrictions on property, to be the counterbalance for the extended use of the right to property to protect financial positions (64/1993).

95. 35/1994(VI.24)AB: ABH 1994, 197; MK 68/1994.

96. While the impact of decisions of the U.S. Supreme Court is obvious, for instance, in many cases involving free speech, express citations of foreign cases (except those of the Strasbourg Court) are rare. In my concurring opinion, the following are referred to: *Board of Regents v. Roth* (408 U.S. 564, 1972); *Paul v. Davis* (424 U.S. 693, 1976); and—as illustration—*Holden v. Hardy* (169 U.S. 366, 1898).

97. 29/1992(V.19)AB: ABH 1992, 162; MK 51/1992. For the notion of state property, see note 82.

98. 46/1991(IX.10)AB: ABH 1991, 211, MK 98/1991; 50/1991(X.3)AB: ABH 1991, 251, MK 107/1991; 59/1991(XI.19)AB: ABH 1991, 293, MK 127/1991.

99. The crimes of "careless administration" (of state property) and the damages that related only to state property were annulled. See 6/1992(I.30)AB: ABH 1992, 40; MK 11/1992.

100. Examples are the "management of office or business space" that does not take into account who the owner is (29/1993(V.4)AB: ABH 1993, 227; MK 56/1993) and the "administration of State property" that had been allocated to all state economic units and local councils whose powers in effect amounted to those of an owner (17/1992(III.30)AB: ABH 1992, 104; MK 32/1992).

101. An example is the protection of a public telephone or an ambulance (cf. note 99).

102. The degree of independence of local governments—which took the place of the earlier council system—was the subject of intensive debate throughout the period following the hasty passage of the Act on the Local Government immediately following the free elections of 1990. In reaction to the council system, their independence from the State was

stressed. The 1990 amendments to the Constitution included a list of "fundamental rights of local governments" (Art. 44/A).

103. Advisory opinions, called "abstract interpretations of a constitutional provision," have a binding effect for all, including, of course, Parliament and Government, under the Constitutional Court Act.

104. The largest government party after the first free elections of 1990, the Hungarian Democratic Forum, wanted to guarantee partial compensation for former owners (by means of vouchers with which state property could be acquired) and—separate from this—for specific moral damages. Under this concept, the privatization of state property was kept completely separate from the compensation of former owners. This solution—which implicitly required the legality of existing state ownership—had the advantage that the acquisition of ownership by investors who bought property in the course of the privatization process was completely assured and not burdened with possible claims from earlier private owners. However, the Smallholders Party—which assured a parliamentary majority for the governing coalition—wanted reprivatization: it wanted unconditionally to return the land *in natura* and, to that end, to expropriate the property of the agricultural cooperatives without compensation. This party approved partial compensation only with regard to nonlanded property. Cf. Ethan Klingsberg, "Judicial Review and Hungary's Transition from Communism to Democracy: The Constitutional Court, the Continuity of Law, and the Redefinition of Property Rights," 1992 *BYUL Rev.* 41; and, Peter Paczolay, "Judicial Review of the Compensation Law in Hungary," *Michigan Journal of International Law* 13, no. 4 (Summer 1992): 806.

105. Portions of the earlier property of Jews had been sold by the State (this fact was cleared up by the Constitutional Court in the Jewish possessions case, 16/1993). Possessions of ethnic Germans that were confiscated after the war were distributed, for example, to Hungarian refugees from neighboring countries, but later they were taken away. The same was true of the land of small farmers who had obtained their land in the 1945 redistributions of large landholdings. In the 1980s, the sale of state property to private parties began, primarily apartments and small service facilities.

106. See the later restrictions and obligations of local governments regarding buildings obtained from the State (64/1993; 4/1993).

107. 27/1991(V.20)AB: ABH 1991, 73; MK 53/1991.

108. 15/1993(III.12)AB: ABH 1993, 112. The next two citations are from ibid 114 and 117, per P. Sólyom, MK 29/1993.

109. 28/1991(VI.3)AB: ABH 1991, 88, (94); MK 59/1991.

110. The Court stressed repeatedly that it was not applying *novatio* as a technical term. Without doubt, the Constitutional Court transferred the dogmatic difficulties rather than resolving them; it had to be noted that the state could not "renew" its obligations as it likes. For the limits of the *novatio* see, for example, my concurring opinion in 27/1991, n. 107.

111. "Therefore, there is no need and—in a compensation system based on the injury suffered—legal way to make a distinction, according to which, for instance, death suffered in a Nazi camp should be compensated differently from that suffered in a Soviet camp or in the cellars of the State Security Office [ÁVH]. Such a distinction would anyway be impossible to carry out and would infringe upon human dignity" (22/1996(VI.25)AB: ABH 1996, 89, 101; MK 51/1996).

112. Declarations of special protections for the mother, the child, and the family also occur in Arts. 15, 16, 66(2), and 67.

113. 54/1993(X.13)AB: ABH 1993, 340; MK 147/1993.

114. A very early statement in this sense appeared in my dissent in decision 31/1990(XII.18)AB: ABH 1990, 136 (142); MK 128/1990.

115. See note 114, 772/B/1990/AB: ABH 1990, 520; and 26/1993(IV.29)AB: ABH 1993, 196; MK 51/1993. Again, this was a six-to-four decision.

116. Indeed, the process took more than half a year in 1995. New plans and follow-up laws had to be tested by the Court as well. This volume contains only the first judgment, which outlines the principal position of the Court.

117. Parliament did not elect justices for two places that became vacant at the end of 1994 until mid-1997. Because the terms of the justices of the first Court ended in 1998, and those of other justices in mid-1999, neither these new justices nor those still to be elected had sufficient time to work with justices from the old court. A few months are not enough to share the experience and the "fresh" tradition, which extends not only to the judgments themselves but to attitude and methodology as well. I do hope that by the time this book reaches the reader it will not have become like a remote star whose light, though it has ceased to exist, continues to reach us for a long period of time.

Following the first decisions on the austerity package on 14 September 1995, the Government issued an official statement, claiming that the Constitutional Court had overstepped its authority and hindered the Government in fulfilling its duties. For further details of this controversy and the decisions of the Constitutional Court, see an interview with me in the *East European Constitutional Review* 6, no. 1 (Winter 1997): 71.

118. When the Court exempted the case from Art. 70/E of the Constitution it also noted that social rights had a role there in that, as a result of the withdrawals, the extent of welfare benefits might not be reduced to a level below that required by Art. 70/E.

119. 56/1995(IX.15)AB: ABH 1995, 260, MK 76/1995; 66/1995(XI.24)AB: ABH 1995, 333, MK 101/1995; 46/1995(VI.30)AB: ABH 1995, 219, MK 56/1995.

120. In the Court's examination of European jurisprudence, two countries with extremely different approaches to social rights in their constitutions were chosen: Germany, where no social rights are determined at all; and Italy, which has a detailed list of social rights. The respective constitutional courts, however, developed very similar requirements of constitutionality in cases regarding the reduction of benefits, and this proved to be similar to the Hungarian decisions.

121. These differences are to be seen in the decisions of the Constitutional Courts which developed a principled position on the character of the system change, as the Courts of Hungary, Germany, and the Czech Republic did.

122. In contrast to Hungary, East Germany and post–1968 Czechoslovakia suffered under totalitarian socialism until the last minute of the old regimes.

123. 26/1992(IV.30)AB, ABH 1992, 135, MK 44/1992; 1154/B/1990AB, ABH 1991, 541; 24/1992(IV.21)AB, ABH 1992, 126, MK 41/1992.

124. Terrorism in "old" democracies, as in Germany in the 1960s and 1970s and today in Spain and Northern Ireland, language and autonomy ambitions of minorities in Belgium, France, Spain and, again, Great Britain. Restrictions of social benefits may also lead to serious upheavals.

125. See the cases concerning the austerity package discussed in note 116 and its accompanying text.

126. This occurred first in a concurring opinion of Sólyom, P., in 31/1990(XII.15)AB: ABH 1990, 136, (142); MK 128/1990.

127. "The violation of the principle of the rule of law—a basic value explicitly stipulated in the Constitution—in itself leads to the unconstitutionality of the legal norm" (9/1992(I.30)AB: ABH 1992, 54 (65); MK 11/1992). The market economy and free competition have not been considered as tests for constitutionality since 1993–94. Instead, the violation of particular rights, especially of those to property or the free choice of occupation and enterprise, are reviewed.

128. This was true above all for the tax and fees amendments, which were introduced overnight. This practice—which admittedly was inherited from the previous system—was changed as a result of the ongoing decisions of the Constitutional Court.

129. See note 61 and accompanying text.

130. See note 61 and accompanying text.

131. This principle follows the *Bundestreue,* an unwritten constitutional principle developed by the German Constitutional Court. It was laid down in connection with the question of how long the President might delay deciding on a nomination. The Court spoke only of a "reasonable time" (8/1992(I.30)AB: ABH 1992, 51; MK 11/1992). Parliament was clearly against this principle, as it kept the posts of two judges of the Constitutional Court vacant for three years, endangering the continuity of the jurisdiction of the Court (see note 117).

132. See the decisions on presidential powers cited previously.

133. Of this aspect the Hungarian Court was especially conscious. In the first years after the changes, the future of the new democracy could not be taken as secure (not even on grounds of foreign policy; see the uncertainties in the former Soviet Union). All means had to be used in order to attach the Hungarian constitutional system to Western standards of democracy. The Court accepted all claims suitable, in order to deliver prompt decisions on provisions of the Constitution, while the "window of history" was open. Within five years, a body of work was completed that other Courts, under normal circumstances, might reach within thirty years.

134. Such decisions of the Constitutional Court were especially frequent in the years 1991 and 1992. See, for instance, 23/1992(IV.21)AB: ABH 1992, 346; MK 41/1992.

135. For the more complicated relationship between membership and the right to vote, see 38/1997(VII.1)AB: ABH 1997, 249; MK 58/1997.

136. Act VII/1989 came into force on 15 June 1989. The new Constitution became effective on 23 October 1989.

137. The Court had obliged Parliament to bring the Referendum Act into harmony with the Constitution as well (2/1993(I.22)AB: ABH 1993, 33; MK 6/1993). Parliament, however, had not passed a new law, so the Court had referred back to this interpretation of democracy in favor of its representative form in subsequent cases in which it dismissed the claims. A new obligation for revision of the Act was issued in case 52/1997.

138. In the wording of the reasons to the amending bill, "facultative referendum."

139. The issue was whether restrictions on the acquisition of arable land should be lifted (cf. note 95 and accompanying text). The voters' initiative sought to exclude non-Hungarian citizens, while the Government—saying that it accepted this policy—approached the question from the side of allowing land acquisition for Hungarian corporations. With this, however, even aliens could become landowners. According to polls, both of the questions would probably have gained an overwhelming majority. He who questions, will win.

140. Article 70/A(1) states that the Republic of Hungary shall ensure human and civil rights for everyone within its territory without discrimination of any kind, such as with re-

gard to race, color, sex, language, religion, political or other opinion, national or social origin, property, birth, or any other grounds.

141. 9/1990(IV.25)AB: ABH 1990, 46; MK 36/1990.

142. This was decisive for the distinction, first, between former owners and non-owners and, second, between the landowners entitled to reimbursement and other property owners.

143. 61/1991(XI.20)AB: ABH 1992, 280; MK 117/1992.

144. In the decisive case, the first compensation decision, the Constitutional Court stated clearly that nobody had a right to compensation; nonetheless, the opinion recognized the inadmissibility of discrimination between the owners of land and other assets. Equal treatment was already required in this case with respect to the same, taking into consideration the perspectives of both groups. This procedure was followed in later compensation decisions (15/1993(III.12)AB: ABH 1993, 112, 121; MK 29/1993; 22/1996). In the first decision, however, the Court tried to remain in accord with the text of the Constitution in that it also spoke of a distinction with regard to the right to acquire property. The existence of such a right was later denied; see 35/1994(VI.24)AB: ABH 1994, 197; MK 68/1994.

145. The protection of simple rights and the development of the Constitutional Court's jurisprudence on the equality clause was explained in Decision 35/1994(VI.24)AB: especially in the concurring opinion of Sólyom, P. (ABH 1994, 197; MK 68/1994).

146. The process was not concluded without tension. In the period between October 1989 and August 1990, the procedure for electing the President (direct election by the people or election by Parliament) was the subject of two referenda and two constitutional amendments. By July 1990, when it was time for the election, the originally envisioned parliamentary election, which was in keeping with competences, was reinstated.

147. In this context, the Constitutional Court was asked to review the supervision of the public media (37/1992).

148. Act CVII/1993 on amendments to the Constitution sets out the competencies of the Government and the President in case of an outside attack by armed forces (Art. 19/E of the Constitution).

149. This was the natural result of the lack of success of the previous, general interpretation. Justice Wayne noted with prescience at that time that judicial activism was provoked by the difficulty of enforcing the decision. See "The Two Faces of Judicial Activism," *George Washington Law Review* 61, no. 1 (1992):7.

150. For example, "The President may not impose conditions above and beyond the fulfillment of the statutory requirements for appointment or dismissal. . . . The refusal to confirm an appointment may not be applied to eliminate such abstract dangers existing independently of the specific personal choice for an appointment which arise from the absence of legal guarantees or are attributable to the deficient nature of the legal regulations affecting the democratic functioning of the system of governance. The President has other constitutionally secured instruments for tackling those threats" (36/1992(VI.10)AB: ABH 1992, 207; MK 59/1992).

151. In his position paper for the third case, the President made it clear that as long as a Media Act had not been passed the freedom of the media was guaranteed by an agreement between the political parties. The compliance with a proposal from the Prime Minister, which was not based on such a consensus, contained the serious danger that the fundamental right of freedom of the press would be unconstitutionally restricted. In addition, this danger constituted a severe restriction on the democratic functioning of the State.

The Constitutional Court, in response, established in detail the requirements for the refusal and also determined the "self-evident rules" cited in note 150. Again, three justices wrote dissenting opinions according to which the Court had not remained within its competence when it decided upon too concrete a question in a given dispute. It is to be noted, however, that the Constitutional Court on the same day, and in the same number of the *Hungarian Official Gazette,* published the media decision (37/1992), which expressly stated that the consensus of political parties would not represent a sufficient guarantee of the independence of the public media. This decision, which did not refer to the actual background of the case, was delivered by a unanimous Court.

Two years later, after the elections and the change of government in 1994, the President finally provided his signature. Upon a proposal of the new Prime Minister, he dismissed the old and named the new chairmen of the public media, although the Media Act had not yet been passed or even a bill drafted. The consensus of the parliamentary parties was also missing: the proposal was supported only by the two governing parties.

152. See 48/1991. After the refusal of this position in the first decision, the President repeated the same argument in his position paper with respect to the application in the third decision, where he distinguished between "simple appointments at the level of undersecretary of state" and appointments that require "the presence of a consensus according to the intent of the Constitution."

153. While exercising this method of interpretation, the President "recommended" to the Constitutional Court in his position paper a restrictive interpretation oriented to the text of the Constitution. See note 154.

154. This part of his position was not repeated in the decision, but the concurring opinion returned to it. According to the President, an interpretation that could not be read directly from the text would constitute amendment of the Constitution, for which only Parliament is qualified to act.

155. Act IV/1972 and its amending Act LXVII/1991.

156. ABH 1993, 256; MK 75/1993.

157. On the budget of the courts, see 28/1995(V.19)AB: ABH 1995, 138; MK 39/1995. On decorations and honorary titles, see 45/1994(X.21)AB: ABH 1994, 254 (according to my dissent, a sitting judge must not be honored by other powers at all (259)); MK 103/1994. On the other hand, it is constitutional that the Ombudsman may not carry any investigation into the courts; see 17/1994(III.29)AB: ABH 1994, 84; MK 33/1994; 28/1995(V.19)AB: ABH 1995, 138; MK 39/1995.

158. This amendment is Art. 42. According to the Constitution, the content of this right is the "autonomous and democratic administration of the local public affairs concerning the enfranchised citizens and the exercise of local public authority in the interest of the population."

159. For the fundamental right of local governance, see Art. 44/A and Art. 44/C. For constitutional protection, see Art. 43(2) and for dissolution Art. 19(3)(l).

160. According to Art. 12(2), the State respects the property rights of the local governments. Art. 44/A considers the right to property to be one of the fundamental rights of the local governments.

161. See Brunner's essay, this volume.

162. This is the same situation that exists in the review for consistency of a domestic norm with an international treaty; there, too, the domestic law, the treaty obligation, and the Constitution must be harmonized (see 53/1993; and 4/1997).

163. Local taxes and manipulation of local referenda and petitions for referenda are oft-repeated themes before the Constitutional Court.

164. At the time the new system of local government was established, the new laws were challenged by the opposition parties, which could not enforce their concepts in Parliament. Only later did the communities themselves appear as applicants against the laws that limited their rights.

165. 18/1993(III.19)AB: ABH 1993, 161; MK 31/1993. See also note 134 and accompanying text.

Structure and Proceedings of the Hungarian Constitutional Judiciary

Georg Brunner

I. Preface: Political Upheaval

The constitutional judiciary was introduced to Hungary in the wake of the political upheaval of 1989–90, which brought to the country a constitutional order based on democracy and the rule of law. While this transition proceeded quickly and dramatically in Hungary, it was not as sudden and unannounced as in the majority of Eastern European countries.[1] The transition had some degree of continuity with the limited reform policy of the "Kádár era," itself not free of setbacks, and developed its own high-speed momentum after Kádár was removed as party leader at the National Party Conference of 20–22 May 1988.

On the eve of the Eastern European revolution, Hungary, together with Yugoslavia and Poland, was one of the few "socialist" countries that had already crossed the threshold from a totalitarian to an authoritarian single-party dictatorship. This transformation commenced in the 1960s and was consummated in the constitutional reforms of April 1972.[2] In comparison with other countries in the Soviet sphere, in the 1960s and 1970s the authoritarian "Kádár system," which was already showing elements of the rule of law, distinguished itself with an observable political and economic stability and a certain legitimacy. Nonetheless, from the beginning of the 1980s various signs of crisis began to multiply. Increasing dissatisfaction manifested itself in the founding of small opposition groups within the society, which were largely tolerated by the regime, as was the formation of a reform movement within the party, headed by the then general secretary of the Patriotic People's Front, I. Pozsgay. Pozsgay not only pushed for the decisive continuation of the reform process "from above" but he made sure that discussions with the societal opposition were never abandoned. This had much to do with the fact that in Hungary—unlike the case in the second Eastern European reform country, Poland—there was never an irreconcilable breach between the rulers and the ruled. Thus, continual development was possible within the framework of a broad general consensus.

At the significant party conference of May 1988, which marked the end of the "Kádár era," the moderate, or conformist, reform movement took over the party leadership. It had in mind "reform of the political institutional system" in accordance with a "socialist pluralism based on the leading role of the Party."[3] This meant social but not political pluralism or the recognition of the existence and legitimacy of various group interests. In order to achieve the necessary balancing of these interests, the party had to pay them adequate attention. According to the party conference resolutions, the Constitution also needed to be reviewed with this goal in mind. In the confrontation that followed between the various reform movements within the party, the democratic radical reformers won out over the moderate system reformers in the first half of 1989. They had the decisive support of M. Németh, who had been the head of government since 1988 and under whose leadership the State freed itself from the Party and became an independent political power. A decisive breakthrough occurred in February 1989, when at a plenary meeting of its Central Committee, the Hungarian Socialist Workers' Party renounced its leadership monopoly and accepted the transition to a multiparty system. Thus, the political associations that had been emerging de facto since the end of 1987 could now form political parties and started pressing for the constitutional reforms that were to effect the system's transformation to the democratic rule of law.

In preparation for constitutional reform,[4] various bodies were commissioned following the party conference. Of these, the Ministry of Justice undoubtedly played the most important role. Under the leadership of Minister of Justice Prof. Dr. K. Kulcsár and Deputy Minister of Justice for Public Law Prof. Dr. G. Kilényi, appointed in June and November 1988, respectively, the "review" called for at the party conference was transformed almost overnight into a project to redraft the Constitution. By the end of November 1988, the Ministry of Justice had already presented a "Concept for the Constitution" whose revised second version, based on appropriate consultations, was approved by Parliament in March 1989. According to the timetable as it was originally conceived, a detailed draft of the Constitution was to be prepared by early summer and, after gathering opinions from interested associations, introduced in the Parliament still sitting at the beginning of 1990. Following its parliamentary approval, the new Constitution was to be put to the people in a referendum in early 1990. In the meantime, those rules that were especially urgent for the transition of regimes were to be singled out and the necessary constitutional changes were to be approved prior to redrafting the entire Constitution.

This timetable was not to be realized. Under increasing pressure for democratization, exerted mainly by the Opposition Roundtable, founded in March 1989 as a union of new parties, the political leadership was forced to conclude that accomplishing the change of regimes exclusively "from above" was imprudent and inclusion of the societal opposition in the process of constitutional drafting was essential for the most broadly based support of the constitutional project. Thus, on 13 June 1989 a National Roundtable was established based on the Polish model. The Hungarian Socialist Workers' Party, the Opposition Roundtable, and, as a third negotiating party, the seven established "social organizations" were to negotiate the means of political transformation of the system and thus as well the reform of the Constitution. At the same time, the relevant work on parliamentary legislation was suspended. At this point, it was expected that Parliament would translate the results of the roundtable negotiations, finally reached on 18 September 1989, into the necessary legislative forms. Rather than creating a new constitution, Act XXXI/1989 of 18 October resulted in a complete revision of the old Constitution, which still had its roots in 1949.[5] The reason for this is that at the Roundtable the societal opposition was able to impose its view that a new constitution should be adopted only by a democratically elected Parliament and that the task of the sitting Parliament could simply be to create the democratic rule of law infrastructure necessary for the change of regimes. The democratic parliamentary election, from which the former opposition parties emerged as the biggest winners, took place in March and April 1990. The new Parliament approved further constitutional amendments. The project to draft a new constitution is still on the agenda, but it is no longer so urgent, even given all of the discrepancies in the current Constitution, which are necessarily the result of its dramatic history of revision. The democratically elected government of J. Antall did not pay much attention to the matter, while the socialist-liberal government of Gy. Horn, which took office in June 1994, tried to push the project through but failed.

II. The Founding and Beginnings of the Constitutional Judiciary

Even in the early stages of constitutional reform, it was undisputed that Hungary should have a constitutional court separate from the ordinary court system. The Constitutional Committee established in April 1984 for the purpose of constitutional control in the parliamentary arena had for various reasons proven to be a failure[6] and needed to be replaced with an effective guarantee of constitutional governance. The introduction of a constitutional judiciary was considered to be so urgent that the constitutional basis for the establishment of the Constitutional Court was actually established in the preliminary stages of the constitutional revision by means of the Act amending the Constitution (I/1989 of 10 January 1989). On the basis of the newly introduced Art. 32/A of the Constitution, the details were to be spelled out in an Act on the Constitutional Court. The government introduced the relevant draft in Parliament in May 1989, but it had to be withdrawn in view of the roundtable negotiations, which began shortly thereafter. To put into effect the matters agreed to at the Roundtable, Parliament then amended § 32/A and approved Act XXXII/1989, "On the Constitutional Court" (hereafter CC Act) on 19 October 1989.[7] Its passage required a qualified majority of two-thirds of the MPs present (Art. 32/A(6) of the Constitution).

The disagreements at the Roundtable involved primarily two issues: the appointment of the constitutional judges and the competences of the Constitutional Court.[8] According to the version of Art. 32/A(6) of the Constitution passed in January 1989, the Constitutional Court was to consist of a president and ten members, all of whom were to be elected by Parliament. The government's first draft of the CC Act proposed in addition that the judges be elected for life, that is to say, until the end of their seventieth year. Five judges were to be elected by the old Parliament and five by the new one on the recommendation of a parliamentary nominating committee that was to have as members also representatives of the Academy of Sciences and the Hungarian Lawyers' Association.[9] This proposal was supported by the Lawyers' Association.[10] The opposition feared that this proposal would lead to overrepresentation of the transitional regime and insisted on more judges, a term limit, and a nominating committee consisting exclusively of Members of Parliament, that is to say, a nominating committee determined by party politics. The opposition was able to put the bulk of its ideas into effect and thus in Art. 32/A(4) of the Constitution the number of constitutional judges was set at fifteen and their election was to be at the proposal of a nominating committee consisting of party representatives by a two-thirds majority of all parliamentary representatives. The CC Act limited the term to nine years but allowed the possibility of a single reelection. According to the transition rules, five constitutional judges each were to be elected by the old Parliament in 1989, the new Parliament within two months of its first session, and in the course of 1994, respectively. From the judges so elected, the Vice President was to be chosen after the first round and the President after the second by the judges themselves.

With respect to the competences of the Constitutional Court, it was agreed that its priorities should include review of legal norms. The major topics of discussion were the range of persons entitled to make an application and the introduction of the constitutional complaint. The concept of the Constitution considered the protection of fundamental rights to be an important task of the Constitutional Court but was reserved with respect to the notion of the constitutional complaint. The opposition placed great importance on everybody's right to apply to the Court and was able to carry the day. As will be shown, in the end not only the quasi-constitutional complaint was allowed but also popular action, which meant that any person could request the determination of the constitutionality of any legal norm or administrative provision (!) without having to show an injury to a fundamental right or any other plausible legally protected interest. With this well-intentioned and, for the formative years of a constitutional state, useful provision the overburdening of the Constitutional Court was predetermined.

As was provided for in the transitional rules of the CC Act, the first five constitutional judges were elected in November 1989. With this modest staffing, the Constitutional Court took up its first extremely busy assignment not in the tradition-filled but somewhat dull provincial city of Esztergom—in keeping with the German Karlsruhe tradition of seclusion, as foreseen in § 3 of the CC Act—but rather in the former party building of the Thirteenth District of Budapest.[11] The election of the second group of constitutional judges by the new Parliament took place in July 1990. On 30 July, the ten constitutional judges elected as their President the Budapest civil lawyer Prof. Dr. László Sólyom,[12] who had been the opposition's leading figure in constitutional debates during the roundtable negotiations and had served until then as Vice President. Later he was reelected as President for second (1993) and third (1996) terms. At the same time, the judges elected as their new Vice President the Pécs public international lawyer Prof. Dr. Géza Herczegh, who in May 1993 renounced his post upon being called to the International Court of Justice at the Hague. Prof. Dr. Tamás Lábady, a former judge at the County Court of Pécs, followed him in the office; he was also reelected in 1996. The third round of elections due in 1994 did not take place because Parliament, in light of experience, changed the Act and reduced the number of judges to eleven in November 1994. Due to political quarrels, it was more than two years before the vacant posts could be filled by electing new judges in November and June 1997.

Because the provisions of the CC Act had peculiar gaps (due to the time pressures of the political collapse), it was provided in § 29[13] that the finer details of the court's constitution and procedures would be covered in "Rules for the Constitutional Court" [hereafter Court Rules], which were to be passed as a formal law at the proposal of the Constitutional Court itself. While the full session of the Constitutional Court had agreed upon a draft of these rules and had presented it to Parliament, at that point differences of opinion surfaced that still have not been resolved. The situation is complicated by the fact that in practice some regulations of the CC Act had already proven themselves in need of adjustment, giving rise to disputes over the degree and direction of the necessary changes. Thus, the passage of the Court Rules is inseparabely tied to the passage of an amended CC Act, for which the Constitutional Court has likewise prepared a draft.

The most important concern of the forthcoming amendments is scaling back the far too broadly conceived competences in the CC Act, which not only have imposed upon the Court a barely sustainable work load but also have led to the unavoidable criticism that the Court is too involved in the political-parliamentary decision-making process in contradiction of the fundamental principle of the separation of powers. Details of these matters will be discussed subsequently. At this point, by way of introduction, the case load is summarized statistically in table 1.[14]

III. Court Structure

The Constitutional Judges

The Constitutional Court (Alkotmánybíróság), at full complement, is to have eleven judges, including the President and Vice President. Their election is accomplished by Parliament, with a two-thirds majority of all representatives (Art. 32/A(4), Constitution), which qualified majority requires that the parties must agree in advance of the vote. This usually occurs in the Nominating Committee, to which all factions send one representative (§ 32/A(4), Constitution; § 6). The proposed candidates receive a hearing before the Legal Committee of Parliament (§ 6) and are then voted upon by the Plenum (full Parliament) in light of the opinion of the Legal Committee (§ 8(1)). If a candidate does not receive the necessary majority, the Nominating Committee must present a new proposal within fifteen days (§ 8(2)). Judges are elected for nine-year terms but only until they reach the end of the seventieth year; a one-time reelection is allowed (§ 8(3), § 15(3)). The President and Vice President are elected by the judges from among themselves for three-year terms, and reelection is possible without restrictions (§ 4(2)).

To stand for election (§ 5) a judge must hold Hungarian citizenship, have no previous convictions, be at least forty-five years old, and have completed a legal education. Further professional qualifications differ for the "theoretician" and the

TABLE 1. The Constitutional Court Caseload

	1990	1991	1992	1993	1994	1995	1996	1990/96
Preventive review of legal norms	—	3	1	4	1	—	2	11
Posterior review of legal norms	584	734	408	350	295	397	402	3,170
Review of conformity with treaties	1	2	1	—	—	1	3	8
Constitutional complaints	12	6	21	17	7	20	19	102
Unconstitutional failure to act	174	49	6	17	5	9	16	276
Conflicts of competence	—	—	1	—	1	1	3	6
Interpretation of the Constitution	8	4	4	—	1	2	—	19
Cases provided for by special acts	13	29	81	41	85	42	83	374
Miscellaneous	833	1,475	1,177	894	703	1,029	1,003	7,114
Total submissions	1,625	2,302	1,700	1,323	1,098	1,501	1,543	11,092
Carryover from previous years	—	343	395	519	542	524	606	—
Total pending proceedings	1,625	2,645	2,095	1,842	1,640	2,025	2,149	11,092
Proceedings completed	1,282	2,250	1,576	1,300	1,116	1,419	1,447	10,390
Proceedings pending	343	395	519	542	524	606	702	702

Source: See note 14.

"practitioner." A theoretician must either be a university professor or have earned the academic degree "Doctor of Government and Legal Sciences" (not to be confused with the title Dr.jur.), which can be compared with the German Habilitation or the American Ph.D. A practitioner must have at least twenty years of experience in a professional practice in a specialized field for which the recognition of a completed legal education is necessary. For appointments of judges to date, preference has been shown for theoreticians. Half of the fourteen judges sitting between 1990 and 1997 have had exclusively academic careers and the other half have close ties to scholarship in that most have been active academically on the side or in teaching or research. Of these seven "half-practitioners," at the time of their election, three were civil judges, two were practicing lawyers, one had once worked as public prosecuter but for many years had been active in legal academic research, and the seventh had served the Constitutional Court as general secretary for six years before being elected judge at the end of 1996. In terms of professional specialization, civil lawyers (eight) and public lawyers (five) dominate the Court, whereas criminal law is represented by only one judge. This unusual makeup of the Court can be explained by the fact that in Hungary legal scholars were the driving force behind the liberal-democratic reforms and within legal scholarship civil law was the field in which one could work relatively undisturbed by political pressure.

It is worthy of note that the political independence of the constitutional judges is assured through strict provisions regarding exclusion and conflicts of interest. These are designed especially to prevent leading officials of the old regime from gaining entry to the Constitutional Court. Thus, nobody is eligible for election as a constitutional judge who in the last four years has been a member of the government or a party or has held a leading position in the government administration (§ 5(3)). Indeed, the Constitution provides that party membership and political activity are inconsistent with the position of constitutional judge (Art. 32/A(5)). Further incompatibilities are set forth in § 9: being a Member of Parliament or of a local government, holding any other government office or an executive position in an interest group, and any gainful occupation that is not scientific, educational, literary, or artistic. If one of the elected constitutional judges falls into any of these specified categories, he has ten days in which to desist from such activities; otherwise, a full session of the Constitutional Court sets a date for termination of the judgship before it has even begun (§ 10, § 15(5)).

The office of a constitutional judge ends (§ 15), other than for the causes already discussed, through resignation, discharge, or removal. Resignation from office is possible at any time and must be submitted in writing to the President of the Court. Discharge results when a judge, for reasons beyond his control, cannot fulfill his official duties. Removal, on the other hand, requires a violation of duty, which arises when the judge does not carry out his duties in a timely manner, is convicted of a criminal offense, or otherwise shows himself to be unfit for the position. A judge who does not participate in the activities of the Constitutional Court for one year must be removed. The Constitutional Court decides on matters of discharge and removal in full session.

Two matters are worth mentioning regarding the legal status of a constitutional judge. For purposes of remuneration, judges have the same status as ministers, which means that according to the official explanation of § 13 they may also take advantage of the privileges that ministers enjoy.[15] Second, constitutional judges enjoy the indemnity and immunity privileges of a Member of Parliament (§ 14). They cannot be held responsible for statements or voting positions made while they are in office. Arrest or prosecution and subjection to coercive measures by the police, unless caught in the act of a criminal offense, are only allowed if a full session of the Constitutional Court waives immunity.

Every constitutional judge has at his disposal a support staff of two research assistants at the level of counsellor or senior counsellor, a personal assistant, and a secretary.

The President and the Vice President of the Court

The powers of the President of the Court (§ 17(1)) are organized above all else as those of a *primus inter pares:* he represents the Court in external affairs, coordinates its activities, and chairs the full sessions. He does not participate in the sessions of the three-judge panels (cf. sec. III), which is a reasonable relief from duties in light of his responsibilities with respect to the administration of justice. In addition to purely management-related activities, the President enjoys other rights under the CC Act that assure him a certain seniority in the dispensing of justice: he can dismiss obviously groundless applications (§ 23(1)) and in full sessions has the determining vote in case of a tie (§ 30(3)). In practice, however, obviously groundless applications are dismissed by the responsible body. President Sólyom has never made use of the tie-breaking vote because he considers it to be incompatible with the equality of constitutional judges.[16] Of greater political significance is the power of the President of the Court to appoint individual rapporteurs, whose function will be mentioned in the final section. In exercising this authority, he can also retain for himself the preparation of important cases. The President of the Court receives the same salary as the prime minister and may even, according to protocol, rank above him (after the Presidents of the Republic and Parliament) in that the Constitution discusses the Constitutional Court before it discusses the government. When the President of the Court is unavailable, he is represented by the Vice President, who otherwise possesses no independent authority.

Full Sessions, Three-Judge Panels, and Committees

The Court may pronounce decisions en banc (full session) or in panels of three. The full session, whose competences are listed in detail in § 30(1), consists of all of the judges. A quorum requires the presence of eight judges, including the President or the Vice President. Decisions are reached with a simple majority. In case of a tie, the President (or Vice President) casts the deciding vote. Because the current President—as mentioned—makes no use of this provision, a tie in effect means denial of the application. "Separate opinions" are possible under § 26 and can be "appended to the file." The term *separate opinion* has been understood in the sense of a dissenting opinion, but concurring opinions have been admitted from the beginning. Since its inception, the Court has maintained the practice of publishing both and has provided for this in its draft Court Rules. Individual constitutional judges often make use of this option. The full session has jurisdiction over decisions in proceedings involving preventive review, review of Acts of Parliament for constitutionality and compatibility with treaty obligations, and for interpretation of the Constitution. In addition, the full session has jurisdiction if the President or three other constitutional judges invoke it.

In addition to deciding cases, the full session decides upon matters involving the status of constitutional judges (termination of office, discharge, removal, or the lifting of immunity) and conflict of interest applications. It determines the Court Rules, elects the President and the Vice President, appoints the General Secretary of the Court, and involves itself with all important matters that arise from the autonomy of the Court.

The three-judge panels are the deciding bodies for less important proceedings, which are identified in § 31 as posterior and treaty reviews of norms other than laws, constitutional complaints, legislative omissions, and conflicts of competence. The panels are established at the beginning of each calendar year by the full session. A quorum requires all three judges to be present and decisions are made by majority vote. The respective rapporteur also serves as chair of the panel. The panels' draft decisions are circulated among the other judges so that the cases can be brought before a full session if three judges deem it advisable.

The active standing committees are the Committee for Court Rules, the Committee for Budget and Personnel, and the Agenda Committee. They are obliged to prepare the decisions of the full session or the President in their respective subject areas, but they can also be invested with the power of decision. The committees consist of three judges, who are elected to three-year terms by the full session at the recommendation of the President.

The Administrative Apparatus

According to § 18, internal administrative tasks are to be carried out by an "office" whose organization and function are to be regulated by the Court Rules. While the Court Rules exist only in draft form, as mentioned, they reflect the administrative structure that has developed in practice. Following this practice, the highest administrative official of the Constitutional Court is the Secretary General, whose activities extend to the area of deciding cases (cf. sec. V). He both serves as press secretary and participates in the full sessions. His office consists of a department for analysis and information, a group that prepares the sessions, a group for data processing, a business office, and a library. Additional administrative units are the President's Secretariat and the Budget Office, which are staffed with the appropriate personnel. The judges themselves participate in administrative matters in connection with the committees on which they serve.

IV. Competences and Types of Proceedings

General Overview

There is no blanket clause for the Constitutional Court. Nonetheless, according to the general description of tasks in Art. 32/A(1–3) of the Constitution and to the individual competences listed in § 1 of the CC Act, it is clear that the abstract review of legal norms is to stand at the center of the practice of Hungary's constitutional judiciary with special consideration given to the protection of fundamental rights. Presumably, this profile was not consciously planned by the framers of the CC Act, who shaped it at the Roundtable.[17] Before discussing the individual competences and types of proceedings, by way of introduction three aspects of the review of legal norms will be presented.

The term *legal norm* (*jogszabály*), uncommon in the United States, covers all rules abstract and general in nature, that is, valid for an indefinite number of cases and addressed to an indefinite number of persons. They constitute a hierarchy, at the top of which the Constitution (Alkotmány) resides. Further levels of the legal hierarchy are, in descending order, Acts of Parliament (*törvény*), regulations (*rendelet*) of the government and individual ministers, ordinances (*rendelkezés*) of state secretaries, and regulations of local governments.

Second, the Court's standard of review must always be the Constitution, not other legal norms. This is clearly more easily said than done. As was shown very early on in the case law involving the priority and proviso of Acts of Parliament, if one accepts the binding nature of the hierarchy of legal norms as a constitutional principle one cannot avoid drawing on Acts of Parliament and even delegated legislation as standards when reviewing the constitutionality of legal norms below the level of an Act. This renders every violation of a higher norm unconstitutional. The Constitution itself provides specifically for the priority of superior legal norms as follows: Acts of Parliament have priority over governmental regulations and resolutions, according to § 35(2), which in turn, together with Acts of Parliament, have priority over regulations of the Prime Minister and members of government, § 37(3); and superior legal norms take precedence over regulations of local governments, § 44/A(2). With respect to other sources of law, the Constitution contains no rules of priority but provides in § 7(2) that the order of lawmaking is to be regulated by legislation. Such a law actually exists in the form of Act XI/1987,

"On Lawmaking." This Act is, of course, not part of the Constitution, and as a consequence it cannot serve as a standard of judgment per se. Nevertheless, in the first years at least, the Constitutional Court[18] took the basic provisions of this Act into consideration with reference to Art. 7(2) of the Constitution, with the result that each violation of the rules on legal priority and provisos of legality was considered to be unconstitutional.[19] Recently, a shift in emphasis has occurred,[20] and the Court now tends to rely on explicit priority provisions of the Constitution when declaring subordinate legislation unconstitutional.[21] In any case, in one way or another each legal norm has been transformed into a standard of review available to the Constitutional Court.

Not only all legal norms but all "other legal instruments of public administration" are considered subject to constitutional review. The sources of law in this category and their hierarchy are to be found in Act XI/1987. What is meant by this terribly drafted term is essentially administrative provisions that are classified as follows:

(a) decisions (organizational provisions received from peer organs)
(b) instruction (administrative guidelines for conduct received from ministers and central agencies)
(c) central bank instructions (binding legal provisions for monetary institutions received from the Chairman of the Hungarian National Bank)
(d) statistical information (statistical rules received from the Director of the Central Statistical Office)
(e) legal guidelines (directives for the interpretation of norms and the exercise of discretion).

Subjecting all of these administrative provisions to constitutional review gave rise to a limitless category of objects of review, which, after the popular action, is the main reason for the Constitutional Court's excessive work load. It is obvious that this disastrous liberality requires legislative correction. In the draft of an amendment to the CC Act presented by the Constitutional Court, it is further proposed that review of local government regulations be transferred to administrative jurisdiction and only the review of parliamentary and governmental legislation remain at the Constitutional Court. On the other hand, the Constitutional Court is striving for a very specific broadening of objects of review, in that it wants to extend its review to leading decisions of the Supreme Court. These acts are "judicial instructions," which are binding on all courts and are decreed by a full session of the Supreme Court—independently of individual cases—to standardize judicial decisions or organize them in terms of legal policy.[22] While these decrees have no direct external effect in a technical sense, practically they function like legal norms. The fact that—unlike other administrative provisions—they cannot be reviewed by a court certainly provides justification for including them in the process of constitutional review.

Preventive Review of Legal Norms (§§ 33–36)

Preventive review of legal norms means a review that occurs before the norm being challenged has taken effect. In this context, four case groupings must be distinguished:

(a) review of draft Acts of Parliament at the request of Parliament, a standing parliamentary committee, or fifty Members of Parliament
(b) review of parliamentary rules of procedure before their adoption at the request of Parliament
(c) review of Acts of Parliament before their promulgation at the request of the President of the Republic
(d) review of international law treaties before their confirmation by Parliament at the request of the President of the Republic or the Government.

A determination of unconstitutionality is binding and creates for the affected party the obligation to remove the unconstitutionality should the norm ever come into force. Until the unconstitutionality has been eliminated, the President of the Republic in type (b) cases and Parliament in type (d) cases are forbidden to confirm the matter in question.

In the practice of the Constitutional Court, cases in groups (a) and (c) have played a role, and in the first group (a) case the basic problems of this type of proceeding came to light at once. It involved the draft of the Compensation Act, which was to regulate reparations for expropriations made during the communist era. The concept for regulation was heavily debated and occupied the public to a very large extent. Therefore, it is not surprising that in Parliament countless applications for amendment to the Government's proposal were submitted by individual Members of Parliament. At the peak of the parliamentary debate, fifty-two MPs called for the Constitutional Court to review various provisions of the government proposal and of the applications for amendment, which placed the Court in the unpleasant position of becoming involved in the political decision-making process. To make things even more difficult, the final version of the text was not yet firm, and as a result the Court was forced to review single, isolated provisions in an overall normative framework that had not yet been determined. The Constitutional Court removed itself from the role of arbitration panel by invoking the principle of separation of powers.[23] This clearly stood in opposition to the unambiguous text of the provisions of the CC Act regarding preventive legal review. A compromise solution was reached through which the Court rejected the application but in addition set forth its basic position on the most important constitutional questions that appeared in the disputed provisions. Of course, the reasons for the decision had no binding effect, but it was possible to give Parliament certain indications as to the direction in which the Court would go should the occasion arise. In a second case, initiated by a standing committee of Parliament, which concerned a draft law on the compensation of victims of communist political repression, the Court specified its point of view by requiring for its preventive review a final draft either already voted upon by Parliament or put to the parliamentary vote but not yet promulgated.[24] In spite of this prudent "judicial restraint," the criticism remained among certain sectors of the public that the Constitutional Court was involving itself in legislative activity. Indeed, politically and constitutionally the preventive review is not unobjectionable and for this very reason the Constitutional Court has proposed in its draft for the amended CC Act that category (a) of cases be dropped.[25] Eventually, in February 1998, Parliament passed an amendment to this effect, which came into force immediately. Five other, no less politically volatile cases fall into group (c). In the first case, the President of the Republic applied for review of the Compensation Act finally agreed to by Parliament, part of which was then found to be unconstitutional.[26] Even more dramatic was the fate of a parliamentary attempt to lift the statute of limitations for specific communist crimes. The President of the Republic opposed all three versions approved by Parliament by calling upon the Constitutional Court to review them. The Court rejected the first two versions as unconstitutional and let the third stand.[27] Finally, the President of the Republic challenged, without success, several provisions of the draft of a new Land Act restricting the acquisition of agricultural land.[28] Unlike the cases in category (a), in these instances the debates in Parliament were already concluded so that the basic concept behind a preventive review of a legal norm, namely, preventing an unconstitutional law from coming into force, could be considered without having to raise the touchy opposing argument of separation of powers. The decision to call on the Constitutional Court is exclusively reserved to the President of the Republic, who in case of objections to Acts presented to him for signature and promulgation has fifteen days in which to call on the Court (Art. 26(4) of the Constitution), while in the case of political objections he may return the Act to Parliament within the same number of days for new consultations and adoption (Art. 26(2) of the Constitution).

Interpretation of the Constitution (§ 51)

According to the scanty terms of § 51(1) of the CC Act, the Constitutional Court is to interpret the Constitution upon the application of Parliament or its standing committees, the President of the Republic, the Government or any of its members, the President of the State Audit Office, the President of the Supreme Court, or the Chief Public Prosecutor. What the legislature intended with this broad competence of interpretation is not made any more clear by reading the official statement of reasons, where it can only be concluded that in practice the necessity could also arise for an abstract interpretation of constitutional provisions, that is, independent of the review of a specific legal norm.[29] In practice, such "necessities" have been claimed in various functional contexts by those constitutional agencies that are entitled to bring applications.

The first cases were related to doubts about the law applicable to the organization of government. Given the uncertainties that characterized the transition to democracy, it made sense to clarify these questions in a binding fashion: the binding effect of a referendum on the framers of the Constitution,[30] the constitutionally required majority for passage of an Act,[31] and who would act as provisional head of state until the constitutional election of a president.[32] Such questions also arose later. Can the positions of commander in chief and chief of staff of the army be held by one and the same person?[33] Can Parliament be dissolved as a result of a referendum?[34] A second group of cases gave rise to more serious problems in that the executive wanted the constitutionality of specific regulatory concepts clarified before a draft law had been introduced, that is, it wanted to bring about a preventive review for cases it could not request reviews for in an actual court proceeding. In the first case, the Constitutional Court, with no hesitation, proceeded to interpret the question of the equality principle in the context of the Government's draft of the Compensation Act. It determined that it would be unconstitutional to choose whether proper redress would be return of the property or compensation, according to the type of expropriated property.[35] The political value of this constitutional interpretation related to a heavily debated dispute within the government coalition: while the dominant Democratic Forum and the Christian Democrats sought general compensation—as did all opposition parties—the Smallholders Party wanted to create an exception for expropriated agricultural real property and have it returned to its original owners. Because the Smallholders Party had to give in to the Constitutional Court rather than to the pressure of its coalition partners, this groundbreaking decision also saved the coalition. In a second case, in which the Finance Minister wanted to know how interest for guaranteed long-term construction loans could be raised constitutionally, the Constitutional Court put on the brakes.[36] It rejected the request with reference to the principle of separation of powers and set forth the requirement, as a condition of admissibility, that the constitutional question to be answered had to be derivable directly from the Constitution, that is, without the intermediate involvement of another legal norm. In this way, the functional competition with the procedure for preventive review of norms was practically eliminated, and since 1993 the Constitutional Court has rarely been confronted with such questions. In one of the two cases worth mentioning, it refused to answer a question posed by the Judicial Committee of Parliament as to the admissibility of a referendum and the powers of the President of the Republic.[37] In the other case, it considered that an application of the President of the Supreme Court fulfilled the requirements for admissibility and construed the relevant provisions of the Constitution concerning the protection of children and the freedom of association in view of legal regulations of children's membership in homosexual organizations.[38] Finally, a third group of cases involved a controversy between constitutional organs that is not provided for in the CC Act as a special type of proceeding. The decision issued in this case dealt with the constitutional legal status of the President of the Republic (especially command of the armed forces and the authority to appoint), which the Constitutional Court interpreted restrictively in the sense of a parliamentary system of government, as was desired by the applicants (the Ministers of Defense and Finance, the Prime Minister, and a parliamentary committee).[39]

Posterior Review of Legal Norms (§§ 37–43)

As was shown in the statistical overview, posterior review of legal norms, that is, of norms that have already taken effect, is the Constitutional Court's daily bread, which at the same time threatens to choke it. The reason is that "anyone" is entitled to bring an action (§ 21(2) CC Act) without limitation; there are no deadlines to be observed, nor is the applicant required to show any impact or other legally protected interest. This means that all legal norms and administrative provisions are subject to legal review. In addition, various kinds of proceedings are hidden in the blanket concept of the "posterior review of legal norms," for which the CC Act and other Acts contain in part special provisions.

It is self-evident that in the loose procedural framework of *abstract legal review* the *popular action* has the largest practical significance. The overwhelming majority of legal review proceedings fall in this category.[40] This is, above all, an encouraging sign that the citizenry willingly accepted the legislature's offer to allow it to play a part in the objective enforcement of a constitutional order. In this way, the Constitutional Court had the opportunity, in the early stages of the new democracy, to review almost the entire legal order for unconstitutionality and to establish guiding standards for the Hungarian constitutional state. Over the long run, however, this work load cannot be sustained; thus, authoritative voices immediately increased, calling for an end to or at least a radical limitation of popular action,[41] the current Hungarian variation of which is unique in the world. The proposal of the Constitutional Court contained in a draft of the revised CC Act addresses itself to reducing the circle of persons entitled to bring a complaint in a "classic" proceeding for abstract norm review to specified constitutional agencies.[42] In addition, popular action would not be entirely eliminated but tied to such restrictive conditions of admissibility that functionally it would resemble—in an admittedly atypical way—a concrete norm review proceeding. According to the Constitutional Court's conception, an individual should be able to apply to initiate a proceeding for posterior review of a norm if it can be shown that his or her fundamental rights were violated as a result of the application of an unconstitutional legal norm and if he or she has exhausted all of the legal remedies available. The deadline for a claim would be sixty days from the issuance of the legally valid decision or from the applicant's awareness of the violation of the right, but no more than one year. In the absence of these conditions, the Constitutional Court would nonetheless retain the right to accept an otherwise inadmissable application if it appears to be justified by the constitutional importance of the question arising from it. This construction distinguishes itself from the constitutional complaint in that the object of review is not the decision of the court or an administrative decision that directly encroaches on a fundamental right but rather the legal norm applied. However, the practical difference is not too great in that the successful complainant can apply for reconsideration by the court or for a new administrative proceeding in which the norm that has been declared unconstitutional may not be applied.

Posterior review of norms also includes the concrete review of norms. According to § 38(1) of the CC Act, a judge who finds that a legal norm or administrative provision to be applied is unconstitutional must stay the proceeding and obtain a decision on the matter from the Constitutional Court. At the same time, this regulation also clarifies the issue of the judicial right of review, much disputed in Hungarian legal literature and, for formal Acts, unanimously rejected[43] (a broad judicial right of review exists, but the Constitutional Court's monopoly on dismissal was firmly established by the inclusion of administrative provisions). This may not have been necessary at the time in light of the public mistrust of judges, which was perhaps still justified. This mistrust was based on the fact that during the communist era judges seldom made use of judicial review and today only cautiously use the existing possibility of presenting a question to the Constitutional Court. In the period 1990–96, only 140 judicial requests were forwarded to the Constitutional Court. In the beginning, most of them were not at the initiative of the judge but rather based on the authority of the parties to the proceeding to propose to the judge that the Constitutional Court be consulted, which is specifically identified in § 38(2).[44] Nonetheless, it appears that the reserved attitude of the judiciary is gradually changing, since the number of proceedings to review concrete norms continues to increase.

Finally, two special proceedings, which have a particular proximity to concrete review of norms but are not capable of being categorized exactly in any one typology, also fall under posterior review of norms. They relate to two specific institutions of judicial review of administrative activities. The first relates to the "general legality review," which originated in the communist era. In theory, the public prosecutor functions as a general agency for legal review of administrative activities and, inter alia, is to oversee the legality of lawmaking acts of the executive below the level of government regulations. Thus, the public prosecutor can "protest" legal or administrative provisions that are unconstitutional or violate a higher ranking law, in response to which the respective lawmaking body must, within thirty days, review the provision objected to and either repeal or amend it. If the lawmaking body believes that the public prosecutor's complaint is unfounded, at this point it can no longer uphold on its own authority the law that it enacted but instead must forward the matter to the Constitutional Court.[45] In practice, the procuracy does not use this instrument. The second variation is of much more importance and relates to the supervision of local authorities by the State, which, with the introduction of local government in 1990, was limited to a purely legal review of administrative activities. State supervisory authorities of local governments were originally the "Republic agents" appointed by the President of the

Republic and subordinate to the Minister of the Interior. As of 1995, the heads of administrative agencies at the regional level have replaced them. The (state) supervisory agencies can object to illegal regulations of the local governments (their bylaws). If the affected local governmental organs do not respond to the objections before the established deadline, the supervisory authorities can ask the Constitutional Court to annul the objectionable legal norm.[46] This happens quite often. On the other hand, local communities can also appeal to the Constitutional Court when their right to self-government has been violated by a legal norm. Furthermore, the language of Art. 43(2), sentence 2, of the Constitution indicates a kind of community constitutional complaint, but the official explanation for the provision inserted into the Constitution in 1990 was that communities could apply for the constitutional review of legal norms and administrative provisions,[47] which is more similar to the acceptance of a proceeding for posterior review of a norm. The undeveloped legal regulation does not provide for a clear qualification of the community right to file a complaint.[48] The Constitutional Court itself considered it insufficient and rejected the possibility of a special community complaint.[49] Apart from these two special proceedings, there is possibly a particular remedy for universities attempting to protect their autonomy against not only legal norms but individual administrative acts.[50]

If the Constitutional Court determines that a legal norm or administrative provision is unconstitutional, it annuls it (§ 40), usually with the result that it becomes inoperative on the day the decision is published in the *Hungarian Official Gazette* (§ 42(1)), and from that point on it may no longer be applied (§ 43(1)). Thus, the invalidity comes into effect *ex nunc.* This theory of nullification, which corresponds to the Austrian approach (Art. 140(5) B-VG) but contradicts the theory of nullity applied in Germany, is at least expedient in that it renders superfluous any complicated provisions as to the legal effect and avoidance of undesired consequences of an *ex tunc* nullity. *Res judicata* decisions of a court and administrative acts that are no longer subject to appeal basically will not be affected by the declaration of nullity. A single exception is made for *res judicata* criminal convictions, whose review in a retrial will occur for the benefit of the convicted person (§ 43(3)). Otherwise, the Constitutional Court is empowered to deviate from the *ex nunc* rule and for reasons of legal certainty or in especially important interests of the applicant to determine an earlier or later time for the commencement of invalidity (§ 43(4)). The Constitutional Court has already made frequent use of this option, usually in the sense of a *pro futuro* nullity to avoid gaps in the law. However, no small number of cases can be listed in which the continued effect of unconstitutional violation of fundamental rights has been avoided by means of a retroactive declaration of nullity.

A legal norm can be open to various interpretations. It is also conceivable that of the various interpretation options some can be considered constitutional and others unconstitutional. Confronted with this situation, only in the summer of 1993 did the Constitutional Court apply the technique of "interpretation in accordance with the Constitution" in order to protect questionable provisions of the Judicature Act from the abrupt consequences of nullity and to allow them to continue in force with constitutional content.[51] This technique, controversial among judges, at the beginning at least, has paved the way for a more subtle control of regular court practice, just as the functionally similar concept of "living law" (*diritto vivente*) was borrowed from Italy and applied simultaneously.

Constitutional Complaints (§ 48)

The arrangements for a constitutional complaint constitute the most unsuccessful provision of the CC Act. A complaint can be brought by any person who claims that his or her fundamental rights have been injured through the application of an unconstitutional legal norm. The right to a complaint is apparently not limited to natural persons but is also available to an association of persons that has no legal capacity and to legal persons to the extent that they have the capacity for fundamental rights.[52] Further conditions of admissibility, in addition to standing, are the exhaustion of remedies and the meeting of the deadline for complaint of sixty days from the issuance of the nonappealable decision. The heart of the regulation consists of the fact that the subject of challenge and constitutional review is not the decision that embodies the direct violation of the fundamental right but the legal norm on which it is based. It is correctly observed that the Hungarian constitutional complaint is not a true constitutional complaint at all but rather a variation of the posterior review of norms in which violation of an individual right is required.[53] This is also confirmed by the fact that the effects of the decisions themselves are the same as in the proceedings for posterior review of norms (§ 48(3)). But because the individual can also achieve these results through the much simpler route of popular action, for which no special standing is required, it is little wonder that the number of constitutional complaints pales in comparison with the posterior norm review.[54]

Nevertheless, under certain circumstances the constitutional complaint can serve a useful purpose. This is the case with a challenge to a legal provision that has been repealed but still exerts a legal effect on affairs that took place in the past and resulted in present claims. Such a situation arises quite often in tax law, which is being changed incessantly. For example, by way of popular action a tax provision valid for 1996 only could not be challenged by a taxpayer who receives his or her tax assessment for 1996 in 1997 when he or she thinks that the underlying provision was unconstitutional. In proceedings of posterior review, the Constitutional Court exclusively reviews legal norms still in force. In such a case, the constitutional complaint may help, but it does not help necessarily. As has been explained, the subject of the constitutional complaint would be the tax provision, not the tax assessment. Should the Court declare the tax provision unconstitutional, this decision would not affect the validity of the tax assessment by necessity. For a success, a second factor is needed, and this is the good intention of the Contitutional Court itself. Section 43(4) of the CC Act gives the Court the discretionary power to annul an unconstitutional provision retroactively or prohibit its application in the special case under consideration if it thinks that this decision would serve the reliability of the legal order or an important interest of the applicant. In the few cases it has dealt with to date, the Court has been reluctant to use its power in favor of the complainant, but sometimes it has done so.[55] In one famous but early case decided in November 1991, the Court even overstepped the boundaries of its legal power and annulled the decision of an ordinary court based on an unconstitutional legal provision.[56] It characterized the constitutional complaint as a legal remedy and concluded from this that in the absence of express legal regulation the Constitutional Court had the following task: to determine the way and manner in which a correction of the challenged violation of a right could validly be accomplished in a specific case of the inherent identification of a legal remedy. The decision was reached by a vote of eight to two, with the dissenting judges Kilényi and Schmidt complaining that the Court had exceeded its legal competencies.[57] This criticism found support in the literature.[58] Specific authorizations cannot be inferred from the CC Act, which limits the functions of the Constitutional Court to the review of legal norms. The only argument in favor of the Court's decision is the absurdity of the legal regulation that makes the constitutional complaint almost superfluous in relation to popular action. There is no reasonable doubt as to the urgent need for a legal revision. Authoritative voices, including some from the Constitutional Court itself, are promoting the introduction of a true constitutional complaint whose subject would be individual acts of the public authorities.[59] This would be useful, indeed. For the time being, however, the Court has to work with a constitutional complaint as it was conceived by the legislature in 1989. It can be assumed that the decision of November 1991 will remain an isolated one and the Court, also impressed by criticism, will refrain from repeating it.

Unconstitutional Omission to Legislate (§ 49)

In the first year of constitutional practice, the second most frequent type of proceeding—after the posterior review of norms—was the proceeding to determine an unconstitutional legislative omission to legislate. Since 1992, its significance has decreased substantially, but it nonetheless remains considerable. In fact, the proceeding involves a type of negative review of legal norms in which the Constitutional Court must determine whether a state authority has neglected to fulfill a legally required lawmaking mandate and has thus prompted an unconstitutional situation. If the Court reaches this conclusion, it sets a specific deadline within which the dilatory state authority must enact the unadopted legal norm. As with popular actions, any person may apply to commence a proceeding; in addition, the Court can officially reach a corresponding determination. It is unlikely that this latter authorization means that the Court can commence a declaratory proceeding on its own. In its practice to date, it has only made use of this authorization when it has been necessary to decide a proceeding for legal review or a constitutional complaint begun by an application that did not include within it a claimed failure to act.[60]

Whether a lawmaking mandate is fulfilled or not is comparatively easy to determine. It is quite clear that the mandate may result, directly or indirectly, from a provision of the Constitution,[61] an Act of Parliament,[62] a piece of delegated legislation,[63] or even an annulment of a legal provision by the Constitutional Court that leads to a gap in the system.[64] The Constitutional Court did not stop here, however. It stated in one of its earliest decisions that an explicit mandate to legislate was not necessary if the competent authority had to notice the existence of a problem in want of legislative solution.[65] In the same decision, the Court addressed the much more difficult question of when legislative inactivity gives rise to an unconstitutional state of affairs. It answered this question in the sense that not every instance of legislative inactivity is unconstitutional but it is when the need for regulation resulted from governmental interference in social conditions with the effect of depriving citizens of the ability to assert their constitutional rights.[66] It seems that the Court confines this requirement to situations in which there is no explicit lawmaking mandate. In all other cases, it tends to assume the unconstitutionality of a state of affairs from the fact that an explicit lawmaking mandate has not been fulfilled, disregarding the political circumstances. Thus, for example, it determined an unconstitutional omission of Parliament to legislate because it had not carried out the constitutional mandate to enact a law for the protection of national minorities within the two and a half years of the adoption of the relevant constitutional provision.[67] The reasons made no mention of the political difficulties (resulting from the Government's good intentions) of introducing before Parliament a bill that had the approval of the associations of national minorities. In fact, the consultations between the Government and the minority associations had commenced quite early but were delayed by controversies, not the least of which were between the individual minority associations. At the time of the proceeding before the Constitutional Court, the pre-parliamentary negotiations were in full swing and the generosity of the Government's endeavors to come to terms with the social forces concerned for reasons of political wisdom and without any legal obligation to do so resulted finally in the qualification of Parliament's omission to adopt a law, whose draft was not yet even submitted to it, as unconstitutional. In this case, the Constitutional Court was somewhat overzealous in promoting the rule of law construed in a very strict manner. On the other hand, there have been several cases in which legislative delay obviously was caused by party quarrels within Parliament and the Constitutional Court's verdict of unconstitutional omission to legislate has been fully justified. The most notorious of these involved the fate of the Radio and Television Act. Its adoption was ordered by the Constitutional Court in June 1992, with a deadline set for 30 November 1992.[68] After the deadline expired, the Court twice more called for suitable legislation.[69] An Act was finally passed in December 1995.

Review of Conformity with Treaties (§§ 44–47)

Pursuant to Art. 7(1) of the Constitution, the compatibility of treaty obligations assumed by Hungary with its internal legal order must be guaranteed. To this end, the CC Act provides for a special proceeding in which the Constitutional Court reviews the conformity of a legal norm or an administrative provision with an international treaty, either at the Court's own initiative or upon the application of Parliament or its standing committees, the President of the Republic, the Government or any of its members, the President of the State Audit Office, the President of the Supreme Court, or the Chief Public Prosecutor.

If an internal legal provision contradicts a treaty, two types of cases are to be distinguished. If the legal provision under review has the same or a lower rank than the legal norm under which the treaty has been promulgated, according to the provisions regarding posterior review, it will be annulled (§ 45). If the norm in question, however, has a higher rank, even an interpretation of the internal norm hierarchy in a manner extremely friendly to international law cannot help resolve the conflict in favor of the treaty. In this case, the Constitutional Court can choose between two options: it can require the body responsible for the execution of the treaty to change the treaty within a specific time period or it can require the responsible lawmaking agency to conform the internal legal norm to the treaty within a certain time period (§ 46). It is noteworthy that in this sensitive matter the Constitutional Court is expected to make the final political determination as to whether international or domestic law should take priority.[70] Finally, it is conceivable that the responsible lawmaking body neglected to adopt the legal regulations necessary to implement the treaty obligations domestically. In this case of legislative inactivity, the responsible government body is obligated to perform its lawmaking duty within a certain time period (§ 47).

Review of conformity with international treaties has not yet achieved any notable practical significance. In this context, another situation, not covered by the proceeding according to §§ 44–47 CC Act, is worth mentioning: review of conformity of international treaties with the Constitution. As has been explained (cf. sec. IV), preventive review of international treaties not yet confirmed by Parliament is provided for expressly. Less clear is the answer to the question of whether a posterior review of the act transforming the international treaty into domestic law is possible. Until recently, the question did not play a major role in the Court's inconsistent practice. While at the end of 1990 the Court's plenary session answered in the affirmative on the ground that the transforming act was part of the Hungarian legal order and as such a legal norm in the sense of posterior review,[71] in early 1993 a three-judge panel refused to accept a similar case and denied the Court's jurisdiction over international treaties irrespective of their becoming part of domestic law.[72] In 1997, the dormant question abruptly gained political significance when a provision concerning European competition law of the Europe Agreement associating Hungary with the European Community was challenged by way of popular action. The substantive matter is still pending, but from the procedural point of view the Court has already clarified its position and stated that posterior review of conformity of international treaties embodied in an Act of Parliament with the Constitution is within its competence.[73]

Conflicts of Competence (§ 50)

While deciding competence conflicts between courts and administrative bodies is a task for the ordinary courts,[74] the Constitutional Court must decide on all applications for every type of competence conflict between the national government and local administrative agencies. To date, only five cases of this kind have come before the Constitutional Court; two were decided by resolving the conflict,[75] while three were dismissed in the absence of a conflict.[76] Their lack of importance notwithstanding, it is evident that these primarily administrative matters are being dealt with at too high a level and burden the Constitutional Court. In its draft of a new CC Act, the Constitutional Court has expressed its desire for a limitation of its jurisdiction over conflicts of competence to those cases in which the Parliament, the President of the Republic, or the Government are involved.

Other Competences

Some competences of the Constitutional Court are established independently of the CC Act. Of these, the so-called constitutional complaints concerning *people's initiatives* and *referenda* play the largest role; they have been widely permissible since 1989 at both the state[77] and local[78] levels. The "constitutional complaints" that have been raised countless times since 1991 affect exclusively plebiscites at the local level, which deal mostly with communities merging or becoming independent. On the national level, at this point there has been one unsuccessful constitutional complaint against Parliament's rejection of a people's initiative for a referendum on Hungary's NATO membership.[79] In contrast, election challenges fall under the jurisdiction of the ordinary courts.[80]

Community Councils may be *dissolved* by Parliament at the request of the government for unconstitutional activities. Before the government files the relevant application, however, it must obtain the opinion of the Constitutional Court.[81]

Only in June 1990, by constitutional amendment, was *presidential impeachment* transferred to the jurisdiction of the Constitutional Court.[82] According to the original version of the constitutional revision of 1989, for this purpose a special chamber was to be appointed each time with the same number of judges from both the Supreme Court and the Constitutional Court under the chairmanship of the President of the Supreme Court. Now the Constitutional Court decides upon the President's removal from office for violation of the Constitution or the law. The charge is brought by Parliament upon a two-thirds majority vote of all MPs, but the request to bring a charge can be effected by one-fifth of the MPs.

Strikingly, *banning of parties* does not fall under the jurisdiction of the Constitutional Court; indeed, it is not even under the jurisdiction of the Supreme Court. A political party whose activities are aimed at the violent overthrow of the government, the exercise or exclusive possession of governmental power, or the commission of crimes may, like any association, be prohibited by the locally responsible regional or the metropolitan court upon application of the public prosecutor.[83] The appeals route leads to the Supreme Court. This provision, which is unique in Eastern Europe, can be explained by the specific phase of reform during the period of transition in Hungary. It clearly does not fit into the otherwise broad political balance of interests according to which the Constitutional Court's areas of responsibility are determined.

V. Procedural Operation and Principles

Legal Bases

The CC Act does not regulate all aspects of proceedings before the Constitutional Court, leaving gaps that can be only partially covered by ordering the application of corresponding provisions from the Code of Civil Procedure regarding legal representation, the use of one's mother tongue, and the exclusion of judges (§ 19). Details are to be governed by the Court Rules, which, although it has not yet occurred, must be promulgated in the form of a legislative act (§ 29; cf. sec. II). However, the proposed draft Court Rules contain detailed procedural provisions in clauses 27–65, which also make reference to the Code of Civil Procedure with respect to expert evidence, witnesses, and documentary evidence. The Constitutional Court follows these draft Court Rules in practice. Whether it has thereby claimed procedural autonomy for itself is an idle question. The insufficient legal regulations leave the Court no choice other than to shape the procedures itself. There appears to be a tendency toward an independent law of constitutional procedure, though some of the constitutional judges prefer the model of the civil procedure laws.[84] In any event, the Constitutional Court is striving *de lege ferenda* for procedural autonomy. It proposes in its draft for a revised CC Act that the Court should approve the Court Rules itself, without parliamentary participation.

Initiation of a Proceeding

A proceeding is basically commenced by means of application (§ 20), which must meet the usual requirements. Entitlement to submit an application is specially regulated for each type of proceeding and has already been discussed. It should be emphasized that, apart from the constitutional complaint, a specific standing of the applicant is not required because the Constitutional Court as a rule does not decide controversies affecting rights of a party but has the main task of reviewing the conformity of legislation to the Constitution in order to contribute to ensuring the constitutionality of the legal system. No statutory requirement of representation by a lawyer currently exists, but it is to be introduced for private persons under the Constitutional Court's plans for reform. Officially, the Court may only commence proceedings for review of treaty norms and for determination of an unconstitutional omission to legislate (§ 21(7)).

The extent to which the *application principle* also covers completion of the proceeding and the determination of its subject, and thus strengthens the *maxim of party disposition,* cannot be inferred from the CC Act. All that can be said with certainty is that this cannot be the case for the two types of proceedings, just named, that the Constitutional Court may initiate on its own. An application possesses no binding effect either for the resolution of a conflict of norms between treaty law and domestic law or for the determination of a constitutional failure to act. Otherwise, the Constitutional Court presumes that the withdrawal of an application is allowable and must lead to the suspension of the proceeding.[85] Only a few early decisions to suspend contained the added feature that the three-judge panel could find no reasonable cause to refuse consent and officially continue the proceeding.[86] Thus, the matter can be considered to have been decided. On the other hand, with respect to determining the subject of the proceeding, in denying the application's binding effect the Constitutional Court appears to be relying on the ex officio maxim. The Court also considers itself authorized to review terms of a legal norm for which a review has not been requested by application.[87] This opinion corresponds somewhat to the German approach contained in § 78(2) of the Federal Constitutional Court Act. The Hungarian Constitutional Court, however, takes this even further. It also annuls provisions in legislative acts not mentioned in the application if there is a close factual relationship between these provisions and those in the law challenged by the applicant, so that in case of the unconstitutionality of the latter, standing on their own, the former would make no sense.[88]

Once submitted, the application is first reviewed by the *Secretary General* for its general admissibility. Pursuant to § 36 of the draft Court Rules, this review extends to the questions of (1) whether the petition qualifies as an application at all, (2) whether another authority (especially the public prosecutor) is responsible for handling the matter, (3) whether the Constitutional Court has already decided on the matter, and (4) whether the application meets all legal requirements. If the Secretary General concludes that commencement of the proceeding is not admissible, he or she makes the appropriate disposition and notifies the applicant. If the application contains deficiencies, he requires the applicant to remove them and advises him or her that otherwise the proceeding cannot commence. In this manner, of the 10,390 matters handled in 1990–96, 7,366 (70.9%!) were concluded by means of an informal letter from the Secretary General.

If an application makes it through the screening of the Secretary General or the applicant is not convinced by the warning letter, the President of the Constitutional Court names a special rapporteur. At the same time, the President decides whether the full session or a three-judge panel is competent, although he or she may convene a full session at any time.

Preliminary Proceedings

The special rapporteur prepares the case to the point that, based on his proposal, the respective deciding body can make a procedural decision (rejecting the claim for inadmissibility or for failure to show sufficient cause, consolidation, separation, discontinuance, or suspension of the proceeding) and can commence with the factual discussion of the case. To this end, the deciding body may draw up the orders necessary to establish the direction of the proceedings. It is considered a weakness that individual judges are not authorized to make these procedural decisions under existing law. The Constitutional Court has thus proposed an appropriate amendment to the CC Act.

Collegial Proceedings

A collegial proceeding, as it is called in the draft Court Rules, is carried out in the full session or in the respective three-judge panel. It is basically a written proceeding. Pursuant to clause 46(2) of the draft Court Rules, an oral hearing is only required if the applicant is the Parliament, one of its standing committees or an individual representative, the President of the Republic, the Government or any of its members, the President of the State Audit Office, the President of the Supreme Court, or the Chief Public Prosecutor. Otherwise, the Constitutional Court can set a date for an oral hearing at its discretion. In principle, the hearing is not public. A public hearing is only to take place as an exception, and its time is to be made public. The President of the Republic, the Prime Pinister, the President of Parliament, the President of the Supreme Court, the Chief Public Prosecutor, the Minister of Justice, and the applicant may participate in the nonpublic hearing and may make oral statements (§ 30(4)). In addition, the president of the Constitutional Court may invite individuals whom he feels should be heard. Only individuals who have been summoned may participate in hearings before three-judge panels, which are chaired by the special rapporteur (§ 31(3)).

For the investigation of information necessary to the decision of the case, the investigation principle apparently applies. Although this is not absolutely clear from the CC Act, the resulting official gathering of evidence is appropriate to the unique character of the constitutional procedure, which is centered on the review of legal norms. It also corresponds to the practice of the Hungarian Constitutional Court. This practice is reflected in clause 43(1) of the draft Court Rules, which provides that the Constitutional Court is free to gather all evidence necessary to reach a decision in the case. This contradicts the text of the law in that the CC Act mentions only requests for information (§ 24), written files, personal hearings, and the calling of expert witnesses (§ 25(2), sentence 1). It specifically forbids other forms of proof (§ 25(2), sentence 2). This rigid legal rule, pursuant to which, for instance, the admissibility of witnesses or documentary evidence would be doubtful, is certainly unreasonable and should be amended according to the wishes of the Constitutional Court. Of greatest importance is the obtaining of position papers from constitutional agencies that are involved in the matter.

Consulting and voting take place, of course, only among the participating judges. Competence to decide, majority requirements, and separate opinions have already been discussed (cf. sec. III). It should be added that the draft decision prepared by the special rapporteur of the case is circulated among the judges ten days in advance so that all of them have time to get acquainted with the facts and legal considerations and form their own opinions. Deliberation on the case is intense, may be controversial, and can result in refusing or changing the draft. The order of voting is also organized according to criteria similar to those found in § 197 of the German Judicature Act: first, the reporter votes; then the remaining judges vote according to age, the younger judges voting before the elder; and, finally, the chair votes. In practice, however, informal voting by a show of hands seems to be preferred. Concurring and dissenting opinions are used quite often if no unanimity can be reached, and it is interesting to observe that it often happens that a new legal concept is expounded first in a separate opinion and adopted later by the majority. Thus, for example, the basic concept of "proportionality," which plays a central role in the Court's jurisprudence today, first emerged in a separate opinion of President Sólyom in February 1990[89] and was adopted by the plenum seven months later.[90]

The *decisions* of the Constitutional Court are "binding on everybody" (§ 27(2), CC Act) and thus apply *erga omnes.* As a rule, they are not orally pronounced and are only delivered to the applicant and—at the discretion of the Constitutional Court—to other interested persons. However, as an exception the Court may pronounce an oral decision in a public or closed session. Decisions in which legal norms or administrative provisions are declared to be unconstitutional and annulled or are issued in a proceeding for constitutional interpretation are published in the *Hungarian Official Gazette* or the journal in which the annulled constitutional provision was published (§ 41; § 51(2)), in full text, including the reasons and separate opinions. Although there is no legal basis for it, the Constitutional Court has also directed the publication of other decisions, those in which the Constitutional Court confirmed the constitutionality of a legal provision or found an unconstitutional omission to which the Court attributed particularly great importance. Thus, in the 1990 *Hungarian Official Gazette* 33 decisions were published. There were 67 in 1991, 74 in 1992, 63 in 1993, 62 in 1994, 81 in 1995, and 60 in 1996. In addition, the Constitutional Court publishes a collection of decisions. The first volume, for 1990, contained 114 decisions, the second (1991) 276, the third (1992) 196, the fourth (1993) 252, the fifth (1994) 226, the sixth (1995) 253, and the seventh (1996) 239.

Costs

Proceedings are cost free and require no fees, but the Constitutional Court can pass on the costs of the proceeding to the applicant if his or her "bad faith" can be established (§ 28). The Constitutional Court has never made use of a possible "misuse" fee because it takes the position that as objective procedures all proceedings serve the public interest and therefore the subjective motive of the applicant is unimportant. On this basis, the Court has requested that the relevant provision be removed from the CC Act.

Provisional Orders?

According to current law, the Constitutional Court is not authorized to regulate a situation in advance. In the Court's view, this should be changed. In its draft for an amended CC Act, it foresees the initiation of a provisional order through which the enforcement of a challenged legal norm can be suspended if this appears to be urgently needed to prevent great disadvantage or for other important reasons.

VI. The Hungarian Constitutional Court in Comparative Perspective

The Hungarian Constitutional Court, which commenced its activities[91] on 1 January 1990, is not the first, but beyond any doubt it is the most active and influential example of its species in Eastern—and perhaps Western—Europe.[92] Constitutional courts have been active in the former Yugoslavia and its federal units since early 1964 and in Poland since the end of 1985. In the aftermath of the unsuccessful Prague Spring of 1968, the former Czechoslovakia, the only country with even a faint prewar tradition of the kind, undertook an abortive attempt to establish a Constitutional Court. All these precursors, however, had a much more limited dimension than the ascent of the constitutional judiciary that began in Hungary and spread all over Eastern Europe in the following years of systemic change.

This is easy to understand. The intended change from communist dictatorship to constitutional democracy involved a demand for efficient legal safeguards for the supremacy of the rule of law. It is no wonder that in looking around for an appropriate device all eyes were fixed on Germany and the impressive performance of its Federal Constitutional Court (Bundesverfassungsgericht) in stabilizing and developing constitutional democracy after a war lost under the aegis of the national-socialist dictatorship. The idea that the supremacy of a constitution, developed in the United States by the Supreme Court, that country's highest ordinary court, ought to be secured by a special court placed outside and above the ordinary court system and assigned the specific function of constitutional review was an Austrian one originally. It was in Vienna in 1920 that, according to Hans Kelsen's vision, the first separate and specialized constitutional court, the Verfassungsgerichtshof, was established immediately after the collapse of the Austro-Hungarian monarchy. Under comparable conditions after World War II, Germany and Italy took up the Austrian idea; their constitutional courts were convened in 1951 and 1956, respectively. The main German contribution to the further development of the idea was the invention of the constitutional complaint (*Verfassungsbeschwerde*) entitling anyone to call on the constitutional court if he or she has exhausted all the legal remedies available and can show that his or her fundamental rights may have been infringed by a public action. The German, Austrian, and Italian experience has proved to be especially attractive for countries confronted with the task of transition from dictatorship to democracy, and special constitutional courts were established in Turkey in 1962, Spain in 1980, and Portugal in 1983. In the case of Eastern Europe, the basic orientation of this model suggested itself also because the legal traditions of the region have been closely related to the German civil law system. In some countries, the influence of French law could be felt, too, but the modest power of the Conseil Constitutionnel, established in 1958, did not offer a model suitable for the purpose of systemic change. Even Romania, with its traditional preference for French solutions, deviated from custom and created a constitutional court, although its comparatively limited competences reflect French influence. Since the most recent courts (those of Ukraine and Latvia) commenced operations in early 1997, almost all of the twenty-eight countries that have emerged from the Soviet orbit have constitutional courts of the German type. There are but three exceptions. Estonia, apparently under Scandinavian influence, assigned the restricted task of constitutional review to a special chamber of the State Tribunal functioning at the top of a unitary court system. The second exception is Kazakhstan, which was not an exception in the beginning but became one as a result of its second Constitution, adopted by referendum on 30 August 1995. At that time, a real Constitutional Court had been active for three years, though not to the liking of its autocrat, President Nazarbaev. The Court's ruling on the invalidity of the manipulated parliamentary elections of March 1994 caused the President to downgrade the Court to a Constitutional Council with limited jurisdiction on the French model. Finally, there is Turkmenistan, whose autocratic President Niyazov considers any kind of constitutional safeguards superfluous. This is quite honest insofar as he is the only one among the dictatorial presidents dominating the Islamic region of the former Soviet Union who does not even pretend to harbor the desire to see his country become a democracy ruled by law.

As a result of these developments, on the geographical map of today Central, Southern, and Eastern Europe have become by and large the homeland of constitutional courts. Their common features and differences may be summarized as follows.

The constitutional court is a unique court, independent of the ordinary court structure and established for the special purpose of deciding matters of constitutional law.

The selection process for constitutional judges may differ. The prevalent method is election by Parliament, although the state president is usually involved in some way, for example, by having a right of nomination or appointment. Occasionally, the lower courts, too, have a role in selecting their "elder brethren." An ingenious equilibrium of the three public powers has been reached in Italy, where one-third of the constitutional judges are elected by the legislative, executive, and judicial branches of government, respectively. This model has been adopted by Bulgaria, Moldova, Ukraine, and Georgia. The term of office is usually limited, with a preference for nine years. Reelection for a second term is partly allowed and partly excluded. Only Serb and Armenian judges have lifetime tenure. High professional qualifications are required everywhere but are defined in different ways.

The powers of the constitutional courts are listed in different catalogs, but the main task everywhere is constitutional review of legal norms. The courts must safeguard the constitutional order for the sake of the body politic. As to type of proceedings, a distinction should be made between previous and posterior review, abstract and concrete review, whether the review concerns legislation in the making or legislation that has already been promulgated, and, in the latter case, whether review is asked for without a specific reason or in connection with a constitutional problem arising from an individual case in an ordinary court. Without going into further detail, it should be noted as a general tendency that posterior and abstract reviews dominate the scene. Preliminary review is used in Hungary, Poland, Estonia, Romania, and Kazakhstan. In the latter two countries, this is the only means of obtaining an abstract review, although a concrete posterior review is possible.

One disputed question is whether constitutional courts should be assigned the additional task of protecting individuals against infringment upon their fundamental rights by public authorities (adding, thus, a further echelon to the hierarchy of the ordinary courts).[93] The question has been answered in the affirmative hesitantly in Austria and decisively in Germany with the introduction of the constitutional complaint as a legal remedy for individual acts, primarily court decisions. This example has been followed by Spain, Croatia, the Czech Republic, and Slovenia, where this type of proceeding has achieved enormous practical significance. Recently, in Macedonia, where the situation is far from clear on that point, the Constitutional Court has admitted the constitutional complaint as well, and apparently citizens there are slowly getting acquainted with it. On the other hand, the constitutional complaint has gained hardly any importance in Slovakia, the Federal Republic of Yugoslavia, and Montenegro, where it is provided for but only as a subsidiary instrument in cases in which no protection by court would otherwise be available.

Some legislatures, apparently, uncertain as to the answer to the disputed question, have tried to find a compromise solution. Typical of this ambiguity is the kind of individual complaint that can be made by a party showing that his or her rights may have been affected, only, but whereby not the public act allegedly violating rights but the underlying legal norm is being challenged. Examples for this hybrid of protecting individual rights and the constitutional order equally are the infrequently used Hungarian "constitutional complaint" discussed in section IV, the rather popular Russian "individual complaint," and the Romanian "objection of unconstitutionality," which can be raised by parties to a litigation in an ordinary court. In all these proceedings, the constitutional court reviews, and if necessary annuls, the legal norm to be applied, but it does not decide the individual case. Even more restricted are the effects of the newly introduced "constitutional petition" in Ukraine, which is directed at the mere interpretation of a constitutional provision in conjunction with an individual grievance. The Hungarian "popular action" (cf. sec. IV) falls into a category all its own. As has been shown, it is a special type of abstract and posterior review not requiring any individual standing but considering the individual person as a trustee of the public good. In this invention lies one of Hungary's major contributions to the spectrum of the constitutional judiciary. It has been a debatable contribution, it is true, since it has resulted in an enormous work load for the court concerned. Nevertheless, in the formative period of a new democracy based on the rule of law, at least, it has proved itself to be a most effective means to that end.

To what effect can a constitutional court declare a legal norm unconstitutional? It will annul it. But what does annulment mean? It can mean that the unconstitutional legal norm is to be considered null and void from its inception. This is the kind of logical concept that Chief Justice John Marshall might have had in mind when he stated that "an act of legislature, repugnant to the constitution, is void,"[94] and it has been embodied by law in Germany (Art. 78; Art. 95(3) B VerfGG). On the other hand, the consequences of this logic may turn out to be extremely unpleasant should all the legal relationships based on a law whose unconstitutionality is discovered many years after its adoption be declared null and void as well. In the course of time, the U.S. Supreme Court has become aware of this fact, and it tries to tackle the problem pragmatically under the heading of retroactivity.[95] The framers of the Austrian Constitution made up their minds in favor of ineffectiveness commencing only at the moment of the court's decision (Art. 139(2); Art. 140(2) B-VerfG) unless the Verfassungsgerichtshof sets a later date within the period of one year. Unlike most of the Western European countries that followed the German path of *ex tunc* nullity with some adjustments (Italy, Spain, Portugal, and Belgium), Turkey and all the former communist countries have been attracted to the Austrian concept of *ex nunc* invalidity. In practical terms, at least, they seem to be right. Even more expedient is the solution arrived at in some countries that state the *ex nunc* invalidity as a general rule only and empower their constitutional courts to deviate from the rule at discretion and determine an earlier (*ex tunc*) or later (*pro futuro*) date for the annulment to take effect (Hungary, Croatia, Czech Republic, and Slovenia).

As can be seen, within one general type of constitutional judiciary several variations are conceivable and many points of technical detail are open to debate.

What matters is the general conclusion that can be drawn from seven years of constitutional development in the former communist world. In eastern Central Europe, at least, the model of separate constitutional courts has stood the test of time and made a significant contribution to developing a government of laws and not men.[96]

NOTES

1. For a thorough and comprehensive study of the whole process, see Rudolf L. Tőkés, *Hungary's Negotiated Revolution: Economic Reform, Social Change, and Political Succession, 1957–1990* (Cambridge, 1996).

2. Cf. Georg Brunner, "Die Verfassungsentwicklung in Ungarn seit der Verfassungsrevision von 1972," *Jahrbuch des öffentlichen Rechts der Gegenwart* NF 30 (1981): 279–344.

3. The quotation is from the conference's closing resolutions, published in *Népszabadság,* 23 May 1988, supplement.

4. For more detail, see Géza Kilényi, "Hungary's Road to a Democratic State of the Rule of Law," in *Democratic Changes in Hungary,* edited by Géza Kilényi and Vanda Lamm, 5–34 (Budapest, 1990); András Bozóki, "Political Transition and Constitutional Change in Hungary," *Südosteuropa* 39 (1990): 538–45; and Georg Brunner, "Die neue Verfassung der Republik Ungarn: Entstehungsgeschichte und Grundprobleme," *Jahrbuch für Politik—Yearbook of Politics* 1 (1991): 297–318.

5. See the announcement of the revision in *Magyar Közlöny,* 1989, 1244. The most recent consolidated text of the Constitution is in *Magyar Közlöny,* 1990, 1741. Cf. Ferenc Majoros, "Ungarns neue Verfassungsordnung: Die Genese einer neuen demokratischen Republik nach westlichen Maßstäben," *Osteuropa-Recht* 36 (1990): 85–99, 161–74; and Georg Brunner, "Die Verfassungsordnung," in *Ungarn auf dem Weg der Demokratie,* edited by Georg Brunner, 42–86 (Bonn, 1993).

6. Regarding the conception and activities of the Constitutional Committee, see György Jutasi, "Az Alkotmányjogi Tanács tevékenységének néhány elvi problémája" (Some Problems of Principle in the Activities of the Constitutional Committee), *Állam és Igazgatás* 36 (1985): 520–35; Albert Takács, "Problems of the Protection of the Constitution, with Special Regard to the Constitutional Law Council," *Acta Juridica Scientiarum Hungaricae* 29 (1987): 165–91; Georg Brunner, "Das Regierungssystem. Verfassung und Verwaltung," in *Südosteuropa-Handbuch. Vol. V Ungarn,* edited by Klaus-Detlev Grothusen, 213–249 (226) (Göttingen, 1987); and Géza Kilényi, "Parliament," in *Parliamentarism and Government in a One-Party System,* edited by Géza Kilényi and Vanda Lamm, 57–98 (76 ff.) (Budapest, 1988).

7. *Magyar Közlöny,* 1989, 1283.

8. The diverging positions and the course of the negotiations are described in detail in Tamás Bán, "Az Alkotmánybíróság létrejötte" (The Establishment of the Constitutional Court), *Világosság* 34, no. 11 (1993): 32–40.

9. Kilényi, *Hungary's Road,* 31 ff.; Bán, *"Az Alkotmánybíróság létrejötte,"* 37.

10. "A Magyar Jogász Szövetség észrevételei az alkotmány szabályozási elveihez" (Comments of the Hungarian Lawyers' Association on the Principles of Regulation of the Constitution), *Magyar Jog* 36 (1989): 845–67 (857 ff.).

11. Amusing details about the difficulties involved in the search for the appropriate building are to be found in Géza Kilényi, "Gondok az Alkotmánybíróság házatáján" ("Constitutional Court Concerns"), *Magyar Jog* 37 (1990): 391–98 (393 ff.).

12. See the biographical sketch in *Frankfurter Allgemeine Zeitung,* 15 July 1991.

13. Sections (§§) cited hereafter without reference to a specific source refer to the CC Act.

14. I am indebted to the former general secretary and present judge of the Constitutional Court, Dr. András Holló, for the provision of these figures.

15. *Magyar Közlöny,* 1989, 1292. In July 1997, this was clarified in the Law when § 13 was amended to this effect by Act LXXIX/1997 on the Legal Status and Responsibilities of Members of the Government and State Secretaries.

16. László Sólyom, interview with *Népszabadság,* 14 November 1991; László Sólyom, interview with Gábor Attila Tóth, *Fundamentum* 1, no. 1 (1997): 31–44 (35).

17. László Sólyom, "Az Alkotmánybíróság hatáskörének sajátossága" (Peculiarities of the Constitutional Court's Competences), in *Tanulmányok Benedek Ferenc tiszteletére* (Essays in Honor of Ferenc Benedek), 5–30 (13) (Pécs, 1996). This essay is a profound analysis of the topic to be discussed here.

18. Hereafter the decisions (*határozat*) and resolutions (*végzés*) of the Constitutional Court will be cited using the citation form typically used in Hungary according to the official reporter *Az Alkotmánybíróság határozatai* (Decisions of the Constitutional Court), published for each year in separate volumes: ABH vol., p. Apart from that, the most important decisions are published immediately in the *Official Gazette,* the *Magyar Közlöny.*

19. See Dec. 17/1990(VII.31)AB (ABH 1990, 173 [177]); Dec. 54/B(1990)3AB (ABH 1990, 274 [275]); and especially Dec. 60/1992(XI.17)AB (ABH 1992, 275 [277]), where it is stated that subordinate legislation contrary to the basic provisions of the act on lawmaking violates the constitutional principle of the rule of law.

20. So Dec. 50/1993(IX.14)AB (ABH 1993, 410 [411]) and Dec. 42/1995 (VI.30)AB (ABH 1995, 185 [186]) emphasize that a mere contradiction to the Act on Legislation does not result in unconstitutionality of the subordinate legislation.

21. In some cases, this even happens with respect to legal norms not mentioned in any priority provision of the Constitution. Cf. Dec. 13/1994(III.2)AB (ABH 1994, 407 [409]); and Dec. 18/1996(V.10)AB (ABH 1996, 253 [254 ff.]).

22. The function of these peculiar acts has been changed recently and serves to maintain the unity of law application by the courts. Cf. Art. 47(2) of the Constitution as amended by Act LIX /1997; and §§ 27–33 of Act LXVI/1997 on the structure and administration of the courts.

23. Dec. 16/1991(IV.20)AB (ABH 1991, 58).

24. Dec. 22/1996(VI.25)AB (ABH 1996, 89 [94]). In the present case, this requirement was fulfilled and the Court satisfied the standing committee partly.

25. See, in agreement, Antal Ádám, "A jogszabályok alkotmánybírósági ellenőrzéséről" (On the Review of Legal Norms by the Constitutional Court), *Jogtudományi Közlöny* 42 (1992): 523–31 (527); Géza Kilényi, "Hogyan tovább, magyar alkotmánybíráskodás?" (Which Way Now, Hungarian Constitutional Judiciary?), in *Alkotmánybíráskodás* (Constitutional Judiciary), edited by Géza Kilényi, 267–301 (274 f) (Budapest, 1993); Imre Takács, "A magyar alkotmánybíráskodás időszerű problémái és továbbfejlesztésének lehetőségei" (Topical Problems of the Hungarian Constitutional Judiciary and the Possibilities of Its Further Development) in *Alkotmányfejlődés és jogállami gyakorlat* (Constitu-

tional Development and Practicing the Rule of Law), edited by Antal Ádám, 93–115 (110) (Budapest, 1994); and Albert Takács, "Az Alkotmánybíróság Magyarországon—tegnap és holnap között" (The Constitutional Court in Hungary—between Today and Tomorrow") in: Ádám, *Alkotmányfejlődés*, 117–47 (128 ff.). On the other hand, for an argument for retention of category (a), with some limitations, see András Bragyova, *Az új alkotmány egy koncepciója* (A Concept of the New Constitution) (Budapest, 1995), 201 ff.

26. Dec. 28/1991(VI.3)AB (ABH 1991, 88).

27. Dec. 11/1992(III.5)AB (ABH 1992, 77); Dec. 42/1993(VI.30)AB (ABH 1993, 300); Dec. 53/1993(X.13)AB (ABH 1993, 323).

28. Dec. 35/1994(VI.24)AB (ABH 1994, 197).

29. *Magyar Közlöny,* 1989, 1297.

30. Dec. 1/1990(II.12)AB (ABH 1990, 13).

31. Dec. 4/1990(III.4)AB (ABH 1990, 28).

32. Dec. 7/1990(IV.23)AB (ABH 1990, 40).

33. Dec. 63/1992(XII.11)AB (ABH 1992, 284).

34. Dec. 2/1993(I.22)AB (ABH 1993, 73).

35. Dec. 21/1990(X.4)AB (ABH 1990, 73). The substance of the whole compensation issue is discussed at some length by Ethan Klingsberg in "Safeguarding the Transition," *East European Constitutional Review* 2, no. 2 (Spring 1993): 44–48 (45 ff.).

36. Dec. 31/1990(XII.18)AB (ABH 1990, 136).

37. Dec. 25/1995(V.10)AB (ABH 1995, 427).

38. Dec. 21/1996(V.17)AB (ABH 1996, 74).

39. Dec. 48/1991(IX.26)AB (ABH 1991, 217); 8/1992(I.30)AB (ABH 1992, 51); 36/1992(VI.10)AB (ABH 1992, 207).

40. The available statistical files do not show to what extent the 3,170 preliminary reviews of 1990–96 relate to popular action. Of the 11,092 total pending constitutional proceedings, however, 8,369 (75.5 percent) were introduced through the application of individuals. If one considers further that of the remaining 2,723 proceedings interest groups and lawyers were the applicants in 1,345 cases, it can be concluded that almost 90 percent of the proceedings were initiated by independent societal forces.

41. András Holló, "Alkotmánybíráskodás Magyarországon" (Constitutional Judiciary in Hungary), *Magyar Közigazgatás* 41 (1991): 10–17 (16); Gábor Halmai, "Az alkotmányvédelem: az állami hatalom korlátozása" (Constitutional Protection: Limitations on State Power), *Társadalmi Szemle* 45, no. 5 (1991): 65–69 (69); László Sólyom, "Az Alkotmánybíróság önértelmezése" (Auto-interpretation of the Constitutional Court), *Jogtudományi Közlöny* 42 (1992): 272–75 (273); Kilényi, 288 ff.; László Sólyom, interview with Andras Mink, *East European Constitutional Review* 6, no. 1 (Winter 1997): 71–77. For extensive and balanced proposals for reform, see Tamás Lábady, "A populáris akció és az egyéni jogvédelem biztosítása az alkotmánybírósági eljárásban" (The Popular Action and the Guarantee of the Protection of Individual Rights in Constitutional Proceedings), *Magyar Jog* 38 (1991): 385–90 (388 ff.). For an argument in favor of popular action with the proviso that representation by a lawyer be compulsory, see Imre Takács, in *Alkotmánytan* (Constitutional Theory), 291 (Budapest, 1992).

42. The following applicants were contemplated: Parliament, its standing committees, the President of the Republic, the Government and any of its members, the President of the State Audit Office, the President of the Supreme Court, the Chief Public Prosecutor, and the Ombudsmen.

43. Cf. Georg Brunner, "Rechtsprechung und Richterrecht in Ungarn" (Judicature and Judge-made Law in Hungary), *Osteuropa-Recht* 26 (1980): 1–30 (24 ff.); and Brunner, "Die Verfassungsentwicklung," 331 ff., with additional references.

44. Lábady "A populáris akció," 386.

45. See § 39, CC Act; and § 13/A(3), Act V/1972, on the Procuracy of the Republic of Hungary, introduced by Act XXXII/1989.

46. See § 99(2)(a), Act LXV/1990, on Local Governments.

47. *Magyar Közlöny,* 1990, 1591.

48. This applies for § 1(3) and § 3 of Act LXV/1990, where it is stated that the rights of local governments are protected by the Constitutional Court and the courts.

49. Dec. 37/1994(VI.24)AB (ABH 1994, 238 [248 ff.]). President Sólyom ("Az Alkotmánybíróság," 27 ff.), criticizes the decision as a missed chance.

50. Again, § 65(2) of Act LXXX/1993 on universities is rather imprecise concerning the applicant. In Dec. 40/1995(VI.15)AB (ABH 1995, 170 [172]), the Constitutional Court dealt with the matter but was not forced to decide it.

51. See Dec. 38/1993(VI.11)AB (ABH 1993, 256), with the dissenting opinion of Vörös, who sees an overstepping of the legal competence and the danger of "governance by the Constitutional Court" in such constitutional interpretations.

52. In this sense, the official reasoning to § 48 of the CC Act (*Magyar Közlöny,* 1989, 1297). According to the standard practice of the Constitutional Court, legal persons can claim, as a general rule, the same fundamental rights as natural persons can and consequently have the same standing in proceedings of constitutional complaints. Cf. Dec. 21/1990(X.4)AB (ABH 1990, 73 [82]); Dec. 34/1994(VI.24)AB (ABH 1994, 177 [183]); and Dec. 24/1996(VI.25)AB (ABH 1996, 107 [111 ff.]).

53. Lábady, "A populáris akció," 387; Gábor Szekfű, "Alkotmány és alkotmánybíráskodás. Az alapjogok értelmezése és védelme az Alkotmánybíróság határozatainak tükrében" (Constitution and Constitutional Judiciary: Interpretation and Protection of Fundamental Rights as Reflected in the Decisions of the Constitutional Court), *Jogtudományi Közlöny* 42 (1992): 52–61 (55); Takács, "Az Alkotmánybíróság Magyarországon," 131; Sólyom, "Az Alkotmánybíróság," 25.

54. In 1990/96, only 102 constitutional complaints were filed, but 3,170 preliminary review proceedings were initiated.

55. Cf., for example, Dec. 38/1992(VI.22)AB (ABH 1992, 355); Dec. 3/1994(I.21)AB (ABH 1994, 59); Dec. 7/1994(II.18)AB (ABH 1994, 68); and Dec. 30/1995(V.25)AB (ABH 1995, 155).

56. Dec. 57/1991(XI.8)AB (ABH 1991, 272).

57. ABH 1991, 284 ff.

58. Károly Törő, "Az Alkotmánybíráskodás és a 'láthatatlan Alkotmány'" (Constitutional Judiciary and the 'Invisible Constitution'), *Magyar Jog* 39 (1992): 85–90 (86); Péter Szigeti, "Hatalommegosztás—Alkotmánybíróság" (Separation of Powers—Constitutional Court), *Világosság* 34, no. 1 (1993): 54; Gábor Halmai, "Tiszta Amerika? Alkotmánybíráskodás nálunk és más nemzeteknél" (America Pure? Constitutional Judiciary at US and at Other Nations), *Világosság* 34, 11 (1993): 22–31 (27); Péter Szigeti, "Alkotmánybíráskodásunk négy éve (1990–1993)" (Four Years of Our Constitutional Judiciary [1990–1993]), *Politikatudományi Szemle* 4, no. 2 (1995): 19–42 (36).

59. László Sólyom, interview with *Népszabadság,* 21 March 1992; László Sólyom, interview with *Fundamentum,* 1, no. 1 (1997): 31–44 (44); Halmai ("Az alkotmány-

védelem"), 69; Ádám ("A jogszabályok"), 529; Lábady ("A populáris akció"), 390, if not with the limitation to occasions of fundamental constitutional significance; Imre Takács, 104; Bragyova 207 f.

60. Cf., for example, Dec. 30/1990(XII.15)AB (ABH 1990, 128); Dec. 32/1990(XII.22)AB (ABH 1990, 145); Dec. 155/B/1990AB (ABH 1990, 198); Dec. 54/B/1990/3AB (ABH 1990, 274); Dec. 60/1994(XII.24)AB (ABH 1994, 342); Dec. 72/1995(XII.15)AB (ABH 1995, 351); Dec. 14/1996(IV.24)AB (ABH 1996, 56).

61. Dec. 35/1992(VI.10)AB (ABH 1992, 204 [205]); Dec. 61/1995(X.6)AB (ABH 1995, 317 [320]); Dec. 14/1996(IV.24)AB (ABH 1996, 56 [58 ff.]); Dec. 49/1996 (X.25)AB (ABH 1996, 150 [154 ff.]).

62. Dec. 1/1995(II.8)AB (ABH 1995, 31 [50]).

63. Dec. 155/B/1990AB (ABH 1990, 198 [200]); Dec. 54/B/1990/3AB (ABH 1990, 274 [275]); Dec. 551/B/1995AB (ABH 1995, 954 [956]).

64. Dec. 29/1991(VI.5)AB (ABH 1991, 419 [420]); Dec. 28/1994(V.20)AB (ABH 1994, 134 [145]).

65. Dec. 22/1990(X.16)AB (ABH 1990, 83 [86]). Cf. Dec. 72/1995(XII.15)AB (ABH 1995, 351 [354 ff.]).

66. Dec. 22/1990(X.16)AB (ABH 1990, 83 [86]).

67. Dec. 35/1992(VI.10)AB (ABH 1992, 204).

68. Dec. 37/1992(VI.10)AB (ABH 1992, 227).

69. Dec. 17/1993(III.19)AB (ABH 1993, 157); Dec. 61/1995(X.6)AB (ABH 1995, 317 [321]).

70. Even if the wording of the relevant provision is not without uncertainty, according to the official statement of reasons this is the intent of the legislature (*Magyar Közlöny,* 1989, 1296).

71. Dec. 30/1990(XII.15)AB (ABH 1990, 128 [131]).

72. Res. 61/B/1992AB (ABH 1993, 831).

73. Dec. 4/1997(I.22)AB, (ABH 1997, 41 [49]).

74. See § 5(1), Act IV/1972, on the courts.

75. Dec. 444/F/1992AB (ABH 1992, 743); Dec. 645/F/1996AB (ABH 1996, 771).

76. Res. 581/B/1994AB (ABH 1994, 956); Dec. 6/B/1994AB (ABH 1995, 848); Dec. 737/F/1995AB (ABH 1996, 706).

77. Articles 28/B–28/D, Constitution, inserted by Act LIX/1997. See Act XVII/1989 regarding referenda and people's initiatives (amended several times). The "consitutional complaint" is covered by § 32.

78. See §§ 45–51, Act LXV/1990 on Local Government. The "constitutional complaint" is covered by § 51.

79. Dec. 3/1996(II.23)AB (ABH 1996, 361).

80. See § 43, Act XXXIV/1989 on the Election of Members of Parliament; and §§ 51–52, Act LXIV/1990 on the Election of Representatives in Local Governments and of Mayors, as amended by Act LXII/1994.

81. See Art. 19(3)(1), Constitution; and § 93(2), Act LXV/1990 on the Local Government.

82. Article 31/A(5), Constitution, inserted by Act XL/1990.

83. See § 16(2)(d), Act II/1989 on the Right of Association. The requirements for prohibition are listed in § 2(2) of this Act in conjunction with Art. 2(3) of the Constitution.

84. Holló, "Alkotmánybíráskodás," 11; Daisy Kiss, "Kérdések és válaszok az Alkot-

mánybíróságról" (Questions and Answers regarding the Constitutional Court), *Magyar Jog* 38 (1991): 419–22 (419).

85. See Res. 544/B/1990/6AB (ABH 1990, 273); Res. 859/E/1990/4AB (ABH 1990, 267); Res. 125/B/1990AB (ABH 1990, 361); Res. 514/B/1990AB (ABH 1990, 372); Res. 1141/B/1990/5AB (ABH 1990, 392); Res. 1149/D/1990/8AB (ABH 1990, 393); and countless other resolutions.

86. Res. 280/B/1990/10AB (ABH 1990, 363); Res. 772/E/1991/4AB (ABH 1991, 946).

87. Dec. 14/1990(VI.27)AB (ABH 1990, 170), strongly criticized in Törő, "Az Alkotmánybíráskodás," 86; Dec. 9/1992(I.30)AB (ABH 1992, 59); Dec. 25/1993(IV.23.).AB (ABH 1993, 188); Dec. 31/1994(VI.2)AB (ABH 1994, 168); Dec. 45/1994(X.21)AB (ABH 1994, 254); Dec. 46/1995(VI.30)AB (ABH 1995, 219); Sólyom, "Az Alkotmánybíróság," 273.

88. Dec. 6/1992(I.30)AB (ABH 1992, 40); Dec. 28/1994(V.20)AB (ABH 1994, 134); Dec. 31/1995(V.25)AB (ABH 1995, 158).

89. Dec. 2/1990(II.18)AB (ABH 1990, 18, 22 [23]).

90. Dec. 20/1990(X.4)AB (ABH 1990, 69 [71]).

91. They are dealt with in the contribution of President Sólyom to this volume. See also the in-depth analysis of Spencer Zifcak in "Hungary's Remarkable Radical Constitutional Court," *Journal of Constitutional Law in Eastern and Central Europe* 3 (1996): 1–56.

92. For comparative studies, see for example, Karl-Georg Zierlein, "Die Bedeutung der Verfassungsrechtsprechung für die Bewahrung und Durchsetzung der Staatsverfassung," *Europäische Grundrechte-Zeitschrift* 18 (1991): 301–41 (concerning Eastern Europe, 326–37); Georg Brunner, "Development of a Constitutional Judiciary in Eastern Europe," *Review of Central and East European Law* 18 (1992): 535–53; Georg Brunner "Die neue Verfassungsgerichtsbarkeit in Osteuropa," *Zeitschrift für ausländisches öffentliches Recht und Völkerrecht* 53 (1993): 819–69; and Herman Schwartz, "The New Courts: An Overview," *East European Constitutional Review* 2, no. 2 (Spring 1993): 28–32, with special emphasis on the differences from the U.S. Supreme Court.

93. For a comparative analysis of the problem, see Georg Brunner, "Grundrechtsschutz durch Verfassungsgerichtsbarkeit in Osteuropa," in *Verfassungsstaatlichkeit: Festschrift für Klaus Stern* (Munich, 1997): 1041–58.

94. *Marbury v. Madison* (5 U.S. [1 Cranch] 137/1803), 177.

95. Cf. the cases *Linkletter v. Walker* (381 U.S. 618 [1965]); *Stovall v. Denno* (388 U.S. 293 [1967]); and *Williams v. United States* (401 U.S. 646 [1971]).

96. In accordance with Schwartz, "New Courts," 32, I think that Stephen Holmes, in "Back to the Drawing Board," *East European Constitutional Review* 2, no. 1 (Winter 1993): 21–25 (23), was definitely wrong when he warned that overlegitimizing constitutional courts in Eastern Europe would discredit the nascent idea of parliamentary representation.

Selected Decisions of the Constitutional Court of the Republic of Hungary

DECISION 8/1990: 23 APRIL 1990

ON TRADE UNION REPRESENTATION

In this very early case, the Court expounded its view on the right to human dignity as "the general right to personality." This concept of a "mother right"—that is, a subsidiary fundamental right that may be relied upon by the Court for the protection of individual autonomy when none of the named rights is applicable for a particular case—is similar to the wide use of the "penumbras" of constitutional privacy and to the German allgemeines Persönlichkeitsrecht. *The Hungarian Court derived from it, for example, the right to know one's parentage, the right to marry, and the right to domestic partnership with no regard to the sex of the partners. Along with the right to life and human dignity, it played a key role in the decision abolishing the death penalty and also in the abortion case. On the other hand, critics of the Court consider this practice of invoking the right to human dignity to be a symbol of the Court's activism.*

The petitioner sought a ruling on the constitutionality of a 1967 Labour Code provision giving trade unions the right to represent employees without their authorization.

The petitioner submitted that representation of employees had previously fallen within the exclusive competence of the trade union in the particular sector of the economy. Under the Labour Code, art. 15(2), the trade union in employment-related issues had the right to act in the interests, in the name, and on behalf of the employees in the absence of any special authorization to do so. Following the process of political transformation, the representation of employees' interests had been placed on a more pluralist basis, reflected in the Constitution, Arts. 4 and 70/C(1). As a result, he contended, representation by trade unions was permissible only in respect of their members without special authorization and not non-union member employees unless so authorized.

Held, granting the petition:

(1) The Labour Code, art. 15(2), was unconstitutional, as it could potentially infringe an employee's right to self-determination, which formed an integral part of the right to human dignity in the Constitution, Art. 54(1). It was not inconceivable that the trade union might choose to exercise its right of representation in spite of an employee's explicit request to the contrary. Such potential infringement of the employee's right to self-determination could not be alleviated by taking into account the employee's interest, which could only be assumed by the union. Indeed, the risk of infringing the employee's interests was at its greatest where the personal matters of non-member employees were concerned. Once the disputed provision had been annulled, the Labour Code would then retain consent as the sole basis for representation.

(2) The right to human dignity in Constitution, Art. 54(1), was a natural right of which no one could be deprived. Such right included, inter alia, the right to free personal development, to self-determination, to privacy or the general freedom of action. It was a "mother

right," a subsidiary fundamental right, which might be relied upon to protect an individual's autonomy when no particular, specified, fundamental right was applicable.

IN THE NAME OF THE REPUBLIC OF HUNGARY!

Concerning the petition of *N.N.* to abolish the right of trade unions to represent employees without authorization to do so, the Constitutional Court of the Republic of Hungary has made the following

DECISION.

The Constitutional Court holds that sentence 2 in art. 15(2) of Act II/1967 on the Labour Code, which states that in employment-related issues the trade union "has the right to act in the interest of, in the name of and on behalf of the employees in the absence of a special authorization to do so"—to be unconstitutional and therefore hereby invalidates it.

The invalidated provision becomes ineffective on the day when this Decision is published in the *Hungarian Official Gazette.*

REASONING

Opinion by the Court: [....]

III

[....]

The Constitutional Court did not find the disputed provision unconstitutional either under Art. 4 or Art. 70/C(1) of the Constitution: Art. 4 extends the trade unions' right to engage in the protection of interest and representation, which appears also in the former Constitution, to other organizations formed for the protection of interests. Neither this rule nor the provision of Art. 70/C(1) pertaining to the freedom of forming trade unions and other organizations for the representation of interests prescribe what interest protection and representation activities include.

On the other hand, the trade union's right under the disputed provision of the Labour Code to undertake the representation without authorisation may infringe upon the employees' right to self-determination, which is an integral part of the right to human dignity declared in Art. 54(1) of the Constitution as a natural right of which no one may be arbitrarily deprived.

On the basis of the disputed provision, it may not be ruled out that the trade union may choose to exercise its right of representation in spite of an employee's explicit request to the contrary. This potential infringement upon the right to self-determination may not be eliminated even by the fact that a representation without authorization must take into account the employee's interest, since the interests of the individual employees are only presumed by the trade union.

The risk of infringing upon the employee's interest in the course of the application of the disputed provision is at its greatest when the non-trade-unionist employee's personal matters are concerned. That was the primary reason why the provision in question had to be annulled. As a result of this annulment, however, the Act has retained only consent as a way of trade union representation. If the right of trade unions to represent their members either without authorization or in capacities which employees may not effectively estop seems justifiable, such a gap should be overcome by creating new legal regulations. [....]

The Decision of the Constitutional Court is based on the interpretation of the right to human dignity. This right at the beginning of the Chapter about fundamental rights and obligations in Art. 54(1) of the Constitution is declared as an inherent right. The Constitutional Court regards the right to human dignity as another phrase for a "general right of personality." In modern constitutions and in the practice of constitutional courts, the general right to personhood encompasses various aspects, such as the right to free personal development, the right to free self-determination, general freedom of action or the right to privacy. The general right of personality is a "mother right"—*i.e.,* a subsidiary fundamental right which may be relied upon at any time by both the Constitutional Court and other courts for the protection of an individual's autonomy when none of the concrete, named fundamental rights is applicable for a particular set of facts.

DECISION 21/1990: 4 OCTOBER 1990

ON COMPENSATION FOR EXPROPRIATED PROPERTY: "COMPENSATION CASE I"

None of the new democracies—from South Africa to Germany—have been able to avoid the settlement of the status of property taken by the authoritarian regimes. This, at the same time, determined a total reallocation of the national wealth, especially in states with socialist planned economies. The present case opened the series of "compensation cases" that resolved the dilemma of returning nationalized property to the original owners, that is, reprivatization, or yielding the way for the privatization of state-owned property on a commercial basis. The decision provided for the constitutional possibility of commercial privatization by denying a subjective right of the former owners to compensation. Although not fully developed, the Constitutional Court also launched here its "legal continuity theory," recognizing legal ownership by the state of "legally sound" nationalized property. The "continuity principle" later became decisive for the constitutional evaluation of the "transition," as in the cases of retroactive punishment (11/1992, 53/1993). Of further significance is the elaboration of a test for positive discrimination, which has remained the basis of the equal protection jurisdiction of the Constitutional Court.

The Prime Minister petitioned for an advisory opinion on the interpretation of certain legal provisions concerning the Government's privatization programme.

He requested (a) whether compensation procedures to provide for certain people's former property to be reprivatized while other people's property would not be returned to them amounted to discrimination contrary to Constitution, Art. 70/A. According to the Government, the general principle of privatization was that state property was sold to new owners in exchange for payment while former owners received partial compensation. The settlement of land ownership would be an exception to these principles because in such questions either the original land would be returned in kind or other land offered in exchange; and (b) whether, in the context of the Constitution, Arts. 12 and 13, it was constitutional to take land from co-operatives without expropriation proceedings and compensation. Within the government's framework of reprivatization, arable land in the possession of the co-operatives, which had not been acquired in the manner prescribed by the Civil Code, would serve as the source for reprivatization without any compensation.

Held, giving the following opinion:

(1) According to Art. 70/A(1) and in the absence of constitutional reasons, if the property of certain people was to be reprivatized while that of others was not—depending on the object of property—this would amount to discrimination in relation to the acquisition of property. In examining the Government's privatization programme, it was necessary to clarify the conceptual uncertainty concerning the relationship between privatization, reprivatization and compensation. Privatization involved the assignment of state property into

private ownership while reprivatization was the return of assets formerly owned by private persons but currently in the possession of the State. The term "compensation" was, however, used in a special sense by the Government: the sole legal basis for the partial compensation was fairness, the State was not obliged to pay such compensation and no former owner had the right to receive it since it depended solely on a sovereign state decision.

(2) It was then necessary to consider two types of discrimination, first between the former owners and non-owners and then between the former owners according to the type of property. The constitutionality of the discrimination between former and non-owners depended on whether the interests of these two groups had been weighed with the same degree of prudence and impartiality. If it were the case that, with the preferential treatment of former owners, the distribution of state property would produce a more favourable overall social result as regards the constitutionally mandated "market economy" than equal treatment would, then this would be permissible. In the latter situation, it was necessary to ascertain whether the other former owners had had their interests considered as thoroughly and impartially as those of former landowners in order to reveal the objective basis of the discrimination between former owners. Further, it had to be proved that former non-landowners had to be put into a disadvantageous position in order to achieve equality of persons as completely as possible in the future market economy. On its interpretation of Art. 70/A, the discrimination in the Act under consideration would accordingly be unconstitutional.

(3) The taking of property from co-operatives, even by virtue of law, without immediate, unconditional, and full compensation violated the Constitution, Arts. 12(1) and 13. The recognition by the State under Art. 12(1) that co-operatives were autonomous included the recognition that they had the right to property, although the Constitution did not expressly provide for co-operative property. Article 9(1) provided a prohibition of discrimination ("the equal protection clause") against any forms of ownership and further, under Art. 13, constitutional protection was also extended, inter alia, to the unnamed property of business associations. As co-operatives and agricultural co-operatives were a form of business association, irrespective of the fact that they were not regulated by the Act on Business Associations, the property of agricultural co-operatives (including arable land) enjoyed constitutional protection similar to that of the property of business associations. Consequently Arts. 12(1) and 13(1) read together guaranteed the right to property including the right of agricultural co-operatives to the arable land they owned. Since property could be taken by a single official decree or by virtue of law only with immediate, unconditional and full compensation, the Government's proposal was therefore unconstitutional.

IN THE NAME OF THE REPUBLIC OF HUNGARY!

Concerning the petition of the Prime Minister made on behalf of the Government on the interpretation of the Constitution, the Constitutional Court has made the following

DECISION.

The Constitutional Court interprets Art. 70/A of the Constitution—with regard to Arts. 9 and 13(1)—to mean that according to Art. 70/A(1) there is discrimination against persons if, in the absence of constitutional reasons, the property of certain persons is reprivatized while the property of others is not, depending on the object of property. Such discrimination is unconstitutional.

The Constitutional Court interprets Art. 13(1) in conjunction with Art. 12(1) to mean that the Republic of Hungary guarantees for agricultural co-operatives, the right to the arable land they own. Article 13(2) of the Constitution on expropriation is a guarantee provision that is applicable to the taking of property not only by a single official decree but also by virtue of law. Property may be taken either by a single official decree or by virtue of law only with immediate, unconditional and full compensation. Takings without immediate, unconditional and full compensation are, therefore, unconstitutional.

REASONING

Opinion by the Court:

I

Under s. 1(g) of Act XXXII/1989 on the Constitutional Court, the Prime Minister of the Republic of Hungary on behalf of the Government petitioned the Constitutional Court to interpret the following:

1. Article 70/A of the Constitution—with regard to Art. 9 and Art. 13(1): whether it constitutes discrimination according to Art. 70/A of the Constitution if certain persons' former property will be reprivatized, depending on what they owned, while other people's property will not be returned to them because of the different privatization and compensation principles.

According to the petition, the Government from the viewpoint of the transformation of the ownership system considers privatization to be its basic goal, the achievement of which requires the enactment or revision of several Acts. In this sphere the Government, following the general principle of privatization, considers new owners receiving property from state property in exchange for payment, while former owners receive partial compensation. The settlement of land ownership would be an exception to these principles, because in such questions either the original land would be returned in kind—*i.e.,* the original ownership would be restored—or other land would be offered in exchange.

2. Article 13 of the Constitution in conjunction with Art. 12 of the Constitution: whether it is possible by virtue of the law to take land from co-operatives without expropriation proceedings and compensation.

According to the petition, within the framework of the reprivatization of arable land, arable land in the possession of the co-operatives which was not acquired in the manner determined by the Civil Code would serve as the source for reprivatization without any compensation.

A

II

According to Art. 70/A(1) of the Constitution, the Republic of Hungary shall ensure the human rights and civil rights for all persons on its territory without any kind of discrimination, such as on the basis of race, colour, gender, language, religion, political or other opinion, national or social origins, financial situation, birth or any other grounds whatsoever.

Paragraph (2) says: "Any kind of discrimination described in paragraph (1) shall be strictly penalized by the law."

Paragraph (3) provides: "The Republic of Hungary shall promote the equality of rights for everyone through measures aimed at eliminating the inequality in opportunity."

Article 9(1) says: "The economy of Hungary is a market economy, in which public and private property shall have equal rights and be granted equal protection," while according to para. (2): "The Republic of Hungary recognizes and supports the right to enterprise and the freedom of economic competition."

According to Art. 13(1): "The Republic of Hungary shall guarantee the right to property."

III

In its *Dec. 9/1990 (IV.25) AB* (MK 1990/36; ABH 1990, 46), the Constitutional Court has interpreted the prohibition of discrimination contained in Art. 70/A(1) of the Constitution. It established, among other principles, that "the prohibition of discrimination does not mean that any discrimination, including even discrimination intended to achieve a greater social equality, is forbidden. The prohibition of discrimination means all people must be treated as equal (as persons with equal dignity) by law—*i.e.,* the fundamental right to human dignity may not be impaired, and the criteria for the distribution of the entitlements and benefits shall be determined with the same respect and prudence, and with the same degree of consideration of individual interests."

In the quoted Decision, the Constitutional Court also expressed its view that—

"the right to equal personal dignity may occasionally result in entitlements according to which goods and opportunities must be distributed (even qualitatively) equally to everyone. If, however, a social purpose not in conflict with the Constitution or a constitutional right may only be achieved if equality in the narrower sense cannot be realized, then such a positive discrimination shall not be declared unconstitutional. The limitation upon positive discrimination is either the prohibition of discrimination in its broader meaning, *i.e.,* concerning equal dignity, or the protection of the fundamental rights which are positively expressed in the Constitution. Social equality as a purpose or as a social interest may take precedence over individual interests but not, however, over the constitutional rights of the individual."

The Constitutional Court also adhered to this interpretation when making this Decision.

IV

Point 1 of the Government petition asks whether it constitutes discrimination between the former owners when, depending on the kind of property, some of them are given back their former properties, while others are not, during the process of reprivatizating state property.

The permissibility of any limitations upon constitutional rights may be judged only on the basis of arguments which address the unavoidability of the limitations in a particular case. Arguments in support of the discrimination between the former owners are not included in the petition.

However, the Constitutional Court has taken into consideration that the question itself implies that it should be examined in relation to the Government's privatization programme; furthermore, that the privatization of state property through sale, to anyone theoretically, is a principal rule in this programme. The former owners of assets that are now in the property of the State will receive partial compensation. Land ownership is an exception to these principles because the original ownership would be restored in kind.

From the wording of the petition it may be inferred that in the case of former owners of assets other than land, the return of assets in kind would be substituted by partial compensation: "their property will not be returned to them due to the different privatization and compensation principles."

These explanations do not contain an assessable cause for the discrimination; moreover, they reflect conceptual uncertainty concerning the relationship between reprivatization, privatization and partial compensation.

Because of the foregoing, the Constitutional Court will first clarify the concepts utilized for the interpretation of the Constitution.

(a) Privatization involves the assignment of state property into private ownership. Reprivatization is the return of assets formerly owned by private persons but presently in the possession of the State. Both privatization and reprivatization may be either gratuitous or in exchange for payment; the difference is among those who are entitled.

The State may privatize or reprivatize those assets that are in its possession. Both privatization and reprivatization are decisions of the owner. It follows from Art. 10(2) of the Constitution that the right of the State to privatization and reprivatization is theoretically unlimited, and this right derives solely from its freedom of ownership. Therefore, no one has the right to privatization or reprivatization without a relevant State decision or under conditions other than those contained in such a decision.

The interpretation of the Constitutional Court concerns legally sound state property.

The Constitutional Court notes that a case is in progress before it concerning the constitutionality of the different legal rules on nationalization. The Constitutional Court refers to ss. 40–43 of Act XXXII/1989 on the Constitutional Court, especially to the provision that—as a principal rule—the annulment of a legal rule does not affect legal relations and the rights and obligations deriving therefrom that came into effect prior to the publication of the decision. Any deviation from this rule may be declared only by the Constitutional Court on the basis of its discretionary powers, if it is justified by legal certainty or if a particularly important interest of the petitioner is attached to it.

(b) Compensation, according to general legal usage, is the remedy for lawfully caused disadvantages and damages, including the remedy for the taking of property, as opposed to the payment of indemnification for unlawfully caused damages. One that causes damage is legally obliged to pay indemnification, while the person suffering from damage has the right to receive indemnification. The word "compensation" is not used in this usual sense in the Government's petition for the interpretation of the Constitution.

The sole legal basis for the partial compensation planned by the Government is equity: the State is not obliged to pay such compensation, and no one has the right to receive such compensation. Just as reprivatization is not a claim resulting from nationalization or the organization of co-operatives, compensation is not that either; it solely depends on a sovereign state decision.

It is not only the seized property that is the basis for the compensation planned by the Government but also the injuries sustained in general. Gratuitous reprivatization and compensation may be different versions of political compensation; however, they are legally independent and their legal settlements occur in completely different contexts (the establishment of the market economy as opposed to the mitigation of damage sustained). Discrimination within one may not be counterbalanced by reverse discrimination in the other. Therefore, during the assignment of state property into private ownership, the preference of the former landowners may not be equated with the fact that they do not receive compensation. The restoration of original ownership of land and the partial financial compensation of the owners of other assets may not be regarded as different methods of the same compensation.

(c) The question to be answered is whether the reprivatization of landownership, with regard to the reprivatization of other state-owned assets, involves discrimination that conflicts with Art. 70/A of the Constitution.

The position of the Constitutional Court is that, in this particular case, differentiating on the basis of the type of property becomes discrimination against persons since it relates to the acquisition of property.

The question includes two partially overlapping kinds of discrimination: discrimination between the former owners and non-owners, on the one hand, and discrimination between the former owners according to the object of property.

V

In *Dec. 9/1990 (IV.25) AB* (MK 1990/32; ABH 1990, 46), the Constitutional Court declared that the prohibition of negative discrimination included in Art. 70/A of the Constitution was not absolute: departure from it is allowed according to the stipulations of that Decision.

(a) Article 70/A of the Constitution prohibits discrimination in connection with human rights and the rights of citizens. In the Constitutional Court's opinion the State's guarantee of the right to property [Art. 13(1) of the Constitution] also embraces the right to acquire property. In the given context, the right to enterprise must also be taken into consideration because privatization, including the privatization of land, primarily serves the formation of farm enterprises.

(b) The question of whether discrimination remains within constitutional limits may only be examined in the objective and subjective context of the current rules because the same criterion—*e.g.*, "landowner"—may constitute discrimination, depending on the context. Equality shall exist in reference to the essential element of a given state of facts. If, however, a different rule applies to a group within a given regulatory scheme, this will be in conflict with the prohibition of discrimination, unless there is sufficient constitutional justification for the difference.

By assignment of state property into private ownership, the State fulfills the duty to create a social market economy, set forth as an aim in the Preamble to the Constitution. However, as an owner, the State acts freely in deciding how to support private property, even when it comes to assigning its own property.

If, however, during the assignment of state property into private ownership, the State differentiates between and treats the former owners differently from others by establishing different conditions for the acquisition of property and, what is more, it further differentiates within the group of former owners, then it will violate Art. 70/A of the Constitution unless its grounds meet the conditions of permissible positive discrimination.

The constitutionality of the discrimination depends on whether the discrimination between owners and non-owners is realized in a procedure where the interests of former owners and non-owners have been weighed with the same degree of prudence and impartiality. In the review of such a possibility, former owners just like non-owners do not have a right to a share in the state property but are entitled to equal treatment and to have their interests judged with the same degree of attention and equity. Without this, the discrimination violates the Constitution.

Even if the above considerations are flawless, the discrimination is constitutional only if the gratuitous property acquisition, granted to former owners, and property acquisition by others in exchange for payment, establishes equality between the private owner participants in the market economy to be developed. If it can be proved that with the preferential treatment of former owners the distribution of state property will yield a more favourable overall social result than equal treatment would, and if it follows inexorably from the facts that another non-discriminatory procedure against the non-owners would be far from this result, then non-owners could not claim their rights ensured by Art. 70/A of the Constitution were violated. The criterion of discrimination—*i.e.,* the former ownership situation—would not be unconstitutional if it logically followed from the above arguments.

The same examination must be made in order to decide whether discrimination between the former owners by the object of property—*i.e.,* if only real property is reprivatized—is in conflict with Art. 70/A of the Constitution. First, it must be ascertained whether the right of the other former owners to have their interests considered as thoroughly and impartially as those of the former landowners has been satisfied in the enactment of the discriminatory regulation. The objective basis of the discrimination between the former owners must be shown. In addition, it must be proved that it was necessary to put non-landowners into a disadvantageous position in order to achieve the equality of persons as completely as possible in the future market economy and that the initial conditions of the market economy would be much more unfavourable if the other former owners were not put into a disadvantageous position.

While proving whether discrimination against certain persons or groups is a condition for achieving a more complete social equality, the Constitutional Court may not accept arguments concerning a preferred group which are valid in relation to other groups as well (*e.g.,* the establishment of farm enterprises, the remedying of injustice). On the other hand, to prove equal treatment, it is necessary to give a complete account of the interests of both the preferred and discriminated groups together with the method of evaluation.

VI

In conclusion: the Constitutional Court holds that the reprivatization of land and "partial compensation" appear in a different economic and political context. They are based on different criteria and there is no legal relationship between them; therefore they may not be interpreted in their correlation with regard to the equality required under Art. 70/A of the Constitution. As to the constitutionality, based on the above criteria, of discrimination between the former owners and non-owners and of discrimination by the object of property, these discriminations are not supported either by the petition or by the documents at the Constitutional Court's disposal. Therefore the Constitutional Court interpreted Art. 70/A of the Constitution to mean that it amounts to discrimination against persons if certain persons' former property is reprivatized while other persons' property is not returned to their possession, and it proclaimed this discrimination unconstitutional.

B

VII

In Point 2 of the petition for the interpretation of the Constitution, the Government requested the Constitutional Court to interpret Art. 13 of the Constitution in conjunction with Art. 12: whether it is possible to take land from co-operatives by virtue of the law but without expropriation and compensation procedures. The petition suggests that the question concerns the reprivatization of land owned by agricultural co-operatives. In view of this, the Constitutional Court has interpreted the above provisions of the Constitution with regard to the property belonging to agricultural co-operatives, irrespective of the fact that there are several other kinds of co-operatives.

VIII

According to Art. 13 of the Constitution the Republic of Hungary guarantees the right to property, and it adds that property may be expropriated only exceptionally when this is a matter of the public interest, and only in the manner prescribed by law, with full, unconditional and immediate compensation.

Under Art. 12(1) of the Constitution, the State supports co-operatives based on voluntary association and recognizes their autonomy. That provision of the Constitution, therefore, concerns those co-operatives which exist on the basis of voluntary association—irrespective of the circumstances of their foundation. The only organ competent to decide whether a co-operative exists on the basis of voluntary or involuntary association is the general meeting of the co-operative. Accordingly, the Constitutional Court has not found any constitutional justification for depriving, with universal validity of law, the agricultural co-operatives of the protection guaranteed under Art. 12(1) of the Constitution.

When formulating its opinion, the Constitutional Court has paid special attention to the current legal rules in force on agricultural co-operatives which allow the winding up of a co-operative upon the decision of the general meeting, and for a member to leave, but which do not allow the distribution of the co-operative's property. Since the petition for the interpretation of the Constitution does not require interpretation of this problem, the Constitutional Court will not examine this issue on its merits. However, it points out that—considering Art. 9 of the Constitution—the property of agricultural co-operatives is not entitled to greater protection than that of other participants in the economy, or than property in general. (The Constitutional Court notes that the problem of distributing co-operative property may be resolved by amending Act I/1987 on Land as well as Act III/1967 on Agricultural Co-operatives.) Further, the Constitutional Court took into account the fact that under Act III/1967 it is also possible for co-operatives to transform themselves into another type of business association.

IX

The recognition by the State that co-operatives are independent includes the recognition that they have the right to property, although the Constitution does not provide explicitly for co-operative property. The Constitutional Court, therefore, found it necessary to interpret Art. 12 of the Constitution in light of Art. 9(1).

According to Art. 9(1) of the Constitution, in the Republic of Hungary public and private property shall have equal rights and shall receive equal protection under the law. The clause, however, may not be viewed, as the public and the private property constituted an exhaustive list of kinds of property protected by the Constitution and, accordingly, to be classified in one of these would be a precondition for constitutional protection. It is not certain kinds of ownership that the Constitution distinguishes between but, on the contrary, it provides a prohibition of discrimination against any forms of ownership. Accordingly, Art. 9(1) of the Constitution is an expression of the proposition of equality before the law, referred to in Art. 70/A(1), as well as the general proposition of the right to enterprise and freedom of competition contained in Art. 9(2), with regard to the right to property.

Article 9(1) of the Constitution is, therefore, not related to Art. 13, which guarantees the right to property without the distinction (between private and public property) set forth in Art. 9(1). On the basis of Art. 13, constitutional protection is extended, among others, to the unnamed property of business associations as well. Co-operatives, therefore, agricultural co-operatives, are a form of business association, irrespective of the fact that—because of political reasons existing at the time of the enactment of the Act—they are not regulated by the Act VI/1988 on Business Associations.

Based on the above, the Constitutional Court does not attach importance to the question of whether or not the name of co-operative property explicitly appears in the text of Constitution. The Constitutional Court, therefore, takes the position that the property of agricultural co-operatives, including arable land, enjoys constitutional protection similar to that of the property of business associations.

Consequently, Art. 13(1) in conjunction with Art. 12(1) shall be understood to mean that the Republic of Hungary guarantees the right to property including the right of agricultural co-operatives to the arable land they own.

X

In accordance with the petition for the interpretation of the Constitution, the Constitutional Court examined the possibility of taking land from co-operatives by virtue of law but without an expropriation procedure and compensation. Article 13(1) of the Constitution on expropriation is a guarantee provision that applies to the taking of property not only by a single official decree but also by virtue of law. Property may only be taken either by a single official decree or by virtue of law—with regard to Art. 13(1) of the Constitution—with immediate, unconditional and full compensation.

Accordingly, the Constitutional Court took the position that the taking of property from co-operatives—even by virtue of law—without immediate, unconditional and full compensation, violates Art. 12(1) and Art. 13 of the Constitution, and is, therefore, unconstitutional.

XI

The Constitutional Court finally points out that the taking of property from co-operatives without immediate, unconditional and full compensation violates the principle included in Art. 9(2) of the Constitution, according to which the Republic of Hungary recognizes and supports the right to enterprise and the freedom of economic competition. At the same time, such an action means the violation of the principle of equality before the law included in Art. 70/A of the Constitution, since this principle concerns not only natural persons but legal entities as well.

DECISION 23/1990: 31 OCTOBER 1990

ON CAPITAL PUNISHMENT

The Capital Punishment *Decision, delivered in the tenth month of the existence of the Constitutional Court, signaled the real power and significance of constitutional review and shocked an unprepared Parliament and the general public as well. The Court declared capital punishment unconstitutional and abolished it. The reasoning of the Court was rather summary, and the justices enlarged upon their own theories in concurring opinions. Nevertheless, it is clear that the Court did not want to follow either the U.S. Supreme Court or the usual arguments on the deterrent effect of the death penalty. The new line of reasons analyzes the very nature of and the connection between the right to life and the right to human dignity and declares them inviolable. This reasoning was also subsequently taken up by the South African Constitutional Court and became the basis of the abortion decision in Hungary (64/1991). The dissent of Schmidt, J. was the first open clash between the "activist" and the restraining wing of the Court, a difference that soon culminated in the presidential power cases (48/1991).*

The petitioner sought a ruling to declare unconstitutional the various provisions of the Criminal Code and related regulations which permitted the imposition of the death penalty as a punishment for breach of criminal law.

The petitioner submitted that the said provisions were unconstitutional on the grounds, inter alia, that (a) they violated Art. 54, which guarantees that no one can be arbitrarily deprived of the right to life; and that such punishment (b) could not be justified ethically; (c) was generally incompatible with fundamental rights as specified in Art. 8; and (d) amounted to an irreparable and irreversible means of punishment unsuitable for preventing or deterring the commission of serious crimes.

Held, granting the petition:

(1) Capital punishment was unconstitutional when assessed against a reading together of Arts. 8(2) and 54(1). The relevant provisions of the Criminal Code and other related legal rules which permitted capital punishment as a criminal sanction conflicted with the prohibition against any limitation on the essential content of the right to life and to human dignity. From an examination of the Constitution, human life and human dignity formed an inseparable unity, having a greater value than other rights, and thus being an indivisible, absolute fundamental right limited the criminal power of the State. It was the inherent, inviolable and inalienable fundamental right of every person in Hungary, irrespective of citizenship, for which the State had a primary responsibility to respect and protect.

(2) Article 8(2) did not permit any limitation upon the essential content of fundamental rights even by way of legislative enactment. Since the right to life and human dignity was itself the "essential content," the State could not dispose of it. Consequently any de-

privation of it was conceptually "arbitrary." The State would come into conflict with the whole concept of fundamental constitutional rights if it were to authorize deprivation of the right by permitting and regulating capital punishment. Therefore Art. 54(1) could not be construed as allowing capital punishment even if imposed on the basis of legal proceedings, *i.e.,* non-arbitrarily, since the possibility of any kind of limitation on any basis of the right to life and human dignity was theoretically excluded. Since capital punishment resulted not merely in a limitation upon that right but in fact the complete and irreversible elimination of life and dignity together with the guarantee thereof, all relevant provisions providing for capital punishment were therefore declared null and void.

(3) Moreover, it followed from the fact that as the sanctions provided for in the Criminal Code constituted a coherent system the abolition of capital punishment—which previously formed a component thereof—would necessarily result in a complete revision of the entire system. Such a revision, however, was beyond the jurisdiction of the Court.

IN THE NAME OF THE REPUBLIC OF HUNGARY!

In the matter of the petition of Dr. Tibor Horváth on behalf of the League against Capital Punishment seeking the criminal regulations providing for capital punishment to be declared unconstitutional and abolished, the Constitutional Court, with the dissenting opinion of Schmidt, J., and with the concurring opinions of Lábady and Tersztánszky, JJ., further of Sólyom, P., Szabó, J., and Zlinszky, J., made the following

DECISION.

The Constitutional Court declares capital punishment to be unconstitutional.

Article 38(1)(i), arts. 39 and 84 in Act IV/1978 on the Criminal Code, art. 399 in Act I/1973 on the Code of Criminal Procedure, paras. 17 and 18 in Law Decree 11/1979 on the Execution of Punishments and Criminal Measures, and paras. 151, 152 and 153 in the Ministry of Justice Decree 8/1979 (VI.30) IM on the Rules of Execution of Punishment, are unconstitutional and are therefore declared null and void.

The indication of "capital punishment" as an applicable kind of punishment, in the provisions of the Criminal Code—art. 155(1); art. 158(2); arts. 160 and 163; art. 166(2); art. 261(2); art. 262(2); art. 343(4); art. 346(1); art. 347; art. 348(3); art. 352(3) and (4); art. 354(3); art. 355(5); art. 363(2); and arts. 364 and 365—is also unconstitutional. The Constitutional Court therefore declares that the provisions in the above-mentioned articles of the Criminal Code, indicating "capital punishment" as an applicable kind of punishment, are also null and void.

The Constitutional Court publishes this Decision in the *Hungarian Official Gazette.* The annulment of the provisions will become effective on the day of the publication of this Decision in the *Hungarian Official Gazette.* In accordance with s. 43(3) of Act XXXII/1989, the Constitutional Court orders the revision of those criminal proceedings which have been completed with a final judgment and which have imposed capital punishment under the annulled provisions on capital punishment and where the sentence has not yet been executed.

REASONING

Opinion by the Court:

I

When petitioning the Constitutional Court to establish the unconstitutionality of legal rules providing for capital punishment, the petitioner pointed out that these rules violate the provisions of Art. 54 of the Constitution, according to which: "In the Republic of Hungary, every human being has the inherent right to life and to human dignity of which no one can be arbitrarily deprived" [para. (1)]; and "no one shall be subjected to torture, to cruel, inhuman or degrading treatment or punishment" [para. (2)].

The petitioner claimed that capital punishment might not be justified ethically, that it was incompatible with human rights, and that it was an irreparable and irreversible means of punishment which was unsuitable and inexpedient for the prevention of severe crimes, or as a deterrent against the commission of such crimes.

II

1. In response to the request of the Constitutional Court, in his opinion dated 19 March 1990 the Minister of Justice considered the provisions on capital punishment to be unconstitutional. He found capital punishment to be an unnecessary and inhuman punishment which might not be justified on moral grounds, it did not serve the purpose of punishment, and was unsuitable both for the protection of society, and as a deterrent against the commission of crimes by members of society.

He pointed out that Act XVI/1989 was a significant step towards the elimination of capital punishment from the Criminal Code since it removed capital punishment from the sentences imposable for crimes against the State.

He also suggested that the abolition of capital punishment was in harmony with European legal development. In Western European countries, the possibility of capital punishment either has been entirely eliminated or may only be applied to military crimes or in wartime.

2. The Constitutional Court requested Dr. József Földvári, Dr. László Korinek and Dr. András Sajó to submit expert opinions.

On the basis of the purpose of punishment, József Földvári finds capital punishment unjustified. However, he considers the abolition of capital punishment to be part of an all-encompassing revision of criminal law. According to András Sajó, capital punishment is unconstitutional because it is arbitrary and cruel, infringes upon human dignity, and is contrary to the idea of the rule of law. László Korinek examined the statistical and criminological aspects of capital punishment and found it neither a suitable nor a necessary means of fighting crime.

3. The President of the Supreme Court, Dr. Pál Solt, and the Chief Public Prosecutor, Dr. Kálmán Györgyi, spoke at the Plenary Session in accordance with s. 30(4) of Act XXXII on the Constitutional Court.

The President of the Supreme Court expressed a legal and ethical view that capital punishment no longer had a place in general, nor here and now in Hungary. In his view, capital punishment is unjustifiable from the perspective of criminal law, and it is unconstitutional considering the relation between criminal law and the Constitution.

The Chief Public Prosecutor, while emphasizing his personal commitment to the abolition of capital punishment, called the attention of the Constitutional Court to the fact that capital punishment may not be declared arbitrary solely on the basis of Art. 54(1) of the Constitution and that such a decision required a comprehensive consideration of Art. 8(2) and Art. 54(1) and (2) of the Constitution with special regard to their relationship to each other.

He believes that the most appropriate forum to make this decision would be Parliament: however he admits that, in the present constitutional situation, the Constitutional Court by virtue of law may not avoid answering the question on its merits.

III

The Chapter on "Penalties and Measures" at art. 38(1) of the Criminal Code mentions capital punishment as the first item on the list of primary penalties. In art. 39, the legislature stipulated the subjective criteria for the imposition of capital punishment, the applicable secondary punishments and certain legal consequences.

The Chapter on "Imposition of Punishments" at art. 84 states that "capital punishment may only be imposed in exceptional cases and—with respect to the extreme danger presented by the perpetrator and the crime as well as to the especially high degree of culpablility—the protection of society can only be secured with the application of this punishment."

Article 399 of the Code on Criminal Procedure, which also concerns capital punishment, establishes the most important procedural rules concerning the granting of a pardon, pregnant and mentally ill convicts as well as those who are sentenced to death in their absence.

Sections 17 and 18 of Law Decree 11/1979 specify the circumstances for execution of capital punishment.

The provisions of the Rules on the Execution of Punishments that have been declared unconstitutional contain the rules for enforcing the punishment in relation to those condemned to death and prescribe the measures to be taken after the execution.

Until the publication of the present Constitutional Court decision, the Criminal Code allowed capital punishment for those who committed the following crimes:

—from among the crimes against humanity: genocide [art. 155(1)], aggravated cases of violence against a civilian population [art. 158(2)], aggravated cases of criminal warfare [art. 106] and violence against an envoy of war [art. 163(2)];

—from among the crimes against individuals: aggravated cases of homicide [art. 166(2)];

—from among the crimes against public order: aggravated cases of terrorist activity [art. 261(2)] and aggravated cases of seizing control of an aircraft [art. 262(2)];

—from among military crimes: specially aggravated cases of desertion [art. 343(4)], the aggravated case of escape from service [art. 346(1)], objection to service [art. 347], the specially aggravated case of breach of duty in service [art. 348(3)], the specially aggravated case of mutiny [art. 352(3) and (4)], the aggravated case of disobedience of orders [art. 354(3)], the specially aggravated case of violence against a commander or an officer in service [art. 355(5)], the aggravated case of jeopardizing combat alertness [art. 363(2)], a commander's breach of duty [art. 364] and escape from performing combat duty (desertion) [art. 365].

IV

The Constitutional Court based its decision to declare the rules on capital punishment unconstitutional and therefore null and void on the following considerations:

Chapter I of the Constitution, entitled "General Provisions," states that "the Republic of Hungary recognizes the inviolable and inalienable fundamental rights of man; to respect and protect these rights is a primary obligation of the State" [Art. 8(1)]. The Constitution states in the first place in Chapter XII, "Fundamental Rights and Duties," that "In the Republic of Hungary, every human being has the inherent right to life and to human dignity, of which no one can be arbitrarily deprived" [Art. 54(1)]. According to Art. 8(4), the right to life and human dignity are considered fundamental rights, whose exercise may not be suspended or limited even in a state of national crisis, emergency, or danger.

It can be concluded from the comparison of the quoted provisions of the Constitution that, irrespective of citizenship, the right to life and human dignity is an inherent, inviolable and inalienable fundamental right of every human being in Hungary. It is a primary responsibility of the Hungarian State to respect and protect these rights. Article 54(1) of the Constitution stipulates that "no one can be arbitrarily deprived of" life and human dignity. The wording of this prohibition, however, does not exclude the possibility that someone shall be deprived of life and human dignity in a non-arbitrary way.

Nevertheless, when judging the constitutionality of the legal permissibility of capital punishment, the relevant provision is Art. 8(2) of the Constitution which was introduced by s. 3(1) of Act XL/1990 passed on 19 June 1990 and entered into force on 25 June 1990, replacing the former Art. 8(2), enacted on 23 October 1989. Under the current provisions of Art. 8(2) of the Constitution, "in the Republic of Hungary rules pertaining to fundamental rights and duties shall be determined by statute which, however, may not limit the essential content of any fundamental right."

The Constitutional Court found that the provisions in the Criminal Code and the quoted related regulations concerning capital punishment breached the prohibition against the limitation of the essential content of the right to life and human dignity. The provisions relating to the deprivation of life and human dignity by capital punishment not only impose a limitation upon the essential content of the fundamental right to life and human dignity, but also allow for the entire and irreparable elimination of life and human dignity or of the right ensuring these. Therefore, the Constitutional Court established the unconstitutionality of these provisions and declared them null and void.

V

After listing the reasons for the Constitutional Court's decision to declare the quoted provisions of the Criminal Code and other regulations unconstitutional and therefore null and void, the Constitutional Court considers it necessary to refer to the following:

1. Article 8(2) of the Constitution as amended on 19 June 1990 conflicts with the text of Art. 54(1). It is the responsibility of Parliament to harmonize them.

2. Human life and human dignity form an inseparable unity and have a greater value

than anything else. Accordingly the rights to human life and human dignity form an indivisible and unrestrainable fundamental right which is the source of and the precondition for several other fundamental rights. A state under the rule of law shall regulate fundamental rights stemming from the unity of human life and dignity with respect to the relevant international treaties and fundamental legal principles and in the service of public and private interests defined by the Constitution. The right to human life and dignity as an absolute value creates a limitation upon the criminal power of the State.

3. The Constitutional Court finds that consideration should be given to the criminological and statistical findings, based on the experience of several countries: the application or abolition of capital punishment have not been confirmed to influence either the total number of crimes or the incidence of the commission of crimes that were formerly penalized by capital punishment.

4. Article 6(1) of the International Covenant on Civil and Political Rights—which was signed by Hungary and promulgated by Law Decree 8/1976—declares that "every human being has the inherent right to life. This right shall be protected by law. No one shall be arbitrarily deprived of his/her life." Paragraph (6) of the same article states that "[n]othing in this article shall be invoked to delay or to prevent the abolition of capital punishment by any State Party to the present Covenant."

The Covenant, therefore, recognizes a development towards the abolition of capital punishment. While art. 2(1) of the European Convention on the Protection of Human Rights and Fundamental Freedoms, signed in Rome on 4 November 1950, had recognized the legitimacy of capital punishment, art. 1 of the Sixth Additional Protocol thereto adopted on 28 April 1983 provides that "[t]he death penalty shall be abolished. No one shall be condemned to such penalty or executed." Also, art. 22 of the Declaration "On Fundamental Rights and Fundamental Freedoms" adopted by the European Parliament on 12 April 1989 declares the abolition of capital punishment. Hungarian constitutional development moves in the same direction since, after the formulation of Art. 54(1), which did not clearly exclude capital punishment, a subsequent modification of Art. 8(2) proscribed limitations by law upon the essential contents of fundamental rights.

5. Since the punishments included in the Criminal Code form a coherent system, the abolition of capital punishment, which is a part of this system, requires the revision of the entire penal system; this does not, however, fall within the competence of the Constitutional Court.

SCHMIDT, J., dissenting: Articles 8 and 54 of the current Constitution in force contain conflicting provisions. While Art. 54(1) prohibits the arbitrary deprivation of one's life and thus fails to repeal the possibility of capital punishment, the subsequently introduced Art. 8(2) does not allow any limitation on the essential contents of fundamental rights even by law. The prohibition of capital punishment may be derived from this latter provision.

While the interpretation of the Constitution falls within the competence of the Constitutional Court, it is the right and obligation of Parliament, the body empowered to frame or to change the Constitution, to resolve the conflict between the provisions of the Constitution. Such powers may not be assumed by the Constitutional Court.

Therefore, in my opinion, the Constitutional Court should state that it lacks such a power and should call Parliament's attention to the necessity of eliminating the conflict. This would not exclude the possibility for the Constitutional Court to list all the current arguments against capital punishment.

LÁBADY and **TERSZTYÁNSZKY, JJ.**, concurring:

1. By recognizing international conventions on human rights, Hungary has assumed an obligation to recognize general human rights as fundamental values. Under Art. 7(1) of the Constitution, the legal system of the Republic of Hungary accepts the universally recognised principles of international law and secures the harmony of domestic law with the obligations assumed under international law.

2. The starting point of current documents on human rights in international law is human dignity. The International Covenant on Civil and Political Rights refers to "the inherent dignity of all members of the human family" and regards human dignity as a paramount source of rights as it points to the recognition that "human rights derive from the inherent dignity of the human person."

3. Human dignity, as the integrity of personality, means along with human life the essence of man. Dignity is the elevating quality of our human existence and value: it is worthy of an unconditional respect, the honour of our human essence. It is an a priori value in the same way that life is, and it expresses the human dimension of life. Being a human and human dignity are inseparable from one another. Both are inalienable, immanent, essential properties of man. To be worthy of life means to be worthy of being a human person, and that is why human life and human dignity may in fact not be handled separately.

4. The existence and dignity of man, as the unity of man, is not really a right, because human essence is in fact transcendent for the law—*i.e.,* it is beyond the reach of the law. Human life and dignity are, therefore, included in the catalogue of human rights and in modern constitutions as the sources of rights or as values beyond the reach of law which are inviolable, rather than as fundamental rights. Law should ensure that such inviolable values are respected and protected.

This—and only this—protection is already a dimension of law. The law involved at this point creates prohibitions and guarantees to differing extents for everyone, including the State.

5. Thus, when Art. 54(1) of the Constitution stipulates the inherent right to life and dignity—as well as with regard to the adjectives "inviolable and inalienable," in Art. 8(1)—it provides for categories that are superior to legal values and must be given the fullest possible legal protection; the standards for the protection of these values (as real legal prohibitions) are unlimited and consequently binding upon the State. The State, therefore, may not use its criminal power to deprive a human being of his/her life and human dignity because, by capital punishment, it would arbitrarily restructure the above values protected by the Constitution. Arbitrarily, because human life and dignity are superior to any other values, they are the source, origin and basis of human rights—*viz.,* they are values inviolable and inalienable by law. Capital punishment is, therefore, arbitrary and consequently unconstitutional.

6. Since Art. 54(1) of the Constitution prohibits the arbitrary deprivation of one's life and human dignity, there must be room, according to the Constitution, for non-arbitrary deprivation. Consequently, it may not be stated that any deprivation of one's life is illegitimate or arbitrary.

Deprivation of one's life is only impossible in law; however, similar values—*i.e.,* another person's life and dignity—may compete with one another. In this case, law structures situations rather than restructuring the values: in the case of defensive actions justifiable under the law or other non-arbitrary deprivations, it protects the quality of non-arbitrariness of the defence against arbitrariness rather than recognizing the right to capital punishment.

SÓLYOM, P., concurring:

1. *Freedom of the Constitutional Court in formulating its Decision*

According to the Constitution, no one may be arbitrarily deprived of his/her right to life and human dignity. Accordingly, the formal key to the constitutionality of capital punishment seems to be the interpretation of arbitrariness. As no one obviously may be "arbitrarily" deprived of any right, our task is to identify the special conditions of the deprivation of one's right to life and human dignity—*i.e.,* to interpret arbitrariness with a view to the attributes of such rights. The decision concerning the constitutionality of capital punishment should, therefore, be based on the explanation of the contents of the right to life and human dignity. The Constitution declares that the law pertaining to fundamental rights must not impose limitations on their essential content. First of all the content of these rights must be made clear before deciding whether the provisions on capital punishment impose a limitation upon the essential contents and meaning of the rights to life and human dignity and are, therefore, unconstitutional.

The right to life and the right to human dignity are the most fundamental rights. As understood by the Constitutional Court, the right to human dignity is a "mother right"—*i.e.,* the source of not yet expressly stipulated fundamental freedoms. The interpretation of the right to human dignity, therefore, may have an impact on the limitations placed upon individual autonomy in the cases of other human rights in the same way as the interpretation of the right to life may influence decisions about other controversial issues concerning the disposal of life (*e.g.,* abortion or euthanasia).

Before such a highly important decision is made, first the freedom of and constraints upon the Constitutional Court in forming the contents of its decision must be made clear.

As far as its grounds and finality are concerned, the decision of the Constitutional Court on the constitutionality of capital punishment considerably differs from the abolition of capital punishment by a legislative act. When deciding, Parliament is free to use any arguments, scientific, practical, criminal policy or other current political considerations or reasons. (See the abolition of capital punishment in 1989 for political crimes.) The publicity surrounding the legislative process provides an opportunity to introduce and compare as many arguments as possible and at the same time prepares the public for the decision. Another reason why it is easier to make a parliamentary decision is that a law abolishing capital punishment does not have any compelling consequences with regard to additional aspects of the right to life. On the other hand, Parliament is under public pressure. Parliament may maintain, abolish or restore capital punishment at its discretion until the Constitutional Court renders a final decision on the constitutionality of this punishment.

By contrast, the Constitutional Court may only make constitutional arguments to justify its decision. In particular, it may not be satisfied with the usual criminological argument that capital punishment cannot be proved to have an effect on the prevention of crimes. The Constitutional Court is not bound by the intent of the legislature since it may review the constitutionality of the Criminal Code and it may interpret the Constitution. A Constitutional Court's decision is final. The Constitutional Court is not bound either by the will of the majority or by public opinion. It is not bound either by any ethical or scientific trend.

The Constitutional Court has to develop its own interpretation of the right to life.

In this context, the starting point is the Constitution as a whole. The Constitutional

Court must continue its effort to explain the theoretical bases of the Constitution and of the rights included in it and to form a coherent system with its decisions, which as an "invisible Constitution" provides for a reliable standard of constitutionality beyond the Constitution, which nowadays is often amended out of current political interests; therefore this coherent system will probably not conflict with the new Constitution to be established or with future Constitutions. The Constitutional Court enjoys freedom in this process as long as it remains within the framework of the concept of constitutionality.

The drafters of the Constitution worked with the pluralism of values, characteristic of a society and state after a change of regime; the modification of the Constitution promulgated on 23 October 1989 (by Act XXXI/1989) broke with the "official" ideology which had formerly served as the basis of the State and with the requirement that the rights shall be interpreted in accordance with this ideology. The various intellectual trends suggested to be listed during the drafting of the Constitution illustrates this diversity of values, as does the reference to "the values of bourgeois democracy and democratic socialism" that remained from these in the modification of October 1989. Since then this reference has also been removed from the Constitution by Act XL/1990. The quite abstract wording of constitutional rights provides no indication that the legislature has committed itself to a given interpretation of these rights. Even if that had been the case, such a legislative commitment would not be a starting point for the Constitutional Court: the Constitutional Court is independent of the legislature's intent, and it would also be disquieting to rely on the argument that the social changes of the past year have discredited the Constitution drafters' original concept. This would mean that the Constitutional Court is compelled to alter the meaning of the Constitution. However, that does not fall within the competence of the Constitutional Court. The interpretation of the Constitution shall be based on the concept of the rights to be interpreted as neutral categories, the limits of which may be established with a high degree of consensus, while their content may be filled with many different value concepts. If we proceed accordingly, the wide definitions of the Constitution also include moral questions to be answered. It belongs to the essence of a pluralist society that these questions may be answered in many different ways—*i.e.,* the rights may encompass a variety of values while the whole constitutional system of rights remains coherent and operative. The Constitutional Court has to intervene in borderline cases to draw the line beyond which a given concept about the content of a right ("answer") may not be brought into harmony with the whole system (basic principles) of the Constitution. The equality of citizens, for example, may be interpreted in a variety of ways; the Constitutional Court had to declare that this equality might not be limited to mechanical equality with regard to the distribution of material wealth and had to clarify the conditions under which positive discrimination is permissible. In other cases, the Constitutional Court may establish that a given concept about the content of a constitutional right fits into the conceptual framework of the Constitution even though the legislature wished to exclude it. In exceptional cases, a constitutional right can bear only a single interpretaton. Of course, it is a value judgement. This is, however, the very thing for which the Constitutional Court has authorization: to enforce its own concept on the content in order to maintain the Constitution. The Constitutional Court has to make the choice in borderline cases or when incompatible concepts come into conflict. The concept of the right to life may not encompass two concepts, one of which allows, while the other excludes, capital punishment. The Constitutional Court shall declare the interpretation binding that it considers to be in harmony with the whole Constitution.

Such a simultaneous freedom and obligation to decide burden the Constitutional Court with an immense responsibility. Though starting from the Constitution as a whole, it is the Court itself that defines the standard of interpretation, with its continuous interpretation. As the decision is final, the judge must accept responsibility before his/her own conscience and before the public, primarily before the scientific community. We must, therefore, face the fact that one of the possible meanings of a constitutional right will become binding (which might be corrected in a later decision by the Constitutional Court or be derogated from due to desuetude). The correct professional reasoning gains ground already within a prior choice of value as well.

In terms of the above framework, the decision of the Constitutional Court is deliberately subjective and tied to history: even if the Constitutional Court proclaims absolute values, it reveals their meaning in and for its own age; its decision, for example, in the questions of capital punishment or abortion should theoretically lay no claim to eternity. The Constitutional Court's image of man, choice of philosophy and conception of a judge's role are all subjective features. That is why it is desirable for the Constitutional Court to consider the contemporary international approach to capital punishment as an objective criterion; the evaluation of this subject already belongs to the Constitutional Court's permissible realm to consider political arguments.

In 1972 the U.S. Supreme Court proclaimed that all laws on capital punishment were unconstitutional and set an example as a liberating effect for other countries. Since 1976, however, we have witnessed the restoration of capital punishment. On the other hand, the Council of Europe—based on a development in most of the Member States—considered the abolition of capital punishment as a general trend, and in 1983 it attached a protocol on the abolition of capital punishment to the European Convention on Human Rights 1950. (Of the 22 Member States, 15 have signed and 12 have ratified this Sixth Protocol—but, *e.g.*, in the non-ratifying Federal Republic of Germany, there is no capital punishment.) Article 22 of the Declaration on Fundamental Rights and Fundamental Freedoms, adopted by the European Parliament on 12 April 1989, declares the abolition of capital punishment. This made most of the European nations go beyond the compromise included in the International Covenant on Civil and Political Rights allowing capital punishment: nevertheless, this compromise was followed by the Hungarian Constitution as late as October 1989 when only the prohibition against arbitrary deprivation of life was included.

The Constitutional Court has good reasons to rely on our own historical situation when it increases the respect of the right to life through the abolition of capital punishment and drives back the criminal power of the State from this field. It is more than a symbolic opposition to a political system that sacrificed human life for its political purposes, without restraint; the abolition of capital punishment for political crimes could have been on the agenda in 1960, in the same way as a similar motivation for the prohibition against capital punishment in the *Grundgesetz* of the Federal Republic of Germany was opportune in 1949. The current historical task now is to establish with binding force for the legislature that in the constitutional order that is interpreted and protected by the Constitutional Court, the State cannot deprive someone of his/her life.

2. *The right to life in the Constitution*

In this point, I will examine the location of the right to life in the Constitution, its qualifications and its relations to other provisions pertinent to it, without outlining the concept of the content of the right to life.

According to Art. 54(1) of the Constitution: "In the Republic of Hungary every human being has the inherent right to life and to human dignity of which no one can be arbitrarily deprived."

Questions to be interpreted:

(a) the specific position of and the relation between the rights to life and to human dignity.

(b) the qualification of those rights as "inherent" and, under Art. 8 of the Constitution, "inviolable" and "inalienable."

(c) the provision "no one may be arbitrarily deprived," under Arts. 8 and 54 of the Constitution.

(a) In the 18th century, it was usual in natural law to trace back natural rights to some primary or fundamental rights. Such a starting point was the right to life. Nowadays, human dignity plays the similar role of a basic norm in both constitutions and international conventions. In this capacity, it is a descendant of "natural freedom" in natural law. The right to human dignity is an express "mother right" in German, American and Hungarian Constitutional Court practice; to protect the freedoms of action and self-determination, the Court derives ever newer fundamental freedoms therefrom. Nevertheless, the right to life has not lost its specific role either. There are opinions that continue to regard it as the basis of other rights. It is more widespread that the right to life follows the right to dignity at the head of the catalogue of fundamental rights, but there are cases, such as in the Hungarian Constitution, where they appear in the same Article. It is a usual practice today that the right to life is related to physical integrity and health, on the one hand, and, influenced by international law, to the prohibition of torture and cruel or degrading punishment, on the other hand. The two rights seem to live separate lives while retaining their importance. A closer analysis, however, can demonstrate their interrelation in substance, that only in their unity may they define the legal status of man and may serve as a real basis of fundamental rights. It is the unity of the right to life and dignity that distinguishes man from other persons, that is, legal entities having legal capacity, on the one hand, and from other living creatures on the other. The separate historical role of these two aspects of the status of man is not inconsistent with the concept that the present historical moment, especially with regard to the acute question of disposal of one's life by a third party, requires a uniform approach to the right to life and dignity. To prove all this, the characteristics of these two rights have to be examined in detail, as I will do in Point 3 below.

(b) According to Art. 54 of the Constitution, human beings have the "inherent" right to life and to the dignity of man. Based on the title of Chapter XII, these rights are "fundamental rights." Under Art. 8, the Republic of Hungary recognizes "the inviolable and inalienable (fundamental) rights" of human beings.

The interpretation of these adjectives does not provide sufficient basis for the decision on the constitutionality of capital punishment. With regard to inalienability for example, there is a classical theory that the right to life may not be assigned to the State in the social contract; consequently the State may not take it away. A similar explanation could be developed for inviolability or for the inherent nature of this right, too, but one can do without these adjectives to argue that the State may not impose limitations upon the right to life (see Point 3). To be inherent can be interpreted as an expression of the fact that life (and dignity) are a priori values, from which the rights that protect them originate. However, legal history and present-day constitutions as well as international conventions show a range of examples that the declaration of inalienability of the right to life has not excluded capital punishment. Article 54(1) of the Hungarian Constitution is also aimed at allowing the deprivation of one's inalienable and inviolable inherent right to life and dignity if it is not an arbitrary deprivation. Therefore, without the interpretation of arbitrariness, no opinion may be formed about the inalienability of the right to life and dignity.

(c) Accordingly, the limits upon the right to life are dependent on how "arbitrariness" is interpreted.

The imposition of a punishment may be considered arbitrary when it allows the judge to be excessively subjective in making his/her decision. Though capital punishment was declared unconstitutional in the USA because of its unusualness and cruelty, the real objection to the statute in question was that the preconditions of the imposition of capital punishment had been imprecisely defined. András Sajó brings up a similar argument in Point 1 of his expert opinion. The provisions of the Criminal Code concerning the imposition of capital punishment, however, do not differ substantially from the provisions concerning the imposition of other kinds of punishment, consequently their "arbitrariness" may have a bearing on the imposition of other punishments. In my opinion, however, the arbitrariness referred to in Art. 54 of the Constitution calls for a special interpretation that has no bearing other than on the right to life and dignity.

Another approach suggests that arbitrariness means the absence of a lawful procedure. It is supported by the European Convention on Human Rights 1950, art. 2, which says that the only permissible deprivation of one's life is the execution of a death sentence imposed according to law. (In 1983, however, the Sixth Protocol abolished capital punishment.) In a state under the rule of law, no punishment may be imposed except for reasons defined in law and on the basis of lawful proceedings. This rule is accurately stipulated in the Constitution with regard to the deprivation of one's freedom (Art. 55). Comparison of Art. 54(1) with Art. 55(1) suggests that the arbitrariness of the deprivation of life and dignity is not precluded if carried out for reasons defined in law and on the basis of lawful proceedings. This is a necessary but insufficient condition. The difference is explained by the qualitatively different nature of the deprivation of life and freedom respectively (see Point 3).

But if the formal legality of capital punishment does not necessarily preclude arbitrariness, the only question left to be answered about its contents is whether or not capital punishment itself as a kind of punishment is arbitrary.

According to a widespread view, capital punishment is arbitrary because no evidence may be found that it is suitable for achieving the aims of punishment which are in accordance with the Constitution. (This is also mentioned in the reasons of this decision.) Human life and dignity enjoy preference over this uncertainty. It is true that a punishment unable to serve its purpose is unconstitutional. It is also true that because the deprivation of fundamental rights is in question here, evidence must be found that the punishment is suitable for the purpose. However, I do not think that the mere argument over effectiveness is sufficient to establish the unconstitutionality of capital punishment. It might be suggested that we also do not have reliable evidence of the preventive effect of other punishments, *e.g.*, of imprisonment. Again, the difference between loss of life and loss of freedom would have to be explained (*i.e.*, the special nature of the right to life) to prove that we can be satisfied with the (high) probability of the appropriateness or effectiveness of the punishment in the case of imprisonment or fines but not in the case of capital punishment. My second objection is that, according to the argument mentioned above, it follows that capital punishment would be constitutional if the punishment was sure to achieve its purpose. The usual reassuring answer is that the purpose of punishment will never be achievable with full certainty in the case of capital punishment for the very reason that the possibility of human error cannot be eliminated. So, the argument remains pragmatic. It is difficult to break out of this circle because we are questioning the practical effectiveness of punishment rather than proving that capital punishment is theoretically unsuitable. This question leads us further to the peculiar nature of capital punishment. With this, we switch over to a theoretically different line of argument: the special nature of capital punishment is based on the peculiarity of the right to life. Therefore it would be better to start from the peculiarity of the right to life and prove that life may not be taken away even if that appears to be reasonable.

(d) According to Art. 8(2) of the Constitution, the laws regulating fundamental rights may not impose any limitations upon the essential contents and meaning of the fundamental right to life and dignity. The question, compared to what do we determine the limitation on a fundamental right is of particular importance in our case. Capital punishment does not come into conflict with the right to life per se, but with the right to life as a right of which "no one can be arbitrarily deprived." So, whether or not the Criminal Code imposes limitations at all upon the constitutional right to life depends on the interpretation of "arbitrary deprivation" included in Art. 54(1) of the Constitution. If the deprivation of life is *per definitionem* and in any case considered arbitrary, *i.e.,* the right to life is considered absolute, then capital punishment is a limitation upon this right. But if the right to life in the Constitution itself is thought to be limited by supposing that certain non-arbitrary cases of the deprivation of life—provided, *e.g.,* that they are based on lawful proceedings—are consistent with the nature of the right to life, then the Criminal Code does not limit the right to life, and whether the Constitution itself may impose a limitation upon the essential content of a fundamental right does not belong to the investigation of the unconstitutionality of the Criminal Code.

3. *The peculiarity of the rights to human dignity and life*

The right to human dignity is not merely a declaration of a moral value. The concept that human dignity is a value a priori and beyond law, and is inaccessible by law in its entirety does not preclude this value from being regarded as the source of rights—as many international conventions and constitutions do by following natural law—or the law from requiring the respect of dignity or the transformation of some of its aspects into a real right.

The right to human dignity has two functions. On the one hand, it expresses that there is an absolute limit which may not be transgressed either by the State or by the coercive power of other people—*i.e.,* it is a core of autonomy and individual self-determination withdrawn from the control of anybody else by virtue of which, according to the classical wording, man may remain a subject and will not be changed into a tool or object. The same is expressed by the approach, shared by the Constitutional Court, that the right to human dignity is a "mother right," the source of ever newer freedoms, with which we continuously safeguard the sphere of self-determination against (state) control. This approach to the right to human dignity is what distinguishes man from legal entities having legal capacity, that may be entirely controlled and do not have any "untouchable" essence. (And that is the theoretical difference between man [as a natural person] and a legal entity [as a legal person], rather than the suggestion that certain rights "because of their nature, may only be attached to man." Based on the latter model analogous rights for legal entities may always be created.)

We shall see that the right to human dignity will fulfill its function only if it is interpreted in unity with the individual person's right to life; if we leave this out of consideration, abstract dignity will allow treatment of a concrete individual as an object.

The other function of the right to dignity is to ensure equality. The historical achievement of "everyone's equal dignity" meant equal legal capacity—*i.e.,* a formally equal chance. In the context of the present decision, we have to emphasise the characteristic of equality that upon this right other rights may be built (*e.g.,* equal dignity, when transformed to legal capacity, serves as a basis for acquiring all other rights); but from equal dignity nothing can be taken away. This means that dignity is indivisible and irreducible—*i.e.,* it is the minimum condition of human status of which no one may be deprived.

The right to equal dignity, in union with the right to life, must ensure that bare lives of different value are not to be treated differently by the law. No one is more or less worthy of life. Because of equal dignity, the life and human dignity of a disabled person and a moral monster are equally untouchable. Human dignity is shared by every human being, no matter to what extent he/she has achieved the inherent possibilities of human beings and the reason therefor. As a result of the unity of the right to life and dignity, not only in death is everybody equal: the equality of lives is guaranteed by dignity.

The right to (bare) life was absolute only in certain natural law theories (*e.g.,* in Hobbes) inasmuch as the authority to dispose of it might not be transferred to the State. Until capital punishment (or war) became questionable or, on the other hand, until other living creatures' right to life emerged, it had not become pressing to figure out what causes the right to life to be a special human right. The dignity of man and its relation to life are what distinguish the right of man to life from any other rights. The right to life without dignity is not the right to human life. In the natural law approach already mentioned, the right to life is a residue of the natural state, the ranking of survival over everything, which right—as has already been written by Spinoza—"is granted to animals as well." Today the right of man to life is made specific by its relation to the right to dignity, as compared to "the rights of animals and trees." The obligation of the State to protect life (each life) and to protect dignity must be distinguished from man's subjective right to life and dignity. The "rights of animals and trees" are not mere metaphors; the State has indeed an obligation to maintain the natural bases of each life, and to safeguard each life from the moss through the embryo to man, but this protection is relative except with regard *stricto sensu* to individual human life, and only man has a subjective right to it.

What today defines the relationship between the right to life and dignity? Before a constitutional court makes a decision about life and death it must first elucidate its image of man. Today the dualistic approach is predominant: the various secularised versions of the different statuses of body and soul. The rather concrete and individual "bodily" rights seem to be inferior to the more abstract right to dignity which is connected with the—from the concrete individual easily separable—"soul." It is, though, common to start from man as a biological and social being. Such a linkage, however, does not have any consequences in law, since the right to life is conceived as "the right to biological-physical existence"; that is why the right to physical integrity and health is traditionally linked to it. In most constitutions, these (individual) "bodily" rights do not enjoy absolute protection, as opposed to the right to dignity by which man has a share in the dignity of the human race and which is, therefore, untouchable. This right survives man in the eyes of those who—like many—view the rights concerning a deceased person (*e.g.,* his/her honour) as the dead person's right.

Such a hierarchy in the rights to dignity and life carries grave consequences. This is because the dualistic approach may be a justification for sacrificing the individual man for public purposes. In such a case, a criminal may be executed for the purposes of general prevention because his/her dignity will not suffer damage anyway. (Hegel honours criminals through punishment. In my opinion this argument may only be accepted for punishments other than capital punishment.) With the dualistic value order, it would also become easy to justify disposal of life by a third party in cases where a loss of dignity is claimed—*e.g.*, in the case a disease resulting in the final loss of clear consciousness. In other words, if because of this dualism the protection of man is restricted to the untouchability of abstract dignity, the life of the concrete person will be at the mercy of others.

The Constitutional Court is free to decide to start from a homogenous and indivisible image of man, rejecting the dualism of body and soul—*i.e.*, to view man in the unity of his/her life and dignity. Accordingly, only the unity of the right to life and to dignity will provide the status that is specifically related to the concrete individual: it is the untouchability and equality contained in the right to human dignity that results in man's right to life being a specific right to human life (over and above animals' and artificial subjects' right to being); on the other hand, dignity as a fundamental right does not have meaning for the individual if he or she is dead. (The possible moral value of his/her death is the concern of survivors, disregarding of course the fact that this value might motivate his/her action, even his/her self-sacrifice.) Human dignity is a quality of human life which naturally accompanies it. The right to human dignity does not allow the individual to be deprived of his/her dignity. Man, however, can only be deprived of human dignity by the taking of his/her life, causing both to come to an end once and for all.

According to the above approach, the right to human dignity and life essentially differs from any other rights.

This right concerns the undivided and complete man—while all other rights regulate abstract "roles," partial aspects. (Even personal rights—such as privacy—concern only those with average, "normal" sensibility.) The right to life and dignity, as the basis of man's legal status, is the most personal and most general at the same time.

The other rights may be limited, then restored; their withdrawal can only be partial also because their limitation does not preclude the effectiveness of other rights. Several rights may be taken away entirely, then granted again. The ultimate limit of their withdrawal is exactly the right of man to life and dignity (which does not mean that reaching this ultimate limit would be constitutional in all cases). In contrast, the right to life and dignity can be taken away only irreversibly, causing any other rights to cease. Due to its indivisibility, the right to life and human dignity is theoretically unlimitable and constitutes a theoretical boundary for the limitation of any other rights. (If the unity of these two rights is recognised as the basis of the individual's legal status, it will be possible to make different decisions about the extent to which other rights based on them may be limited. The limitation of personal freedom for the purposes of punishment, for example, may take a variety of forms. Within the given legal system, a limit must be defined which even punishment by imprisonment may not exceed. This may range from an open prison to custody "in irons," from country to country, and from constitution to constitution. In the meantime, the various derivative rights deducible from the right to life and dignity may also be limited—*e.g.*, in respect of the outward appearances of dignity. The condemned, however, continues to be entitled to several other rights and when his/her sentence has been served his/her right to personal liberty is also restored. The limitations, however, may not concern the fundamental right to life and dignity, not only because it is forbidden but also because law is not able to impose such limitations. It is easy to admit, for example, that as long as the prisoner is conscious, he will possess the possibility of autonomous reaction to his condition, whether it is internal resistance, repentance or any other decision. And while he is alive, there is no doubt about his/her human status. The uniform approach to life and dignity is an even more complete safeguard for man: his/her dignity does not depend on his/her state of consciousness and morality; it is given by his/her life. His/her human status is therefore indisputable, because his/her life is untouchable due to his/her dignity.)

Article 8 of the Constitution restricts the possibility of limiting fundamental rights. It withdraws at the outset their "essential content" from the control of the legislature—*i.e.,* the State—and it forbids the suspension or curtailment of the exercise of the most important fundamental rights even in times of emergency, national crises or state of danger. But the right to life and dignity are conceptually unlimitable. Man can only be deprived of those completely and once and for all—*i.e.,* no distinction may be drawn between the part that may be limited and the "essential content." The right to life and human dignity constitutes the essential content itself, and that is why the State may not dispose of it. These rights also form a part of the essential contents of all other fundamental rights, since they are the source and the condition of, and serve as the absolute boundaries upon the limitability of, all of the other fundamental rights.

It follows from this that the deprivation of the right to life and dignity is conceptually "arbitrary." The State will come into conflict with the whole concept of the Constitution concerning fundamental rights if it authorizes the deprivation of the right to human life and dignity by allowing and regulating capital punishment. Consequently, Art. 54(1) of the Constitution may not be construed as allowing capital punishment as a "non-arbitrary" deprivation of life. On the contrary, capital punishment is unconstitutional.

Thus, capital punishment is arbitrary not because it limits the essential content of the right to life but because the right to life and dignity—due to their characteristics—is from the outset unlimitable. That is why the modification of Art. 8(2) and (3) of the Constitution by Act XL/1990 was not necessary to render capital punishment unconstitutional. When Art. 8(3) of the Constitution still allowed limitation upon the exercise of a fundamental right "necessary in the interests of national security, internal order, public safety, health and morals or for the protection of the fundamental rights and freedoms of others," the term "arbitrariness" in Art. 54(1) of the Constitution could not be construed to allow capital punishment if imposed on the basis of lawful proceedings—*i.e.,* non-arbitrarily. Capital punishment was unconstitutional even at that time because, in terms of the right to life and dignity, the possibility of any kind of limitation on any basis is theoretically precluded.

4. *The dilemma of justifiable defence*

The Constitutional Court considered it necessary to note that the entire penal system will need to be revised after the abolition of capital punishment. The serious problems concerning the system of punishments are considerably decreased by the fact that capital punishment has always been an alternative penalty in the Criminal Code. The uniform approach to right to life and dignity, however, has indeed made a new explanation for justifiable defence unavoidable, at least in cases where the person attacking life is killed. (What follows will concern exclusively this case of justifiable defence.) If the deprivation of one's right to life is arbitrary per se, no one may have a right to deprive another person of life under any circumstances. The problem of justifiable defence applies to all other cases when the law "allows" the deprivation of his/her life: for example, in extreme necessity or under the orders of a principal.

Although the Constitutional Court is not required to draw these conclusions, I will briefly summarize what follows from Point 3 above with regard to justifiable defence. The deprivation of life cannot be supported by the usual explanation for justifiable defence according to which "the prosecuting authorities of the State are not present at the scene of the unjustified attack, and thus the victim (or the person acting in support of the victim) accomplishes the defence of society against the assailant." The State may not assign a power for the implementation of justice that it itself lacks: the assailant could not be sentenced to death by a court either.

Due to the absolute approach to the right to life, the range of justifiable defence will narrow. Life can only be proportional to life. If an attack against material goods or public interest is repelled by killing the assailant, then criminal responsibility may not be precluded under the rules of justifiable defence. But the question still remains: why cannot the person be punished who repels an attack against his/her life by killing the assailant?

When the person assaulted kills his/her assailant, the law does not recognize the legality of the deprivation of life by non-punishability, ensured by "justifiable defence," but it recognizes that the situation in which the attack and its repelling occurred is beyond the reach of law. The situation of justifiable defence is present only if there is a choice between lives, "the redistribution of death," because the life of the person assaulted may be saved only if the assailant's life is lost. However, the law may not divide and distribute death. In this borderline case, law does not oblige and does not entitle the assaulted person to anything. It may not grant a right to kill the assailant, just as it may not require the assaulted person to bear the attack, since this would mean the power of disposing of his/her life. Therefore, the natural state prevails in those moments in which the situation requires a choice between lives. That is the case from a psychological perspective as well: the manifestation of the instinct for life, which can break through any barriers of civilization—*i.e.,* the characteristically non-human "right" to survival (a right "granted to animals as well"). Upon the end of the situation of choice law regains control, but only to the extent that it examines the limits of its competence—*i.e.,* whether the conditions of the "justifiable defence situation" were present, without assessing what happened in this situation.

SZABÓ, J., concurring:

1. The expert opinions outlined above have examined the inefficiency and unsuitability of capital punishment for achieving the purposes of punishment, as well as its arbitrariness in light of the inconsistencies in the decisions of criminal courts. In my opinion, these arguments are incapable of deciding the question as they concern not only capital punishment but in fact all other kinds of punishment. The conclusion drawn from them, however, is that neither the lack of efficiency nor the unsuitability for serving its purpose nor the variations and inconsistencies in the courts' rulings question the raison d'être of punishment in general. It is well known that criminal reprisal is unable to influence the formation of criminality as it is basically dependent on the current social situation. This does not mean, however, that punishment in general should be given up because of its inefficiency and unsuitability for serving its purposes or because of the variations and inconsistencies in the decisions of the courts. The imposition of punishment is based on the principle that no crime may remain unpunished or that crime deserves punishment, rather than on the efficiency, the appropriateness to fulfill its purpose and the uniformity of punishment. And if these arguments do not question criminal punishment in general, they do not question the raison d'être of capital punishment either. In this system of arguments, the unsuitability for serving the purposes of punishment would question the constitutionality of punishments in-

cluding capital punishment only if the purposes of punishment were defined in the Constitution. However, there are no constitutionally legitimated purposes for punishment. Therefore, the constitutionality or unconstitutionality of capital punishment—as a kind of punishment—depends solely and exclusively on how the right to life is regulated in the Constitution. This right is defined in Art. 8 as a fundamental right to be protected by the State, the essential content and meaning of which may not be limited even by law.

When the Constitutional Court eliminated capital punishment from our legal system, it relied solely and exclusively on the Constitution rather than on criminal or criminological considerations. It maintained the principle that crime deserves punishment, but—worthy of a state under the rule of law—it did not deduce the State's right to punishment from unlimited state authority. The right to punishment is not unlimited. We must, therefore, give up capital punishment as a licence for punishment stemming from an unlimited power.

2. The Constitutional Court established in the reasoning of its decision that the punishments included in the Criminal Code constitute a coherent system, and the abolition of capital punishment as one of its elements requires the revision of the entire penal system, which, however, does not fall within the duties of the Constitutional Court.

I consider this revision necessary for the following reasons:

—in the present system of criminal law—irrespective of the opinion of experts and the explanations of criminal law theories—capital punishment is justified on the basis of the purposes of punishment, *i.e.,* with general and special prevention;

—the removal of capital punishment from the penal system therefore, necessarily has an influence on the Criminal Code's interpretation of the social purpose of the penal system;

—since within the penal system capital punishment has found its justification in the purposes of punishment, in the pursuit of these purposes, these must also necessarily be considered unconstitutional.

—punishments in the penal system need not be bound to the pursuit of purposes, or to the suitability for the achievement of the purpose, since the fact that it is not effective or that it does not fulfill certain purposes does not mean that its use is not necessary, fair and justified. The principle that crime deserves punishment may come true without the pursuit of purposes, effectiveness or efficacy;

—the social purpose of criminal law is to become a sanctional cornerstone of the legal system as a whole. It does not have an independent sphere of action as have the other branches of law. That is why a criminal sanction differs from the sanctions of other branches of law which are aimed at repairing, restoring, or setting of obligations. A criminal sanction is, therefore, a punishment; it causes disadvantages. Its role and intention is to maintain the soundness of legal and moral norms when the sanctions of other branches of law fail;

—a punishment intended to maintain the soundness of law has a symbolic function: the orders of criminal law may be contravened with impunity neither when there are good reasons to transgress those nor when the punishment fails to achieve any purpose or the punishment is unsuitable for achieving a definite aim. The aim of punishment is within itself: in the public declaration of the soundness of law, in the reprisal that does not consider the purpose;

—a symbolic retaliatory punishment, which leaves the purpose out of consideration and intends to maintain the soundness of law, is the same as the principle of proportional punishment. The principle of proportional punishment precludes punishment on the basis of purpose because punishment on the basis of purpose requires and allows proportioning to the purpose instead of proportioning to the weight of the deed. If, for example, education or treatment was viewed as a purpose, a serious crime would be assessed in the light of bad education or curability rather than the seriousness of the crime. However, the perpetrator's personal condition may not be the basis of punishment in a state under the rule of law. A punishment intended to maintain the soundness of law—a retaliatory proportional punishment—is much more humane than a seemingly humane, educational punishment because it does not concern my personality, personal autonomy and freedom of conscience. The logic of imposing a punishment in criminal law may not be substituted with the logic of education and treatment if it wants to remain within the framework of justice;

—another reason why the principle of proportional punishment is the only possible constitutional punishment in a state under the rule of law is that nothing else is compatible with the idea of equality before the law. Any other approach would be a declaration of inequality before the law as it would necessarily proportion punishment to the individual's personal condition or status instead of the deed.

The removal of capital punishment from our legal system has the paradoxical consequence that the idea of punishment intended to maintain the soundness of law—*i.e.,* retaliatory punishment—is confirmed, not the idea of revenge that corresponds to the principle of *talion—i.e.,* "an eye for an eye, and a tooth for a tooth." Historically, reprisal is the rationalization and moderation of revenge. It maintains moral indignation as a motive while, in its standard, it induces moderation, self-control and the causation of just and well-deserved *malum.* In the future, the most serious punishment replacing capital punishment will be the standard of comparison. A retaliatory punishment respects personality because it does not assume the role of psychotherapy, curing, social or mental care and, therefore, does not make these obligatory as punishment. These functions must and can be offered as a service in the course of the punishment being enforced.

The power of the State to sentence establishes no right to take away life. There are no hangings in a state under the rule of law! However, a state under the rule of law is entitled to employ retaliatory, proportional punishment that maintains the soundness of the law. A proportional punishment may be imposed without capital punishment. As mankind has given up mutilative or bodily punishments, it can give up capital punishment as well. The principle of proportional punishment will not suffer damage if, next to the whipping bench, the gallows and guillotine are put in criminal museums.

ZLINSZKY, J., concurring:

1. *Capital punishment and the text of the Constitution*

From the point of view of the unconstitutionality of capital punishment, Art. 8(1) and Art. 54(1) of the Constitution must be examined in relation to the entire text and basic trend of the Constitution.

The provision in Art. 54(1), according to which no one can be arbitrarily deprived of life, is obviously adopted from the Universal Declaration of Human Rights, and both texts were formulated for the situation where law still recognizes capital punishment. That capital punishment is "arbitrary per se" may not be derived from the Constitution: with regard to capital punishment, originally, the Constitution did not consider capital punishment arbitrary provided it was imposed for reasons defined by law and on the basis of lawful proceedings. (The text of the Constitution is imprecise in its meaning as well: instead of "can not be," one obviously must not be arbitrarily deprived of one's life.)

The later amended Art. 8(1) prohibits the limitation of a fundamental human right even by law: if the right to life is recognized as a fundamental right—and it is undoubtedly recognized as a fundamental right in our Constitution—then this right may not be limited by the Criminal Code. The question is whether the deprivation of life means its limitation. Since more includes fewer, and complete deprivation is more than limitation, the answer to the above question seems to be affirmative.

2. *The right to life*

Law, however, is not able to provide man with eternal life. It merely aims to create and maintain a social order where the individual is free to fulfill his/her life and human dignity without doing harm to others. The fulfillment of human dignity includes the free decision to accept and fulfill moral values. Any legal barrier directly or indirectly forcing moral decisions on people in fact hurts their dignity, because it reduces and, in the worst case, deprives them of the freedom of taking their own moral decisions. In pursuit of the possible respect for the freedom of man, the law establishes such norms for coexistence which are intended to resolve the frictions between individuals; at the same time, it seeks to guarantee the individual's safety so that he/she can freely form his/her life in accordance with his/her own goals.

The limit of human freedom is where this freedom comes into conflict with the freedom of others. If the free decision of a person is directed against another person's life, dignity or freedom of action, it will be the responsibility of the society and, within this, of the State to help the victim. In the legal system, the State promises this assistance and at the same time prohibits individual defence against attack or threat (at least it allows a very narrow range of justification when the attack is direct and may not be repelled in another way).

3. *The criminal power of the State*

The criminal power of the State serves to protect the individual's safety. Partly by punishing the attack or injury and inducing the offender to change his/her position, partly by threatening with punishment in order to hold others back from causing similar injuries, and finally by eliminating or minimizing the situations in which somebody's life and dignity can be threatened.

The criminal power of the State undoubtedly restricts people in their freedom of decision; therefore, it imposes to a certain extent limits on human dignity. At the same time it provides the possibility for making a new positive moral decision, since the legally formed norm may be freely accepted and abided by; and such a decision has moral value. It is still a fact, however, that while living in a society is at the same time a limitation on and a prerequisite for human freedom, a norm protected by the State is a limitation upon the moral value, and therefore it only has a place there and to the extent that is necessary for the protection of the individual's life and freedom (life is to be understood here as encompassing all of the prerequisites of social existence). Therefore, according to my opinion and contrary to the concurring opinion of Szabó, J., punishment is acceptable only if directed to an objective and it immediately loses its justification as soon as it becomes unsuitable for achieving its objectives. Society after all is not entitled to form an opinion about the individual's morality or acceptance or rejection of values.

4. *Conclusion*

As even the members of the Constitutional Court have different opinions about the interpretation of the criminal power of the State, no conclusion may be drawn from the criminal jurisdiction itself or from its bounds about the permissibility or impermissibility of capital punishment. I think it has been an implicitly accepted principle—a constitutional principle—in criminal law for centuries that punishment has preventive purposes: it serves to deter attacks against protected social values. It may prevail only where it fulfills its objective; it loses its legal basis when it can no longer serve its purpose or can serve that only at the expense of causing a more serious injury than that which it prevents.

The general preventive effect of capital punishment may not be proved by present scientific knowledge. It would probably have a preventive effect in a part of the cases if the criminal was sure to count on being punished; but regarding another criminal it would not have such an effect, as some of the crimes threatened with capital punishment are committed as emotional act or by deviant persons. Because criminal prosecution is often unsuccessful, the preventive effect of capital punishment does not prevail even where there would be a theoretical possibility for it; and it may not be proved whether in these cases other serious but non-lethal threats bound to ensue would not have the same degree of preventive effect. Thus, in this regard, the necessity of capital punishment is not confirmed today; therefore, the use of capital punishment is based either on the prerogative decision-making power of the legislature or on the maintenance of the status quo: it is arbitrary.

There is no doubt that capital punishment precludes the risk of repeated crime. The latter is quite frequent, and that is why capital punishment seems to create a certain social security. The risk of repeated crime, however, may be controlled by other means as well; in the meantime, the preconditions of crime are reproduced by society and capital punishment diverts attention from the fact that society does not pay the required attention to the elimination of the preconditions and to the creation of the prerequisites of safe coexistence. From this point of view, the maintenance of capital punishment is definitely harmful because it disguises the delay in absolutely necessary steps to be taken by the State. Besides, capital punishment eliminates the still occasional—even though highly probable—risk of repeated crime by an action that results in the certain termination of life, whereas the right to life—because of its nature—may not be limited or terminated in order to prevent or lessen presumed but uncertain risks.

Today in Hungary, social sentiments towards criminals often call for retaining capital punishment. It is quite common, however, that such sentiments are also directed towards crimes which are not threatened with capital punishment, as for example in the case of fatal car accidents when they demand death for the person who caused death. The Constitutional Court, however, does not hunt for popularity in society; its only competence is to ensure the coherence and constitutionality of the legal system: deprivation of life by the State is forbidden even according to the strict text of our Constitution and may not be justified by the constitutional principles of criminal law either.

DECISION 15/1991: 13 APRIL 1991

ON THE USE OF PERSONAL DATA AND THE PERSONAL IDENTIFICATION NUMBER

The PIN case constitutes, again, one of the early, "symbolic" Decisions of the Constitutional Court, which provoked long-term criticism and bitter resistance from the side of the data-gathering and data-processing state bureaucracy. The Court declared the unlimited use of the uniform personal identification number to be unconstitutional. It was more than five years before the decision was fully implemented by way of new legislation. The decision laid down the principles of protection of personal data that underlay the Data Protection Act passed two years later. On the other hand, the Constitutional Court discussed in depth the dangers for the "right to informational self-determination" that made the unlimited use of the PIN unconstitutional.

The petitioner sought constitutional review of several legal rules on the grounds that they violated the right to the protection of personal data under Art. 59 of the Constitution.

Law Decree 10/1986 on the State Population Register provided, inter alia, that under (a) s. 1(1) the objective of the Register was to promote the enforcement of the citizens' rights and the fulfillment of their duties to provide assistance for the activity of state and private organizations; (b) s. 1(2) the duty of the Registrar was the collection of data necessary for unified personal data records and the keeping and supply thereof; (c) s. 3 there was an obligation to supply data on education and professional training; (d) s. 4 the Register was to contain the citizen's personal identification number (PIN), and basic identification and residence data, the scope of which data to be recorded being delegated to the Council of Ministers; (e) s. 6(2) for the compulsory introduction of the PIN into the Register and into the procedures for the administration of the State and the judiciary; (f) s. 7(1) the Register (for its services) could use data from other records if the organization concerned approved; and (g) s. 7(2) a private person could request another person's data to which he/she was entitled or had a lawful interest, such application being certified by his/her own statement or by an official document. The Register was to supply data to state and private organizations to facilitate the performance of their duties; (h) s. 7(3) the mandatory regular data supply to certain organizations for the performance of their basic tasks, such organizations to be determined by decree of the Council of Ministers; (i) s. 8, provision of data could be refused if it violated a citizen's personality rights; (j) s. 10(2) the citizen had the right to correct the data on himself or herself; and (k) s.10(3) personal data could only be made public in cases specified by a statute or by decrees of the Council of Ministers.

Two Decrees of the Council of Ministers were also issued to execute various provisions of the Law Decree: Decrees 25/1986 (VII.8) MT and 102/1990 (VII.3) MT. Under the former, it was provided, inter alia, that (a) in para. 1(1)(o) the registration of the PIN for the father, mother, children and spouse of the person in question was required; and (b) in para. 5(2) the person/organization requesting data from the Register could only use it for the purpose indicated in its application therefor.

The petitioner submitted that (a) the Law Decree was unconstitutional because it did not fulfill the Constitution or the regulatory level necessary for the regulation of fundamental rights as required by Act XI/1987 on Legislation; (b) the provision of mandatory data was prescribed in such a way that the scope of data to be provided was to be determined by the Council of Ministers, which also conflicted with Act XI/1987. The authorization did not specify the subject or the limit of its scope. Consequently the Council regulated fundamental rights and duties for which it could not be authorized; and (c) it was unconstitutional for a Decree of the Council of Ministers to determine who received the mandatory data and who, based on such data, established rights and duties; moreover the protection of personal data in the hands of such recipients could not be guaranteed.

Held, granting the petition:

(1) In the absence of a definite purpose and for arbitrary future use, the collection and processing of personal data were unconstitutional. The right to the protection of personal data, the so-called right to informational self-determination, as guaranteed under Art. 59, permitted everyone the freedom to decide about the disclosure and use of their personal data to the extent that the approval of the person concerned was generally required to register and use it. In addition Art. 59 ensured that such person could monitor the entire route of data processing thereby guaranteeing the right to know who used the data and when, where and for what purpose it was used. A statute could exceptionally require the compulsory supply of personal data and prescribe the manner of its use provided it complied with Art. 8.

(2) In addition the principle of adherence to the purpose to be achieved was a condition of and the guarantee for exercise of the right to informational self-determination. Personal data might therefore only be processed for a definite and legally justified purpose to which every stage of the process had to conform. The person concerned was to be informed of the purpose for the data processing in a manner which allowed him/her to assess its effect on his/her rights, to make a well-founded decision on its provision and to enforce his/her rights were the use of such data to deviate from the original purpose. If there were any possible alteration in the purpose, the person was to be notified unless a statute permitted otherwise.

(3) The definition by the Law Decree of the purpose and scope of collection of data and data processing violated a person's right to human dignity. The protection of the right to informational self-determination in the process of data forwarding was to be ensured through guarantee-based regulations and the adherence to the purpose to be achieved, which had to be present at every stage from the supply to the elimination of such data from a record. Since the Register the data processing for which was "for the purpose of storage" lacked any tangible objective, this resulted in a gap in continuity in purpose from the data-forwarding stage onwards as well as the lack of legitimacy of an alteration in the purpose thereof. Moreover it was clear that a data user with an undefined scope for data collecting would become familiar with personal data in their entirety and in their context. Taken out of its original context, the data used to create a "personality profile" violated the personality rights of the person concerned.

(4) The main legal provisions on the population Register, with respect to the collection of data and its processing, were unconstitutional. Section 1 of the Law Decree provided

a definition of the objective of the Register and its duties which were inadequate and vague, incapable of guiding data processing in a definite direction or restricting it in any way. In addition, under s. 4, data collection for storage purposes had no definite purpose or scope: there was no detailed list of the data to be included in the Register and instead the Law Decree gave a broad authorization to the Council of Ministers to draw up such a list. However it had gone beyond its authorization under ss. 3–4 when it included for compulsory registration the PIN of the person's father, mother, children and spouse, thereby violating the personality rights of the person since it used relationships without his/her knowledge.

(5) Further, s. 7 was unconstitutional since it gave unlimited freedom to the data processing of the Register. The person concerned was not required to give his/her approval to the processing, neither was there a duty that once the specific service had been completed the data was to be deleted or that a record of such amendments was to be kept with the data. Moreover, when combined with data from other sources, the data in the Register could provide different information on a person, who would be ignorant of its provision. Consequently, in order to render constitutional the acquisition of data from other records or its forwarding, the data would have to be used solely for the purpose of original record keeping and made available only to the audience with whom the person would have to deal in connection with the original record keeping. Data outside the collection remit of the Register would have to be deleted after forwarding while the request and forwarding of data would need to be documented.

(6) In addition, different stipulations under s. 7 provided for data supply or forwarding to private persons, *i.e.,* having a "lawful interest" in another person's data, or to organizations "to facilitate the performance of their duties," which did not sufficiently take into account a person's right to data protection. These objective conditions were of themselves incapable of providing the requisite basis for protection under s. 8, according to which subjective criterion, supply could be refused if it might violate personality rights. The supply of personal data for the performance of a specifically defined task and the performance of which possibly justified the risk involved in the supply alone complied with personality rights protection. Only organs of state administration and the judiciary were given such tasks so that identical restrictive conditions were to be imposed on providing data to these "organizations" other than the aforementioned organs and to private persons—the right to informational self-determination could be enforced if based on a right documented and certified in writing on the same footing as private persons. Finally the requirement of mandatory regular data supply in s. 7(3) to local governments and to ministries for the performance of "their basic tasks" was insufficient to permit constitutional data forwarding, and those entitled could only be determined by statute not merely by executive decree.

(7) The express guarantees of personality rights in the Law Decree failed to meet all the criteria of constitutionality. For instance, s. 10(2) only provided the right to make corrections for the person concerned. Since the essence of the right to informational self-determination was that the party concerned might know and follow the route and circumstances of the use of his/her personal data, the preconditions necessary for the exercise of this right were to be ensured: applications for data on certain subjects were to be officially documented in the Register, *i.e.,* records on whose data was supplied to whom, when and for what purpose, as well as the use of other data systems. Certification would also facili-

tate possible corrections which would need to be made in all registers receiving the wrong item of data. Further the right to correction should also be extended to deletions. By s. 10(3), personal data could only be made public in cases specified by statute or government decree, which general authorization, in view of the current Decision, was also unconstitutional. The right to informational self-determination might be limited only in unavoidable situations, the justified exceptions to the rule being determined by statute. Therefore only where the person concerned could forbid the provision of his/her data recorded in the Register would the protection of personality rights satisfy the Constitution.

(8) Finally the universal and unified PIN available for unlimited use was unconstitutional. Section 6(2) permitted the use of PINs in any official document and record or computerized register system and was thus broader in scope than the Register: indeed, it failed to limit or impose conditions on the use of PINs. The PIN threatened personality rights particularly where data were acquired from various data bases without informing the person concerned: he/she was therefore limited in or deprived of the possibility of monitoring the data flow. Further this mass of interconnected data, of which the person generally had no knowledge, rendered him/her defenseless and created unequal communication conditions so that one party possessed information giving a particular (distorted) image of which the other party concerned was unaware. The power of the state administration in using PINs was also markedly extended. Where they were used outside the ambit of the administration, this increased the power not only of the data user over the parties concerned but also of the State since it further broadened (possible) control through use of such data. Taken together, they seriously jeopardized the right to self-determination and human dignity. Accordingly PINs remained contrary to the right to data protection, to the principle of divided information systems with adherence to the purpose to be achieved and to the main rule that data were to be acquired from persons with their knowledge and consent.

IN THE NAME OF THE REPUBLIC OF HUNGARY!

On the basis of a petition seeking an ex post facto review of the unconstitutionality of legal rules currently in force, the Constitutional Court has made the following

DECISION.

The Constitutional Court holds that the collection and processing of personal data in the absence of a definite purpose and for arbitrary future use are unconstitutional.

The Constitutional Court holds that the universal and unified personal identification number (PIN) available for unlimited use is unconstitutional.

The Constitutional Court holds that Law Decree 10/1986 on the State Population Register as well as Decree 25/1986 (VII.8) MT issued by the Council of Ministers for the execution of this Law Decree and Decree 102/1990 (VII.3) MT issued by the Council of Ministers are unconstitutional; accordingly, the Court annuls the Law Decree and the decrees on its implementation.

The legal rules will lose force as of 31 December 1991, with the exception of the provisions listed hereunder, which will lose force on the day of the publication of the present Decision in the *Hungarian Official Gazette:*

In the Law Decree: the second sentence of s. 4; s. 5(2); the second and third sentences of s. 6(2); s. 6(3); the second sentencc s. 7(1); in s. 7(2): "unless otherwise regulated by the law . . .," "or its lawful interest . . .," and "or by one's statement . . ."; and s. 7(4); as well as, in s. 10(3), the words: "by Law Decree or decree of the Council of Ministers . . ."

Accordingly, in the period between the publication of the Constitutional Court Decision and 31 December 1991, ss. 4, 6(2), 7(1) and (2), and 10(3) of the Law Decree shall remain in force with the following texts:

"*Section 4:* The State Population Register contains the citizen's PIN, his/her basic personal identification data and the address of his/her residence."

"*Section 6(2):* The PIN shall be used for the purposes of identification in the computerized registers which contain, among others, personal data as well."

"*Section 7(1):* The State Population Register provides private persons, and organizations with data for the performance of their duties.

(2) A private person may request from the State Population Register data and issue of documents pertinent to other persons to which he is entitled. The applicant shall verify this entitlement by a 'written deed.'"

"*Section 10(3):* Data related to the citizen's person, family status and other circumstances may be made public only with the approval of the citizen concerned, or in cases determined by statute."

The Constitutional Court orders the publication of its Decision in the *Hungarian Official Gazette.*

REASONING

SÓLYOM, P., delivering the Opinion of the Court: [....]

II

According to Art. 59 of the Constitution in the Republic of Hungary everyone is entitled to the protection of his/her reputation, and to privacy, including privacy of the home and to the protection of personal secrets and data.

The Constitutional Court, continuing to adhere to *Dec. 20/1990 (X.4) AB* (MK 1990/98; ABH 1990, 69), does not interpret the right to the protection of personal data as a traditional protective right, but as an informational right to self-determination, with regard to the active aspect of this right.

Thus, the right to the protection of personal data, as guaranteed by Art. 59 of the Constitution, means that every person has the right to decide about the disclosure and use of his/her personal data. Hence, approval by the person concerned is generally required to register and use personal data; the entire route of data processing and handling shall be made accessible to everyone, *i.e.,* every person has the right to know who, when, where and for what purpose uses his/her data. In exceptional cases, a statute exceptionally requires the compulsory supply of personal data and prescribes the manner in which these data may be used. Such a statute restricts the fundamental right to informational self-determination, and it is constitutional only if it is in accordance with the requirements specified in Art. 8 of the Constitution.

Any legal rule [....] is in conformity with Art. 59 of the Constitution if it contains guarantees that the person concerned is able to monitor the route of his/her data during the processing and to enforce his/her rights. [....]

Adherence to the purpose to be achieved is a condition of and at the same time the most important guarantee for exercising the right to informational self-determination. [....] It follows from the principle of adherence to the purpose to be achieved that collecting and storing data without a specific goal, "for the purpose of storage," for an unspecified future use are unconstitutional.

The other basic guarantee is the restriction on the forwarding and publication of data. [....]

Personal data may be made accessible to a third party, other than the concerned party and the original data user, and thereby to link up data-processing systems, only if all the conditions required for data forwarding are fulfilled in relation to each item of data. [....]

III

The contested Law Decree is unconstitutional because it fails to meet the basic requirement of the adherence to the purpose to be achieved. Particularly,

—it does not specify the objective of data processing;

—in connection with this it does not determine precisely the scope of data to be processed;

—it allows the use of other unspecified records and registers for services related to the population register;

—it does not ensure adequately the rights of the affected person; in particular it does not contain sufficient guarantees for the protection of the affected party concerning data forwarding. [....]

2. The main provisions of the legal rules concerning the State Population Register are in themselves also unconstitutional.

2.1. The definition of the objective specified in the Law Decree (s. 1(1): "to promote the enforcement of the citizens' rights and the fulfillment of their duties, is to provide assistance for the activity of state organs, economic and social organizations, associations and associations of private persons [hereinafter 'organizations']") is completely inadequate in light of the fact that the establishment of a data-processing system affecting the entire population of the country is in question, and, furthermore, this system fundamentally affects personal data and the course of the rights related to it (see: PIN). This vague text is incapable of guiding data processing in a definite direction or of restricting it in any manner, *i.e.,* it does not allow at all for the mention of any adherence to a purpose to be achieved. [....]

2.2. The scope of the registered data is determined by s. 4 of the Law Decree: "The State Population Register contains the citizens' personal identification number, his/her basic identification and residence data. The scope of the data to be recorded is to be determined by the Council of Ministers."

This authorization is unconstitutional. [....]

Concerning the importance of a State Population Register, the Law Decree should have given a detailed list of the data to be included therein. Instead, the detailed determination of these data was left to the Council of Ministers in such a way that the scope of this authorization in its contents has not been determined. The term "basic personal identification data" is not specific enough to act as a guarantee. [....]

3. The universal and unified personal identification code (PIN), the use of which is unrestricted (*i.e.,* the PINs assigned to all the citizens and residents of the country according to the same principle), is unconstitutional.

Section 6(2) of the Law Decree states: "The personal identification numbers shall be used as identification data in the computerized register system which contain other personal data; it shall be entered into official documents and records, and shall also be used in state administration and judicial procedures."

According to the restrictive interpretation of this passage the PINs shall be stored in the computers of the Population Register as identification codes, and that these PINs shall be entered into the files and records of the State Population Register. In its wider sense, however, this passage allows the use of PINs in any official document and record; moreover, these code numbers have been used for every sort of computerized register system on the grounds that s. 6 is made up of provisions broader than the scope of the State Population Register. The provision of the Law Decree concerning PINs is, thus, ambiguous; as indicated by actual experience, this provision has failed to restrict unambiguously the obligatory use of PINs.

This ambiguity, however, is only a consequence of the much more serious shortcoming of the regulation from the aspect of constitutional law: this is that s. 6 imposes no limitations or conditions whatsoever on the use of PINs.

3.1. The PIN, as regulated in the Law Decree, is a universal, multi-purpose identification code that may, in principle, be used in any register. It is in this sense that the Constitutional Court applies the concept of PIN in the reasoning of this Decision, also in those parts not strictly related to the Law Decree. (Another type of PIN is an identification number which serves only the purpose of a given data processing and which may be used only for that, such as the pension number or account number. These personal numbers of limited use raise other legal problems related to data protection. The current legal problem of the relationship between the two types of personal numbers is that legislation prevents the general use of such one-purpose personal numbers.)

The significance of the unified personal identification code is that it allows an easy and reliable identification of personal data of an individual as well as their collection by means of a short and technically easily manageable code which is invariable and may not be interchanged. Thus, the personal number is an obvious concomitant of any sort of integrated record-keeping system; its introduction, both in Hungary and abroad, was a part of the plan to install large, central storage data banks. In addition, the unified personal code is perfectly suitable to the occasional link of personal data available in different registers. Through its use, the data are easily accessible and may be checked against one another.

These technical advantages enhance the efficiency of data-processing systems utilizing personal numbers and of the related administrative or service operations. Likewise, this system saves time and money for those subject to data supply because it makes the repeated furnishing of data avoidable.

These advantages, however, involve serious risks for personality rights, particularly from the aspect of the right to informational self-determination. The PIN is particularly dangerous to personality rights. If the data are acquired from various data bases, without "informing" the person concerned, bypassing him, then this person is precluded from the data flow, and he is either limited in or deprived of the possibility of monitoring the route and use of his/her data. This method contradicts the basic principle of data protection that data should be obtained from the person concerned with his/her knowledge. The widespread use of PINs results in impairing the private sphere because even data from the remotest data storage systems established for different reasons may be used to establish a personality profile, which is an artificial image extending to an arbitrarily wide activity of the person and penetrating into the person's most private matters; this image, due to its construction from data torn out of their context, is most likely to be a distorted image as well. In spite of this, the data user will make its decisions on the basis of this image, will use this image to produce and forward further information concerning the person in question. The large amount of these interconnected data, of which the person in question generally has no knowledge, renders the person defenceless and creates unequal communication conditions. Where one party cannot know the information the other party possesses about him/her, this creates a humiliating situation and prevents free decision making. The power of the state administration in using PINs is markedly increased. If PINs may be used in areas outside the ambit of the administration, this increases the power not only of the data user over the parties concerned but also of the State because it further broadens the possible control through the use of such data. Taken together, they seriously jeopardize the right to self-determination and human dignity. The unlimited use of PINs might become a tool for totalitarian control.

The logic of PINs is thus contrary to the constituent elements of the right to data protection, to the principle of divided information systems with adherence to the purpose to be achieved and to the principal rule that data should be acquired from persons concerned with their knowledge and consent. If the principles of data protection are applied consistently, the personal identification number loses its significance because the "advantages" inherent in it cannot be utilized.

The PIN is the technically most advantageous tool to achieve reliable linkups of personal data as far as currently existing data-processing techniques are concerned. Personal data may, of course, be connected to names, and, if necessary, to supplementary identification items like mother's name and residential address. Given the computer capacities available today, the extent of these shall not create a serious problem. "Natural" data might, however, change (*e.g.,* names by marriage or name changes), and it might happen that further data are needed to make distinctions; furthermore, in case of variable data (like residential addresses), the permanent updating and monitoring of data are necessary. The difficulties and expenditure involved might constitute a significant item in the cost-and-benefit analysis of data processing, thus creating a natural brake on unjustified data collection which might otherwise be encouraged by the readily available PINs. The limitations arising from the right to informational self-determination apply, of course, to any data acquisition and processing. Due to their technical perfection, the PINs require the introduction of special safeguards in accordance with the increased risks. If personal data are updated by a central record-keeping system available through the PINs, then the data-processing body in charge of this operation, like the Population Register, acquires a key position, which, therefore, requires an especially precise regulation of guarantees.

3.2. The PINs, therefore, by their very nature pose a particular danger to personal rights. It follows from the primary duty of the State concerning the protection of fundamental rights (Constitution, Art. 8) that this risk shall be reduced to a minimum, *i.e.,* the use of the PINs shall be restricted by security regulations. This can be done in two ways: either the use of the PINs is to be restricted to precisely defined data-processing operations, or strict conditions and controlling measures are to be imposed on the availability of information connected to PINs and on the linkup of record-keeping systems using PINs. On the other hand, it must not be ignored that any limitation of the unified and universal code results in losing the essence of the code. A PIN available only for limited use is no longer a PIN in the sense of the Law Decree.

3.3. The use of PIN varies widely from country to country. In a number of countries there are de facto universal PINs as a result of the unhindered introduction and application of an identification code originally adopted for definite purposes. The number itself was originally introduced for the purposes of the population register or as a social security number. Examples for the former one are Belgium, Denmark, Iceland, the Netherlands and Norway, while for the latter Finland or Switzerland. The Swedish personal number, considered as a copybook example of the universal personal number, was originally a registration number in the birth certificate records.

In other countries, personal numbers are forbidden or even considered unconstitutional. In Portugal, a 1973 Act of Parliament ordered the introduction of the universal PIN starting in 1975. On the other hand, Art. 35(2) of the 1976 Constitution, issued after the downfall of the fascist regime, forbids the linkup of personal data storage systems, and according to para. (5): "It is forbidden to assign nationally uniform personal numbers to citizens." In France and in the Federal Republic of Germany, public opposition to the idea of a population register using PINs led in 1978 to the promulgation of the Law Decrees on Data Protection and to the abandonment of integrated data storage systems and PINs.

The German Federal Constitutional Court declared as early as in 1969 that the "registration and catalogue listing of citizens which affect the entire person of those citizens" are incompatible with the fundamental right to human dignity to which the State has no right even under the anonymity of statistical data acquisition (BVerfGE 27, 1, 6); the so-called population census decision, which in 1983 formulated the right to informational self-determination, considers PIN as a "decisive step" leading to personality profiles the avoidance of which shall be accepted even by other means of limitation on informational self-determination (BVerfGE 65, 1, 27, 53, 57).

Between the two extremes are those states where some personal numbers serving certain purposes are used for purposes other than the original one: however, these were successfully prevented from becoming universal codes. (This was the case in France, for example, where the identification number assigned to everyone born in France by the National Economic and Statistical Research Centre did not become a universal PIN; similar legal constraints were imposed on the use of social security numbers in Canada.)

The dangers of electronic data processing to the autonomy of personality became widely recognized in the 1970s. From this time on, the PIN became a symbol for the total control of citizens, for an approach to efficiency alone and for the treatment of persons as objects.

Although the PIN is only a tool, and its role may only be appreciated in the entire context of data-processing regulation, its introduction or application was sufficient to trigger the clash of the two value systems, the preference of technical possibilities or of personality rights. This resulted in the precise legal regulation, that is, the limitation of the use of PINs becoming a general requirement, and this process started even in countries where the PINs had been introduced before the age of consciousness of data protection. (See, *e.g.*, the report of the Data Protection Expert Committee of the Council of Europe: "Introduction and Use of Personal Identification Number: Issues of Data Protection," Strasbourg, 15 December 1989.) Even the application of the general principles of data protection similar to any other personal data present a limitation of the use of PINs. This means that legal authorization is required for anybody who demands the disclosure of the PIN; in the absence of such, no one may be disadvantaged for refusing to disclose his/her PIN. The PIN must not contain sensitive data (*e.g.*, ethnicity or religion), but there is an increasing demand that it should not be a "talking number" either, *i.e.,* one that provides such information as the date or place of birth.

The use of personal numbers shall be exactly specified and limited by statute, and its use shall be controlled and supervised by an independent data protection commissioner. However, beyond these general requirements, the risks inherent in PINs must be counterbalanced by separate safeguards as well. For example, the establishment of data and record storage units operating with PINs is subject to a special permission in Norway, and in certain record-keeping units the use of this number is forbidden. The linkup of registers operating with PINs shall be subject to particularly strict conditions and supervision and shall be made accessible to the persons concerned as well. These safeguards were introduced, *e.g.,* by the Swedish data protection office.

The safeguards related to PINs shall prevail in case of identification documents that may be used similarly (*e.g.,* identity card, passport or driving licence number), and with adequate modifications in case of personal codes used in other special areas (pension and social security numbers).

3.4. The current regulation of the PINs is unconstitutional because s. 6 of the Law Decree allowed their unlimited use or made their unlimited use compulsory for state organs without providing safeguards against the dangers inherent in them.

Hungarian law allowed for all the dangers arising from the nature of PINs to be realised when it failed to regulate the use of such numbers and introduced them in an unconditional way into such a legal environment where the fundamental guarantees of the right to data protection were unknown. (Only one of these safeguards, the right of inspection by the person concerned, was regulated: however, this being out of its context, it has never become a "living" right.) The issue of the possibility of limiting the data flow within the state administration has never been raised by officials, and the handing out of PINs was made a condition for the availability of services even outside the state sphere.

These circumstances resulted in a multitude of registers operating with PINs, frequently without the knowledge of the persons concerned, and with unimpeded communication between the various systems; today no one can know who, where and to what of his/her personal data someone has access.

In the face of such dangers the Civil Code and other legal provisions on the protection of personality and secrecy are insufficient. It was with regard to the Population Register and PIN system set up in 1974 that a modification of the Civil Code in 1977 introduced a general clause according to which no computerized data processing may violate personality rights and further established the right to correction of the person concerned, together with forbidding the information supply to unauthorized persons (Civil Code, art. 83). However, up to the present time there has not been a single legal rule or court decision which gave substance to the above-mentioned general clause or indicated the constituent elements of the right to informational self-determination or of the right to data protection. Data users were not, therefore, impeded either by adherence to the purpose to be achieved or by rules on data acquisition or forwarding, and the persons concerned could not be aware of their rights either. (The persons concerned have no legal possibility even today to learn about which registries they might be recorded in, and hence the practice of the right of inspection is illusory.) The independent control and supervision of data processing have been completely missing. Only the Law Decree contained provisions concerning the more detailed regulation of the flow of personal data and of their protection. This Law Decree has, however, been proved by the Constitutional Court to fall short of the requirements of constitutionality. The above-mentioned, and generally insufficient, safeguards are in no way capable of counterbalancing the peculiar risks inherent in the nature of the PINs. Neither the Law Decree nor other legal rule in Hungarian law contains measures directed at fending off the dangers inherent in PINs either by prescribing conditions for their use or by allowing the control of the use of such numbers.

Based on these considerations, the legal rules in force concerning the use of PINs violate the Constitution: these provisions are contrary to the right to the protection of personal data (Constitution, Art. 59) and limit these rights in a disproportionate and unnecessary manner.

3.5. It is the duty of the legislator to create an Act, in accordance with Arts. 59 and 61 of the Constitution, concerning the protection of personal data and the accessibility of information of public interest, and to give a concrete form in so-called area-specific statutes to the basic principles laid down in the above-mentioned Act. It is the legislature's responsibility to decide whether to introduce, within certain limitations, the PINs which were annulled in their current form, and to specify the limitations and special controlling measures on the use of these PINs. In the present case, the Constitutional Court has declared the PIN-system to be unconstitutional because the Law Decree contains no limitation whatsoever on the use of PINs. This, however, does not mean that any sort of restriction or limitation is sufficient to render the use of PINs constitutional. The Constitutional Court, therefore, summarizes its opinions expressed above on the limits within which personal identification codes are considered to be in conformity with the Constitution.

The Constitutional Court establishes that the universal personal identification number is, by its very nature, contrary to the right to informational self-determination. Only the use of an identification number limited for data processing with a specific purpose is, therefore, compatible with the Constitution. An Act introducing such "personal numbers" limited in use shall provide regulatory and control guarantees that preclude the use of this number for other purposes and in other contexts. Neither the "state sphere" nor the entirety of state administration may be considered a unity within which a single, unified personal identification code shall be introduced or used.

4. The Law Decree and its executing decrees create or maintain such a seriously unconstitutional situation as to justify their immediate invalidation. On the other hand, the Constitutional Court has taken into account the fact that an abrupt reorientation of the registers created by these legal rules into a personal identification system which conforms to the Constitution would present a transitional but significant setback to the operation of the state administration. In addition, the Constitutional Court has also considered the fact that the reform of these systems is already under way, and that the Act on Data Protection will be enacted within a foreseeable time. In order to facilitate the switch to a personal registration system that is constitutional, the Constitutional Court decided that those parts of the Law Decree on the basis of which the State Population Register may perform data furnishing absolutely necessary for the protection of citizens' rights and the operation of administration will remain in effect until the end of this year. Data service may continue on a provisional basis to private persons if they certify in writing their entitlement to the data and to administrative bodies entitled by the decrees of the Council of Ministers to regular data supply. (See Point 2.3 above for the reasoning behind this.) Data forwarding to private persons claiming only lawful interests, or unable to certify their right in writing, and to any organizations other than the above-mentioned is, however, discontinued with immediate effect.

In order to allow the performance of this limited scope of duty and to facilitate the reorganization, the decision leaves the scope of data acquisition intact until the end of this year, only the potential to expansion of this activity by a decree has been made impossible with immediate effect.

Due to the seriously unconstitutional character of the current use of PINs, the Constitutional Court annuls with immediate effect the provision making the use of PINs compulsory in official documents, registers, during administrative and judicial proceedings as well as the provision which had prescribed the entry of PIN into the identity cards. From the time of publication of this Decision, no one has the right to require the furnishing of the PIN or to make the exercise of any right or the grant of a service dependent on the furnishing of such number.

The Constitutional Court takes into account that the already existing PINs will not be deleted from the state-managed registers before the introduction of the new codes by an Act. It points out, however, that new persons may no longer be registered with PINs, and that the linkup of various registers by the PINs is beyond the limit of tolerance within which the already existing PINs, used solely as internal indicators, are not to be deleted in the interim period. The danger involved in such limited use of the otherwise unconstitutional PIN is offset by the fact that, by its nature, this usage is doomed to be phased out: since the unified character of the systems is necessarily destroyed by the ban to register new data with the PIN and by the fact that the persons concerned will not supply their former PINs.

The abolition of the unconstitutional situation is the duty of everyone who kept PINs on record; this applies to both the state-run and the non-state-run data users; the latter have thus far used the PINs at their own risk theoretically depending on the consent of the persons concerned.

Only the State Population Register is entitled to issue new PINs until 31 December 1991 and to use them, along with the existing ones, as internal identification codes. This is necessary in order to keep the data base intact until the legislature makes its decision concerning the constitutional successor of the Population Register.

5. This Decision of the Constitutional Court will be published in the *Hungarian Official Gazette,* in accordance with s. 41 of Act XXXII/1989 on the Constitutional Court.

DECISION 16/1991: 20 APRIL 1991

IN THE MATTER OF THE PETITION ON COMPENSATION: "COMPENSATION CASE II"

Although the case has commonly been referred to as "Compensation Case II," its first part, concerning the competence of the Constitutional Court to preliminary review of bills, is of equal significance. The Court excluded the use of the review of bills during the parliamentary debate and stated that only the review of the final text, before the final vote, was in accordance with the role and functions of the Constitutional Court. Thus, the Court wanted to avoid being involved in the political process and, indeed, this competence was not used until 1997. From here stems the frequently cited statement: "The Constitutional Court is not an adviser to the Parliament but the judge on its legislation." The Court, however, was unsure whether such a restrictive interpretation had not gone too far; therefore it made in the second part of the judgment principled statements as to the constitutional issues raised by the draft Compensation Act. These statements became fundamental for the special "dogmatics" of the Court in all subsequent compensation issues.

During the parliamentary debate on the draft Bill on the Settlement of Ownership Issues by providing Partial Compensation for Damages unjustly caused by the State to the Properties of Citizens after 8 June 1949 (hereinafter: the Compensation Bill), 52 Members of Parliament petitioned for the preliminary review of certain provisions.

The petitioners submitted, inter alia, that the Bill (a) did not provide a right to full compensation for the damage sustained nor for the equal treatment of victims; (b) unconstitutionally permitted the State to make non-state-owned arable land acquirable with compensation vouchers and to limit the circle of those entitled thereto; (c) with the option of the right to purchase, either by contract or by law, amounted to an expropriation of property under Art. 13(2); and (d) in permitting Parliament to distribute social property to private persons and to local governments, did not have any regard to the previous title to the former socialized property.

Held, rejecting the petition:

(1) Preliminary review could not be used to review the provisions of a bill which had still to be voted on by Parliament. If the constitutionality of a bill was disputed during the legislative process, then such review might prevent the later annulment of an enacted statute already put into practice and, at the same time, protect the prestige of Parliament. Act XXXII/1989 on the Constitutional Court did not restrict the Court's jurisdiction to reviewing only the final text of the Bill but made preliminary review possible at any stage of the legislative process. Thus, by its rulings, the Court could determine the course of the parliamentary debate while concurrently ensuring the constitutionality of the process. Such a role was irreconcilable with its legal status since it was not an adviser to Parliament but the judge of the results of its legislative work. The current Act concerning preliminary review of bills

had to be interpreted by the Court in accordance with the principle of separation of powers. Only through amendment by Parliament could the purpose of such review (preventing enactment of an unconstitutional statute) be finally reconciled with the Court's judicial role by permitting review on the merits of the final text of a bill either prior to voting or after voting but before promulgation.

(2) However, without rendering a decision on the constitutionality of the Bill's provisions, the Court would summarize its theoretical stance on the issue of their constitutionality. The proposed Bill had abandoned the idea of reprivatizing land, replacing it—similarly to all other assets—with the remedy, through a unified "partial compensation," the "unjust" damages caused in private property by the enumerated legal rules within the given period of time. The general justification of the Bill emphasized that the State acted solely out of moral obligation and that the extent of compensation might not be full. Within the new concept, Parliament had excessive freedom in making distinctions in the details primarily because the State, instead of fulfilling legal requirements, would grant goods to the beneficiaries on the basis of fairness. Within such a scheme, reasonable cause would need to be shown for any unequal treatment, *i.e.,* that it was not arbitrary: no one was entitled to be granted a definite form of ex gratia benefit although the Constitution Art. 70/A was also applicable in the controlling of ex gratia benefits.

(3) The discretion of Parliament in drafting the Bill was limited by constitutional considerations. In the legislation providing for the scheme of compensation, the State could make non-state-owned arable land (for practical reasons, land possessed by co-operatives) purchasable with compensation vouchers and limit the circle of those entitled to acquire such property thereby. It was also permissible in this process to lay down, in respect of such property, priorities which did not violate the rights of others: indeed priorities based on economic policy considerations could create sufficient grounds where such priorities specifically referred to land. However it would be unconstitutional for the State, were it ultimately to provide compensation by land, to determine the distribution of non-state-owned arable land in a manner different from that of other property assets serving as a basis for compensation.

(4) The option of the right to purchase, either by contract or by law, was not an expropriation of property subject to Constitution, Art. 13(2), but rather an encumbrance on the right to property and so subject to Art. 8(2) and Art. 13(1). The change in ownership depended on whether or not the holder of the right to purchase exercised this right. The owner could still be released from his obligation arising out of the option, under the Civil Code, art. 375(3), if he could prove that since the establishment of the right a substantial change had occurred in his circumstances so that he could not now be expected to comply with such obligation.

(5) Further, in conformity with current political and economic objectives, Parliament could distribute the burdens or renew the obligations resulting from the different transformations in property ownership. In the course of breaking down social property, statutes transformed ownership patterns by dividing up the burdens arising from the earlier creation of social property and also the obligations among those acquiring such property free of charge. Both the conversion of co-operative property to the private ownership of former co-

operative members and the creation of property of local governments conformed with current objectives. While the transformation of ownership remained incomplete, a future owner had no right to have his former social property transformed into private ownership or to gain new property without bearing the burden of social transformation. However, once completed, the new property would be fully protected and therefore free of any constitutional possibility, subsequently or retroactively, of being subject to distribution of the burden of transformation.

IN THE NAME OF THE REPUBLIC OF HUNGARY!

Based on a petition for the preliminary review of the constitutionality of certain provisions of the Bill, together with the concurring opinion of Zlinszky, J., concerning Point III.3 of the Reasoning, the Constitutional Court made the following

DECISION.

The Constitutional Court rejects the petition for the preliminary review of certain provisions of the Bill submitted under No. 1020 and aimed at the settlement of ownership by providing partial compensation for damages unjustly caused by the State to the properties of citizens after 8 June 1949.

This Decision will be published by the Constitutional Court in the *Hungarian Official Gazette*.

REASONING

SÓLYOM, P., delivering the Opinion of the Court:

I

In the course of the debate on the Bill, fifty two Members of Parliament proposed that the Constitutional Court review the unconstitutionality of the following provisions of the Bill (hereafter the Bill) submitted under No. 1020 and aimed at settling ownership issues by the compensation of damages unjustly caused by the State to the property of citizens after 8 June 1949: s. 14; s. 3(1) and (2); s. 8 and s. 1. Furthermore, the Members of Parliament also proposed a preliminary review of points 1, 3 and 8 of the proposal for modification, submitted under No. 2089 by the leaders of the parliamentary groups of the government coalition concerning s. 4(3), the new s. 8(2) and (3), and s. 12(2) of the Bill.

II

1. The preliminary review belongs to the exceptional jurisdiction of the Constitutional Court and serves to prevent the possibility of Parliament enacting an unconstitutional statute. If the constitutionality of a bill is questioned during the legislative procedure, then a preliminary review may prevent the annulment of a promulgated legal rule which has still been put into practice, and, as a main point, it protects the prestige of the legislature. In countries where there is preliminary review, the review is most often formal, *i.e.,* it is aimed

exclusively at examining the constitutionality of the legislative procedure and the question of legislative authority. The possibility for a review of the merits of a bill is much rarer.

In the course of a preliminary review of constitutionality during the legislative process, the Constitutional Court might come into conflict with the principle of the separation of powers. The only case in which this conflict does not arise is when such an abstract problem of constitutional law emerges which may be made independent of the context of the provisions of the bill and it, in fact, necessitates the interpretation of the Constitution. In this case, however, the Constitutional Court's jurisdiction to interpret the Constitution is available. In all other cases, by exercising preliminary review, the Constitutional Court becomes a participant in the legislative process, thereby limiting the power of Parliament to decide and sharing the responsibilities of the legislature.

In resolving the conflict between the purpose of preliminary review and the enforcement of the separation of powers, the stage at which the Constitutional Court conducts the preliminary review and whether the review is directed at formal issues or that of substance has a decisive role.

2. This was the first time that a petition for preliminary review of a bill was submitted to the Constitutional Court, and thus the Constitutional Court had to face the contradiction inherent in the nature of review. This contradiction is particularly deepened by the shortcomings of Hungarian legal rules.

Section 1(a) of Act XXXII/1989 on the Constitutional Court (hereafter the Constitutional Court Act), determines the jurisdiction of the Constitutional Court for the preliminary review of certain provisions of bills. Section 33 lists those entitled to submit such petitions and lays down the consequences if the unconstitutionality is established by the Constitutional Court: "the organ or the person submitting the bill shall provide for the termination of the unconstitutionality." By virtue of these measures, the procedure is directed at reviewing the constitutionality of the content of the bill, and it may be requested at any time from the date when the bill was submitted to Parliament.

This solution in the Constitutional Court Act may permit the Constitutional Court to be involved in the legislative process at any stage and on any number of occasions. This way, the Constitutional Court, by its decision, influences, and, by excluding certain solutions, even determines the course of the debate in such a way that at the same time it secures the constitutionality of the legislative process. However, such a role is irreconcilable with the legal status of the Constitutional Court. The Constitutional Court is not an adviser to Parliament but the judge of the result of the legislative work. The purpose of preliminary review, *i.e.,* preventing the enactment of an unconstitutional statute, and the judicial function of the Constitutional Court may be reconciled in case of a review on the merits if the final text of the bill is submitted to the Constitutional Court either prior to voting on the bill or after voting but still before promulgation.

This is how the preliminary review is exercised in every legal system which has adopted the institution of preliminary review. (Art. 61 in the French, Art. 278 in the Portuguese, Art. 26 in the Irish Constitutions: prior to promulgation, Art. 127 of the Italian Constitution makes similar provisions for review in case of violations of legislative competences. For the preliminary review of international treaties, Art. 78 of the Spanish Act on the Constitutional Court requires that the text of the treaty is previously finalized; similar conditions and regulations applied to the preliminary review of bills until 1985 when this jurisdiction of the Constitutional Court as an intervention in the legislative process was revoked.)

Only the Constitutional Court Act does not contain such restrictive conditions. The object of review in Hungary is a bill the text of which may be reformulated by those submitting it until the end of the general debate. If modifications of the bill are also submitted to Parliament, then the subject of the voting remains uncertain until the beginning of the voting, and the final text of the future statute is formulated definitively only after the voting on the proposals for amendment. The constitutionality of "certain provisions" which are subject to review may not be adjudicated upon by being taken out of the context of the bill. The result of such an isolated investigation might lose its validity when considered in another context. Review of the constitutionality on such an uncertain and isolated basis of comparison involves particularly great dangers in Hungarian parliamentary practice, where concepts contrary to, or radically different from, the original bill are also presented as suggested amendments rather than alternative bills. The Constitutional Court also observes in the present case, that the proposals for amendments involve the most divergent concepts and that even in case of a judgment on the discriminative character of the various provisions solely qualitative amendments might lead to different results. According to the rules of the Constitutional Court Act, nothing can guarantee that the preliminary review undertaken by the Constitutional Court will in effect fulfill its purpose of preventing the enactment of an unconstitutional statute.

In the course of its practice hitherto, the Constitutional Court has taken meticulous care to maintain the principle of the separation of powers and interpreted its own jurisdiction accordingly. In its *Dec. 31/1990 (XII.18) AB* (MK 1990/128; ABH 1990, 136), the Constitutional Court laid down the principles that in interpreting the jurisdiction of the Constitutional Court to interpret certain provisions of the Constitution, "primary consideration should be given to the principle of the separation of powers, which is the most important organizational and operational principle of the Hungarian state organization," and consequently, "the jurisdiction of the Constitutional Court referred to should be interpreted in a restrictive manner." The broad interpretation would "inevitably result in the Constitutional Court assuming the responsibility of the legislative, and even of the executive, powers and thereby some sort of governance by the Constitutional Court would be created which is in utter contradiction with the principles of state organization as specified in the Constitution." The Constitutional Court has, therefore, defined the conditions necessary for a procedure of interpreting the Constitution. The Constitutional Court follows this principle in the case of the preliminary review as well.

According to the legal rules currently in force, the Constitutional Court may not bind the preliminary review to a "final text," *i.e.,* to that stage of the legislative process which is prior to the final voting on the whole of the bill. This could only be made possible by amending the Constitutional Court Act. The Constitutional Court should also acknowledge the fact that the Constitutional Court Act includes a review which is possible at every, though not defined, stage of the legislative process. In view of all these considerations, the Constitutional Court performs the preliminary review of certain provisions in the Bill in such a way as to minimize the contradiction between its own legal status, particularly its position within different branches of power and the preliminary review provided by the Constitutional Court Act and to prevent the results of its own review from becoming disfunctional. For this reason, the Constitutional Court limits itself in this Decision to summarizing its theoretical stance on the issues of constitutionality of the provisions of the Bill in question in the reasoning of the Decision without rendering a decision on the constitutionality of these provisions.

III

1. The Constitutional Court draws again attention to *Dec. 21/1990 (X.4) AB* (MK 1990/98; ABH 1990, 73) concerning the issue of the Bill. According to the petition adjudicated upon in that Decision, the original ownership of arable land would have been restored in kind, while the other earlier owners and parties suffering damages would have received partial financial compensation. The Constitutional Court ruled that these two solutions may not be considered as different methods of the same compensation. The Constitutional Court also stated that the issue of whether the discrimination remains within the constitutional bounds may only be examined in the objective and subjective context of the prevailing regulations.

The present Bill concerns something different. "The given regulatory concept," within which, according to the Constitutional Court, constitutional reasons are required for justifying distinctions, is narrower and more homogeneous. The proposed Bill abandoned the idea of reprivatizing land and intends instead to remedy, through a uniform "partial compensation," all kinds of "unjust" damage caused in private property by the enumerated legal rules within the given period of time. The general justification of the Bill emphasizes that the State is acting solely out of moral obligation and that the extent of compensation may not be full.

The Constitutional Court points out that within the new concept the legislature has considerable freedom in making distinctions in the details, primarily because the State, instead of fulfilling legal requirements, grants goods to the beneficiaries on the basis of fairness. Thus, if the distinction is not among a priori entitled parties, then the limitation of this distinction is the theoretical limit of positive discrimination: the unconditional observance of the treatment of people as having equal dignity and the non-violation of the fundamental rights defined in the Constitution (see *Dec. 9/1990 (IV.25) AB:* MK 1990/36; ABH 1990, 46). Within this scheme, the only thing which may be required is that a reasonable cause for any unequal treatment shall be shown, *i.e.,* to show that such treatment does not qualify as arbitrary. It shall be taken into consideration that no one is entitled to be granted a definite form of ex gratia benefit. On the other hand, the contents of Art. 70/A of the Constitution are also applicable in and determinative of the ex gratia benefits.

2. Legislation shall provide for the coverage of the compensation scheme. If it is feasible in a constitutional manner, there may be no objection made to the State making arable lands not in state ownership obtainable with compensation vouchers. If the State provides a possibility for compensation, ultimately, by land then it is in itself not unconstitutional if the distribution of this limited coverage with special legal status is determined in a way different from other property assets serving as the basis for compensation. In itself, it is not unconstitutional either if the circle of those entitled to acquisition of property through the system of compensation vouchers is limited when arable lands not in state ownership are involved. In the course of this, no objection can be made against the drawing up of priorities for groups of would-be landowners which do not violate the rights of others. By virtue of legislative discretion, such preferences based on economic policy considerations, for example, might create sufficient grounds if these preferences specifically refer to land.

The Constitutional Court emphatically draws attention to the condition stipulated in its *Dec. 21/1990 (X.4) AB* (MK 1990/98; ABH 1990, 73) that in support of the constitutionality of a discrimination the Constitutional Court "may not accept arguments concerning a preferred group which are valid in relation to another group as well (*e.g.:* the establishment of an entrepreneurial economy, remedying injustice). On the other hand, to prove equal treatment, it is necessary to give a complete account of both the preferred and the discriminated groups together with the method of evaluation."

3. *Decision 21/1990 (X.4) AB* stated that Art. 13(2) of the Constitution is a rule of guarantee which controls the expropriation of property not only by the individual administrative act but also through law. The right of purchase, either by contract or by law, however, is not an expropriation of property subject to Art. 13(2) of the Constitution but it is an encumbrance on the right to property.

Article 13(2) of the Constitution applies to expropriations, and is applicable only as regards such legal institutions where the expropriation of property is accomplished either through an individual act of the authority or by legal provision. Such legal expropriation of property is, for example, nationalization. Through the expropriation of property under Art. 13(2), the property generally goes into public ownership, and only in exceptional cases may the property be taken into private ownership, but even in this case, only for use in the public interest.

The right of purchase, on the other hand, is a limitation of the right to property. The change in ownership depends on whether or not the holder of the purchasing right exercises this right. The courts may release the original owner from his obligation arising out of the purchasing right of the other party if the owner proves that since the establishment of the right of purchase such a substantial change occurred in his circumstances that it may not be expected from him to comply with this obligation (art. 375(3) of the Civil Code).

The constitutionality of the right of purchase shall be judged according to Art. 13(1) and Art. 8(2) of the Constitution. Even if it were unconstitutional, the right of purchase based on a statute would not qualify as expropriation or into some other legal institution of the same effect; in such cases, the statute establishing the right of purchase should be repealed.

The Bill grants the right of purchase to a defined circle of entitled parties for acquiring arable lands owned by the State or by co-operatives, lands which were expropriated by laws defined in the Bill. The constitutionality of this right of purchase in terms of the co-operatives shall be adjudged in the following context:

"Social property" constituted the economic and political basis of the earlier political system (see Art. 6(1) of the Constitution [of 1949, as] amended by Act I/1972). The Constitution currently in force is the constitution of a "peaceful political transition into a state under the rule of law realizing a social market economy" (Preamble). A necessary precondition to this transformation is the dismantling of the social property, *i.e.,* the creation of ownership patterns of equal rights from it and in its place. This process naturally involves mostly the transformation of the earlier social property into private property, but new forms of ownership will be created as well, the source of which will also be provided to a significant extent by social property, *e.g.,* the property of local governments.

There is no constitutional obstacle to the procedure such that, in the course of breaking down social property, the statutes aiming at the transformation of ownership patterns divide up the burdens arising from the earlier creation of social property and also the obligations which are due as a result of the constitutional amendment of 23 October 1989 among those who acquire former social property free of charge. This allocation of burdens is, of course, neither a civil law legal succession—since only a part of the burdens is legal obligation and the other part is the social cost of transformation; furthermore, nor is it an automatic or mechanical process because it is to be implemented by legislation transforming the ownership pattern according to its current political and economic objectives. Such an objective is, for example, the conversion of the present co-operative property to the private property of former co-operative members; the creation of the property of local governments is a similar task. As long as the transformation in respect of the property concerned is not completed, the future subject of the new ownership has no right to have this former social property transformed into his/her private ownership or to gain new property without bearing the said burden. Once the process of transformation is completed, the new property is, naturally, fully protected, that is, in this respect there is no longer any constitutional possibility to distribute the burden of social transformation subsequently or in a retroactive manner.

The burdens that might be considered include, for example, the compensation envisaged in the legal rules on nationalization as well as the burdens arising from property expropriation increasing co-operative property executed according to the legal rules appearing in the Annex of the Bill. The legislature may distribute the different burdens resulting from the different ownership transformations in a variety of ways. The legislature may also renew the obligations of different bases, according to the pattern of novation: essentially the same debt is preserved but under a new legal title and new conditions and to a new extent. Such a novation is also suggested in the Bill where equity constitutes the new legal ground. This, therefore, excludes reference to the old legal titles.

4. Because of the ex gratia character of compensation, no constitutional complaint may be made if the process of compensation takes place in different phases.

5. A statement concerning the unconstitutionality of the possible discrimination arising from the extent of compensation may be made only with the knowledge of the final context of the wording of the Bill. Since the property assets affected by the Bill are different, the different methods of calculation used to establish the value serving as the basis for compensation is not unconstitutional in itself. If, however, the different methods of calculation result in striking differences in the compensation for the various property assets, then this might lead to the finding of unconstitutionality.

ZLINSZKY, J., concurring: Referring to the statements in *Dec. 21/1990 (X.4) AB* (MK 1990/98; ABH 1990, 73), it should be emphasized again that the opinion expounded therein concerns public property which was nationalized in accordance with legal rules. In respect to the illegal expropriation of property, the legal remedy is within the competence of the ordinary courts; this remedial procedure has been available since 1 April 1991 and may be initiated at any time within the statute of limitations. The civil law regulations provide the possibility to reclaim property illegally expropriated from both the State and from public institutions or private persons who acquired such property from the State free of charge. From the principle of constitutional equal protection for state, co-operative, municipal and private property it follows that: the party acquiring property free of charge which was illegally expropriated and gratuitously granted to him has to bear responsibility towards the former owner of this property. According to Art. 13(2) of the Constitution, a full and unconditional compensation may not be considered in the case of a party acquiring the property for free because the party acquiring the property free of charge suffers no damage upon the return of the property.

In protecting co-operative and municipal properties, a distinction should therefore be drawn between property acquired for valuable consideration and property acquired free of charge. The protection of the former and the latter is the same as that of the similarly acquired private property, the property burdened being protected by its own right, while the freely acquired property is protected by the right to legal succession of the original owner.

DECISION 48/1991: 26 SEPTEMBER 1991

ON PRESIDENTIAL POWERS

This case is the most significant and elaborate of the five cases defining presidential power in the new parliamentary democracy. Both the competences of the President as commander in chief of the armed forces and his power of appointment were interpreted restrictively as followed from the systematic interpretation of the Constitution, which clearly provides for a pure parliamentary system. The decision was born in times of intense political conflict between the Prime Minister and the President and despite the self-understanding of the President, who claimed rights of the executive for himself. For today, the benefits of a principled clarification of the role of the President in the parliamentary system remain the most lasting effect of the decision. No less interesting are the dissenting and the concurring opinions concerning the role of the Constitutional Court itself in the interpretation of the Constitution. While in the even more "activist" formation of the Court's competences in the preliminary control case (16/1991) the Court was unanimous, here it became extremely divided.

The petitioners sought an advisory opinion on the interpretation of the Constitution in relation to the position of the President of the Republic vis-à-vis the armed forces.

The first petitioner, the Minister of Defence, sought the interpretation of those constitutional provisions on the governance of the activities of the armed forces and to establish the interrelation between the institutions of the President, Parliament and Government as laid down in Art. 40/B(3) with regard to their authority on governance of the armed forces. He submitted that the governance, in peacetime, of the armed forces was for the exclusive authority of the Government; the President or Parliament could not determine directly the forces' activities outside the area specifically assigned to them by law.

The second petitioner, the Parliamentary Committee on Cultural, Educational, Scientific, Sport, Television and Press Affairs, requested the interpretation of the question of the President's power of appointment pursuant to the various statutes governing appointments adopted in accordance with Art. 30/A(1)(m). They further requested interpretation of the question of ministerial countersignature pursuant to Art. 30/A(2), with particular reference as to whether the President (a) could refuse the appointment of a duly submitted nominee; (b) could challenge the grounds of the position to be filled; (c) had to take into account the view expressed by the parliamentary committee which interviewed the nominee; (d) whether the President's consideration had to include practical and political purposes besides considering the existence of the necessary legal conditions; and (e) at what stage the Government's responsibility commenced when countersigning the President's action.

The third petitioner, the Minister of Justice, submitted for interpretation Art. 31/A(1) particularly whether the President's personal inviolability (*i.e.,* to be protected from criminal prosecution) included, narrowly speaking, the strengthened criminal protection of his life and personal safety or, broadly speaking, the protection of his reputation and dignity.

Held, granting the petition:

(1) The current separation of powers over the armed forces under the Constitution was the natural result of every parliamentary system. Both governing and commanding functions over the armed forces were activities directed at their successful operation: the governing authority stood above (outside) the forces while the commander was situated inside, being not only the head but also part of the organization. The relative independence of the armed forces within the executive branch and the establishment of governing authorities which fell outside the executive power's jurisdiction were political rather than constitutional questions for which the Constitution set the framework. Under Art. 40/B, the Parliament, the President and the Government had the sole right to participate in directing the armed forces according to their respective constitutionally-established powers and without infringing on those of the other two institutions. No command role could be established under the Constitution independent of the directing powers stipulated for the three institutions. The commander of the Hungarian Army might exercise his leading powers exclusively in accordance with the directing actions of the said institutions and within the limits of the established rules.

(2) Parliament could establish new, unspecified powers for directing the armed forces without amending the Constitution only where such a constitutional Act of "power creation" did not infringe the directing powers vested in the other institutions in Art. 40/B. However, were Parliament to seek to redistribute the various powers provided for in the Constitution, it would then be necessary to amend it.

(3) Through Art. 29(2), the President was vested with the authority of a traditional commander in chief of the armed forces. This supreme command function was a constitutional one and did not thereby give him a rank or post in the Hungarian armed forces. Since the commanders in chief was outside the structure of the forces, being its director but not its leader, he therefore did not act as superior officer in respect of the armed forces since the commands (which had to be issued in accordance with his governing authority/action) were issued by the commanders of the Hungarian Army and the Border Guard respectively. The President's power of direction over the armed forces, being exclusively determined by the Constitution and legislation enacted thereunder, was similar to those which he possessed in respect of other institutions in the exercise of the powers of appointment, approval and confirmation.

(4) The Government was the sole executive branch which possessed all governing authority over the armed forces accorded to it under the Constitution and which did not fall within the competence of the President or Parliament. Thus, under Art. 35(1)(h), it had the power to regulate and supervise the operation of the armed forces. Although no law could deprive the Government of its supervisory authority in the field of the armed forces, it was still theoretically possible to widen the authority of the President or Parliament.

(5) The President's governing actions in respect of the armed forces during peacetime were all subject to countersignature. In fact all appointments and approvals effected by the

President according to the Constitution or other laws (except appointing judges) were subject to the countersignature of the Prime Minister or the relevant competent minister. Such countersignature validated the President's action, on the one hand ensuring that this action would not conflict with government policy while on the other hand making the Government assume political responsibility for such action before Parliament.

(6) The President was required to reject the appointment or approval if he were of the opinion that the necessary legal preconditions for such appointments were absent. Such prerequisites included Hungarian citizenship; professional qualification; age; or procedural conditions, which included, inter alia, the interviewing of the nominee by a competent organ, *e.g.*, the relevant parliamentary committee. Both the interview and opinion of such an organ/committee amounted to procedural validating instruments. Indeed the President, if legislation expressly so determined, was required to take the opinion into consideration in his deliberations, but it did not bind him in his decision.

(7) In other situations, the President might reject the appointment of a candidate on the grounds of merit only if he had a well-founded conclusion that his compliance with the proposal could seriously endanger the democratic functioning of the State according to Art. 29(1). By rejecting a formally correct nomination, the President directly intervened in the merits, thereby preventing the politically responsible organ from fulfilling its duty without his assuming that responsibility. His refusal served as a final guarantee, an extraordinary measure the exercise of which was to be based on grounds similar to those which lead to the extraordinary convening or dissolving of Parliament.

(8) As part of his constitutional status, the inviolability of the President expressed the principles that he bore no political responsibility before Parliament and that his legal responsibility was limited; moreover his protection from criminal prosecution, according to Art. 31(1), was to be provided for in separate legislation. According to Arts. 31, 31/A and 32, the President was legally responsible for actions while in office which amounted to a premeditated breach of the Constitution or other legislation. For acts committed outside his official activities, he might be held criminally responsible after the end of his term in office. Consequently his complete non-responsibility existed only vis-à-vis acts committed while in office but being of a non-official type. As regards his immunity from criminal prosecution, it was for Parliament to decide on the scope of such protection with regard to his life, good health, honour and dignity and to the extent thereof including severity or leniency of the punishment.

IN THE NAME OF THE REPUBLIC OF HUNGARY!

Following the petition submitted by the Minister of Defence, the Minister of Justice and the Parliamentary Committee on Cultural, Educational, Scientific, Television and Press Affairs on the interpretation of the Constitution, the Constitutional Court, with the dissenting opinion of Kilényi, Schmidt and Vörös, JJ., on Point 2 of Section B of the Decision, and with the concurring opinion of Ádám, Herczegh, Lábady, Szabó, Tersztyánszky and Zlinszky, JJ., made the following

DECISION.

A

On the basis of the interpretation of Art. 40/B(3) of the Constitution, with regard to the interpretation of Art. 19(3), Arts. 29 and 30/A, as well as of Art. 35(1) of the Constitution, on the powers of the Parliament, the President of the Republic and the Government over the armed forces, the Constitutional Court states the following.

1. All institutions provided for in Art. 40/B(3) of the Constitution shall participate in directing the activities of the armed forces according to their respective powers stipulated in the Constitution and without infringing those other powers. No other institutions except those laid down in Art. 40/B(3) have exclusive powers over the armed forces. Leadership roles, independent of those of direction cannot be established constitutionally. The commander of the Hungarian Army may exercise his power of leadership exclusively in accordance with directive actions of the directing organizations and within the limits thereof. Orders based on the respective directive actions of the Parliament, of the President, and of the Government may be issued by the commander of the Hungarian Army or the commander of the Border Guard.

2. Without amending the Constitution, Parliament may provide new powers for directing the armed forces to another organization only if this does not limit the powers of those organs entitled to direct according to Art. 40/B(3) of the Constitution.

3.(a). Article 29(2) of the Constitution, by providing that the President of the Republic is the commander in chief of the armed forces, does not determine his sphere of power. Within his sphere of power, the Constitution fails to determine the rights and duties of the President as commander in chief of the armed forces. The constitutional significance of Art. 29(2) lies in the obligation that the President must be vested with at least one power of a traditional commander in chief.

The President's status as commander in chief is part of his constitutional legal status and does not result in his having any rank or commission in the Hungarian Army or in the Border Guard.

The commander in chief is outside of the structure of the armed forces; he is the director of the army but not its leader. Therefore, the commander in chief does not act as a superior officer in respect of any of the military organizations. The Constitution and other laws based thereon exclusively determine the power of direction of the commander in chief; further rights do not derive from Art. 29(2) of the Constitution.

(b). The President's power of direction over the armed forces is similar to that he has in respect of other institutions; he can exercise appointment and approval rights in the same manner he generally exercises appointment, approval and confirmation rights.

4. It is the Government that has the power to regulate the functioning of the armed forces. Article 35(1)(h) of the Constitution speaks about the Government's direction of the operation of the armed forces, which determines those parts of the power of direction that belong to the executive branch. The Government, being the sole executive branch under the Constitution, possesses in accordance with its constitutional position all powers of direction over the armed forces that do not fall expressly under the power of the Parliament or the President according to the Constitution and the legislation in force. These three institutions together shall fully encompass the power of direction over the armed forces.

Statutes cannot deprive the Government of its power to direct the operation of the armed forces; at the same time within the limits of the separation of powers among the branches of government and within the President's legal status, as well as without prejudice to the Government's legal status and power, it is theoretically possible to broaden the President's or the Parliament's power.

B

The Constitutional Court on the basis of the interpretation of Art. 30/A(1)(h), (i), (m) and (2) of the Constitution, on the President's power to appoint and on the ministerial countersignature, rules as follows:

1. With the exception of the President's right to appoint as determined in Art. 48 of the Constitution, all appointments, promotions, confirmations or dismissals (hereafter appointments) and approvals effected by the President pursuant to the Constitution or other legislation are subject to the countersignature of the Prime Minister or of the competent minister. The countersignature is the validating instrument of the President's action. By countersigning the President's action, the Government undertakes the political responsibility for the action before Parliament.

2. The President must reject the appointment or approval if he is of the opinion that the proposed action fails to fulfill the necessary legal preconditions. On all other occasions his rejection of an appointment or approval will be constitutional only in those cases when he comes to a well-founded conclusion that his compliance with the proposal would seriously disturb the democratic functioning of the State. In the case of an appointment only the person in question, and in the case of an approval only its respective content, may be examined by the President.

3. Should legislation require that in the course of the appointment the nominee be interviewed by an organ—*e.g.*, the competent parliamentary committee—or such committee express its opinion, these actions shall be considered by the President as being among the validating instruments of the appointment or approval, *i.e.*, as one of the necessary legal preconditions to be met before he takes action. The opinion expressed by an organ participating in the procedure must be taken into consideration by the President only in cases when legislation expressly so requires. Consideration means the weighing of the opinion expressed, but it does not bind the President in his decision.

C

On the basis of the interpretation of Art. 31/A(1) of the Constitution, the Constitutional Court states:

1. The personal inviolability of the President is part of his constitutional legal status. Being inviolable in person, the President bears no political responsibility before Parliament; he has legal responsibility exclusively under Art. 34(4), Art. 31/A(2)–(6) and Art. 32 of the Constitution.

2. The President's protection under criminal law shall be subject to separate legislation. The content of this legislation shall be decided upon by Parliament.

The Constitutional Court shall publish this Decision in the *Hungarian Official Gazette.*

REASONING

SÓLYOM, P., delivering the Opinion of the Court: [....]

4. The President expressed his opinion in writing. In his opinion in most cases the Constitution fails to determine or gives only partial, contradictory determination on the separation of powers within the executive between the President and the Government. Pending the resolution of these conflicts of competence in a new Constitution, a proper constitutional practice should be established through arrangements made between the President and the Prime Minister establishing constitutional conventions. The President has interpreted his own power to appoint in the sense that he does not consider on their merits nominations concerning the heads of administrative departments working directly under the Prime Minister's remit. However, under the respective political arrangements or legislation adopted following the change of system, should an institution be of a non-administrative type or fall only partially under the Government's remit, the President reserves the right to exercise fully his power to appoint. Therefore, in the public service media or in the armed forces, appointments may be effected only under an agreement between the President and the Prime Minister to that effect. The President's deliberative power is based upon the fact that it is the President who exercises the right to appoint. He carries legal responsibility for his actions: according to Art. 31(4) of the Constitution, the President may be removed from office if he has deliberately flouted the legislation in force. The President's status as commander in chief (by making a simple grammatical interpretation) necessarily includes the right to give commands. From the commander in chief status it follows that the President of the Republic is the official superior of the armed forces' commander.

On Art. 31/A of the Constitution the President has emphasized that he does not intend to have wider or more guarantees for his inviolability than those accorded to other citizens.

A

I

According to Art. 40/B(3) of the Constitution, unless a valid international treaty otherwise provides, the direction of the armed forces is within the framework of the Constitution and other separate laws, the exclusive province of the Parliament, the President of the Republic, the National Defence Council, the Government and the responsible minister. Art. 40/A(1) provides that the armed forces are: the Hungarian National Army and the Border Guard.

[....]

III

Separation of powers in the direction of the armed forces and the Constitution

[....]

IV

The powers of the Parliament

[....]

The powers of the President of the Republic

[....]

The powers of the President in case of the incapacitation of Parliament

[....]

The commander in chief function

According to Art. 29(1) the President of the Republic is Hungary's head of state; according to para. 2 of the same Article he is the commander in chief of the armed forces.

None of these paragraphs can be interpreted as rules on competence. They designate the President's two functions. The constitutional provision that provides that the President is Hungary's head of state and the commander in chief of the armed forces does not establish competences but calls for adequate legislation on authorizing the President to fulfill at least one duty corresponding to the content of these functions. (Similarly, Art. 19(1) of the Constitution, stating that "Parliament is the supreme body of state authority and popular representation," is not a rule on competence. These functions naturally establish certain powers that are laid down in detail in other provisions.)

There are strong historical ties between the functions of a head of state and a commander in chief. The commander in chief function is typically part of the ruler's rights; even in republics it is listed among the president's rights. The Constitution does not designate the head of state rights and the commander in chief rights among the President's powers.

[....] The Constitution automatically limits the range of powers with which the President can be endowed from these traditional rights through separate legislation, by institutionalizing a parliamentary republic on the one hand and on the other hand by giving power of direction to the President over the armed forces but sharing this power among the President, the Parliament and the Government. The President as commander in chief (if Parliament is not incapacitated) can exercise neither the principal rights of direction given to the Parliament (use of the armed forces, declaration of the state of war or conclusion of peace) nor the armed forces' management materializing in command because the Government possesses these rights. The directive position precludes the possibility of the commander in chief having powers of command. The President's endowment with powers of command is contradictory to his legal status: being commander in chief he would be subordinate to the orders of the other institutions having directing authority over the armed forces. From among the traditional rights of a supreme commander—in peacetime and not deputizing for Parliament—the President may be given only personnel and representation powers under the Constitution. Should there be at least one commander in chief power among the President's rights, the function established by Art. 29(2) of the Constitution is made material.

[....] Article 40/B of the Constitution ties direction competences to the presidential, not to the commander in chief, function. This at the same time underlines the natural condition that the constitutional requisites for the commander in chief function are the same as those for the presidential powers of a similar nature. It means that the same rules apply to appointment, approval or countersignature irrespective of the President. *e.g.,* as head of state appointing a university professor or as commander in chief appointing a general.

The competences of the commander in chief according to the current law

[. . . .]

In summary: The President's supreme command function is a constitutional function and not a rank or post in the Hungarian Army or the Border Guard. The commander in chief of the armed forces is outside the structure of the armed forces; he may direct them but does not lead them. Thus the commander in chief is not the official service superior of the armed forces. The commands on the basis of his direction act just as in the case of the other organs having powers of direction and are issued by the commander of the Hungarian Army and of the Border Guard, respectively.

The commander in chief's powers of direction are determined exhaustively by the Constitution and relevant legislation adopted in accordance with the Constitution. Besides those determined in the Constitution and other laws, no further powers derive directly from the commander in chief function.

Limits to the powers of the commander in chief

Besides the ministerial countersignature, there are several limitations to the power of the commander in chief stemming from the Constitution:

Such powers of direction of the armed forces may only be established for the President by laws which do not restrict the powers of Parliament or the Government as provided by the Constitution.

Further, the President's powers as commander in chief have to be in line with his constitutional status in a parliamentary system. No statute can determine such decision-making powers connected to the commander in chief status that differ substantially from similarly applied decision-making powers established by the Constitution for the President's comparable powers. For the powers of the commander in chief to differ significantly from the typical presidential powers, they should have been expressly so laid down in the Constitution, and in this way the President's legal status would be different from his present status. Limitations on the President's powers in a parliamentary republic have special significance in those cases in which the usually applicable mechanisms on the political responsibility for the President's action (prime ministerial or ministerial countersignature) fail to function. Our interpretation of the Constitution dealing with such cases is in Part B of the present Decision.

The powers of the Government

[....]

B

[....]

II

1. The Constitution has given four types of decision-making powers to the President: (a) the validity of the President's decision is dependent on the assent of another organ; (b) the President initiates the decision of another organ—the final decision, binding on the President as well, is taken by another organ; (c) the President's decision is decisive, final, no organ can revise it, and no other organ takes over political responsibility for the action—such decisions are referred to in the Decision as independent political decisions; and (d) independent decisions, in which case the Constitution sets only a final deadline.

(a) The President may exercise the majority of his powers dependent on other decisions. Since the President bears no political responsibility for his actions, but only criminal responsibility for premeditated breach of the Constitution or other legislation while in office (Arts. 31(4) and 31/A), political responsibility is assumed by the Government before the Parliament through countersignature by the Prime Minister or the competent minister. Besides countersignature, there exist other solutions for relieving the President of his political responsibility. In case of the Parliament's incapacitation the President may exercise his powers under Art. 19/A(11) of the Constitution only after the Speaker of Parliament, the President of the Constitutional Court and the Prime Minister together have established that the circumstances necessary for declaring a state of war, a state of national crisis or a state of emergency exist. These preliminary or confirming decisions are validating instruments of the President's actions.

(b) The President's independently exercised powers are mainly of an initiating type; in the decision-making chain further decisions are possible that also bind the President. One of these powers is to send back for reconsideration by the Parliament laws with which the President disagrees but the Parliament's repeated positive decision binds him to promulgate. Another such power is the initiation of a preliminary review by the Constitutional Court (Art. 26(2)–(5)). The President may submit a petition for the holding of a referendum (Art. 30/A(1)(g)), but he cannot order it. It is the President who nominates the President of the Supreme Court, the Chief Public Prosecutor, and ombudsmen, but it is Parliament which elects them (Art. 48(1); Art. 52(1); Art. 32/B(4)). It is a special transitory power between an independent political decision and initiation which allows the President to adjourn—for no more than 30 days—the Parliament's session on one occasion during any given session. One-fifth of the MPs, however, may revise this decision, and on their request the Parliament shall be convened (Art. 22(4)–(5)).

(c) In exceptional cases the President is entitled to take final, non-revisable decisions, for which neither the President, nor any other organ bears political responsibility before the Parliament ("independent political decisions"). [....]

The President may take such an independent political decision in cases, as shown by the cases of empowerment in the Constitution—when serious disturbances in the State's democratic functioning require his intervention. By his exceptional measure the President may remove the state mechanism out of the cul-de-sac to enable it to resume normal functioning. With such intervention the President fulfills his duties set out in Art. 29(1): "guards the democratic operation of the State." The Constitution does not require other organs to bear responsibility for the President's decision, since it is precisely the State's democratic functioning which is being endangered. According to the Constitution such cases may arise if the Parliament has at least four times within twelve months during its own mandate withdrawn its confidence from the Government, or if within forty days after the Government's mandate has ended the Parliament fails to elect a new Prime Minister. In the above cases the President may dissolve the Parliament while simultaneously setting the date for new elections (Art. 28(3)). A Parliament that has dissolved itself or been dissolved may be reconvened by the President in a state of war, in danger of war or in a state of emergency. (On the extension of its mandate the Parliament makes its own decision: Art. 28/A(3).) The President may convene the Parliament for an extraordinary sitting (Art. 22(3)).

In the Court's interpretation, there are similar independent political decisions when the President exercises his powers of appointment or confirmation by rejecting it on the grounds of merit. Such a decision is decisive, final and non-revisable. No one bears political responsibility for it; *i.e.,* it meets the criteria set out for independent political decision.

(d) Of a different character are decisions concerning duties of the President to which the Constitution provides only for deadlines (*e.g.*, promulgation of laws). [....]

2. [....] Countersignature is the validating instrument of the President's actions. In one respect, the countersignature ensures that the President's action will not contradict the Government's policy; in another it includes the President's action within the system of parliamentary responsibility through the assumption by the Government of the political responsibility for this action.

The President's action being subject to countersignature does not mean that the President's powers of appointment are a mere formality. Appointing is part of the head of state's or the commander in chief's competence; by exercising these powers the President—among others—fulfills his duties under Art. 29 of the Constitution. When exercising these powers the President is entitled to refuse the appointment; in this case there is no legal possibility for countersignature. Countersignature may be effected exclusively for accomplished appointments.

The constitutional concept of the President's power of appointment includes his right to refuse the appointment. Through this right, a competence which by virtue of the Constitution's special provisions on countersignature is closely related to bearing the responsibility before the Parliament becomes the President's power of independent political decision. It is obvious that the conditions and limits of such decisions cannot be wider than of those "independent political decisions" enumerated by the Constitution that have no aspect of responsibility.

On the other hand, the decision is limited by the correctly interpreted content of the power of appointment. Therefore, the President's power of appointment is a power which is restricted; the right to initiate does not belong to the President but to other organs defined by law.

The appointment's execution means the acceptance of the choice of the nominated person and its confirmation. A negative decision—the appointment's refusal—can be based solely on the choice of the person, unless it is based on the lack of procedural conditions. The appointment's practicability, its maturity, and consideration of the position to be filled shall fall outside the power to make this decision.

The President must reject the appointment if he is of the opinion that it fails to fulfill the necessary legal preconditions. (Such preconditions can be, *e.g.*, Hungarian citizenship, professional qualification, age or procedural conditions, among them the interviewing of the nominee by the competent parliamentary committee.)

The President may reject the appointment on the grounds of merit only if he has well-founded convictions that the appointment might seriously disturb the "democratic functioning of the state organization" (Art. 29(1) of the Constitution).

By rejecting a formally correct nomination, the President definitively intervenes in the merits of the case and prevents the politically responsible organ from fulfilling its duties without taking over this responsibility from that organ. According to the preconditions for independent political decisions as specified in the Constitution (see Point (c) above) and based on his constitutional status, the President's refusal based on grounds of merit serves as a final guarantee; it is an extraordinary measure that is to be applied only to a serious disturbance in the functioning of the organization of the State. It means that the rejection of the nomination shall be based on very serious objections to the nominee or that a series of perilous appointments shall reach a point when to safeguard the democratic functioning of the State's organization the President must stop the process. A constitutional rejection of the appointment shall be based on as serious grounds as are necessary for the extraordinary convening or dissolving of the Parliament.

Everything that has been stated concerning appointments is naturally valid in case of promotions, dismissals, confirmations and the President's rights of approval. [....]

KILÉNYI, SCHMIDT and **VÖRÖS, JJ.,** delivered a dissenting Opinion: While agreeing with the other Points of the Decision, on the constitutional limits of the President's power of appointment (Point B/2) we hereby state our separate opinion. [....]

The present Hungarian situation is very peculiar: the Prime Minister has come from the ranks of the government coalition, while the President has come from the opposition, and since, in its present form, the whole Hungarian state structure is being newly created, there exist no established procedural methods or guiding principles to resolve the internal problems related to their functions. [....]

Bearing the above in mind, the principal question of the present interpretation of the Constitution is whether the question, unregulated by the present Constitution, can be resolved through interpreting the Constitution or whether it requires legal regulation, in our case, by amending the Constitution. We—disagreeing with the majority opinion expressed in this Decision—have come to the conclusion that in this case only legal regulation can provide a constitutionally clear solution. Within the framework of an interpretation of the Constitution one can only come to such a general conclusion that, *e.g.*, the President may not deprive the Government of its powers to nominate an individual or of its responsibility for the appointment; therefore the nomination's rejection can be a "final remedy" only very rarely used on extraordinarily serious grounds.

All attempts to establish positively those grounds that can legally empower the President to reject a nomination fall under writing the Constitution, not under interpreting it, and they are therefore outside the Court's competence. [....]

ÁDÁM, HERCZEG, LÁBADY and **TERSZTYÁNSZKY, JJ.**, concurring: We agree with the provisions of and reasoning adduced to the Decision of the Court. [....]

3. The Court's powers to interpret abstractly the Constitution mean that on the basis of the current Constitution in force the Court may authoritatively explain the content of its provisions and the interdependence among the provisions. This activity shall be based on the presumption that the Constitution—like law itself—constitutes a unifed system without internal contradictions. All provisions shall have a defined purpose and sense; no contradictions or loopholes causing dead ends for solving constitutional questions can exist. In its interpretation the Court does not establish new rules but clarifies their inner meaning as if opening up the text and with due regard to their content and interrelationships. When exercising its rights on interpretation, the Court carries out cognitive and qualifying activities and establishes the constitutional content of the text of the Constitution. This duty definitely falls within the Court's jurisdiction. During these activities the Court shall rely on the well-established methods of grammatical, logical, systematic and historical interpretation used in the legal sciences and legal practices. [....]

SZABÓ and **ZLINSZKY, JJ.**, concurring: Under the purpose of the present petition, the Constitutional Court has to decide whether there can be constitutional loopholes in a state under the rule of law. Is it theoretically possible that state power in certain cases does not rest on constitutional provisions but that its exercise can be guided by "customary law" to be established by those exercising power? This would mean that the Constitution would be adopted, formulated and amended by those who exercise power and not by the Parliament through a two-thirds majority vote or—in extraordinary cases—through the will of the people by popular referendum.

In a strict grammatical interpretation, the Court could have established that, if the Constitution fails to provide guidance in questions related to the basic principles of the state organization or to the basic rights of the citizens, there is a legal loophole. But such an interpretation would mean the denial of the Court's principal duty. The Court's interpretive power is aimed at ensuring the unity of the constitutional system. [....]

[....] Public power shall always be based on law. There is no room in this field for loopholes; it would contradict Hungarian statehood established by the Constitution. Constitutional provisions to be interpreted cannot gain practically accepted essence through agreement between the institutions exercising power. The Court must clarify the methods of exercising public power and its limits in accordance with the Constitution in force; should the legislature disagree with the expressed interpretation, it can give new meaning to the provisions in question by amending the Constitution. [....]

Neither the Constitutional Court nor the President is accountable before the political power: they are subjected solely to the Constitution and other legislation. [....] They are independent, bear no political, only legal, responsibility, and they take their decisions according to their convictions. But they have to respect the Constitution and other laws and base their decisions on them even in those cases in which their individual conscience or conviction would suggest something else. Through them constitutional legislation is expressed.

All such efforts which wish to burden the President, the Constitutional Court or the judicial organization with decisions entailing political responsibility contradict the constitutional principles of a state under the rule of law. Anybody who intends to use these organs for political control—even being guided by the best intentions—damages their constitutional significance or dignity. This conviction—deriving from the Constitution—has inspired the Court's present Decision.

DECISION 57/1991: 8 NOVEMBER 1991

ON LEGAL GUARDIANS AND ON THE FAMILY ACT

The decision establishes a "right to know one's ancestry," which—like the "penumbra" of the constitutional privacy in the United States—has been derived from the right to human dignity. This right the Constitutional Court understands to be a "general right of personality," including the right to self-determination (8/1990) and, in this case, to self-identification. The Court eliminated procedural rules that deprived a child from challenging the presumption of paternity. With this case, the Constitutional Court introduced the concept of "living law" into its practice. The concept—borrowed from the Italian Constitutional Court—means that the Court reviews not the normative text itself but the norm that prevails, becomes effective, and is realized by the established practice of the ordinary courts or administrative agencies. No doubt, the "living law" extends constitutional review beyond the mere control of the legislature.

The petitioner sought an ex post facto constitutional review of certain statutory provisions.

Act IV/1952 on Marriage, Family and Guardianship (the "Family Act") provided under s. 43(5) that a challenge to the presumption of paternity may be brought by the child within one year of attaining majority and by other parties with standing to sue within one year of the notification of birth. Under s. 44(1) the action must be initiated personally by the party with standing, but, with the approval of the Court of Guardians, the action may be commenced (if the person with standing were totally incapacitated) by a statutory agent [*e.g.*, parents are "statutory agents" of their children while minors]. Further, Act III/1952 on the Code of Civil Procedure, art. 293(2), provides that a judgment against a defendant in an action challenging the presumption of his paternity does not allow a retrial if following such a judgment the child is legally recognized by someone conferring on him/her the full force of parental authority. Nor did an appeal lie against the overturning of the presumption.

The petitioner, Mr. Jánosi Antal, father of the child in question, submitted, inter alia, that (a) the above-mentioned legal rules violated the child's constitutional right to ascertain his/her family law rights and parentage and were thus contrary to Art. 67(1). As a result of their application his son (who was under the legal age of majority), through a guardian *ad litem* appointed by the Court of Guardians, had initiated proceedings leading to a judgment overturning the presumption of his paternity and to the removal of his son whom he alone had raised for several years; (b) a child due to incapacity arising from his minority could not be included in the category of total incapacitation under s. 44(1) for otherwise the child's right to initiate proceedings under s. 43(5) became a mere formality. This was the case because if the child's mother (who had no right to bring an action) or the Court of Guardianship commenced proceedings which resulted in overturning the presumption of paternity then the prohibition against seeking a new trial or other legal remedy deprived the child of the right to initiate personally such a paternity suit within one year of attaining majority.

Further, (c) such reasoning was based on incorrect judicial interpretation and practice vis-à-vis s. 43(5), in which the year after majority also amounted to a final deadline for a challenge to be brought (via the Court of Guardianship) at any time during the child's infancy; and (d) such interpretation in practice led, upon the mother's initiative, to the child securing a nineteen-year period in which to start a challenge whereas other eligible parties were limited to one year. This amounted to an unconstitutional interpretation.

Held, granting the petition in part:

(1) Before examining the substantive content of the case, it was necessary to determine the principles applicable in respect of a statutory text, which possessed a variety of putative interpretations. If the practice of the ordinary courts and generally accepted methods of statutory interpretation had led to one specific, defined meaning and content to gain permanent and uniform acceptance in legal practice, and that interpretation contained and gave effect to an unconstitutional content, then the unconstitutionality of that content had to be reviewed.

(2) In the present case, legal practice interpreted the second sentence of s. 44(1) of the Family Act to permit the guardian *ad litem* to have standing to bring proceedings in the name of a minor. Consequently the child (in practice, on the mother's initiative) had nineteen years from birth to commence an action as opposed to the one year of other parties entitled. Where the challenge to the presumption of paternity was successful and the presumption was overturned, such judgment could not be set aside on appeal challenging the legality of the rule nor was a retrial permitted. Therefore the child upon attaining majority had no legal possibility of establishing or clarifying its family law situation.

(3) The scope of "general right of personality" in Art. 54(1) and within it the right to self-determination and self-identification included the right to ascertain, discover or question one's parentage and to demand that no one (except directly affected blood relatives) make their origins subject to debate. Forfeiture of that right on account of legal proceedings initiated by third parties, the outcome of which was not subject to challenge, violated not only a child's right to identity but also his general right to personality. Consequently the irrevocable forfeiture of a child's right to ascertain its parentage by conferring upon a statutory agent an unqualified right to sue was unconstitutional and the relevant provision would therefore be declared null and void.

(4) As a result the reinstatement of Jánosi Antal as the designated father on his son's birth certificate would be ordered. The constitutional complaint used by the petitioner gave no general right to legal redress since it could be used only in exceptional circumstances, on the basis of a violation of a fundamental right and only after the offending provision had legal effect. The only remedy available in the case of such a complaint was the invalidation (not modification) of the rule violating the fundamental right. Its specific and particular nature thereby distinguished it from the petition for ex post facto review for which anyone had standing. In the present case the appropriate remedy would be to annul the previous modification of the son's birth certificate. The minor's rights to self-determination and self-identification would thereby be restored so that on attaining his

majority he would be able to initiate, on his own decision, an enquiry into his family status and parentage.

IN THE NAME OF THE REPUBLIC OF HUNGARY!

In the matter of a constitutional complaint and a petition seeking an ex post facto determination of the unconstitutionality of the legal rule and its annulment, the Constitutional Court—with a dissenting opinion of Kilényi and Schmidt, JJ., regarding Part A/1—has made the following

DECISION.

A

1. The Constitutional Court holds that the final and irrevocable forfeiture of a child's right to ascertain his or her consanguineal descent ("parentage") through the application of a statutory agent's unrestricted standing to sue is unconstitutional.

The Constitutional Court holds that the following provision of s. 44(1) of Act IV/1952 on Marriage, Family and Guardianship is unconstitutional: "a totally incapacitated person may be represented—subject to the approval of the court of guardianship—by a statutory agent." Accordingly, this provision is declared null and void, effective 31 March 1992.

The declaration of the provision null and void leaves the following text of s. 44(1) in force: "The paternity and maternity, and the judicial determination of the consequences of a marriage taking place after the birth of an offspring may be requested by filing suit, and the presumption of paternity may also be challenged by filing suit. The action must be initiated personally by the party with standing to sue."

2. The Constitutional Court rejects the petitions seeking to declare s. 43(5) of Act IV/1952 on Marriage, Family and Guardianship, and art. 293(2) of Act III/1952 on the Code of Civil Procedure unconstitutional and null and void.

B

The Constitutional Court holds that the legal provisions declared null and void cannot be applied in the case of the Budapest resident, Jánosi Antal. Accordingly, the partial judgment of the Buda Central District Court, No. 2.P.XII.30.004/1984/66, and the judgment on appeal to the court of second instance, the Budapest City Court, No. 54.Pf.25.286/1986/5—affirming the reversal of the presumption of paternity of Jánosi Antal—is hereby vacated.

The Constitutional Court hereby orders the reinstatement of Jánosi Antal as the designated father on the birth certificate of the child, named László Antal, born on 15 September 1979 to Erzsébet Alice Takács, in the IXth District, Budapest, registered in the birth certificate under No. 3223/1979.

The Constitutional Court hereby publishes its Decision in the *Hungarian Official Gazette.*

REASONING

LÁBADY, J., delivering the Opinion of the Court: [....]

A

IV

The Constitutional Court holds that the constitutional complaint and the petitions are partially well founded and are partially unfounded for the following reasons:

1. First the Constitutional Court had to determine what principles and considerations to apply in conducting its constitutional review when faced with a legislative text having a variety of possible interpretations.

1.1. According to s. 1(g) of Act XXXII/1989 on the Constitutional Court (hereafter referred to as the Constitutional Court Act), the expressly specified competence of the Constitutional Court is limited to interpreting the provisions of the Constitution. In the absence of an independent interpretive authority for statutory interpretation, therefore, the constitutional review cannot address the interpretation and determination of the possible different meanings and contents of a legislative text, in itself; such a review may be conducted only in connection with a question falling within the scope of the Constitutional Court's jurisdiction. If judicial practice of the ordinary courts and generally accepted legal interpretation apply a legislative text, possessing a variety of possible interpretations, in a uniform manner with a specified and determined meaning, then the Constitutional Court must scrutinize the constitutionality of the legislative text based on that meaning and content. If the normative content prevailing in practice can be determined, then the constitutional review must commence from the fact that the meaning and content of the legal rule is what the uniform and permanent legal practice deems it to be.

1.2. The constitutionality of any legal rule can evidently only be judged upon its textual interpretation and normative content. Accordingly, in the process of the so-called abstract norm control the Constitutional Court compares not merely the black letter of the legal rule but also its determined meaning and textual content, with the content of the constitutional norm determined and interpreted by it as well. If a legal rule with two or more meanings exists only in one sense in legal practice, and it exclusively prevails with that content, then the Constitutional Court is not required to bring within its scope of enquiry the (several) other textual meaning(s) and normative content(s), because in this respect no constitutional question even arises. In addition, the determination of the unconstitutionality of a norm-content which exists only in the books cannot be the subject of proceedings before the Constitutional Court in the absence of a petition in s. 20 of the Constitutional Court Act.

Following the above, the Constitutional Court should not compare the normative text in itself with the content of the provisions of the Constitution, but the norm which prevails, becomes effective and is realized—namely, the "living law."

1.3. In the opinion of the Constitutional Court, the "living law" must be understood to comprise the text and both the interpretive and applied content of a legal rule.

According to the Constitutional Court Act, the Constitutional Court has no jurisdiction to review the constitutionality of the judicial application of the law. On the one hand, this means that if a legal rule has several interpretations and even the legal practice does not agree upon a single interpretation then the Constitutional Court cannot make a binding interpretive decision, for such a decision would encroach upon the jurisdiction of the Supreme

Court. On the other hand, it also means that if a legal rule, having numerous possible interpretations, is applied with one single content in legal practice then only that normative content may serve as the basis for constitutional review. Were this otherwise, in the course of proceedings, the Constitutional Court would be engaged in an independent statutory interpretation falling outside its competence and would indeed exceed the boundaries of its competence by disputing the appropriateness of the interpretation of a legal rule determined by the ordinary courts' practice. If, however, the given interpretation of the legal rule is dependent upon the guiding determination of the Supreme Court—as is also the case with the legal rules challenged by the current petitions—then a determination of the normative content diverging from the Supreme Court's interpretation would encroach upon the Supreme Court's competence.

Therefore the same conclusion may be drawn, since the practice of the laws cannot be made the subject of the Constitutional Court's constitutional review in the absence of the relevant competence; the content of the legislative text must be examined by the Constitutional Court in light of the meaning attributed to it by the uniform legal practice. In the event that a legal rule possessing a variety of possible interpretations gains a permanent and uniform interpretation in legal practice with an unconstitutional content, then the unconstitutionality of that content must be determined in the proceedings before the Constitutional Court.

2. For these reasons, the Constitutional Court examined the constitutionality of the challenged legal rules in the context of the meaning attributed to them by legal practice.

According to the challenged regulations, a challenge against the presumption of paternity may be brought without any legal limitation in the name of child who has not yet reached the age of legal majority by a guardian *ad litem* appointed by the court of guardianship. Although according to the second sentence of s. 44(1) of Act 10/1952 on Marriage, Family and Guardianship (hereafter: Family Act) the action must be initiated personally by the party with standing to sue, a totally incapacitated person may instead be represented by a statutory agent—subject to the approval of the court of guardianship. Given that according to art. 295(2) of the Civil Procedure Code the action against the father must be initiated by the child, and furthermore as s. 87(1) of the Family Act prohibits a parent from representing his or her child in a case whose subject matter is the determination of the child's family law rights, the statutory agent of a child under the legal age in such an action may not be either the father or the mother. For this reason—in practice upon the mother's initiative—the suit is filed by a guardian *ad litem* appointed by the court of guardianship who is conferred, under art. 225(3) of the Civil Code, with the powers of a general guardian. Since according to the Act the statutory agent of a child under the legal age is the parent or the guardian, and given that the guardian *ad litem* is endowed with the powers of a general guardian, the uniform legal practice has always been—on the basis of the guiding decision referred to by the Supreme Court—to interpret the second sentence of s. 44(1) of the Family Act to permit the guardian *ad litem* to have standing to sue in the name of the child under the legal age.

As a consequence, the child and (in the interest of the child) the mother, who is legally not entitled to initiate the proceedings otherwise, have a nineteen year time frame from the birth of the child to bring suit, in contrast to other parties entitled, whose opportunity is limited to one year. In the event that the challenge to the presumption of paternity is successful and the court overturns the presumption, the part of the judgment declaring that the presumption of paternity is overturned may not be set aside on a retrial pursuant to art. 293(2) of the Code of Civil Procedure or by a legal protest. This therefore means that the child has no legal possibility whatsoever upon reaching the age of majority to establish or clarify his or her family status.

According to the petitions and the constitutional complaint, this legal arrangement violates Art. 67(1) of the Constitution because the provisions therein state that a child has a right to receive that degree of protection and care from the family, the State and society which is required for an appropriate physical, intellectual and moral development.

3. In the Constitutional Court's opinion the provisions of Art. 67(1) of the Constitution may not be interpreted to contain a child's right to ascertain his or her parentage. From the aforementioned constitutional provision only a right to receive actual family care can be derived. And this encompasses not only the consanguineal but also the so-called sociological family unit and protection and care from that family.

However, the Constitutional Court points out that the right to ascertain one's parentage, and to challenge and question the legal presumption relating to it, are everyone's most personal rights which fall within the scope of "general right of personality" found in Art. 54(1) of the Constitution. According to Art. 54(1) of the Constitution, in the Republic of Hungary everyone has the inherent right to life and human dignity, of which no one can be arbitrarily deprived. [....]

According to the Constitutional Court's view, the right to self-determination and self-identification is also part of the "general right of personality." And the right to self-determination and self-identification encompasses that most personal right of every person to ascertain, discover or question his or her parentage and to demand that nobody—apart from the directly-affected blood relatives—should question his or her origins. Depriving him/her of this right by legal proceedings initiated by third parties, having unquestionable and unreviewable consequences, violates the child's right to identity and therefore concurrently results in the violation of the constitutional general right of personality. For this reason the Constitutional Court holds that the irrevocable forfeiture of a child's right to ascertain his or her parentage by conferring upon the statutory agent an unqualified right to sue is unconstitutional. [....]

KILÉNYI, J., in whose dissenting opinion **SCHMIDT, J.,** concurred: [....]

I cannot accept the "living law" theory advanced by the Reasoning of the Constitutional Court Decision for the following reasons:

(a) According to Art. 2(1) of the Constitution, the Republic of Hungary shall be an independent democratic state under the rule of law. In a state under the rule of law, the will of the legislature must be respected and given effect. Thus, if an unconstitutional interpretation of a legal rule by the courts places them in confrontation with the law, it is the courts which must be compelled by the use of the appropriate legal instruments to interpret and apply the statute or some other legal rule in a constitutional manner, and it is not the legislature which is to be "punished" for the unconstitutional interpretation by the courts applying the law by declaring null and void a regulation which would not be unconstitutional according to a proper interpretation.

(b) [....] In its Reasoning the Constitutional Court may expound that meanings of the challenged legal rule according to which it is not regarded as being unconstitutional. The fact that a certain legal rule can be interpreted differently and that one of such interpretations is unconstitutional does not in itself render the legal rule in question to be unconstitutional as such.

(c) A legal rule is the will of the legislature stated and declared in an appropriate manner, and not the will of the executive and judicial branches expressed through the application of the law. Accordingly, the legal rule—which is subject to an ex post facto norm control by the Constitutional Court—is the text published in the *Hungarian Official Gazette* and not the version corrected and thereby distorted by the practice of its application. Any contrary interpretation amounts not only to a recognition of the legitimacy of a customary law to corrupt and amend the law but also deprives citizens and legal persons of the possibility of acquainting themselves with the laws in force. [....]

(e) If the Constitutional Court accepts the theory of "the living law," the necessary repercussion of that will be that practically it can never decide on the basis of a published statutory text but will always be compelled to examine the application of the law in practice, at the very least with the view to determine whether or not such application is "permanent and uniform." The court has neither competence nor technical resources for this purpose.

DECISION 64/1991: 17 DECEMBER 1991

ON THE REGULATION OF ABORTION

The abortion case struck down the then valid—and quite liberal—regulation by the Minister of Health on formal grounds: fundamental rights shall be regulated exclusively by an Act of Parliament. On this occasion, the first part of the decision discusses at length the constitutional dividing line between statutory and governmental regulation. This was necessary given the trend after the system change, when—as a reaction to the former "government by decree"—almost all subjects were to be regulated by statute and the burden on the Parliament grew unbearable. In the second part, the Court laid down guiding principles for the future abortion law. The decision was unable to follow the usual worldwide reasoning, which rendered the "right to life" of the fetus dependent on its maturity. Instead of this, the Court radicalized the question: if the fetus is a person, then his/her right to life deserves absolute protection, if not, it enjoys only relative protection. The Court drew attention to the new phenomenon that due to technical means available the fetus was becoming gradually better known in his/her personal capacities and this "personification" might even lead to his/her being recognized as a person in the legal sense as well. But the decision on whether this time has come or whether the fetus is or is not a person is in the competence of Parliament.

Two groups of petitioners sought to challenge the constitutionality of various statutory and non-statutory provisions regulating abortion.

The basis of both petitions was that the governmental and ministerial decrees on abortion were contrary to the Constitution, Art. 8(2), and to various provisions of Act XI/1987 on Legislation since such decrees constituted non-statutory regulation of issues involving fundamental rights and duties which could only be regulated by statute. The decrees were also contrary to Arts. 35(2) and 37(3), which prohibited the Government and ministers from issuing unlawful decrees.

The first group of petitioners contended that the decrees were unconstitutional since they permitted or insufficiently restricted the availability of abortions. They submitted inter alia that (a) since human life began at conception and any restriction on the substantial content of fundamental rights and duties, being contrary to Art. 8(2), was equally applicable to a fetus as to a fully grown human being, the decrees violated Art. 54(1) under which no one can be arbitrarily deprived of their right to life and human dignity; (b) failure to protect the life of the fetus to the same extent as that conferred on other lives was discriminatory and therefore breached Art.70/A(1); (c) consequently permitting abortion also violated Art. 56, which guaranteed the right to legal capacity; and (d) the decrees did not guarantee doctors and other health care workers the right to refuse termination of a pregnancy, thereby violating their right to freedom of conscience in Art. 60.

The second group contended that, since abortion was a matter of conscience to be resolved by the woman concerned, any external regulatory interference is unconstitutional. They submitted inter alia that (a) the right to terminate pregnancy sprang from the woman's fundamental right to human dignity under Art. 54(1) and consequently any restriction on this right by decree was contrary to Art. 8(2); and (b) were the decrees to be annulled, the Constitutional Court should therefore declare an unconstitutional omission to legislate since the provisions remaining in force would prohibit abortion in all circumstances, thereby violating those rights of women which, according to Art. 8(2), could not be restricted.

Held, granting the petitions in part:

(1) The non-statutory-based regulation of abortion was unconstitutional. Statutory regulation is required for any direct and significant restriction of fundamental rights and, in certain instances, the determination of the content of such rights and the manner of their protection. However where the relationship with fundamental rights is indirect and remote, administrative/executive (*i.e.*, non-statutory) regulation is sufficient, as otherwise everything would have to be regulated by statute. The need for statutory regulation depends on the particular measure and the intensity of its relationship to fundamental rights. In the case in question, the regulation of abortion concerned the fetus's right to life, and since this raised the question of its legal status such regulation undoubtedly pertained to the fetus's right to legal capacity. This right was the prerequisite for the fetus's right to life and human dignity as a legal subject. Therefore a decision as to whether the fetus is a legal subject would determine whether it is a human being in the legal sense. The connection between abortion regulation and the rights to life and legal recognition was necessarily predicated by the prior determination of the existence of these rights: since these rights could not be limited, for they either did or did not exist, the regulation of abortion was fundamentally related to them.

(2) In order to determine whether these rights were affected by abortion regulation to an extent which rendered statutory intervention necessary, a balancing test had to be employed. It was necessary to weigh the woman's right to self-determination (dignity) against the question of whether the State's duty to protect life extends to the fetus the right to life. Only if the fetus has no right to legal recognition and is therefore not a legal subject could it be maintained that abortion complies with the right to life under Art. 54. In contrast, if the fetus has a right to life and human dignity then this right could not differ from those accorded to others and the rights of the unborn, when conflicting with those of the mother, had to be weighed no differently than would be the case with children already born. The right to dignity of the fetus in such circumstances would prohibit the termination of a pregnancy. Consequently abortion always requires statutory regulation because any ruling on the matter implies the resolution of the question of the fetus's legal status. Based on this reasoning the executive decrees in question were unconstitutional since by regulating abortion they also determined that question, a decision which according to Arts. 8(2), 54 and 56 could only be made by statute.

(3) Article 8(2) was also violated by the Health Act 1972, s. 29(4) and s. 87(2). These subsections authorized the regulation of abortion by measures which did not have the full force of law. No decree could be elevated to the status of a law by another law, *i.e.*, the mere possibility to regulate was superfluous, since the decrees in question could not be construed to mean that the Health Act exclusively authorized statutory regulation of abortion in a manner consistent with the Constitution and the Act on Legislation. Both subsections were necessarily unconstitutional since they permitted regulation of a fundamental right by decree and not by statute.

(4) Although the question of whether the fetus is a legal subject could not be resolved by constitutional interpretation, nevertheless it was possible to evaluate both the constitutionality of the restriction and the extension of its scope. According to the Constitution and international human rights agreements, every human being is unconditionally entitled to be recognized as a legal subject, *i.e.,* a person in the legal sense of the word. The substantive rights to life and to human dignity which supplement a human being's basic legal status fulfilled formal requirements of the right to legal capacity while giving content to a person's human quality. The right to human dignity meant that the individual possessed an untouchable core of autonomy and self-determination beyond the reach of all others, whereby the human being remained a subject not amenable to transformation into an instrument or object, whereas entities having legal capacity remained susceptible to total regulation, lacking an inviolable substance. Human dignity was a quality coterminous with human existence indivisible and unlimitable, thus belonging equally to every human being. Consequently the right to equal dignity coupled with the right to life ensured that the value of human life could not be legally differentiated. A person's dignity and life is inviolable irrespective of development or conditions or fulfilment of human potential. Based on these most important fundamental rights, which form the foundation of a person's legal status, the Constitution does not permit the revocation or restriction of any part of the legal position already attained by a human being. Conversely only a constitutionally mandated change in the scope of entitlement to legal status and, correspondingly, in the legal concept of personhood, can permit its extension to the pre-natal stage.

(5) Further it was also possible for the Court to consider whether such an extension modified the basic characteristics of the legal concept of man and assess whether its interpretation of the right to life complies with such a modification. The realization of this extension would be permissible provided it did not contradict the existing constitutionally validated legal concept of man. The most important substantive component of such concept was equality in the abstract, which, being the legal equivalent of the ethical concept of man guaranteed by substantive law, is not affected by the extension of legal capacity to the unborn. Consequently the fetus's legal status did not have to be recognized nor was it impossible to accord it legal capacity since such an extension did not substantially affect the important elements of the legal concept of man. Within such a framework, it was for Parliament to legislate on the matter.

(6) The abortion regulations which also authorized their practice were to be annulled prospectively from 31 December 1992. Under such circumstances an unconstitutional omission on the part of the Parliament to enact legislation on the provision of abortion would only arise were it to fail to determine the fetus's legal status and were there to be no Act passed within the time limit. Until such time, there was accordingly no unconstitutional violation of women's right to self-determination.

(7) The abortion regulations in force guaranteed doctors and other health care professionals the possibility, on grounds of conscientious objection, of refusal to perform or to assist in abortions. The State's duty to uphold the doctor's right to freedom of conscience was met by the Constitution and by existing rules in the Labour Code, which permitted exemption from work-related obligations or permitted the doctor to create a work environment where he/she was not forced to undertake an abortion contrary to his/her convictions.

(8) Subject to Parliament's determination on whether the fetus was a legal subject, there were constitutional boundaries limiting the opportunities for abortion. Were the legislature to decide that the fetus was not legally a person, a legal subject entitled to the right to life and dignity, then abortion was permissible only in those situations in which the law tolerated a choice being made between two lives and therefore did not punish the extinction of human life. Were the legislature to decide otherwise, the State would be compelled to balance its duty to protect life against the woman's right to self-determination. An outright ban would be unconstitutional since this would completely negate the mother's right to self-determination, as would rules which exclusively favoured that right. The State's duty was to protect human life from its inception, and so the right to self-determination could not be dispositive even at the earliest stages of pregnancy. This duty meant that the State could not lawfully permit unjustified abortions. Justifications deemed adequate by Parliament had to be incorporated into a new abortion law as conditions with which to be complied. In the ultimate analysis, it was for Parliament to decide where to draw the line between the two unconstitutional extremes of total prohibition and unrestricted availability of abortions.

IN THE NAME OF THE REPUBLIC OF HUNGARY!

On the basis of petitions seeking an ex post facto review of the constitutionality of laws and regulations and the establishment of unconstitutional omissions to legislate, the Constitutional Court, with concurring opinions of Ádám, Herczegh, Kilényi, Lábady and Zlinszky, JJ., has made the following

DECISION.

The Constitutional Court holds that determination of the rules regulating the termination of pregnancy in a decree is unconstitutional. Accordingly, the first sentence of s. 29(4) of Act II/1972 on Health, according to which "termination of pregnancy is permitted only in circumstances and in the manner set forth by legal rules," s. 87(2) of the aforementioned Act, as well as Council of Ministers Decree 76/1988 (XI.3) MT on the termination of pregnancy, and Minister of Health Decree 15/1988 (XII.5) SZEM enacted for its implementation, are therefore found to be unconstitutional, and the Constitutional Court declares them to be null and void as of 31 December 1992.

Petitions calling for the establishment of an unconstitutional omission to legislate are dismissed.

This Decision of the Constitutional Court is hereby published in the *Hungarian Official Gazette.*

REASONING

SÓLYOM, P., delivering the Opinion of the Court: [....]

C

According to Art. 8(2) of the Constitution "in the Republic of Hungary rules pertaining to fundamental rights and duties shall be determined by statute. [....]" Thus, in order to judge the constitutionality of the challenged provisions, one must first identify those fundamental rights and duties which are affected by the abortion regulations. [....]

2. Undoubtedly, the regulation of abortion rights is closely related to the aforementioned fundamental rights. However, not every kind of relationship calls for statutory regulation. The determination of the content of a certain fundamental right and the establishment of the essential guarantees thereof may only occur in statutory measures; moreover the immediate and significant restriction of a fundamental right calls for statutory measures as well. However, where the relationship with fundamental rights is indirect and remote, administrative regulation is sufficient. If it were otherwise, everything would have to be regulated by statute.

Thus it follows that whether there is a need for statutory regulation should be determined on the basis of the particular measure, depending on the intensity of its relationship to fundamental rights.

3. Regulation of the termination of pregnancy affects a number of fundamental rights. [....] However, the relationship between abortion regulation and the right to life is qualitatively different from those pertaining to all other fundamental rights. Abortion being the disposal of the fetus's life, it is always in need of legal qualification; its regulation "pertains to" the fetus's right to life and—since this raises the prior question of the fetus's legal status—such regulation undoubtedly also "pertains to" the fetus's right to legal capacity. [....]

(a) The woman's right to self-determination is the most persuasive and best known, indeed classic, argument in favour of abortion—one which has also been voiced by decisions of numerous foreign constitutional courts. In contrast, the classic argument in favour of the fetus is that the State's duty to protect life can be extended to the fetus without deciding the question of its legal status.

The connection between abortion and the right to life and the right to dignity (self-determination) undoubtedly requires that abortion shall be regulated by law. This is so, since regulating abortion substantially affects these two fundamental rights in every case, given that both the argument for the right to self-determination as well as the invocation of the objective obligation to protect human life tacitly presuppose the denial of the fetus's legal personality. For, if the fetus does have a right to life, then the mother's right of self-determination cannot be considered, or only to the extent that it could be weighed against the right to life of any other human being imposing a comparable burden on the mother. Further, in this case a relative protection of the right to life is no longer adequate. The obligation of the State to protect life or the right to self-determination necessitates the statutory regulation of the abortion only in this context.

(b) If the relation with the fetus's legal status is left aside, the strength of the connection between the mother's right to self-determination and the regulation of abortion, thereby the necessity of statutory regulation, remains doubtful, at least theoretically. [....]

(c) Article 54(1) of the Constitution states that the right to life is guaranteed to "every human being," on the one hand, and—in harmony with Art. 8(1)—that the "respect and protection" of human life shall be "the primary obligation of the State"—on the other. The State's duty to "respect and protect" these fundamental rights is not exhausted by the duty not to encroach on them but incorporates the obligation to ensure the conditions necessary for their realization. [....]

Due to the differences between the entitlement to fundamental rights, on the one hand, and the State's various considerations and duties, on the other, the individual's subjective right, as one aspect of the fundamental right, is not necessarily of the same extent as its objective aspects. On the basis of its general and objective considerations the State may exceed the province protected by the subjective right while determining the boundaries of the objective, institutional protection of the same fundamental right.

This is the situation, for instance, when the individual's exercise of a civil liberty does not appear endangered but, adding the individual cases on the whole, the institution guaranteed by the fundamental right will be threatened. A single occurrence of an expropriation, for example, does not threaten the right to property, yet such a threat to the institution of property would clearly emerge if dispossession beyond some threshold level were to become systematic.

The situation with respect to the right to life is similar. For the individual, this right serves to ensure his/her own life. However, the duty of the State goes beyond its obligation not to violate the individual's right to life and to employ its legislative and administrative measures to protect this right. It must also protect human life and its condition of existence in general. This latter duty is qualitatively different from aggregating the right to life of individuals; it is human life in general, consequently human life as a value, that is the subject of protection. Hence, the State's objective and individual duty to protect human life extends to those lives which are in their formation, no less than it has a duty to secure the conditions of life for the future generations. This duty, in contrast with the right to life, is not absolute. Accordingly, it is possible that this duty is restricted by other rights. Thus, the State's duty to protect the life of the fetus may be restricted by the mother's right to health or her right to self-determination.

But there is no general guiding principle which can be derived from the State's duty to protect life—the most frequently cited argument in favour of protecting the fetus—which can explain why the law does not protect every fetus equally or why it protects the fetus only to a certain extent, beyond which infringement upon its prospects for life is permitted. It is not readily apparent why the State's interest in a pregnancy which has progressed beyond the third month is more compelling than its interest in protecting a fetus less than three months old—which if protected would also develop into a viable being. Since the fetus's human potential is constant throughout the pregnancy, on what basis can one grade the intensity of protection afforded to it? If it is said that the *nasciturus* is accorded the right to life, then on what principled grounds can one distinguish between the protection of lives of the born and still unborn? Other countries' constitutional courts do employ these questionable distinctions, albeit that they are always based on pragmatic considerations which are debatable in principle.

The State's duty to protect life, derived from Art. 54, does not call per se for any statutory regulation. On the basis of Art. 54, the State has to provide for the protection of life by institutions in a general and impersonal manner with respect to "every human being"—as a statistical multitude of people. Traffic regulations, environmental emissions limits, and technical safety regulations do not require regulation by statutes despite the fact that all of these regulations clearly touch upon the objective aspect of the right to life and the State's duty to protect it. This is the case, since such regulations seek to protect life only to a limited extent and, beyond that, knowingly risk human lives, for they accept that some loss of life is inevitable in improving overall social welfare.

However, in contrast with the situation where human life in the abstract is exposed to risk, in the case of abortion it is always a specific individual life that is deliberately singled out for termination. This is so, even if, for the sake of circumspection, one were to talk of "potential" life.

Therefore abortion may only be taken as falling under the relative institutional protection of life, pursuant to Art. 54, if the individuality of the fetus were not legally recognized. Since the deliberate and specific nature of abortion as an act cannot be eliminated, the depersonalization of the other side must be increased in the extreme. Abortion may only "pertain to" the objective side of the right to life guaranteed by Art. 54 of the Constitution—thus this right should not be taken into account as a subjective right—if legally the fetus is not considered to be a human being. In contrast, if the fetus has a right to life and dignity then this right cannot differ from those accorded to other human beings; therefore it has to be contrasted with the fundamental rights of the mother, no differently than in the case with children already born. [....]

4. [....] Based on this reasoning, Council of Ministers Decree 76/1988 (XI.3) MT and Minister of Health Decree 15/1988 (XII.15) SZEM are hereby held to be unconstitutional, given that by regulating abortion they also decide on the question of the fetus's status, so pertaining to Arts. 54 and 56 of the Constitution, a decision which pursuant to Art. 8(2) of the Constitution can only be made by statute.

The Constitution is also violated by the first sentence of s. 29(4) of the 1972 Health Act, which states that abortion is permitted only in circumstances and in the manner set forth by legal rules. This provision authorizes the regulation of abortion by measures ranking lower than statutes in the hierarchy of sources of law. [....] As a result, the first sentence of s. 29(4) of the Health Act 1972 is contrary to Art. 8(2) of the Constitution. [....]

The Constitutional Court declared the regulations null and void, which for formal reasons are deemed to be unconstitutional. The Constitutional Court has refrained from making a determination of the merits of the constitutionality of the regulations of abortion for the reasons discussed below.

D

1. The question of whether the fetus is a legal subject cannot be resolved by interpretation of the Constitition. Accordingly, only after the legislature's decision concerning the fetus's legal personality and depending thereon would the Constitutional Court be able to make a substantive evaluation of the constitutionality of abortion regulations.

The fact that according to the current law the fetus is not a legal subject does not advance the resolution of the problem. A group of petitioners precisely questions the constitutionality of this situation by arguing that the fetus also belongs to the subjects of fundamental rights, whenever possible under the Constitution when it refers to "everyone" or "every human being."

In examining whether the fetus is a legal subject, one is not confronted with the usual task of constitutional interpretation. This is not a case in which one can apply a generally accepted and value free notion in order to determine which of the possible interpretations are, and which are not, compatible with the Constitution. Whether or not the fetus is a legal subject gives rise to fundamentally different legal situations. The two interpretations are mutually exclusive yet both of them can be reconciled with the present Constitution. Interpretation of another fundamental right secured by the Constitution cannot help the Court to decide in favour of one or the other. The Constitutional Court can interpret the meaning of the right to life and human dignity, as well as the right to be a legal subject [the right to legal capacity, Art. 56], but their efficacy—whatever their content—hinges on who is considered to fall within the category of "every human being."

The decision on whether the fetus is a legal subject is tantamount to the redefinition of the legal status of human beings. But such a determination, which must precede any interpretation of fundamental rights, cannot be derived from the inner logic of the Constitution and is not to be found therein; it is an external decision—due to the drafters of the Constitution—that would most appropriately be regulated by incorporation into the Constitution itself. The Constitutional Court can contribute to the making of this decision by evaluating the relationship between the decision about redefining the category of legal subjects, on the one hand, and the present Constitution, as well as the interpretation of fundamental rights by the Constitutional Court, on the other hand: what changes, if any, are needed and the possibilities and limits of redefining the institution of legal capacity. The Constitutional Court will state its view regarding the constitutionality of restricting the scope of the institution of legal subjectivity and, second, whether the extension of its scope alters the basic characteristics of the legal concept of a human being (a natural person) and whether the Constitutional Court's interpretation of the right to life accords with such a modification.

2. According to Art. 54(1) of the Constitution in the Republic of Hungary every human being has the inherent right to life and to human dignity of which no one can be arbitrarily deprived. Article 56 declares that in the Hungarian Republic every human being has legal capacity.

According to art. 6 of the Universal Declaration of Human Rights everyone has the right to recognition everywhere as a person before the law. Article 16 of the International Covenant on Civil and Political Rights declares that everyone shall have the right to recognition everywhere as a person before the law.

(a) International agreements on human rights state—accordingly the Constitution as well—that every human being, everywhere, unconditionally has legal capacity, thus she/he is a person in the legal sense. This recognition represents the universal triumph of the goals sought throughout a long historical process—stretching back at least 200 years: human beings, not only in their "natural state" but also before the law, have become equal. The legal capacity is conferred on every human being, thus precluding slavery; and being not only universal but also equal to everyone, it excludes any further differentiations (*e.g.*, feudal ones) which are based on the gradation of legal status. Once every human being's legal capacity is recognized, "human being," "legal subject," "everyone" and "person" all become synonyms legally. As a result "human being" has become a normative concept. At the time when every individual acquired this legal status, the divergence between biological and legal conceptions of humanity and the ethical views on the determination of human beings did not create the sort of tensions which characterize the contemporary debate. On the contrary, the plurality of concepts of human beings came into accordance at that time. The normativity of the "person before the law" was hidden by the unproblematic conception of the "natural" human being. The legal concept was synchronized to the latter, the proposition that everyone is equally entitled to legal personality being derived from moral values. It was taken for granted that everyone is a human person who is born as such.

(b) Legal capacity is such an abstraction which no longer contains anything necessarily restricting its application to humans. It is a formal quality. Every human being must be so endowed but those other than human beings can also be bestowed with this right. The law can designate anything as a legal subject, that is, a "person."

Accordingly there are two substantive fundamental rights that supplement a human being's basic legal status, which give content to the formal requirements of the right to legal capacity and express a person's human quality: the rights to life and human dignity. The right to human dignity means that the individual possesses a core of autonomy and self-determination beyond the reach of all others, whereby—according to the classical formulation—the human being remains a subject, not amenable to transformation into an instrument or object. This concept of the right to dignity distinguishes human beings from legal entities, having legal capacity, the latter being amenable to total regulation, lacking an untouchable essence. Dignity is a quality coterminous with human existence, a quality which is indivisible and cannot be limited, hence belonging equally to every human being. The right to equal dignity, coupled with the right to life, ensures that the value of human life cannot be legally differentiated. The human dignity of life is inviolable of anyone who is a human being, irrespective of physical and intellectual development and condition and irrespective of the extent of fulfilment of the human potential. We cannot even talk of a human being's right to life without positing that person's individual subjective right to life and dignity. The State's duties to secure the right to life merely contribute to this, but are not a substitute for subjective rights, and without respecting the subjective right to life and human dignity, those objective duties are meaningless with respect to living human beings.

(c) During the second half of this century the relationship between the biological and legal conception of human beings became problematic once again. Given the plurality of equally prevalent moral views in society we cannot even discuss a generally accepted moral concept of man. The multifaceted and diverse situations as a third party disposes of the life of another person must all confront the legal concept of man and its fundamental legal status, as discussed above: hence the death penalty, euthanasia, abortion and every regulation pertaining to the fetus outside the womb are inevitably constitutional problems.

Judging from the perspective of fundamental rights there is a substantial difference between the death penalty and euthanasia, on the one hand, and abortion on the other hand.

With respect to the death penalty or euthanasia there is no question that it is the life of a human being which is being disposed of. The constitutionality of these acts can be determined by interpretation of the rights to life and dignity without necessarily having to inquire into the formal legal concept of man.

That the death penalty is deemed unconstitutional in a growing number of countries is a clear indication that the development whereby everyone, purely by the virtue of being human, is to be accorded full legal status of a human is approaching its culmination. This will occur if the unconditional right to life and dignity, akin to that of legal capacity, is recognized. In contrast, those countries which have the death penalty and permit euthanasia regard the rights founding the uniquely human legal status as revocable or subject to limitations on the basis of specific criteria (such as guilt, quality of life, physical or conscious state) to this concept. The basic question of the death penalty and euthanasia is accordingly the decision on the unconditionality or the restrictability of the right to life and dignity.

However, with respect to abortion the question is not whether the fundamental rights shaping the uniquely human legal status are unconditional or subject to limitations but concerns the preliminary question of whether the fetus is a human person and thus capable of becoming a subject of these rights.

According to Hungarian law the fetus is not a legal subject. That the Criminal Code protects the interest of the fetus by declaring abortion to be a crime is a different question. Likewise, that the Civil Code provides for the interests of the unborn child, technically by recognizing the fetus's conditional right to legal capacity, subject to its live birth, is a different question. This method of a conditional right is appropriate to ensure the property interests of the child until birth. But such a conditional legal capacity is not appropriate for solving the problem of abortion. The fetus's right to life—in effect its right to be born—cannot be made dependent on the condition of its being born.

(d) Two conflicting developments regarding the concept of man compels a determination of whether the fetus is a legal subject. Both developments alter the traditional thinking about the fetus.

On the one hand, abortion has reached a historically unprecedented magnitude, having become one of the main forms of contraception, while its directly associated health risks have become insignificant. Related to this trend, the negative moral evaluation of abortion which characterized previous eras is becoming increasingly neutral. The decriminalization of abortion has commenced. Social movements press for the total liberalization of abortion. The practice of abortion on a mass scale and its accompanying rationalizations and justifications mitigate the public's concerns about the disposal of the fetus. The precondition of the sought-after permissibility of abortion is the continued non-recognition of the fetus as a human being and its right to life. As a result of these changes, in the majority of states under the rule of law the constitutionality of applying penal sanctions to abortions were challenged before constitutional courts, hence raising the questions of the legal conditions of abortion as well.

On the other hand, as a result of scientific progress, birth is no longer an obviously natural and qualitative line separating the life of a fetus from a "human person's life." Biological, and especially genetic, opinions maintain that individual human life is a uniform progression from conception, not from birth, to death. Within this progression several stages can be distinguished, with birth not necessarily being the most important dividing line during the early stages of human life. The social position of the fetus is also changing. It participates in society on account of its independent physical presence and, increasingly, on its individual attributes, rather than on the basis of its impending social position (by conditional property rights). The progress of medical technology and the application of other technical devices now permit the gathering of much information about the fetus within the womb: its gender and physical characteristics can be known; it can be cured and manipulated; it can be made visible to the mother and her family, allowing them to follow its progress. The individuation of the fetus is intensifying. Outside the womb, the fetus also appears independently in societal affairs—this is the basis, for instance, of surrogate motherhood. These changes are the direct outcome of technological advancement, and their dissemination and growing popularity is thus irreversible. This transformation means that the conception of the fetus as a person will become increasingly self-evident in public opinion. These changes therefore point to a direction, leading toward the incorporation of the fetus into the everyday "self-evident" conception of man, thereby brings the latter into harmony with those moral and biological viewpoints, which posit that humans must be so recognized from the moment of conception.

The two conflicting trends can be made seemingly compatible by positing—as tradition would also have it—that the concept of man can be extended only to the matured (viable) fetus. (Even abortion advocates limit their demands for the freedom to choose within the first three months of pregnancy.) However, intervention with the fertilized cells or during the initial stages of fetal development would require a uniform determination of the fetus's legal status based on a single principle. If the law at all extends human status prior to birth, and provided it maintains its existing principles, then the fetus must be recognized as a legal subject irrespective of its stage of development. This follows from the fact that the law does not distinguish—and cannot, while remaining within this conceptual framework—between those born on the basis of physical state, mental functioning or by any similar criteria.

Nonetheless, the legislature can decide that only the fully matured fetus is entitled to legal status with its concomitant absolute right to life, or can, alternatively, create a special legal status for the fetus within which one can distinguish on the basis of age, maturity or even the "domicile"—inside the uterus as opposed to outside in artificial conditions. Both solutions can increase the protection accorded to the fetus, but theoretically the same problems of reasoning arise, which characterize the relative protection extended to the fetus by the well-known existing regulations. That is, determination of why the legal recognition of the fetus as a human person commences at a given certain moment, and not before, cannot be supported by any principle. Conversely, creating a special legal status does not extend to the fetus the absolute protection of the right to life and dignity just as present regulations fail to do so. From the perspective of the law the fetus is either a human person or not. The relativity and restrictability of protection that would be accorded to the life of fetus by making it a special legal person, enjoying sui generis legal protection, would not result in more protection in practice than that already extended by the State on the basis of its objective duty to protect life.

3. The question is whether human legal status should follow the aforementioned changing trend—in natural and social sciences and in public opinion—of the concept of man, thus extending the legal concept of man before birth all the way back to conception. The nature of such an extension of the scope of legal capacity is comparable only to the abolition of slavery, but it surpasses even that event in significance. With this measure the legal capacity of man would reach its theoretically feasible final limits and completeness: the differing concepts of man would again coincide.

(The question raised by the other tendency, how to ensure the greatest possible disposal of the fetus, would reduce the protection afforded to the fetus without effecting any change in its current legal status or requiring any review thereof.)

Interpretation of the current Constitution cannot furnish a resolution of the question whether the fetus is a legal subject.

Interpretation of the right to life and dignity can only be applied by the Constitutional Court to determine whether these bases of the legal status of man can be constitutionally limited. The interpretation of the proposition that "every human being has legal capacity" can only answer the question—if seeking to avoid a tautology—of whether legal capacity can be revoked. Nonetheless, such an interpretation by the Constitutional Court of these fundamental rights touches on the dispute concerning the concept of man, given that the normative concept of the human person whose substance is not constitutionally defined, and the image of man applied by the Constitutional Court in interpreting fundamental rights, must have common roots. The Constitutional Court holds that, based on its interpretation of the most important fundamental rights which form the foundation of a person's legal status, the Constitution does not permit the revocation of any part of the legal status already attained by a human being. Accordingly, the scope of legal capacity cannot be restricted. (Thus, the enactment of a law recognizing personality subject to the appearance of a specifically human characteristic, hence conferring the legal status of being a person on an infant when he/she is about one and a half years old—a view that accords with some theories expressed in discourse on ethics—would be held unconstitutional.)

In contrast, the expansion of the legal concept of man is a question which the Constitutional Court can only address to the extent of declaring its position regarding the constitutional requirements of such an expansion. From what has been stated above, it follows that the only constitutional change in legal capacity and, correspondingly, in the legal concept of man would be its expansion to the pre-natal stage. The realization of this goal is constitutional—but only if it does not contradict the presently recognized legal concept of man in the constitutional order. The most important substantive component of that concept is equality in the abstract; in contrast, the beginning of legal capacity rests on a much less principled basis.

It is characteristic of a person's basic legal status that legal capacity is independent of that person's qualities. This is so with respect to the right to life and dignity as well. (The debate concerning the recognition of the unconditional nature of these rights equally affects "everyone.") If the rights representing the human quality of the born are affected neither by his/her unique characteristics nor his/her circumstances (as for instance his/her age) then the fetus's development and its specific qualities could likewise prove irrelevant to his/her legal capacity and to the right to life and dignity. Equality in the abstract, the legal equivalent of the ethical concept of man guaranteed by the rights to life, dignity and legal capacity, is not affected by the extension of legal capacity to the unborn.

The other main contemporary component of the concept of man is that it begins at birth. This element was principally significant when it could harmonize differing conceptions of man while justifying the equality of every human being. Whether it continues to achieve this end is doubtful given that the biological concept of man is expanding.

It is the legislature which must evaluate the ethical and scientific viewpoints about the fetus, weigh its changing conceptualizations in the context of conflicting social trends, and decide whether these changing conceptualizations should be followed by the law. From what has been discussed above, it neither follows from the Constitution that the fetus's legal capacity must be fully recognized nor that it is impossible legally to accord it as a human person. Such an extension does not substantially affect the important elements of the legal concept of man, such as equality and the absolute nature of the right to life and dignity.

E

[....]

2. Other petitioners alleging an unconstitutional omission contend that abortion regulations in force do not guarantee doctors and other health care professionals the possibility, on grounds of conscientious objection, to refuse to perform or assist in abortions.

The right to freedom of conscience pertinent in connection with this regulation means that the State cannot compel anyone to accept a situation which sows discord within, or is irreconciliable with, those fundamental convinctions which mould that person's identity. The duty of the State extends beyond refraining from such compulsion to the safeguarding—within reasonable limits—the exercise of alternative behaviour. Sacrifice required of a person in pursuit of the dictates of his/her conscience is not unconstitutional, provided that the burdens imposed are not disproportionate. [....]

With regard to the doctors opposed to abortion, the State's duty to uphold the right to freedom of conscience is met if exemption from obligations under labour law is granted or, alternatively, if the obstetrician/gynaecologist is afforded an opportunity to create a work environment where he/she is not forced to undertake an abortion contrary to his/her convictions. Existing regulations permit these options.

The execution of legally permitted abortions, and participation therein, is an activity falling within the scope of the work of the doctors and health care workers specializing in the field. The general provisions prescribing performance duties, compliance requirements and sanctions imposed for the refusal thereof are contained in the Labour Code (art. 34). According to the Code, a worker is obliged to follow the instructions of his/her superiors unless the undertaking of those orders would gravely and directly endanger health or physical well-being or would encroach upon the employee's legally protected interests. [....] Even less conceivable would be to allow the order of the employer to impede the exercise of fundamental rights, including the right to freedom of conscience. Restricting the freedom of conscience can proceed only when dictated by the interest of some other fundamental right or constitutionally mandated duty, and even then such restriction must be necessary and proportionate. Hence the worker can refuse to carry out instructions which violate his/her freedom of conscience. Such a refusal is judicially protected. The Constitutional Court notes that judicial protection of the right to freedom of conscience would apply even in the absence of the Labour Code provision to the same effect. That is, even without this provision the judiciary could always invoke in a labour suit Art. 60 of the Constitution, providing for the exemption from the duty to carry out orders. Hence there is no basis for asserting a failure to legislate; the petition is especially groundless with respect to existing regulations.

[....] It is groundless to invoke the freedom of conscience when the activity objected to—in general or in the workplace chosen by the employee—is inherent in that sphere of work. In principle, the conduct of abortions which do not conceivably serve a medical purpose do not form a necessary part of the occupational sphere of an obstetrician/gynaecologist. For this reason a doctor opposed to abortion can invoke, in general, the right to freedom of conscience (unless he/she is employed at an abortion clinic). The State also has a duty to make it legally possible and, if need be, to participate actively in the creation of a work environment where the obstetrician/gynaecologist is not forced to conduct abortions against his/her conscience. Whether there are sufficient numbers of such workplaces being formed, whether the burdens imposed on a doctor thus required to shift workplace are excessive, and the degree of protection which freedom of conscience is to receive in work-related proceedings are all questions concerning the individual's ability to exercise his/her human rights, questions whose investigation according to existing law does not fall within the jurisdiction of the Constitutional Court.

3. Based on the aforementioned reasoning, petitions seeking the establishment of an unconstitutional omission to legislate are rejected by the Constitutional Court.

F

Finally, the Constitutional Court points to those constitutional boundaries which—subject to the legislature's decision concerning the legal capacity of the fetus—limit the opportunities for abortion.

1. If the legislature decides that the fetus is legally a person, that is a legal subject entitled to the right to life and dignity, then abortion is permissible only in those situations where the law tolerates a choice being made between lives and accordingly does not punish the extinction of human life. Such is the case, for instance, if abortion is required to save the mother's life.

2. If the legislature decides that the fetus is legally not a person, not a legal subject un-

der Art. 56 of the Constitution, and therefore does not have the right to life and dignity, then the State is compelled to balance its duty to protect the fetus's life against the mother's right to self-determination and her every other fundamental right. The answer to the question of the extent to which constitutional rights, primarily the mother's personality rights, impose limitations on the State's duty to protect the fetus cannot be directly derived from the Constitution itself. Thus the Constitutional Court can only designate the constitutional boundaries of the freedom of the legislature, wherein the law must lie; alternatively it can determine that an unconstitutional omission to legislate has occurred if the legislature fails to extend the minimum constitutionally required protection either to the mother's right or to the fetus.

Accordingly, if the fetus's legal personality were not recognized, the legislature—when called upon to designate conditions authorizing abortion—cannot ignore either of the two most important rights in conflict: it must weigh both the woman's right to self-determination and the State's duty to protect life. An outright ban on abortion would not be constitutional, for this would completely negate the mother's right to self-determination (and her right to health as well). Such a ban does not follow from the Constitution, given that in this scenario the fetus does not have the right to life according to Art. 54 of the Constitution. It would likewise not be constitutional if regulations would favour exclusively the mother's right to self-determination. The State has a duty to protect human life from the moment of its inception and hence the right to self-determination cannot prevail alone even in the earliest stages of the pregnancy. This duty to protect life means that the State cannot constitutionally permit unjustified abortions. Justification is especially necessary in the case of abortion as the State's duty to safeguard human life now serves the purpose, not of averting or minimizing anonymous statistical risks but the wilful termination of the life of an individual human fetus. Justifications deemed adequate by the legislature must be incorporated into abortion law as conditions with which to be complied.

Where the law should draw the line between the unconstitutional extremes of total prohibition and unrestricted availability of abortions and what indications it requires is the responsibility and the competence of the legislature to decide. However, specific conditions cannot violate other constitutional rights. Every condition necessarily differentiates—for instance, on the basis of age, health, social position or ethical perspectives—but such a differentiation cannot conflict with Art. 70/A, *viz.,* that it must comply with the constitutional requirements for positive discrimination. Attention must likewise be paid to ensure that no one is compelled to act contrary to the dictates of his/her conscience and that the exercise of other abortion-related rights are duly respected.

G

The Constitutional Court declared the regulations indicated in the operative part of this Decision null and void effective from 31 December 1992. If the Constitutional Court's decision to strike down these regulations were to be effective from the date of its publication, then every abortion would become a criminal act. But in this Decision the Constitutional Court expressed no opinion on the substantive issues of abortion. Accordingly, it did not determine a date for invalidating regulations which, for all practical purposes, would be tantamount to taking a position on these substantive issues. There is ample time for the legislature to make its determination and enact a law on abortion and the legal status of the fetus.

ÁDÁM, J., concurring: [....]

Hence, the circumstance that neither the Constitution nor the law recognizes the fetus as a legal subject does not permit indifference or neutrality toward the life and fate of the fetus. The general and individual protection accorded to the fetus serves to secure the birth of a healthy human being. This statement makes sense only if it includes the fetus's right to be born. But from this it does not follow that the fetus's right to be born is identical with the right to life accorded to those already born. It depends on the legislature's determination that under which conditions does it allow priority to the exercise of mother's right to life, health, dignity, self-determination and her and her family's right to social security and other fundamental rights against the competing right of the fetus's right to be born. [....]

These statements are placed on the record to emphasize that the fetus is entitled to some rights even if the law does not recognize it to be a human being legally. The legal situation thus brought about, stipulating duties of the State and other legal subjects, does not, however, make it impossible for the law to determine the conditions under which the realization of fundamental rights which compete with the fetus's right to be born may have priority. This is the case given that the fetus's right to be born is not an absolute right within the existing constitutional framework but is instead a derivative right which is not identical with its source, *viz.,* the right of a thus legally recognized person to life and dignity.

HERCZEGH, J., concurring: [....]

In regulating abortion the legislature can never omit to investigate whether a repetitive surgical intervention undermines the health of those operated on, and whether such procedures increase the frequency of premature births and the number of physically and mentally impaired survivors. On the basis of the constitutional provisions referred to, especially those dealing with duties pertaining to the provision of health care, the State in pursuing birth control regulation must balance the feasibility of providing medical advice reducing the risks to women, consider the possibility of providing appropriate medical information and supervision for those desiring to avoid unwanted pregnancies without worsening domestic and social problems, while intensifying the protection afforded to children and families and generally improving the level of health awareness. [....]

KILÉNYI, J., concurring: [....]

On my part, I cannot identify with those petitioners' reasonings which, in effect, reduce the question of the legality of induced abortion to a technical problem of genetics, arguing that according to the present scientific position the fetus becomes a human being of full value from the moment of conception, and thereby the prohibition contained in Art. 8(2) of the Constitution automatically extends to it. In my view, the genetic definition of the human essence of the fetus is one issue and the law's determination of the moment whence the human being is recognized as a legal subject is another matter. There is no necessarily automatic link between these two things. [....]

On the basis of this reasoning, it is my view that the legislature would not find itself in conflict with the Constitution even if it were to limit legal capacity to the already born, while treating the life of the fetus as sui generis amenable to legal protection but not falling within the ambit of Art. 8(2) of the Constitution. That sui generis legal protection is not constant throughout the duration of the fetal existence but grows in accordance with the fetus's natural progression, or is conferred on the fetus periodically in a manner which does not correspond with any material change from the genetic viewpoint, is also compatible with such a legislative position.

2. The relation between religious beliefs and doctrines and secular laws is inevitably raised in connection with this affair which, in light of Art. 60(1)–(3) may even become a constitutional problem. With respect to this, my opinion is the following:

The task of the secular law is the governance of the life of society by imposing behavioural rules backed by the police powers of the State. For this reason, secular laws apply to all, irrespective of one's denomination. But this does not relieve the legislature of its duty to consider its citizens' religious beliefs—or other principles, be it pacifism, vegetarianism or something else—when making law. This is so, given that according to the provisions of Art. 60(1) the State is required to its utmost ability to refrain from imposing a pattern of behaviour on its citizens which is in conflict with their convictions. (Of course, not even the State can tolerate all convictions.) [....]

[....] [T]here need not be any conflict where the State does not deem illegal behaviour which is prohibited by any church. For in this case the State merely provides the legal possibility for surgically induced abortion to take place which the mother—according to her convictions—may use or refuse. The freedom of conscience confers on every citizen the undisputed right to adopt a stricter moral standard than the State imposes on the rest of society and to decide, accordingly, not to take advantage of the possibility of procuring an abortion even though the law does not prohibit it. [....]

LÁBADY, J., concurring:

Concurring with the holding concerning the determination of the unconstitutionality and the annulment of abortion regulations, my opinion is that these regulations are also substantively unconstitutional.

1. I do not share the position of the majority view that the question whether the fetus is a legal subject cannot be resolved by constitutional interpretation. This viewpoint sees a possibility for the legislature to establish the fetus's legal status differing from that of man. Such "segregation," however, has no constitutional basis.

2. No doubt, the Constitution does not define the normative concept of man. It does not shed light either on the exact beginning or ending of human life and legal capacity. However, as the majority view indicates, the concept of man—along with its philosophical, ethical, moral, scientific and natural concepts which developed during the course of history—has also become a normative value. But if the concept of man is a normative one, it cannot fall outside the Constitution—the normative universe of the country's fundamental law—and its constitutional place must be located by the Constitutional Court, in accordance with constitutional values, on the basis of constitutional interpretation. [....]

[...] Hence, the Constitutional Court must interepret the commencement and termination of human life and legal capacity and the concept of man in its entirety on the basis of the Constitution. [....]

4. The truly problematical, scientific dilemmas of a few decades ago which influenced formal legal thinking and normative construction of the legal status of man have now been decided unambiguously. We know that from the moment of the union of male and female spermatozoa the individual is genetically fully complete. [....]

Hence the fetus is biologically human, and not a thing, not an object; it is a genetically complete being: individual; between conception and biological death the life of the individual human being is a continuum.

5. The life of the fetus prior to birth (inside and outside the womb) does not (and cannot) have a special legal status because birth is an artificial as well as arbitrary and normatively determined boundary within the biological continuum. The claim that the fetus is an integral part of the woman's body cannot be validated by genetic, physiological and morphological studies. On the contrary, the fetus is independent, an individual separate from the person of the mother, with its individual heart function, circulation, nervous system and unique features.

If the law could differentiate between the post- and pre-natal phases; moreover if with respect to the latter it could further articulate distinctions on the basis of whether the fetus is capable of surviving outside the womb, or according to temporal proximity to birth, whether it is genetically healthy or damaged and the like, then—in principle at least—the same normative distinctions could be applied, based even on the same criteria (the newborn's viability, quality of life, state of mind and physical well-being and so on), to those already born. This would, however, give rise to an apartheid normative concept of man.

The argument provided by the majority to the effect that no part of the legal position already secured by Constitution cannot be taken back, while irrefutable, does not advance the position since the debate surrounding the commencement of the legal subjectivity, the regulation as a person, *viz.,* the normative concept of human being, is not resolved in the Constitution by express provisions. It resolves only that a human being has unconditional legal capacity and, furthermore, that its life and dignity is inviolable. However, the qualification as a human being, as a person existing at birth (at the separation from the mother's body) in any case was made on the basis of legislative enactment and constitutional interpretation by the Court.

6. Undoubtedly, birth represents a qualitative change in the continuum of human development. This, however, cannot be the basis of a different, divergent normative system of the value of human life. Article 54(1) extends absolute protection to human life and dignity, not to human life that has separated from the mother's body. [....]

7. On the basis of Art. 56 of the Constitution every human being in the Republic of Hungary has legal capacity. Since the fetus is human, legal subjectivity commences at conception not at birth. He or she who is conceived has legal capacity; its human existence and dignity gives rise to its legal subject's right to be born.

Hence the fetus is not simply genetically, biologically (and ethically) human but also, in the legal and the constitutional sense, it is a legal subject and accordingly its legal position, human status, that is its constitutional status, falls within the scope of Art. 54(1) of the Constitution.

8. In our concurring Opinion—with Tersztyánky, J.—in this Court's Decision concerning the unconstitutionality of the death penalty (*Dec. 23/1990 (X.31) AB:* MK 1990/107; ABH 1990, 88), we adopted the opinion that the right to life and human dignity are [....] not fundamental rights, but [....] categories preceding legal values, sources of the rights to be found in the catalogue of human rights and in modern constitutions.

But the a priori positing of values regarding human life and dignity means that, on the one hand with respect to the legal protection of human life we cannot discriminate between the pre-natal and post-natal phases and, on the other hand, that the State is precluded from using not only its punitive powers in depriving a person of life or dignity but also its other legal instruments, including the "right to abortion," because the value under consideration is inalienable and inviolable even by law (not transferable to woman, mother, spouse or the State); the value in question is untouchable by legal means.

9. [....]

Given that the fact of human existence is the basis for, and condition of, the appearance of legal subjectivity (and subjective rights), and as the concept of life encompasses all values, the legal values forming part of the totality of human life do not compete with the whole. The mother's personality rights accordingly cannot restrict the fetus's right to be born, because such a restriction means the destruction of the fetus as human life, that is, it amounts to an arbitrary deprivation of its life.

Accordingly, the legal regulations governing abortions challenged by the petitioners are substantively unconstitutional (Art. 8(2) of the Constitution).

10. The life of a human being can only compete with that of another human being. Article 54(1) of the Constitution only prohibits the arbitrary deprivation of life. Evidently, deprivation of life is not arbitrary if the same values compete against one another, if the law has to make a choice between lives. If one person drifts into mortal danger and can be saved only by sacrificing the life of another (for instance, the life of the mother in case of an ectopic pregancy) then the arbitrariness of deprivation of life is suspended by the objective of saving a life. Here the law must stipulate an exculpatory reason (which does not mean a right to kill). The impending statutory provisions must regulate this non-arbitrary quality and restrict it within the framework of appropriate legal guarantees.

ZLINSZKY, J., concurring: [....]

II

[....] National and international jurisprudence and legal practice restrict the retroactive right of legal capacity to the moment of birth by a fiction. According to our current laws, the right to birth and to legal capacity cannot be derived from this fiction. According to current Hungarian law, the fetus is not a legal subject under the civil law. [....] On the basis of existing civil law provisions, the legal scenario that a conflict of interest concerning property law between parent and child can be traced from the moment of conception, is applicable only to children already born. The very fact that a curator is conferred with the power of a legal guardian, rather than having a guardian appointed for the fetus, indicates that what is at stake is not the need for personal care but the securing of contingent birth-dependent property rights.

[....]

According to the two pertinent constitutional provisions, Arts. 54 and 56, every human being has an inherent right to life and every human being is endowed with legal capacity. However, the Constitution uses the word "human" in a normative and not a scientific sense. The legislature evidently considers the recent determination of the natural sciences in the process of its legislation but the Constitutional Court is not the legislature and its task is the precise determination of the content of the Constitution. Viewed from this perspective, the concepts of "man" and "inherent rights" can be interpreted, and are to be interpreted consistently with the prevailing legal system unless or until the moment when it becomes clear that the Constitution seeks to go beyond the existing system, or that the legal system is in open conflict with the Constitution.

In the process of legal development—as our reasoning above indicates—the legal concept of "man" has never fully acquired the biological sciences' concept of humanity. The concept of inherent right, both as a civil and a criminal law category, is tied to the separation from the mother's body, and not to the moment of conception taking place within her body. The legislature can decide differently but the Constitutional Court cannot do so in light of the current law. Otherwise, both the Civil Code's conditionality pertaining to the legal capacity of the fetus as well as the criminal law's distinction between abortion and manslaughter would lose its rationale, and the legal system would be mired in self-contradiction. [....]

In the provisions of the Constitution, according to current law, "man" refers to the born, separated from the mother. Every human being born has legal capacity, every born person is endowed with legal capacity. I do not share the view that one cannot derive from the Constitution a position regarding the status of the fetus. A grammatical, literal interpretation of the Constitution would not be incompatible with the conceptualization of fetus as a "human person." But given that this would prompt an essential modification to the approach of the Hungarian legal system, such an interpretation would require a firm and certain pronouncement. [....]

[....] The existing Hungarian legal system—consistent with the Constitution—treats the fetal life as a value to be protected, but it does not recognize the fetus as a legal subject, viewing it instead as an independent and unique object of public law. Our legal system does so by statutory regulation (Civil Code, Criminal Code, Health Act). Hence, this is not a preliminary question to be addressed in order to analyze further the conflicts. [....]

5. The Constitutional Court accordingly must conclude on the basis of the text of the Constitution and the context of the Hungarian legal system that the fetus is not a legal subject, though biologically human, and it is not recognized as a "man" in the constitutional sense. Accordingly, the fetus has no independent, inalienable and inviolable rights stemming from personality.

In the view of the Constitutional Court, Art. 54(1) does not preclude the legislature from conferring human rights on the fetus. But in so doing, it must be aware that the relationship of the mother and the fetus is a special one—precisely because of their physical interconnection—and it is not susceptible to the kind of legal regulation traditionally applied to the relationship of two independent persons; their confrontation can only be comparative, and in any case it requires specific statutory regulation.

6. In fact, precisely on account of human dignity, the legislature ought to reflect on the ramifications of recognizing the fetus as a human being, an independent legal subject. For in this case it must ensure that this independent legal subject is protected by society—even in opposition to the other legal subject carrying it in the womb—to afford legal protection and representation to the fetus in the event of its rights conflicting with those of others, and in order to do this the institutions entrusted with the protection of the fetus would have to be convinced of the existence of the fetus as a first step. The ancient laws which posited that the foetus was part of the mother did not espouse a biological position. The most ancient Babylonian laws treated the fetus as an independent life form susceptible to being violated by the intervention of a third person. But they recoiled from establishing a legal relationship between the mother and the fetus, since the inner family circle itself was deemed legally unitary and the intra-familial relationships were only morally regulated. Even today it is not devoid of risks to go beyond this—despite the expansion of the "individualization" of the fetus. The administrative, artificial and repetitive intervention into the family circle which would be required, poses a great danger to the sphere of family intimacy, not only for the

mothers but for the children as well. In this case the "medicine" may do more harm than good. [....]

III

[....]

2. (a) [....] Thus, fetal life does not carry with it legal subjectivity but it is a protected, indeed an exaltedly protected "legal object" within society. This is illustrated by the prohibition of abortion by criminal law, by the various constitutional provisions protecting the pregnant mother, as well as a host of social legislation, including the aforementioned provisions of the Health Act. Through its regulations concerning the mother, the legal system exalts the protection of the fetus, endeavouring to secure the conditions required for its healthy development and to ensure that it can be born, thus becoming a legal subject, a human being in the legal sense. [....]

(b) The compatibility between the protection of human life as a social value and the mother's human dignity can only be brought about if the mother has an unrestricted freedom in deciding whether she wants to have a child. If as a consequence of the mother's voluntary act a child is conceived, even if that was not the goal intended and the possibility was not perhaps carefully contemplated, the determination of the fetus's fate can no longer be based on the mother's human dignity. Carrying the child to its full term is the human moral duty of the mother. The law can transform a moral duty into a legal one. Such a statutory regulation would not be in conflict with the text of the Constitution, but this duty can only be eventually derived (Art. 54(1) of the Constitution read in conjunction with art. 169 of the Criminal Code and s. 29(4) of the 1972 Health Act), thereby requiring legislative resolution. In case the legislature were to treat the fetus as a human being, then based on the traditional legislative logic every artifically induced abortion would have to be criminally punished, and only a conflict between the mother and child's life could provide a basis for precluding criminal liability. But the special relationship between the mother and the fetus would also justify the attempt to create special regulations within this area. For the prohibition of surgically induced abortion does not merely limit the opportunities for freedom of action of select individuals in favour of other interests; this prohibition at the same time imposes an affirmative duty, the carrying and giving birth to the child, thus subjugating a human's life and personality to the service of another interest to an extent which has no analogy in society.

(c) Arising as a separate question is the constitutionality of the content of the Council of Ministers Decree 76/1988 (XI.3) MT, para. 2(d): in the event that the act leading to conception was not voluntary on the part of the mother, but forced, does it not follow from the mother's dignity that she should decide freely whether or not she keeps and gives birth to the child. If the freedom to give birth is viewed as an essential human right with its substantive content not amenable to restriction, then in this instance we must provide for a contingent-free determination, and if the pregnancy is evidently the outcome of an involuntary act then the mother's decision in the negative following that cannot be considered, from the constitutional perspective, as necessarily illegal. The extent to and the conditions under which the mother's decision would be permitted is dependent on the positive regulations enacted by the legislature. In so doing, the legislature must balance the conflict between the mother's fundamental right stemming from her human dignity and the life of the fetus constituting an object of general protection.

(d) It is a generally accepted legal principle that no one has the right to dispose of human life. (Human life cannot be property. The fetus, even when construed as a legal object is not an object of exchange.) Thus the mother has not only no exclusive right to dispose of the fetus residing in her womb—as claimed by proponents of unrestricted abortion rights—but she has no disposal rights whatsoever. Fetal life is human life, valued as such, and its disposal inside or outside the uterus as an object or property is not condoned by the law.

Since the mother has no right of disposal over the fetus, there is no legal order that could prescribe the sharing of this right of disposal with the father. The negative disposal of the fetus, *viz.,* whether to keep it or not, is not a right conferred on either the father or mother as legal subjects.

In enacting new laws the legislature, in light of Arts. 8(1), 66, 67 and 70/D of the Constitution, cannot resolve the issues by a complete abandonment of the protection of fetal life; it cannot make surgically induced abortion to be dependent solely on the unrestricted decisions of the mother or the parents. Such statutory regulation would be unconstitutional. Given that the current regulation and the practice based thereon approaches that extreme position, its substance, too, is constitutionally doubtful.

3. In what way could surgically induced abortion be constitutional?

[....]

For a law to accord fully with the Constitution it would have to recognize the fundamental value of the life of a child from the overall perspective of society. Welfare, economic and moral assistance conferred upon parents supporting children can be made into a right of the parents. It must be conferred not as a privilege but as a constitutional right within the boundaries of social possibilities. [....] (Cf. Arts. 66–67 of the Constitution).

In the current state of society, it is an indisputable fact that there are situations in which the nurturing of a child would raise serious social problems for a woman. These could be health related or originating from the social position hence worsening not only the mother's but also her family's material situation. In these cases the mother's indisputable right to life, health and social success conflicts with the mother's moral obligation and the State's duty under public law to protect every human life. The boundaries of this conflict must be defined by the legislature, which, when the need arises, must also attempt to balance the conflicting interests.

(a) [....] The life of the fetus can be sacrificed to save the mother's life.

(b) A harder question is when the duty to protect the life of the fetus conflicts with the duty or right to protect the mother's health (Council of Ministers Decree 76/1988 (XI.3) MT, para. 2(a)). Legal systems and judicial practice in general interpret "health" broadly to mean a right to complete physical and psychological well-being. But in any given case, to determine whether and the extent to which the life in the process of creation would endanger the well-being of the mother is not easy even for medical science, while proving almost impossible for the law. [....] This question involves the mother's moral responsibility on the one hand, and the professional and ethical responsibility of the doctor on the other hand, though the legislature need merely to restrict or make available, within the boundaries it deems fit, the freedom for the realization of the intention and the enforcement of legal duties, dissolving the conflict between the protection of life, based on Art. 54 of the Constitution, and the individual right to health, derived from Art. 70/D(1) of the Constitution.

(c) Undoubtedly, it is possible that in a given case the birth of a child can result in difficulties with regard to the self-assertion and conduct in a woman's life and can lead to a major alteration in her social situation and relations. (Council of Ministers Decree (XI.3)

MT, para. 2(c) and (e)–(i) sought to redress this problem.) But the human right to social fulfillment can never be classified as a fundamental human right which justifies risking human life. [....]

(d) [....] According to the Constitutional Court, these latter social welfare considerations must be contemplated by the mother and her family prior to deciding whether to have a child. To allow surgically induced abortion on the basis of material considerations cannot under any circumstance be viewed as a constitutional right. (At most, the material consideration may, within narrow limits, constitute an excuse from the duty to protect life.) In view of the mother's guaranteed right to freedom of conscience, the use of the Criminal Code to pressure her to fulfill her moral and human duties may not necessarily be needed; however, the protection of life and the risk to the health of the pregnant woman, as well as the placing of the unborn child at risk, should spur the legislature to alleviate the financial and social burdens imposed by child rearing rather than loosening the restraints on the availability of surgically induced abortions. [....]

DECISION 9/1992: 30 JANUARY 1992

ON THE PROTEST OF ILLEGALITY

The decision abolished a kind of extraordinary appeal, inherited from the socialist legal system, the admissibility of which was dependent on the free discretion of the President of the Supreme Court or the Chief Public Prosecutor. The case is one of the first applications of the "living law" conception (57/1991), having considered the factual use of the "protest of illegality" as a substitute for the second-level appeal. The case is also the starting point for the new conception of the Constitutional Court on the rule of law clause of the Constitution: from now on any violation of the rule of law clause in itself—without encumbrances on other, named constitutional rights—is a sufficient basis for unconstitutionality. This was made possible by the elaboration of the content and tests of the rule of law. The most important among these is legal certainty, the career of which also began with this decision. Finally, the case is the first in the series of decisions preparing the way for the retroactive criminal legislation case (11/1992).

The petitioner sought a determination of the unconstitutionality of the legal rules governing the protest of illegality.

The protest of illegality permitted the President of the Supreme Court or the Chief Public Prosecutor to lodge a protest against any final judgment of a court, whether civil or criminal, if they deemed such judgment to be unfounded or a violation of the law. Such protest, for which there was no limitation period in lodging, was decided upon by a panel of three Supreme Court judges or, if the protest were against a Supreme Court judgment, by the Presidential Panel of that Court. Their decision could either reject the protest or hold that the challenged judgment was unfounded or violated the law. Such decision bound the parties to the action subject to certain qualifications, *viz.,* that (i) in a criminal case a heavier punishment could not be imposed through a protest after a year of the coming into force of the challenged final judgment; (ii) in a civil case only a protest lodged within a year of the final judgment could give rise to a decision binding the parties; and (iii) in respect of a civil procedural matter, the challenged final judgment might be annulled, partially or totally, only if the effect of the judgment extended to the parties and the violated procedural rule had no substantial impact on the judgment of the merits.

The petitioners submitted, inter alia, that (a) the protest violated the principle of the rule of law under Art. 2(1): in particular it was discretionary in nature thereby rendering it possible for illegal judgments to remain in force; further such a protest could be decided by the President of the Supreme Court or the Chief Public Prosecutor without reasons; and (b) art. 270(1) of the Code on Civil Procedure permitted these two named persons to lodge a protest against any final judgment in a civil action. Such provision violated Arts. 35(1)(a) and (b) and 51(1) and (3) since parties to the action were not forced to lodge a protest even if a violation of the law had occurred.

Held, granting the petitions:

(1) The protest of illegality was unconstitutional. Although in principle applicable only in extraordinary cases to obtain a ruling on legal uniformity, the protest of illegality had through judicial practice also to come to fulfill the function of a legal remedy. On the one hand, in respect of its latter function, the protest would have been constitutional if it had conferred on the parties affected a defined and qualified right of standing so that the Supreme Court would have been able to judge the alleged violation of law and so render a decision on the merits which bound the parties. In fact the parties had no rights at all to have the Chief Public Prosecutor or the President of the Supreme Court lodge a protest on their behalf who alone had the standing, guided by their discretion, to decide in which cases to lodge and to initiate a protest. On the other hand, uniform court practice, which offered appropriate guidelines on legal principles, required a right to choose between cases; such a function could not be fulfilled through a review mandatory upon a party's request. A decision on the uniformity of the courts' practice neither invalidated nor arbitrarily modified one judgment among the many because a decision had to be made; further its aim was not to provide a legal remedy in the individual case neither could it consider the constitutional dimensions thereof. Consequently the introduction of constitutional requirements necessary to protect one function of the protest necessarily precluded the other.

(2) The protest of illegality was also contrary to the principle of the rule of law, and in particular legal certainty under Art. 2(1), which formed a part thereof. The whole of the legal proceedings were clouded by uncertainty since the two entitled persons might change the final judgment independently of the wishes of the parties, based on deliberations lacking any objective restrictions. Following a final judgment (itself perhaps the result of an appeal) proceedings might be recommenced: indeed, on the basis of repeated protests of illegality, such proceedings could in practice be recommenced several times. Since legal certainty embodied predictability in the application of the laws and in legal proceedings, the protest rendered it fundamentally uncertain.

(3) Moreover the protest was contrary to the institutions of the finality of judgments. A necessary requirement for the overturning of a final judgment is that the criteria for so doing are predictable and determined by law. The protest failed to satisfy this criteria: the "violation of the law" and the "unfoundedness" of the challenged judgment were themselves vague concepts and subject to broad interpretation. But what above all rendered it vague was that the Chief Public Prosecutor and the President of the Supreme Court had the discretion to refuse to lodge the protest even if by their own interpretation there had been such a violation or the decision was unfounded. It was not certain therefore in which case a protest would be lodged and since the parties to the proceedings had themselves no right to lodge a protest, there was no need to give a reason for its rejection. There was also a possibility that a very serious violation of criminal law, revealed in judging the protest, would result merely in a declaration that such a violation had occurred; alternatively, the final judgment might be modified to impose a harsher punishment on the convict.

(4) The forfeiture of the parties' right to decide with regard to the lodging of a protest violated not only the right to self-determination under Art. 54(1) but also within the right of a party to civil dispute to litigate the matter under Art. 57(1), the freedom not to exercise that right. In civil proceedings the protest thus violated the parties' right to instruct since it

could be lodged in any case without regard to the particulars thereof and could result in a modification of the final judgment with binding effect on the affected parties, independent of or even contrary to their wishes. This violation of basic principles of civil procedure consequently amounted to a violation of the right to self-determination.

(5) The legal regulation of the protest also violated the principle of judicial independence under Arts. 50(3) and 57(1). The lodging of the protest gravely interfered with judicial decision making because the discretionary determination by the authorized persons disturbed a case already subject to a final judgment. The Chief Public Prosecutor could suspend or stay the execution of the challenged judgment and order the necessary urgent relief. A protest lodged by the President of the Supreme Court was determined by a committee under his direction: thus a protest against a Supreme Court decision would be adjudicated upon by the Presidential Panel of the Supreme Court the head of which was the President himself. Such procedures were necessarily incompatible with the independence of the judiciary.

(6) The protest of illegality lodged against a convicted person or because of the prosecutor's dismissal of a case violated legal certainty and the rules according to which a criminal prosecution had to proceed within strict substantive and procedural limits, with the risk of failure or commission of errors resting with the State. With the lodging of the protest against him, the burden was arbitrarily shifted onto the criminal. The risk of failure to prosecute or of errors was therefore also shifted onto the accused and opened up the possibility that a harsher sentence would be imposed on him.

IN THE NAME OF THE REPUBLIC OF HUNGARY!

In the matter of the petitions seeking an ex post facto review of the unconstitutionality of legal rules, the Constitutional Court has made the following

DECISION.

The Constitutional Court holds that the legal institution of "the protest of illegality" [the discretionary ex officio and ex parte challenge of a final judgment] is unconstitutional. For this reason the Constitutional Court declares the legal rules pertaining to the lodging of such a protest null and void, effective from 31 December 1992. Those rules of criminal procedure according to which a protest of illegality may impose a more disadvantageous treatment on a convicted person than was imposed by the final judgment are declared by the Constitutional Court null and void effective from the date of publication of this Decision.

Accordingly, with the date of publication of this Decision the following provisions of Act I/1973 on the Code of Criminal Procedure (hereafter referred to as the Code of Criminal Procedure) shall no longer have any effect:

—The second and third sentences of art. 285;

—The clause of art. 287(3), which states that "after the passing of one year from the entry into force of the challenged judgment";

—The first sentence of art. 288(6) and part of the second sentence, stating that "if subpoenaed, in any event, and if notified," and part of the third sentence, stating that "or the protest of illegality was lodged against the convicted person";

—The clause of art. 288(8) which states that "the subpoenaed accused in custody or";

—The clause of art. 290(4) which states that "if the accused is at large the requisite coercive measures may be ordered";

—The first sentence of art. 290(5) and part of the clause stating "in other cases" from the second sentence therein.

These rules remain in effect until 31 December 1992, with the following text:

Article 285. A protest of illegality has no delaying force; however, the President of the Supreme Court or the Chief Public Prosecutor may suspend or interrupt the execution of a challenged judgment pending the adjudication of the protest.

Article 287(3). No graver punishment may be imposed on a convicted person pursuant to a protest of illegality than was determined by the challenged final judgment, and only the existence of an illegality may be determined; this limitation applies to a procedure initiated anew because of a prior vacating of a final judgment pursuant to a successful protest of illegality.

Article 288(6). An accused person in custody must be arraigned upon his or his defence lawyer's request. The defence lawyer must be subpoenaed to attend the arraignment hearing if defence was obligatory in the procedure.

Article 288(8). The hearing may not take place in the absence of the Chief Public Prosecutor or his representative and the subpoenaed defence lawyer.

Article 290(4). If the Supreme Court invalidates the final judgment and the convicted person is in custody, the Supreme Court must make a decision on the matter of bail.

Article 290(5). The cost of the criminal procedure is borne by the State.

With the publication of this Decision, arts. 284(2), 288(2)(b) and 290(2)(d) of the Code of Criminal Procedure are likewise declared null and void.

Effective from 31 December 1992 the following shall no longer have any effect:

—Article 270 of Act III/1952 on the Code of Civil Procedure;

—Section 10(2) of Act IV/1972 on the Judiciary, and that part of s. 33(2) thereof which states that "a protest of illegality may be brought against the final judgment of any court";

—Section 33(2)(a) remains in force with the following text: "(2) The President of the Supreme Court (a) may request the files of any court during any stage of its proceedings; he may order the case for hearing to the Supreme Court as an appellate court";

—Section 5(2)(f),(g) of Act V/1972 on Prosecution;

—Article 284(1) of Act I/1973 on the Code of Criminal Procedure.

The Constitutional Court orders the review of all those criminal proceedings in which the convicted person received a harsher punishment pursuant to a protest of illegality than was originally imposed by the final judgment, provided that the convicted person has not already been relieved of all disadvantageous consequences of being sentenced.

The Constitutional Court rejects the petition seeking the vacating of final judgments.

The Constitutional Court publishes its Decision in the *Hungarian Official Gazette.*

REASONING

SÓLYOM, P., delivering the Opinion of the Court: [....]

II

The essence of the current regulation of the protest of illegality is that the President of the Supreme Court or the Chief Public Prosecutor may lodge a protest against any final judgment of a court if that judgment is deemed to be unfounded or in violation of the law. The protest is judged by a panel of three sitting judges of the Supreme Court or by the Presidential Panel of the Supreme Court if the protest is lodged against a judgment of the Supreme Court. In the judgment made pursuant to such a protest of illegality, the Supreme Court either rejects the protest as being without merit or holds that the challenged judgment violates the law or is unfounded. There is no limitation period for lodging such a protest of illegality. The effect of the judgment made pursuant to a protest of illegality binds the parties to the action with the following qualifications. In a criminal matter, after one year of the entry into effect of the challenged final judgment, no punishment more burdensome to the convicted person may be imposed by a judgment made pursuant to a protest of illegality. In a civil matter, only protests of illegality lodged within one year of the final judgment may result in decisions binding on the parties. In a civil procedure, the challenged judgment may only be partially or fully vacated if the effect of the judgment extends to the parties, except when such a procedural rule was violated which had no substantial impact on the judgment on the merits of the case. [....]

IV

This protest of illegality, in principle applicable only in extraordinary cases, has in fact become "a third-instance safety valve" of the theoretically one-level system of appeal or an unacknowledged substitute for a second appeal. Individual legal protection, originally purely supplementary and infrequently applied, has become in practice the first-order priority. This is demonstrated by the number of petitions for protest of illegality, the absolute number of protests lodged, their numbers relative to the cases in which final judgments have been entered, as well as by the fact that the number of protests of illegality lodged in the interest of uniformity in court practice more than one year after the entry of final judgment are negligible, comprising less than 1 percent, further that the so-called principled protest—those lodged within a year but without a binding effect on the merits—exists only in theory. By virtue of its use, the protest of illegality is of the nature of a legal remedy.

The Constitutional Court—in accordance with its position expounded in its reasoning of *Dec. 57/1991 (XI.8) AB* (MK 1991/123; ABH 1991, 272)—does not examine the text of the norm itself, not even in a case of a protest of illegality, but takes judicial notice of the content of that norm as consistently and uniformly construed by judicial practice, and it is this "living" norm content which it then compares with the Constitution. Therefore, in the course of examining the constitutionality of the protest of illegality, the Constitutional

Court gave appropriate weight to the fact that in judicial practice this institution invariably fulfills a legal remedy function as well.

V

1. In the case of the institution of the protest of illegality, the functions of legal remedy and the uniformity of the courts' practice combine in a manner whereby neither one meets the constitutional requirements and, indeed, the realization of the constitutional requirements necessary for one task is not made possible by the other. For the protest of illegality to fulfill its function as a legal remedy in a constitutional manner, it would have to confer on the affected parties a defined and qualified right to call upon the Supreme Court to adjudicate the alleged violation of the law in a manner that would permit a decision on the merits to be reached with binding effect on the parties. In contrast, the parties have no rights whatsoever to have the Chief Public Prosecutor or the President of the Supreme Court lodge a protest of illegality on their behalf. These entitled persons, guided by their discretion, choose the cases in which a protest of illegality is lodged, although the majority of cases they choose are ones in which the parties have sought a review of the final judgment and a modification of the judgment affecting them. But the decision delivered pursuant to a protest of illegality may only have binding effect on the parties if the protest were lodged within one year of the final judgment coming into force, and the timing of the initiation of the protest of illegality likewise depends on the will of the parties with standing to lodge a protest. But the introduction of the safeguards conceptually required for the legal remedy is precluded by the legal uniformity function of the protest of illegality. For decisions on the uniformity of court practice—offering guidelines on legal principles when deemed appropriate—the right to choose among the cases is required. Such a function could not be maintained, even in principle, by a review which is mandatory upon a party's request. By its nature, a decision on the uniformity of court practice does not invalidate the finality of judgments and it may not arbitrarily modify one judgment among the many falling within its scope simply because the necessity of rendering a decision has been determined in connection with this case. In general, the moulding of uniformity in court practice has nothing to do with a protest of alleging the judgment to be unfounded. Indeed, the remedy of unlawful judgments may also be unrelated to the problem of uniformity in court practice. The aim of a decision on the uniformity of court practice is not to provide a legal remedy in the individual case, neither can it consider the constitutional dimensions of the latter. And even if the protest serves neither uniform court practice nor individual legal remedy but another distinctly conceived goal—"the guarantee of legality"—the functions of the institutions sketched above may still not be reduced to a common denominator, and rather than supplying the missing requirements this third goal impedes in a further way the creation of the requirements necessary for either objective. It is a self-contradictory institution which makes the redress of violations of law, and its binding effect on the parties, dependent on the discretionary decision of the two entitled persons, the exercise of which is not obligatory even in the event of a manifest violation of a law, even where a criminal conviction arose therefrom to the disadvantage of the accused.

The institution of the protest of illegality is also contrary to the principle of legal certainty making up the content of the principle of the rule of law (Art. 2(1) of the Constitution), the institution of finality of judgments and—in civil cases—the parties' right of disposal.

2. Article 2(1) of the Constitution states that the "Republic of Hungary is an independent, democratic state under the rule of law." This general provision of the Constitution declares the basic values of the republic: independence, democracy and the rule of law. The principle of the rule of law is expounded in further detail by other provisions of the Constitution, although these provisions do not comprise the whole content of this fundamental value, and hence the interpretation of the notion of the rule of law is one of the Constitutional Court's important tasks. The principles comprising the fundamental value of the rule of law are expounded by the Constitutional Court on a case-by-case basis. Although in the constitutional review the Constitutional Court primarily examines the compatibility of the challenged regulations with specific provisions of the Constitution, this does not mean that the general provisions are seen as formal declarations and that the fundamental principles are consigned to a secondary, mere auxiliary role. The violation of the fundamental value of the rule of law enumerated in the Constitution is in itself a ground for declaring a certain legal rule unconstitutional.

3. Legal certainty is an indispensable component of the rule of law. Legal certainty compels the State—and primarily the legislature—to ensure that the law in its entirety, in its individual parts and in its specific legal rules, are clear and unambiguous and that their operation is ascertainable and predictable for the addressees of the norm. Thus, legal certainty requires not merely the unambiguity of individual legal norms but also the predictability of the operation of the individual legal institutions. It is for these reasons that procedural guarantees are fundamental for legal certainty. Only by following the formal rules of procedure may a valid legal rule be created, only by complying with the procedural norms do legal institutions operate in a constitutional manner.

4. Notwithstanding this, the principle of legal certainty leaves ample room for balancing and decision-making opportunities for the legislature since the rule of law also demands the realization of other principles, some of which may conflict with the requirement of legal certainty. For instance, the doctrine of equity enabling the making of a just decision in an individual case is contrary to legal certainty in principle. Yet legal certainty is not breached because the scope and conditions of specific exceptions are clarified in advance by the law. This applies both to specific applications of the doctrine of equity (for instance, equitable compensation as contained in art. 347(2) of the Civil Code) and to all those concepts which provide a great margin of appreciation for judges (the predictability of the latter is ensured in a state under the rule of law by a variety of institutions, including those of legal uniformity). The requirement of the rule of law as to substantive justice may be attained within the institutions and guarantees ensuring legal certainty. The Constitution does not confer a right for "substantive justice" in the same way it does not guarantee a right to ensure that no judicial decision shall be unlawful. These are the goals and duties of the state under the rule of law for the realization of which it must establish the appropriate institutions—primarily those providing procedural safeguards—and guarantee the implicated rights. The Constitution therefore confers the right for procedures necessary and, in the majority of cases, appropriate for the realization of substantive justice. Article 57 of the Constitution confers a right for access to justice but does not guarantee that its outcome shall be correct in every instance. But the Constitution contains further procedural safeguards to ensure a fair and lawful judicial decision: the constitutional right to a legal remedy. If a legal institution aimed at the realization of substantive justice or the elimination of errors made in the application of the law operates without precise procedural safeguards comparable with those of ordinary and extraordinary legal remedies, then legal certainty is violated.

The requirements of substantive justice and legal certainty are brought into harmony by the finality of judgments—once more on the basis of the priority of legal certainty. The finality of judgments, in its precise formal and substantive determination, is a constitutional requirement being part of the rule of law. [....] Legal certainty demands that the final judgment—within the scope of the *rationae materiae* and *rationae personae* of the decided issue—shall be binding on both parties involved in the dispute as well as subsequent courts or other authorities. If the requirements for the finality of a judgment have been met, it takes effect irrespective of the correctness of its content.

5. The protest of illegality violates the requirement of legal certainty as judicial proceedings become uncertain in their entirety since a protest by the Chief Public Prosecutor or the President of the Supreme Court may change the final judgment without any objective restrictions and on the basis of deliberations also independent of the parties' will. Following a final judgment—perhaps a result of an appeal itself—proceedings recommence, and, indeed, on the basis of repeated protests of illegality, they may be reinitiated several times in practice. [....]

The protest of illegality is especially contrary to the finality of judgments. A necessary but not sufficient constitutional requirement for the vacating of a final judgment is that the criteria for doing so be precisely determined by law and that they be predictable. The institution of retrial meets this criterion where it is known in advance, in which cases and within what time frame there may be a new trial once the final judgment is entered in a civil case or a criminal matter. With respect to the protest of illegality there is no comparable predictability and certainty: the "violation of the law" and the "unfoundedness" of the challenged judgment are themselves anyhow subject to broad interpretation and are, in fact, vague concepts (which may not be compared with the objective requirements of the discovery of new evidence, for example). Besides that, what makes the institution of the protest of illegality fundamentally vague is that the parties entitled to lodge such a protest are not required to do so even if on their own interpretation there has been a violation of the law or an unfounded decision. It is totally uncertain in which case a protest would finally be lodged. Since the parties to the actions do not have a right to a protest to be lodged, there is no need to give reasons for the rejection of their petition for a protest. But this circumstance, logical in itself, highlights the great extent to which the practical operation of the protest of illegality as a kind of appeal is inconsistent even with the minimum requirement of legal certainty. The discretionary right to lodge the protest—given that it is used for individual legal protection—also violates equality before the law whenever one of the two authorized persons lodges a protest in one case, while in another comparable situation fails to do so, or when he lodges a protest on behalf of one party while ignoring the other party's request without an explanation. [....]

6. [....] The root of the unconstitutionality of the protest of illegality is the discretionary power conferred on those entitled to lodge a protest. But this characteristic feature cannot be altered within the framework of the institution because the function of uniformity in court practice, which confers its legitimacy, would be incompatible with a compulsory protest, based on fixed criteria and without the possibility of the selection of cases and it would especially be contradictory to the parties' right to lodge such a protest.

7. In conclusion it can be stated that the legal institution of the protest of illegality is contrary to legal certainty comprising the rule of law and the finality of judgments serving that end. Although in practice it is used for the purposes of a legal remedy, the protest lacks the basic constitutional guarantees of the right of legal remedy. The violation of these rights

may not be justified by the fact that such a restriction may be unavoidably necessary in the interest of the realization of other constitutional rights and that the magnitude of the violation would be proportional. On the contrary: discretionary power can never be in principle a pressingly necessary means to realize either legality or substantive justice at the expense of fundamental values giving stability to the rule of law. The realization either of legality or substantive justice through an arbitrary selection is not constitutional. [....]

DECISION 10/1992: 25 FEBRUARY 1992

ON POWERS *EX NUNC*

Seemingly only dealing with a dogmatic question of the effect of Constitutional Court decisions, this case is decisive for the theory of the Constitutional Court on the constitutional meaning of the system change. Its reinforcing the role of legal certainty has been important both for compensation cases and for the continuity theory, fully developed in the immediately following case on the statute of limitations (11/1992).

The petitioners sought constitutional review and annulment of s. 43 of Act XXXII/ 1989 in the Constitutional Court.

Section 43(1) provides that a legal rule declared null and void by the Constitutional Court may not be applied commencing from the date the Court's decision is published in the *Hungarian Official Gazette* (*i.e.*, it is effective prospectively, *ex nunc*).

The petitioners submitted that, on the basis of legal certainty, a violation of the Constitution could only be remedied by a retroactive (*i.e., ex tunc*) nullification. Legal certainty was infringed by an *ex nunc* invalidation since this left intact legal relationships which had come into existence on an unconstitutional basis.

Held, rejecting the petition:

(1) Legal certainty, as part of the rule of law under Art. 2(1), was not violated by *ex nunc* invalidation of an unconstitutional legal rule, which thereby left intact those legal relationships which had come into existence on a (now) unconstitutional basis. Considerations of legal certainty were separate from those of the nullity of a legal rule especially concerning legal relationships created on the basis of unconstitutional legal rule. The individual legal relationships and legal facts became independent of the underlying norms: thus they did not share automatically the fate of those norms, otherwise every change in a legal rule would involve the review of all relevant legal relationships.

(2) Legal certainty had been borne in mind when drafting the Constitutional Court Act. In harmonizing the principle with the constitutional reviewability of all laws in force, the Act provided that legal rules would lose their validity upon the date of publication of the decision determining their unconstitutionality and that legal relationships created prior thereto were to remain intact. Intervention into the latter relationships was legally permitted only if such intervention was demanded by another rule of law principle competing with that of legal certainty. For example, in harmony with fundamental principles of constitutional criminal law, s. 43(3) of the Act mandated the review of a final judgment in criminal proceedings for the benefit of a convicted person. In principle this would be detrimental to legal certainty were the provision not to state that it was applicable only if the detrimental consequences of the punishment were still in force.

IN THE NAME OF THE REPUBLIC OF HUNGARY!

In the matter of a petition seeking an ex post facto review of the unconstitutionality of a legal rule, the Constitutional Court has made the following

DECISION.

The Constitutional Court rejects the petition seeking a determination and declaration of nullity of s. 43 of Act XXXII/1989 on the Constitutional Court.

The Constitutional Court rejects the petition seeking a modification of its *Dec. 27/ 1991 (V.20) AB* (MK 1991/53; ABH 1991, 73) and, furthermore, the retroactive nullification of previously invalidated legal rules.

The Constitutional Court orders the publication of this Decision in the *Hungarian Official Gazette.*

REASONING

SÓLYOM, P., delivering the Opinion of the Court:

I

The petitioners consider unconstitutional that regulation of s. 43(1) of Act XXXII/1989 on the Constitutional Court (hereafter referred to as the Constitutional Court Act), which stipulates as the principal rule that a legal provision declared null and void by the Constitutional Court may not be applied commencing from the date of the decision's publication in the *Hungarian Official Gazette* (*i.e.,* it is effective *ex nunc*). It is the petitioners' contention that a violation of the Constitution may only be effectively remedied by a retroactive (*i.e., ex tunc*) nullification of the legal rule violating the Constitution. In their brief the petitioners do not cite particular constitutional provisions which, in their view, contradict the legal rule they challenge but, instead, they invoke the principle of legal certainty. It is their contention that legal certainty is violated by the fact that an *ex nunc* invalidation of an unconstitutional legal rule leaves intact legal relationships which came into being from an unconstitutional foundation.

II

1. The Constitutional Court holds that the consequences of the unconstitutionality of a legal rule, as defined by s. 43 of the Constitutional Court Act are, indeed, connected with the requirement of legal certainty, which is to be regarded as part of the rule of law declared by Art. 2(1) of the Constitution. The question is, therefore, whether s. 43 of the Constitutional Court Act is contrary to Art. 2(1) of the Constitution.

2. According to Art. 32/A(2) of the Constitution, in the event of a determination of unconstitutionality, the Constitutional Court nullifies the statutes and other legal rules. The Constitutional Court Act defines the consequences of the determination of unconstitutionality by using three different terms: the Constitutional Court annuls the legal rule (s. 40), in which case the legal rule loses force on the day of the publication of the decision (s. 42(1)), and from that day onward it must not be applied (s. 43(1)). The principal rule, therefore, is invalidation *ex nunc;* s. 43(2) supports this conclusion by stating separately that the nullification of a legal rule does not affect the legal relationships arising prior to the publication of the decision or the rights and duties arising therefrom.

As an exception from this rule, s. 43(4) of the Constitutional Court Act renders it possible for the Constitutional Court to invalidate a legal rule *ex tunc,* that is, retroactively, or even to determine invalidation as being effective from a future date.

The same paragraph also provides that where the application of an unconstitutional legal rule to a concrete dispute is in question the Constitutional Court may decide on the applicability contrary to the principal rule, that is, it may determine the consequences of the unconstitutionality for certain legal relationship on a case-by-case basis, retroactively as well as prospectively. However, concerning the consequences of an unconstitutional legal rule serving as the basis for a final judgment in a criminal proceeding, the Constitutional Court is compelled to arrive at a single conclusion: the court must order a review of the judgment if the convicted person has not yet received relief from the detrimental repercussions of having been sentenced and if the nullification of the legal rule applied in the case would lead to a reduction or setting aside of the punishment or an exculpation from criminal liability (s. 43(3)).

3. The Constitutional Court Act regulates the consequences of the unconstitutionality of a legal rule with respect to the unconstitutional legal rule itself as well as concerning the legal relationships previously created thereon. This topic is not identical to the problem of nullity. (Such a question of nullity is, for instance, whether a legal rule contrary to the Constitution is, in principle, null and void or merely voidable; whether a legal rule contrary to the Constitution, upon its enactment, comes into being as a legal rule at all; whether a Constitutional Court decision merely declares the existence of nullity; [...] *etc.*) Since nullity differs from annulment, petitioners' reasoning that annulment must conceptually be exclusively retroactive is not sound. Annulment, which in legal parlance always means a constitutive decision, may be either *ex nunc* or *ex tunc,* and, indeed, it may even designate a date subsequent to the publication of the decision. In contrast, nullity is a quality which exists *ab initio,* with respect to which it is meaningless to pose questions concerning the timing of a legal consequence.

The Constitutional Court Act takes no position on theoretical and legal dogmatic problems concerning nullity. Nor is there a need to do so in the Constitutional Court's view since a dogmatic classification of nullity has no decisive influence on the issue whether deriving legal consequences from unconstitutionality is itself constitutional. Different considerations govern the theoretical classification of nullity than the practical arrangement of the consequences of nullity in a manner which leave intact where possible the existing rights and concluded legal relationships. The consequences of the unconstitutionality of a legal rule must be ordered in such a way that it really results in legal certainty and this constitutional requirement is more important than the consistent application of theories on nullity. Following a given doctrine of nullity serves legal certainty at most in principle only by being suitable for some non-contradictory descriptive theory of the legal system. Considerations of legal certainty diverge from that of the nullity of a legal rule especially concerning legal relationships created on the basis of the unconstitutional legal rule. The individual legal relationships and legal facts become independent of the underlying norms and they do not automatically share the fate of the latter. Were this otherwise, every change in a legal rule would involve the review of the multitude of legal relationships.

This is the reason why foreign laws on constitutional courts either address only the legal consequences of unconstitutionality, or—if a theoretical position concerning nullity may be discerned in their regulation—they do not address every conceivable consequence of this theoretical position and, in the interest of legal certainty, they have separate provisions addressing those legal relationships which came into being from the null and void legal rules. In the area of the Constitutional Court's review the requirement of legal certainty may be satisfied in a variety of ways. One may imagine a system where only the constitutionality of "new" legal rules may be examined, that is, only a short period of time is provided for challenging a legal rule upon its coming into force. It is possible that a law permits only a prospective invalidation of a legal rule. Another known solution is whereby the Constitutional Court Act mandates that the constitutional court declares the "nullity" of a legal rule but the Act does not permit the consequences of this decision to be given effect to already-concluded legal relationships.

4. The regulation by the Constitutional Court Act is in harmony with the requirement of legal certainty. The Constitutional Court Act does not impose restrictions on the challenging of legal regulations by their date of coming into force, the constitutionality of any legal rule may be subject to enquiry irrespective of the duration of its being in force or the multitude of legal relationships which were built upon them. In the interest of legal certainty such a free hand in intervening in past legal situations must be counterbalanced by some restrictions. Such a treatment of the past is made especially justified by the fact that almost simultaneously with the passing of the Constitutional Court Act the Constitution was comprehensively amended; thus the legislature had to be aware that the Constitutional Court would also review legal rules enacted prior to the constitutional amendment, based upon the new Constitution. Yet it would work to the detriment of legal certainty if as the chief rule the Constitutional Court would nullify such legal rules with retroactive force which came into being prior to the Constitution now in force, and if as a result of this retroactivity such legal relationships would have to be regarded as invalid which came into being at a time when the divergent value system and rules of the Constitution now in force were not foreseeable. Thus, it was precisely legal certainty which the Constitutional Court Act considered, and regulated in harmony with the constitutional reviewability of all the laws in force, when it made the principal rule that unconstitutional legal rules lose their validity upon the day of publication of the decision determining their unconstitutionality and that legal relationships created previously would remain intact.

Concurrently, the Constitutional Court Act renders it possible for the Constitutional Court to diverge from the rule of *ex nunc* invalidation if in a given case a different date would better serve legal certainty. For instance, in order to avoid a legal vacuum the Constitutional Court frequently provides time for the enactment of new regulations with its prospective nullifications. The Constitutional Court has an opportunity to exercise *ex tunc* invalidation as well, just as it may apply the consequences of unconstitutionality individually to legal relationships. Thus, by law the Constitutional Court may exercise these prerogatives in the interest of legal certainty and it may consider the especially important interests of a petitioner—the latter evidently employed in the event of a constitutional complaint. Intervention into already concluded legal relationships is prescribed by law only in the event such intervention is demanded by another rule of law principle competing with that of legal certainty. It is in such a manner, in harmony with the fundamental principles of constitutional criminal law, that s. 43(3) of the Constitutional Court Act mandates the review of a final judgment in criminal proceedings for the benefit of a convicted person. In principle this is detrimental to legal certainty. The contradiction is solved by the Constitutional Court Act in stating that s. 43 is applicable only if the detrimental consequences of the punishment are still in force.

III

With respect to the petitioners' request that the Constitutional Court modify a previously delivered decision, the Constitutional Court declared that it lacks jurisdiction. According to s. 27 of the Constitutional Court Act a decision of the Constitutional Court may not be appealed and the decision of the Constitutional Court is binding on everyone. In the event the Constitutional Court's position changes regarding some legal question this will be expressed in a new decision delivered on another occasion. It is an entirely different matter that with respect to certain mistakes (misspellings, for instance) the Constitutional Court has an opportunity for correcting its decision (*Dec. 20/1990 (XI.27) AB:* MK 1990/98; ABH 1990, 69). But the petitioner here requests the Constitutional Court to review its position on a legal question in the form of modifying a previous decision. For this reason the Constitutional Court rejects this part of the petition.

The petitioners sought the *ex tunc* nullification of the previously invalidated legal rule affecting detrimentally the property and personality of Hungarian citizens who have left the country illegally. The jurisdiction of the Constitutional Court in the event of an abstract norm control extends only to a constitutional review of those legal rules which are in force at the time of the proceedings. A constitutional review of a legal rule already invalidated is possible only if in a concrete case such an enquiry is initiated by a judge, pursuant to s. 38 of the Constitutional Court Act, concerning the constitutionality of a case pending before him or her (*Dec. 34/1991 (VI.15) AB:* MK 1991/65; ABH 1991, 170) or if the question of the applicability of the already invalidated legal rule is raised pursuant to a constitutional complaint. In the present case neither condition is met, and for this reason the Constitutional Court rejected the petition seeking a review of the constitutionality of previously invalidated legal rule and its retroactive nullification.

DECISION 11/1992: 5 MARCH 1992

ON RETROACTIVE CRIMINAL LEGISLATION

All new democracies have to face the problem of the prosecution and punishment of politically motivated crimes committed—and not prosecuted and even encouraged or promoted—during the former nondemocratic regimes, as was and has been the case from Argentina to South Africa and the postcommunist states. Here the natural demand for justice may conflict with constitutional boundaries of the applicability of criminal law, especially the retroactive amendment of statutory limitations. Under the special circumstances of the transition to democracy in Hungary, especially with regard to legal continuity, the special importance of the formal procedural guarantees, and legal certainty, the Constitutional Court gave priority to the constitutional prohibition of retroactive criminal legislation. In this case, the Court defined its theory of the constitutional meaning of the transition, the concept of the "revolution under the rule of law"—keeping in mind that there are constitutional means for rendering justice other than setting aside the rule of law. Later, the Court helped to resolve the problem by the means of international law (53/1993).

The President of the Republic, having declined to promulgate Act IV/1991 on the Prosecution of Serious Criminal Offences not previously prosecuted for Political Reasons, petitioned for a preliminary review of its constitutionality.

He sought to know whether s. 1 of the Act violated the principle of the rule of law under the Constitution, Art. 2(1) and, further, Art. 57(4). In particular, he petitioned, inter alia, as to whether (a) the recommencement of the statute of limitations conflicted with the principle of the rule of law, an essential component of which was legal certainty; (b) s. 1 of the Act amounted to an unconstitutional retroactive criminal law which violated the doctrine of *nullum crimen sine lege,* especially since the statute of limitations for acts criminalized by the section might have already expired according to the Criminal Code in force at the time the acts were committed; (c) the recommencement of the statute of limitations, which had already expired, violated the rule of law, especially legal certainty; (d) overly general provisions and vague concepts violated the principle of legal certainty, *e.g.*, "the State's failure to prosecute its claim was based on political reasons"; and (e) the distinction drawn by the law among perpetrators of the same offence on the basis of the State's reason for prosecuting such offences violated the prohibition of arbitrariness under Art. 54(1) and equal protection of citizens under Art. 70/A(1).

Held, granting the petition:

(1) The ambiguity and vagueness of the Act offended the principle of legal certainty and was accordingly unconstitutional. Since the change of system had proceeded on the principle of legality as imposed by the rule of law, the old law had thereby retained its validity and thus, irrespective of the date of enactment, every law had to comply with the present Constitution. It was possible, however, to give special treatment to the previous law where

legal relationships created by the old (now unconstitutional) law could be harmonized with the new Constitution or where, in judging the constitutionality of new laws intended to remedy unconstitutional measures of the previous systems, the unique historical circumstances of the transition should be taken into consideration. Such matters were to be resolved in conformity with the fundamental principle of the rule of law, of which legal certainty formed a part, that required, inter alia, the protection of vested rights, the non-interference with legal relations already executed or concluded, and the limitation of the possibility of modifying existing long-term legal relations. As a consequence of legal certainty, already concluded legal relations—as a rule—could not be altered constitutionally either by enactment or by invalidation of existing law. Retroactive modification of the law and legal relations were permitted within very narrow limits. Exceptions to legal certainty were permissible only if the constitutional principle competing against it rendered this outcome unavoidable, provided that in fulfilling its objectives it did not impose a disproportionate harm. Accordingly, reference to historical situations and the rule of law's requirement of justice could not be used to set aside legal certainty as a basic guarantee of the rule of law.

(2) As a result, the Act on the recommencement of the statute of limitation overstepped the limits of the State's criminal power. These were guaranteed rights the restriction of which Art. 8(4) did not permit even if other fundamental rights could constitutionally be suspended or restricted. The constitutional guarantees of criminal law could neither be relativized nor be balanced against some other constitutional right or duty since they already contained the result of a balancing act, *i.e.,* the risk of unsuccessful prosecution was borne by the State. The presumption of innocence could not therefore be restricted or denied full effect because of another constitutional right: as a result of the State's inaction, once the time limit for prosecution expired the non-indictability thereby acquired was complete. Considerations of historical circumstances and justice could not therefore be used to gain exemption from the guarantees of criminal law since any such exemption would completely disregard those guarantees, a result precluded by the rule of law.

(3) The Act was also contrary to the principle of the legality of criminal law. Article 8(1) and (2) required offences and their punishment and that the declaration of criminality of an act be regulated only by statute and imposition of punishment had to be necessary, proportional and used only as a last resort. It followed from Art. 57(2), on the presumption of innocence, that only a court of law establishing the defendant's guilt could convict him and from Art. 57(4) that such conviction and punishment could only proceed according to the law in force at the time of commission of the crime. The court was therefore required to judge the offence and punishment in accordance with the law in force when the crime was committed unless a new law was passed subsequent to the offence which prescribed a more lenient punishment or decriminalized the act. This was the necessary result of the prohibition on retroactivity embodied in the principle of legal certainty (foreseeability and predictability), which, in turn, stemmed from the rule of law.

(4) The reimposition of criminal punishability for a crime the statute of limitations for the prosecution of which had already expired was contrary to Arts. 2(1) and 57(4). With the expiration, the criminal responsibility of the offender was irrevocably extinguished and he acquired the right not to be punished since the State was unable to punish him during the period prescribed for the exercise of its punitive powers. It did not matter which method

was used to reimpose punishability (whether the statute of limitations recommenced or ex post facto legislation was imposed to toll the statute) since their constitutionality had to be viewed in the same light as a law retroactively imposing punishment on conduct which, at the time of its commission, did not constitute a criminal offence.

(5) The statutory extension of a statute of limitations which had not yet expired was also unconstitutional. According to law, the prosecuting authorities could suspend and recommence its running with regard to the offender without informing him, with the result that the duration of the suspension extended the statute of limitations: this latter would then represent the minimum rather than the actual time required for termination of the offender's responsibility. Although the statute of limitations did not guarantee that punishability would be extinguished within the initially prescribed time frame, it did ensure the methods of calculating the time expired did not change in a manner detrimental to the offender: the State's punitive powers therefore had to be the same at the time of punishment as at the time of the offence. Consequently the extension of the as yet unexpired statute of limitations was unconstitutional since it would always impose a more onerous burden on the offender. Moreover determination of whether or not the period had expired could not be decided retroactively by the legislature: no law could therefore retroactively declare that the period was "tolled" for reasons which the law in force at the time of the offence and during the running of the statute of limitations did not acknowledge as applicable to that criminal offence. The legal facts determining the commencement and duration of the statute of limitations had to exist during the running of the period, and what did not constitute a legal fact warranting the tolling of the period could not be declared so retroactively.

(6) The incorporation of the condition that the statute of limitations recommenced "if the State's failure to prosecute its claim to punish was based on political reasons" into the Act was unconstitutional. Legal certainty required the predictability of the behaviour of other legal subjects as well as of the authorities themselves, and the condition failed to satisfy this requirement since it did not allow for a meaning which could be determined with sufficient certainty. Further the differentiation contained in the law allowed the recommencing of the statute of limitations for only three of many non-prosecuted crimes and then only for non-prosecution of those three crimes based on political reasons: such differences could only be justified if Parliament sought to apply positive discrimination in favour of those offenders whose actions, while not covered, could have fallen within the scope of the Act. As the Act revealed no reason which could satisfy the constitutional requirement for positive discrimination, it was accordingly contrary to Art. 70/A(1).

IN THE NAME OF THE REPUBLIC OF HUNGARY!

Pursuant to the petition submitted by the President of the Republic seeking a preliminary review of the Act passed by Parliament but not yet promulgated, the Constitutional Court has made the following

DECISION.

The Constitutional Court holds that the Act passed during the 4 November 1991 parliamentary session concerning the Prosecution of Serious Criminal Offences Committed between 21 December 1944 and 2 May 1990 that had not been previously prosecuted for Political Reasons (hereinafter the Act) is unconstitutional.

The Act violates the principle of legal certainty by reason of vagueness and ambiguity in definition.

The Act violates the requirement of constitutional criminal law that the statute of limitations—including the interruption and tolling of the statute of limitations—must be governed by the law in effect at the time of the commission of the crime except that if, during the running of the statute of limitations, laws more favourable to the defendant came into force.

Concerning the question of the constitutionality of the specific provisions of the Act, the Constitutional Court declares the following:

1. Reimposition of criminal punishability for offences whose statutes of limitations had expired is unconstitutional.

2. Extension of the statute of limitations defined by law for criminal offences whose statute of limitations has not yet expired is unconstitutional.

3. Enactment of a law to interrupt the running of the statutes of limitations for criminal offences whose statute of limitations has not yet expired is unconstitutional.

4. The determination of causes for tolling and interruption of the statute of limitations by a retroactive law is unconstitutional.

5. With respect to the running of the statute of limitations, there is no constitutional basis for differentiating between the State's failure to prosecute for political or for other reasons.

6. The vagueness of the statutory definition stating that the "State's failure to prosecute for criminal offences was based on political reasons" is repugnant to the principle of legal certainty, and as a result the tolling of the statute of limitations on such a basis is unconstitutional.

7. It is unconstitutional for the Act to incorporate the crime of treason within its scope without consideration of the fact that the legally protected subject matter has undergone numerous changes under different political systems.

8. Restrictions upon the right of pardon for a partial or total mitigation of punishments, imposed on the basis of the Act, is unconstitutional.

This Decision of the Constitutional Court shall be published in the *Hungarian Official Gazette.*

REASONING

SZABÓ, J. (Parts I, II and IV), and **SÓLYOM, P.** (Parts III and V), delivering the Opinion of the Court:

I

1. The Act adopted at the 4 November 1991 session provides as follows:

Section 1(1). On 2 May 1990, the statute of limitations shall recommence for the prosecution for criminal offences committed between 21 December 1944 and 2 May 1990 which constituted criminal offences under the law in force at the time of the commission of the said offences and are otherwise defined in Act IV/1978 as treason (s. 144(2)), voluntary manslaughter (s. 166(1) and (2)), and infliction of bodily harm resulting in death (s. 170(5)), provided that the State's failure to prosecute the said offences was based on political reasons.

(2) The punishment prescribed under paragraph (1) can be mitigated without any restriction.

Section 2. This Act shall come into force on the day of its promulgation.

2. The President of the Republic did not promulgate the Act and on 16 November 1991 petitioned for the preliminary review of its constitutionality. The petition set forth the following:

> The substance of the [constitutional] concern is whether s. 1 of the Act violates the principle of the rule of law contained in Art. 2(1) of the Constitution and whether it is in violation of Art. 57(4) of the Constitution.
>
> Specifically:
>
> Is not the provision to recommence the period of limitation in conflict with the fundamental constitutional principle stated in Art. 2(1) of the Constitution, according to which the Republic of Hungary is a state under the rule of law? Legal certainty is namely an indispensable component of the rule of law, without which there can be no rule of law.
>
> Does not the language of s. 1 constitute an unconstitutional retroactive criminal law and does it not violate the historically developed legal doctrine of "*nullum crimen sine lege,*" which is internationally recognized as protecting human rights, especially in light of the fact that the statute of limitations for acts punishable by s. 1 may have already expired according to the Criminal Code in force at the time of their commission?
>
> Does the "recommencement" of the statute of limitations, which had already expired, violate the principle of the rule of law? Does not the aforenoted provision contradict the requirement of the rule of law according to which, after the expiry of the statute of limitations, the State promises immunity from prosecution to everyone, and does not the revocation of that promise offend the basic constitutional principle that every citizen can have faith in the trustworthiness of the law and the State?
>
> Is the constitutional principle of legal certainty violated by the overly general provisions and vague concepts contained in the Act such as, inter alia, that "the State's failure to prosecute its claim was based on political reasons"; that the Act refers to high treason and grievous bodily harm without referring to their basic definition; further, that it declares the possibility of unrestricted mitigation of punishment for every case? Finally, can the tolling of the statute of limitations be constitutionally applied to the Criminal Code by way of analogy in view of the fact that the Code's substantive provisions do not permit the use of the doctrine of analogy?
>
> Does not the Act make an arbitrary and unreasonable distinction among perpetrators of the same criminal offence on the basis of the State's reason for the prosecution of such offences? Does not this provision violate the prohibition of arbitrariness under Art. 54(1) of the Constitution, and the rule of the equal protection of citizens under Art. 70/A(1)?

II

The Constitutional Court holds that the provisions of the Act are not unambiguous.

1. The vagueness of the statutory text allows the following conclusions:
—the statute of limitations shall recommence for crimes the statutes of limitations of which have already expired;
—as of 2 May 1990, the statutes of limitations for crimes whose time limits have not yet expired are uniformly extended—irrespective of the time which has already elapsed; and
—with respect to some criminal offences, the statute of limitations has been tolled and its running is to continue on the basis of the Act.

2. The Act defines the criminal offences falling within its scope pursuant to Act IV/1978, thus ignoring the fact that the legal definition of these offences has changed on a number of occasions and in a variety of ways not only between 1944 and 1978 but also since 1978.

The overall ambiguity and vagueness of the Act violates the principle of legal certainty and hence is unconstitutional.

III

The Act under review illustrates with unusual sharpness the relationship between the law of the preceding political systems and the principle of the rule of law declared by the new Constitution. For this reason, a separate summary of the Constitutional Court's viewpoint on this matter is warranted.

1. With the enactment of the constitutional amendment of 23 October 1989, in fact, a new Constitution came into force, which, with its declaration that "the Republic of Hungary is an independent democratic state under the rule of law," conferred on the State, its law and the political system a new quality, fundamentally different from that of the previous regime. In the constitutional law sense, this is the substance of the political category of the "change of system" or "transition." Accordingly, any evaluation of state actions necessitated by the transition cannot be separated from the requirements of the rule of law, as crystallized during the history of constitutional democracies and also considered by the 1989 Hungarian constitutional revision. The Constitution provides for the basic institutions of the state under the rule of law and defines the human and civil rights together with their basic guarantees.

That Hungary is a state under the rule of law is both a statement of fact and a statement of policy. A state under the rule of law becomes a reality when the Constitution is truly and unconditionally given effect. For the legal system the change of system means, and the change of the legal system is possible only in that sense, that the whole body of law must be brought into harmony—and new legislation must be kept in harmony—with the new Constitution. Not only must the legal provisions and the operation of state organs comply strictly with the Constitution but the Constitution's values and its conceptual culture must permeate the whole of society. This is the rule of law, and this is how the Constitution becomes a reality. The realization of the rule of law is a continuous process. For the organs of the State, participation in this process is a constitutional duty.

2. The Constitution created the Constitutional Court in order to review the constitutionality of laws and to invalidate unconstitutional laws. The Constitutional Court was the first new organ of the state under the rule of law to commence operations. In its first Decision (*Dec. 1/1990 (II.12) AB:* MK 1990/12; ABH 1990, 13—concerning the effect of the

26 November 1989 referendum on the possibility of constitutional amendment) and with respect to other matters of political significance prior to the convening of the first freely elected Parliament (*e.g.,* concerning presidential powers or the electoral law), the Constitutional Court made it clear that political endeavours of any kind must be realized within the constitutional framework and that everyday political considerations are precluded from the adjudication of the constitutionality of the laws. From the beginning, the Constitutional Court has not distinguished in its constitutional review between laws enacted before or after the new Constitution.

3. The change of system has been carried out on the basis of legality. The principle of legality imposes on the state under the rule of law the requirement that legal regulations regarding the legal system itself should be abided by unconditionally. The politically revolutionary changes adopted by the Constitution and all the new fundamental laws were enacted, in full compliance with the old legal system's procedural laws on legislation, thereby gaining their binding force. The old law retained its validity. With respect to its validity, there is no distinction between "pre-Constitution" and "post-Constitution" law. The legitimacy of the different (political) systems during the past half century is irrelevant from this perspective; that is, from the viewpoint of the constitutionality of laws, it does not comprise a meaningful category. Irrespective of its date of enactment, each valid legal rule must conform with the new Constitution. Likewise, constitutional review does not admit two different standards for the review of laws. The date of enactment can be important insofar as previous laws may have become unconstitutional when the new Constitution entered into force.

Special treatment accorded to the law of the preceding systems—even when legality and legal continuity are recognized—can arise in two respects. The first question is: what could be done with the legal relations created on the basis of the old and now unconstitutional laws—could they be put into harmony with the Constitution? The second question is whether in judging the constitutionality of new laws intended to remedy the unconstitutional measures of the previous systems, one should consider the unique historical circumstances of the transition. These questions, too, must be answered in a manner which conforms with the requirements of the rule of law.

4. A fundamental principle of the rule of law is legal certainty. Legal certainty demands, inter alia, the protection of vested rights, non-interference with legal relations already executed or concluded and limiting the possibility of modifying existing long-term legal relations. As the Constitutional Court held in *Dec. 10/1992 (II.25) AB* (MK 1992/19; ABH 1992, 72), the consequences of the unconstitutionality of a law must be evaluated primarily with reference to their impact on legal certainty. This is the guiding principle for determining the date of invalidation for an unconstitutional law and especially for the invalidation of the legal relations arising therefrom. This is so because the individual legal relations and legal facts become independent of the statutory sources from which they emerge and do not automatically share their fate. Were this otherwise, a change in the law would necessitate in every instance a review of the whole body of legal relations. Thus, from the principle of legal certainty, it follows that already executed or concluded legal relations cannot be altered constitutionally by enactment of a law or by invalidation of a law by either the legislature or the Constitutional Court.

An exception to this principle is permissible only if a constitutional principle competing with legal certainty renders this outcome unavoidable and provided that in fulfilling its objectives it does not impose a disproportionate harm. The review of a final crimimal court decision, if the decision had been based upon a law which was subsequently declared unconstitutional, is an example of such an exception. A constitutional criminal justice system demands this exception. However, the unjust result of legal relations does not constitute an argument against the principle of legal certainty. As the Constitutional Court's Decision (*Dec. 9/1992 (I.30) AB:* MK 1992/11; ABH 1992, 59) stated: "[T]he requirement of the rule of law as to substantive justice may be attained within the institutions and guarantees ensuring legal certainty. The Constitution does not and cannot confer a right for substantive justice."

As far as the protection afforded to already concluded legal relations is concerned, no distinction can be made according to the time of and reasons for striking down a law as unconstitutional. With respect to every legal relation, the legislature is constrained by the restrictions imposed on retroactive legislation; the Constitutional Court is even further constrained as it cannot even establish the unconstitutionality of the substance of norms with effect for the time before the entry into the force of the new Constitution.

Retroactive modification of the law and legal relations is permitted only within very narrow limits. The problems created by unconstitutional laws can be constitutionally remedied by the enactment of new, prospective laws.

5. It is to be decided whether the unique historical circumstances of the transition should be considered in reviewing the constitutionality of new laws pertaining to the unconstitutional acts and measures of the former regime.

Within the framework of the rule of law, and in order to further its development, the given historical situation can be taken into consideration. However, the basic guarantees of the rule of law cannot be set aside by reference to historical situations and to justice as a requirement of the state under the rule of law. A state under the rule of law cannot be created by undermining the rule of law. Legal certainty based on formal and objective principles is more important than necessarily partial and subjective justice. In its practice, the Constitutional Court has already given effect to this principle.

The Constitutional Court cannot ignore history since it has to fulfill its task embedded in history. The Constitutional Court is the repository of the paradox of the "revolution under the rule of law": in the process of the peaceful transition, beginning with the new Constitution, the Constitutional Court must, within its competences, in all cases unconditionally guarantee the conformity of the legislative power with the Constitution.

The Constitutional Court has always considered the important historical circumstances of specific cases. The Court is aware that its decisions are constrained by history: even in those cases where the Constitutional Court declares absolute values, it reveals their meaning for its own age. In the abortion case (*Dec. 64/1991 (XII.17) AB:* MK 1991/139; ABH 1991, 297), the Constitutional Court's Decision that the legislature must expressly decide on whether the fetus is a person having full legal capacity was based on the recognition of the historical expansion of the legal status of human beings and on the fact that the traditional conceptualization of the fetus was changing in two opposite directions. Several decisions adjudicate upon the constitutionality of laws restricting the freedom of contract or property, with regard to whether the restriction is necessary and proportionate, in light of the factual development of the market economy (as a constitutional goal). The constitutional review of laws on nationalization and compensation was expressly related to the change of property system. However, the Constitutional Court never regarded these situations as exceptional from the point of view of the Constitution, that is, the suspension of the constitutional requirements was never contemplated. The question asked by the Constitutional Court was "[h]ow could the unique and specific historical requirements of the transition be realized on the basis of legal continuity in a manner which conforms with constitutional requirements?" (*Dec. 28/1991 (VI.3)* AB: MK 1991/59; ABH 1991, 88).

In contrast to the Compensation Act, in the present case the legislature has less constitutional discretion for manoeuvre. Regulating property relations is prospective. The Compensation Act confers rights, and where it restricts rights it is linked to the acquisition of future property rights. The possibility of the "novation" of state duties is also prospective, though this is not necessarily and unconditionally constitutional; not even in extraordinary circumstances can the State arbitrarily modify the legal basis, conditions or scope of its duties.

In contrast, the law providing for the recommencement of the statute of limitations oversteps the limits of the State's criminal powers. The guarantees concerned here cannot be restricted according to Art. 8(4) of the Constitution even in cases when other basic rights can be constitutionally suspended or restricted. In contrast to the restriction on property rights, the basic institutions of constitutional criminal law cannot even be relativized theoretically, nor is it possible to balance them against some other constitutional right or duty. This is so because the guarantees of the criminal law already contain the result of a balancing act, namely, that the risk of unsuccessful criminal prosecution is borne by the State (*cf. Dec. 9/1992 (I.30) AB:* MK 1992/11; ABH 1992, 59). Hence, the presumption of innocence cannot be restricted or denied full effect because of another constitutional right; as a result of the State's inaction, once the statute of limitations expires, the non-indictability acquired is complete, amenable neither to subsequent "reduction" nor resuscitation; nor can the condition of "*nullum crimen sine lege*" be substituted by, for instance, the pursuit of some other constitutional goals seeking the protection of the rights of others. Simply put, historical situations, justice, *etc.,* are of no consideration in this matter. Exemptions from the guarantees of criminal law are only possible with their overt disregard, an outcome precluded by the principle of the rule of law.

IV

[....]

In the Constitutional Court's opinion, in a state under the rule of law the violation of rights can only be remedied by upholding the rule of the law. The legal system of a state under the rule of law cannot deprive anyone of legal guarantees. These guarantees as basic rights are due to everyone. Wherever the value of the rule of law is entrenched, not even a just demand can justify the disregard of these guarantees. Justice and moral argument may, of course, motivate penal sanction but its legal foundation must be constitutional.

1. [....] [T]he principle of the rule of law, in comparison with the specific constitutional provisions, is not a mere auxiliary rule, nor a mere declaration, but an independent constitutional norm, the violation of which is itself a ground for declaring a law unconstitutional. In the Constitutional Court's practice, legal certainty is closely interconnected with the constitutional law principle of the rule of law.

According to the Constitutional Court's interpretation, legal certainty requires of the State, and primarily the legislature, that the law as a whole, its specific parts and its provisions, including the Criminal Code, be clear, unambiguous, their impact predictable and their consequences foreseeable by those to whom the laws are addressed. From the principle of predictability and foreseeability, the criminal law's prohibition of the use of retroactive legislation directly follows, especially ex post facto legislation and analogy.

The procedural guarantees follow from the principles of the rule of law and legal certainty. These are of fundamental importance from the perspectives of predictability and foreseeability of the operation of legal institutions. Only by following the formalized legal procedure can there be valid law; only by adherence to the procedural norms can the judiciary operate constitutionally. The statute of limitations in the criminal law guarantees lawful accountability for criminal liability by imposing a temporal restriction on the exercise of the State's punitive powers. Failure to apprehend or the dereliction of duties by the authorities which exercise the punitive powers of the State is a risk borne by the State. If the statute of limitations has expired, the person has a right to immunity from criminal punishment.

2. Under the rule of law, the State does not and cannot have unlimited punitive powers. This is especially so because the sovereign power itself is not limitless. Given constitutional rights and liberties, the sovereign power can interfere with individuals' rights and freedoms only on the basis of constitutional authorization and constitutional reasons.

Article 8(1) and (2) of the Constitution is also applicable to the constitutional requirements imposed on criminal law. [....] The criminal law, and especially its penalties, touch upon fundamental rights or constitutionally protected values. Their unavoidable, necessary and proportional restriction by law form the basis and constitutional meaning of the justification of criminal punishment as the final instrument under the legal sanctions.

The Constitutional Court emphasizes that the Act under review is unconstitutional not simply because it violates the constitutional prohibition on retroactive punishment (Criminal Code, art. 2), thus contradicting the principle of legal certainty (its predictability and foreseeability) contained in Art. 2(1) of the Constitution, but also because the Act does not conform with the constitutional requirements of unavoidability, necessity and proportionality for the imposition of a criminal punishment. Not even in a state of national crisis, a state of emergency, or a state of danger does the Constitution permit the restriction or suspension of the criminal law's constitutional fundamental principles (Arts. 54–56, 57(2)–(4)).

3. The criminal law of a liberal, democratic state construes—which constitutes the classical criminal law—the principles of "*nullum crimen*" and "*nulla poena sine lege*" (prohibition of retroactivity) as a (constitutional) duty imposed on the State: the conditions of the exercise of its punitive powers must be determined prospectively by law. In the process of exercising these punitive powers, this principle has become more and more complex. This trend is exemplified by the expansion of the requirements of criminal liability going beyond the rules contained in the provisions of the Criminal Code which lay down the specific criminal offences.

The Constitutional Court interprets the principles of *nullum crimen* and *nulla poena sine lege* on the basis of the constitutional principle of the legality of criminal law. In connection with this task the Court has undertaken a comparative review of the constitutions of other constitutional democracies. The Court has concluded that these constitutions do not merely state that criminal offences must be prohibited only by statute, and the threat of punishment must likewise be determined by statute, but they require that criminal responsibility, sentencing and punishment must all be lawful and based on statute. That is, they all do what Art. 57(4) of our Constitution prescribes. This, in turn, declares that the right of the individual to lawful sentencing and punishment is a fundamental right. The Constitution states that "no one shall be declared guilty and subjected to punishment [for an act which did not constitute a criminal offence under Hungarian law at the time it was committed]." Thus, the issue is not simply that the State prescribes by statute the criminal offences and their punishment, but that the individual has the right to be subjected exclusively to lawful judgment ("declared guilty") and that his/her punishment be prescribed by law ("subjected to punishment").

In a state under the rule of law, criminal law is not merely an instrument but it protects and embodies values: the principles and guarantees of constitutional criminal law. Criminal law is the legal basis for the exercise of punitive powers as well as a guarantee of freedom for the protection of individual rights. Though criminal law protects values, as a guarantee of freedom it cannot become an instrument for moral purges in the process of protecting moral values.

"*Nullum crimen sine lege*" and "*nulla poena sine lege*" are fundamental constitutional principles whose legal content is determined by a number of criminal law provisions. Such a regulation is the Criminal Code's definitions of the elements of a criminal offence, the legal concepts of the penal system and punishment. The concept of a criminal offence, as well as the concept of punishment, are crucial from the perspective of determining individual criminal liability and prosecution. The individual's constitutional rights and freedoms are affected not only by the elements of an offence and the sanctions of the criminal law but also by the interconnected and closed system of regulation of criminal liability, punishability and determination of penalty. Modification of every regulation of criminal liability fundamentally and directly affects the individual's freedom and constitutional position. Statutes of limitation can be modified only if they remain in conformity with the basic constitutional requirement of criminal liability.

4. To summarize: the principles of "*nullum crimen sine lege*" and "*nulla poena sine lege*" are part of the constitutional principle of the legality of the criminal law but do not comprise the only criteria for the constitutionality of criminal liability. In the Constitutional Court's view, the constitutional principle of the legality of criminal law incorporates the following:

—Article 8(1) and (2) of the Constitution requires that punishable offences ("punishability") and their punishment ("threat of punishment") be regulated by statute and not by regulation of a lower level. (Articles 1 and 10 of the Criminal Code are to the same effect.)

—Declaration of the criminality of an act and the imposition of the threat of punishment must be based on constitutional reasons: they must be necessary, proportional and be used only as a last resort (Art. 8(l) and (2) of the Constitution and the corresponding provision, art. 10, of the Criminal Code).

—Declaration of guilt (conviction) can only be undertaken by a court of law through establishing the defendant's guilt in a formal decision. This follows from Art. 57(2) of the Constitution declaring the presumption of innocence.

—Conviction (declaration of guilt) and punishment can only proceed according to the law that was in effect at the time of the commission of the crime. This requirement is imposed by Art. 57(4) of the Constitution, echoed by the Criminal Code's prohibition of retroactivity (art. 2). The court must judge (determine criminal liability, convict and pass sentence for) the offence in accordance with the law in force at the time of its commission, and the punishment is also so determined unless a new law is passed subsequent to the offence which prescribes a more lenient punishment or decriminalizes the act, thus making the action unpunishable by criminal law. This is the necessary result of the prohibition of retroactivity embodied in the principle of legal certainty (foreseeability and predictability), which, in turn, stems from the principle of the rule of law whose logical precondition is the public availability of the law at the time of the commission of an act (Criminal Code, art. 2). In addition to the express prohibition of retroactivity, the requirement of the application of the more lenient regulation also springs from the constitutional requirement of the rule of law: the Constitution cannot permit the application of norms which are alien to its basic principles (such as the imposition of the death penalty), even when at the time of the commission of the offence that regulation was the applicable rule.

On the basis of the foregoing, the Constitutional Court holds that the Act under review is unconstitutional because it is repuguant to the constitutional principles of the legality of the criminal law.

V

The constitutional problems of the Act under review were examined separately and without consideration of the possibility that adoption of a viewpoint regarding one issue may render the resolution of another superfluous. The Constitutional Court desires to address every conceivable interpretation of the Act under review and examine some of its conceptual components in light of the fact that Parliament will necessarily deal with the Act once again.

[....] The Constitutional Court concluded [in Part IV] that the requirements of the rule of law for the criminal law, especially legal certainty, cannot be limited to the determination of the elements of a crime and the punishment. The same constitutional requirements are imposed on every aspect of criminal liability—from the conditions of punishability to the regulation of sentencing. [....]

The constitutionality of criminal laws must be scrutinized not merely by reference to the criminal law guarantees expressly determined by the Constitution. The criminal law of itself implies many other fundamental principles and rights. Thus, for example, there is no specific provision in the Constitution prohibiting the imposition of objective [strict] liability in criminal cases, but from the right to human dignity may be derived the principle that only the person who is guilty may be punished. Another constitutional principle giving content to the rule of law is that the conditions and restrictions on the State's punitive powers determined by law cannot be modified to the detriment of the individual whose act is being judged. No additional burden can be imposed on the perpetrator on account of a change in public policy relating to criminal punishment or due to a mistake or dereliction of duty by the authorities. From this principle derives the unconstitutionality of any retroactive measure imposing a harsher sentence; [....]

The running of the statute of limitations is a matter of fact, but the period itself is a matter of legal determination. Only a court can determine with final effect, whether the statute of limitations for the punishment of a specific criminal offence has expired. [....] The legislature's only constitutionally permitted discretion to interfere with the statute of limitations is to enact a more lenient standard. However, legislation seeking the opposite goal is unconstitutional for a variety of reasons, depending on whether or not the statute of limitations had already expired.

1. The re-imposition of criminal punishability for a crime for the prosecution of which the statute of limitations had already expired violates the Constitution.

With the expiration of the statute of limitations, the criminal punishability of the offender is irrevocably extinguished. The primary reason for the State's termination of punishability is the restriction on its own punitive powers. These reasons have nothing in common with the determination of criminal liability and guilt; these reasons do not alter the nature of the act since the criminal offence remains criminal. The reasons for the termination of punishability are independent of the offender's will and it always remains uncertain as to whether the punishability will be terminated. The perpetrator of a crime may hope for pardon, a change in criminal policy or that the statute of limitations will expire but he/she can never be sure that he/she will benefit from these events. (Under the conditions excluding punishability there is only one that will certainly be fulfilled: the offender will definitively die.) The perpetrator of an offence acquires the right to be free of accountability only if the reasons for the termination of punishability in fact materialize.

Hence, if the statute of limitations has already expired, the offender would acquire the right not to be punished. This right commences when the State's claim for punishment ceases to exist due to its inability to apprehend and punish the offender during the time prescribed for the exercise of its punitive powers. The principle of reliance requires that once a reason for the termination of punishability is realized there may be no new statute making the same offence punishable once again. The legal technicality employed to reimpose criminal punishability—whether the statute of limitations recommences or ex post facto legislation is imposed to toll the statute—is a matter of indifference; its constitutionality must be viewed in the same light as a law retroactively imposing punishment on conduct which, at the time of its commission, did not constitute a criminal offence. From the perspective of punishability, an offence whose statute of limitations has run its course must be treated—given that the State's claim for punishment has been extinguished—as never having been punishable.

The statute of limitations cannot be recommenced for an offence the statute of limitations for which statute has already expired. This conforms with the Constitution's express criminal law provisions, which limit the State's punitive powers and never permit the shifting of the burden upon the perpetrator due to the State's failure to prosecute lawfully. Just as the presumption of innocence protects persons other than the innocent, the statute of limitations also extinguishes punishability irrespective of the reasons for not prosecuting the offender; the offender cannot be burdened by the State's dereliction of its duty. (The guarantee—as always—prevails irrespective of whether the reasons for enacting statute of limitations are appropriate in the specific case. That a person is obviously guilty matters not; he/she remains innocent if the guilt cannot be legally established. It does not matter that all the evidence is available and that there is a demand of society for punishment if the State does not prosecute—the statute of limitations continues to run.)

Hence, the Act making offences punishable whose statutes of limitation have already expired is contrary to Art. 2(1) of the Constitution because it violates legal certainty, it infringes the principle of limits of the State's punitive powers and, further, it is also contrary to Art. 57(4) by retroactively imposing criminal liability.

2 and 3. The statutory extension of a statute of limitations which has not yet expired presents different constitutional problems than those posed by the reimposition of criminal liability for offences whose statutes of limitations have already expired.

With the expiration of the statute of limitations the State's claim for punishment is extinguished and the offender acquires the right not to be punished. But while the statute is running it serves as a reminder to the investigating authorities who control the process: according to the Act, the authorities can interrupt and recommence the running of the period without the offender having to receive notice of this change. Under the Act, whenever the authorities suspend criminal proceedings, the statute of limitations is extended by the duration of the suspension. (Apart from some statutory exceptions, the statute of limitations is "tolled" during the suspension of the proceedings.) Thus, the "normal" statute of limitations applies only if no criminal proceedings are instituted against the offender. This is an exceptional case, however, an operational failure of law enforcement. Hence the offender does not have the right to have his/her punishability extinguished within the "normal" duration of the statute of limitations and he/she cannot expect as a matter of right that no criminal action will be brought against him/her. He/she only has the right not to be prosecuted and punished once the legally mandated statute of limitations has expired. Thus, the statute of limitations represents the minimum rather than the actual time required for the termination of the punishability.

Although the statute of limitations does not guarantee that punishability will be extinguished within the initially prescribed time frame, it does ensure that the methods of calculating the time expired do not change in a manner detrimental to the offender. This follows from the principle that the limits of the State's punitive powers must be the same at the time of the punishment as at the time the offence was committed. Hence the unconstitutionality of a law extending the statute of limitations for offences the period of which has not yet expired depends on whether such an extension imposes a more onerous burden on the offender than would be the case if the statute were tolled—even if it were unknown to the offender—due to an individual criminal measure. [....]

[....] [T]he statutory extension of a currently running statute of limitations would always impose greater burdens. Statutory extension of the time frame for criminal punishability does not merely replace the [individually] interrupted or tolled statute of limitations, but has a wider impact.

On the one hand it affects every offender, irrespective of whether criminal proceedings are contemplated against that person. [....]

Likewise, in each individual case a heavier burden is imposed if the tolling or interrupting of the statute of limitations pursuant to the initiation of some action by the authorities is substituted by a new statute. [....]

4. The constitutional concern presented by retroactive legislation for the extension of the statute of limitations cannot be avoided by the explanation that the period has been "tolled." If the period had indeed been tolled under the law in force at the time of the commission of the offence, then a new statute prescribing the tolling is unnecessary. Determination of whether or not the period had expired—by application of the law concerned—is left exclusively to the prosecutor and, in the last instance, to the courts. The legislature cannot retroactively decide this question. [....]

5 and 6. The statute of limitations for the punishability of the criminal offences set out in the Act under review recommences "if the State's failure to prosecute its claim to punish was based on political reasons." This condition is unconstitutional per se.

Legal certainty demands the clear and unambiguous formulation of legal rules. [....] Not even with the knowledge of the special purpose of this Act can the meaning of "failure to prosecute its claim to punish" be determined with sufficient certainty. Failure to initiate proceedings and termination of criminal proceedings in the absence of legal justifications fall within the ambit of this concept, but so does, for instance, the conclusion of proceedings with an unlawfully lenient punishment such as a warning. Likewise, what constitutes "political reasons" and what criteria are to be applied cannot be determined unequivocally—especially in light of the political changes which have taken place during the long period of time covered by this Act. [....]

With regard to the Act under review, the statute of limitations for the criminal offences committed between 21 December 1941 and 2 May 1990 could have been tolled only on the basis of reasons which were recognized by the law in effect at the time the offences were committed. That "the State's failure to prosecute its claim to punish was based on political reasons" did not exist as a justification for tolling the statute of limitations. Although s. 9 of Act VII/1945 on the people's tribunal retroactively tolled the statute of limitations for all criminal offences committed in 1919 and thereafter, "whose prosecution was prevented by the ruling regime," and decreed its date of commencement as of 21 December 1944, the periods covered under that law and the Act under review are different.

After 21 December 1944, there were legal directives by the Attorney General and the Minister of Interior, which carried out the resolutions of the [Communist] Party's central organs, such as Directives 6/1955, 1/1961, 2/1966, and 1/1985 of the Attorney General and Directives 8/1966 and 22/1985 of the Minister of Interior—according to which, with respect to a certain (changing) group of people and criminal offences, criminal proceedings could only be initiated with the approval of the relevant Party organs. These legal regulations were fashioned after the right of immunity conferred on Members of Parliament. It is now a task of the judiciary to judge in each case what effect these directives may have had on the statute of limitations. But the Act under review has no influence on this matter.

7. Treason is a crime against the State. The subject matter protected by this category alters with the changes in political systems and thus takes on formal and textual similarities; different meanings notwithstanding, treason is treated differently in different political systems. Failure to prosecute an act of treason for "political reasons" is typically an ex post facto classification, constituting a retroactive determination of the legal fact. [....]

DECISION 30/1992: 26 MAY 1992

ON THE FREEDOM OF EXPRESSION

This case opened the "Hungarian First Amendment jurisdiction" of the Constitutional Court, laying down at the start a liberal, extensive interpretation of the right to the freedom of expression. The Court asserted for free speech a privileged rank in the hierarchy of rights: it was protected regardless of its content, and all other rights conflicting with it had to be interpreted restrictively. The Court kept in line not only with the U.S. Supreme Court but the German and Spanish Constitutional Courts and the European Court of Human Rights as well. Nevertheless, public opinion and the legislature could hardly accept that even unpleasant, hurtful, or offensive speech was protected by the Constitution (to the extent drawn by the Court in this decision). Parliament soon restored the crime of incitement, abolished in this case, now in alleged conformity with the requirements of the Constitutional Court. This new provision of the Criminal Code was again challenged before the Court. The case is still pending. The principles of this decision have been followed in the cases concerning public service media (37/1992) and government defamation.

The petitioners sought an ex post facto review of the constitutionality of art. 269 of Act IV/1978 on the Criminal Code (as amended).

Article 269 provides under para. 1 that anyone who, before a large public audience, incites hatred against the Hungarian nation, any other nationality, people, religion or race, or certain groups among the population commits an offence punishable by up to three years' imprisonment. Under para. 2 anyone in the same circumstances who uses an offensive or denigrating expression, or commits similar acts, against the groups above, commits an offence punishable by up to one year's imprisonment, corrective training or a fine.

The petitioners submitted, inter alia, that art. 269 was unconstitutional because it punished behaviour which fell within the scope of the freedom of expression of opinion and freedom of the press under Art. 62, freedom of thought under Art. 60 and the right of asylum under Art. 65.

Held, granting the petition in part:

(1) In approaching the question of the constitutionality of Criminal Code, art. 269, it was necessary to examine the dividing line between the freedoms of expression and of the press on the one hand, and behaviour prohibited as criminal and subject to criminal sanction on the other. It was important to determine whether and on what terms a constitutional fundamental right might be limited or restricted and if two such rights conflict on what criteria would one take priority. The right of expression was the "mother right" of the fundamental rights of communication. Free expression of ideas and beliefs, free manifestation of even unpopular or unusual convictions, is fundamental to a pluralist, democratic society. The State could only restrict a fundamental right in order to protect or realize another if such restriction were proportional, and even then the legislature was required to use the least restrictive means available for the achievement of its objective. A restriction on the content

of a right was impermissible if it were arbitrary, without a necessary reason or if its size were disproportionate to the desired objective. Finally the constitutional boundary of the freedom of expression had to be drawn in such a way that, in addition to the individual's subjective right to free expression, it was necessary to consider the (free) formation of public opinion as an indispensable democratic value.

(2) The restriction of the freedom of expression and the freedom of the press under art. 269(1) was justified by the historically proven harmful effect on certain groups of incitement to hatred, the protection of fundamental constitutional values and the fulfillment of international treaty obligations by Hungary. Further, the impact and consequences for an individual and society of the prohibited behaviour were so grave that other forms of accountability (*e.g.*, civil liability) were inadequate to deal with persons who publicly incited racial hatred. Consequently since only a criminal sanction was sufficient to respond effectively to the behaviour, defining the scope subject to punishment by law had to be scrutinized strictly: thus criminal sanction could only be applied when absolutely necessary and only as justified by proportionality if, as in the present case, there were no other means of protecting the state under the rule of law and its social and economic aims and values.

(3) Moreover art. 269(1) was sufficiently definite and did not define too broadly the scope of behaviour subject to criminal sanction. Constitutional criminal law required that the provision designating a type of behaviour against which criminal sanctions may be applied must be specific, clearly defined and demarcated. Thus a clear expression of the legislative intent concerning the content of the unlawful act was also necessary. The definition of the crime had to contain an unequivocal message putting a person on notice as to when he would commit the crime while simultaneously minimizing the opportunity for arbitrary interpretation by those applying the law. "Incitement to hatred" included behaviour which was capable of whipping up intense emotions in the majority of the people, which, upon giving rise to hatred, might result in the disturbance of social order and peace which latter also contained the danger of the large-scale violation of individual rights. Bearing in mind the danger to individual rights and through this the threat to public peace, the restriction on the freedom of expression in art. 269(1) was to be regarded as necessary and proportionate and accordingly constitutional.

(4) Article 269(2) of the Criminal Code however was unconstitutional. The freedom of expression had only external boundaries: unless and until it clashed with such a constitutionally drawn external limit, the opportunity and fact of the expression of opinion was protected irrespective of the value or veracity of its content. The Constitution guaranteed free communication—as an individual behaviour and social process—and it was not to the content that the right of free expression related. Although everyone was entitled to support or oppose an opinion provided that some other right was not violated to such an extent that freedom of expression was pushed back, art. 269(2) did not establish an external boundary; rather in reality it classified opinion on the basis of content. The message conveyed by certain words was so clearly linked to a given situation and cultural context (which was subject to change) that the abstract, hypothetical definition of an offensive or denigrating expression—in the absence of an actual breach of the (public) peace—was a mere assumption which did not sufficiently justify the restriction of the external boundary, *i.e.*, the violation of another right, itself uncertain.

(5) Moreover a further distinction had to be made between incitement to hatred under art. 269(1) and the use of offensive or denigrating expressions under art. 269(2). Apart from public gatherings the "public at large" effectively meant the press. The freedom of the press now meant that anyone speaking out publicly could not invoke external compulsion, and any journalist or writer risked his entire moral credibility through his writings. Anyone known for using scurrilous or derisive language would earn a reputation for this: such abusive language needed to be answered by sanctions for which the payment of a large sum of damages would be considered as adequate. Criminal sanctions, as previously indicated, could be applied for the defence of other rights and only when unavoidably necessary; they were not to be used as a means with which to shape public opinion or the manner of political debate. Consequently, art. 269(2) would be declared null and void.

IN THE NAME OF THE REPUBLIC OF HUNGARY!

In the matter of the petitions seeking an ex post facto review of the unconstitutionality of a legal rule, the Constitutional Court has made the following

DECISION.

The Constitutional Court rejects the petitions seeking the determination of unconstitutionality and the annulment of art. 269(1) of Act IV/1978 on the Criminal Code (hereafter referred to as the Criminal Code).

The Constitutional Court holds that art. 269(2) of the Criminal Code is unconstitutional and therefore annuls it effective from the date of publication of its Decision.

The Constitutional Court orders that the final judgments entered in criminal proceedings conducted on the basis of art. 269(2) of the Criminal Code be reviewed if the convicted person has not yet been relieved of the unfavourable legal consequences.

The Constitutional Court publishes its Decision in the *Hungarian Official Gazette.*

REASONING

SÓLYOM, P., and **SZABÓ, J.,** delivering the Opinion of the Court: [....]

II

1. The definition of incitement against the community, the present art. 269 of the Criminal Code, is given by s. 15 of Act XXV/1989 on the amendment of the Criminal Code in the following manner:

"(1) A person who, in front of a large public gathering, incites hatred

(a) against the Hungarian nation or any other nationality,

(b) against any people, religion or race, further against certain groups among the population,

commits a criminal offence and is to be punished by imprisonment for a period of up to three years."

"(2) Anyone who in front of a large public gathering uses an offensive or denigrating expression against the Hungarian nation, any other nationality, people, religion or race, or commits other similar acts, is to be punished for the offence by imprisonment for up to one year, corrective training or a fine."

2. During the regulatory history of the criminal rules investigated at present, both the scope of statutorily protected targets and the behavioural means of commission of the offence have been modified. What remains the same is the goal of the declaration of punishment: the statutory demarcation of the boundary where the freedom of expression—and freedom of speech embodied in the former—ends and the behaviour prohibited by criminal law begins.

According to the provisions of Act V/1878 on the Hungarian Criminal Code (the *Codex Csemegi*) relevant to the facts of the case examined by the Constitutional Court, a person who in a meeting publicly and orally, or who by the distribution or public exhibition of a publication, writing or illustration, incites any class, nationality or religion for the hatred of another is guilty of incitement: art. 172(2). [....]

In 1989, in the interest of the creation of guarantees for the rule of law, criminal offences of a political nature received top priority among the regulations singled out for urgent modification. Act XXV/1989 lifted incitement from the category of crimes against the State and, with its criminal liability greatly restricted, placed it among the offences against public peace, defining it as "incitement against the community." The reduction of criminal liability was achieved by narrowing the scope of the definition and, secondly, by imposing the requirement of publication before a larger audience.

3. [....] [T]he demarcation of the boundary between incitement, arousal of hatred and expression of opinion remains hotly contested even internationally.

III

The petitions concerning the definition of criminal offences in art. 269(1) of the Criminal Code are unfounded. However, art. 269(2) of the Criminal Code—in light of the provisions of Art. 8(1) and (2) of the Constitution—restricts the freedom of expression and the freedom of the press guaranteed in Art. 61(1) and (2) of the Constitution to an unnecessary and disproportionate degree and is therefore unconstitutional. [....]

2.1 [....] [T]he right of expression has a special place among the constitutional fundamental rights, in effect amounting to the "mother right" of the so-called fundamental rights of communication. Enumerated rights derived from this "mother right" are the right to free speech and the freedom of the press, the latter encompassing the freedom of all media, as well as the right of freedom of information—the right to be informed and to acquire information. In a broader sense, the freedom of expression includes artistic and literary freedoms, the freedom to distribute and disseminate works of art, the freedom of scientific research and the freedom to teach. These latter rights are expressly provided for by Art. 70/G of the Constitution. Other rights related to the freedom of expression are the freedom of religion and conscience (Art. 60 of the Constitution) and the right of assembly (Art. 62).

It is this combination of rights which renders possible the individual's reasoned participation in the social and political life of the community. Historical experience shows that on every occasion when the freedom of expression was restricted social justice and human creativity suffered and humankind's innate ability to develop was stymied. The harmful consequences afflicted not only the lives of individuals but also that of society at large, inflicting much suffering while leading to a dead end for human development. Free expression of ideas and beliefs, free manifestation of even unpopular or unusual ideas, is the fundamental requirement for the existence of a truly vibrant society capable of development.

2.2. [....] In addition to the right of the individual to the freedom of expression, Art. 61 of the Constitution imposes the duty on the State to secure the conditions for the creation and maintenance of democratic public opinion. The objective, institutional aspect of the right to freedom of expression relates not only to the freedom of the press, freedom of education and so on, but also to that aspect of the system of institutions which places the freedom of expression, as a general value, among the other protected values. For this reason, the constitutional boundary of the freedom of expression must be drawn in such a way that in addition to the person's individual right to the freedom of expression, the formation of public opinion, and its free development—being indispensible values for a democracy—are also considered.

Given that the subject of this inquiry is the restriction of the freedom of expression by the use of criminal sanctions, the constitutional demands imposed on the constitutional criminal system on the whole must be given effect. [....]

IV

With respect to the behaviour subject to criminal sanctions contained in art. 269(1) the Constitutional Court has made the following determination:

1. The potential harms resulting from incitement to hate, the subjecting of certain groups in a population to denigrating and humiliating treatment, is amply documented in the annals of human experience.

The power of words was previously noted in the 1878 *Codex Csemegi,* in whose accompanying annotation the Minister of Justice stated the following:

> The free communication of ideas, to which mankind owes its greatest achievements, becomes just as dangerous as fire, which gives light and warmth, but which, when raging uncontrollably, very often becomes the cause of great misfortune, much suffering and destruction.

The tragic historical experiences of our century prove that views preaching racial, ethnic, national or religious inferiority or superiority, the dissemination of ideas of hatred, contempt and exclusion, endanger the values of human civilization. [....]

2. To afford constitutional protection to the incitement of hatred against certain groups under the guise of the freedom of expression and freedom of press would present an indissoluble contradiction with the value system and political orientation expressed in the Constitution: the democratic rule of law, the equality of human beings, equality of dignity, as well as the prohibition of discrimination, the freedom of religion and conscience, the protection of national and ethnic minorities—as recognized by the various Articles of the Constitution. [....]

Incitement to hate is the negation of this aforenoted content, the emotional preparation for the use of violence. It is an abuse of the freedom of expression; it is an intolerant classification of a group, which is the characteristic of dictatorships, not democracies. To tolerate the exercise of the freedom of expression and the freedom of the press in a way which art. 269(1) prohibits would contradict the requirements springing from the democratic rule of law.

According to Art. 54 of the Constitution, everyone has the inherent right to human dignity. Accordingly, human dignity may restrict the freedom of expression.

3. The necessity of restricting the freedom of expression and freedom of the press also follows from the international obligations of the Republic of Hungary. [....]

4. Criminal law is the *ultima ratio* in the system of legal responsibility. Its social function is to serve as the sanctioning cornerstone of the overall legal system. The criminal sanction, the role and function of punishment, is the preservation of legal and moral norms when no other legal sanction can be of assistance. [....]

In the Constitutional Court's view, the impact on and consequences for an individual and society of the previously analyzed behaviour, prohibited by art. 269(1) of the Criminal Code, is so grave that other forms of responsibility, such as the application of the instruments of civil law liability, are inadequate for dealing with the perpetrators of such behaviour. The emphatic expression of disapproval and condemnation of such behaviour, the fortification of those democratic ideas and values which are attacked by the perpetrators of these activities, and the restoration of the violated legal and moral order require the application of the instruments of criminal law.

5. Finally, the question whether art. 269(1) is restrained and provides an appropriate response to the phenomenon deemed undesired and dangerous must be looked into, that is, whether this article, in accordance with the authoritative requirement in restricting a constitutional fundamental right, confines itself to the narrowest possible subject to achieve its objective. [....] It must be determined, therefore, whether art. 269(1) is sufficiently definite and does not define the scope of behaviours subject to criminal sanctions too broadly.

Article 269(1) meets the requirements imposed on restrictions of fundamental rights. As the historical review in Part II/2 of the present Decision demonstrates, the 1989 amendment considerably narrowed the scope of offences for which criminal liability is incurred in a number of ways:

—The scope of offences was narrowed by the exclusion of the constitutional order, as well as the State's alliances, friendship, co-operation or other international relations from the category of protected legal subjects. Accordingly, incitement to hatred against these institutions was eliminated from the category of criminal behaviour. The instrumentalities of the criminal law are triggered only if someone engages in conduct qualifying as conspiracy against the constitutional order (art. 139/A of the Criminal Code), rebellion (art. 140 of the Criminal Code) and treason (art. 141), all of which require conduct which goes considerably beyond incitement to hatred.

—The formerly first-degree (the most serious gradation) incitement to hatred, the commission of the incitement in front of a large public audience, became the basic definition of the offence of incitement against the community. [....] The content of this concept has long been formed in the case law of the criminal courts.

On the other hand, incitement against the community undoubtedly broadened the scope of criminal liability relative to the original offence of incitement insofar that the new definition requires no intent as regards the result, that is, an express purpose to incite hatred is no longer required for a finding of criminal liability and it is sufficient that the perpetrator is merely conscious of the fact that his behaviour is capable of triggering hatred.

One phrase of the legal definition requiring interpretation is that of "certain groups in the population." This expression reveals the intention to protect people of divergent viewpoints (members of political parties, societies, movements, *etc.*) or individuals differentiated from others by virtually any criterion.

The conduct constituting the offence in the definition of incitement also requires interpretation. The words themselves convey generally understood meanings. Hatred is one of the most extreme, negative feelings, defined by the dictionary as an intense, hostile emotion. One who incites provokes, encourages and urges hostile behaviour and hostile actions resulting in harm against some individual, group, institution or regulation. Given that in the *Codex Csemegi* incitement to hatred was already conduct constituting the commission of the offence, the criminal courts could draw on more than a century of interpretive experience. The Curia [the Supreme Court] at the turn of the century defined the concept of incitement with great precision on a number of occasions (Curia, 7 *Crim. Law Reports* 272):

> According to law, this expression "incitement" is not the expression of some unfavourable and offensive opinion, but such virulent outbursts which are capable of whipping up such intense emotions in the majority of the people which, upon giving rise to hatred, may result in the disturbance of the social order and peace.

And (Curia, 1 *Crim. Law Reports* 124):

> Thus criticism, disapproval, objections or, indeed, offensive declarations do not constitute incitement; incitement occurs only when the expression, comments, *etc.*, address not reason but seek to influence the world of emotions and are capable of arousing passions and hostile feelings. For the concept of incitement it is totally immaterial whether the stated facts are true or not; what matters is that they, true or false, are capable of arousing hatred.

The more serious version of the incitement against community, the definition of the incitement to hatred, therefore complies with the requirement of proportionality: it extends only to the most dangerous behaviour and may be unambiguously applied by the courts. The fact that the original definition of the Criminal Code permitted even in the recent past such a restriction on the freedom of expression which is not acceptable by the democratic value system is not an argument for the unconstitutionality of the definition itself. It merely proves that precise legal definitions provide only a limited protection against the abuse of the instruments of criminal law. The real protection is provided by the operation of the institutions of the democratic rule of law, the genuine independence of the judiciary and the creation of a society committed to democratic values.

V

1. According to what has been said above, the right to the freedom of expression is not merely an individual fundamental right but also the recognition of the objective, institutional aspect of that right which concurrently means protecting public opinion as a fundamental political institution. Although the privileged place accorded to the right of freedom of expression does not mean that this right may not be restricted—unlike the rights to life and human dignity, which are absolutely protected—but it necessarily implies that the right to free expression must only give way to a few rights; that is, the laws restricting this freedom must be strictly construed. The laws restricting the freedom of expression are to be assigned greater weight if they directly serve the realization or protection of another individual fundamental right, a lesser weight if they protect such rights only indirectly through the mediation of an institution, and the least weight if they merely serve some abstract value as an end in itself (public peace, for instance).

2. The behaviour defined as an offence punishable by law in art. 269(1) is "incitement to hatred." The definition of incitement contained in the Curia decision cited above makes it abundantly clear that such behaviour falls within this category, which "is capable of whipping up such intense emotions in the majority of the people which, upon giving rise to hatred, may result in the disturbance of the social order and peace." (Curia, 7 *Crim. Law Reports* 272.) The disturbance of the social order and peace—"public peace" to use the Criminal Code's terminology—also contains the danger of the large-scale violation of individual rights: the whipped-up emotions against the group threaten the honour, dignity (and life, in the more extreme cases) of the individuals comprising the group and by intimidation restricts them in the exercise of their other rights as well (including the right of freedom of expression). The behaviour criminally sanctioned in para. (1) contains such a danger to individual rights as well, which gives such weight to public peace that—according to the argument set out in Part IV—the restriction on the freedom of expression may be regarded as necessary and proportionate. Although the actual outcome of the examination is the same, this reasoning considered not only the intensity of the disruption of public peace which—above and beyond a certain threshold ("clear and present danger")—justifies the restriction of the right to freedom of expression. Here, what is of crucial importance is that which has become threatened: the incitement endangers individual rights also accorded prominent places in the constitutional value system.

In contrast, in the case of "denigration" (according to para. (2)), it is not an element of the legal definition that the offending or denigrating expression or similar activity be capable of disturbing the public peace. In contrast with "incitement to hatred," nor does the behaviour constituting the offence permit the drawing of such a conclusion. The Criminal Code assumes that the use of an expression offensive to a national or religious community is generally contrary to the desired peace of society. Thus, this legal definition of the criminal offence amounts to an abstract protection of the public order and peace as an end in itself.

The criminal offence is committed even if under the given circumstances the utterance of the offending statement does not result in even the threat of violating an individual right. But such an abstract and removed threat to public peace is not sufficient justification to permit constitutional authorization for the use of sanctions of the criminal law to restrict the freedom of expression.

3. The right to free expression protects opinion irrespective of the value or veracity of its content. Only this approach meets the requirement of ideological neutrality phrased by the constitutional amendment of Act XL/1990 and expressed by the expunging from Art. 2 of the Constitution that provision inserted in October 1989—precisely as an example of pluralism—which contained major ideological trends. The freedom of expression has only external boundaries: until and unless it clashes with such a constitutionally drawn external boundary, the opportunity and fact of the expression of opinion is protected, irrespective of its content. That is to say, it is individual expression of opinion, further the public opinion formed by its own rules, and, related to it, the opportunity of the formation of an individual's opinion built upon as broad a knowledge as possible which are what the Constitution protects. The Constitution guarantees free communication—as an individual behaviour and social process—and it is not the content to which the right of free expression relates. Every opinion, good and damaging, pleasant and offensive, has a place in this social process, especially because the classification of opinions is also the product of this process.

Everyone—including the State—may support opinions he finds agreeable, may act against them if deemed misguided or wrongheaded, provided that in doing so he does not violate some other right to such an extent that the freedom of expression is forced to retreat. But art. 269(2) of the Criminal Code does not establish an external boundary; in reality, it classifies opinion on the basis of its content—and the violation of public peace is related to this only as a hypothetical or a statistical probability.

The qualification of an expression as offensive or denigrating is always relative, and so it constitutes a question of criminal law rather than one of constitutional law. The message conveyed by certain words is so closely linked with a given situation and cultural context (and it changes, too) that the abstract, hypothetical definition ("is capable of") of offending public peace by "denigration"—in the absence of an actual breach of that peace—is a mere assumption which does not sufficiently justify the restriction of the freedom of expression. For in this case the existence of the external boundary, that is, the violation of another right, is itself uncertain. Accordingly, the examination of the necessity and unavoidability of restricting the right to the freedom of expression is premature.

Moreover, "public peace" itself is not unrelated to the condition of the freedom of expression. Where one may encounter many different opinions, public opinion becomes tolerant, just as in a closed society an unusual voice may instigate much greater disruption of the public peace. In addition, the unnecessary and disproportionate restriction of the freedom of expression reduces the openness of a society.

The Constitutional Court takes note of the historical circumstances of certain cases. The recent change of the political system is inevitably accompanied by social tensions. These tensions are undoubtedly exacerbated if people can give vent with impunity before the public to their hatred, enmity and contempt of certain groups.

But the unique historical circumstances give rise to another effect, and it is precisely for this reason that a distinction must be made between incitement to hate and the use of offensive or denigrating expressions. The "public at large"—apart from meetings—means the press, in effect. With the freedom of the press having become a reality no one speaking out publicly may invoke external compulsion, and with every line penned he gives himself and risks his entire moral credibility. Only through self-cleansing may a political culture and a soundly reflexive public opinion emerge. Thus one who uses scurrilous or derisive language stamps himself as such and in the eyes of the public he will become known as a "mudslinger." Such abusive language must be answered by criticism. The payment of a large amount of compensation may also be considered in this process. But criminal sanctions must be applied for the protection of other rights and only when unavoidably necessary, and they should not be used for shaping public opinion or the manner of political discourse. This latter option is that of a paternalistic approach.

4. According to the aforementioned reason, art. 269(2) of the Criminal Code is unconstitutional and therefore the Constitutional Court annulls it. For the maintenance of public peace the application of criminal sanctions for the public utterance, or similar conduct, offending, disparaging or denigrating the Hungarian nation, other nationalities, peoples, religion or race is not unavoidably necessary. The legal definition of the offence restricts unnecessarily and, in light of the desired objective, disproportionately the right to the freedom of expression. The abstract, hypothetical threat to public peace in itself is not a sufficient justification to permit criminal regulation and restriction by art. 269(2) of the fundamental right of the freedom of expression, a right whose exercise is indispensable for the functioning of a democratic state under the rule of law.

According to the Constitutional Court's Decision, the dignity of communities may be a constitutional limit to the freedom of expression. Thus, the Decision does not pre-empt the legislature's ability to extend the scope of criminal sanctions beyond incitement to hatred. Nonetheless, there are other means available, such as expanding the possible use of moral damages, to provide effective protection for the dignity of communities.

5. The review of criminal proceedings in which final judgments have been entered according to art. 269(2) is ordered, pursuant to s. 43(3) of the Constitutional Court Act.

DECISION 37/1992: 10 JUNE 1992

ON THE MEDIA

The broadcasting decision was born out of the "media war" concerning the Government's influence on the state-run nationwide radio and television. The holdings of the Court, however, survived these struggles in which real constitutional rights issues merged inseparably with political and business interests disguised as constitutional problems. The Court developed here in detail the idea of the State's responsibility for "the conditions for the creation and maintenance of a democratic public opinion," already laid down in the leading free speech case, 30/1992. The regulatory duty of the State—in the interest of enforcing "neutrality," that is, comprehensive, balanced, and accurate reporting—regarding public radio and television was based on their monopoly position and the limited number of frequencies. The principles of impartiality remained valid even after (at the end of 1997) more nationwide commercial television stations commenced broadcasting.

The petitioners sought an ex post facto review of the constitutionality of para. 6 of Council of Ministers Decree 1047/1974 (IX.18) MT and a declaration of the said para. 6 to be null and void and a declaration of an unconstitutional omission to legislate.

Paragraph 6 of the said Decree provided that Hungarian State Radio and Hungarian State Television were under the supervision of the Council of Ministers and subject to its approval of their corporate and operational regulation.

It was submitted that para. 6 violated Art. 8(2), Art. 61(2) on the freedom of the press and Art. 61(4), which only permitted regulation by a two-thirds majority Act of the supervision of public radio and television and the appointment of their heads. In the absence of such an Act, such regulation at the level of Council of Ministers engendered an unconstitutional situation since it afforded the Government an exclusive opportunity to exercise a determining influence over news content, thus violating the right to freedom of the press.

Held, granting the petition:

(1) Freedom of the press is a fundamental right derived from the mother right of all rights of communication, the freedom of expression under Art. 61. The State had to guarantee press freedom cognizant that the press was the pre-eminent tool for disseminating and moulding views and for the gathering of information necessary for the formation of opinion. Since the freedom of the press was subject only to external limits, the freedom was primarily guaranteed by the State's non-intervention with respect to its content, ensured, *e.g.*, by the prohibition of censorship and the opportunity of the free establishment of newspapers. The protection afforded to the right to be informed, namely, the substantive and procedural safeguards for freedom of information, was developed by the State in connection with regulating access to data not only for the press but for everyone. Since a democratic public opinion was formed on the basis of an objective and comprehensive dissemination of information, the right to information indispensable to such opinion formation was constitutionally recognized as a restriction on press freedom only to the extent it was unavoid-

able: statutory regulation would therefore be required to prevent the emergence of information monopolies.

(2) The freedom of expression in radio and television imposed requirements beyond those secured for the freedom of the press. As a result, in the present case, para. 6 of Council of Ministers Decree 1047/1974 (IX.18) MT was contrary to Art. 61(1) and (2) because it did not contain any substantive, procedural or organizational regulation which would preclude the possibility of the Government from using its licence to assert (even indirectly) a controlling influence on programme content. The protection of the freedom of expression of opinion for radio and television required extensive legally regulated organizational solutions able to guarantee comprehensive, balanced and accurate reporting of the views prevailing in society and to give effect to unbiased reporting about facts and events in the public interest. Any future Act on radio and television would have to ensure that neither organs of the State (legislature or Government) nor specific interest groups could, directly or indirectly, exert a formative or undue influence on the content of public radio and television broadcasting, thereby rendering biased the subject matter of programmes.

IN THE NAME OF THE REPUBLIC OF HUNGARY!

In the matter of petitions seeking an ex post facto review of the unconstitutionality of a legal norm, and a procedure initiated ex officio for the declaration and termination of an unconstitutional omission to legislate, the Constitutional Court has made the following

DECISION.

The Constitutional Court holds that para. 6 of the Council of Ministers Decree 1047/1974 (IX.18) MT is unconstitutional. The Constitutional Court suspends its proceedings concerning the determination of the date of annulment of the unconstitutional legal norm until 30 November 1992.

The Constitutional Court holds that Parliament has failed to fulfill its legislative duty as enshrined by Art. 61(4) of the Constitution. For this reason the Constitutional Court calls upon Parliament to enact, by 30 November 1992, the law or laws on the supervision of public service radio and television, the licensing of commercial radio and television and the prevention of the emergence of information monopolies in radio or television broadcasting. In the event the deadline set herein expires without legislative action having taken place, the Constitutional Court shall recommence the suspended proceedings.

The Constitutional Court publishes this Decision in the *Hungarian Official Gazette.*

REASONING

SÓLYOM, P., delivering the Opinion of the Court: [....]

II

1. According to its established practice, the Constitutional Court does not establish formal unconstitutionality and does not annul a legal norm if a subject of legislation according to the Act XI/1987 on Legislation (hereafter referred to as the Act on Legislation)

was regulated by a lower-level norm coming into force prior to the Act on Legislation. According to s. 5(d) of the Act on Legislation, beginning in 1988 the regulation of the press must be made by statute. [....]

Council of Ministers Decree 91/1990 (V.2) MT [amending the challenged Decree of 1974] introduced the regulation currently in force, and Council of Ministers Decree 92/1990 (V.10) MT, in force as from 2 May 1990, retroactively dissolved the "Supervisory Committee" and ordered the retransfer of all of its supervisory authority to the Council of Ministers.

These changes in the supervisory authority occurred after the new Constitution came into force. Since the Decrees regulate a legislative subject, they are contrary to the provisions of the Act on Legislation and, therefore, Art. 35 of the Constitution. What is more, since the amendment of the Constitution by Act XL/1990, they also contradict Art. 61(4) of the Constitution. According to this latter provision, the supervision is to be regulated by a statute adopted by a qualified majority. In spite of this, the supervision and the right of approval of the rules of organization and operation existing throughout the history of the legal norm have been regulated by the Council of Ministers—even under the force of the [new] Constitution. Thus the text of the challenged provision was formally enacted unconstitutionally, and this error was repeated after the constitutional amendment's imposition of more stringent requirements. Thus para. 6 of the Council of Ministers Decree is formally unconstitutional and must be declared null and void by the Constitutional Court.

2.(a) The Constitutional Court stated in its *Dec. 30/1992 (V.26) AB* (MK 1992/53; ABH 1992, 167) that freedom of expression is the "mother right" of all rights of communication; among others, the fundamental right of the freedom of the press may be derived therefrom. The Constitutional Court expounded that the Constitution guarantees and protects free communication—as individual behaviour and social process—irrespective of its content. The decision held that the pre-eminent role of the freedom of opinion required that other rights balanced against it be interpreted narrowly. The Constitutional Court also made clear with respect to the expression of opinion that in addition to the protection of the fundamental rights of individuals the State is burdened, where appropriate, with an affirmative duty of institutional protection. From Art. 61 of the Constitution is thereby derived the fundamental right to the freedom of expression, on the one hand, and the State's obligation to secure the conditions necessary for the creation and maintenance of the functioning of democratic public opinion on the other hand. According to another Constitutional Court decision [*Dec. 64/1991 (XII.17) AB:* MK 1991/139; ABH 1991, 297], in the process of the objective protection of fundamental rights the State examines the values attached to a specific fundamental right in relation to other fundamental rights, and the protection of fundamental rights is embedded in the State's protection and maintenance of the constitutional order as a whole.

(b) With respect to the freedom of the press, the freedom of expression is given effect in a unique manner. The State must guarantee the freedom of the press cognizant of the fact that the press is the pre-eminent tool for disseminating and moulding views and for the gathering of information necessary for the formation of opinion. As the right of the freedom of press can be derived from the "mother right" of freedom of expression, the pre-eminent status conferred on the freedom of expression relates to the freedom of the press to the extent that it serves the former constitutional fundamental right.

The press is an instrument of information, not merely one of free expression since it plays a basic role in the process of gathering the information necessary for the formation of opinions. Article 61 of the Constitution, too, enumerates separately the right of the freedom of expression and the right of access to and dissemination of data of public interest.

The freedom of the press is primarily subject to external limits (which may also take the shape of special institutional features appropriate for the press's uniqueness, such as right of reply or the criterion of "a large public audience" [for incitement] in criminal law). Still, the freedom of the press is primarily guaranteed by the State's non-intervention with the content; this is assured, for instance, by the prohibition of censorship and the opportunity of the free establishment of newspapers. With this self-restriction, the State makes it possible in principle for the whole spectrum of opinions existing in society, as well as all the information of public interest, to appear in the press. The substantive and procedural safeguards of the right to be informed, that is, the freedom of information, is primarily developed by the State elsewhere, in connection with regulating access to data with respect to everyone including the press. But a democratic public opinion may only come about on the basis of an objective and comprehensive dissemination of information. Accordingly, the right to information, which is indispensable to opinion formation, is recognized by the Constitution as a boundary of the aforementioned concept of the freedom of the press, but only to the extent that is unavoidable: it expressly compels Parliament to prevent by statutory regulation the emergence of information monopolies.

(c) The service of the freedom of expression and the right to information in radio and television imposes requirements above and beyond those arising from the uniqueness of the freedom of the press. Here, the exercise of the fundamental right must be reconciled with the restricted technical means for its realization, that is, the finiteness (within the foreseeable future) of broadcast frequencies. In contrast with the printed press, this technical limitation does not permit establishment of broadcasting stations without constraints.

(d) Further unique solutions are required concerning the (at the time) practically monopolized national public service radio and television. With respect to them, the legislature is obliged to enact such laws the substantive, procedural and organizational regulations of which render both possible and obligatory a comprehensive, balanced and accurate reporting by these institutions and ensure their continued operation in such a manner.

3. The unique guarantees required by radio and television are in principle not restricted to a specific organizational solution or legal form. However, the protection of the freedom of expression for radio and television does require extensive legally regulated organizational solutions. Such solutions can be qualified as constitutional if they are able to guarantee a comprehensive, balanced and accurate reporting of the views prevailing in society and to give effect to an unbiased reporting about facts and events of public interest.

Of course, the nature of the organizational and legal solutions depends upon the country's existing structure of radio and television: whether and to what extent there are local public radio and television, as well as commercial radio and television, stations augmenting the national public service radio and television. The requirements for the presentation of views and reporting of information shall be ensured with respect to the radio and television sector as a whole; it is up to the legislature to decide the extent to which commercial and local public stations should assist the national public service radio and television, which bear the brunt of this duty. To pass constitutional muster, the Act on Radio and Television must ensure that neither organs of the State nor specific interest groups will be able to exert a formative influence on the content of public radio and television programmes.

The Constitution thus demands that the State engage in affirmative protective action on the one hand and self-restraint on the other hand. Parliament is obliged to enact a statute concerning the guarantees of the freedom of opinion, in addition to those identified in Art. 61(4) of the Constitution, as long as they are necessary for the attainment of the aforementioned goal.

Further, the appropriate regulations for the attainment of this aforementioned positive result must ensure that neither the organs of the State nor a specific group of society be able to influence the content of the programmes in such a way as to injure the comprehensiveness, balance in the scope of coverage, and accuracy in presenting the opinions prevalent in society, as well as the non-bias of the reporting. The Constitution demands that radio and television be free from the State and from individual groups in society. They cannot have a licence to make the subject matter of programmes one sided or exert undue influence on their content. This prohibition extends to indirect influence as well as to its possibility.

The requirement of freedom from "state organs" with respect to content of the programmes applies equally against the legislature and the Government. Both are subject to criticism and supervision through public scrutiny. Therefore none of them may be permitted to have instruments to influence opinions disseminated by radio and television. Formative influence by Parliament on the content of radio and television programmes is no less unconstitutional than that by the Government.

The same applies to local governments, political parties and other social organizations, groups representing particular interests and other groups.

It is the legislature's duty to specify the legal solution which is capable of guaranteeing the unbiased reporting and comprehensive, balanced and accurate presentation of prevailing opinions; within these limitations it is also the legislature which determines what role is to be given to public service radio and television. Given the present [technical] limitation on the possibility of radio and television broadcasting, statutory creation of specific social representation for making basic decisions on organization and structure and for supervising the balance of the content of programmes has become a widespread means of guaranteeing the freedom of expression. (Article 61 of the Constitution permits but does not mandate this solution.) The Constitutional Court points out that a full or partial reconstitution of political representation is alien to the institution of this unique social representation guaranteeing the freedom of expression. Political parties' consensus is not appropriate (and even less so where the consensus is limited to parties represented in Parliament) for extending constitutional protection to all aspects of freedom of expression. On the contrary: freedom from the State demands that neither Parliament nor Government be in a position to exert influence over programme content; just like political parties, groups created for the same purpose or for the representation of the same interests must likewise be denied a controlling influence.

4. The content of para. 6 of Council of Ministers Decree 1047/1974 (IX.18) MT is unconstitutional not because it entrusts the Government with the supervision—including the rules on organization and operation—of Hungarian [State] Radio and Hungarian [State] Television but because it does not contain any financial, procedural or organizational regulation which would preclude the possibility of the Government using its power to assert—even indirectly—a controlling influence on programming content. For this reason the norm violates Art. 61(1) and (2) of the Constitution.

III

The Council of Ministers Decree does not contain even the minimum guarantees of the freedom of opinion and the press and is therefore unconstitutional. But there is no other legal norm which provides any legal and organizational guarantees in connection with the freedom of expression with respect to radio and television. The absence of the regulation—especially in light of Art. 61(4) of the Constitution—has created an unconstitutional situation. Because of the features outlined in Point II.2 of this Decision, freedom of expression in the field of radio and television may only be realized under present conditions with the requisite degree of security if its method and organizational framework is prescribed by specific and positive regulation. According to Art. 61(4) of the Constitution, the adoption of the Act on the supervision of public radio and television, appointment of their heads and the licensing of commercial radio and television stations requires the majority of two-thirds of the votes of Members of Parliament present.

The Constitutional Court may establish an unconstitutional omission to legislate if the legislature has failed to fulfil its legislative duty mandated by a legal norm and this has given rise to an unconstitutional situation. In the present case the Constitutional Court emphasizes the unconstitutionality of the current situation. (The enactment of the statutes necessary for the execution of the Constitution is mandated by Art. 78 of the Constitution itself, and the duty to act is further emphasized by Art. 61, specifically dealing with radio and television.) The realization of the fundamental rights of the freedom of expression, freedom of the press and freedom of information is impeded by the absence of regulations inevitably necessary to give them full effect.

The Constitutional Court is also authorized to initiate ex officio a procedure for the determination of the legislature's unconstitutional omission to legislate and to call upon the legislature to comply with its duties within a deadline determined by the Court. In its practice thus far the Constitutional Court has declined to declare such an unconstitutional omission and to issue an instruction, provided that Parliament has already commenced deliberations concerning the requisite law. But the Constitutional Court points emphatically to the principle that the legislature's duty is dispatched upon the enactment of the Act and not with the commencement of its deliberations. Therefore, in the event that the omission to legislate has caused a serious violation of the Constitution and the completion of the deliberations on the bill may not even approximately be forecast, the Constitutional Court may establish an omission and may set a deadline for its rectification.

In the present case the omission inhibits the realization of a fundamental right which has a pre-eminent role in the functioning of a democratic society. For this reason the Constitutional Court has established the legislature's omission to legislate and has called upon Parliament to enact by 30 November 1992, in accordance with the requirements enumerated in the holding of this Decision, all those laws which are prescribed by Art. 61(4) of the Constitution.

IV

The Council of Ministers Decree is unconstitutional because of the absence of guarantees against government influence. The situation in general is unconstitutional because of the absence of a law containing guarantees against undue influence from any source. Since there is no qualitative difference between unconstitutional influence emanating from the Government, Parliament or political parties, the Constitutional Court had to weigh whether the preservation of the former or latter unconstitutionality would pose a lesser danger to legal certainty.

If the Constitutional Court were to strike down the Council of Ministers Decree effective immediately, public service radio and television broadcasting would fall completely outside legal supervision, that is, from that sphere of relations of political responsibility which may be legally enforced. In that case only in the event of a serious abuse of the freedom of expression would there be a possibility for the application of the instruments of criminal law or of the protection of personality. Consequently, the media would be totally at the mercy of political party struggles and the factional struggles carried on therein; this condition would explicitly militate against the freedom of expression.

With the suspension of the decision concerning the date of nullification, the Constitutional Court leaves in force the Council of Ministers Decree until the enactment of the statutory regulation. With this move the Constitutional Court maintains the possibility of legal handling of the situation. The supervisory rights can be applied to the benefit or detriment of the freedom of the press. It is true that, according to the Constitutional Court's present Decision, even the existence of this ambivalence is unconstitutional, meaning that of the two aforementioned possibilities the possibility of governmental influence over the content of programmes would have to be foreclosed. Nevertheless, the protection of the constitutional order and the protection of citizens' rights is the Government's constitutional duty (Art. 35(1)), for which it may be held accountable. One can no more assume that the Government will not stand up to protect the freedom of the press than that it will restrict it. Numerous questions concerning the supervisory right may be clarified by judicial remedies (*e.g.*, employment rights). For this reason, the Constitutional Court regards the future invalidation of the Council of Ministers Decree as comprising the lesser threat to legal certainty. The Constitutional Court's choice was influenced by the consideration that this Decision concurrently established Parliament's unconstitutional omission to legislate, compelling it to rectify the unconstitutional situation within a short time period by enacting a law providing for the constitutionally mandated freedom of the radio and television. But if Parliament fails to pass the Act by the expiration of the deadline, it becomes warranted to continue this procedure and determine the date of invalidation of the Council of Ministers Decree based on a new evaluation of the aforementioned reasons.

DECISION 4/1993: 12 FEBRUARY 1993

ON THE RESTITUTION OF CHURCH PROPERTY

Although the petitioners simply challenged the constitutionality of the Act, which provided for returning some real estate—among them school buildings—to certain churches (their owners before the communist nationalization), the decision embraced all basic questions of the freedom of religion. The first part of the decision clarifies all the relevant notions. After decades of socialism, it was important to stress that the neutrality of the State was not the same as indifference; then the Court applied the neutrality principle to state-run schools. The separation of State and church has not been resolved in the spirit of the establishment clause; in harmony with the Hungarian tradition, it also contained elements of cooperation. This amounted in the third part of the decision to a constitutional justification for restoring parts of former church property on the basis of functionality (as opposed to the "compensation" in compensation cases 21/1990 and 16/1991). This kind of interplay of the "state support" necessary to guarantee "free exercise" might not seem strange to American readers. The case also gave the Court an opportunity to rule on the frequently politically misused question of the need for a qualified majority to pass laws on certain subjects enumerated in the Constitution. The interpretation of the Court restricted the necessity of such qualified majority voting.

The petitioners sought constitutional review of Act XXXII/1991 on the Settlement of the Ownership of the Real Estate Formerly Owned by Churches (hereafter the Act).

The Act, passed by a simple majority of votes, aimed at providing a partial remedy for the very serious injustices experienced by the Churches during nationalization between 1948 and 1953 and at ensuring the necessary objective and financial conditions for their operation. Sections 1 and 2 permitted the transfer of buildings which had served certain church activities before nationalization, *e.g.*, under s. 2(2), religious life, operation of a monastic order, education, health and social care, youth and child welfare, and cultural purposes. According to s. 15, the Government and the interested church might conclude an agreement in order to create sufficient material conditions for church activities which were useful for society and provided for a partial compensation for church-owned buildings nationalized after 1 January 1948 (with the exception of property returned under ss. 1 and 2). The amount to be used as compensation was to be fixed annually by the State Budget.

The petitioner submitted, inter alia, that the Act was contrary to the Constitution: (a) Art. 60 because it did not guarantee the existence of a non-ideological (neutral, public or state) school in each settlement; and (b) Art. 60(4) because it was not passed by the votes of two thirds of the MPs present. The need for such a qualified majority referred to the freedom of conscience and religion as a legislative subject including regulation connected with institutions of religious freedom. Since the Act rectified the financial conditions fundamentally of the institutional framework of religious freedom and thereby determined it for the future, it required a two-thirds majority to be passed; and (c) Art. 70/A, since it drew a distinction between the compensated churches and the other churches as well as organizations having suffered similar property loss. Moreover the way the Act reprivatized the property of the churches was also unconstitutional.

Held, granting the petition only in part:

(1) The State was to remain neutral in cases concerning the right to freedom of conscience and religion, from which right it was required to guarantee the possibility of the free formation of personal convictions. Article 60 guaranteed freedom of conscience and religion, which formerly comprehended the freedom to choose or adopt a religion or a personal conviction; freedom of its exercise, including the negative freedom of religion being the right not to manifest any conviction; and the right to religious association and assembly. On the one hand, religion was part of the right to human dignity so that the guarantee of its freedom ensured free expression of a human being's personality, which itself could not be limited by law. Thus, from the freedom of religion, the State had a duty to abstain from interference in its exercise. On the other hand, there was also a close relationship between the right to free exercise of religion and freedom of expression. Since the manifestation of this freedom was the exercise of religion or worship, any laws limiting such freedom had to be as strictly construed as those in respect of freedom of expression. The State was to protect the freedom of conscience and religion without considering its value or its content (thus the right could only have external limits), and it was from such a position that the State drew its neutrality, as underlined by Art. 60(3).

(2) From a reading of Arts. 60(3) and 70/A, the State was not to favour any church or influence its internal workings, particularly in matters of religious truths. Rather it was required to treat all churches equally and provide everyone with the opportunity to exercise their freedom of conscience. However, the separation of Church from State did not mean that the State ought to ignore the characteristics of religion and church in its legislation: for instance, it could take into consideration everything that differentiated churches and religious communities with respect to their history and social role, from those other social organizations, associations, unions and chambers of commerce, the establishment of which was governed by Arts. 3, 63 and 70/C. Such roles included school education, tending to the sick and charity, once exclusively church duties that became state ones at the time of nationalization. Further the neutral state legal system ensured that religious communities could freely use the legal form of "church" as defined by the State's secular laws. Provided the community fulfilled the criteria in such laws, it would obtain its legal status according to the legal form chosen by itself and could enforce its special characteristics within this sphere and so fit into the legal system in a way provided by the State. Its neutrality in connection with the right to freedom of religion therefore did not mean inactivity. In fact the State was bound to ensure the circumstances under which different ideas could be formed and developed, and to enable the free formation of personal convictions.

(3) A neutral (public or state) school could not be committed to any religion or worldview but had to provide a comprehensive, balanced and unbiased expression of the prevailing ideas in society, offering the possibility of a free and well-founded choice. Where a school was sponsored by the State or local government which permitted education committed to a religion, then such a school had to be considered a "committed" school like other church schools; otherwise the requirement of religious neutrality would not have made sense. In the exercise of the freedom of religion, parents had the right to have their children

attend church schools and not to have them attend schools that are contrary to their world-view. In acting according to their conscience, it was not unconstitutional for such persons to be constrained to make a sacrifice, albeit a proportionate one. Thus, while the State was to ensure the legal possibility for establishing non-neutral schools, it was not obliged to establish them. Where, however, the church or parents established or ran committed schools, the State was required to support them to the extent of their fulfilling the State's obligations in them.

(4) Consequently the Act did not infringe the various principles derived from the freedom of conscience and religion in Art. 60. Moreover it provided sufficient guarantees in the transfer of erstwhile state school buildings to the church for the protection of the rights of parents and children not wanting to attend church school. The State was bound to provide a viable alternative by making possible attendance at neutral state schools, for those refusing to attend church schools, without discrimination or imposition of an undue burden for them. Consequently whereas the State and local governments were not obliged to establish a church school for those choosing it, they were required to make a neutral school available where demanded even in cases in which the number of pupils was low.

(5) The Act involved detailed regulation of various matters and did not involve the direction and defence of the right to freedom of conscience and religion: its passing by a simple majority in Parliament was therefore in accordance with Art. 60(4). The constitutional requirement of a two-thirds majority of MPs present to pass an Act on fundamental rights referred to freedom of religion, rights of ethnic and national minorities, and citizenship. The current emphasis on the two-thirds majority revealed the political importance of such rights when broad consensus was needed to amend them in the Constitution. The fundamental right was not a legislative subject in every detail: an Act, even if a qualified voting one, was needed only to define the content of the fundamental right, its substantial guarantees and its direct and significant restriction. Such an Act would therefore determine the direction of the enforcement and protection of such right, directly implementing a specific constitutional provision: lawful regulation pertaining to a fundamental right with its particular, detailed rules therefore required only a simple majority. Moreover the protection and realization of fundamental rights would be restricted unjustifiably if every change and development, or partial guarantee which did not determine the regulatory concept, were attached to a two-thirds majority.

(6) There was no unconstitutional discrimination between the churches and other legal entities on the basis of ss. 1 and 2 of the Act. The aim of the Act and the nature of the return of buildings differed fundamentally from the concept of the partial compensation for unjust harm done to citizens. This derived from the difference between the function of the property of individuals and legal entities pursuing commercial activity or representing certain interests and the functions of church property as listed in s. 2(2). However the historical social role of the churches and the inseparability of their operation from the right to freedom of religion offered a satisfactory basis for the classification of churches as being among organizations supported by the State: in other words it was the State's constitutional duty not only to privatize a particular part of its property but also to establish and promote public organizations and, in order to fulfill their obligations and to strengthen their autonomy, the State also transfers property to them. Nevertheless in the broad group of comparable or-

ganizations, the transfer of property was at different stages, and, provided such transfer was in conformity with the function of the organization, it was not arbitrary. Further it was logical that churches which either were not operating at the relevant time or had suffered no loss remained unentitled since the present transfer was of buildings previously used by the entitled churches for implementation of their right to exercise freedom of religion and which could now be reclaimed for the same purpose in conformity with the churches' real needs.

(7) Section 15 of the Act was unconstitutional. The rule contained therein supported the activities of churches generally and was not bound, like the benefits listed under ss. 1 and 2, to the needs of the churches' specified activity. Its legal title was the "partial compensation" of the properties which had been nationalized: other provisions of the Act redressed the damage caused by deprivation of the objective and financial conditions for the real exercise of religion on the ground of the principle of function. After the restitution of function, no additional differentiation between the churches was necessary to promote the freedom of religion and thus the possibility of state support for the material independence of churches could not constitutionally be limited to those which lost their property after 1948. The characteristics of churches justified the transfer of property to them on the principle of function which differed from compensation given to remedy only past violations of property rights. Additional property to guarantee uninterrupted operation could only be provided as compensation if the transfer of property for churches and other autonomous public bodies had already been formed: therefore, compensation did not mean unreasoned discrimination in such a system compared to other benefits supplied to other bodies in which there was a public interest during the course of their becoming autonomous. Accordingly, in the absence of the conditions necessary for supporting affirmative discrimination, s. 15 remained contrary to the Constitution.

IN THE NAME OF THE REPUBLIC OF HUNGARY!

On the basis of petitions seeking an ex post facto review of unconstitutionality of a statute and its annulment, the Constitutional Court—with the dissenting opinions of Schmidt, J., regarding Point I of Part B of the Decision, and of Vörös, J., regarding Part B and Point 2 of Part C, and further with the concurring opinion of Herczegh, J., regarding the reasoning to Point I.2(b) of Part A—has made the following

DECISION.

A

1. The State must remain neutral in matters concerning the freedom of religion and other questions concerning conscience. From the right to freedom of religion follows the State's duty to ensure the possibility of free formation of personal convictions.

The separation of church and State does not mean that the State must disregard the special characteristics of religion and church.

2. A state school must not be committed to any religion.

The State shall ensure the legal possibility for establishing church schools, but the State itself is not required to establish such schools.

Where the State transfers school buildings to serve as a church school, for those who do not want to attend a church school the State must provide for a viable alternative by making the attendance at a state school possible in such a way that attending the state school must not be an undue burden for them.

3. The Constitutional Court rejects the petitions challenging Act XXXII/1991 on the Settlement of the Ownership of Real Estate Formerly Owned by Churches on the basis that the Act would violate Art. 60 of the Constitution because, in cases where erstwhile state school buildings are transferred to the church, it does not guarantee a free choice of schools based on the freedom of conscience and religion.

B

1. The Constitutional Court holds that where the Constitution requires the votes of a two-thirds majority of Members of Parliament present to pass an Act on a fundamental right, the requirement of qualified majority does not refer to any statutory regulation on that fundamental right but only to an Act which directly implements the given specific constitutional rule. Such an Act determines the basic direction of the enforcement and the protection of the given fundamental right. The requirement of a qualified majority to pass an Act on fundamental rights does not exclude detailed rules necessary to implement the given fundamental right which can be determined by a simple majority.

2. There was no need for the votes of a two-thirds majority of the Members of Parliament present to pass Act XXXII/1991 on the Settlement of the Ownership of Real Estate Formerly Owned by Churches. The Constitutional Court rejects the petitions which contended that the Act was contrary to Art. 60(4) of the Constitution because of the absence of a two-thirds majority.

C

1. The Constitutional Court declares that s. 15 of Act XXXII/1991 on the Settlement of the Ownership of Real Estate Formerly Owned by Churches (henceforth the Act) is unconstitutional and therefore annuls it. Section 15 of this Act will lose force on the day this Decision is published in the *Hungarian Official Gazette.*

2. The Constitutional Court rejects the petitions which contend that s. 1(2) and (4); s. 2(2)(a), (e); s. 12(2); s. 13; s. 16(5); s. 17(2); and s. 22 of the Act are unconstitutional.

The Constitutional Court publishes this Decision in the *Hungarian Official Gazette.*

REASONING

SÓLYOM, P., delivering the Opinion of the Court:[....]

A

I

According to the petitions the Act is contrary to Art. 60 of the Constitution because it does not guarantee the existence of ideologically non-committed schools in each settlement.

1. Article 60(1) of the Constitution guarantees the right to freedom of thought, con-

science and religion for everyone. Paragraph 2 lays down the traditional meaning of freedom of religion, extending it to freedom of conscience; freedom to choose or accept a religion or a personal conviction; freedom of its exercise, including the negative freedom of religion, namely, the right to omit manifestation of conviction; and finally it contains—not as a special rule but through the liberty of exercising religion "collectively" and "publicly"—the right to religious association and assembly.

The (traditional) free exercise is the most important of the three aspects of the freedom of religion and it stands closer to other rights and liberties, and through this the freedom of religion fits into the "fundamental rights of communication." The law can ensure it the most completely: and it is also the basis of other components of the freedom of religion. For example, the freedom of religion (thoughts and beliefs) is ensured through communication in the Constitution when it declares the meaning of freedom of religion with the freedom of choosing and accepting a religion. On the other hand in the Constitution the free exercise does not mean only liturgical actions and teachings but more: religion can be manifested in "any other ways."

The element of freedom of religion that everyone is allowed to follow in his lifestyle his own convictions should be considered differently to the classical "religious acts and observance" related to freedom of expression. But the realization of freedom of conscience in social life is also a symbolic expression having the same characteristics as communication-related freedoms.

To clarify the meaning of freedom of religion, we should enlarge on its relationship to other basic rights with special regard to the limits of rights and the objective duties of the State to guarantee them.

Article 60(1) of the Constitution declares the freedom of thought, conscience and religion. From para. (2) on, the Constitution does not contain any provisions concerning freedom of thought but determines the meaning of freedom of conscience and religion. According to the Constitutional Court, Art. 61 on the freedom of expression covers the expression of thought. Article 60 is a special rule of the general Art. 61, and, like the freedom of conscience and religion, is a special field of freedom of thought. That is why the Decision does not consider freedom of thought but freedom of religion; however, its statements also refer to personal convictions unless they do not expressly indicate the differences.

(a) The freedom of religion and the right to human dignity

The Constitutional Court laid down two aspects of the right to human dignity. On one hand the right to human dignity—together with the right to life and legal capacity—is considered as a right which determines the person's legal status (See *Dec. 64/1991 (XII.17) AB:* MK 1991/139; ABH 1991, 297). On the other hand according to the practice of the Constitutional Court—from *Dec. 8/1990 (IV.23) AB* (MK 1990/35; ABH 1990, 42)—the right to human dignity is the "general right of personality," which includes the right to free development of one's personality. The Constitutional Court also interpreted the freedom of conscience in *Dec. 64/1991 (XII.17) AB* as a right to personal integrity. (The State cannot compel anyone to accept a situation which sows discord within, or is irreconcilable with, those fundamental convictions which mould that person's identity.)

The freedom of conscience and religion acknowledges that the person's conviction and, within this, in a given case, religion, is a part of human quality, so their freedom is a pre-condition for the free development of personality.

Personality itself is untouchable by the law (this is expressed by the unlimited right to life and human dignity); the law can only help to ensure this autonomy by guaranteeing its external conditions. Therefore the right to freedom of conscience and religion—even if we do not consider now the right to free exercise of religion—includes the State's duty not to take a stance in matters of truthfulness of religious faith and other personal convictions. The Constitution—because of historical reasons—only makes a declaration on this with regard to the freedom of science (Art. 70/G(2)), but according to the Constitutional Court, the State has the same obligation concerning the freedom of religion.

The close relation between freedom of religion and right to human dignity should also be considered when we are talking about the other two elements of freedom of religion, worship or acting and living according to one's convictions. It gives special emphasis to the freedom of action based on the general right of personality if the action is derived from the person's religious and conscientious convictions. (This is acknowledged by the right to refuse military service by referring to conscientious objections.)

(b) The right to freedom of religion and freedom of expression

The special protection of the freedom of religion also derives from the close relationship between the right to free exercise of religion and freedom of expression.

According to *Dec. 30/1992 (V.26) AB* (MK 1992/53; ABH 1992, 167) the freedom of thought and the freedom of religion also belong to the "fundamental rights of communication." The "mother right" of these rights, the freedom of expression—in the Constitutional Court's practice—enjoys a privileged position among fundamental constitutional rights. The above-mentioned decision declares that "the laws restricting the freedom of expression must be strictly construed." This also refers to laws restricting the freedom of religion.

The laws can influence freedom of thought and religion only if the thought or the conviction is expressed. This expression is the exercise of religion. The State can defend the "free choice and acceptance of a religion or any other personal convictions" (Constitution, Art. 60(1), first indent) through ensuring the free flow of ideas. Because of the nature of the freedom of thought, conscience and religion and because of the possibilities offered by the law, the competence of the State can only be limited to the process of communication, which is significant to the formation and manifestation of convictions. From this position of the State also comes its neutrality.

According to *Dec. 30/1992 (V.26) AB* (MK 1992/53; ABH 1992, 167) the right to the freedom of expression protects the opinion irrespective of the value or the veracity of its content. The Constitution guarantees free communication—as individual behaviour or a public process—and the fundamental right to freedom of expression does not refer to the content of the opinion. This statement is also valid for the freedom of religion. Further, it can only have external limits.

(c) The separation of church and State

The neutrality of the State is explicitly ordained and guaranteed by Art. 60(3) of the Constitution, which states that in the Republic of Hungary the church shall operate in separation from the State.

From the principle of separation it follows that the State must not be institutionally attached to churches or any one church; that the State must not identify itself with the teachings of any church; and that the State must not interfere with the internal workings of any church, and especially must not take a stance in matters of religious truths. From this (as well as from Art. 70/A of the Constitution) it follows that the State must treat churches equally. Because the State is required not to take a stance exactly in matters that make a religion a religion, concerning churches and religion the State can only create an abstract legal framework that applies to every church or religion equally and allows them to fit into a neutral legal order; in matters of substance, the State has nothing to go by but the interpretations of the churches and religions themselves. [....]

It is exactly by way of a neutral and general legal framework that the separation of church and State can provide the fullest possible freedom of religion.

The separation of church and State, however, does not affect the duty of the State to provide both positive and negative freedom of religion without discrimination, based on Art. 60 of the Constitution. Positive and negative rights to the freedom of religion are equally important: neither is a general rule to which the other would be an exception. From the neutrality of the State it does not follow that the State should endorse the negative right to the freedom of religion, let alone religious indifference. The State violates its duty deriving from the freedom of religion if it does not engage itself in providing everyone with the possibility of an informed and well-founded choice in these questions.

Nor does the separation of church and State mean that the State must disregard the special characteristics of religion and church in its legislation. The Constitution forbids only limitations which are effective exclusively for religious convictions or the practice of religion. It is not forbidden for the State to take the characteristics of religion and the churches into consideration when shaping the laws that make the freedom of religion prevail.

The church is not the same for religion and for state law. The neutral State must not follow the different religions' differing ideas on the church. The neutral State can consider everything that differentiates religious communities and churches in general, with respect to their history and social role, from other social organizations, associations, organizations representing particular interest groups that can be established under the Constitution. [Arts. 3, 63 and 70/C of the Constitution]. The Constitution ensures that religious communities can freely use, besides the organizations that can be established on the basis of the right of association, the legal form of "church" as defined by secular law. The State considers the churches' characteristics with this legal institution and ensures they fit into the legal system. The religious community obtains its legal status according to the legal form chosen by itself and can enforce its special characteristics within the framework of that form. In what way the separation of church and State occurs and how strict and consequential it is depends on the historical conditions of each and every country. The present interpretation of Art. 60(3) of the Constitution cannot be separated from the role of the churches in Hungarian history (including the process of secularization), nor from their present functions, nor from the current process of societal transformation. It is a general phenomenon that a number of tasks formerly carried out by the churches (*e.g.,* school education, tending to the sick, charity) have become the duties of the State, while the churches have also maintained their activity in these domains. In these fields separation does not exclude co-operation, even though it must take place under rigorous guarantees. Also, treating the churches equally does not exclude taking the actual social roles of the individual churches into account.

(d) The State's duty to "respect and protect" the fundamental rights (Art. 8(1) of the Constitution) concerning the freedom of religion is not totally fulfilled by not violating individual liberties: the State also has to guarantee the conditions that are necessary for the freedom of religion to prevail [....] (see *Dec. 64/1991 (XII.17) AB:* MK 1991/139; ABH 1991, 297).

The State's neutrality in connection with the right to freedom of religion does not mean inactivity. It is the State's obligation to ensure a field for manifesting, teaching and following in life one's religious convictions, for the operation of churches as well as for rejecting religion or keeping silent on it. In this field the different ideas can be formed and developed and enable the free formation of personal convictions. On the one hand the State shall ensure this process of communication, which actually derives from the right to freedom of thought and freedom of expression. On the other hand it shall protect other fundamental rights against the freedom of religion as well. Finally there could be a need for the positive regulation of the right to freedom of religion. Wherever it is the State itself that creates a situation in which the freedom of religion and the freedom to refuse it are limiting each other, the State has to strike a regulated compromise. Subjects involving matters of ideology in obligatory education are an instance of such a situation.

2. The realization of freedom of religion in compulsory school education.

(a) In order to implement Art. 60, Parliament passed Act IV/1990 on the Freedom of Conscience and Religion, and on the Churches. Section 5 of this Act states that the parent or guardian has the right to decide on and provide for the moral and religious education of the minor child. According to s. 17, churches in the capacity of legal persons can carry out any educational or instructional activity that no Act restricts to be carried out by the State alone. In institutions of education and instruction run by the State, the church can teach religion as an elective subject.

These regulations partially implement Art. 60 of the Constitution but are not sufficient implementations of the full obligation of the State concerning the freedom of religion. Moreover, Hungary assumed more than this in international agreements. [References were made to the relevant articles of the European Convention on Human Rights (First Protocol, art. 2), the International Covenant on Civil and Political Rights (arts. 2 and 18(4)), and the New York Convention on the Rights of the Child (art. 14), all of which had been promulgated into Hungarian law.]

(b) The State should guarantee the legal and institutional conditions needed for the realization of fundamental rights so that duties also arising from other basic rights and constitutional requirements, shall be considered (*Dec. 64/1991 (XII.17) AB:* MK 1991/139; ABH 1991, 297). So the realization of freedom of religion should be harmonized with those fundamental rights which should also be realized in educational affairs. The State shall set up free and compulsory primary schools (Art. 70/F), and the parents and guardians are obliged to ensure the education of their children under the legal age (Art. 70/J). The parents have the right to choose the kind of education their children are to receive (Art. 67(2)). The State should respect and support the freedom of learning and teaching (Art. 70/G).

The terms "public school" and "church school" are used in this Decision to denote the different types of schools that comply with different aspects of the freedom of religion. The schools that satisfy the conditions of being a "public school" generally correspond to the "institutions of instruction and education run by the State." These are set apart from the schools in which educational activity is "carried out by a church" under s. 17(2) of Act IV/1990. At present, the institutional separation of public and church schools is not fully complied with as required by the Constitution. Provisional arrangements, however, can be steps toward a full institutional separation. The Decision differentiates between public and church schools according to the different constitutional requirements deriving from the concept of the freedom of religion. The difference between public and church schools is that—even if both should give an objective knowledge in a tolerant way and respecting the freedom of conscience of the pupils—while church schools identify with the teachings of a church, public schools cannot do that; they must remain neutral in matters of worldview. [....] [A] school run by the State (or the local government) in which the State allows education committed to a religion to take place is not a "public school." If religious education only takes place in separate classes, the requirement of the religious neutrality of public schools does not apply to those. Whatever is said in this decision about church schools also refers to every school where education "committed" to any worldview takes place. Such schools are termed church schools and also "committed" schools by this decision in order to differentiate them from "neutral" public schools.

The State must remain neutral in matters of religion. Therefore public schools must also be neutral. The State realizes through these public schools, which are open to all children, the right to education and ensures the conditions of compulsory schooling. Neutrality requires that the State shape the syllabi and organize and supervise its schools in such a manner that information on and knowledge about religion and worldview be transferred in an "unbiased, critical and pluralist fashion." The public school must not carry out education in a manner that can be considered to disregard the convictions of the parents (and the child) (see the judgment of the European Court of Human Rights in *Kjeldsen, Busk, Madsen and Pedersen,* Judgment of 7 December 1976, Series A, No. 23). These conditions correspond for public schools to the requirements the Constitutional Court set forth for the nationwide public television and radio monopolies in the interest of guaranteeing the freedom of speech. In that case, organizational arrangements are constitutional if, in principle, they can ensure the comprehensive, balanced and unbiased expression of the opinions prevailing across Hungarian society (*Dec. 37/1992 (VI.10) AB:* MK 1992/59; ABH 1992, 227). *Mutatis mutandis,* these conditions also apply to public schools. That is, the neutral public school cannot be committed to any religion or worldview; rather, it must make free and well-founded choice possible. It is in the way the whole school functions that the comprehensive, balanced and unbiased transmission of knowledge about matters of worldview must show: as long as he/she teaches in an unbiased manner, the State cannot force any teacher to conceal his/her convictions.

By establishing neutral public schools the State has not done everything necessary to ensure that the "conditions necessary for the freedom of religion" prevail. Parents have the right to have their child attend the church school of their choice. Within the limits of parental guidance, the child has the same right.

The complement of the parent's right to choose is the State's obligation to protect certain institutions. The State must not legally prevent schools committed to any religion or atheism from being founded: the necessary statutes must be passed. But the State is not required to establish non-neutral schools. If, however, the church or the parents establish and run a committed school, the State has to support them inasmuch as these institutions fulfill state obligations; moreover, support cannot be denied if the State is already supporting a comparable committed institution and the discrimination has no constitutional reason.

Even though parents are not entitled to expect the State to establish schools committed to the worldview of their wish, they do have the protective right not to have their children attend schools that are contrary to their worldview. Likewise the Constitutional Court stated in connection with the freedom of conscience, the State must refrain not only from a compulsion like this but also within reasonable bounds it must render an alternative attitude possible. It is not unconstitutional if, for the sake of the latter, those who would like to act according to their conscience are constrained to make a sacrifice, which is not a disproportionate one (*Dec. 64/1991 (XII.17) AB:* MK 1991/139; ABH 1991, 297). The alternative to all types of committed schools which satisfies the freedom of conscience is the neutral public school. Attending neutral school with whatever conviction means much less of a burden on one's conscience (if it is a burden at all) than going to a differently, moreover contrarily devoted, one.

For those who do not want to attend a committed school, it is not just the legal opportunity to act according to their conscience that the State must provide; it must in fact make attending a neutral public school possible.

(c) [....] As follows from the above, even where it transfers the ownership of the (major part of) the former building of the public school to the church, for those who do not want to attend a church school the State must provide for a viable alternative by making the attendance of a neutral school possible; making use of the alternative of attending a neutral school must not be an undue burden for them. [....] Since the transfer of ownership of buildings to churches is based on the principle of functionality, the building transferred is in fact used to practise the religion in question; usually it is a church school that replaces the public school. However, the constitutional solution is not a ban on the transfer of ownership to the church—for such a ban would restrict the fundamental rights of those who want their children to receive a religious education; rather, the solution is that the State should take affirmative steps to ensure the freedom of conscience and religion of the parents and children rejecting the church school. (A limitation of rights would only be acceptable if that were inevitable to guarantee either the positive or the negative right to the freedom of religion. This is not the case: the State is always capable of establishing a neutral school.)

The transfer of the building that theretofore served as a public school to serve as a church school does not legally mean closing the public school. According to s. 100(2) of Act XX/1991 on the Competences of Local Governments, the local government can only close or reorganize its mandated institutions if it continues providing the activity or service in question at the same level of quality. Under s. 2(1) of the Act under review, the transfer of buildings happens to the extent and when it is necessitated by the real activity of the church as well as considering the financial situation of the local government. Both provisions guarantee that the transfer of ownership of the buildings must not infringe on the local government's complying with its obligations. The Constitutional Court points out, however, that the local government will not comply with its obligations if the local school continues to function as a church school. The school cannot operate in a neutral and a religious spirit at the same time since ideological education belongs to the substance of both types of school—indeed, of each school. The set of provisions in the Act which guarantee for the local government the right to receive a substitute piece of real estate or financial compensation from the central State also ensures that the neutral public school continues functioning. The State and the local government must make schooling possible for children who choose to attend a public school just as much as if there had not been any transfer of ownership, even if the number of such children is low. [....] Attending the neutral school should not be an undue burden for those who choose to practise their right to do so. What an undue burden is must be determined based on the merits of the actual case.

The Act contains satisfactory guarantees to ensure that the transfer of ownership of buildings to the church—if in compliance with the Act—does not violate the right to the freedom of religion and conscience of the parents and children who refuse to attend church schools. Therefore the petitions that appeal to the Constitutional Court to declare the Act unconstitutional for the reason given above are rejected by the Constitutional Court.

B

II

According to the petitions, the Act is contrary to Art. 60(4) of the Constitution because it was not passed by the votes of two thirds of the Members of Parliament present. In the opinion of the petitioners the need for a qualified majority is not concerned with the Act "on Freedom of Conscience and Religion, and on the Churches" but refers to freedom of conscience and religion as a legislative subject which includes all regulations in connection with the institutions of religious freedom. Since the Act "fundamentally rectified the financial conditions of the institutional framework of religious freedom and thereby determined it for the future," it requires a two-thirds majority to be passed.

1. The text of the Constitution as amended by Act XXXI/1989 introduced the concept of a "constitutional act." Under Art. 24(3) of the Constitution, which came into force on 23 October 1989, for amendment of the Constitution, for passing certain decisions defined in the Constitution and also for passing constitutional acts, the affirmative votes of two thirds of the Members of Parliament are required. According to Art. 8(2), laws pertaining to fundamental rights and obligations must be determined exclusively by a constitutional act. As it appears from the wording of the norm in force at that time, there was no difference between the Constitution and the constitutional act regarding the formal conditions for passing these acts. Moreover, as for the content, according to the Preamble to Act XXXI/1989 "constitutional acts together with the Constitution form the highest level of substantive legal regulations in public law." The constitutional act serves to "relieve" the Constitution by not burdening it with detailed regulations that are important from the point of view of constitutional law. In *Dec. 4/1990 (III.4) AB* (MK 1990/19; ABH 1990, 28), in accordance with the conception of the Constitution in force at that time, the Constitutional Court declared that the demand for regulation in a constitutional act applies to all laws on fundamental rights and duties. According to the "direction" or "character" of these rules, one must not make a distinction between regulation in an "ordinary" or a constitutional act; the latter is obligatory in each case.

In June 1990, however, by Act XL/1990, which amended the Constitution, the situation fundamentally changed. The category of constitutional act was eliminated. According to the then introduced Art. 8(2) of the Constitution currently in force, rules pertaining to fundamental rights and duties are determined by statute. The exclusivity of regulating fundamental rights and duties in statutes which required a qualified majority to be passed was also repealed. Since that time, some fundamental rights can be regulated in statutes passed by a simple majority. However, in several cases concerning fundamental rights, a new rule replaced the one which had made possible the regulation thereof solely in a constitutional act. Thus the votes of two thirds of the Members of Parliament present are now required to pass a statute on rights, obligations or institutions provided for in the given Article of the Constitution.

The current system theoretically differs from the previous one which comprehended constitutional acts. The constitutional acts referred to every fundamental right, as well as to any regulation of them, with the obligation of exclusivity. The Constitution and constitutional acts, on the one hand, and statutes passed by a simple majority on the other hand, created a clear hierarchical order concerning their content and form.

Since the current Constitution required a two-thirds majority for statutes to be enacted on particular fundamental rights, several different orders of importance can be established among the fundamental constitutional rights, which do not overlap. Among the statutes to be passed by a qualified majority, the regulations concerning the most important fundamental rights do not appear: neither that on the right to life and human dignity, nor that on legal capacity, nor the guarantees of personal freedom and safety, including the deprivation of one's freedom. The right to trial before a court, as well as the right to a legal remedy, is missing from them, and the basic guarantees of criminal law, like the presumption of innocence, the right to defence, the principles of *nullem crimen* and *nulla poena sine lege,* and, further, the right to property, are missing from them. Therefore all these rights can be regulated by a simple majority.

The two-thirds majority concerns only three of the rights (freedom of religion, the rights of national and ethnic minorities, and citizenship—Arts. 60, 68 and 69 of the Constitution) protected by special guarantees in Art. 8(4) of the Constitution (the observation of these rights cannot be suspended or their exercise curtailed, even in case of emergency), while in the case of other fundamental rights falling within the scope of Art. 8(4) a simple majority is sufficient (Arts. 54–56, Art. 57(2)–(4), Art. 66, Art. 67, Art. 70/E). The present rule on the two-thirds majority does not establish a theoretically based hierarchy among fundamental rights; it only reveals their political importance for the political factors in agreeing to amend the Constitution.

Because of the theoretical change outlined above, the statement of the Constitutional Court in *Dec. 4/1990 (III.4) AB* (MK 1990/19; ABH 1990, 28) and *Dec. 5/1990 (IV.9) AB* (MK 1990/32; ABH 1990, 32) in connection with constitutional acts is no longer applicable to laws passed by a two-thirds majority under the Constitution currently in force.

2. [....] Obviously, the subject matter of the two-thirds statute cannot mandatorily be bound to more than the statutes in general, namely, to the content of the affected fundamental right, its substantial guarantees and its direct and significant restriction. The question remains whether, concerning the rights where the Constitution speaks of a qualified majority, everything should be regulated by a statute passed by a qualified majority, where otherwise the Constitution requires a simple majority statute. In some cases, the Constitution declares not only that the statute on the fundamental right in question must be passed by the votes of two thirds of the Members of Parliament present but it also specifies particular topics connected with the fundamental right, on which a two-thirds statute must be enacted. Thus, according to Art. 61(3), the Act on the Freedom of the Press must be enacted by a qualified majority. Yet para. (4) stipulates four subjects in the sphere of the mass media which also require a two-thirds statute. A similar technical solution can be found concerning questions of state organizations. [....]

If the regulation on the fundamental rights in question were the subject of a two-thirds statute, there would be no sense in raising the aforementioned partial topics to a qualified level of voting. For example, the freedom of the press relates not only to the printed press but also to the radio and television. There can be no doubt about the fact that organizational guarantees belong to the "substantial guarantees" which must be regulated by statute (at least by a statute passed by simple majority) with respect to the press as a whole, but from these only those mentioned in para. (4) obligatorily concern a two-thirds statute. [....]

Hence, from the text and the structure of the Constitution, it does not follow that only two-thirds statutes could dispose of all aspects of the fundamental rights, that for the statutes on them the Constitution ordains a qualified majority.

The examination of the function of the qualified majority does not promote this view either. Both the absolute demand for a constitutional act for each regulation relating to the fundamental right and the current, huge number of Acts to be passed by a qualified majority were rooted in the peculiar political circumstances of the transition. The Constitution currently in force expresses the aim that the regulation of certain basic institutions and certain—mainly political—fundamental rights should be realized with a broad consensus. This aim is achieved if—in conformity with the text of the Constitution—the Act on the basic institution or fundamental right is passed with a two-thirds majority. However, that kind of interpretation would be contrary to the substance of parliamentarianism, as, outside the conceptional questions relating to two-thirds statutes, it would prevent the simple majority from regulating the fundamental rights in question in accordance with its political conceptions: to regulate their implementation, to build further guarantees, and to adjust their realization to the given conditions according to its own concepts. The protection and realization of fundamental rights in the system of the Constitution, based on parliamentary principles, would suffer an unjustifiable restriction if every change and improvement, or partial guarantee which does not determine the regulatory concept, would require a two-thirds majority. The way provided for extending the guarantees can be contrary to the political interest of the minority and to its view concerning the right in question. The Constitutional Court recalls that the Court considered decisive the functioning ability of the parliamentary system, and within this the maintenance of the decision-making ability of the Parliament as well as stable and effective government (*Dec. 3/1991 (II.7) AB:* MK 1991/13; ABH 1991, 15). [....]

The question is not finally solved if Parliament decides separately in each case on what to include in a two-thirds statute. In other words, if a simple majority decides upon it, those who think that a two-thirds statute should be passed would ask for the Constitutional Court`s interpretation; if this decision needed a two-thirds majority, in case of a debate an agreement could not emerge. Parliamentary groups have already asked the Constitutional Court in a number of petitions to interpret the Constitution related to whether each legal regulation on the fundamental right in question or only the statute "pertaining to it" requires a two-thirds majority; in addition several petitions have asserted that some of the statutes are unconstitutional since the Act in question should have been passed with a qualified majority.

Parliament can resolve these arguments by amendment of the Constitution. The other possibility is the interpretation of the Constitution binding on everyone, which is within the jurisdiction of the Constitutional Court. The Constitutional Court interpreted in its decision that those "regulations pertaining to fundamental rights and duties" require a statute in accordance with Art. 8(2) of the Constitution (*Dec. 64/1991 (XII.17) AB:* MK 1991/139; ABH 1991, 297). There is a necessity and a possibility for a similar interpretation to separate the questions to be regulated by qualified-majority statutes from those to be regulated by a simple majority.

On the basis of the foregoing, the Constitutional Court held that not all of the statutory regulations pertaining to a fundamental right require two thirds of the votes of the MPs present. Among the rules concerning fundamental rights, there are some which concern two-thirds statutes and there are others related to statutes to be passed by a simple majority; these two groups can be distinguished according to their substantive characteristics.

The sphere of statutes which should be passed by a qualified majority cannot fully be determined with the help of formal and procedural features.

The Constitution distinguishes two-thirds statutes from other statutes concerning fundamental rights only from a procedural point of view by the qualified majority necessary for their enactment; in the hierarchy of norms, the qualified Act is not superior to the other statutes. The specific procedure is, however, a constitutional requirement also in case of the amendment of these statutes. [....]

Considering that in the system of the current Constitution the scope of the two-thirds statutes cannot be traced back to a theoretical basis, specifically that these statutes do not stand above the other Acts in the hierarchy of norms but according to the Constitution each law is equal, regardless of the fact of whether it was passed by a simple or a qualified majority, moreover that the function of laws passed by a two-thirds majority must be interpreted by placing them into the whole parliamentary system, according to the Constitutional Court's interpretation, the constitutional purpose of laws to be passed by a two-thirds majority will be realized if it requires that these laws determine the direction of the regulation of the fundamental right in question. It must be judged separately in the case of every single fundamental right as to whether an Act determines the direction of the protection and realization of that fundamental right or it contains such detailed rules that do not define it.

Hence the Constitutional Court found that, where the Constitution ordains the votes of two thirds of the Members of Parliament present, the obligation for a qualified majority statute does not concern any legal regulation of the fundamental right in question but only the statute passed as the direct implementation of the given constitutional provision. Such a statute determines the direction of the enforcement and the protection of the fundamental right in question.

The requirement of a qualified majority concerning an Act on a fundamental right does not exclude the fact that the detailed rules necessary for the enforcement of the fundamental right require only a simple majority. A statute passed constitutionally by a qualified majority cannot be amended by a statute passed by a simple majority. [....]

3. Parliament passed the Act on the Freedom of Conscience and Religion, and on the Churches prescribed by Art. 60(4) of the Constitution, by a two-thirds majority: that is, Act IV/1990. For the constitutional enactment of the present Act in question, a simple majority was also sufficient. On the one hand, since the Act regulates significant safeguards related to the freedom of practice of religion, because it concerns the right to property of local governments and also speaks about expropriation, it needs to be at the level of statutory regulation. The rules of the Act are not contrary to the concept laid down in Act IV/1990 on the Freedom of Conscience and Religion, and on the Churches. Moreover the Act provides further guarantees for the realization of the freedom of religion. The Constitutional Court therefore rejected the petition directed at establishing the unconstitutional character of the Act on the basis of the absence of a two-thirds majority.

C

III

The petitions dealt with in this section claim that the Act violates Art. 70/A because they claim it discriminates between the churches which are indemnified and the other churches or between the indemnified churches and the different associations that also suffered. They claim the reprivatization of the belongings of churches under the Act violates the Constitution.

1. The Act, according to its Preamble, has two objectives: "to remedy partially the infringement of lawful rights" and "to ensure the objective material conditions necessary for the churches to carry out their activity." [....] These ends are served by the Act in different

proportions and different ways. Therefore, in order to rule about whether an unconstitutional discrimination is taking place, we have to consider the transfer of ownership of buildings under ss. 1 and 2 and the partial compensation under s. 15 separately.

2. The buildings to be transferred under ss. 1 and 2 of the Act used to serve the ends stipulated in s. 2 before nationalization and are necessary for serving those ends at present. [....] Even though transferring ownership of real estate to churches also partially remedies past infringements of churches' property rights, the emphasis is on the principle of functionality, *i.e.*, guaranteeing the material conditions necessary for the churches to fulfill their missions.

Unconstitutional discrimination can only take place between subjects that are comparable. Thus the notion that there could be discrimination between the churches covered by the Act on the one hand and other organizations that suffered infringements of their property rights in the past (*e.g.*, the Incorporated Law Society or political parties) on the other, or the notion of discrimination between churches and individuals, are both flawed *ab ovo*. The purpose of the Act and the returns of ownership under it are radically different from "partial compensation for unjust harm done to citizens." [....] The ends to serve by the property returned to the churches are: religious life, the functioning of monastic orders, instruction, education, health and social ends, protection of the young and of children, and cultural activities. It is not as much the infringements of property rights as the infringements of the constitutional right to practise one's religion that are remedied by the Act.

The churches that are the beneficiaries of the Act are not comparable to any non-business legal person; they are only comparable to legal persons of comparable function, role, magnitude and autonomy, whose property is also closely connected with exercising a fundamental right. Churches are not organized to represent well-defined interests as do businesses, associations, political parties or unions, but to practice religion. (Religion, in turn, is, for the individual believer, something that concerns and defines all of his/her life and his/her personality.) [....] Based on their different but just as comprehensive need for legal regulation and their autonomy *vis-à-vis* the State, local governments are somewhat comparable to churches. Local governments also implement a fundamental right, the right of communities of citizens to self-government (Art. 42 of the Constitution).

While fulfilling its obligations set forth by the Constitution, the State does not just privatize a part of its property; it also establishes and promotes public organizations and, in order to help them fulfill their obligations and strengthen their autonomy, the State also transfers property to them. The historical and social role of the churches and the impossibility of separating religion from the church and therefore the impossibility of separating the right to the freedom of religion from the operation of the church are enough to justify the inclusion of churches, especially the "historical churches" covered by the Act, among the public organizations promoted by the State.

The transfer of property to local governments was partially completed when they were first elected or is under way, whereas for churches the Act will be implemented in ten years. Since other organizations are not automatically entitled to be given property by the State, only arbitrary discrimination against any of them would be unconstitutional. (See *Dec. 21/1990 (X.4) AB:* MK 1990/98; ABH 1990, 73). [....]

Based on the above, the Constitutional Court rules that ss. 1 and 2 of the Act do not represent unconstitutional discrimination.

Given that the buildings whose ownership is to be transferred had formerly also been used to implement the right to practise one's religion, and that churches can only reclaim buildings in order to serve the self-same end and not exceeding their actual needs, there is a legitimate reason for not transferring ownership of buildings to those churches that did not exist or were not harmed at the time of the infringements. The general problem of state support of churches is different from what is covered by the Act: the Act aims at the restitution of the constitutional right to practise one's religion after former government infringements and not at a simple restitution of property rights.

3. Under s. 15 of the Act, the Government and the church in question can come to agreement over partial indemnity for church property taken without compensation by the State after 1 January 1948 (excluding real estate returned under the Act); the indemnity provides the material conditions for the socially beneficial activity of the church. [....]

[Section 15] of the Act provides general support for the functioning of the churches in question; unlike the transfers under ss. 1 and 2, it is not tied to requirements as to designated activities of the churches. The title of the church to receive indemnity is "partial compensation" for property that was nationalized without compensation. The two titles of this transfer and the fashion in which it is allotted raise different questions.

If we consider the aspect of s. 15 which makes way for state support to make churches more autonomous, then there is no constitutional reason why only the churches that lost property after 1948 should benefit from it. Past violations of the constitutional right to practise one's religion (the State having cut off the material conditions necessary to exercise it) are remedied by other portions of the Act in accordance with the principle of functionality. [....] After the restitution based on function, no additional discrimination between churches is necessary to promote the freedom of religion.

If, on the other hand, we consider s. 15 a compensation statute, it would be necessary to justify why the churches are singled out for compensation of all the legal persons and other organizations that had been harmed. The special characteristics of the churches covered by the Act—as explained above—are sufficient to justify a transfer of property based on their function. But that is fundamentally different from compensation that is simply aimed at remedying past violations of property rights. Whether a discrimination on that head is justified under the Constitution can only be determined considering the full set of persons that was harmed that way, concentrating on violations of property rights only, and taking all the Compensation Acts passed so far into account. At present, the justification for affirmative discrimination in this respect [....] is lacking. [....]

[Considering] the importance of the freedom of religion and the obligation to separate church and State, the priority of restitution to churches and the affirmative discrimination in favour of them under ss. 1 and 2 of the Act, based on the principle of functionality only, is justifiable under the Constitution. Further compensating funds to provide for the undisturbed functioning of churches can only be transferred if there is a legal framework in place providing funds to and supporting and promoting the economic autonomy of churches and self-governing public purpose organizations in general. The compensation must fit into that framework so that it does not unjustly discriminate against other public purpose organizations.

IV

[....]

1. The petitions indicate that the substantive violation of property rights of local governments is in the prohibition on alienation and encumbrance. [....]

2. [....]

(d) The practice of the Constitutional Court has interpreted the content of the fundamental rights of local governments as rules which contain legal regulations determining the direction (concept) of the enforcement and protection of fundamental rights. The Constitutional Court has interpreted the "fundamental rights of local governments" in Art. 44/A of the Constitution as sets of jurisdictions which are essential for the autonomy of the local governments, especially for their independence from the Government. The Constitutional Court has decided on the grounds of characteristics of specific cases whether the certain fundamental right of the local government sustains a conceptual harm caused by the real restrictive effect of different acts.

The fundamental right to property of local governments must also be interpreted in conformity therewith. According to Art. 44/A(1)(b) of the Constitution the local representative body exercises ownership in the assets of local government, independently manages local government revenue and may undertake business activities at its own liability. This fundamental right ensures the ownership position and thus the autonomy of the local governments with regard to the fact that the property of local governments was created by the Constitution and the Act on Local Government at the time of the formation of local governments instead of the (state property) trustee rights of the former "local councils." Act LXV/1990 on Local Government expresses this fundamental right very clearly: "The local government freely disposes of the assets of local government within the limits of the law" (s. 1(6)(b)). This new situation interprets the provisions of Art. 12(2) of the Constitution: "The State shall respect the property of local governments." The fundamental right therefore ensures full rights of ownership but does not provide privileged protection for local government property. It cannot even do so because that would be contrary to Art. 9(1) of the Constitution, which provides for equal consideration and protection under the law for each kind of property. So by a correct interpretation the restriction of the fundamental right of the local government is applied when it is aimed at the position of the local government as owner. Therefore no two-thirds majority is required for statutory restrictions which also affect the other owners or restrict partially the property of the local government but do not limit the autonomy of the local government as owner. [....]

3. The Constitutional Court holds that the Act contains no restrictions concerning the position as a property owner of local governments. The scope of the Act nevertheless covers real estate which is owned—among others—by local governments. The Act is neither related in general to property of local governments nor restricts in general the right of disposal of the local representative body, yet it contains—as it derives unavoidably from the aim of the Act—limitations on every person who is an owner of the formerly nationalized property of churches.

The Act is in fact an Act that facilitates expropriation of real estate that is owned by private persons or local governments. Expropriation is a process which is strictly limited by constitutional guarantees. This process—as it is similar in the case of other rules containing restrictions on property—may be regulated by an Act passed by a simple majority. *Dec. 16/1991 (IV.20) AB* (MK 1991/42; ABH 1991, 58) on expropriation declares that "expropriation as set forth by Art. 13(2) of the Constitution transfers property as a rule into public property; it may however be transferred exceptionally into private property to serve exclusively the public interest."

Sections 9 and 10 of the Act contain the rules on how the provisions on compensation in case of expropriation shall be applied. Compensation for expropriation of real estate of local governments therefore meets the constitutional requirements. [....]

SCHMIDT, J., dissenting: [....]

My opinion dissents from the opinion expressed by the majority decision as concerns the demarcation of the field of regulation of Acts requiring a qualified majority and Acts requiring a simple majority under the Constitution.

1. The claim for so-called two-thirds majority acts was guaranteed in Hungary by the character of the transition. The point under the circumstances of the peaceful transformation was that the political opposition had to gain a more decisive (public) legal role compared to its weight in the Parliament. This compromise was also accepted during the roundtable negotiations by the political forces at that time. The Constitution requires a two-thirds majority in approximately 30 legislative subjects.

2. The legislation of a two-thirds majority formed in this way, led to significant public legal deadlock—regardless of the fact of whether the two thirds concerned the whole body of Members of Parliament or only the Members present. The importance of this constitutional construct today is that a government coalition not having at its disposal a two-thirds majority or more is forced to compromise with the opposition in the most important legislative matters, without which it is unable to govern. In case the political battle intensifies between Government and opposition, *i.e.,* they are unable to reach a compromise (*e.g.,* in the case of the Act on the Mass Media), this constitutional construct may become the source of ungovernability of the country.

On the one hand there is a historical reason for creating two-thirds majority legislation; on the other hand today it facilitates stable government neither politically nor legally. It is not easy to find a solution to the problem. Under these circumstances political forces in the Government want to limit the extent of legislative subjects that require a two-thirds majority or try to limit them through interpreting the Constitution. The opposition on the other hand wants to maintain, even strengthen, the two-thirds majority legislation in order to protect its position. This political deadlock resulting from two-thirds majority legislation endangers even future drafting of the new Constitution. The legal solution may well be created by a new Constitution abolishing the two-thirds majority legislation and simultaneously embodying the most important guarantees in the Constitution—which also means they would become rules of a two-thirds majority. As concerns fundamental rights this could mean that the Constitution would not only declare these rights, as it is the case today, but would also contain the most important guarantees.

3. The Constitutional Court was set up to protect the Constitution. In case of such political and legal disputes, there is a burden on the Constitutional Court since on the one hand it shall ensure that the political system remains stable, and on the other hand it must comply with the provisions of the Constitution, *i.e.,* it shall protect decisions to be passed by a two-thirds majority.

4. Chapter XII of the Constitution on "fundamental rights and obligations" requires two-thirds majority voting in 11 cases. Nearly all of them—as it is stated in the reasoning—are in the field of civil liberties. In one of these cases—related to mass media—the Constitution provides rules on the content of an Act which is to be passed by a two-thirds majority. In all other cases it merely states that any statute regulating the related civil liberties shall be passed by a two-thirds majority of the Members of Parliament present.

5. The provision shows that Parliament was given broad discretionary powers so as to

decide the issue as to what extent it should regulate the related legislative subject with a two-thirds majority and to what extent with a simple majority. It follows that it would be equally constitutional if the Act on Freedom of Conscience and Religion and on the Churches contained a single section only and also when all social relations related to freedom of religion were regulated by a statute passed by a two-thirds majority.

6. If this discretion of the Parliament was limited by the Constitutional Court, *i.e.,* it would regulate the extent of matters subject to a two-thirds majority, then it would exceed its powers since it is to be regulated by the Constitution. That would also be so if it merely defined the contents of statutes to be passed by a two-thirds majority in general principles (such as "direct execution," "concept of enforcement and protection of fundamental rights," *etc.*). The Constitution however—except for its provisions on freedom of the press concerning the Act on Mass Media—contains no such rules, and further such rules may not be deduced from the Constitution by way of interpretation. Such general principles may only be drawn up by way of logical reasoning, and, according to my opinion, the Constitutional Court has no power to do that.

7. Such extension of reasoning would lead to a decision by the Constitutional Court on political issues that are in fact beyond its competence. The reasoning put it correctly that such an interpretation would mean that all disputes between the government coalition and the opposition related to a two-thirds majority would unavoidably reach the Constitutional Court since such a decision would transform political debates under the interpretation of the Constitutional Court into public legal issues.

8. I agree on the statement of the Decision which provides that the enactment of the Act did not require the votes of two thirds of the Members of Parliament present since it is not contrary to the fundamental rules on freedom of religion. According to my opinion, with that statement the Constitutional Court would have provided a response to the petitions and it was not unavoidably necessary to extend the petitions so far as to interpret the constitutional provisions concerning legislative subjects requiring a two-thirds majority voting.

9. Being aware of the fact that the Decision judged the petitions in the above-mentioned expansive way, I am of the opinion that formulation of a further requirement should be necessary in the part of the Decision concerning the two-thirds majority statutes.

A simple-majority statute may only be passed in the field of constitutionally two-thirds majority statutes if a compromise has already been reached in the passing of the two-thirds majority statute, *i.e.,* if the Act concerning the related fundamental rights has already been passed by a two-thirds majority by the Parliament. As the Constitution grants a discretionary power regarding the content of two-thirds majority statutes, without the above-mentioned rule the constitutional provision on two-thirds majority statutes could practically be terminated by a simple majority. And that would be unconstitutional. [....]

HERCZEGH, J., concurring: [....]

Both "state" and "church" schools are bound to a factual and tolerant transfer of knowledge which respects the pupils' freedom of conscience. The larger part of the knowledge taught there lacks any religious content or even any religious reference. Therefore schools owned by the church cannot identify themselves entirely with the doctrines of a particular religion. Statements of the truth of religious doctrines may and have to take place within a framework of religious studies which may be organized as an extracurricular activity. Schools run by the church do not differ from those run by the State in terms of the knowledge taught or in the methods of education; the difference between the two is that the latter establishes its education on its particular ethical religious scale of values; it is exercized in a manner which prevents it from becoming a burden or, respectively, a conflict of conscience neither for students observing other religions nor for those not observing any religion. [....] A sharp distinction between the two types of schools is not justified by historical experience. [....]

DECISION 16/1993: 12 MARCH 1993

ON THE RESTITUTION OF JEWISH POSSESSIONS

The Jewish compensation case constitutes a special chapter in the compensation cases series. This was the only case in which the Constitutional Court took factual evidence in an extensive manner; indeed, the Court inquired into the fate of Jewish gold and jewelry from its being "taken into custody," through its way abroad after the war, until its return to Hungary. The Court revealed the fact that some of these valuables had been sold by the socialist State to foreign buyers as recently as 1981. The section describing these facts could not be reproduced here. The second peculiarity of the decision is that the Court held admissible a positive discrimination in favor of the National Jewish Compensation Fund: although the compensation is only for natural persons, an exception concerning the Fund was found not to be contrary to the nondiscrimination principle.

The petitioners sought determination of an unconstitutional omission on the part of successive governments in their failure to discharge their obligations under the Paris Peace Treaty of 1947.

According to Decree 1600/1944 ME, the Jewish population of Hungary was required to register all its valuables above a certain figure. These registered items were to be sequestered and deposited in bank safes. The Minister of Finance was authorized to take an inventory of the contents of these safes and to deposit there cash and other paper assets as well as jewelry and valuables belonging to Jews.

This confiscation, extended by subsequent decrees, was to be remedied by Act XXV/1946 on the Condemnation of the Persecution of Hungarian Jewry and the Mitigation of its Consequences. Section 2(1) provided that where the State had acquired, or would acquire because of the absence of heirs or beneficiaries, the inheritance of Jewish people who died as a result of persecution between 1941 and 1946, then this inheritance would be assigned to a separate fund. Section 2(3) stated that where confiscated property was returned from abroad and the "lawful owners" could not be determined, then this property would also go to the fund.

When the National Jewish Restitution Fund was established, the items under Decree 1600/1944 ME were outside its scope since they were still abroad, pending a decision on their return. Moreover although the process of returning confiscated assets was regulated, no ministerial decree was ever issued to lay down the manner in which "lawful owners" under Act XXV/1946, s.2(3), were to be determined.

Under the Paris Peace Treaty of 1947, art. 27(1), Hungary assumed the responsibility for restoring the possessions, legal rights and interests, or, if the restoration were impossible, the payment of appropriate compensation, to the Jewish people affected by the confiscations. Article 27(2) provided that when no heir or beneficiary came forward within six months or no other claims were submitted, any such unclaimed assets were to be transferred by the Hungarian Government, in effect, to the Fund. The Treaty was promulgated by Act XVIII/1947.

Nevertheless, Jewish assets returned from abroad and those without heirs or beneficiaries ultimately ended up in the possession of the State in the National Bank under the authority of the Ministry of Finance in what amounted to de facto nationalization.

The petitioners submitted inter alia that (a) Jewish property confiscated according to Decree 1600/1944 ME should have been returned to the original owners or their heirs and beneficiaries. In the absence of the latter, jewellery and valuables or the equivalent in compensation should have been distributed to the Fund. The failure by the State to enact a legal rule to discharge these obligations under Act XXV/1946 and the 1947 Treaty gave rise to an unconstitutional omission to legislate; and, since the injured parties claimed return of their valuables on the basis of the original custody or deposit agreement, Act XXIV/1992 (the Second Compensation Act), ss. 1 and 3, were therefore unconstitutional and contrary to the 1947 Treaty, and consequently ought to be annulled.

Held, allowing the petition in part:

(1) Following the enactment of the Second Compensation Act, the statutory provision of compensation to satisfy the claims arising from the compelled depositing and sequestration of valuables according to Decree 1600/1944 ME did not violate the Constitution or the Paris Peace Treaty. In the light of official state actions and legal rules in the late 1940s and early 1950s, the State had come to treat these valuables as its own property thereby injuring the proprietary rights of the former owners. Accordingly the State was burdened with the responsibility to make amends for the injuries thus inflicted not only according to art. 27 of the Treaty but also Act XXV/1946, such responsibility being independent of whether or not the valuables became state property. "Payment of appropriate compensation" under the Treaty, art. 27(1) did not necessarily mean full compensation but could also be satisfied by partial compensation provided that former owners received such compensation without discrimination. This formerly unimplemented duty under domestic legislation had consequently been discharged with the coming into force of the said Compensation Act. In this respect, no constitutional omission of the duty to enact legislation existed.

(2) However, such a constitutional omission did exist in respect of the State's failure to issue or enact legal rules which would have given effect to the provisions of art. 27(2). The State thereunder had been required to assume the duty of transferring to interest groups working on behalf of Jewish victims deprived of their property the claims of former owners without legal heirs or beneficiaries as well as all those inheritances and bequests of deceased individuals targeted by laws of racial persecution which, in the absence of heirs or beneficiaries, had been or would be passed onto the State. Although the still in force Act XXV/1946, s. 2(1)–(3), contained provisions closely related to art. 27(2), the State failed to act upon them: it did not proceed with the probate procedures defined by s. 2(1); the Ministry never issued the regulations under s. 2(3) on the method of determining the "lawful owners" of the valuables; and the State did not transfer either probate estate (inheritance and bequests) or other valuables to the National Jewish Restitution Fund. Partly because of an omission to legislate and partly because of the executive's failure to act, the State did not fulfill the obligation imposed on it in respect of those legal persons (organizations) defined in art. 27.

(3) In rectifying this omission, the action to be taken by Parliament, *e.g.,* enactment of a statute or negotiated settlement, had to remain in harmony with the founding principles

of the previously enacted Compensation Acts. Thus provision by the State of partial compensation for the organizations in the same manner and to the same extent as the first two Compensation Acts would be constitutional. Although these Acts only extended to natural persons, the State had previously provided by statute the opportunity for legal redress for property damages to legal persons, *viz.,* local governments and churches. The enactment of legal rules allowing redress were justified in the latter cases since it amounted to the realization of the opportunity to exercise a fundamental right guaranteed by the Constitution while in the case of Jewish interest groups the basis for such rules was an international treaty. The differentiation in enacting legislation in favour of such groups, with respect to other persecuted persons, was not contrary to Art. 70/A and in fact amounted to a partial counterbalancing of previous negative discrimination suffered by Jewish people and their property: thus in its ultimate result it effectively amounted to a positive discrimination in favour of the members of such groups, whereas no ground existed to justify conferring positive discriminatory treatment on natural persons who had suffered deprivation of property right on account of their Jewish religion or ancestry.

IN THE NAME OF THE REPUBLIC OF HUNGARY!

In the matter of petitions seeking a review ex post facto of the unconstitutionality of a legal rule, and the establishment of an unconstitutional omission to legislate, the Constitutional Court has made the following

DECISION.

1. The Constitutional Court holds that an unconstitutional situation has arisen due to Hungary's failure to comply with the provisions of art. 27(2) of the Paris Peace Treaty.

Accordingly, the Constitutional Court requests Parliament to undertake the necessary steps for the implementation of the said provisions of the Peace Treaty by 31 December 1993.

2. The Constitutional Court rejects the petition seeking a determination that Act XXIV/1992 is in conflict with an international treaty. The Court determines ex officio that the challenged Act is not in conflict with an international treaty.

3. The Constitutional Court rejects the petition seeking a determination of unconstitutionality and annulment of ss. 1 and 3 of Act XXIV/1992 and their supplementary regulations.

The Constitutional Court publishes this Decision in the *Hungarian Official Gazette.*

REASONING

KILÉNYI, J., delivering the Opinion of the Court: [....]

III

[....]

In the Constitutional Court's view, the documents indicate that the valuables sequestered and deposited under Decree 1600/1944 ME were sorted by category with the identifying labels containing names removed and discarded upon their shipment abroad. This is why when the shipment was returned from Paris in 1948 the accompanying lists described them by categories as goods in bulk. The possibility of identifying their owners no longer existed. [....]

By the processing (melting down and sale) of the gold, silver and other valuables, the ordering of an inventory system by categories of goods in 1951 and the political decisions made in 1948–49, the State came to treat these valuables as its own property. In light of this, the Constitutional Court holds that the former owners of the gold, jewellery and other valuables, whose possessions had been sequestered and deposited by Decree 1600/1944 ME, confiscated or hauled abroad and subsequently returned to Hungary, have suffered injury to their property rights inflicted by the legal rules—invalidated in the meantime—and official actions of the Hungarian State.

Yet, for the same reason as noted above, it is impossible to return the valuables in their original state to their former owners. [....]

During the past decades, millions of citizens suffered deprivation of their property rights, partly as a result of nationalization and partly due to unlawful deprivation of property rights. That in the latter case the ownership was not always transferred to the State was irrelevant for the former owners' grievances.

[....] Accordingly, compensation laws consider not the acquisition of property by the State but deprivation of property by the State. [....]

IV

The Constitutional Court did examine ex officio the compatibility of the legal regulations currently in force with the Paris Peace Treaty and the question of an unconstitutional omission to legislate.

According to the petitioners, it is both unconstitutional and a violation of the Paris Peace Treaty that the provisions of s. 2(2) and (3) of Act XXV/1946 concerning the rights of the National Jewish Restitution Fund have not been implemented.

The Constitutional Court had already ruled and addressed in its previous decisions, that a petition for the determination of a conflict or incompatibility with an international treaty may only be submitted by parties and institutions authorized pursuant to s. 21(3) of Act XXXII/1989 on the Constitutional Court. The individuals submitting this petition do not belong to this group. Accordingly, the court rejected the petition concerning their question.

However, s. 44 of the Constitutional Court Act confers on the Constitutional Court the authority to initiate ex officio an examination of the possible conflict between a legal rule and an international treaty.

Pursuant to the exercise of this right, the Constitutional Court holds that in art. 27(1) of the Paris Peace Treaty Hungary had assumed the responsibility for "restoring the possessions, legal rights and interests, or if restoration is impossible, the payment of appropriate compensation" concerning the issue under examination.

The Constitutional Court's position, expounded in this Decision and already described in detail in a prior decision (*Dec. 15/1993 (III.12) AB:* MK 1993/29; ABH 1993, 112), is that the "appropriate" compensation referred to in an international treaty does not necessarily mean full compensation but may also be satisfied by "partial compensation measured according to the country's ability to pay, provided that the people who have suffered deprivation of their possessions and violations of their legal rights and lawful interests receive such compensation without discrimination."

For this reason, in the Constitutional Court's view, the statutory provision of compensation for settling the claims arising from the compelled custodial depositing, sequestration and confiscation of valuables arising from Decree 1600/1944 ME violates neither the Constitution nor the provisions of the international treaty.

Thus, concerning the citizens' personal grievances, the duty which the State had assumed in the international treaty and domestic legislation still in force, but which for decades remained unimplemented, has now been finally discharged with the enactment of the Second Compensation Act.

With this action, the decades-old violation of the Constitution and the international treaty has now been rectified. Thus, no unconstitutional omission to legislate exists.

Accordingly, the Constitutional Court rejects the petitions in this regard.

The situation is different concerning the assumption of the duty according to which the claims of former owners without legal heirs or beneficiaries are transferred by the State to the interest groups working on behalf of victims deprived of their property, as well as the transfer to those groups all those inheritances and bequests of deceased individuals targeted by laws of racial persecution, which, in the absence of heirs or beneficiaries, have been or will pass to the State.

According to art. 27(2) of the Paris Peace Treaty, promulgated by Act XVIII/1947:

> All rights, possessions and interests of all individuals, organizations or communities located in the territory of Hungary which individually or collectively were subjected to harassing legal regulation of a fascist spirit on account of racial, religious or any other reasons, if within six months of this Agreement having entered into force are not claimed by an heir or beneficiary and if no other claims have been submitted, shall be transferred by the Hungarian Government to the organizations representing such individuals, organizations or communities. The possessions thus transferred shall be used by these organizations for the support and restitution of the surviving members of the aforementioned groups, organizations and communities. These transfers must be carried out within twelve months of this Agreement having entered into force, and they include the rights, possessions and interests to be returned in accordance with section 1 of this article.

Neither the Hungarian Government nor the Hungarian legislature ever issued or enacted legal regulations to execute the provisions cited above from the Peace Treaty. [....]

What is missing, however, is the legal regulation concerning the organizations defined in art. 27(2) of the Paris Peace Treaty, and the Constitutional Court determines the existence of an unconstitutional omission to legislate in this regard. The actions taken for the termination of this situation must be in harmony with the founding principles of the previously enacted Compensation Acts.

Parliament may satisfy the Constitutional Court's request to rectify the unconstitutional situation manifested in the omission in a number of ways—such as by the enactment of an Act or by authorizing the Government to terminate the unconstitutional situation through a negotiated settlement. With respect to these possible solutions, the Constitutional Court points to the following issues:

(a) Everything that has been stated by the reasoning of this Decision in connection with the "appropriate" compensation of natural persons amounting to partial compensation necessarily applies to the compensation of organizations as well. Therefore, it is not unconstitutional if the State provides for the compensation of the organizations and funds in the same manner and to the same extent as has been done in the First and Second Compensation Acts.

(b) Although the ambit of the Compensation Acts extends only to natural persons, this does not mean that the State *ab ovo* deprives legal persons of the opportunity of seeking redress from the State—depending upon its ability to pay—for at least partial compensation for the damage inflicted on their property. Such legal redress has been implemented, for instance—although it did not proceed under the title of compensation—by Act LXV/1990 on Local Government and Act XXXII/1991 on the Settlement of the Ownership of Real Estate Formerly Owned by Churches, while redress for property damages inflicted on other types of legal persons is in the process of drafting and preparation. Accordingly, the resolution of the claims of Jewish interest groups does not give rise to a discriminatory situation between these organizations and all other legal persons. In the cases of churches and local governments, it was the exercise of fundamental rights guaranteed by the Constitution, while in the case of the Jewish organizations it is an international treaty, which justifies the issue of legal regulations related to and seeking redress for the grievances. The Constitutional Court also considered the following: although Jews were not the only group of people which was persecuted in past decades for racial, religious or national reasons and subjected to legal discrimination in Hungary, as a result of the mass destruction of their members they have suffered more grievous harm than other groups. Hence, if the Hungarian State complies with the Paris Peace Treaty and executes its provisions concerning the Jewish interest groups, this would amount to such a discrimination with respect to other persecuted groups of people which is not merely not contrary to the provisions of Art. 70/A of the Constitution but would serve as a partial counterbalancing of previous negative discrimination. There is no logical contradiction in the Constitutional Court's position on the method and extent of compensation, stating that while the Constitutional Court has found no constitutional justification to confer positive discriminatory treatment on natural persons who suffered property losses on account of their Jewish religion or origin, such a discrimination is constitutionally permitted with respect to the compensation of Jewish interest groups. The explanation is that, although organizations are the ones entitled to the compensation, they—in accordance with the provisions of the Peace Treaty—use those funds for the support of surviving members of the persecuted group and its communities. Thus, in the case at hand, the positive discrimination in favour of the organization is tantamount, in terms of its final result, to a positive discrimination in favour of the members of this group of people subjected to grave persecution, and it was in light of this fact that the Constitutional Court did not deem constitutionally permissible the double-edged positive discrimination, favouring both the interest organizations and the individual members of the community.

(c) Upon undertaking the measures indicated in the Constitutional Court's holding, Parliament shall not merely discharge an international legal obligation, but shall concurrently give effect to the will of Hungary's democratically elected People's Assembly, manifested in ss. 1 and 2 of Act XXV/1946.

DECISION 53/1993: 13 OCTOBER 1993

ON WAR CRIMES AND ON CRIMES AGAINST HUMANITY

With this case, the Constitutional Court resolved the intense conflict between the demand for "just punishment" of those who had committed politically motivated crimes under the previous dictatorships and the constitutional limitations of the applicability of criminal law after the statute of limitations has run out. The method the legislature had chosen—prosecution based on international law—proved to be constitutional in principle; the technical realization of this idea, however, was erroneous in many respects. The Court, on the one hand, showed how to correct these mistakes. Because the subsequent legislation did not produce the correct regulation either, the ordinary courts followed the thesis of the Constitutional Court (at the end of the reasoning) on the direct applicability of generally accepted principles of international law. On the other hand, the Constitutional Court had to clarify the relationship between the absolute prohibition of retroactivity for domestic law and the exception according to international law.

The President of the Republic sought a preliminary examination of whether the unpromulgated Act on Procedures in the Matter of Certain Criminal Offences committed during the 1956 October Revolution and Freedom Struggle (the Act) complied with the Constitution and two international agreements.

Act IV/1978 on the Criminal Code, art. 33(2) provides that no statutory limitation on the time for punishment may be applied inter alia to (a) war crimes or (b) other crimes against humanity.

Section 1 of the unpromulgated Act provided that in relation to limitation periods for the punishment of criminal offences, art. 33(2) of the Code was to be applied to such offences committed during the 1956 Revolution and Freedom Struggle. Further, s. 2 of the Act provided inter alia that art. 33(2) also applied to "grave breaches" during the stated period, as defined and governed by the 1949 Geneva Convention on the Protection of Civilians in Time of War.

Before promulgating the Act, the President submitted a petition contending that (a) the Court had previously examined the same subject matter which had already been addressed in a former Act; and for that reason (b) it was necessary to determine whether the Act complied with (i) the International Covenant on Civil and Political Rights; (ii) art. 7(1) of the European Convention on Human Rights; (iii) Constitution Arts. 2(1), 7(1), 8(1) and 57(2), (4); and (iv) the constitutional principles concerning the legality of criminal law, *viz.*, the limited criminal power of the State, faith in the law, legal certainty and, taken together, the rule of law.

Held, allowing the petition in part:

(1) The Court has no jurisdiction to undertake constitutional review of an unpromulgated Act of Parliament vis-à-vis an international agreement. Section 44 of Act XXXII/1989 on the Constitutional Court only permits review of legal rules which attained that qual-

ity solely on promulgation, and there appeared therefore to be no basis to conduct a review of an international agreement contained in a pre-promulgated Act. However in the constitutional review of a bill, unpromulgated Act or legal rule which gave effect to international obligations, and in particular if it were aimed specifically at harmonizing domestic with international law (as required under Art. 7(1)), then it was necessary to raise and answer questions as to whether the domestic norm conflicted with the international legal obligation and whether the latter was in harmony with the Constitution. Different standards applied to the examination of constitutionality of an internal legal rule related to international law than to a purely domestic norm. Since the recognition or not of international law might lead to different outcomes in the constitutional review of a challenged domestic norm, it was also necessary to take Art. 7(1) into consideration in that review, as the consonance between international and internal law required thereunder also formed part of the requirement of constitutionality of the legal rules giving effect to international obligations. Consequently it did not matter whether the review was preliminary or ex post facto; the limitations on jurisdiction meant, at most, that a preliminary review should not contain any formal finding on the relations between the international agreement and the unpromulgated Act.

(2) The first indent of Art. 7(1) amounted to an act of transformation of the generally recognized rules of international law into the Hungarian legal system and according thereto such rules did not form part of the Constitution but were "assumed obligations." Although the assumption and transformation were contained in the Constitution, this did not affect the hierarchical relationship of the Constitution, domestic and international law, nor did it preclude certain "generally recognized" rules from being defined by specific international agreements, regarding which a separate act of transformation was needed. The participation of Hungary in the community of nations, expressed under Art. 7(1), entailed a constitutional command for domestic law, from which it followed that the Constitution and domestic law had to be interpreted in a manner whereby the generally recognized rules of international law were truly given effect. Further Art. 7(1) required the harmony of the Constitution, the obligations derived from international law whether directly assumed under the Constitution (general transformation) or undertaken by treaty (specific transformation), and domestic law. In guaranteeing their harmony attention had to be paid to their particular characteristics.

(3) In the present case, interpretation of both the Constitution and domestic law had to take into account the fact that the international norms regulating war crimes and crimes against humanity related not only to the issue of responsibilities of nations *inter se* but also to the determination of obligations and imposition of criminal responsibility on individuals. Thus international law touched upon an area which otherwise fell within the domestic criminal jurisdiction of the State. The particular characteristics of such criminal offences were that they did not originate from and were not classified under domestic criminal law but rather it was the international community which qualified them as criminal offences. The international community prosecuted and punished such crimes by international tribunals and by insisting that States wishing to be members of such a community prosecute these offences. The States, in prosecuting and punishing those crimes, acted upon the mandate from the community of nations according to the parameters of international law. The international community might claim (through the action of international organizations) to

overturn national practices failing to comply with international law. The prosecution and punishment of these crimes might only proceed within a framework of legal guarantees which could not be replaced or substituted by those of domestic law. International law applied the principles of *nullum crime sine lege* and *nulla poena sine lege* to itself. Lastly, by reason of its accession to the 1968 Convention, Hungarian statutory limitations did not apply to the prosecution and punishment of such crimes under international law.

(4) Since the regulations concerning war crimes and crimes against humanity were among "the rules generally recognized by international law" under Art. 7(1), they fell within those assumed international legal obligations the harmony of which with the Constitution and domestic law was required by Art. 7(1). By virtue of Art. 7(1), certain rules of international law had to be given effect concurrent with domestic law. Through the State's penal power, that of the international community was executed within the framework of conditions and guarantees provided by international law. Domestic substantive law might be applied only to the extent that international law expressly commanded it (*e.g.*, imposition of sentence), and no domestic law which conflicted with an express peremptory rule of international law (*ius cogens*) could be given effect. The absence of any interpretive provision in the Constitution with regard to the integration of an international rule into the national legal system, *i.e.*, its "harmony" or "consonance," required domestic constitutional interpretation of international law according to Art. 7. Thus Arts. 57(4) and 7(1) had to be interpreted in the light of each other and therefore, together with the unconditional application of *nullum crimen* to domestic law, Art. 7(1) brought about the constitutional realization of international criminal law relating to war crimes and crimes against humanity.

(5) In applying the principles already outlined to the determination of the present case, the criminal offence defined in s. 1 of the Act did not constitute a war crime according to international law. With respect to such an offence, which belonged merely to the sphere of domestic criminal law, the retroactive application of art. 33(2) of the Criminal Code was therefore unconstitutional since it could only be applied if, at the time of the commission of the criminal offence, Hungarian law then in force had declared the non-applicability of statutory limitations. As this was not the case in relation to the period covered by the Act, s. 1 sought an unconstitutional application of art. 33(2) to offences listed in the section: Parliament could not determine the expiration date of certain criminal offences, and s. 1 was accordingly contrary to Arts. 57(4) and 7(1).

(6) However the application of s. 2 of the Act was constitutional since it fell within the limits determined by the present Decision. Article 33(2) could be applied to the offences listed under s. 2 without regard to the domestic limitation period in force at the time of the commission of the said offences since they amounted to "grave breaches" or prohibited acts in non-international armed conflicts as laid down in the 1949 Geneva Conventions and interpreted by the International Court of Justice and therefore the 1968 Convention rendered possible the non-applicability of domestic limitation periods and Hungary had assumed the obligation thereunder according to international law. Accordingly the retroactive non-applicability of limitation periods contained in the 1968 Convention applied exclusively to criminal offences defined by international law and listed in the Convention and which were punishable irrespective of whether or not they violated the laws of country in which they

were committed. Such crimes therefore were to be distinguished from similarly defined domestic criminal offences.

IN THE NAME OF THE REPUBLIC OF HUNGARY!

On the basis of the petition submitted by the President of the Republic concerning the constitutional review of the provisions of the law passed by Parliament but not yet promulgated, the Constitutional Court has made the following

DECISION.

1. In the application of s. 33(2) of Act IV/1978 on the Criminal Code (hereafter referred to as the Criminal Code), it is a constitutional requirement that the non-applicability of statutory limitations may only be determined with respect to those criminal offences the punishability of which was not subject to the statute of limitations according to Hungarian law in effect at the time of the commission of the offence unless international law classifies the offence as a war crime or crime against humanity, declares or makes possible the non-applicability of statutory limitations, and Hungary is under an obligation by international law to preclude the applicability of statutory limitations.

2. The Constitutional Court holds that it is consistent with the Constitution if art. 33(2) of the Criminal Code is applied without regard of the Hungarian statute of limitations in effect at the time of their commission to the following offences defined by international law:

—"grave breaches" as defined by the Geneva Conventions of 12 August 1949 on the Protection of War Victims, committed in an international armed conflict which might arise between two or more of the High Contracting Parties, according to art. 2 common to the Geneva Conventions:

—prohibited acts committed in an armed conflict of non-international character in the territory of one of the High Contracting Parties as determined by common art. 3.

3. Section 1 of the Act on the Procedure in the Matter of Certain Criminal Offences committed during the 1956 October Revolution and Freedom Struggle, passed by Parliament on 16 February 1993, is contrary to Arts. 57(4) and 7(1) of the Constitution.

The application of s. 2 of this Act is constitutional within those constraints, which the Constitutional Court defined above in paragraph 2 of this Decision.

The Constitutional Court publishes this Decision in the *Hungarian Official Gazette.*

REASONING

SÓLYOM, P., delivering the Opinion of the Court: [....]

III

The relationship between domestic and international law according to Art. 7(1) of the Constitution

(a) The first sentence of Art. 7(1) of the Constitution, according to which the legal system of the Republic of Hungary accepts the generally recognized rules of international law, states that these "generally recognized rules" are part of Hungarian law, even without separate (further) transformation. An act of general transformation—one without a definition or enumeration of the rules—was performed by the Constitution itself. According to it, the generally recognized rules of international law are not part of the Constitution but are "assumed obligations." The fact that the assumption and transformation are contained in the Constitution does not affect the hierarchical relationship of the Constitution, international and domestic law. This general internalization of assumed obligations absolutely does not preclude certain "generally recognized rules" from being defined by specific international agreements (as well), and that regarding those a separate act of transformation takes place. The United Nations Charter and the Geneva Conventions, for instance, may contain such rules.

Article 7(1) of the Constitution also means that by the Constitution's command, the Republic of Hungary participates in the community of nations; this participation, therefore, is a constitutional command for domestic law. It follows therefrom that the Constitution and domestic law must be interpreted in a manner whereby the generally recognized international rules are truly given effect.

(b) The second sentence of Art. 7(1)—the harmonization of the obligations assumed under international law and domestic law—applies to every "assumed" international obligation, including the generally recognized rules. In addition, the harmony must be achieved for the whole of domestic law, the Constitution included. Thus, Art. 7(1) of the Constitution requires the harmony of the Constitution and the obligations derived from international law—assumed directly under the Constitution or undertaken in treaties—as well as domestic law; in ensuring their harmonization attention must be paid to their particular characteristics.

IV

The particular characteristics of war crimes and crimes against humanity

In the present case, the interpretation of both the Constitution and domestic law must proceed in light of the fact that the norms regulating war crimes and crimes against humanity comprise a particular part of international law, one which involves not merely responsibilities of States with respect to one other but also the determination of obligations and imposition of criminal liability on individuals as well. By this action, therefore, international law touches upon such an area which otherwise falls within the sovereign State's domestic punitive power, and it does so, with respect to war crimes and crimes against humanity, in a manner which, in many respects, diverges from the principles of domestic criminal law and the regime of application of the domestic punitive power.

1. War crimes and crimes against humanity are such criminal offences which did not arise as part of the domestic criminal law but are deemed to constitute criminal offences by the international community which defines their elements.

These criminal offences—according to the prevailing legal standard of international law, having evolved since the Second World War—are not simply offences punishable by the domestic law of most countries. (Therefore, homicide may not, in itself, be classified as a crime against humanity.) Their international status is linked with their definition on a supranational level, either on the basis of natural law [....], or by reference to the protection of the "foundations of the international community," or by citing the threat posed by these activities for all of humanity: their perpetrators are "enemies of the human race." Thus, the significance of these offences is too great to permit their punishment to be made dependent upon their acceptance by or the general penal law policy of individual States.

2. It is the international community which prosecutes and punishes war crimes and crimes against humanity; it does so by international tribunals and by insisting that those States which desire to be members of the international community prosecute such offenders.

The Nuremberg and Tokyo trials introduced and laid the foundation of international criminal justice; following in their footsteps, the 1948 Convention on the Prevention and Punishment of the Crime of Genocide also provided for the creation of an international criminal tribunal, which, however, was never established. The States committed themselves by international agreements to the punishing of such crimes. During the past ten to fifteen years, the activities of international organizations (committees and tribunals) established to monitor and ensure compliance with the comprehensive human rights conventions have come to articulate with increasing vigour the condemnation of those States which in their domestic law fail to comply with their international obligations. (It is primarily the decisions and resolutions of the Inter-American Court of Human Rights and the Inter-American Commission of Human Rights which developed the international-law-based duty of States to initiate criminal prosecution which may not be avoided even by amnesty.) The idea of international tribunals also appeared during the Gulf War, while the U.N. Security Council recently established an international tribunal to punish those persons who are responsible for the serious violations of international humanitarian law in the territory of the former Yugoslavia after 1991 (Sec. Con. Res. 808 (1993), Sec. Con. Res. 827 (1993) U.N. SCOR). U.N. Security Council Resolution 808 requested the Secretary-General to prepare the material necessary for the implementation of the Resolution, this being in fact the Statute and the Explanatory Memorandum (Report) of the International Tribunal.

The special significance of the Statute and Report of 3 May 1993 is that—precisely because of the requirement of *nullum crimen sine lege,* included in paras. 2–5 of the Statute—it determines and describes in detail the international humanitarian law the rules of which are "beyond any doubt part of customary international law so that the problem of adherence of some but not all States to specific conventions does not arise" (Report, para. 34). Thus, the law to be applied is independent of the individual States' domestic law. [....]

3. The State which prosecutes and punishes war crimes and crimes against humanity acts upon the mandate given to it by the community of nations according to the conditions determined by international law. The community of nations occasionally may also claim, through the action of international organizations, to overturn that domestic legal practice which does not comply with international law. The punitive power of the community of nations functions under different conditions and within different constraints than that of individual States; the differences are attributable to the specific characteristics of these criminal offences prosecuted by the international community, especially to the dangers inherent for the whole of humanity, which lead to detachment from national assessment.

4. The prosecution and punishment of war crimes and crimes against humanity may only proceed within a framework of legal guarantees; it would be self-contradictory to protect human rights without such guarantees. But these international guarantees cannot be replaced or substituted by the legal guarantees of domestic law.

(a) International law applies the guarantee of *nullum crimen sine lege* to itself and not to domestic law. "Customary international law," "legal principles recognized by civilized nations," and "the legal principles recognized by the community of nations," are such a *lex,* which classifies certain behaviour prosecutable and punishable according to the norms of the community of nations (through international organizations or the State members of the international community), irrespective of whether the domestic law contains a comparable criminal offence and whether the respective treaties have been incorporated into domestic law. The gravity of war crimes and crimes against humanity, and the fact that by their commission international peace, security and, indeed, humanity itself are placed in danger, cannot be reconciled with making their punishment subject to domestic law. The independence of the definition of the crime against humanity from domestic law was articulated by art. 6 (c) of the Statute of the Nuremberg International Military Tribunal; the activities enumerated therein are classified as crimes against humanity "whether or not in violation of the domestic law of the country where perpetrated"; the 1968 New York Convention added the following clause to the definition of crimes against humanity: "even if such acts do not constitute a violation of the domestic law of the country in which they were committed." In a similar vein, the Principles of International Co-operation adopted by the U.N. General Assembly in 1973 (on the prosecution and punishment of war criminals) ordered the punishment of crimes against humanity "wherever they are committed." In defining the applicable substantive law for the International Tribunal to punish the crimes committed in the former Yugoslavia in violation of international humanitarian law, it was expressly rejected that domestic law incorporating international humanitarian customary law also be considered as norms applicable, reasoning that those rules of international humanitarian law which undoubtedly became part of customary law "provide [in that capacity] a sufficient basis for subject-matter jurisdiction" (Report, para. 36). This, too, reinforces the separateness of the two legal systems.

Article 15(1) of the International Covenant on Civil and Political Rights—which, in its content, matches art. 7(1) of the European Convention for the Protection of Human Rights and Fundamental Freedoms—obliges member States to uphold unconditionally the principles of *nullum crimen sine lege* and *nulla poena sine lege*. The reference by international law to the criminal offence defined ("[n]o one shall be held guilty of any criminal offence on account of any act or omission which did not constitute a criminal offence, under national or international law, at the time it was committed") has been interpreted by legal scholars to refer only to those criminal offences which are undoubtedly punishable by domestic law, either through ratification or direct application.

According to art. 15(2) of the Covenant "[n]othing in this article shall prejudice the trial and punishment of any person for any act or omission which, at the time when it was committed, was criminal according to the general principles of law recognized by the community of nations." (The content of art. 7(2) of the European Convention is similar, with the distinction that the latter substitutes "civilized nations" for the term "community of nations.") This separation makes possible the prosecution of the previously noted sui generis criminal offences defined by international law even by those State members of the community of nations whose domestic system of law does not criminalize and does not punish that action or omission. It follows logically, therefore, that such acts are permitted to be prosecuted and punished in accordance with the conditions and requirements imposed by international law. The second paragraphs of both the Covenant's and the European Convention's relevant articles evidently break up the guarantees of domestic penal law, all the more so since art. 4(2) of the International Covenant and art. 15(2) of the European Convention both imperatively require the prevalance of the principles of *nullum crimen-nulla poena,* even in situations of war or in states of emergency. For those States which incorporate into domestic law the international legal norms concerning war crimes and crimes against humanity subsequent to the commission of these crimes, para. 2 of the aforementioned articles equals authorizing retroactive criminal legislation in the State's domestic legal system. The types of conduct had to be criminalized at the time of their commission by international, and not domestic, law.

Historically, the distinction has been applied with respect of war crimes and crimes against humanity committed during the Second World War. But the development of international law since has continuously separated the sphere of "international humanitarian law" from the war context and made the prosecution and punishment of these crimes independent of the requirements and conditions of the domestic criminal law system, also with regard to statutory limitations, inasmuch as two conventions on the non-applicability of statutory limitations for war crimes and crimes against humanity have been concluded.

(b) Neither of the international legal documents defining international substantive or procedural law contains any time limitation on prosecution and punishment of war crimes and crimes against humanity. In the aftermath of the Nuremberg and Tokyo trials, however, States prosecuted war crimes on the basis of their domestic law, and prior to the expiration of the domestic-law-based limitation period statutory measures were taken to extend or to lift the limitation period. The aim of the 1968 New York Convention [Convention on the Non-Applicability of Statutory Limitations to War Crimes and Crimes against Humanity, 754 U.N.T.S. 73] was precisely the termination of the uncertainties and randomness associated with various domestic laws when the Convention declared that "no statutory limitations shall apply to" the war crimes and crimes against humanity enumerated therein, "irrespective of the date of their commission." From the Convention's Preamble it is evident that war crimes and crimes against humanity, on the one hand, and "ordinary crimes" determined in domestic laws, on the other hand, cannot be treated in an identical manner.

The New York Convention came into being at a period when the ideal of the "collective" international prosecution of crimes against humanity was receding into the background. The Convention's signatory States assume the obligation that "any legislative or other measures necessary to ensure that statutory or other limitations shall not apply to the prosecution and punishment of" war crimes and crimes against humanity therein defined.

Article 7(2) of the European Convention and art. 15(2) of the International Covenant permit in principle signatory States not to apply the domestic statutory limitations for crimes defined by the community of nations. In contrast to this permissive provision, the New York Convention provides for an obligation to that effect. Moreover, the New York Convention is retroactive.

The New York Convention was ratified basically only by the so-called Third World countries and the then socialist States. But this fact, which can be traced to then prevailing political conditions, did not make the regulation of the non-applicability of statutory limitations any less topical. In 1974, the Council of Europe prepared and opened for signature the European Convention on the Non-Applicability of Statutory Limitations to War Crimes and Crimes against Humanity. The scope of this Convention, in addition to covering the crimes against humanity enumerated in the Convention on the Prevention and Punishment of the Crime of Genocide, and the war crimes defined by the Geneva Conventions, also extended to "any comparable violation" of the law of war, but no such extension was applied with respect to crimes against humanity. As a general rule, the non-applicability of statutory limitations is applied prospectively for activities committed subsequent to the Convention's entry into force in the signatory State. Retroactivity is permitted only where the limitation period has not yet expired; therefore the [1974] European Convention only permits an extension of the limitation period. The Convention was ratified only by the Netherlands (1981) and signed only by France (1974) and Belgium (1984). The majority of European States solved the non-applicability of statutory limitations for war crimes by resorting to domestic law.

V

Criminal offences defined by international law and the Constitution

1. The definition and conditions for punishing war crimes and crimes against humanity is provided by international law; these crimes—directly or indirectly through the obligations imposed on the States—are prosecuted and punished by the community of nations. The rules on the punishment of war crimes and crimes against humanity—since these crimes threaten the foundations of humanity and international coexistence—constitute peremptory norms of general international law (*ius cogens*). Those States which refuse to assume these obligations cannot participate in the community of nations.

The norms on war crimes and crimes against humanity are undoubtedly part of customary international law; they are general principles recognized by the community of nations; in the parlance of the Hungarian Constitution, they belong to "the generally recognized rules of international law." The Hungarian legal system accepts these rules, according to the first clause of Art. 7(1) of the Constitution; therefore they fall, without separate transformation or adoption, within those "assumed obligations under international law" whose harmony with domestic law is required by the second clause of the aforementioned Article of the Constitution.

The international obligation to punish perpetrators of war crimes and crimes against humanity encompasses the whole of the relevant international *ius cogens.* Thus, it cannot be assumed without the international law conditions of the imposition of punishment being accepted by Hungarian law. If any rule unequivocally comprizing part of the international customary law on war crimes and crimes against humanity were to be interpreted differently by Hungarian law, then the offences qualified and prosecuted by domestic law would cease to be war crimes or crimes against humanity according to international law. Such a procedure by the Hungarian State would not, however, alter the command of international law, nor would it modify the State's obligation, nor would it change the international law imposed criminal liability of the perpetrators of such acts.

2. The international law of war crimes and crimes against humanity pays no heed to the principle of *nullum crimen* prevailing in domestic law when it makes the punishment of these offences independent of whether or not they constituted a criminal offence in the domestic penal law at the time of their commission. This statement is contradictory only if the harmony of international and domestic law would result in the accommodation of international law to the conditions of domestic law. But in the case at hand what is at stake is not simply that with respect to war crimes and crimes against humanity an exception is made to the otherwise unconditionally applied domestic rule of *nullum crimen sine lege.* Thus, the question cannot be limited as to whether the particular rules aimed at redressing the violations of international humanitarian law may be integrated into Art. 57(4) of the Constitution. The constitutional question must be raised and answered by considering that Art. 7(1) of the Constitution mandates that, alongside the domestic law, rules of another legal

system, those of international law, shall prevail concurrently. It is the condition for participation in the community of nations that international law concerning these crimes be given effect, which the Constitution expressly recognizes, requires to apply and to harmonize with domestic law, and the domestic treatment of which in a divergent manner would not alter the State's obligations in international law. It is isolation from international law that would be contrary to Art. 7(1) of the Constitution. It is not the principle of *nullum crimen* that is abandoned, but its relevance exclusively in the sphere of domestic law is denied. Within its own system, international law demands that certain criminal acts be classified based on general principles recognized by the community of nations and prevailing at the time the act was committed—in the sense of the rules referred to above as international customary law—as war crimes or crimes against humanity. Through the punitive power of the Hungarian State it is, in fact, the punitive power of the international community which is given effect within the framework of conditions and guarantees provided by international law. Domestic law may be applied only to the extent international law expressly commands it (for instance, as is the case with the determination of sentences). No domestic law in conflict with an express peremptory rule of international law (*ius cogens*) may be given effect.

The harmonization of domestic and international penal law may proceed in numerous ways. It is possible expressly to provide for the independence of the two systems. This is what the International Covenant and European Convention did in their own sphere of application, stating that the international obligation for the unconditional application of the principle of *nullum crimen* in domestic criminal law does not become redundant by giving effect to rules of international law on war crimes and crimes against humanity. The permissive provisions of the International Covenant and the European Convention facilitate the integration of the international rule into the domestic legal system—what the Hungarian Constitution labels "harmony." [....]

On the basis of the reasoning above, there is no contradiction between Art. 57(4) and Art. 7(1) of the Constitution, and instead they must be interpreted in light of one another. Alongside the unconditional applicability of the principle of *nullum crimen* to domestic law, as guaranteed in Art. 57, Art. 7(1) brings about the constitutional endorsement of rules of international criminal law pertaining to war crimes and crimes against humanity.

3. The international conventions and documents which define war crimes and crimes against humanity, and which undoubtedly form part of the generally recognized and imperatively applied rules of international law, do not regulate the statute of limitations. For this reason, those States which prosecute these crimes on the basis of international customary law may apply their own domestic penal laws concerning the statute of limitations and are not compelled to declare that statutory limitations may not apply. The 1968 New York Convention on the Non-Applicability of Statutory Limitations for the Punishment of War Crimes and Crimes against Humanity, as well as the 1974 European Convention addressing a similar subject, may not be regarded as part of customary international law or a generally recognized rule of international law. But those States which ratified either of the two conventions assumed, with respect to the war crimes and crimes against humanity enumerated therein, an international obligation to declare, even with retroactive force, that statutes of limitations may not apply.

With Act I/1971, Hungary incorporated the New York Convention. Thereby it not only assumed the international obligation concerning the non-applicability of statutory limitations but also recognized a broader concept of crimes against humanity than is "generally" recognized by international law. This is the case, as according to the Convention apartheid and exile by use of armed force or occupation are also deemed to constitute war crimes or crimes against humanity.

In deciding the question of whether the obligation assumed by the Convention is to be given the same weight for the interpretation of Art. 57(4) as the general rules of international law, what matters is that the rules of non-applicability of statutory limitations are closely related to the nature of war crimes and crimes against humanity and that in this regard we may characterize the development of international law as a clear, but yet incomplete, process. International law itself does not contain any regulation of the statute of limitations. The New York Convention—according to its Preamble—merely restates this international legal situation and makes it impossible for signatory States to apply statutory limitations in domestic law. Thus the Convention extends the defining characteristic of the international legal regulation of these criminal offences—the rendering of prosecution and punishment independent of domestic law—to the period during which prosecution and punishment may be initiated. If with respect to the fundamental question—the application of sui generis international legal conditions alongside domestic law—unconstitutionality could be excluded, then that verdict perforce applies to the similar and auxiliary obligation of the same nature. In its *Dec. 11/1992 (III.5) AB* (MK 1992/23; ABH 1992, 77), the Constitutional Court interpreted the entirety of the constitutional requirements on criminal responsibility within domestic law. The Constitutional Court proceeded the same way with respect to international law's criminal liability as well.

4. Constitutionalism demands that criminal rules of international law be given effect according to the acts defined and conditions contained in international law.

(a) The criminal offence defined in s. 1 of the Act does not constitute a war crime according to international law. [....]

(b) [....] [Section 2 of the Act] conflates several regulations of the Geneva Conventions addressing different subject matters and categories of protected persons and creates a connection between them which does not appear in the Conventions. Domestic regulation may not alter the content of an international agreement. Hence, the constitutional concerns raised concerning the text of the Act are justified. [....]

5. [....] In its *Dec. 38/1993 (VI.11) AB* (MK 1993/75; ABH 1993, 256) the Constitutional Court stated that the Court avoids the annulment of a legal rule if the requirements of constitutionalism in the legal system and legal certainty may be secured without recourse to such a measure. In such case, the Constitutional Court defines, setting out constitutional requirements, that sphere of interpretation which, if complied with, permits the legal rule to be in harmony with the Constitution (Part IV.(2)(a)).

Consonant with this position, and also in order to dispel possible doubts of the prosecutors and the courts, the Constitutional Court found it necessary to apply the constitutional requirements imposed in connection with the application of art. 33(2) of the Criminal Code, defined with binding force by the first part of the operative part of this Decision, explicitly and with binding force to the international law criminal offences contained in s. 2 of the Act by the second part of the operative part of the Decision. By this resolution the declaration of unconstitutionality of s. 2 of the Act became avoidable, and s. 2 of the Act merely became part of that broader framework in which—irrespective of the pace of future legislative action, by the binding force of the Constitutional Court's Decision—the provisions of the Geneva Conventions may be applied constitutionally in the criminal courts.

DECISION 64/1993: 22 DECEMBER 1993

ON LOCAL GOVERNMENT APARTMENTS

The review of the "tenants' right to purchase," by force of which the tenants of former state-owned flats, now in the possession of local governments, could obtain the ownership of the flats through unilateral declaration at a price and under conditions prescribed by law, constitutes the most celebrated case of the implementation of the principles laid down in the second compensation case (16/1991) on the distribution of the social costs of the transformation. The long-lasting effect of the decision lies, however, in the redefinition of the concept by the Court on the constitutional right to property. The Court extended the protection of property beyond the civil law notion of ownership to rights and entitlements of economic value on the one hand. On the other, however, it made this protection relative by recognizing the restriction on property in the public interest, in certain cases even without compensation.

The petitioners sought constitutional review of certain provisions in Act LXXVIII/1993 on Certain Regulatory Aspects of Leasing and Alienating Apartments and Commercial Premises (the Real Property Act).

Under a previous statute, Act XXXIII/1991 on the Conferral of Certain Assets to Local Government (the Assets Act), mixed-function and non-residential buildings, state-owned rental apartments and other state-owned non-residential spaces contained therein became the property of local governments (s.1(1)). According to s. 2(7), a separate Act was to regulate the distribution, lease, rent and privatization of such apartments and non-residential space, which was enacted as the Real Property Act.

This latter Act encumbered local government ownership of apartments with the tenant's right to purchase. Such right could be exercized annually for a period of five years. The ceiling of the purchase price could not exceed 50 percent of the apartment's market value (s. 49) and acceptance of payment by installments was made obligatory (s. 50).

Certain petitioners sought inter alia a constitutional review of Chapter III, ss. 45–61 of the Act regulating the rights to purchase. They submitted that (a) the rules governing such rights violated Art. 8(2) because they were a disproportionate restriction on the owner's right to dispose of the property. For this reason, the tenant's right violated Arts. 9(1) and 13(1) as well as Art. 12(2), which mandated respect for local government property; and (b) ss. 49 and 50 were matters which would usually be at the discretion of the parties concerned. Determination of these matters by law infringed the constitutionally guaranteed principle of personal autonomy.

Held, allowing the petition in part:

(1) Constitutional protection similar to that provided for expropriation under Art. 13(2) could also extend to property burdened with an encumbrance. Even where such a restriction was necessitated by the public interest, other identifiable constitutional considerations supported compensation or at least mitigation for the owner of the loss sustained. In

such cases, it was necessary to investigate the proportionality between the public interest justifying intervention in property rights and the forced violation/restriction of the owner's property right in order to establish whether the latter, under the circumstances, was entitled to compensation. In considering proportionality, it was permissible for the Court generally to determine the criteria which decided whether or not an intervention was constitutional, *e.g.*, the extent of the encumbrance (disproportionate if its duration were indeterminate); the law forced only one group of owners to bear such a burden and not others in a similar position; and compensation may be necessary for the proportionality of the restriction on the use of the property. Thus in approaching the present case it had to be resolved whether the particularities of the right to purchase provided by the Real Property Act (including the creation and burdening of local government property) rendered the statutory foundation of that right unconstitutional per se or whether the right to purchase local government apartments in exchange for compensation could be deemed to constitute a proportional encumbrance.

(2) Legal certainty demanded a limit on the distribution of the burdens of the transformation: if transformation of a specific property were complete, *i.e.*, the transition from social to either private or local government property, then the protection afforded to the "new" property was naturally complete. Thus there was no constitutionally permissible possibility for a subsequent or retroactive distribution of the burden of such transformation. In respect of local governments, the transformation had been completed and so the constitutionality of the imposition of burdens or encumbrances on their property could only be evaluated on the basis of the considerations contained in the present Decision. Thus, even if the imposition of the right to purchase was a constitutionally permissible restriction on local government property rights, the details of such restriction had to be examined in order to see whether or not they satisfied the requirements of proportionality.

(3) The right to purchase was a grave burden per se. Even if the person authorized were not to exercise the right, its existence meant the prohibition of the apartment's alienation. The uncertainty caused by the fact that tenants could declare their intention to purchase annually for a five-year period rendered local government marketing of apartments extraordinarily difficult. If the said person exercized his right, then the local government lost its right of ownership to the apartment. The right to purchase amounted to a restriction on the right to property which might lead to the termination of that property right. Consequently, given the weight of this burden, the five-year "window of opportunity" opened by the Real Property Act was disproportionate in its duration.

(4) Since the exercise of the right to purchase was accompanied by the loss of property, proportionality between the public interest and expropriations demanded compensation. Such right could only be constitutional if accompanied by a guarantee of value being given effect. For this reason the compensation given by the Real Property Act had to approximate to full compensation applied to expropriation. In the present case, therefore, for the loss of apartments sustained by local governments in the exercise of the right to purchase, they had to receive remuneration or compensation which would ensure their retaining that value represented by the apartments transferred to them under the Assets Act. Provided this result was adhered to and that the provisions of the Real Property Act would be considered, it was for Parliament to establish the method of providing the necessary value

guarantees. Parliament had as yet failed to provide for full compensation and instead had merely fixed price ceilings. In the present case, therefore, the provision and amount of value guarantees were disproportionate and accordingly unconstitutional.

(5) In respect of non-residential property, however, even with the provision of a full-value guarantee, the right to purchase was an unnecessary and disproportionate burdening of local government property. There was no constitutional justification with respect to the Real Property Act to burden such local government property assets—belonging to the sphere of free enterprise—with such a right to purchase. Thus the disproportionality in the price ceiling was merely an additional reason for the finding of unconstitutionality, which would exist even without it.

IN THE NAME OF THE REPUBLIC OF HUNGARY!

In the matter of petitions seeking an ex post facto review of the unconstitutionality of a legal rule, the Constitutional Court—with the concurring opinions of Szabó and Vörös, JJ.—has made the following

DECISION.

The Constitutional Court holds that the right to purchase established by ss. 45(1) and 54(1) of Act LXXVIII/1993 on Certain Regulatory Aspects of Leasing and Alienating Apartments and Commercial Premises is unconstitutional; consequently, ss. 45–63, the second sentence of s. 83(1) and s. 89(3) and (4) of the aforementioned Act, are declared null and void as of the date of the publication of this Decision.

The Constitutional Court rejects the petitions seeking a determination of unconstitutionality and nullification of ss. 20(2), 34, 35, 43(1), 75(1) and 76(2) of the Act.

The Constitutional Court orders the publication of this Decision in the *Hungarian Official Gazette.*

REASONING

SÓLYOM, P., delivering the Opinion of the Court: [....]

III

The provisions of [Act LXXVII/1993 on Certain Regulatory Aspects of Leasing and Alienating Apartments and Commercial Premises, hereafter] the Real Property Act concerning the privatization of apartments and non-residential premises—the third and fourth Chapters of the Act—seek, according to the legislative intent, to conclude the "change of the system of property rights" with respect to real property, thereby creating the legal environment for a freely functioning real estate market and terminating the contradictions of the system of rented apartments. (See the Preamble to the Real Property Act.) [....]

The "transition" is taking place within constitutional bounds. The constitutional requirements determined in relation to certain transition-oriented regulations bind the subsequent measures as well. Corrections of possible conceptual errors may proceed only by paying due regard to these restrictions and by respecting acquired rights. In the process of examining the Real Property Act one must be aware that the privatization of the former socialized property is just as much part and parcel of the "change of the system of property rights" as is the creation of local municipal property—largely deriving from the same sources—and its express protection by the Constitution. [....]

3. [....]

The local governments did not and do not have a right to acquire specified assets or to obtain certain objects under specified conditions (*Dec. 1582/B/1990 AB:* ABH 1991, 605). The provision of the local governments with property from state property was a gratuitous acquisition to which the rules developed in *Dec. 16/1991 (IV.20) AB* (MK 1991/42; ABH 1991, 58), concerning the encumbrances on such property, apply.

[....] However, making an encumbrance more onerous may always become the subject matter of constitutional review since, in this case, what is at stake is no longer the encumbrances associated with the acquisition of property but the burdens placed on the property already acquired.

Constitutional review may also be conducted with respect to the concretization of abstract encumbrances. Indeed, the subject matter of this case is precisely whether the "abstract" encumbrances provided for by s. 2(7) of the Assets Act, that "a separate Act determines the regulations concerning the privatization" of apartments and non-residential premises, may constitutionally encompass the right to purchase by the tenants.

4. The Real Property Act made the burdens of the apartment privatization greater for the local governments compared to those burdens already existing at the time of acquisition of the property.

The right to purchase established by the Real Property Act is a greater burdening of local government property than the "right to buy apartments" regulated by Council of Ministers Decree 32/1969 (IX.2) MT. [....]

IV

1. According to Art. 13(1) of the Constitution, the right to property is a fundamental right. The sphere and means of constitutional protection of property does not necessarily follow the legal concepts of civil law. That is so, as the necessary and proportional restriction and the essential content of the right to property are concepts which have no civil law analogies. The bundle of property rights [under civil law, that is possession, use and disposal of assets]—which even by civil law are not necessarily vested in the property owner and in some instances are vested in others by law—may not be identified as the constitutionally protected essential content of the right to property.

In the field of protection of fundamental rights, the encumbrance of property by public law may lead either to the declaration of unconstitutionality of the intervention of the public authorities, and therefore to the nullification of the legal rule on which it was based, or to an acknowledgement of the constitutionality of the burden imposed, and at most to the substitution of a legal remedy (monetary compensation), that is, guaranteeing the value of the property, for guaranteeing the physical integrity of the property. Expropriation is the extreme case of the application of the latter remedy expressly regulated by Art. 13(2) of the Constitution, but there are other instances in which monetary compensation arises.

The expropriation of property in the constitutional sense does not necessarily mean the loss of the property right in the civil law sense; however, the Constitution does not provide unconditional protection against physical loss of property.

Thus the scope of the constitutional protection of property may not be identified with the protection of the abstract civil law property, that is, neither with the bundle of rights of possession, use and disposal, nor with its determination as a negative and absolute right. The content of property as a fundamental right must always be understood within the framework of (constitutional) public and private law restrictions. The extent of the constitutional protection of property is always concrete; it depends upon the subject, object and function of the property as well as the nature of the restriction. Viewed from the other side, the constitutional permissibility of the intervention of the public authorities into the property right varies according to these considerations.

Property is afforded constitutional protection in its capacity as the traditional means of securing an economic basis for the autonomy of individual action. The constitutional protection must track the changing social role of property so as to fulfill the same task. Thus, when the protection of individual autonomy is at stake, the constitutional protection of property extends to rights with an economic value which today perform this former role of ownership, including public law entitlements (for instance, to entitlements from the social insurance). On the other hand, however, the social burdens of property make constitutionally permissible a far-reaching restriction on the autonomy of the property owner. The means of constitutional protection is determined by that particularity of property—which does not arise with other fundamental rights—that as regards its constitutionally protected role it may be substituted. The object of the constitutional protection is primarily the physical object of property. But it is the Constitution itself which permits expropriation in the public interest, indicating that the limit of constitutional guarantee of property is the guaranteeing of the compensation of its value for the owner.

In accordance with the present state of the protection of the fundamental right of property, the Constitutional Court has already extended this protection to certain rights previously not recognized as property by civil law (*Dec. 17/1992 (III.30) AB:* MK 1992/32; ABH 1992, 104) and permitted for the purpose of protecting property its functional differentiation, for instance for the intensified protection of property serving the public good (*Dec. 6/ 1992 (I.30) AB:* MK 1992/11; ABH 1992, 40).

The Constitutional Court's conception of the protection of property accords with that of the European Convention on Human Rights and the case law of the European Court of Human Rights. [....]

2. In protecting the fundamental right of property the demarcation line is no longer between the "restriction" of property and its "taking" in the civil law sense. What has become the constitutional question is in which cases a property owner must accept restrictions by the public authorities without compensation and in which cases he can claim indemnification for the restriction on his property rights. In response to the multiplication of legal restrictions, the concept of the classic "taking" has become broader, a concept applied by the State to acquire property (usually realty) deemed indispensable for the public good whenever a civil law transaction proved ineffective in acquiring that property. But, just as more and more property restrictions merit protection analogous to that afforded in cases of expropriation, also a growing number of restrictions must be borne without any compensation at all. Rights to real property are especially impinged upon by the restrictions, with respect to which public use or public purpose giving content to "public interest" changes in that the restriction or expropriation of property now often serves the benefit of other private

persons (and serves the "public" only in the sense that social problems are solved)—such as the case in many instances of town planning, land reform, rent control and security of tenure.

3. Article 13(2) of the Constitution permits expropriation only in exceptional cases in the public interest, in cases and in the manner stipulated by law, and only if full, unconditional and immediate compensation is provided. This provision refers to that traditional concept of expropriation which involved the taking of the whole of the property. But a heavy burdening of the property may also qualify for constitutional protection similar to that provided in cases of expropriation. Even in the event of a restriction necessitated by the public interest there may be other constitutionally cognizable considerations which speak in favour of compensating the owner for his loss or at least mitigating the damage. Such a consideration may be the extent of the burden or the fact that the law only forces one group of property owners to bear the burden whereas others similarly situated remain exempt. In these cases, the requirement of proportionality between the necessitated intervention with the owner's property right and the public interest justifying the intervention compels compensation.

Because of the particularities of the nature of property protection the central point of the enquiry into the constitutionality of state intervention, the field of the constitutional review, has become the adjudication of proportionality between the ends and the means, *viz.*, the public interest and the restriction on property. At the outset of an enquiry into the necessity and unavoidability of restricting a fundamental right, it must be borne in mind that Art. 13(2) of the Constitution merely requires the "public interest" to justify expropriation; that is, if monetary compensation is provided, a more compelling and justified "necessity" need not be established for constitutional purposes. Anyway, the social and economic role of property, especially the way in which specific regulatory measures fit into the given political economic tasks, renders the determination of necessity or unavoidability more difficult than is the case with other fundamental rights, where it may be more possible to make comparisons of general validity. In a democratic society it is natural that the "public interest" is evaluated in significantly divergent ways. Accordingly, the constitutional review of the "public interest" determined by the democratically elected legislature does not focus upon the question of whether such legislation was unavoidably necessary; rather—though formally it is not directed at ascertaining the existence of the "public interest" but applies the criterion of "necessity-proportionality"—it confines its enquiry to the question of whether the invocation of the "public interest" is justified and whether the solution adopted for the "public interest" violates some other constitutional right (such as the prohibition of negative discrimination). It was in this spirit that the Constitutional Court proceeded in the matters decided by its *Dec. 7/1991 (II.28) AB* (MK 1991/22: ABH 1991, 22) and *Dec. 13/1992 (III.25) AB* (MK 1992/30; ABH 1992, 95). [....]

Nevertheless, in investigating the proportionality of public interest and the restriction on property rights, the Constitutional Court may generally decide upon those criteria which determine the constitutionality of an intervention. This method militates against the unavoidable loss suffered by legal certainty on account of the limited review to which the "necessity" of public interest may be subjected. For instance, the Constitutional Court considers disproportionate a property restriction if its duration cannot be estimated. (See also, in addition to the aforementioned cases, *Dec. 24/1992 (IV.21) AB* (MK 1992/41; ABH 1992, 126).) In other cases compensation may be necessary for the proportionality of the restriction on property. According to Art. 13(2) of the Constitution expropriation demands immediate, unconditional and full compensation. But the Constitutional Court may hold in other instances of property restriction as well that proportionality requires the payment of compensation.

In the case at hand what must be decided is whether the particularities of the right to purchase provided by the Real Property Act, including the history of the creation of the burdens on local municipal property, render the statutory foundation of the right to purchase per se unconstitutional or whether in exchange for compensation (and for what sort of compensation) the right to purchase may be deemed to constitute a proportionate encumbrance.

V

[....]

The imposition of the burden concomitant with the transfer of property [the transfer of previously state-owned apartments to the local governments under "the continuation of the legal regulation of alienation"] renders unnecessary the examination of whether the social burdens on the ownership of rental apartments would anyhow render constitutional the significant legal restriction imposed on the property owners (landlords') right of disposition. The permission of the regulation (but not its content) is an original encumbrance on the property. [....]

VI

Thus, the legislature is entitled to regulate the alienation of apartments; at the outset, local governments, to which the apartments were transferred pursuant to the Assets Act, acquire the right of disposition with this restriction.

1. The reservation of the right to "regulate alienation" by separate Act embodies in principle every aspect of alienation, from the prohibition of sale to its compulsion. [....]

The fact that the legislature reserved the right to regulate alienation also means conceptually that the State transferred the property to the local government with the burden imposed that the State could not guarantee its physical integrity in the possession of the local governments. On the basis of the legislative reservation, the local governments had to anticipate a state housing policy which would compel them to alienate the apartments. The conferral of the purchase right of the tenants is undoubtedly a direct, grave and legally conceivable manifestation of this policy. Leaving in force the previous rules concerning the alienation of apartments—with the express retention of the possibility of amendments—is another indisputable sign of the State's privatization policy.

In case of the reservation "to regulate alienation" it is necessary that the broader concept of the protection of property comes into play which guarantees for the value of the property, that is, which guarantees the value of the transferred property rather than the specific property itself, whose status is uncertain from the beginning. This is the last line of defence and guarantee of property protection by the Constitution as well.

2. The right to purchase of apartments as provided by law and the protection of property rights may be constitutionally reconciled within the Real Property Act by a significant reduction in the duration of the right to purchase and by giving effect to the value guarantee. [....]

3. [....]

(b) Since the right to purchase, if exercized, leads to the loss of property, proportionality between the public interest and the intervention with the right to property demands compensation. The right to purchase may only be constitutional if accompanied by a value guarantee being given effect. For this reason the compensation foreseen by the Real Property Act must approximate the constitutionally demanded full compensation applied in the classic case of expropriation. Other conditions, such as the immediacy of compensation, are to be regulated in accordance with the nature of the case at hand. For the loss of apartments inflicted by the exercise of the right to purchase, local governments must receive such consideration or compensation so as to ensure that they retain in their possession the value represented by the apartments transferred to them under the Assets Act.

The way of providing value guarantees is for the legislature to establish. In so doing attention must be paid to all of the provisions of the Real Property Act. It is, however, not required that the full amount of compensation shall be paid by the tenants entitled to purchase. [....]

VÖRÖS, J., concurring, in whose Opinion **SZABÓ, J.,** joined: [....]

In my judgment, it is of pivotal importance to separate clearly the two institutions [the right to property and the expropriation] from the perspective of the unconstitutionality of the right to purchase contained in the Real Property Act. For if a "unique" way of expropriation can be read into the right to property, then the boundary between right to property and expropriation becomes blurred. In the future it cannot be known how far the constitutional guarantee of the right to property will extend and from what the conditions imposed on expropriations as guarantees are to protect. The reduction of the right to property to a value guarantee, resulting from the stipulation of the interchangeability of the actual object and the value of the property, makes the right to property relative and its content uncertain, and this without transforming it into an expropriation: it loses the protection of the former without falling under the protective wings of the latter constitutional institution. That property right to which neither the right to property nor the expropriation guarantee attaches, that is, one whose deprivation is possible only subject to compensation for its market value and without the public interest rationale justifying expropriation, is no longer a property right.

DECISION 21/1994: 16 APRIL 1994

ON THE FREEDOM OF ENTERPRISE ON THE LICENSING OF TAXIS

Imposing a numerus clausus *on taxicabs is not unusual in metropolises from New York to Vienna, and more than once it has raised constitutional issues. In this case, the Constitutional Court did not find the arguments of the Budapest local government compelling enough for the constitutionality of such a restriction. Nevertheless, the case provided an opportunity for the Court to clarify fundamental notions of the new, constitutionally mandated "market economy." The Court held that neither the "market economy" nor "the freedom of economic competition" constituted a fundamental right. In contrast, "the right to enterprise" was seen as a true constitutional right, which the Court considered in many respects to be the same as the "right to work" and the "right to choose [one's] job and profession." By this, the Constitutional Court also abandoned the former "socialist" notion of the right to work. This case, together with the local government apartment case (64/1993), defined the concept of the Constitutional Court regarding property and other economy-related rights.*

The petitioners sought an ex post facto examination of the constitutionality of certain legal rules.

Section 19(2) of Act I/1988 on the Traffic on Public Roads authorized local governments, subject to consultation with professional advocacy groups, to regulate by decree the number of taxis licensed within their jurisdiction.

The petitioners submitted, inter alia, that s. 19(2) was contrary to the rights of free enterprise and free competition under Arts. 9(2), 70/A, 70/B and 70/C and accordingly sought a determination of its unconstitutionality.

Held, allowing the petition in part:

(1) The fundamental right to work contains the freedom to choose and practise every type of occupation, of which the freedom of choice (Art. 70/B) and the right to free enterprise (Art. 9(2)) are merely aspects: an unconditional constitutional requirement of this right is that the State cannot prevent a person from becoming an entrepreneur. Although the right to work (occupation, enterprise) received the same protection from state intervention and restriction accorded to other freedoms, the constitutionality of such restrictions was evaluated by different standards depending upon whether it was the practice or free choice of occupation which was restricted by the State and further whether the State conditioned the choice of occupation by subjective or objective criteria. The quotas imposed on certain occupations on the basis of objective criteria was such a restriction: if the quota had been filled, it rendered impossible the choice of that profession irrespective of the individual's personal characteristics. It was necessary to scrutinize strictly the constitutionality of such objective restriction, primarily its necessity and unavoidability and whether it represented the least

restrictive means of achieving the given regulatory objective. Moreover, as such an objective restriction involved a total negation of the fundamental right to work, it could not be applied to regulate competition or for planning needs. As regards the fulfillment of subjective requirements, this was available to everyone in principle and Parliament had a greater leeway in respect of subjective restrictions. On such a basis, restricting the practice of occupations might generally be justified on grounds of profession and efficiency and gives rise to fundamental rights concerns only in extreme cases.

(2) The objective restriction of the freedom of choice of an occupation by authorizing local governments to regulate by decree the number of licensed taxis under s. 19(2) of the Act was unconstitutional. Although the number of taxis and entrepreneurs was not necessarily identical, nevertheless the limitation of taxis evidently resulted in the restriction on the number of entrepreneurs. There was no constitutional right or interest which could have made the objective restriction on the choice of occupation necessary and proportionate in the taxi industry. The restriction on the right to free enterprise by quotas was not a constitutional instrument of competition regulation. It could not be used to raise the quality of the service or as a substitute for tax collection: the public administration had to find other means to achieve such ends. Further the statutory authorization permitting local governments to limit by decree the number of taxis was also unconstitutional because it did not contain any criterion for issuing the restrictions. Since a restriction of an essential component of a fundamental right could only be provided by law and constitutionally justifiable means and manner, the *numerus clausus* scheme set out in the Act, on the one hand, and the giving of carte blanche to local governments for such a restriction on the other, were constitutionally precluded.

IN THE NAME OF THE REPUBLIC OF HUNGARY!

In the matter of the petitions seeking an ex post facto review of the unconstitutionality of legal rules, the Constitutional Court—with the concurring opinions of Tersztyánszky and Zlinszky, JJ.—has made the following

DECISION.

The Constitutional Court holds that s. 19(2) of Act I/1988 on Traffic on Public Roads is unconstitutional and accordingly annuls this provision effective from the date of publication of this Decision.

The Constitutional Court rejects the petitions seeking the determination of unconstitutionality and the declaration of annulment of paras. 5/A(2) and 5/B(2)(a) of Government Decree 89/1988 (XII.20) MT on Transportation Services on Public Roads and the Maintenance of Vehicles used for Public Transportation, and para. 2 of Ministry of Transport Decree 21/1992 (X.27) KVHM on Certain Requirements for Private Taxi Licensing.

The Constitutional Court publishes this Decision in the *Hungarian Official Gazette*.

REASONING

SÓLYOM, P., delivering the Opinion of the Court: [....]

IV

1. According to the Preamble to the Constitution and Art. 9(1), the economy of Hungary is a market economy. Article 9(2) states that the Republic of Hungary recognizes and supports the right to enterprise and the freedom of competition in the economy.

Concerning the characteristics of the market economy, the Constitution states merely that within it public and private property shall have equal rights and be granted equal protection. The Constitution does not otherwise commit itself to any substantive model of the market economy. The Constitutional Court, in its reasoning of *Dec. 33/1993 (V.28) AB* (MK 1993/68; ABH 1993, 247), stated that the Constitution—beyond its declaration of the principle of the market economy—is neutral in terms of economic policy. The magnitude or extent of state intervention, and especially its prohibition, may not be deduced directly from the Constitution.

For this reason, the Constitutional Court, using abstract and general criteria, can only define those extreme situations in which state intervention reaches such a critical intensity that by violating the principle of market economy it becomes unconstitutional. It is the intervention that conceptually and practically renders the existence of the market economy impossible which is qualified as unconstitutional; such would be the case, for example, with overall nationalization and the introduction of a comprehensive, rigid system of central planning. The interpretation of rights and institutions describing and defining the "economic system" must consider the "market economy" within these constraints. These rights and institutions are: the right to property; the equality of private and public property; the right to enterprise; the freedom of competition; state property; the proprietary independence of state enterprises, co-operatives and local governments; the right to work and choice of occupation; the right to organize interest groups; the right to freedom of movement and settlement; and finally the prohibition of discrimination and the general right to personality deduced from the right to human dignity (Arts. 9–14, 70/B, 70/C, 58, 70/A and 54 of the Constitution). [....]

But apart from such extreme cases, the "market economy" is irrelevant for all constitutional review. No one has a right to the market economy, that is, it may not be classified as a fundamental right; no alleged unconstitutionality of any fundamental right may be decided by asserting a violation of the market economy. The constitutionality of an intervention may not be conditioned on whether or not it facilitates the development of the market economy. Successive governments confronted with changing economic situations freely shape their economic policies; they may liberalize or increase state regulation provided they do not make a market economy manifestly impossible. When freedom must be protected from itself is liberalism's eternal dilemma. While it is true that the restrictions imposed on the free market must also serve to maintain its existence, there is no constitutional criterion for determining when this goal has been reversed; more importantly, the ideal of market freedom varies, reflecting changes in economic policy, and the Constitutional Court is not authorized to replace the legislature's conception of the market economy with one of its own. (However, concerning the question of what makes the operation of a market economy totally impossible, the Constitutional Court is competent to impose its own views.) Finally, restrictive regulation of the market may also be constitutional because of fundamental rights and constitutional values totally independent of the freedom of the market, for instance, environmental, health or national security reasons. But the converse of this statement is also true: the restriction of the market may be unconstitutional—also independent of considerations of the freedom of the market—if it violates some fundamental right. [....]

2. "Freedom of economic competition" is likewise not a fundamental right but such a condition of the market economy whose existence and operation must be ensured by the State pursuant to Art. 9(2) of the Constitution. The State's "recognition and support" of the freedom of competition requires the establishment of an objective, institutionalized protection for free enterprise and the fundamental rights, mentioned in Point 1 above, necessary for the market economy. It is primarily the realization and protection of these fundamental rights that gives rise to free competition, which—similar to the market economy—has no separate constitutional assessment.

3. However, the right to enterprise (Art. 9(2) of the Constitution) is a genuine fundamental right.

According to the Constitutional Court in *Dec. 54/1993 (X.13) AB* (MK 1993/147, at 8802; ABH 1993, 340 at 341–42):

> The right to enterprise is one aspect of the constitutional fundamental right to choose freely one's occupation [Art. 70/B(1)], its manifestation in a specific category [....] No one has a subjective right to engage in entrepreneurial activity in a specific occupation or field, nor to a particular legal form of an entrepreneurial activity. The right to enterprise means only—but this much is posited as a constitutional requirement—that the State may not prevent or make impossible the launching of an entrepreneurship.

The right to work as a subjective (justiciable) right must be distinguished from the right to work as a social right, especially the latter's institutional aspect, namely, the State's duty to engage in an appropriate employment and job-creation policy. This aspect has no relevance to the case at hand, nor to any of the State's duties emanating from the right to enterprise. On the other hand, there is no constitutional justification to limit the subjective right to work only to the formal employer-employee relationships governed by labour law.

There is no hierarchical relationship between the subjective right to work, the right to choose freely one's job and profession (Art. 70/B of the Constitution), on the one hand, and the right to enterprise on the other hand. The right to work must be interpreted as containing the freedom to choose and practise every type of occupation, profession and "work." In this context, the specific mention of the freedom of choice in Art. 70/B of the Constitution and the right to enterprise in Art. 9 of the Constitution is mere repetition or more detailed specification. Work, occupation or enterprise as fundamental subjective rights do not differ from one another.

4. The fundamental right to work (occupation, enterprise) receives the same protection from state intervention and restriction which is afforded to other fundamental freedoms. But the constitutionality of these restrictions is evaluated by different standards depending upon whether it is the practice or the free choice of the occupation which is restricted by the State, and, with respect to the latter, the judgment differs depending on whether the State conditions the choice of occupation by subjective or objective criteria. (For instance, in the case at hand, the practice of the taxi industry is restricted by regulations concerning the se-

curity deposit, the condition and tests of roadworthiness of motor vehicles, *etc.* The subjective restriction, which is dependent on the subject, is the requirement of passing a test for taxi drivers; the objective restriction, which is totally independent of the personal characteristics of the people desiring to engage in this entrepreneurial activity, is the number of licences which may be issued.)

What endangers the right to work (occupation, enterprise) the most is if a person is precluded from engaging in that activity, if he is not permitted to choose that occupation or work. If this were an unenumerated right, it would be given effect on the basis of a violation of the general right of personality. The Constitutional Court (*Dec. 54/1993 (X.13) AB:* MK 1993/147; ABH 1993, 340) has already declared that it is an imperative constitutional requirement that the State desist from preventing a person from becoming an entrepreneur. The *numerus clausus* (quotas) imposed on certain occupations on the basis of objective criteria are precisely such a restriction: if a quota has been filled, it renders impossible the choice of that profession irrespective of the individual's personal characteristics. The constitutionality of such objective restriction, primarily its necessity and unavoidability, whether the restriction is truly the least restrictive means of achieving the given state goal, must be subjected to strict scrutiny.

The prescription of subjective requirements is also a restriction on the freedom of choice. But the fulfillment of these requirements is available to everyone in theory (if not, it is an objective restriction). For this reason the legislature's margin of appreciation is somewhat greater than in the case of objective restrictions. Finally, restricting the practice of occupations may generally be justified on professional and efficiency grounds, and they raise fundamental rights concerns only in extreme cases.

In evaluating the objective restrictions, attention must also be paid to the fact that since this restriction involves the total negation of a fundamental right such an instrument may not be applied to regulate competition. The application of a *numerus clausus* scheme is especially impermissible for the planning of needs, for such a licensing mechanism is the hallmark of central planning and not the market economy. Likewise, the simplification of some administrative tasks (such as, with respect to taxis, the growing danger of traffic chaos because of the rising number of cars and shortage of parking spaces) does not justify the imposition of closed quotas.

V

[....]

3. Consumer protection and the nature of the taxi industry justifies the restriction of the exercise of the occupation by both the security deposit and the stringent technical requirements as to cars. Compliance with the technical requirements is proportionate with both consumer protection and the requirement of a minimal service quality, and it may be seen as necessary for those purposes. [....]

4. In principle, a satisfactory completion of an examination may always be a necessary prerequisite for entering a profession, unless the work is entirely unskilled labour—but even in that case some knowledge of safety regulations may be prescribed. The taxi industry does not require separate vocational training, but its practice may be conditioned on requirements beyond that of a driving licence. [....] The Constitutional Court reviewed the education and testing curricula and found that they may be characterized as constituting a compelling and proportionate restriction on the free choice of work.

5. Section 1(2) of Act LXXVIII/1992, amending s. 19 of Act I/1988, contains objective constraints on the freedom of occupation: it authorizes local governments to regulate by decree the number of licensed taxis within their territories. Although the number of taxis and entrepreneurs is not identical, since a single entrepreneur may operate several taxis or a taxi may be used by several entrepreneurs, the regulation of the number of taxis evidently results in the restriction on the number of entrepreneurs.

This regulation is unconstitutional on a number of grounds.

(a) The Constitutional Court did not find such constitutional right or interest which could have made the objective restriction on the choice of occupation necessary and proportionate in the case of the taxi industry. The justifications invoked by the legislature are especially inadequate to satisfy the requirement of constitutional restriction of a fundamental right. "The undesired expansion of the supply, the deterioration of the quality of the service, the unduly high price level for the service, the ensuing economic hardship for a large proportion of the entrepreneurs, the non-payment of taxes and service charges"; and their "elimination and consumer protection—given the absence of self-regulating mechanism in the taxi market—requires purposive intervention" wrote the Minister for Transport, Communication and Water. But this "intervention" cannot amount to the violation of the essential content of a constitutional fundamental right. The restriction on the right of enterprise by *numerus clausus* is not a constitutional instrument of competition regulation; it may not be used to raise the quality of the service, not to mention its use as a substitute for tax collection. The anomaly of the taxi market—the squeezing out of competitors, *etc.*—can and must be solved by using other administrative means. (For instance, payment of public charges should be assured by the prescription of mandatory issuance of receipts and the installation of taxi meters instead of restricting entry into the occupation, as has been the case.) Public administration may not lighten its burdens at the expense of such a restriction of fundamental rights.

(b) The statutory regulation authorizing local governments to limit by decree the number of taxis is also unconstitutional because this authorization does not provide any criterion for the restrictions. [....]

TERSZTYÁNSZKY, J., concurring (in whose Opinion **ZLINSZKY, J.,** also concurred): [....]

I do not agree, however, that s. 19(2) of Act I/1988 is unconstitutional because the limitation on the number of taxis per se violates the right of enterprise.

The Act refers to the protection of legal interests related to traffic on public roads. The service of transporting passengers by car on public roads is a form of enterprise for the general public. On the basis of the meaning attributed to the challenged regulations in the process of analyzing the regulatory environment, it cannot be excluded that for reasons of safety and flow of traffic it is necessary to restrict within a locality the number of motor vehicles offering the service of passenger transportation to the public.

Nor can the possibility be excluded that the unrestricted expansion of the supply side of the service—precisely because of its particular characteristics—may result in the bankruptcy of the taxi industry as a whole. [....]

DECISION 28/1994: 20 MAY 1994

ON ENVIRONMENTAL PROTECTION

Here, again, a complicated and originally well-intentioned side effect of compensation and privatization—efforts to secure enough land to be distributed—led to a fundamental decision on another question, the nature of the right to a healthy environment. This case is a sister of the other avant-garde decisions of the Constitutional Court, such as the PIN (15/1991), abortion (64/1991), and the same-sex partnership (14/1995) cases. As a result of the analysis of the peculiarities of the right to a healthy environment, the Court spelled out the nonderogation rule: the legally secured level of nature protection may be reduced only under conditions that are valid for the restriction of any fundamental right.

The petitioner requested ex post facto constitutional review of certain laws concerned with landownership and the environment.

He sought annulment of s. 13(7)(4) of Act II/1993 on Land Reallocation and Land Distribution Committees (the Land Reallocation Act). This provision had repealed s. 19 of Act II/1992 on Transitional Rules and on the Entry into Force of Act I/1992 on Co-operatives (the Transitional Rules Act). Section 19 had prescribed that protected areas under the ownership of agricultural co-operatives were to be transferred to state ownership and the management of the environmental protection authorities (EPA). In view of the rules concerning the acquisition of protected natural areas by the State, he submitted that the repeal violated Art. 70/D since the transfer of such areas into private ownership and the management of co-operatives led to the dismemberment of those areas and the destruction of natural treasures. Annulment thereof would then leave an unconstitutional situation amounting to an unconstitutional omission to legislate, which Parliament would be required to rectify.

Held, granting the petition:

(1) The right to a healthy environment under Art. 18 was not an individual fundamental right nor merely a constitutional duty or state goal for which the State might freely choose any means of implementation. Nor did it amount to a social right but rather to a distinct fundamental right exceedingly dominated and determined by its objective aspect of institutional protection. The right raised the guarantees for the implementation of state duties in the area of environmental protection, including the conditions under which the degree of protection already achieved might be restricted, to the level of a fundamental right. In fact the right to a healthy environment was a part of the objective, institutional aspect of the right to life. In determining the degree of protection as the key factor, one had to consider three matters—the limited resources of the natural basis of life, the irreversibility of a substantial part of environmental damage, and the fact that these marked the conditions for the continuance of human life. The right to environmental protection guaranteed the physical conditions necessary to implement the right to human life. Thus extraordinary rigour was called for in protecting such a right through legislative acts.

(2) It therefore followed that the State could not reduce the degree of protection of nature as guaranteed under law unless this was necessary to realize other constitutional rights or values and even then only in proportion to the set goal. The State was not free to allow any deterioration of the environment or risk thereof. Since environmental damage destroyed non-renewable resources, was often irreparable, and the neglect of environmental protection set in motion irreversible processes, prevention took precedence over all other means to guarantee the right to environmental protection because subsequent penalties for irreparable damage could not guarantee restoration of the original condition. In implementing the right, the State was thus constitutionally required not to regress from the degree of protection already achieved unless the conditions were such that would also allow restrictions on individual fundamental rights. By upholding this degree of protection in the enforcement of the right, the State could not turn from preventative rules of protection to protection ensured by sanctions although any state action contrary thereto might be compelled by unavoidable necessity and proportionate with this necessity. Increased severity of prohibitions and sanctions was insufficient, and instead preventative guarantees were needed that excluded the possibility of damages with the same probability as if the area were owned by the State and managed by environmental protection authorities. Indeed the higher class of protection to which a given area belonged, the lower the possibility of substituting other protective methods for the transfer of ownership to the State and that of management to the said authorities.

(3) The reduction in the degree of environmental protection guaranteed by law violated the right to a healthy environment as guaranteed by Arts. 18 and 70/D(2). The amendments to the Transitional Rules Act and the Land Reallocation Act which caused this reduction were motivated by the circumstance of the expansion of lands to be allocated, in view of the expected large number of claims for land under the Compensation Act and the compensation in kind of the joint landowners. This circumstance though could not be set against the constitutional duty of the State to protect the environment. As a result of the amendments, forests were included among the areas which could be incorporated into the land fund with permission from the environmental protection authorities, and the allocation of arable lands located within present and prospective national parks was also allowed. Making ministerial permission a condition of the latter was insufficient as an increase of severity to balance the reduction of protection, since it did not exceed the restrictions already available under the current environmental protection legislation. Moreover it contained no provisions beyond mere authorization with which to enforce stricter conditions.

(4) In the interest of environmental protection, the relevant provisions were annulled retroactively as of the date they entered into force, but this did not automatically affect the property rights obtained under the now unconstitutional provisions or the in-kind designation of the share of property. The constitutional and mandatory degree of protection (now being that which was originally stipulated by s. 19 of the Transitional Rules Act) posed no obstacle to the expropriation of present and prospective protected natural areas which had meanwhile passed into or had been designated as private property. Although expropriation was not the only means of restoring the degree of protection originally determined by the transfer into state ownership and management by the relevant authorities, practically strict preventative supervision could substitute state acquisition only with respect to lower-class protection areas.

(5) The enforcement of the right to environmental protection and in particular the prevention of irreparable damage to nature required a consistent legal regulation which mandated the restoration of the original degree of protection. However, due to the final changes in ownership which had occurred since the amendment to s. 15 and the repeal of s. 19, even the retroactive nullification of the unconstitutional provisions and restoration of s. 19 was no longer sufficient to re-establish the original degree of environmental protection. Accordingly, with respect to all areas under protection and targeted for protection, the absence of rules that prescribed their acquisition by the State and management by the relevant authorities or that guaranteed an equal degree of protection gave rise to an unconstitutional situation for which Parliament was called upon to enact the necessary provisions.

IN THE NAME OF THE REPUBLIC OF HUNGARY!

In the matter of a petition seeking the ex post facto review of the unconstitutionality of a legal rule as well as its annulment, the Constitutional Court, with the dissenting opinion of Ádám and Tersztyánszky, JJ., has made the following

DECISION.

(1) The Constitutional Court declares that the right to a healthy environment, as defined in Art. 18 of the Constitution, incorporates inter alia the responsibility of the Republic of Hungary to ensure that the State does not reduce the degree of the protection of nature as guaranteed under law, unless this is unavoidable in order to enforce any other fundamental right or constitutional value. Even in the latter event, the point to which the degree of protection is reduced cannot be disproportionate to the goal to be achieved.

(2) The Constitutional Court declares that the admission of "forest" land-use areas into the categories of arable land that can be designated [for privatization] with the permission of the environmental protection authority, as provided by s. 15 (1)(i) of Act II/1992 on Transitional Rules and on the Entry into Force of Act I/1992 on Co-operatives, and s. 15(4) of the same Act, are contrary to the Constitution, and therefore annuls retroactively the said provisions of the Act as of the date they entered into force. Section 15 (1)(i) remains in force as follows:

> [Lands as defined under s. 13(a), (b), and (d) of s. 13(2) must, above and beyond the provisions of s. 14, be designated so that—]
> (i) they include no other protected natural areas, with the exception of arable land belonging to inhabited farms, whose designation requires permission by the environmental protection authority, no national parks, nor areas under special protection and those protected under international convention, and, further, no arable land—including ploughed fields, orchards, gardens and vineyards—whose designation likewise requires permission from the environmental protection authority.

(3) The Constitutional Court declares that s. 13(7)(4) of Act II/1993 on Land Reallocation and Land Distribution Committees, is contrary to the Constitution; thus it annuls retroactively this provision of the Act as of the date it entered into force.

(4) The Constitutional Court declares that with respect to all areas under protection

and targeted for protection—those upon which the provisions of Points 2 and 3 of this Decision do not result in the re-establishment of the original degree of environmental protection—the absence of rules that prescribe their acquisition by the State and management by environmental protection authorities, or the absence of rules guaranteeing an equal degree of protection, where possible, gives rise to a situation contrary to the Constitution. The Constitutional Court therefore calls upon Parliament to meet its legislative responsibility by 30 November 1994.

The Constitutional Court publishes this Decision in the *Hungarian Official Gazette.*

REASONING

SÓLYOM, P., delivering the Opinion of the Court: [....]

III

1. Article 18 of the Constitution stipulates that the Republic of Hungary recognizes and shall implement the right of all individuals to a healthy environment. It follows from Art. 70/D(2) that one way in which the Republic of Hungary implements the human right to "the highest possible level of physical and mental health" [Art. 70/D(1)] is the protection of the built and natural environment.

In *Dec. 996/G/1990 AB* (ABH 1993, 533), the Constitutional Court ruled that from a reading of the above constitutional provisions the State was to establish and operate specialized institutions to enforce environmental rights. It declared furthermore that neither the wording of Art. 18 (the right to a "healthy environment") nor the embedding of the duty of the State to protect the environment among the means to enforce the right to health could be interpreted as a restriction on the right to a healthy environment. The duties of the State must include the protection of the natural basis of life and must extend to the establishment of institutions for the management of non-renewable resources (*Dec. 996/G/1990 AB:* ABH 1993, 533 at 535).

Concerning the objective, institutional protection of fundamental rights, *Dec. 64/1991 (XII.17) AB* (MK 1991/139; ABH 1991, 297) declares that the range thereof may exceed the protection guaranteed by the given fundamental right when operative as an individual right. This objective protection both goes beyond and differs qualitatively from the sum of the protection of the individual rights. The State's objective and institutional duty is to protect human life in general—consequently human life as a value—and this includes securing the conditions of life for future generations (*Dec. 64/1991 (XII.17) AB:* MK 1991/139 at 2812–13; ABH 1991, 297 at 303).

2. The right to a healthy environment differs from all other fundamental rights and state goals due both to its particular relation to individual rights and its specific subject.

(a) The right to a healthy environment in its present form is not an individual fundamental right, nor merely a constitutional duty or state goal for which the State may freely choose any means of implementation whatsoever.

As generally recognized, the right to a healthy environment cannot be included among the classic, protective fundamental rights. It is classified as a "third-generation" constitutional right, the character of which is still under debate and which has been adopted only by a few contemporary constitutions. This right, however, goes beyond the bounds of a constitutionally mandated state goal. The right to a healthy environment is named as a "right" in the Constitution, and is respected and protected by the State as such exactly as the inviolable and inalienable fundamental human rights are in Art. 8(1); whereas the Republic of Hungary "protects," "acknowledges," "supports" and "respects" state goals—according to the wording of the Constitution—without classifying them as rights. What are called state goals are realized primarily through the enforcement and state protection of the specific individual rights stipulated in the Constitution. However, the right to a healthy environment cannot be interpreted as a state goal because it could not be filled out by fundamental rights in the same manner as—for instance—the content of a market economy as a state goal was constituted by numerous fundamental rights (see *Dec. 21/1994 (IV.16) AB:* MK 1994/40 at 1407; ABH 1994, 117 at 119).

(b) The right to a healthy environment cannot be compared to social rights, either. Although the latter primarily entail the duty on the State to take adequate measures in areas such as social welfare, job creation, and the establishment of educational and cultural institutions, the relations between such state responsibilities and individual rights are both close and extensive. Social rights are implemented both by the formation of adequate institutions and by the rights of individuals to have access to them, which rights are to be specified by the legislature. In a few exceptional cases, however, certain social rights to be found in the Constitution have an element of a subjective (justiciable) right.

(c) Hence, although "everyone" or at least every citizen is entitled to social rights, in the course of their implementation it is possible to identify the persons holding the individual rights that provide for their enforcement. This is true even in the case of state goals included in the Constitution, which prescribe the establishment of complex institutions (*e.g.*, a "market economy"), for in this case there are persons entitled to the individual fundamental rights that implement the state goal. Both the individual fundamental rights and the individual rights of access to the social, cultural, and other institutions the State is constitutionally obliged to establish are necessary instruments to implement the given constitutional task and social right; the institutional guarantees provided by the State and the individual rights have approximately equal weight and complement each other.

3. In contrast to the preceding examples, the right to environmental protection primarily constitutes the independent and self-contained institutional aspect in itself of the protection of that right, or it is a distinct fundamental right exceedingly dominated and determined by its objective aspect of institutional protection. The right to environmental protection raises the guarantees for the implementation of the state duties in the area of environmental protection to the level of a fundamental right, including the conditions under which the degree of protection already achieved may be restricted. Due to the distinctive features of this right, what the State ensures by the protection of individual rights elsewhere it must ensure in this case by providing legal and organizational guarantees.

(a) Naturally, individual rights must also be estabished by the legislature to ensure enforcement of the right to a healthy environment, but most of these are only indirectly related to environmental protection. For example, the right to compensation for environmental damage gives a remedy at the same time for violation of property rights. There are individual rights related explicitly to environmental protection, but they are primarily of a procedural nature, such as the right to participate in the licensing procedure. The majority of the individual rights utilized in the area of environmental protection do not serve specifically the purpose of environmental protection but can be employed for this purpose among many others. Such a right is a civil action to prohibit conduct involving the risk of damages or the constitutional right of access to information of public interest.

The right to environmental protection is most closely related to the right to life, for the right to a healthy environment is, in fact, a part of the objective, institutional aspect of the right to life. The responsibility of the State to maintain the natural basis of human life is isolated and named as a separate constitutional "right." If Art. 18 of the Constitution were absent, the state duties in the area of environmental protection could also be deduced from a broad interpretation of Art. 54(l) of the Constitution.

The express declaration of the right to a healthy environment bestows a special constitutional weight upon the consequences which necessarily follow from the State's objective responsibility to protect life. These objective state duties are broader than the sum total of the individual rights to life. The right to environmental protection formally detaches these duties from the individual right to life and through this makes it easier for the environmental right to encompass state responsibilities of other origins necessary for the implementation of these duties and facilitates the adaptation of those duties to the special area of environmental protection.

The right to a healthy environment is unique in that its proper subjects could be identified as "mankind" and "nature."

Efforts to bestow "rights" upon "nature" or its representative elements—such as animals and plants—and the assertion of the "rights of yet-unborn generations" are eloquent illustrations of the same problem. However, legal responsibilities toward "nature" and "present and future mankind" can be determined without resorting to figurative language and legal constructs of this sort.

(b) The constitutional right to a healthy environment entails the responsibility of the State to protect the environment and maintain the natural basis of life. At present, specific individual rights are only incidental to the implementation of this right; their role is quantitatively negligible even when compared with the corresponding role of individual rights in the implementation of social rights. The State must therefore provide additional legislative and organizational guarantees to substitute for the function of individual rights. Providing such guarantees is not simply more important in the area of environmental protection than in the case of other constitutional rights where the court (including the Constitutional Court) may provide direct protection of individual rights. Instead, the legislature must provide all the institutional guarantees which are—within the limits of dogmatic possibility—functionally equivalent to those granted by the Constitution in the area of individual rights.

(c) Hence, the degree of institutional protection of the right to a healthy environment is not arbitrary. Besides the dogmatic peculiarities outlined above, the key factor in determining the degree of protection is the three-pronged raison d'être of environmental protection—the limited resources for the natural basis of life, the irreversibility of a substantial part of environmental damages and, finally, the sheer fact that these mark the conditions for the continuance of human life. The right to environmental protection guarantees the physical conditions necessary to implement the right to human life. In light of the above, extraordinary rigour is called for in protecting the right to a healthy environment by legislative acts.

IV

It follows from both the subject and the dogmatic peculiarities of the right to environmental protection that the State must not reduce the degree of protection of nature as guaranteed under law unless this is necessary to realize other constitutional rights or values. Even in the latter case, however, the degree of protection must not be reduced disproportionately with the goal set forth.

1. The practice of the Constitutional Court has allowed the legislature relatively great liberty in determining the methods and degrees by which it enforces constitutionally mandated state goals and social rights. A violation of the Constitution may arise only in borderline cases when the enforcement of a state goal or a protected institution or right is clearly rendered impossible by either interference by the State or, more frequently, by its omission. Above that minimal requirement, however, there are no constitutional criteria—except for the violation of another fundamental right—to determine whether legislation providing for a state goal or a social right is constitutional or not.

The right to a healthy environment differs from state goals and social rights in this respect as well. *Decision 996/G/1990 AB* declares (ABH 1993, 533 at 535) that the State may freely choose the principles and methods by which it protects the environment; the State is free, moreover, to determine what specific legislative and governmental measures are to follow from the particular state responsibility to assure a healthy environment. It follows, however, from the distinctive features of the right to a healthy environment, as stated in the present Decision, that the State is not free either to allow any deterioration of the environment or a risk thereof.

Indeed, there are objective criteria—a range of which is defined as mandatory by international norms—which in effect prescribe the necessity of the protection of nature. Environmental damage destroys non-renewable resources, is often irreparable, and the neglect of environmental protection sets in motion irreversible processes. The enforcement of the right to environmental protection thus cannot be subjected to such quantitative and qualitative fluctuations caused by economic and social circumstances as those of social and cultural rights, in the case of which restrictions arising from circumstances may subsequently be redressed. Due to these distinct features, prevention has precedence over all other means to guarantee the right to a healthy environment, for subsequent penalties for irreparable damages cannot ensure restoration of the original condition. The enforcement of the right to a healthy environment constitutionally obliges the State—so long as legal protection is indeed necessary—not to regress from a degree of protection already achieved unless the conditions are such that would also allow restrictions of individual fundamental rights. The enforcement of the right to a healthy environment by upholding the degree of protection also compels the State not to regress from preventive rules of protection to protection ensured by sanctions. Similarly to the previous rule, any action by the State contrary to this requirement must be compelled by unavoidable necessity and proportionate with this necessity.

2. The Constitutional Court notes that several means of guaranteeing the given degree of legal protection are known with respect to individual rights, such as the protection of vested rights and the protection of legitimate expectations. The practice of the Constitutional Court has seen numerous examples of the above. [....] The non-derogation of the degree of protection is even more relevant to the right to a healthy environment where the matter at issue is not a protection of legitimate expectations but the execution of a special state responsibility arising from a particular fundamental right—a responsibility which embraces all the guarantees of fundamental rights in the form of special duties of the State.

3. The Constitutional Court places great emphasis on the fact that it declared the responsibility to guarantee the status quo of protection in consideration of the protection of

nature—based on the distinctive features of the right to a healthy environment; hence, the same responsibility, due to the differences identified above, does not apply to social rights. [....]

ÁDÁM and **TERSZTYÁNSZKY, JJ.,** dissenting: [....]

As provided by Art. 18 of the Constitution, the State unequivocally upholds its right to implement the right to a healthy environment. The relevant provision of Art. 18 directly authorizes and requires the State to pursue action on this front. This right gives rise to the articulation of state goals and the acceptance by the State of its responsibility for enforcement. Its implementation requires material resources. It is the Act on the State Budget that allots these material resources for the use of the relevant state organs.

Article 18 of the Constitution requires neither the maintenance of a given degree of duties the State accepted and enforced voluntarily in the past, nor that of a standard that arose from a system of conditions.

Within the domain of environmental protection, the constitutionality of legislation concerning the protection of the natural environment—beyond the necessity of meeting international obligations, as prescribed by Art. 7(1) of the Constitution—can come into question only in extreme cases. Such an extreme case would arise especially if there is reasonable cause to believe that the effect of the regulation would summon forth a considerable and irreversible deterioration in the natural basis for life.

A change in duties undertaken previously by the State, as it appears in a reduction in the degree of protection, thus does not provide due grounds to declare the contested provisions of law unconstitutional. [....]

DECISION 60/1994: 24 DECEMBER 1994

ON BACKGROUND CHECKS FOR THOSE IN PUBLIC OFFICE

Unveiling the activities and identification of agents of the secret services under the socialist regime has not only plumbed the moral depths of new democracies but it has been of practical importance. The replacement or elimination from consideration for key positions of persons who formerly acted against the principles of the constitutional state reduces the influence of those who might endanger or pose a risk to the transition to democracy. The Hungarian law, which was passed unduly late, in the fifth year and so at the end of the system change, did not fulfill the second task. The law was repeatedly challenged before the Court, and its implementation was unsatisfactory. The Constitutional Court reviewed the Act in terms of balancing, on the one hand, access to public and personal data and, on the other, data protection. This is one of the very rare cases in which the Court uses the phrase "political question" as regards the definition by the legislature of positions for which "lustration," that is, accounting for the past, is obligatory. In this regard, the Court required the strict application of the nondiscrimination clause. It is also to be noted that in this decision the Constitutional Court felt it necessary to stress that the changes in 1989–90 were of a revolutionary nature and the distiction between the previous regime as nondemocratic and the present regime under the rule of law might not be made relative.

The petitioners sought constitutional review of certain provisions of Act XXIII/1994 on Background Checks for Individuals Holding Certain Key Offices and to establish constitutional omissions on the part of Parliament.

Sections 1 and 2 of the Act required background checks to be run on certain listed public officials and others occupying key positions in public life. The aim of such checks was to discover whether such persons prior to the establishment of a state under the rule of law had carried out activities for state security organs, obtained data therefrom to assist them in making decisions or were members of the Arrow Cross Party. If, during the course of a check, an individual fell into one of these categories the results were to be published unless he or she were to resign from his or her post.

Further, the Committee, established under ss. 5–7 to regulate the background checks, might examine any relevant records without restriction apart from rules on the protection of secrets and obtain information from the Interior or Defence Minister (s. 8). According to s. 9, these two ministers could guarantee the conditions necessary for the checks conducted by the Committee.

The petitioners submitted, inter alia, that (a) ss. 1 and 2 limited the right to privacy of personal information without this being necessary for the validation of any constitutional right, *i.e.,* the limitation did not meet the requirement of proportionality under Art. 8(2); (b) according to the Committee procedure, individuals who might eventually turn out to be innocent could be brought to public attention on the basis of unproven information and this was contrary to Arts. 54 and 59; (c) s. 2 arbitrarily designated those activities and occupations which defined the circle of individuals subject to background checks (officials occupying positions within a predefined level, a set range of ranks in the armed forces and other state authorities authorized to bear arms, and a certain circle of college and university teachers); (d) moreover, under s. 2(18), (23), (24) and (25) individuals with roles in state affairs and the economy were differentiated on the basis of their managing state agencies, organizations under majority-state ownership, privately owned ones, banks, financial institutions or insurance firms; (e) there was a distinction under s. 22(2) between those employed in the print media based on the daily or weekly circulation figures and the position held by the journalist; and (f) no appeal lay against a committee decision although an individual could file a claim before the Budapest City Court. The rules which applied to judicial review of administrative decisions, according to s. 19, served as a guide in such court proceedings. This contradicted Art. 57(5) since the Act provided an insufficient remedy.

Held, allowing the petitions in part:

(1) Data and personal records on individuals in positions of public authority and those who participated in political life which indicate that such persons once pursued, or belonged to state organs or organizations which formerly pursued, activities contrary to the principles of the rule of law, constituted information of public interest according to Art. 61. The fundamental rights to the protection of personal records (the right to informational self-determination) and to have access to information of public interest (freedom of expression, of information) were to be interpreted in light of each other: when there was a conflict between the two competing rights it could not simply be said that the latter always had to be interpreted strictly and had to take precedence. In the present case the right of individuals—especially voters—to have access to information of public interest took precedence over the protection of the personal records of persons in key political roles or other public offices, given that the term "public interest" presumed that the information could be a key factor in evaluating the suitability for further office of those in the latter category. The present Act implemented Art. 61 since it permitted the public to learn of the former anti-constitutional activities of persons now well placed in the establishment. Moreover, the disclosure of this information was necessary because the greater part of such activities occurred secretly and the continued unconditional secrecy of the data in the records listed in s. 1 of the Act was contrary to Art. 61. Were Parliament to limit the mandated disclosure for any constitutionally acceptable reason, then such limitation had to be necessary and proportional.

(2) Parliament, in laying down the constitutional criteria to be used to draw a distinction between private and public information, was not entirely free to decide whether to destroy secret service records (although they created an unconstitutional situation from their very incipience), or to continue handling them as secret, or to disclose their contents and if so to whom. It was a political decision for Parliament to draw the line between information of public interest and the right to informational self-determination, to strike a balance between on the one hand making certain activities completely transparent—in order to strengthen the continued progress of the nation's transition and to carry out its duty to the public—and on the other limiting the right of access to other information and continuing to classify some records as private—in order to ensure a measure of political stability. This political decision could not be based upon the Constitution but rather on the constitutional certainty that the records can neither be kept secret nor brought entirely to light. Thus, once

the political decision was taken, Parliament would circumscribe the records, deeming one part as private and another as of public interest, in a uniform manner using the standard it had defined in constitutionally setting the limits of Arts. 59 and 61.

(3) In applying these criteria, s. 2 of the Act violated Art. 70/A on non-discrimination since it failed to establish consistent constitutional criteria to distinguish between public and private data. This led to an unconstitutional distinction between those who were subject to background checks and those not so subject, even though they would otherwise fall under the same criteria: it was therefore Parliament's obligation to eliminate the discrimination. In particular those subsections of s. 2 were unconstitutional where it was demonstrated that a precisely defined group was either somewhat broader or narrower than would meet the constitutional criterion.

(4) In the first category were the records of university and college officials and the top executives of state- or majority-state-owned enterprises which were not information of public interest since such persons neither exercized public authority nor took part in (public) political affairs. Further the influence of the national public media and their influence on public opinion as estimated on the basis of newspaper circulation did not justify the classification of the personal records of editors and higher-level employees of non-political programmes and newspapers as information of public interest. As a consequence of these broader than necessary criterion, s. 2(18), (21), (22), (23), (24) and (25) were unconstitutional.

(5) In the second category, the Act prescribed background checks only on members of the press and within the press (except for Hungarian Radio and Hungarian Television) exclusively the print media as opposed to the electronic media. The basis for this concerned the responsibility of all individuals who moulded public opinion, but this criterion was not used consistently since others who shaped public opinion such as political parties, church bodies (members) or officials, heads of national bodies and organizations, and trade union leaders were not included. Similarly the principle of equal treatment would require background checks to apply as well to editors and higher-level employees at commercial and non-commercial local radio and television stations with an audience comparable to that of newspapers with circulations over 30,000 and to editors and higher-level employees at non-commercial national or regional radio and television stations if they engaged in activities directly forming public opinion. In these circumstances the failure to prescribe background checks violated Arts. 61 and 70/A: such discrimination could be eliminated by Parliament either by extending the background checks or by introducing a narrower definition of those to be checked, based on consistent criteria.

(6) The Committee was a special administrative body with a specified jurisdiction. In conducting the background check, the Committee was not limited to the use of records specified in s. 1 but to verify such records it was entitled to use any means of legal evidence (s. 12). The verification process under s. 1(b) required the Committee to prove the actual activity in question and in so doing was governed by Act IV/1958 on the General Rules of State Administrative Procedure and Act III/1952 on Civil Procedure, including the appropriate application of presumption of innocence in administrative procedure. Moreover, since the committee procedure was not a judicial one, there was thus no constitutional re-

quirement that the Act provide detailed procedural rules comparable to those Acts on Legal Proceedings: the degree to which the Committee procedure was regulated was sufficient to guarantee legal certainty. Further, the Committee was not a legislative body and so, in applying s. 17 of the Act, the procedural rules were neutral constitutionally speaking and might not impose any obligations on others or assign rights to individuals nor affect the rights of the scrutinized individuals.

(7) By failing in the Act to provide guarantees for the practice of the fundamental right to informational self-determination under Art. 59, Parliament had engendered an unconstitutional omission to legislate. Informational self-determination permitted individuals enjoying constitutional protection to have control over the disclosure and use of their personal records. However s. 25 of the Act only provided for the continued secrecy of information on individuals subject to background checks and made no mention of such persons' rights. Parliament had not resolved the issues of how to guarantee the right of access to (certain) personal records, how to protect the security of further records and also the procedure for destroying them. As a result, Parliament had failed to guarantee, in particular, the right of the scrutinized individuals, on whom the organizations or individuals defined in s. 1(a) and (b) collected information or who appeared in reports they compiled, to review their records and to destroy them once the information had been reviewed and the Act had ceased to be in force.

(8) Moreover, another constitutional omission to legislate had occurred, since Parliament had failed, according to s. 9, to require *all* top authorities who supervized or kept the relevant public records (including the Minister without Portfolio for the Secret Services) to guarantee the requisite conditions for the review of the records of those under scrutiny. Having annulled the unconstitutional limitations contained in s. 8, which revized text permitted the Committee to examine or request any file from any records, it had not been possible to eliminate thereby the provisions of s. 9, under which the conditions for perusal of such records were guaranteed by the Minister of Interior or of Defence, nor was it possible to render s. 9 consonant with s. 8. Consequently Parliament had breached its duty to ensure the effective operation of the procedure and administrative institution which it had created by failing to guarantee the necessary authorization in the form of legal provisions.

IN THE NAME OF THE REPUBLIC OF HUNGARY!

In the matter of petitions seeking the ex post facto review of the constitutionality of a legal rule and of the ex officio proceedings aimed at establishing an unconstitutional omission to legislate, the Constitutional Court, with the concurring opinion of Vörös, J., has made the following

DECISION.

1. The Court declares that data and records on individuals holding positions of public authority and those who participate in political life in the state under the rule of law—including those who develop public opinion by their profession—which reveal that these persons at one time pursued activities contrary to the principles of the rule of law or belonged

to state organs which had at one time pursued activities contrary to the same, count as information of public interest under Art. 61 of the Constitution.

The right of informational self-determination of the affected persons and other rights of those interested may not be limited through the continued secrecy of records established by the political police in a system that did not adhere to the principle of the rule of law, even with regard to information declared not to be of public interest.

2.(a) The Constitutional Court declares that s. 2(18), (23), (24) and (25) of Act XXIII/1994 on Background Checks for Individuals Holding Certain Key Positions (hereafter the Act), s. 4 and the part of the second half of s. 8 of the Act "from the Minister of the Interior and regarding the paramilitary forces from the Minister of the Interior and the Minister of Defence," are unconstitutional.

(b) The Constitutional Court declares that s. 2 of the Act fails to apply consistently the same criteria in order to distinguish between public and personal data, leading to an unconstitutional discrimination between those individuals who are subject to monitoring and those who are not, even though they would otherwise fall within the same criteria. With respect to the groups of individuals referred to explicitly, the Act draws such a distinction between checks conducted on persons in the print media as opposed to those in the electronic media. To eliminate this discrimination, the legislature must establish and enforce a consistent standard within the constitutional framework laid down in para. 1 of the operative part of this Decision based on its own discretion.

(c) The Interior Ministry Order 13/1994.BM (hereafter the Order), on the Implementation by the Interior Ministry of the Act on Background Checks on Individuals Holding Certain Specified Key Offices, is unconstitutional.

3. The Constitutional Court annuls ss. 2 and 4 together with the indicated part of the second half of s. 8 of the Act as well as the Order.

Section 2(18), (23), (24) and (25), s. 4, and the indicated part of s. 8 of the Act cease to have effect, and the Order shall be regarded as revoked, on the day this Constitutional Court Decision is published.

Section 8 will remain in force as follows:

> *Section 8.* Parliament's National Security Committee, according to the provisions for the checks as stipulated by s. 7 of the Act, as well as the committee [of judges assigned by Parliament to conduct the checks stipulated by the Act], are authorized to review documents pertaining to the activities defined under s. 1 of the Act on the scrutinized individuals (hereafter the records) free of all limitations but those in accord with statutes on the protection of secrets, and to request information from the records.

Section 2(1)–(17) and (19)–(22) of the Act will cease to have effect on the day the law amending this section of the Act comes into force.

4.(a) The Constitutional Court declares it to be a constitutional requirement as regards the committee defined in s. 5 of the Act (hereafter the Committee) that it proceed in accordance with the provisions of Act IV/1957 on the General Rules of State Administrative Procedure.

(b) The Constitutional Court declares it to be a constitutional requirement that, in applying s. 17 of the Act, the Committee's rules of procedure may not assign rights or obligations to individuals apart from members of the Committee itself.

5.(a) The Constitutional Court declares that Parliament created an unconstitutional situation by failing to guarantee the practice of the right to informational self-determination, especially the right of individuals concerned, on whom the organizations or individuals defined in s. 1(a) and (b) of the Act collected information, or who appeared in reports they had compiled to review their own records and to delete such records.

(b) Parliament created an unconstitutional situation by failing to guarantee the practice of the right to informational self-determination, in particular the right of individuals scrutinized under the Act to destroy their records once the Act ceases to have effect.

(c) Further, Parliament created an unconstitutional situation with respect to s. 9 of the Act in failing to oblige all authorities who keep public records, including the Minister without Portfolio for the Secret Services, to guarantee the conditions for the examination of the records.

The Constitutional Court calls upon Parliament to meet its legislative obligation as defined by section 5(a)–(c) above of this Decision by 30 September 1995.

6. The Constitutional Court rejects the petitions seeking the establishment of the unconstitutionality of ss. 1(a), 5–7(a), and 10–23(a) of the Act.

7. The Constitutional Court publishes this Decision in the *Hungarian Official Gazette.*

REASONING

SÓLYOM, P., and **TERSZTYÁNSZKY, J.,** delivering the Opinion of the Court: [....]

III

1. "Lustration laws," such as the Act at issue in this Decision, are typical products of the change of system under way in the former socialist countries. The lustration, or background checks, generally served two different purposes, and accordingly the laws come in two types.

(a) The majority of lustration laws lay down rules on incompatibility. Those who held certain state or party positions in the former socialist system, and, further, those who belonged to the ranks of the political police or were to be found among its secret informers, may not occupy certain positions as the change of system unfolds. Particular laws extend to employees of institutions of culture, (higher) education, and academia, public service radio and television, and also to lawyers. (See the Czechoslovak lustration law of 1991 and the Treaty of Unification between the Federal Republic of Germany and the German Democratic Republic of 31 August 1990. Up until the end of 1992, three such laws were passed in Bulgaria, and one in Albania was approved in 1993.) Constitutional court decisions were rendered on each of these Acts in the respective countries. In accordance with the nature of the laws, the constitutional complaints concerned violations of the right to work and to choose freely one's occupation and of international agreements which guaranteed social welfare rights.

(b) A consummate example of the other type of lustration law is Germany's "Stasi Act." In this case, the primary aim was nothing other than bringing completely to the light of day the activities of the former state security organs and secret agents. Calls for the public naming of former agents were to be heard in other countries as well but did not come to pass.

(c) The Hungarian contemporaries of the above-mentioned lustration laws from countries in the region were the bills submitted to the Parliament, and ultimately placed on its legislative agenda, in 1990 (No. 482) and 1991 (No. 2,294). These bills would have required individuals occupying posts defined by law to be called upon to resign if it were proven that they had previously been informers. Were they to refuse, their pasts as informers in the state security apparatus would be made public. The entire procedure—from the call to resign, to the adjudication of possible objections by the given individuals, to the possible decision to forego publicity—would have been in the hands of the President of the Republic, the Prime Minister and the National Security Committee of Parliament, and according to the 1991 Bill in the hands of the President of the Republic, the Speaker of Parliament, the President of the Constitutional Court, and the Prime Minister, with the exclusion of the courts. Both proposals classified information left undisclosed as state secrets.

2. The "lustration" or background check thus came in two types, according to purpose. One aimed to guarantee personnel replacements in certain key positions and at the same time keep the nation's transition as defined in the Constitution from being endangered by those who in the past stood actively and in their professional capacity against the principles of a state under the rule of law. The other aimed toward a genuine public disclosure of the nature of the previous regime, to guarantee a measure of redress, and simultaneously to symbolize the irreversibility of the changes, through revealing the activities of the secret services.

[....]

3. [....]

(b) Even the content of the Act differed from that in other countries; it neither declares incompatibility between personnel in past and present offices nor proposes to unveil the whole of the previous system of political informing, least of all with respect to those who had been under observation.

The Act in fact promotes the transparency of those in prominent political and other public roles, and thus of the life of the nation in general. In it, there is a confluence of the moral obligation that remained in the wake of the transition: the unveiling of deceit, publicity rather than punishment, and the value system normal to a state under the rule of law.

[....]

(d) As opposed to the earlier laws in other countries, in Hungary the order of the goal and the means has been reversed. Elsewhere, the goal was resignation due to incompatibility; the means of compulsion toward this end was the public disclosure of information. In the case of the Act at issue, the priority is rather a general transparency of state and public affairs; and if an individual is unwilling to accept the publicity that accompanies a position, he may elude the bind, logically enough, by leaving the post.

4. The Act must therefore be examined in view of the fact that in a state under the rule of law the fundamental right to the freedom of information presumes that the functioning of the State is transparent to its citizens. For this reason, the scope of private life of individuals who hold positions of public authority or who partake in political life—with respect to aspects in connection with these public activities—is restricted. Entirely independent of the original goals of the lustration laws, "public" information on individuals in certain positions of public authority today necessarily includes information revealing previous activity expressly contradictory to the principles of the rule of law or individuals' memberships in an organization which pursued such activity. In defining the range of such activity, the Constitutional Court must consider the transition as a historical fact. The constitutional is-

sue at the crux of the matter involves striking a balance between circumscribing the circle of individuals at issue and the information of public interest on them.

Nor can it be overlooked that the very system of records at issue, maintained to the present day, is itself unconstitutional, and that these records—both those of the agents who supplied the information and those of the individuals who are the subjects of the files—must therefore be brought into harmony with the Constitution. Continued secrecy, constitutionally speaking, is an insufficient solution.

IV

The petitions are in part justified, for the reasons given below:

1. The most important issue surrounding the constitutional review of the Act may be approached in two ways, depending on whether the starting point is the freedom of information or the disclosure of personal records in the public interest.

(a) The records kept by the oft-cited Department III/III of the Interior Ministry's state security apparatus, and in part the records of the other secret services, by their very nature contradict in view of their aims, content, and secrecy not only every principle of a state under the rule of law but the Constitution in its particulars as well. What, then, can justify their continued secrecy in a state under the rule of law? Further, how can such records be disclosed in such a way that the personality rights of those who enjoy the constitutional protection of these rights are not violated?

These questions bear upon the fate of all the secret service records established and maintained contrary to the Constitution.

(b) Both bills No. 482 and No. 2294, as well as the Act in issue, aimed, however, explicitly to avert this broad approach; the proposals justified the classification of information left undisclosed as secret under certain conditions in the interest of the "need for political stability" and to avoid harassment [against individuals whose names appear therein]. [....]

(c) Both approaches lead to the same decisive questions however: which information kept in records in the public interest may nonetheless be treated as private and which personal information may be classified as "of public interest?" [....]

2.(a) [....]

The shedding of light on the past, and with it an objective evaluation of the importance of the change of regime, presumes the public disclosure of the activities of the former secret services. With regard to such records, even laws which otherwise protect the security of information, personal and otherwise, regularly make exceptions to the rule, given suitable guarantees and in order to serve the interest of public knowledge. This includes Act LXII/1992 on the Protection of Personal Data, s. 32(3)(b) of which allows public access to personal information if necessary to assure that research under way into historical events can reach objective conclusions to be imparted to the public. Just as violations of the right to (informational) self-determination require clarification of who actually may gain access to secret service files which concern them, so that they may understand the true extent to which the past regime influenced their personal fate, and in this way, at least, temper the transgression against their human dignity [...], so too the nagging issue of the past in the larger sense, as it concerns the nation as a whole, can be resolved only if the secrecy of former secret service records is not further maintained.

The unconditional secrecy of the data in the records listed in s. 1 of the Act is unconstitutional, for Art. 61 of the Constitution stipulates their disclosure. Should the legislature limit their mandated disclosure for any constitutionally acceptable reason, the limitation must clearly be necessary and of a degree in proportion to the reason.

[....]

(ba) [....] The fundamental right to the protection of personal data and to access to information of public interest shall be interpreted in light of each other (*Dec. 34/1994 (VI.24) AB:* MK 1994/68 at 2493–94; ABH 1994, 177 at 184–85; *Dec. 36/1994 (VI.24) AB:* MK 1994/68 at 2516; ABH 1994, 219 at 229). This is natural, for informational self-determination and the freedom of information are two complimentary preconditions for individual autonomy.

Owing to the close relationship of the two rights mentioned above, when the freedom of information conflicts with the protection of personal records it cannot simply be said that the latter must always be strictly interpreted and must take precedence. In light of the subject of the Act at issue, the Constitutional Court has established a hierarchy of these two basic rights. Even practice thus far has offered visible landmarks to determine when the freedom of information should be interpreted broadly and the protection of personal data strictly.

The Constitutional Court has also consistently held that in the interest of the democratic functioning of the State, and likewise in the democratic formulation of public opinion, the constitutionally protected "personal space" of public officials and key political players is smaller than that of other individuals, for they must especially allow themselves to be subjected to the criticism of others. [See, most recently, *Dec. 36/1994 (VI.24) AB:* MK 1994/68; ABH 1994, 219.] To this end, it may be necessary to disclose the personal data of public officials that bear upon their present office or political role. [....]

(bb) Section 1 of the Act defines data that may be used in determining whether people who today occupy key public offices or political roles, including those whose responsibilities include developing public opinion, had earlier pursued activities contrary to the principles of the rule of law or belonged to state organs which did so. These are data of public interest as laid down in Art. 61 of the Constitution. [....]

The data defined in s. 1 of the Act refer exclusively to activities which unequivocally contradict the principles of the rule of law. Any law which allows the public to learn that an individual in a position of public authority or with a key political role once pursued activities contrary to the rule of law, or that belonged to such an organization, implements Art. 61 of the Constitution. The disclosure of such information is also necessary because the greater part of such activities occurred secretly. [....] Both the political domain and state affairs in their broadest sense are to be entirely transparent, thus allowing informed judgments to be drawn as to their nature, and require that the constitutional principle of access to information of public interest, in the case of the information defined by the Act, be validated. [....]

(c) [....] As may be concluded from the reasoning above, it would be unconstitutional to accord continued complete secrecy to the records or, by contrast, immediately to destroy them. Similarly, there exist constitutional obstacles to a complete disclosure of records; one such obstacle, for example, is the right to informational self-determination of those individuals on whom files were kept. Drawing the line between information that is of public interest and information that should remain under lock and key is, [...] the sort of "political issue" which offers the legislature a fairly broad margin of appreciation. In this way, the legislature can, as presumably it intends to, strike a balance between on the one hand making completely transparent certain activities—in order to fortify the continued progress of the nation's transition and to carry out its obligation to the public—and on the other hand limiting the right of access to other information and continuing to classify some data as private—in order to assure a measure of political stability. Such a political decision has the power to either circumscribe or expand the borders of public disclosure and, thus, the extent of the probe into the given individual's past. [...]

DECISION 14/1995: 13 MARCH 1995

ON THE LEGAL EQUALITY OF SAME SEX PARTNERSHIPS

On the basis of the equal protection clause, the Constitutional Court recognized, and for practical reasons enforced, the recognition of the same sex partnership in the Civil Code and in all respective laws that had previously provided only for the "domestic partnership" between men and women. By the subsequent amendment of the Civil Code, "men and women" was replaced with "persons." The case demonstrates the established policy of the Constitutional Court, which has linked equality to human dignity. This requires that all persons living together enjoy the same legal status without regard to their gender, save in the legal relationships where the restriction to men and women has a constitutional reason (e.g., concerning the children of a couple). The Court abstained from any direct (moral or other) evaluation of homosexuality, as it would also do in the homosexual associations case (21/1996). On the other hand, the applicants failed in their challenge of the notion of marriage as a union exclusively of a man and a woman.

The petitioner sought constitutional review of legal provisions concerning marriage and domestic partnership which discriminated against him on grounds of sexual orientation.

According to s. 10(1) of Act IV/1952 on Marriage, Family and Guardianship, men and women of legal age may marry. Further, art. 578/G of Act IV/1959 on the Civil Code defines partners in a domestic partnership as a woman and a man living together in a common household in an emotional and economic community outside a marriage.

The petitioner submitted that these two provisions infringed his constitutional rights to equality under Art. 66(1) and to be free from negative discrimination on the grounds of sex under Art. 70/A because (a) they made it impossible for persons of the same sex to marry; and (b) they failed to recognize that such a relationship could amount to a domestic partnership.

Held, giving the following ruling:

(1) The legal provisions did not violate Arts. 66(1) or 70/A. As regards the latter, the institution of marriage had special, express constitutional protection and was generally recognized as the union between a man and a woman. Men and women separately comprized homogenous groups of legal subjects which had to be treated the same in order to prevent negative discrimination. This requirement of equal regulation of the conditions of marriage between persons of different sexes excluded the legal possibility of marriage between persons of the same sex. Moreover, in respect of Art. 66(1), the provision in Act IV/1952 denying marriage to persons of the same sex, prohibited men and women equally from marrying persons of their own sex. Taken together, the legal provisions did not discriminate on grounds of sex or otherwise.

(2) An enduring union of life between two persons, however, might constitute such values that it could claim legal recognition on the basis of the equal personal dignity of the

persons affected, irrespective of their sex. In respect of financial conditions and the benefits which were derived from this type of economic union, there was no constitutional justification which prevented the rules governing domestic partnerships from applying to an enduring union of persons of the same sex. Indeed, the regulation of partners in a domestic partnership and relatives was arbitrary, violating the right to human dignity in Art. 70/A since it excluded those of the same sex from among persons living in a common household and in an emotional and economic union.

(3) The regulations on domestic partnerships and relatives could be rendered constitutional by expanding their scope to include same sex relationships. This could be achieved not only by removing the restriction in the Civil Code, art. 578/G(1), that partners in a domestic partnership must involve only a man/woman relationship but also by providing the same legal standing with a separate legal institution for those of the same sex. Further, the legislature could also re-examine all rules applicable to partners in a domestic partnership and broaden them wherever the restriction to a heterosexual relationship did not have a foundation. In this way each rule would be rendered applicable to all persons living in such an intimate relationship.

IN THE NAME OF THE REPUBLIC OF HUNGARY!

In the matter of petition seeking an ex post facto review of the unconstitutionality of a legal rule, the Constitutional Court has made the following

DECISION.

1. The Constitutional Court rejects the petition seeking a determination of unconstitutionality and annulment of s. 10(1) of Act IV/1952 on Marriage, Family and Guardianship.

2. The Constitutional Court suspends its proceedings concerning the examination of constitutionality of art. 578/G of Act IV/1959 on the Civil Code until 1 March 1996.

3. The Constitutional Court declares that it is unconstitutional that those legal regulations, which determine the rights and responsibilities of persons who live together outside marriage in an emotional, sexual and economic community and who publicly uphold their relationship, specify legal consequences only for those domestic partnerships currently defined in the Civil Code.

The Constitutional Court publishes this Decision in the *Hungarian Official Gazette.*

REASONING

SÓLYOM, P., delivering the Opinion of the Court:

I

The petitioner requested the constitutional review of s. 10(1) of Act IV/1952 on Marriage, Family and Guardianship, according to which "men and women of legal age may get married." The petitioner also initiated the review of art. 578/G of Act IV/1959 on the Civil

Code, which regulates the financial relations of those living in the same household and defines the notion of partners in a domestic partnership as "a woman and a man living together in a common household in an emotional and economic community outside a marriage."

In the petitioner's opinion, the two legal provisions in question constitute a negative discrimination on the basis of sex by making it impossible for persons of the same sex to get married and by not acknowledging their domestic partnership. Accordingly, the provisions in question violate both Art. 66(1) of the Constitution, which declares the equality of men and women, and Art. 70/A, which prohibits negative discrimination on account of any criterion—including sex.

II

The Constitutional Court points out that both in our culture and in law the institution of marriage is traditionally the union of a man and a woman. This union typically is aimed at giving birth to common children and bringing them up in the family in addition to being the framework for the mutual taking of care and assistance of the partners. The ability to procreate and give birth to children is neither the defining element nor the condition of the notion of marriage, but the idea that marriage requires the partners to be of different sexes is a condition that derives from the original and typical designation of marriage. The institution of marriage is constitutionally protected by the State also with respect to the fact that it promotes the establishment of families with common children. This is the reason why Art. 15 of the Constitution refers to the two subjects of protection together: "The Republic of Hungary protects the institutions of marriage and family."

From the wording of the most important international human rights documents, it can also be derived that the family is conceived of as the union of a man and a woman: the right to get married is defined as the right of men and the right of women, while in relation to other rights the subjects of rights are "persons" without any such differentiation (art. 16 of the Universal Declaration of Human Rights, 1948; art. 23 of the International Covenant on Civil and Political Rights, 1966; and art. 12 of the European Convention on Human Rights, 1950). The European Court of Human Rights has confirmed this interpretation (see *Rees,* ECtHR, Judgment of 17 October 1986, Series A, No. 106).

In recent decades in the culture which Hungary also shares, homosexuality has been decriminalized, and movements have been started to protest against negative discrimination with respect to homosexuals. In addition, changes can be observed in the traditional family model, especially in terms of the durability of marriages. All these are not reasons for the law to diverge from the legal concept of marriage which has been preserved in traditions to this day, which is also common in today's laws and which, in addition, is in harmony with the notion of marriage according to public opinion and in everyday language. Today's constitutions—among them the Hungarian concerning its provisions on marriage and the family—consider marriage between a man and a woman as a value and protect it (Arts. 15, 67 and 70/J of the Hungarian Constitution).

The State can offer different legal options for traditional and currently exceptional communities, through which it acknowledges and integrates such communities into different social relations. In doing this, the State does not have to follow the self-interpretation of the communities, but it can maintain and support traditional institutions, as well as create new legal forms for acknowledging new phenomena, and with this it can, at the same time, extend the boundaries of "normality" in public opinion. In determining the notion of marriage, the same requirements are valid, as, for instance, in the case of determining the legal notion of "church": *cf.* Constitutional Court in *Dec. 4/1993 (II.12) AB* (MK 1993/15 at 705; ABH 1993, 48 at 53); and *Dec. 8/1993 (II.27) AB* (MK 1993/29; ABH 1993, 99). In creating these legal institutions, the right of the affected person is not that the same institutions be available to everybody; instead, the constitutional requirement is that those affected are handled as equals and as persons of equal human dignity—that is, their points of view are evaluated with like circumspection, attention, impartiality and fairness (*Dec. 9/1990 (IV.25) AB:* MK 1990/36 at 770–71; ABH 1990, 46 at 48; *Dec. 21/1990 (X.4) AB:* MK 1990/98 at 2082; ABH 1990, 73 at 78). Equality between man and woman has a meaning if we acknowledge the natural differences between man and woman, and equality is realized with respect to this.

The Constitutional Court declares that since the institution of marriage has a special and explicit protection in the Constitution and since, according to the generally accepted legal notion that marriage is the union of a man and a woman, men and women separately constitute homogeneous groups of legal subjects that have to be treated equally in order to prevent negative discrimination as regards marriage. The Constitution only requires equal regulation of the conditions of marriage between persons of different sexes, which excludes the legal possibility of marriage between persons of the same sex. On the basis of the above, the Constitutional Court has arrived at the conclusion that the challenged provision does not discriminate either in terms of sex or in terms of other conditions and thus does not violate Art. 70/A of the Constitution.

The challenged provision cannot be related to Art. 66(1) of the Constitution, since the provision has no reference to the equality of men and women. The provision in the Family Act denying marriage to persons of the same sex prohibits men and women equally from marrying persons of their own sex. Hence, the Constitutional Court rejects the petition seeking to establish the unconstitutionality of and to annul the contested provision of the Act on Marriage, Family and Guardianship.

III

An enduring union for life of two persons may constitute such values that it should be legally acknowledged on the basis of the equal personal dignity of the persons affected, irrespective of the sex of those living together. Equal treatment always has to be interpreted with respect to the social relations that are the subjects of legal regulation—with special regard as to whether the law is taking into account the children born out of this union, the previous or subsequent marriages, or whether the law evaluates the close personal relationship in itself. Especially with respect to financial conditions and benefits that derive from the economic union, the official incompatibility, and the exemptions and restrictions of criminal law and procedure concerning the "relatives," there is no constitutional reason to justify that the respective regulations should never be applicable to a permanent union of persons of the same sex. On the contrary, a constitutional reason is required for any discrimination according to the sex of those living in such a union.

Several provisions in Hungarian law recognize domestic partnership and extend to it the legal provisions concerning marriage; primarily these are the provisions on relatives. The sole legal definition of domestic partnership can be found in art. 578/G(1) of the Civil Code. According to this definition, "the partners in a domestic partnership are a man and a woman living together in a common household, in an emotional and economic community, outside a marriage." In fact a domestic partnership typically exists between men and women, and this is also what public opinion understands by this notion. But the legal recognition of a domestic partnership has an incomparably shorter history than the institution of marriage. Judicial practice began to recognize domestic partnerships in the 1950s, and such partnerships were incorporated into the important legal regulations only between 1961 and 1977. The cohabitation of persons of the same sex, which in all respects is very similar to the cohabitation of partners in a domestic partnership—involving a common household, as well as an emotional, economic and sexual relationship, and taking on all aspects of the relationship against third persons—gives rise today, albeit to a lesser extent, to the same necessity for legal recognition just as it did in the 1950s for those in a domestic partnership. The difference is that in a state under the rule of law the problem also arises from the point of view of fundamental rights, and the Constitutional Court has the opportunity to fulfill its task of minority protection. The Constitution specially protects marriage and not domestic partnership. In the latter case, the question of the partners' sex emerges as a question of negative discrimination.

From the point of view of judging possible discrimination—that is, not treating persons as persons with equal dignity [Art. 70/A of the Constitution]—it is decisive that the legal regulation of partners in a domestic partnership refers to such partners alone only in the most rare cases; it usually encompasses a certain circle of (close) relatives depending on the subject of the regulation. The Constitutional Court examined the legal provisions currently in force which define rights or responsibilities with respect to the partner in a domestic partnership and found that usually it was not relevant whether the relationship was between persons of different sexes. When the law regulates domestic partnership together with relatives, the reason of the regulation is an emotional and/or economic relationship, presumed on the basis of formal family law relations, or, in the absence thereof—like in cases of engaged couples or partners in a domestic partnership—factually existing. The sex of partners and relatives may be significant when the regulation concerns a common child or—more rarely—if it concerns a marriage with another person. However, if these exceptional considerations do not apply, the exclusion from regulations covering both relatives and domestic partnership, living in a common household and in an emotional and economic union, is arbitrary and thus violates human dignity; therefore it is discrimination contrary to Art. 70/A of the Constitution. What is more, the provisions in question can only fulfill their task completely if they expand to cover these kinds of relationships as well. The rules of incompatibility (concerning, for instance, officials in economic chambers, bodies of the local governments, and courts) are incomplete if they do not apply to persons of the same sex who live together according to the critieria of a domestic partnership. The principles upon which one can refuse to give evidence or neglect to report a crime can be invoked in the case of persons in an intimate relationship irrespective of their sex. Similarly, crimes against relatives cannot be judged more leniently just because the injured person is a person of the same sex. The benefits (social and social security) that can be given only on the basis of a domestic partnership cannot depend only on the sex of the two people living together.

The legislature has several options to provide all those who live in a relationship comparable to a domestic partnership with an equal legal position in those legal relations where there is no constitutional reason for discrimination on the grounds of sex among those living in an intimate relationship. In order to achieve this aim, not only could the legislature remove from art. 578/G(1) of the Civil Code the restriction that partners in a domestic partnership must involve only a relationship of a man and a woman, but it could also provide for persons of the same sex the same legal position through a separate legal institution. (An institution of this kind was the one accepted in Denmark in 1989 for homosexuals, called a "registered partnership.") Instead of these general solutions, the legislature could also reexamine all provisions applying to partners in a domestic partnership and expand them to all persons living in such an intimate relationship wherever the restriction to a heterosexual relationship has no legal ground. The legal notion, currently in force, of partners in a domestic partnership is defined by the Civil Code. The constitutionality of this cannot be determined on its own but depends on whether the distribution of rights and duties among those who are in the same situation is done in a manner that respects the right to equal human dignity—that is, realizing the equal treatment of persons and evaluating their points with like circumspection, attention, impartiality and fairness. The legislature can create a situation that is in harmony with the Constitution, while leaving untouched the legal notion of domestic partnership that is currently in force. Thus the Constitutional Court did not decide on the constitutionality and the annulment of the definition in art. 578/G(1) of the Civil Code but instead suspended its proceedings until 1 March 1996. If the legislature does not terminate the unconstitutional situation by this deadline, the Constitutional Court, in the framework of the available ex post facto review, can create a situation that is in harmony with the Constitution through the constitutional review of the Civil Code's notion of domestic partnership or through expanding the constitutional review to all provisions dealing with domestic partnership. The Constitutional Court applied the similar method in *Dec. 15/1993 (III.12) AB* (MK 1993/29; ABH, 1993, 112).

DECISION 43/1995: 30 JUNE 1995

ON SOCIAL SECURITY BENEFITS

This case has been the flagship of a series of cases dealing with the austerity package introduced by the Government in 1995. Most importantly, the Court also insisted here that no exceptional historical situation—except those foreseen in the Constitution—might justify the lifting of constitutional guarantees. So, while the Court was not able to accept claims of the Government concerning an "economic emergency situation," on the other hand it clearly yielded to the necessary reforms of the social security system, striking down, at the same time, all unconstitutional details of this package of laws. The decision determines for subsequent cases the methods for judging the constitutionality of cutting off social benefits: it focuses on the protection of acquired rights, reliance interest, and legal certainty. The Court was very keen to keep itself in line with other European constitutional courts even when acting from different constitutional positions regarding social rights. In these cases, the Court, which has no power to grant an injunction, often helped itself by abolishing the provisions on the coming into force of the given laws and postponing the investigation into the merits.

The petitioners sought annulment of various provisions of Act XLVIII/1995 on the Amendment of Certain Laws to Promote Economic Stabilization (the Economic Stabilization Act).

The State had operated a mixed system of social security for decades, which contained insurance elements as well as welfare elements based on the principle of solidarity. Certain welfare benefits were closely linked to social security benefits and thus guaranteed rights for those eligible to the benefit. In view of the existence of a child, the benefits granted to support the family were provided through a system of several different interrelated institutions comprizing the family allowance, the child care benefit, the child care fee, the pregnancy allowance, the maternity benefit and the child care allowance: together they constituted a calculable, continuous system of benefits.

The Economic Stabilization Act altered this system by transforming it into a "system of assistance" based on the principle of need. The child care fee and the pregnancy benefit were abolished and replaced respectively with a new child care benefit and a non-recurrent maternity grant following delivery. Eligibility for the family allowance, child care benefit and child care allowance was to be based on the principle of need.

The petitioners sought constitutional review of the relevant provisions of the Act concerning the welfare benefits system. They submitted that (a) the Act virtually overnight annulled or altered the conditions of the benefits (which had played a substantial role in the livelihood of the families), which amounted to a violation of acquired rights, constitutionality and legal certainty; (b) the benefits taken together comprized a calculable, continuous system of welfare support (thus the Act violated Art. 70/E and the rights guaranteed to families, children and mothers under Arts. 66 and 67); and (c) the entry into force on 1 July 1995 of the Act promulgated on 15 June 1995 containing such severe changes, together with the belated promulgation of the provisions on execution on 17 June 1995, violated the principle of the rule of law laid down in Art. 2.

Held, ruling in favour of the petitioners:

(1) The challenged provisions of the Economic Stabilization Act were unconstitutional. Although Parliament could transform the welfare benefits system based on the citizen's right thereto into one based on the principle of need, this could only be exercized within very strict constitutional limitations. In deciding which benefits to withdraw, Parliament had to ensure that the extent of such benefits was not reduced below a minimum level required for the protection of social rights under Art. 70/E and that the constitutionality of the changes did not conflict with other constitutional rights and principles, namely, legal certainty, the ban on negative discrimination and, where the benefit included elements of insurance, the protection of property.

(2) Indeed legal certainty was the most substantial conceptual element and theoretical foundation of the protection of acquired social rights. Consequently it was of exceptional significance from the point of view of the stability of the welfare benefit system. The benefits and their related expectations could not be altered constitutionally overnight or without sufficient reason: in particular special reasons were required for changes without a transitional period. The mandatory payment of contribution in the compulsory social insurance scheme gave rise to a personal and pre-determined claim which enjoyed a high degree of state guarantee or protection of legitimate expectations, thus ensuring the stability in the system. Proximity in time to when the benefit would be paid corresponded to the need for greater protection of the certainty in its payment to an entitled recipient. The benefit already acquired and enjoyed necessarily required even greater protection. Consequently benefits provided for a short and determined period, *e.g.,* the child care benefit, child care fee and child care allowance, enjoyed priority protection not only because of their subject but also because of the short foreseeable period of confidence. Their termination during this short period of receipt thus violated the acquired rights constituting legal certainty and were therefore unconstitutional.

(3) However, where the benefit would be of much longer duration, due to the period of entitlement, a change in economic circumstances could constitute a better grounded reason for interim change in the system. The constitutional basis against which to measure the change differed according to whether or not there was an insurance element in the benefit: where such an element had a role, the constitutionality of the State's intervention in the system by reducing or terminating the benefit had to be decided on the basis of the protection of property as a fundamental right; where such an element did not have a role or this role had ultimately ceased, the basis was the requirement of legal certainty.

(4) In the former case, people invested part of their income in social security, the benefits of which perform the function of protecting property taken *stricto sensu* according to the Civil Code, *viz.,* guaranteeing security. If people's "goods" were taken by law for the purpose of social security, then it was the law that had to provide for security comparable to that of property. The protection of property was linked to a person's own property or value-generating work in the social security field and for that reason fuller protection of insurance services paid for through one's own contributions had to be distinguished from

grants of an assistance type. Such protection of property extended until the service or benefit in question performed the same function which the material property would have served, from which it followed that this attribute of social security could not be terminated. However, an exact matching between payments made and benefits received was excluded by the mode of operation of social security (non-capitalized assets), the built-in solidarity element and the long-term risk borne by the contributor. The fundamental right to protection of property could, however, be restricted in the public interest provided that this was proportionate, *i.e.,* did not violate another constitutional right. Within this framework of proportionality, it was possible to take into account the specific features of the legal relationship of social security (insurance element) to match the objective and means of the change of system to the changes themselves. Thus it was possible to make a constitutional appraisal in order to see whether the "public interest" justified the reduction in benefits in the context of the ability to function and survival of the entire system, the increased difficulties for the State in fulfilling its commitment and those inherent in social security, including the impossibility of collecting contributions from employers.

(5) In the absence of an insurance element in the particular benefit, the requirements of legal certainty were to be used to determine the constitutionality of the change in the availability of the benefit. This was particularly true of the family allowance, which according to the Act would be replaced with a system with a different base without any transition. Parliament had ignored the fact that regularly received benefits, the payment of which had already been commenced, and the continued expectation thereof played an important role in the long-term financial planning of families in respect of having children and raising and educating them. Although the family allowance did not cover all such costs, it guaranteed relative stability (by virtue of its calculability) in taking care of children. The Act, in withdrawing or transforming already acquired rights with respect to the family allowance virtually with immediate effect, breached the constitutional requirement of legal certainty.

(6) In determining the constitutionality of the transformation of the welfare benefits system, it was not sufficient to refer solely to the economic reasons for such intervention in the system. It was also necessary to examine the constitutional protection afforded to the mother, the family and the child. Indeed mothers and children were especially protected by the Constitution, so Arts. 15, 16, 66(2) and 67(1) and these provisions, together with the right to life under Art. 54(1), had to be taken into account in order to decide whether the current formulation of a benefit were contrary to another constitutional right. The intermediate termination of the child care fee and the pregnancy benefit upset the balance between the State's obligation to protect life and the acknowledgement of the right of the mother to self-determination and might accordingly be unconstitutional.

IN THE NAME OF THE REPUBLIC OF HUNGARY!

In the matter of petitions seeking an ex post facto review of the unconstitutionality of legal norms, the Constitutional Court—with the concurring opinion of Zlinszky, J.—made the following

DECISION.

1. The Constitutional Court declares that the principle of legal certainty as the most substantial conceptual element of the rule of law and theoretical basis of the protection of acquired rights is of particular significance from the viewpoint of the stability of welfare systems.

In the interest of the protection of acquired rights, legal certainty requires that benefits provided for a relatively short and determined period under the framework of maternity and child support benefits—the pregnancy allowance, the maternity benefit, the child care benefit, the child care fee and the child care allowance—be guaranteed under conditions no less favourable than those specified in legal regulations in force with respect to children already born and children to be born within 300 days as of 15 June 1995.

In the case of a subsidy within the maternity and child support benefits pertaining to a long period—particularly if it does not include an element of insurance—the legislature is entitled to amend the entire legal regulation of the subsidy, including the legal grounds of entitlement and its preconditions, in such a manner that the amendment also affects those who have already acquired a right to the subsidy. In such cases, however, the constitutional requirement flowing from the principle of legal certainty and pertaining to the shift to the new system is to guarantee a period of preparation for those concerned necessary for adjustment to the amended provisions and for the organization of the finances of the family in accordance with the new conditions.

2. In consideration of the above, the Constitutional Court declares that [the following provisions] are unconstitutional: s. 68, s. 79(4) and (5), s. 92(1)(d) and (2), as well as s. 93(1) in the part referring to s. 25(1) and (2) of the Social Security Act, s. 93(3), s. 159(1) and (2) with respect to the sections, subsections and paragraphs listed above and, further, s. 83 of Act XLVIII/1995 on the Amendment of Certain Laws to promote Economic Stabilization (hereafter referred to as the Economic Stabilization Act).

The Constitutional Court declares, with effect from the date of the promulgation of the Economic Stabilization Act, the unconstitutional provisions null and void.

The Constitutional Court declares further, as a consequence of the annulment of the relevant provisions of the Economic Stabilization Act, [that the following provisions issued in the execution of the Act] are unconstitutional: para. 32 of Government Decree 68/1995 (VI.17) Korm. on the execution of Act XXV/1990 on Family Allowance and Family Support; and the part of para. 7 of Government Decree 72/1995 (VI.17) Korm. on the amendment of Government Decree 32/1993 (II.17) Korm. on the Rules for Determining Child Care Allowance and the Evidence Admissible for Claiming Welfare Benefits relating to the child care allowance.

In consideration of this, the Constitutional Court declares these provisions null and void with effect from the date of the promulgation of the Government Decrees.

As a result of the annulment [the following shall not enter into force on 1 July 1995]: ss. 61–68, the provisions of s. 73, the part referring to "maternity benefit" in s. 77, s. 79(4)–(6), and s. 83 of the Economic Stabilization Act;

in close interrelation with s. 83, s. 40 of Act LV/1995 on the Amendment of Act XXII/1992 on the Labour Code; as well as

the indicated provisions of Government Decrees 68/1995 (VI.17) Korm. and 72/1995 (VI.17) Korm. related to the execution of the Act.

In determining the new date of entry into force of the provisions that shall not become effective according to the Decision of the Constitutional Court, the legislature shall also observe the constitutional requirements specified in the Decision of the Constitutional Court.

The Constitutional Court will render a separate Decision on further petitions submitted seeking the establishment of the unconstitutionality of certain provisions of the Economic Stabilization Act—also including the petitions affecting certain partial issues of the new regulation pertaining to the welfare benefit systems.

The Constitutional Court publishes this Decision in the *Hungarian Official Gazette.*

REASONING

KILÉNYI, J., and **SÓLYOM, P.,** delivering the Opinion of the Court: [....]

II

[....]

In Hungary, a so-called mixed system of social security has been in operation for decades, in which, in addition to elements of insurance, welfare elements are also present based on the principle of solidarity.

Certain welfare benefits, however, are closely linked to social security benefits ensuring subjective rights for those eligible to the benefit.

The benefits granted in view of the existence of a child support the families raising children through an intertwined system of several different interrelated institutions.

[....]

As a result of the Economic Stabilization Act, the changes taking place in the welfare benefit system are highly substantial because they replace a well-known and calculable benefit system maintained for decades that families have become used to, and these changes affect rights already acquired and acknowledged according to this former system.

In the course of the interpretation of Art. 70/E of the Constitution, the Constitutional Court has pointed out several times that the State meets its obligation specified in this Article if it organizes and operates a system of social insurance and welfare benefits. Within this, the legislature can itself determine the means whereby it wishes to achieve the objectives of social policy.

In relation to Art. 70/E(1) of the Constitution, the Constitutional Court also declared that "social security means neither a guaranteed income, nor that the achieved living standard of citizens could not deteriorate as a result of the unfavourable development of economic conditions" [*Dec. 772/B/1990 AB:* ABH 1991, 519 at 520].

It follows that the State has a wide margin of appreciation with respect to changes, regroupings and transformations within welfare benefits depending on economic conditions. The right of the State to change, however, is not unlimited [*Dec. 26/1993 (IV.29) AB:* MK 1993/51 at 2862–63; ABH 1993, 196 at 199–200].

The Constitutional Court points out that the constitutional criteria of statutory changes to welfare benefits are partially independent of the question as to what benefits those eligible would be entitled pursuant to Art. 70/E of the Constitution. In determining which of the benefits are actually enjoyed and how they can be withdrawn constitutionally, social rights have a role insofar that, as a result of such withdrawals, the extent of welfare benefits as a whole may not be reduced below a minimal level which may be required according to Art. 70/E. The constitutionality of the individual changes, however, also depends on whether or not they clash with other constitutional principles and rights, thus whether or not they are contrary to the principle of legal certainty, the prohibition of discrimination and, if it is about a benefit including elements of insurance, to the protection of property.

Therefore, within the above limitations, the legislature does have a possibility under the Constitution to transform welfare benefits due as a citizen's right into a benefit based on need.

This change laid down in the Economic Stabilization Act, however, constitutes a substantial modification in comparison with the former system, which has an impact on acquired rights and expectations affecting the existence and livelihood of families and the education of children as well as on additional family decisions.

Hence the competences of the State—the legislature—pertaining to changes can be constitutionally exercized only within the very stringent limits of the principle of the rule of law.

As a matter of principle, the Constitutional Court has already pointed out that the rule of law enshrined in Art. 2(1) of the Constitution presupposes the protection of acquired rights [for instance, in *Dec. 62/1993 (XI.29) AB:* MK 1993/172 at 10760; ABH 1993, 364 at 367].

The protection of acquired rights is a rule in a state under the rule of law. It is not, however, of absolute force that would not allow for exceptions. The decision on the exceptions, however, is only possible on a case-by-case basis. The Constitutional Court must be the ultimate forum in which to decide whether the conditions of an exceptional intervention obtain [*Dec. 32/1991 (VI.6) AB:* MK 1991/61 at 1137–38; ABH 1991, 146 at 154].

Legal certainty—which, in the view of the Constitutional Court, is the most substantial conceptual element of a state under the rule of law and the theoretical basis of the protection of acquired rights—is therefore of exceptional significance from the viewpoint of the stability of the welfare benefit systems.

Under the Constitution, benefits and expectations related thereto cannot be substantially altered without sufficient reason or overnight. Special reasons are required for changes without a transition.

In the case of a mandatory insurance system, the insured may expect a greater stability of the system against the mandatory payment of contributions, that is, against this type of "encumbrance" on his/her property.

In the view of the Constitutional Court, the objectives of Art. 70/E of the Constitution can be equally implemented through mandatory or voluntary insurance [*Dec. 772/B/1990/5 AB:* ABH 1991, 519]. The two systems, however, also imply different obligations for the State.

The mandatory payment of contributions ordained by law—which, in substance, differs from the contribution to public revenues (Constitution, Art. 70/I) because it gives rise to a personal and predetermined claim—can be legitimized only by a high degree of state guarantee (and, from the other perspective, protection of legitimate expectations).

Mandatory insurance draws off the assets which the person concerned could have used to take care of himself/herself and his/her family at his/her own risk and puts these assets in the service of social security so that the insured will also be able to take care of others based on solidarity.

By turning the coverage into a part of the uniform social welfare system, the State collectivizes a typical behaviour of the owner.

The protection of welfare benefits that had evolved within and from a mandatory insurance system is therefore particularly warranted.

Expectations enjoy the greater protection the nearer they are to "fulfillment," that is, to the coming into existence of the right to the benefit falling due. The benefit acquired and already enjoyed should be protected even more.

This is also related to the bearing of risk inherent in long-term continuous legal relationships, to which the Constitutional Court has already referred several times [*Dec. 32/1991 (VI.6) AB:* MK 1991/61 at 1143; ABH 1991, 146 at 166].

The beneficiary must attach particular importance to the historically evolved situation and operation of social security, in the sense that it manages its finances not out of capitalized assets or other assets the value of which can be maintained over time, but it consumes the current payments of the active generations (who can only pin their hopes on the future). That is to say, this type of financing makes the system even more high risk. The further away the due date of the benefits is, the less calculable it is as to what social security will be able to provide for them.

Hence, the duration of the benefit promised must make a difference from the viewpoint of the protection of acquired rights.

Benefits for a short and determined period such as the child care benefit, the child care fee and the child care allowance enjoy a higher degree of protection not only because of their subject but also because the short, foreseeable period, establishing confidence.

Consequently, their termination during this period violates acquired rights constituting legal certainty, hence it is unconstitutional.

Protection has a different mode and extent in the case of the family allowance that is provided for the period of a generation where, in view of the long period of performance, a change in the economic situation may constitute a better grounded reason for the interim change planned by the State.

The protection of expectations and benefits is stronger depending on whether or not they are provided on the basis of financial contributions of the beneficiaries. The withdrawal of a benefit due against contributions or the unfavourable change of its legal basis shall be examined according to the criteria of the impairment of fundamental rights.

This the Constitutional Court has professed to as to the priority of the insurance element within the mixed system of social security. The pension must be disbursed for the period covered by the contribution unconditionally; otherwise the beneficiary would be deprived of an acquired right [*Dec. 11/1991 (III.29) AB:* MK 1991/34 at 725; ABH 1991, 34 at 35]. The nominal pension calculated according to the rules of insurance is inviolable. The arbitrary changing of the ratios of insurance and solidarity is constitutionally excluded [*Dec. 26/1993 (IV.29) AB:* MK 1993/51 at 2863; ABH 1993, 196 at 200].

Changing a benefit without a transition or "degrading" it from an insurance to a form of assistance also brings about an essential change in the legal position in the sense that the person concerned falls into a weaker category of protection of legitimate expectations (the protection of property ceases), and this amounts to an intervention in fundamental rights.

The constitutionality of such a change should also be evaluated accordingly. The unconstitutionality of an arbitrary change in the ratios of the insurance and solidarity elements can be interpreted in this context. In itself, it is difficult to separate the part of the contribution that will be turned into one's own benefit and the part that will be spent on others. It is against the Constitution if the ratios shift to the extent that the level of the protection enjoyed to date deteriorates to a qualitatively weaker one and this is not constitutionally grounded.

The legal relationships in social security must be addressed in their entirety.

The employers (principals, *etc.*) paying the contribution also constitute part of the system. In the technical structure of financing, a part of the contribution is paid by the employer—but based on the personal income disbursed. The direct deduction is like the advance on tax. In principle, it could be disbursed and the beneficiary could be required to pay it in immediately. Therefore, the beneficiary is entitled to all the guarantees concomitant with the insurance element irrespective of who actually pays the contribution in his favour.

In the present system, the employer is obliged to pay the major part of the contribution; it is the employer who has to manage his assets in such a way as to be able to meet this obligation. Protection of legitimate expectations—also as part of the protection of the fundamental right to property—extends to the employer as well.

In the case of social security benefits where the insurance element has a role to play, the constitutionality of the reduction or termination of the benefits should be evaluated according to the criteria of the protection of property.

The extension of the protection of the fundamental right to property to social security benefits and expectations related thereto fits into the conception of the Constitutional Court expounded on the function of property [*Dec. 64/1993 (XII.22) AB:* MK 1993/184 at 11078; ABH 1993, 373 at 380]:

> Property is afforded a constitutional protection in its capacity as the traditional means of securing an economic basis for the autonomy of individuals. The constitutional protection must track the changing social role of property so as to fulfill the same task. [....] [T]he constitutional protection extends to rights with an economic value which today perform this former role of ownership, including public law entitlements (for instance, to entitlements from the social insurance).

It was in that spirit that the Constitutional Court protected the assets of churches, corporations under public law and, most importantly, municipalities on the grounds that that is the basis of their autonomy [*Dec. 4/1993 (II.12) AB:* MK 1993/15 at 711–12 and 714–15; ABH 1993, 48 at 66 and 72]. The change that has taken place in the protection of property has been discussed many times in the literature and is generally accepted.

The vast majority of the people today are not "self-pensioners," and it is not their own material goods that constitute social and economic security in their inactive age; from the outset, they live in such a way that they invest a part of the result of their work in social security, and it is its benefits that perform the function of property taken *stricto sensu* according to the Civil Code, *viz.*, guaranteeing security. If their goods are taken for this purpose by law, it is the law that must provide for a security comparable to that provided by property. The same applies to services due in case of loss of income arising out of illness or other reasons and, further, to the part of the coverage of the additional burden arising from the raising of children that the insured compensates for by the payment of contributions. (From the viewpoint of protection, it is not significant whether or not the benefit was due after or during the period of contribution payment.)

The protection of property does not lose its link to one's own property or value-generating work in the field of social security either. That is why we distinguish the more extensive protection of "insurance" services paid for by contributions of the beneficiaries from the lesser protection for grants of an assistance type. Property protection may extend until a service performs the same function which the material property would serve; it follows therefrom that this attribute of the service cannot be terminated. At the same time, an exact matching between one's own payments and the benefits received is excluded by the mode of operation of social security (non-capitalized assets), the built-in solidarity element and the risk also borne by the contribution payer in the long term.

The Constitutional Court expounded its views on the protection of property as a fundamental right and the social burdens of property in *Dec. 64/1993 (XII.22) AB* (MK 1993/184; ABH 1993, 373). [....]

According to Art. 13(2) of the Constitution, "public interest" is sufficient to allow for restriction [of property]. [....]

[....] The "public interest" justifying the reduction in [social security] benefits, the ability to function and survival of the entire social security system, the increased difficulties in the fulfillment of the commitments of the State due to external reasons and those inherent in social security (also including the impossibility of collecting contributions from the employers) can be appraised in terms of the categories of constitutional law.

In cases, however, in which the insurance element does not have a role or this role has been ultimately terminated, the constitutionality of intervention in welfare benefits must be decided not on the basis of the protection of property as a fundamental right but on the basis of the requirements of legal certainty, which is the most important constituent of the rule of law. The Constitutional Court has expounded the content of legal certainty in a number of decisions. The judgments which specify a period of preparation for the implementation of the new provisions in relation to the coming into force of a legal regulation as a constitutional requirement, represent a substantial portion among these [*Dec. 7/1992 (I.30) AB* (MK 1992/11; ABH 1992, 47); *Dec. 25/1992 (IV.30) AB* (MK 1992/44; ABH 1992, 132); *Dec. 28/1992 (IV.30) AB* (MK 1992/44 at 1607–8; ABH 1992, 155 at 156–59); *Dec. 57/1994 (XI.17) AB* (MK 1994/113; ABH 1994, 324)].

In the case of family allowance, the constitutional problem consists not of the changing of the former system but of the fact that already acquired rights are to be replaced with a system with a different base without any transition period. In drafting the provisions of the Economic Stabilization Act, the legislature neglected the fact that the regularly received benefit already received on a regular basis and the promised expectation play an important role in the long-term decisions pertaining to the livelihood of the family, as regards whether to have a child or children and their schooling and education. Although the family allowance by itself has never covered the financial obligations of the families raising children, by virtue of its calculability, it guaranteed a relative stability in taking care of them. [....]

As the Economic Stabilization Act ordained, virtually with immediate effect, the implementation of the withdrawal or transformation of already acquired rights with respect to the family allowance, this gave rise to an unconstitutional situation. In view of this, the Constitutional Court rendered its Decision on the unconstitutionality of the termination of the family allowance acquired in accordance with earlier provisions, on the provisions bringing into force the Economic Stabilization Act as specified in the operative part of this Decision.

III

Children and mothers are particularly protected by the Constitution [Arts. 15, 16, 66(2) and 67(1) of the Constitution]. Therefore, in judging whether the intervention in already acquired rights has been constitutional or arbitrary, the Constitutional Court is of the view that it is not sufficient to refer to the economic reasons for the intervention. It is also necessary to examine whether the constitutional provisions referred to are abided by. Society has an elementary interest in having an active population in the future, able to realize the commitments of the State.

In its decision on abortion, the Constitutional Court expounded in detail that it is the institutional obligation of the State to protect human life, including human life that is in the process of coming into existence, together with guaranteeing the living conditions of future generations [*Dec. 64/1991 (XII.17) AB:* MK 1991/139 at 2812; ABH 1991, 297 at 303].

In the view of the Constitutional Court, the Constitution makes it possible for the legislature to decide that the fetus is not a person, having no legal capacity. Abortion, however, owing to the obligations concerning the protection of life, cannot be permitted without restriction and without reason (*Dec. 64/1991 (XII.17) AB:* MK 1991/139 at 2819; ABH 1991, 297 at 316). According to the concurring opinions of more Justices in that case, the support and protection due to the mother before the birth of the child [Constitution, Art. 66(2)] and the protection and care due to the child according to the Constitution [Art. 67(1)] must also be included in the examination of the constitutionality of abortion.

Although the maternity benefit, the pregnancy allowance and other benefits or even the concrete regulation or extent of the family allowance cannot be directly derived from the provisions of the Constitution, in order to decide whether the actual formulation of a benefit is contrary to another constitutional right, the provisions of the Constitution on the right to life [Art. 54(1)] must also be taken into account.

The far-reaching consideration of the mother's right to self-determination according to the law in force requires appropriate positive countermeasures that will encourage the willingness to bear children. The institutions of the child care fee and of the pregnancy benefit introduced in 1993 were expressly such encouraging institutions. Their immediate termination—since the new rules of the child care allowance cannot constitute a comparable compensation, neither can the one-off maternity grant available upon delivery replacing the pregnancy allowance guaranteed from the fourth month of pregnancy—upset the balance between the obligation of the State to protect life and the acknowledgement of the right of the mother to self-determination. Through this, an unconstitutional situation may arise.

[....]

As a result of the Decision of the Constitutional Court, some of the provisions of the Economic Stabilization Act providing for the entry into force of the Act, including the section abrogating s. 25/A of the Act on Social Security and the amendment of s. 1 of the Act on the Protection of the Fetus, shall not enter into force on the date originally envisaged: specification of the new date of entry into force is the responsibility of the legislature.

With this Decision, the Constitutional Court also points out that before bringing and implementing decisions pertaining to the transformation of the entire welfare benefit system the State must, in addition to the aspects related to the financial-economic situation of the country, also take into account its obligations to protect the mother, the family and the child as expressly assigned to it by the Constitution.

In implementing and executing the legal regulations aimed at the transformation of the welfare benefit system affecting a substantial portion of society, it is a requirement flowing from the principle of the rule of law as stipulated in Art. 2 of the Constitution that the behaviour of the State be calculable, so that both natural and legal persons will be able to plan with good grounds in making their economic-, family- or livelihood-related decisions and that they will be able to infer the will of the State incorporated into legal regulations. [....]

ZLINSZKY, J., concurring: [....]

The Constitutional Court does not wish to tie the hands of the legislature in the search for appropriate solutions, but in a form more express than that incorporated in the Decision, the Court must call the attention of the legislature to the fact that it can expect the agreement and co-operation of society, which is the necessary precondition of the success of the reforms, only if it chooses and requires restrictive measures which meet the sense of moral and social justice of society. It may well be that the existing welfare benefit system is obsolete. It contains deficiencies and it occasionally provides superfluous support, but as a whole, even to date, it is far from guaranteeing the equal sharing of the burden of social reproduction. In perspective it continues to assist in the continuous deterioration of the social equilibrium, also, in the long run, reducing the quality of society. Rather than providing excessive benefits to the strata which, on the whole, undertakes the reproduction of the population, it provides them with support under the level which could be expected constitutionally.

It seems that the present "package of laws" rather than facilitating stabilization as it promised will further increase these differences, as it makes the conditions of raising children much more difficult. Its provisions that have been promulgated to date are expressly contrary to the requirement and objective of social and economic stabilization in the long run. The legislature should present at least an acceptable plan for long-term settlement to society in order to be able to justify even the maintenance of the existing negative discrimination. Their aggravation, especially for the sake of the apparent advantages of savings, which are of negligible importance in quantitative terms for the entire budget, can hardly be harmonized with the word and the spirit of the Constitution. The Decision of the Constitutional Court provides an opportunity for the legislature to create the missing harmony. There are good reasons to call attention separately to this opportunity also as a necessity.

DECISION 21/1996: 17 MAY 1996

ON THE MINIMUM AGE FOR MEMBERSHIP OF HOMOSEXUAL-ORIENTED ASSOCIATIONS

This case was an advisory opinion on the request of the President of the Supreme Court, and the underlying case of the ordinary jurisdiction—refusing the registration of an association for the rights of homosexuals because its rules did not exclude the membership of minors—attracted nationwide publicity. This decision gives insight into how the "abstract interpretation of constitutional provision" works and to what extent abstract decisions of the Constitutional Court can determine the outcome of concrete cases. Here the Constitutional Court also abstained from any moral judgment about homosexuality; it balanced the rights to association of minors against the State's duty to protect the child from risks in connection with which the immature minor was not able to find out about and evaluate either the possibilities or the consequences of the choice for his or her personality, later life, and social adaptation.

The President of the Supreme Court sought the abstract constitutional interpretation of certain fundamental rights.

The petitioner submitted that there was a concrete constitutional problem in that the rights of the child guaranteed by Art. 67 conflicted with his/her right of association under Art. 63(1) where it concerned the child's membership in an association which presented itself as one protecting the rights of homosexuals as a social group.

Held, ruling accordingly:

(1) The membership of minors in associations related to homosexuality could be excluded or restricted by law or in court decisions. In the conflict between the rights guaranteed under Arts. 63(1) and 67, the different criteria restricting them also had to be harmonized: this meant not only to which protective measures a child had a right under Art. 67, *i.e.,* whether the restriction on the child's membership in such an association formed a part of the constitutionally required minimum protection provided by the State, but also whether this level of protection was a necessary and proportionate restriction on the exercise of the right of association under Art. 63(1). The right of the child to protection and care at the same time established the constitutional duty of the State for the institutional protection of the child's personality development, which protective duty (based on the Constitution) could result in the restriction of the child's fundamental rights by the legislature or courts. Further, the specific qualities of the child's fundamental right legal status would have to be clarified, for these were different from the general precisely because of his/her age.

(2) Consequently, there were several criteria to be considered in determining whether and to what extent the right of the child to protection for his/her development could restrict his/her right of association. These were age, the nature of the association to be joined, the child's ability to understand and evaluate his/her choices with respect to homosexuality and

the consequences thereof for his/her own personality, later adult life and social adaptation, particularly the consequences of membership in a homosexual-related association and the public view of homosexuality therein. Taking these into account and without forming a moral judgment on homosexuality on the basis of the Constitution, it remained harmful for the development of the child's personality (physical, mental and moral) and would decisively affect his/her future were he/she to come onto a path with no alternatives due to the lack of maturity necessary to decide these vital questions. The State, in avoiding the child's exposure to such risk, could set a higher age limit for coming out publicly (if legally possible, *e.g.*, in regulating membership of associations) because a different level of maturity was necessary for evaluating the social consequences thereof. Thus setting an age limit for membership of a homosexual-related association primarily protected the responsible and mature decision of those who would bear its consequences for the whole of their lives. As a result, on the basis of Art. 67, children's membership in such associations could be restricted.

IN THE NAME OF THE REPUBLIC OF HUNGARY!

In the matter of the petition by the President of the Supreme Court seeking the interpretation of constitutional provisions, the Constitutional Court has made the following

DECISION.

1. The right of the child to protection and care necessary for proper physical, mental and moral development to be provided by the State (Art. 67(1) of the Constitution) establishes the constitutional duty of the State to protect the development of the child. This duty of the State serves as a constitutional basis for the legislature or the courts to restrict—primarily in the public sphere—the child in exercising his/her fundamental rights, including the right of association guaranteed in Art. 63 of the Constitution.

Article 67 of the Constitution also means that the State has to protect the child from—besides influences harmful to his/her development—taking risks in connection with which, because of his/her age (presumed to correlate with physical, mental, moral and social maturity), he/she is not able get to know and evaluate either the possibilities or the consequences of his/her choices for his/her own personality, later life and social adaptation.

2. On the basis of the above, the child's membership in associations related to homosexuality can be excluded or restricted in laws or in court decisions. The actual restriction on the child's exercise of his/her right of association has to adjust to the concrete risk endangering the development of the child. In the course of considering whether the right of the child to protection for his/her development may lead to the restriction on his/her right of association, the age of the child and the nature of the association have to be evaluated together and from the point of view of whether the child is able to know and evaluate the choices in connection with his/her relationship to homosexuality and the consequences of his/her choice for his/her own personality, later life and social adaptation, including those consequences which might ensue from membership in the association in question and the public assumption of the concept of homosexuality prevalent there.

The Constitutional Court publishes its Decision in the *Hungarian Official Gazette.*

REASONING

SÓLYOM, P., delivering the Opinion of the Court:

I

1. The President of the Supreme Court petitioned the Constitutional Court, in the framework of abstract constitutional interpretation, to delimit the fundamental rights expressed in Art. 67 and Art. 63(1) of the Constitution. The petitioner found it to be a "concrete constitutional problem" that "the right of the child to protection and care necessary for proper physical, mental and moral development to be provided by the State [Art. 67 of the Constitution] conflicts with his/her right of association [Art. 63(1) of the Constitution] if the question arises about the child's membership in an association which presents itself as the association protecting the rights of homosexual persons as a social group."

2. The petition complies with the conditions set forth by the Constitutional Court in *Dec. 31/1990 (XII.18) AB* (MK 1990/128 at 2503–4; ABH 1990, 136 at 137). The Constitutional Court has always tried to keep abstract constitutional interpretation away from two extremes: on the hand, from "the purely abstract and indeed unbounded interpretation that is disconnected from any concrete problem"; and, on the other hand, from deciding concrete cases or merely interpreting laws by abstract interpretation. By the latter condition the Constitutional Court wanted to keep away from the tasks of other branches of power. The condition of "concrete constitutional problem" expresses the relative generality of the interpretation, and the Court decided from case to case whether "a properly abstract answer to be compulsorily applied in all cases in the future" (*Dec. 36/1992 (VI.10) AB:* MK 1992/59 at 2027; ABH 1992, 207 at 211) could be given, one which went beyond the particular problem that concerned the petitioner.

II

In the present case a classical political liberty, the right of association, conflicts with the right of the child to protection and care necessary for proper physical, mental and moral development to be provided by his/her family, the state and society.

1. The conflict between two fundamental rights cannot possibly be judged completely in an abstract manner. There is a question about whether there is any hierarchical relationship between the two or any difference in their nature which could give a general framework for the judgment.

(a) The permanent practice of the Constitutional Court places "rights of communication" above others in the sense that "laws restricting the freedom of expression have to be interpreted restrictively": (*Dec. 30/1992 (V.26) AB:* MK 1992/53 at 1913; ABH 1992, 167 at 178). The right of freedom of expression is the "mother right" to fundamental rights of communication according to the Constitutional Court. The priority of freedom of expression against other rights does not, however, comprise all fundamental rights of communication. For, if this were the case, almost all classical political liberties would enjoy this special protection, which on the one hand would decrease the real significance of the freedom of expression and on the other hand would make the difference between political and sociocultural rights more distinctive than it actually is by their nature. The prior practice of the Constitutional Court required an especially strong connection with the "mother right" for extending the priority of the freedom of expression over other rights (*cf.*, in connection with the freedom of religion, *Dec. 4/1993 (II.12) AB:* MK 1993/15 at 704; ABH 1993, 48 at 51).

Thus the right of association does not share in the priority of freedom of expression in relation to other constitutional rights.

(b) Classical liberties do not necessarily enjoy priority against social rights or other obligations of the State that do not derive from classical rights. But when rights of the two different types conflict with one another, their peculiarities cannot be disregarded.

2. In the conflict between the right of the child to protection and care necessary for proper development and the right of association, the different criteria restricting the two different rights also have to be brought into harmony.

(a) Thus in the case to be decided not only the question has to be answered in the course of interpretation as to what protective measures the child has a right, taking into consideration only Art. 67 of the Constitution, that is, whether the restriction on the child's membership in an association related to homosexuality forms a part of the constitutionally required minimum protection—but also the Constitutional Court has to define the constitutionally required level of protection with regard to whether this level of protection is at the same time a necessary and proportionate restriction on a classical liberty, that of the exercise of the right of association.

The extent to which a fundamental right can be restricted in the interest of protecting the exercise of another can be determined only in connection with a concrete legal regulation or a concrete case. In the course of abstract constitutional interpretation about the conflict of two fundamental rights, the test of required minimal state measures (in connection with the protection of the child, Art. 67) and the test of proportionality (for the restriction on the right of association, Art. 63) can be applied, with one significant proviso: if the "concrete constitutional problem" is considered as an abstract case as the elements of a rule defined *in abstracto* in a law. In fact, the Constitutional Court has to create a constitutionally perfect statutory rule, to which legislation can adjust or on the basis of which courts can judge constitutionally.

(b) The conflict of the right of the child to protection and the freedom of association can arise in several cases even within the case defined in the petition—"if the question arises about [the child's] membership in an association presenting itself as the association protecting the rights of homosexual persons as a social group"—and these require differing judgments. The constitutional questions are different, on the one hand, according to whether we talk about generally prohibiting or setting conditions for the child's membership or individually exercising the right of association, and, on the other hand, whether the restriction is given by a legal rule or court decision or is enforced by the parent. Restricting the right of association by statutory regulation is, by its nature, general; the courts can generally exclude the membership of children in associations which permit the membership of children by refusing registration and can decide in individual membership cases, while the parent can prohibit the membership of his/her own child.

Nevertheless, the Constitutional Court mentions at the outset that a separate examination of these restrictions will follow depending on what amount of restriction on the right of association the Constitutional Court regards as constitutionally justified in the interest of protecting the development of the child. For, if the Court finds that it is the duty of the State generally to protect the child from risks related to membership in such an association, then courts naturally cannot diverge from this in individual membership cases and the duty of protection will not lie with the parent—in the form of approval of membership in the association.

3. In order to clarify the relationship between the right of the child to protection and the right of association, we have to take into consideration two specific qualities of the right given in Art. 67 of the Constitution. One is that the right of the child to protection and care at the same time establishes the duty of the State for the institutional protection of the child's personality development. This protective duty of the State can result in the restriction of the fundamental rights of the child. The decisive question in the Decision of the Constitutional Court will precisely be about where to draw the line between the child's independent exercise of fundamental rights and the State's or the parent's guardianship over his/her exercise of fundamental rights. On the other hand it will be necessary to clarify those specific qualities of the child's legal status in the system of fundamental rights which are different from the general, precisely because of his/her age. [See, below, Point III.1.]

From the point of view the right of association guaranteed in Art. 63 of the Constitution, we need to indicate that the question in our case is not about the constitutionality of an objective of an association (see s. 2(3) of Act II/1989 on the Right of Association, hereafter the Association Act) but about the restriction on the right of association in the interest of the child (Art. 67 of the Constitution). That is, the present case does not involve the matter of constitutionally qualifying associations related to homosexuality. The constitutional conditions for restricting the exercise of the right of association by legislation follow from the Constitution and its interpretation by the Constitutional Court. The judge refuses to register the social [non-profit-making] association if the founders do not comply with conditions set forth in the Association Act. According to s. 2(2) of the Association Act, exercising the right of association cannot violate Art. 2(3) of the Constitution [cannot aim at the acquisition or exercise by force of public authority, nor at its exclusive possession], cannot amount to committing a crime or encouraging someone to do so, and cannot result in the violation of the rights and liberties of others. This latter condition is also included in art. 15 of the New York Convention on the Rights of the Child—promulgated in Act LXIV/1991—which declares that the signatory States must recognize the child's right of association.

Restricting the right of association in the interest of protecting third persons from the infringement of "their rights and liberties" is constitutional if this restriction is made necessary by the other right and the extent of restriction is proportionate to the desired aim. This other right has to be a constitutional right or may be deduced from such a right. The right of the child to protection and care necessary for development excludes the child's membership in certain associations. If in such an association, according to its statutes, children too can be members, then the association does not comply with s. 2(2) of the Association Act since this violates the right of children guaranteed in Art. 67 of the Constitution. The task of the Constitutional Court in the present Decision is to determine those features in connection with associations related to homosexuality, on the basis of which it can be determined in which cases the child's right to protection and care necessary for his/her development makes the restriction on the exercise of the right of association necessary and proportionate. This abstract constitutional interpretation at the same time determines the constitutional requirements for applying the quoted provision of the Association Act—the exercise of the right of association cannot result in the violation of the rights and liberties of others—for the case defined in the petition.

III

1. According to the Constitution human rights are due to "everyone"; civic rights apply naturally to Hungarian citizens and for certain rights the Constitution itself defines the circle of those eligible (refugees' rights, the right to vote). The Constitution is not consistent in differentiating between a legal capacity for fundamental rights and the right to exercise fundamental rights. (The limits of the right to vote, which theoretically belong to the latter, Art. 70 of the Constitution defines as exclusion, that is, as the lack of legal capacity concerning suffrage.) The conditions for exercising fundamental rights can be defined in laws for certain groups of persons.

The child is entitled to fundamental rights. The Constitution excludes them explicitly only from the right to vote. The child—like everybody else—can exercise fundamental rights under the conditions set forth by the individual spheres of the law. But these restrictions can be the subject of constitutional review.

Where laws do not regulate minors' and juveniles' exercise of rights, it has to be determined from case to case which fundamental rights and in what respect the child can exercise on his/her own, or who should exercise them on his/her behalf and in his/her interest, and whether with regard to his/her age and Art. 67 of the Constitution, the child can be excluded completely from certain spheres of a fundamental right. The possibility of the child's exercise of fundamental rights—including the right personally to exercise them—gradually widens with age and with the development of an ability to make decisions while considering the consequences of exercising a right.

The Constitutional Court has treated this question in two connections. On the one hand the Court declared it unconstitutional that the child could be completely deprived of his/her right to ascertain his/her ancestry because of the unconditional authorization of the officially assigned guardian to initiate paternity suits (*Dec. 57/1991 (XI.8) AB:* MK 1991/123; ABH 1991, 272); on the other hand the Court said that the right of parents to provide the kind of schooling for their children which suits, but at least does not conflict with their consciences, applies to the child as well "within the boundaries of parental guardianship" (*Dec. 4/1993 (II.12) AB:* MK 1993/15 at 706; ABH 1993, 48 at 56). This reinforces the fact that the personal exercise of rights or one which is conducted in the interest of the child by others depends on the fundamental right in question. Moreover it is necessary to make further distinctions. For example, exercising the right of association usually applies to the child too. But the question of whether the parent or the child can decide about it and when the right of association can be restricted or excluded depends on the one hand on age and on the other hand on the aim of the association and the effects of membership on the child's physical, mental and moral development—protected by the Constitution.

2. Whether restricting the exercise of the fundamental right of the child is justified depends on the mutual consideration of two factors: is the child generally mature enough for independent decision making; and, as for the subject of decision, how much maturity is needed in the given case? The "maturity" of participants is usually required in order to preserve the capacity to function of the social institutions involved, that is, it is required by the public interest. But protecting the child against himself/herself—that is, against the consequences of his/her decision—may be a sufficient argument for restriction. Restricting rights for public interest or for the interest of a person overlaps in most cases.

The civil law institutions of limited legal competence and limited liability above all protect, for instance, the security of transactions; but they also protect the minor (his/her property) from careless losses and generally from risks. From this latter point of view, protection is preventive: it restricts the rights of the child during childhood in the interest of the child's future. Setting age limits for the right to vote or for holding certain offices also serves the interest of the optimal operation of certain institutions. The age (or permission) requirement for marriage protects the seriousness and the durability of the institution and at the same time protects the child from the consequences of carelessly changing his/her status. In the listed cases restriction under the age limits applies to positive activities of some sort. Nevertheless, from the point of view of restricting the child's exercise of rights, the quality of the prohibited activity is not decisive.

Restricting fundamental rights does not involve a value judgment about what the child is prohibited or prevented from doing. It is the significance of the decision that justifies the restriction on the exercise of a right by the child until he/she is capable of responsible decision making. The decision can be made weighty by the consequences and risks that the child assumes by the decision.

Article 67 of the Constitution, which compels the State to provide protection and care necessary for the personality development of the child, requires on the one hand the prevention of unambiguously harmful effects and on the other hand also requires averting the assumption of weighty risks that can determine the child's personality and thus the whole of his/her future life.

Everyone can harm himself or herself and can assume risks if he/she is capable of making a free, informed and responsible decision. The law gives a wide range of possibilities for this by its non-interference, and the rights to self-definition and activity (Art. 54 of the Constitution), following from the general right of personality, guarantee this possibility. The restrictive paternalism of the State is a matter of constitutional debate only in borderline cases (from the punishment of drug usage to euthanasia). But in the case of children the Constitution itself and international treaties also compel the State to protect the development of the child from dangers and risks, exactly in order that the child can prepare for responsible and informed decisions once his/her maturity (supposed to correlate with age) renders him/her capable thereof.

3. The duties of the State following from Art. 67 of the Constitution for the protection of the child's development, but its constitutional possibilities too, are present primarily in the public sphere; the child's public activity can be regulated, and also institutional protection can be provided by general regulations. In the private sphere the right and the duty of protection and care are due primarily to the parents. Thus, for instance, a law can prohibit—with a general preventive aim—the selling of alcohol to children in public places, the selling of pornographic printed matter or the opening of sex shops in close proximity to schools. Laws can prohibit children from entering such places. It is the responsibility of the parent, however, to decide whether the child can have access to alcohol or pornography at home. The State intervenes only if the development of the child is seriously and concretely violated or endangered—for instance by suspending parental supervision.

4. The State has to protect the child from taking risks in connection with which, because of his/her age (presumed to correlate with physical, mental, moral and social maturity), he/she is not able to know and evaluate either the possibilities or the consequences of his/her choices for his/her own personality, later life and social adaptation. The State is thus bound, as part of its duty to avert risks, to prohibit the child at least in the public sphere from pursuing activities or taking a stand in matters in connection with which the child is not mature enough in the above sense to develop a responsible position, although taking up

a public position can prove to be decisive for the child's physical, mental and moral development and his/her later life. The risks involved are particularly increased if [the child is] taking up a public position in relation to a question which society judges as controversial in the sense that it is widely judged to be negative.

In restricting the child's exercise of rights on the basis of Art. 67 of the Constitution, the following have to be taken into consideration:

No freedom can be restricted generally but only in those respects of its exercise in which a restriction is necessary for the protection of the child or others' rights.

An abstract endangerment of the physical, mental and moral development is not sufficient for the restriction on a liberty even in the interest of protecting the child. It has to be proven that a certain activity is restricted or prohibited by the law because such an activity carries concrete dangers for the affected age group; the proportionality of the restriction on the right depends on the extent of this concrete danger.

When state intervention prevents the assumption of excessive risks, in qualifying the extent of the risk, the positive, educational effect on the personality also has to be considered, which might be realized by participation in debate since expressing and debating opinions forms part of democracy. Thus it depends on the concrete circumstances as to what extent the child's freedom of inquiry and of expression can be restricted in controversial questions. The child too has to understand that there are disagreeable, provocative, controversial phenomena which might potentially exert harmful influences; he/she has to learn to form a position, have an opinion, debate and hold his/her opinion even against a majority, *etc.* Accessibility can depend, for instance, on whether there is a possibility of putting these effects in a context, to confront them with other opinions—for example, in the framework of education.

At the same time, qualifying risks cannot exclusively depend on the evaluation of a branch of science that is confined to its own specialization, but it has to ponder what effects these risks can have on the development and future of the affected group of children in the given social context. An art critic can give an unambiguously positive aesthetic evaluation of a work of art, and this will not exclude the restriction on access, since the child might not be capable of (exclusively) aesthetic evaluation and the actual effect of the work can be dangerous.

5. A general restriction on the child's right of association could not be justified constitutionally. The question can only be about laying down criteria for or prohibiting the establishing or joining of certain types of associations.

There is no need, in the present Decision, to examine whether the civil law rules of legal capacity to act, especially the approval of the parent (or guardian) of the child's legal statement establishing his/her membership, apply to exercising the fundamental right of association. For, if membership in a certain association constitutes such a weighty risk for the child that a law or the courts can in general exclude it on the basis of the interpretation of the Constitutional Court in the present Decision, then approval is off the agenda.

Thus it is only possible to decide separately, for certain types of risk, the constitutional question of up to what age of the child the parent can exercise the right of association on the child's behalf, when the child is mature enough to decide about exercising this fundamental right, and, further, in which cases parental approval is required because of the extent of risk involved in membership and when the law evaluates this risk so extensive to deprive completely the child and the parent of the decision.

IV

1. The international comparison of (constitutional) court decisions on homosexual discrimination suggests that the "moral judgment of public opinion" plays an increasingly less important role in them. "Public morals" and "majority views" had been driven from the decisive arguments earlier on, through recognition by the courts of self-determination in the private sphere differing from these standards (setting out from the cases on contraception and abortion); later by enforcing the prohibition on discrimination, this protection was expanded to homosexuals too. But the situation, in fact, is much more complicated than that since public morals still remain arguments in many important decisions. Parallel with liberalization, there is another line of decisions present, which—in accordance with public morals—provides protection against the aggressive "self-assertiveness" of others, the provocative propagating of their own moral norms (see, for instance, the restriction on offensive pornography). The subject of these cases is usually the presence of activity in the public sphere that is considered to be immoral by the "majority view" (which is also publicly upheld by those who do not comply with it, that is, by the moral convention).

A further important difference that can be deduced from decisions made abroad is that discrimination "according to sex" can usually be successfully contested while discrimination "according to sexual orientation" is rarely contested successfully.

2. It is a universal phenomenon that a certain part of sexual morals—by recognizing moral plurality—is withdrawn from legal sanction. It is without doubt, though, that criminal law draws the outer limit in the sphere of sexual morals (too) and society does not tolerate going beyond that. Although the definition of crimes is the competence of legislation and thus the sphere where democratic majority opinion—and sentiments—is realized, in exceptional cases constitutional review can be applicable.

There are crimes in the case of which the moral and legal judgment not only coincide but punishability cannot really be questioned morally—as in the case of murder. Likewise, from the point of view of sexual morals, punishing incest cannot be questioned, although theoretical articles have questioned it, just like they questioned—demanding the "sexual rights of children"—punishment for "sexual intercourse with minors." These efforts remained theoretical curiosities without any effect on positive law and adjudication. But if there are several kinds of moral judgments present with significant strength in public opinion—even if artificially reinforced—"public morals" or the "public view" as constitutional arguments lose their strengths and are pushed into the background.

A sphere of previously criminalized behaviour, the crimes against sexual morals—prostitution, "crimes against nature" between consenting adults—are no longer punished in most European countries. But public morals are still there, although they usually disguise themselves as legally more unambiguously protectable values or interests. For instance, prostitution is not a crime. But in case of its administrative regulation—*e.g.*, confinement to a place—the morally motivated objection of the neighbourhood is usually taken into consideration, even if not explicitly. In these cases it is acknowledged that the "neighbourhood deteriorates," but it is not stated why—only the *fact* is noted that the value of flats decreases.

3. The Constitution has broken with the "official" ideology, which was made the foundation of the State, and also with that rights had to be interpreted in harmony with it. By Act XL/1990 amending the Constitution, the last reference to ideologies and values formulated separately—independently of fundamental rights—was dismissed. Constitutional

interpretation has to start from the notion of rights, as a neutral category, the boundaries of which are consensually fixed, but as for its content, there are several concepts with different value contents. The essence of a pluralistic society includes the fact that rights can be realized with different value contents, while the whole constitutional system of rights remains coherent and operative. The Constitutional Court has to intervene in borderline cases and in situations when incompatible concepts clash and has to draw the line beyond which a certain substantial interpretation cannot be harmonized with the system of constitutional rights. The Constitutional Court in the course of this interpretation does not start from the presumed general value structure of the Constitution but expounds the value contents explicable from individual fundamental rights. For interpreting individual fundamental rights, there is comprehensive, comparative international case law and theoretical opinions at hand so that there is no need to turn to directly ideological or political arguments. Constitutional interpretation of such methodology is protected from the direct enforcement of ideologies by emphasizing formal guarantees, and the elaboration on the value content of individual rights provides protection against the abuse of positivism.

The Constitutional Court does not review the content of public morals enforced in law. As the Court basically made it over to legislation to define "public interest" (*Dec. 64/1993 (XII.22) AB:* MK 1993/184 at 11079; ABH 1993, 373 at 382), enforcing public order as well as morals is the right of representatives—until, for other reasons, they come up against the boundaries of the Constitution. These boundaries have to be defined according to the above method so that an independent evaluation of public morals preferably does not occur.

The relationship between persons of the same sex—in its durable and publicly assumed form and confined to certain aspects of life—was recognized to be protected by legal instruments by the Constitutional Court itself, *not because* the relationship was homosexual but because the relationship is such that similar cases are elsewhere recognized by the law and the differentiation had no basis (*Dec. 14/1995 (III.13) AB:* MK 1995/20; ABH 1995, 82). In the course of the so far single judgment on homosexuality, the Constitutional Court remained on a neutral path, disregarding the evaluation of public morals. This neutrality is possible in the course of interpretation carried out for the present case—in spite of the fact that the Constitution explicitly gives a right to protect the proper physical, mental and moral development of the child. There is no reason in the present case for the Constitutional Court to confine itself to certain questions of sexual morals instead of the protection of the child's personality development as a whole. What is more, in the present case the Constitutional Court does not even consider the problem of homosexuality to be a question of sexual morals—although it is generally regarded as such in the public opinion.

4. The causes, the development and what is more the notion of homosexuality are ambiguous or controversial; even in terms of self-definition there are several and contradictory views. One extreme view is that homosexuality is an innate and unchangeable bent, as a "third gender," and according to the other extreme homosexuality is a "social construction"; it does not differ from heterosexual behaviour, and thus this trend rejects as "stigmatization" all forms of differentiation/discrimination and actually even the problematization of homosexuality. An in-between view is the (outdated) illness theory, according to which one can recover from homosexuality, but obviously it cannot be punished. The "neutral" approach, which views all differentiation/discrimination according to sexual orientation as unfounded, is not extreme either. There are also differences among the views according to whether homosexuality is merely a sexual preference or the basis of self-identity and fur-

thermore, in connection with this, whether it is a lifestyle, a peculiar culture. (It is in the latter sense that certain groups in Hungary reject the term "homosexual" for its overemphasis on sexuality, while they are—as they call themselves—*melegek* ["gay"] as regards their whole personality.) Different claims accompany the different theories—*e.g.,* the recognition merely of different and undisturbed sexual behaviour and, on the other extreme, overthrowing the power conditions of the bipolar heterosexual world.

The very boundaries of homosexuality are blurred as well. A gradual transition is presumed today between "clear" heterosexuality and homosexuality. Several forms of interest in and affection for the other or the same sex can pertain to the same person with different intensities, and it depends on innumerable individual and social factors which of these one expresses. From fantasies to hidden affection and bisexuality, and the different types of homosexual behaviour, the scale of behaviour is gradual and not necessarily finite. It is of significance for the Constitutional Court that individual decision plays an important role in homosexual behaviour. Also it depends on decision how one relates to his/her homosexuality, *e.g.,* how much publicity one gives to it, whether one wants to remain hidden, living undisturbed with his/her affections in his/her private life, or wants militantly to go public.

The different interpretations of homosexuality pose different legal requirements. The human rights approach goes best with the "neutral otherness" theory: without evaluating homosexuality it can be determined that in many respects discrimination is unjustified on the basis of constitutional tests. The usual (constitutional) court cases involve denying jobs (especially in schools) to homosexuals and discrimination in flat renting. It is more difficult to avoid the evaluation of homosexuality in the case of restricting the parental rights of the homosexual parent and in examining restrictive adoption cases. The most difficult is criminal law.

That is: discrimination according to sex (sexual role) is indeed impermissible where sexual role is indifferent to the essence of the relation in question, or at least it does not have a constitutionally justifiable weight. But in the case where exactly this gives the essence of the relation in question, it is very difficult to avoid taking a position on homosexuality by some other kind of argumentation. The dream of certain homosexuals to achieve the entirety of their rights, while there is not a word about what they are, is not realizable in these cases. The recognition of the rights of homosexuals (where it is necessary as such) will always reinforce their separateness.

V

1. The Constitutional Court does not qualify homosexuality from a moral point of view. In the present case, however, it cannot disregard either the peculiarities of homosexuality or the current social situation of homosexuals.

The peculiarities of homosexuality cannot be evaded in the present case since in the relations in question the sexual role is not necessarily irrelevant. From among the above listed characteristics of homosexuality for the purposes of constitutional interpretation the following are decisive: the ambiguous boundaries of homosexuality, the many kinds of homosexual roles (both in terms of self-definition and in terms of social representation) and the personal decision about assuming a given role.

Publicly assuming homosexuality, of any kind, is an existentially decisive decision also because of the current social reception of homosexuality by contemporary Hungarian society; there is much to be assumed, and later any change is difficult. The Constitutional

Court does not qualify the problems of homosexuals in terms of social adaptation, acceptance and discrimination—which the homosexuals themselves feel and experience to be more weighty than the objectively measurable social judgment—but takes them into consideration as facts while assessing the weight of the decision of the child.

The Constitution protects primarily not that decision of the child of becoming or not becoming a homosexual, but that he/she can decide with full knowledge of the possibilities and the consequences about how to relate to his/her discovered affections and which role to chose from among the many possibilities. This is the interpretation in harmony with the value content of Art. 67 of the Constitution.

The Constitutional Court thus does not interpret the Constitution to say that the possibility of becoming homosexual would endanger the "moral development" of the child (Art. 67) because the Court cannot form a moral judgment about homosexuality on the basis of the Constitution. But it is harmful for the development of the whole personality (physical, mental, moral) and decisively affects the future of the child if he/she comes onto a path with no alternatives because of the lack of maturity necessary for decision making in such vital questions. The State cannot expose the child to the risk of immature decision for two reasons. Neither of these reasons is related to homosexuality solely.

Psychosexual development is a long process in which premature effects might be seriously harmful; those effects also belong here to which the child cannot adequately relate because of the lack of necessary maturity. Thus the law protects this development even in the private sphere by criminal law sanctions (see sexual intercourse with minors) and can assist it in the public sphere with further limits (for instance, the protection of the child from pornography).

Certain decisions have such consequences for social status that the law sets an age limit. In some of these decisions one assumes a legal status (marriage, change of sex) and the effect of others amounts to the assumption of a certain status (becoming sterile, publicly assuming homosexuality). These roles and/or legal statuses require above all the maturity necessary to bear the consequences, and thus the age limits are always higher than the age of maturity necessary for a sexual role. The development of homosexual identity and coming out, as a path of psychosexual development, itself receives protection (counselling, protection against violence, keeping alternatives open). But the law can set a higher age limit here too for coming out publicly with the role (where the law has a possibility for this—*e.g.*, in regulating membership in associations), because a different kind of maturity is necessary for evaluating the social consequences of the many kinds of homosexual roles.

There is a difference between heterosexual development and homosexual coming out. Homosexual affections (in our society) have to be realized explicitly and accepted by the person, and it depends on him/her as to what extent he/she wants to come out with it. The development of heterosexuals "works on its own" (that is, "naturally"); self-reflection during puberty has to handle the problems within the male or female roles and is not about the roles themselves as optional identities. If somebody has problems in terms of the latter, he/she might become homosexual.

2. On the basis of the above the membership of children can in principle be restricted in homosexual associations on the basis of Art. 67 of the Constitution. But the actual restriction on the right of association has to adjust to the concrete risk endangering the child's development. Legislation or the court deciding on the membership of the child has to consider the age and the nature of the association together and mutually.

First, that age has to be determined by the court at which sexual orientation is usually fixed in Hungary. The age limit necessary for publicly assuming a role—depending on the nature of the association—can be set higher.

It might prove helpful for a minor under 18 years of age struggling with homosexuality if he/she can find company in a regular framework where there are people with similar problems and where he/she can receive psychological, medical or legal counselling if need be.

But an association of adult, practising homosexuals, one which is a part of the homosexual subculture, is different. In this context—completely excluding the criminal law aspect—there is an increased possibility that a minor whose homosexuality has not yet been fixed and who has not chosen a role excludes his/her options by a premature decision.

And, finally, associations that are active towards society, fighting for the rights of homosexuals, demonstrating their presence, represent separateness and a kind of homosexuality that is to be assumed by the whole of the personality. Participation in such an association presses the minor to take a final decision. Not only among minors in their puberty but even among adults homosexual affections are not unambiguous and exclusive. A "campaigning" association does not allow the possibility that a person does not differ completely with the whole of his/her personality from the world of two sexes, that a person chooses to remain hidden or lives a "double" life as a bisexual. Membership of children in such associations is the most problematic since this constitutes the most public commitment, and thus there is hardly any way back from there or any possibility for different roles.

3. The petition questions the constitutionality of restricting the child's *membership* in associations related to homosexuality. The argumentation of the Constitutional Court rests on the affected person's own relation to his/her homosexuality, the choice of roles, and the weight of the decision's consequences. It is a question whether on the basis of these arguments one can make a difference between homosexual or potentially homosexual minors and between children for whom the question of choosing to be a homosexual does not even come up and who would join an association aimed at the protection of homosexual rights out of a pure human rights' motivation.

The second argument expounded above for restricting the public activity of the child in a homosexual association—the immaturity of the child to evaluate the social consequences of publicly taking a position on questions of homosexuality and responsibly to decide—is valid irrespective of the direction of the minor's psychosexual development. This component of the risk is the same since the public will not differentiate among members. Such a differentiation actually would be impossible technically and also because of transitions. The participation of children in public social discourse could be restricted in other cases—not only in questions of sexual roles or sexual morals—and also in the absence of being personally affected.

The first argument of restriction—the protection of mature decision about how to relate to his/her own homosexuality—does not, of course, apply to the minor motivated solely by rights protection. The necessity of restricting the right of association, which was founded by the interest of homosexual or potentially homosexual minors, also extends to them. They have to go along with the age limit exactly in the interest of minors of the same age group which is to be protected, for setting an age limit for membership primarily protects the responsible and mature decision of those who will bear the consequences of their decisions for their entire lives.

DECISION 22/1996: 25 JUNE 1996

ON COMPENSATION FOR PAST INJUSTICES

The Compensation Act of 1992, which provided for damages for loss of life and wrongful arrest, was reviewed on the basis of hundreds of applications in 1995 and found in many respects discriminatory and therefore unconstitutional. Before passing the profoundly amended Act, the Human Rights Standing Committee of Parliament asked for preliminary review. The legislature had satisfied all the demands of the first Constitutional Court decision—these could be followed in the present decision, too. During the debate in Parliament, however, a new question was raised with extraordinary vehemence: whether the groups of injured who had been deported by the Nazis might be treated equally with those deported by the Soviets into gulags or forced labor camps. In accordance with its practice from the beginning (23/1990), the Constitutional Court stressed here the equal dignity of all human beings. The Court not only held the equal treatment of these groups constitutional but noted that there would be no constitutional way to make any distinction according to whether the loss of life had been caused by fascist or communist regimes or according to different ideologies.

The Parliamentary Standing Committee on Human Rights petitioned for preliminary review of the text of a bill before the final vote.

Act XXXII/1992 (the third Compensation Act) regulated the question of compensation for those wrongfully deprived of their lives and liberty for political reasons. The purpose of the Act was to compensate not for property losses or material damage (as had been the aim of previous compensation statutes) but rather for personal injury and loss of life which had occurred under different political regimes. Broadly speaking, one regime had perpetrated such violations on the grounds of racism and nationalism while the subsequent regime followed mostly ideological and political motives.

The Act provided, inter alia, under (a) s. 2, that a one-time compensation of HUF 1 million was to be made to those entitled according to the Act; and (b), s. 3(1), that (i) deportation by either regime was to be regarded as a form of deprivation of liberty, along the lines of unlawful imprisonment, unlawful pre-trial detention, unlawfully imposed forced medical treatment, forced labour, *etc.*, and that the criteria for compensation with respect to these violations of the law were identical; and (ii) the possibility of compensation was restricted to those whose rights had been arbitrarily violated in connection with a formal criminal procedure together with the relatives of those who became victims of crimes for which the State could have been made civilly liable.

These provisions were challenged as unconstitutional on the grounds, inter alia, that they specified in an arbitrary and discriminatory way those who were entitled to compensation, for instance, those killed by Hungarian authorities without any formal judicial procedure, *e.g.*, shot or killed in forced labour camps, were excluded from compensation.

In its decision (*Dec. 1/1995 (II.8) AB:* MK 1995/10; ABH 1995, 31), the Court ruled that the principles underlying the Act were, in general, constitutional: the type of compensation provided through the Act was not based on a legal obligation emanating from the time before the transition. The Government compensated according to equity, and thus no one had an entitlement to compensation.

The Court found, however, an unconstitutional omission to legislate: Act XXXII/1992 provided for an additional Act, which would cover those persons who had not fallen under the previous Compensation Acts. The failure of the Government to comply with this obligation created an unconstitutional discrimination to the detriment of those who had not fallen within the compensation statute, in particular, persons who had been killed without any formal judicial procedure were excluded from compensation, as were their relatives.

Further the provisions of the Act concerning deportation were unconstitutional. During the Second World War, "deportation" to Germany or to the Soviet Union had meant far more than deprivation of liberty. It had amounted to expulsion from the country by force when Hungarian authorities, on racial, religious or political grounds, handed their own citizens to authorities of foreign powers who had them carried off to concentration camps. Leaving these historical circumstances out of consideration violated the constitutional requirement of treating everybody with equal dignity. Deported people formed a clearly defined, specific group that the legislature was bound to respect.

The legislature was therefore obliged to rectify its constitutional omission by passing a further compensation statute before the end of September 1995. This obligation could be met by amending Act XXXII/1992 in the light of the Decision.

The amending legislation in its bill stage provided, inter alia, that (i) by cl. 1, s. 2/A of the Act would include a provision granting one-time compensation to the relatives of those who lost their lives as a result of politically motivated arbitrary conduct of Hungarian authorities or officials but, by virtue of s. 3 of the Act, would not apply to death which had occurred during imprisonment; (ii) by cl. 2, s. 2/B(1) of the Act would define a separate criterion for eligibility for compensation, *viz.,* deportation abroad during the Second World War on racial, religious or political grounds; (iii) by cl. 2, s. 2/C of the Act would define separate rules of compensation for forced labour in the Soviet Union; (iv) by cl. 3, s. 3(1) of the Act would, for the purposes of compensation, put into the same group people whose personal liberty was violated due to internment, forced labour, public security custody, forced resettlement and labour, *i.e.,* outside criminal proceedings; and (v) compensation to the groups of persons entitled, as provided for in ss. 2/A, 2/B and 2/C of the Act, would amount to HUF 300,000, with those deported or carried off to forced labour receiving increased amounts calculated on the basis of the deprivation of liberty.

After the text of the amending legislation had been finalized, but before voting on it, the Standing Committee on Human Rights sought a preliminary review of the Bill on the grounds that it infringed the constitutional prohibition of discrimination ("equal protection clause") as well as the right to equal dignity under Art. 70/A of the Constitution. The Committee submitted, inter alia, that (a) under the same criteria for compensation, the Bill differentiated between the groups entitled on the basis of Nazi deportation and Soviet forced labour; (b) the difference between compensation under s. 2 of HUF 1 million and that introduced by the Bill (under ss. 2/A, 2/B and 2/C) of HUF 300,000 was unconstitutional; and (c) it was also unconstitutional for s. 2/A(1), in cl. 1 of the Bill, to exclude one-time compensation from cases under s. 3(1) if the loss of life resulted from arbitrary conduct and was not covered by s. 2.

Held, granting the petition:

(1) The Court had jurisdiction to review the constitutionality of the bill. Adjudicating

upon the constitutionality of the provisions of a pending bill, the text of which was not definitive, would mean the possibility of the Court becoming involved in the everyday legislative process by being required to choose from among several options. This was the task of the legislature, and any interference in this process on the part of the Court would be incompatible with the principle of the separation of powers. However, in the present case, the Court was able to accept jurisdiction since the legislature had already finalized the text of the bill and had excluded the possibility of any further changes.

(2) Although the legislature had redressed some of its previous omissions by creating new groups of persons entitled to compensation, *e.g.*, by granting one-time compensation for relatives of those who lost their lives as a result of the politically motivated arbitrariness of the authorities, the introduction of s. 2/A(1) would unconstitutionally exclude certain people therefrom. By a reading of ss. 2, 2/A(1) and 3(1) of the Act, persons who lost their lives because of politically motivated arbitrary acts of a Hungarian official or authorities during the restriction of their personal liberty (*i.e.*, outside a criminal procedure) were denied compensation. Since the most important constitutional consideration in the implementation of personal compensation was equal treatment (Art. 70/A(1), together with respect for the equal dignity of persons in Art. 54), which was characterized by distributive justice, from the perspective of equal treatment the persons in question had a constitutional right to be treated equally by the legal provisions and they should be considered with equal care and fairness. Consequently, the loss of life as a result of arbitrariness of the authorities during unlawful imprisonment outside a criminal procedure established for the relatives of the entitled a constitutional claim for compensation to the same extent as for loss of life due to such arbitrariness in a criminal procedure.

(3) Moreover, the legislature had also rectified its omission with respect to those deported by the Nazis to Germany or carried off to forced labour in the Soviet Union. Since the criteria of the Bill for creating the latter two categories remained within the constitutional limits defined by the rule on the distribution of rights as well as the principle of the prohibition of discrimination in Art. 70/A, it was constitutional for the Bill to divide the groups of beneficiaries on the basis of deportation and forced labour while attaching the same legal consequences as regards compensation.

(4) It was unconstitutional, however, if the amount of compensation for those deprived of their lives was substantially unequal for different groups of people. The Bill had established substantially different standards for similar grievances, *viz.*, the loss of life. Loss of life was so serious a grievance that it absorbed all previous injustices. It would be arbitrary and at the same time would violate human dignity to differentiate among the diverse ways of losing life, whether in a Nazi death camp, a Soviet gulag or the cellars of the State Defence Authority. It was thus unconsitutional that the amount of compensation to be awarded in cases falling within s. 2 of the Act was substantially greater than that proposed in the new ss. 2/A, 2/B and 2/C.

(5) If, as a result of this change, the legislature was required to enlarge substantially the range of persons entitled to compensation (because of the stated constitutional requirements), it would remain constitutional to redistribute the overall amount designated for such compensation. In maintaining proportionality, the share in the compensation of

all groups of beneficiaries could be changed as appropriate. In this way, the amount of compensation due on the basis of the same suffered wrong for each individual would be reduced in comparison to the originally declared figure in s. 2 of the Act. Such redistribution did not affect compensation already paid out in accordance with the previous provisions.

IN THE NAME OF THE REPUBLIC OF HUNGARY!

In the matter of the petition seeking the preliminary review of certain provisions of a Bill, the Constitutional Court made the following

DECISION.

The Constitutional Court declares in relation to certain provisions of Bill No. 1268 amending Act XXXII/1992 on the Compensation of Those Illegally Deprived of Life and Liberty for Political Reasons:

1. It is not unconstitutional that the Bill defines compensation for deportation and for being carried off for Soviet forced labour as different categories. The provisions of the Bill attaching to these wrongs the same legal consequences in terms of compensation are not in conflict with the constitutional prohibition of discrimination either.

2. With the introduction of the provision into s. 2/A of the Act by cl. 1 of the Bill the legislature terminates the unconstitutionality resulting from omission and fulfills its constitutional duty to legislate by granting a one-time compensation for the relatives of those who lost their lives as a result of politically motivated arbitrary acts of Hungarian authorities or officials.

3. It is unconstitutional that the amount of compensation stipulated in s. 2 of the Act differs substantially from that in ss. 2/A, 2/B and 2/C. It is a constitutional requirement that in the cases of ss. 2, 2/A, 2/B, and 2/C similar groups of beneficiaries shall be compensated to a similar extent for wrongs defined on similar grounds, as also for the loss of life. Minor differences resulting from calculation methods and from the historical genesis of the regulation are not unconstitutional.

4. The provision in s. 2/A(1) of the Act introduced by cl. 1 of the Bill, according to which the rule concerning one-time compensation cannot be applied to cases of deprivation of freedom falling under s. 3 (1) if the loss of life was a result of politically motivated arbitrary acts of Hungarian authorities or officials and it does not fall under s. 2, is also contrary to the constitutional requirement of everyone being treated as a person of equal dignity under Art. 70/A of the Constitution.

5. In the cases of loss of life defined in Point 3, the beneficiaries shall be determined in the same manner.

6. Should it be necessary to enlarge substantially—to its multiple or in its order—the group of the persons to be compensated in order to ensure compliance of the Act with the constitutional requirements, it is not contrary to the Constitution if the legislature redefines and redistributes the total amount destined to the compensation and as a result the amount due on the basis of the same wrong suffered substantially decreases compared to what has been originally stipulated. With a view to maintaining proportionality in such cases, the share in the compensation of all groups of beneficiaries can be changed as is appropriate.

The redistribution does not affect compensation already paid in accordance with the previous regulations.

The Constitutional Court refuses to examine the petitions stemming from persons not entitled to submit such petitions.

The Constitutional Court publishes this Decision in the *Hungarian Official Gazette.*

REASONING

LÁBADY, J., and **SÓLYOM, P.,** delivering the Opinion of the Court: [....]

V

[....] 1. The Bill, by defining the conditions of eligibility for compensation of those deported during the Second World War for racial, religious or political reasons, as well as of those carried away for forced labour to the Soviet Union, and their relatives, separately from the beneficiaries of the compensation for the loss of life and from those compensated for the different deprivation of liberty, creating separate groups of beneficiaries, meets the constitutional requirement that the legislature, in defining eligibility for compensation, has to determine the criteria for eligibility uniformly, according to characteristics that are identical and most typical of a group and in a manner respecting the equal dignity of persons. According to the regulation in s. 3(1)(b) and (e) of the original third Compensation Act—which has been declared unconstitutional—deportation abroad during the Second World War for racial, religious or political reasons and forced labour for which people were carried off by Soviet authorities are qualified as a serious violation of personal liberty exceeding thirty days. The Act, in respect of compensation, put these violations in the same category with the imposition of unlawful imprisonment, unlawful pre-trial detention, and all other unlawful deprivations of liberty, unlawfully imposed forced medical treatment, forced labour, *etc.,* and defined the criteria for compensation to be identical with these latter violations of the law.

According to the decision of the Constitutional Court [*Dec. 1/1995 (II.8) AB:* MK 1995/10; ABH 1995, 31], the legislature, in defining eligibility for compensation, did not consider with proper circumspection and care the viewpoints of those deported when it qualified deportation as mere deprivation of liberty. The Court stated that historically what deportation during the Second World War meant was a violent carrying off of people in large numbers usually to concentration camps, in the course of which the Hungarian State gathered its own citizens and gave them up under a foreign sovereign's authority (MK 1995/10 at 560; ABH 1995, 31 at 56).

It is thus a constitutional requirement that the legislature should take these specific aspects and historical facts of deportation into consideration and should not identify deportation with mere deprivation of liberty, because by creating homogeneous groups despite divergent characteristics the legislature violates the constitutional requirement of respecting the equal dignity of persons and thereby accomplishes an act of unconstitutional discrimination [Art. 70/A(1) of the Constitution].

The Bill properly meets these constitutional requirements by creating further homogeneous groups. The provision in cl. 2 of the Bill, supplementing the third Compensation Act with s. 2/B(1), provides a separate eligibility for compensation for deportation abroad during the Second World War because of racial, religious or political reasons. Since, according to s. 2/B(2), violations defined in s. 2/B(1) are to be compensated for to a greater extent than the deprivation of liberty, the Bill fulfills the constitutional requirement that follows from the constitutional rule of the distribution of rights and the principle of the prohibition of discrimination, according to which the legislature has to consider from different perspectives the viewpoints of those who suffered different violations under different circumstances. [....]

2. According to the decision of the Constitutional Court [*Dec. 1/1995 (II.8) AB*], the considerations and characteristics related to the deported basically apply to the cases of those carried off for forced labour to the Soviet Union, and the Constitutional Court therefore declared s. 3(1) of the third Compensation Act unconstitutional and null and void (MK 1995/10 at 560; ABH 1995, 31 at 56). The Court also declared that the legislature, at the latest in the course of enacting the new Act on compensation, has to create new provisions that meet the constitutional requirements instead of those declared null and void and that would retroactively settle entitlement to compensation for the particular group of persons carried away for forced labour.

The Bill fulfills this constitutional requirement inasmuch as its cl. 2 amends the third Compensation Act with the provisions of s. 2/C and defines separate rules of compensation for forced labour in the Soviet Union.

These rules of compensation are basically identical to the provisions on compensation for deportation during the Second World War as to the extent and conditions of compensation; but the Bill—by addressing the beneficiaries in the separate parts—puts those entitled to this type of compensation into separate groups. Since the criteria for creating the groups are within constitutional limits, it is not against the Constitution that the Bill—under the same criteria of compensation—divides the groups of beneficiaries on the basis of deportation and forced labour. [....]

3. Section 2/A(l) of the Act, introduced by cl. 1 of the Bill, creates a new basis of entitlement for compensation—and thus a new group of beneficiaries—by granting one-time compensation for the relatives of those who lost their lives as a result of the politically motivated arbitrary acts of a Hungarian authority or official. [....]

In connection with this regulation, the Constitutional Court found the legislation in unconstitutional omission and also that it is arbitrary and thus unconstitutional to set the condition—that the State failed to prosecute the perpetrators of the crime—for bringing a civil law claim because of personal injuries suffered as a victim of those crimes (*Dec. 1/1995 (II.8) AB:* MK 1995/10; ABH 1995, 31).

Although the Constitutional Court has stated that the group of people who suffered personal injuries in the previous regimes is basically undefinable, unassessable since practically anyone who lived in Hungary during the previous regimes might have suffered material or merely personal injuries (*Dec. 28/1991 (VI.3) AB:* MK 1991/59 at 1095–96; ABH 1991, 88 at 96–97), in its decision, which forms the basis of the current case, the Court also stated that the legislature is in unconstitutional omission because the third Compensation Act does not grant eligibility for compensation to a group of beneficiaries defined in the Preamble and s. 1 of the Act. The group consists of people who suffered personal injuries as victims of state arbitrariness outside a criminal procedure. According to the decision, the constitutional requirement of respect for the equal dignity of persons and the prohibition of discrimination in Art. 70/A(1) of the Constitution compellingly requires that the legislature—according to its obligation assumed in the Act—orders the compensation of these victims too.

The last part of s. 2/A(1) of the Act, introduced by cl. 1 of the Bill, contains a restriction on the group of beneficiaries who lost their lives due to the politically motivated arbitrary acts of a Hungarian authority or an official that is constitutionally unjustifiable and violates the constitutional requirement of equal treatment. According to this, the provision cannot be applied when the death occurred, for any reason, during imprisonment (s. 3).

Section 3(1) of the third Compensation Act, to be amended by the Bill, puts, for the purposes of granting entitlement to compensation, in the same group those who suffered grave injuries violating personal liberty exceeding 30 days, whereas these injuries can only in certain cases be attributed to the disfunctional operation of the administration of justice. Those groups of beneficiaries listed in s. 3(1)(b) and (c) whose personal liberty was restricted in the course of the execution of internment, forced labour, public security custody, forced resettlement and labour service based on a public administrative decision—that is, outside a criminal procedure—do not meet or only partly meet the latter qualification. Those persons who lost their lives because of politically motivated arbitrary acts of a Hungarian official in the course of or during the restriction of their personal liberty described above, due to this excluding provision, do not fall under s. 2/A(l) and cannot be grouped with those receiving one-time compensation under s. 2. The loss of life as a result of arbitrariness of the authorities during an unlawful imprisonment or loss of liberty outside a criminal procedure establishes for the relatives of the entitled a claim for compensation, the extent of which should be as large as the compensation for the politically motivated arbitrary acts of an authority or official in a criminal procedure. This follows from the provisions of the Constitution requiring equal treatment and respect for persons of equal dignity (Arts. 70/A (1) and 54 of the Constitution), thus exclusion of these beneficiaries from one-time compensation is arbitrary, and thus unconstitutional.

Since the most important constitutional consideration in the implementation of personal compensation is equal treatment, which is characterized by distributive justice (*Dec. 15/1993 (III.12) AB:* MK 1993/29 at 1571; ABH 1993, 112 at 120), from the point of view of equal treatment, the persons in question have a constitutional right to be treated equally by law and the viewpoints of each of them are to be considered with equal care and fairness. Thus, in determining the group of those receiving one-time compensation, the legislature cannot disregard the viewpoints of those who lost their lives, albeit outside a criminal procedure but undoubtedly because of the intentional act of a Hungarian authority (or official) during an unlawful imprisonment (in labour camps, during forced labour in Hungary, in ghettos in Hungary, during labour service, *etc.*). [....]

4. With respect to the loss of life, the constitutionality of creating groups of beneficiaries cannot be connected with the question of the extent of compensation.

In creating groups, the law determines the conditions of eligibility as well as the extent of compensation and delineates the groups eligible for compensation. The substantial basis for creating these groups is the difference in injuries. Since in Hungarian law compensation—in all previous versions—was based on fairness instead of the liability of the State (and the ex gratia compensation absorbed all possible responsibility-based claims), it is even more justifed that all differentiation in compensation has to adjust to the result, the caused and suffered injury.

Although deprivation of liberty can in general be conceived of as one type of injury, there have been so many different typical modes of captivity in respect of the severity of the injury and the extent of suffering that it renders it not only permissible but constitutionally required that the compensation be different. This was the result of the previous constitutional review of the third Compensation Act.

When, however, captivity caused death, the finality and absolute weight of this "result" minimizes the significance of the difference in injuries and suffering preceding death. This loss absorbs all previous injuries.

From a theoretical point of view, departing from the capital punishment and abortion decisions of the Constitutional Court, the absolute nature of the right to life makes the different appreciation of the loss of life impossible in a system of compensation based not on responsibility but on caused injuries. "The right to equal dignity in unity with the right to life secures that there can be no differences made among the value of human lives" (*Dec. 64/1991 (XII.17) AB:* MK 1991/139 at 2815; ABH 1991, 297 at 309).

Considering the equally immeasurable value of the lives of the deceased, there can be no differentiation made as regards the actual circumstances of their deaths or the ideological commitment of the regimes by which they were killed.

Thus there is no need and—in a system of compensation based on the injuries caused—no legal possibility for a comparison, which is anyhow inexecutable and contradicts human dignity, that different kinds of compensation would be given for death in a Nazi death camp, a Soviet gulag or in the cellar of the AVH [State Defence Authority in Hungary].

If the law grants compensation for the relatives of those who lost their lives, this does not express the worth of life but eases the relatives' loss. With respect to the aim of the process of compensation, after forty years it is especially impossible to differentiate between the pain of the relatives and the possibilities for easing that pain on the basis of how we legally qualify the unlawful circumstances of the injured person's death.

Constitutional objections arise not in case the Bill equalizes the deported and those carried off for Soviet forced labour but if it does not grant equal compensation for the loss of life. [....]

5. [...] (c) The elements of the rules for the four types of compensation for the "loss of life" form a consistent group not only from the perspective of the injuries but also with regard to the contribution of the State or an official person in the incurring of death. There are no constitutional reasons for there to be significant differences within this group in the degree of compensation for the loss of life. Therefore it is unconstitutional that the compensation prescribed in s. 2 is many times greater than that granted in ss. 2/(A), 2/(B) and 2/(C). (At HUF 1 million as opposed to HUF 300,000; in the case of the deported and those carried off for forced labour this benefit increased with the amount calculated for deprivation of liberty.) [....]

Constitutionality requires that for injuries defined on a similar basis in ss. 2, 2/(A), 2/(B) and 2/(C) as also for the loss of life, a similar amount of compensation should be given. Minor differences resulting from calculation methods and from the historical genesis of the provisions are not unconstitutional. [....]

6. The Parliament can remedy the unconstitutionality of the Bill by considering the following.

(a) The legislature was not bound to grant compensation to those who had been deprived of life and liberty. It depends on its decision as to whether or not to give it and on how much money to set aside for this purpose. For the loss of life the legislature from the beginning intended to give a compensation of HUF 1 million. The third Compensation Act attempted to harmonize this amount with the financial endurance of the State by narrowing the group of those to be compensated for the loss of life. The legislature considered the group of those who lost their lives during a criminal procedure to be both small and definable enough to grant compensation to them for the loss of their lives. Together with this, the relatives of those were to be compensated who became the victims of crimes for which the State could have been made liable under civil law. This group of beneficiaries was likewise narrow in the original conception: according to legislative intent the group would have consisted of those deprived of life during the suppression of the 1956 Revolution and Freedom Fight.

The decision of the Constitutional Court on the one hand broadened the group to be compensated and on the other hand required a larger amount of compensation for certain groups. The group increased in number by the inclusion of all those who paid labour service and by the establishment of entitlement to compensation for the victims of arbitrariness of the authorities (well exceeding the original intent of s. 20). (See Points 2, 3 and 5 of *Dec. 1/1995 (II.8) AB.*) In the case of the deported and those carried off for forced labour the obligation of creating a new group self-evidently required the granting of a higher amount of compensation than for the mere deprivation of liberty (*Dec. 1/1995 (II.8) AB:* MK 1995/10 at 560; ABH 1995, 31 at 57).

As for the future regulation of compensation for the deported, those carried off for forced labour abroad and the victims of arbitrariness of the authorities, the Constitutional Court did not state further detailed requirements, and especially did not deal with the amount of money but stressed the liberty of the legislature in designing the new solutions (*Dec. 1/1995 (II.8) AB:* MK 1995/10 at 560; ABH 1995, 31 at 57). Point 1 of the decision, however, stated the constitutional requirement that "the legislation, in defining eligibility for compensation, has to determine the criteria for eligibility uniformly, according to characteristics that are identical and most typical of the group and in a manner respecting the equal dignity of persons."

(b) From the constitutional requirement that in the homogeneous group to be compensated for the loss of life each has to receive a similar amount of compensation it does not follow that the only constitutional solution is to give to everyone the amount of compensation originally defined for a narrower group, *i.e.,* HUF 1 million. There is no constitutional requirement in this regard. If the group of those to be compensated has to be broadened because of constitutional concerns, Parliament can define anew and distribute the amount of money set aside for this purpose. [....]

(c) It is no problem of constitutionality if the legislature defines the amount of money to be used towards compensation in harmony with the financial endurance of the country and other financial responsibilities and tasks. With regard to this framework, the amount of compensation granted to individual persons naturally depends on the supposed number of beneficiaries.

Should it be necessary to enlarge substantially—to its multiple or in its order—the group of the persons to be compensated in order to ensure compliance of the Act with the constitutional requirements, it is not contrary to the Constitution if the legislature redefines and redistributes the total amount destined to the compensation and, as a result, the amount due on the basis of the same wrong suffered substantially decreases compared to what has been originally stipulated. With a view to maintaining proportionality in such cases, the share in the compensation of all groups of beneficiaries can be changed as it is appropriate.

Redistribution does not, naturally, affect compensation paid in accordance with previous provisions: as concluded legal relations, they remain untouched.

(d) The above self-evidently apply to those who are compensated for labour service. Constitutional requirements apply in the respect that there should be no exceptions and differences without rational reasons in the group to be compensated and in the similarity of the amount of compensation granted for the same injuries. The actual amount of compensation however is not a question of constitutionality. Thus it is not the group of those who paid labour service and are to be compensated that has to be adjusted to the funds but rather the reverse. [....]

DECISION 4/1997: 22 JANUARY 1997

ON THE REVIEW OF INTERNATIONAL TREATIES

The case decided a preliminary question to another application challenging a certain provision of the Europe Agreement between Hungary and the European Union. To this case, first the competence of the Constitutional Court was to be established for ex post facto review of international treaties. The Court held that it had the jurisdiction to examine the constitutionality of the (domestic) law promulgating an international treaty and in this case the review extended to the examination of the constitutionality of the treaty as well. This was derived from the analysis of the definition of the Court's competence in the Constitution for the "review of constitutionality of legal norms." The Court used the opportunity and in the reasons enlarged upon the meaning of this provision. It was the first occasion that the Court relied on the legislative history of the Constitution and the Constitutional Court Act. It established that the ex post facto review covered all kinds of legal norms, further that the actio popularis, *the standing of everybody, was an inevitable part of this competence. Because all political controversies on and about the Constitutional Court usually end in questioning its competences and politics regularly threatens to curtail the Court's powers, it was necessary to give an authoritative interpretation of the extent of at least the constitutionally mandated competences of the Constitutional Court.*

The petitioner sought ex post facto review of certain provisions of Act XXXII/1989 on the Constitutional Court which, in part, allegedly prevented constitutional consideration of international treaties promulgated into domestic law.

The Act provides, inter alia, by (i) s. 1(a) that the Court has jurisdiction to conduct a preliminary examination of the constitutionality of international treaties; (ii) s. 21, the Parliament, a standing committee thereof or 50 MPs, or the President of the Republic, or the Government has standing to bring s. 1(a) proceedings; (iii) s. 35(1) the President may request the review of an unpromulgated statute; and (iv) s. 36(1) the Parliament, the President or the Government may seek review of a treaty prior to ratification.

The petitioner submitted, inter alia, that (a) as citizens were not permitted preliminary review of a treaty before ratification under s. 21, the effective denial of an ex post facto review through an *actio popularis* was contrary to the principles of the sovereignty of the people and of the rule of law under Art. 2 of the Constitution; (b) this principle was likewise infringed since the Court could not review a treaty ex officio: the restriction of fundamental rights by international treaties could therefore occur, taking them beyond the control of citizens and the Court. Thus an obligation assumed under a treaty might create the possibility for a concealed amendment of the Constitution; (c) since by Art. 7(1) the Constitution stood above the provision of an international treaty promulgated by a national legal rule, it was within the Court's remit to review this domestic regulation; and (d) the restriction, limiting the right to initiate proceedings before the Court to certain political actors, was in breach of Art. 8.

Held, rejecting the petition:

(1) Restricting the exercise of the right to initiate preliminary review of constitutionality to the persons entitled in s. 21(1) of the Act was constitutional. According to Art. 32/A(1), the Court had a compulsory jurisdiction only for constitutional examination of legal provisions which concept did not include pre-ratification (thus unpromulgated) treaties. Indeed the Constitution had given the legislature discretion both to define the circle of persons entitled to initiate such proceedings and to decide upon ensuring the existence of preliminary constitutional review. The general standing to commence proceedings before the Court (*actio popularis*) was a basic constitutional right under Art. 32/A which did not include preliminary review. Further it could not be derived from the principles of the sovereignty of the people or the rule of law that this realization would be the precondition (concerning preliminary review of treaties) of guaranteeing for every citizen the right to commence proceedings before the Court. Further, a constitutional command for an ex officio procedure did not derive from Arts. 2, 7 or 32/A in any of the Court's competences.

(2) According to s. 1(b) of the Act, the Court had jurisdiction to review the constitutionality of a law promulgating an international treaty, which included examination of such treaty. The Court derived only one function from the Constitution, *viz.,* ex post facto review, which was mandatory and, from the historical perspective of its drafting (and that of the Act), universal. The decisions of the Court in which it interpreted its own jurisdiction were binding on everyone, as with any other decision, including one made on the basis of the competence achieved by that interpretation. Moreover, by examining the constitutionality of international treaties, its constitutional task remained within the limits of ex post facto review: thus the examination of the harmony between the treaty and the Constitution did not interfere with the functions and jurisdiction of the other branches of power.

(3) The constitutional requirement for the examination of the constitutionality of international treaties derived from Arts. 7(1) and 32/A. There was no constitutional basis under which to deal with a law promulgating a treaty differently from any other legal rule when it came to constitutional review. Since it was derived from the Constitution that ex post facto review was to cover all kinds of legal rule, this universality could not be restricted even by statute. In this way the examination of international treaties, after they became part of domestic law, fit into the logic of constitutional review. In those countries where this review process was universal and no specific reference was made to review of international treaties, constitutitonal courts reviewed the latter on the same basis as domestic law.

(4) As a result of the foregoing, were the Court to hold an international treaty or provision thereof unconstitutional, it would declare the unconstitutionality of the domestic law promulgating the treaty. Such a decision would, however, have no effect on the obligation assumed by the State under international law. Following upon such a decision the legislature would be required to harmonize the internal legal norms with Hungary's international

obligations either by annulling the unconstitutional part of the treaty or by the modification thereof or by constitutional amendment.

IN THE NAME OF THE REPUBLIC OF HUNGARY!

On the basis of a petition seeking an ex post facto review of the unconstitutionality of a legal rule, the Constitutional Court, with the dissenting opinion of Vörös, J., has made the following

DECISION.

1. The Constitutional Court declares that according to s. 1(b) of Act XXXII/1989 on the Constitutional Court, the Constitutional Court has jurisdiction to review the constitutionality of the law promulgating an international treaty.

2. The constitutional review includes the examination of unconstitutionality of the international treaty forming part of the promulgating law.

3. If the Constitutional Court holds that an international treaty or any provision of it is unconstitutional, it declares the unconstitutionality of the domestic law promulgating the international treaty.

4. The decision of the Constitutional Court declaring unconstitutionality has no effect on the obligations assumed by the Republic of Hungary under international law.

5. Following upon such a decision of the Constitutional Court the legislature is required to—if necessary, by amendment of the Constitution—achieve the harmony of domestic law and the obligations assumed under international law. Pending this process, the Constitutional Court may suspend its proceedings concerning the determination of the date of annulment of the unconstitutional legal rule for a reasonable time.

6. The Constitutional Court rejects the petition seeking the establishment of the unconstitutionality of ss. 1 (a), 21(1) and 35–36 of Act XXXII/1989 on the Constitutional Court.

7. The Constitutional Court rejects the petition seeking the ammendment of the rules on the jurisdiction of the Constitutional Court in the Act on the Constitutional Court.

The Constitutional Court publishes this Decision in the *Hungarian Official Gazette.*

REASONING

SÓLYOM, P., delivering the Opinion of the Court: [....]

II

[....]

2. The petitioner submits as unconstitutional the provision that the examination of the unconstitutionality of an international treaty prior to its ratification may only be initiated by Parliament, the President of the Republic, and the Government, and there is no *actio popularis* assuring standing to any person to initiate such constitutional review.

According to Art. 32/A(3) of the Constitution, everyone has the right to initiate proceedings before the Constitutional Court in the cases specified by statute. In respect of the *actio popularis*, it follows from the Constitution that the standing of everyone shall relate to the constitutional review defined in paras. (1) and (2) of Art. 32/A. This is a review which may result in declaring the unconstitutionality of a legal rule and its annulment, that is, an ex post facto review. The historical interpretation of Art. 32/A of the Constitution shows unambiguously that the original intent of the Constituent power was to establish popular standing for the ex post facto review.

The first drafts of the Act prepared in May 1989 by the Ministry of Justice did not provide citizens with standing for ex post facto review [reserving this right for certain state authorities, as well as interest groups such as unions]. [....] During the Roundtable talks, one of the major demands of the opposition—which was also a condition for its consent to the Bill's final text—was that every citizen should have the standing to challenge the constitutionality of legal norms, while in force, before the Constitutional Court. [....]

The other important proposal of the opposition groups at the Roundtable was that the Court's abstract norm control and the power of annulment should also extend to Acts of Parliament. The Bill of the Ministry of Justice intended that in case of unconstitutionality of an Act the Constitutional Court was to send the decision back to the Parliament, which, by discussing the decision, either agrees to it or ratifies the Act by a two-thirds majority of its Members (s. 46). In accordance with the proposal of the Opposition, the negotiating parties agreed that the Court's power of annulment extends without exception to all kinds of legal rules including specific legal instruments of state administration. [....]

The third proposal of the Opposition was the system of nomination and election of judges that is provided for in the law currently in force.

All the three modifications obtained were of such significance that the Opposition ensured they had them incorporated into the new Constitution. [....]

Two conclusions can be drawn from the legislative history of Art. 32/A of the Constitution. First of all, Art. 32/A(1) and (2) of the Constitution determine the jurisdiction of the Court incorporating the agreement reached in debates at the Roundtable related to the competence of the Constitutional Court. The incorporation into the Constitution of the rules on competence, which express the genuine characteristics of a constitutional court and its jurisdiction, is indispensable. The reason for the fact that only the most important competence of the Court was incorporated into the Hungarian Constitution may be found in the circumstances of the constitution-making process. The incorporation of other competences into the Constitution—as is generally done in the cases of recently established constitutional courts—is as important as a matter of guarantee and therefore desirable.

The other compelling conclusion to be drawn is the interpretation of Art. 32/A of the Constitution, according to which the legislature must ensure—within the framework of the abstract ex post facto review—general standing before the Constitutional Court. [....]

Thus, it is Art. 32/A of the Constitution that s. 21(2) of the Act executes, providing that the procedure under s. 1(b) may be initiated by anyone. However, it does not follow from the Constitution that the initiation of other procedures within the jurisdiction of the Constitutional Court should also be open to anyone. The Constitution does not require an *actio popularis* in cases other than the ex post facto review of laws in force. [....]

Accordingly, restricting the standing for preliminary constitutional review as set out in s. 21(1) of the Act is not unconstitutional. Further, the Constitutional Court notes that Art. 32/A(1) of the Constitution specifies as its constitutionally mandated competence only the constitutional review of legal norms. An international treaty which is not ratified is not a legal norm. Thereby the Constitution gives the legislature discretion not only in defining the conditions of standing to initiate the procedure but also in the issue of whether or not it provides for the preliminary review of the unconstitutionality at all. [....]

5. Regarding the ex post facto review of the unconstitutionality of international treaties the Constitutional Court declared in *Dec. 61/B/1992 AB* (ABH 1993, 831) that based on s. 1 of the Act the Constitutional Court does not have jurisdiction to review ex post facto international treaties which are "ratified and promulgated" in domestic law. This statement is in conflict with the previous *Dec. 30/1990 (XII.15) AB* (MK 1990/126 at 2441–42; ABH 1990, 128 at 131–32), according to which the domestic law promulgating an international treaty "as a law is not exempted from the reach of constitutional review"; therefore, based on s. 1(b) of the Act, the Constitutional Court has a competence for ex post facto review of the law promulgating an international treaty. The above-cited decision has examined on the merits the constitutionality of certain provisions of the international treaty which constituted a part of the law promulgating the treaty. [....]

[Despite the conduct of this review, in another part of] the reasoning, the Constitutional Court "shared" the views of the ministries that the Constitutional Court has no competence for ex post facto review of international treaties. The statement of the Constitutional Court in this respect is obviously inconsistent since ex post facto review, provided in s. 1(b) of the Act, cannot be divided with respect to international treaties into reviewing the treaty itself, on the one hand, and the treaty "constituting part of" the law promulgating the treaty, on the other; indeed, the Constitutional Court did not make this distinction in its decision either. Hence, upon the current petition, the Constitutional Court had to eliminate the inconsistency present in its previous decisions, and the Court had to make its position clear on the matter of constitutional jurisdiction in respect of international treaties.

Part III of the Constitutional Court's *Dec. 53/1993 (X.13) AB* (MK 1993/147 at 8795; ABH 1993, 323 at 327) contains statements relevant to the Constitutional Court's competence regarding the relationship between domestic and international law. According to this, the first sentence of Art. 7(1) of the Constitution states that "the generally recognized rules" of international law are part of Hungarian law even without separate (further) measures of transformation. Such an act of general transformation was performed by the Constitution itself. According to it, the generally recognized rules of international law are not part of the Constitution but they are "assumed obligations." The fact that the assumption and transformation is contained in the Constitution does not affect the hierarchical relationship of the Constitution, international and domestic law. This general internalization of assumed obligations absolutely does not preclude certain "generally recognized rules" from being defined by specific international agreements (as well), and regarding those a separate act of transformation takes place.

The second sentence of Art. 7(1)—the harmony of the assumed international obligations and domestic law—applies to every "assumed" international obligation, including the generally recognized rules. In addition, the harmony must be achieved for the whole of domestic law, the Constitution included. Thus, Art. 7(1) of the Constitution, requires harmony between the Constitution, the obligations derived from international law—assumed directly under the Constitution or undertaken in treaties—and domestic law; in ensuring their harmony, attention must be paid to their particular characteristics.

According to this decision, in order to fulfill Art. 7 of the Constitution, all three levels—domestic law, international treaties and the Constitution—must be examined together and connected. That is, "the question of whether the international obligation undertaken is in harmony with the Constitution must be raised and answered"; further: "it is irrelevant whether the constitutional review of a legal provision is preliminary or ex post facto; neither may proceed without an examination of the harmony between the domestic legal rule, the international treaty, and the Constitution" (MK 1993/147 at 8794–95; ABH 1993, 323 at 326).

6. As a result of the above-mentioned provisions of the Constitution and the previously cited decisions of the Constitutional Court, the Constitutional Court may examine the constitutionality of an international treaty not only under s. 1(a) of the Act within the framework of preliminary review but also according to s. 1(b) of the Act in the form of ex post facto review. If this were not the case, that would not only entail an eventual irreparable infringement of Art. 7(1) of the Constitution but would also be in conflict with Art. 32/A(1) and (2) of the Constitution.

Only one ground of competence of the Constitutional Court follows from the Constitution itself, namely, the ex post facto review, but this is mandatory and—as it was already referred to in its historical interpretation—extends to all sources of legal provisions. During the drafting of the Act and the Constitution there did not come to light even a single reference on the part of the legislature which would have aimed at excluding any type of legal rule—for instance, laws promulgating international treaties—from ex post facto review. The fact that—under the circumstances of drafting and passing the Act—the legislature did not at that time consider this particular case of ex post facto review separately, does not affect the Constitutional Court's right to interpret its own jurisdiction. The decisions of the Constitutional Court in which the Court interprets its competence are binding on everyone, just like other decisions—including those made on the basis of the competence achieved by such an interpretation. In this interpretive work, the Constitutional Court is led by the object of fulfilling its special task and by the models of other constitutional courts with the adoption of those solutions which were developed in response to the needs of an effective constitutional case law. [....] In accordance with its previous decisions interpreting the jurisdiction of the Court, the Constitutional Court in the present case, besides fully implementing its constitutionally mandated jurisdiction for ex post facto review, takes into account foreign models of examining the constitutionality of international treaties. Finally, the Constitutional Court also refers to the fact that by examining the constitutionality of international treaties the Court remains within the boundaries of its constitutional task, the ex post facto review. Since it examines exclusively the harmony between the international treaty and the Constitution, it does not interfere with the functions and competence of other branches in the separation of powers. The fact that s. 1(b) of the Act does not contain special procedural regulations for cases in which the challenged law promulgates an international treaty does not have an effect on the competence of the Constitutional Court regarding the examination of such laws. Parliament has provided the Constitutional Court with several other competences in statutes other than the Act without actually providing for separate procedural regulations. [....] Concerning the examination of international treaties, general procedural rules of ex post facto review apply, and the Constitutional Court pays attention to the specific characteristics of the international treaty in case of determination of the consequences of the unconstitutionality.

As the examination of the constitutionality of international treaties is required, according to the Constitutional Court's *Dec. 53/1993 (X.13) AB* (MK 1993/147; ABH 1993, 323), under Art. 7(1) of the Constitution, it also derives mandatorily from Art. 32/A. There is no constitutional basis for dealing with the law promulgating an international treaty in a manner different from the regime applicable to other legal rules for the purpose of constitutional review. Since it derives from the Constitution that ex post facto review shall cover all kinds of legal rules, this universality may not be restricted even by an Act of Parliament.

Section 1(a) of the Act, therefore, does not mean that the Constitutional Court may examine only preliminarily the unconstitutionality of certain provisions of an international treaty, but it means that besides the ex post facto review, which derives from the Constitution, the unconstitutionality of an international treaty may also be examined preliminarily on the basis of and under the conditions set out in the Act. From that fact that s. 1(a) of the Act specifies the preliminary examination of international treaties, it does not follow that in sub-s. (b) the legislature should have had to mention the law promulgating a treaty as a special type of law, and the conclusion may not be drawn that the legislature would have aimed to exclude the ex post facto review of this source of law. Regarding the preliminary review of the unconstitutionality, it was necessary to specify the different types of norms which may be examined, because it was not possible to mark under one composite (comprehensive) name the bill, the adopted but unpromulgated statutes, and the Standing Orders of Parliament. To mark international treaties separately was especially required, since treaties do not necessarily appear in the form of a bill, and, contrary to the above-mentioned categories of preliminary review, the legislature intended to restrict the examination only to individual provisions of an international treaty. Also for the same reason s. 30(1)(a) and (b) of the Act specifies the different types of norm falling under preliminary control.

If the international treaty—and so the law promulgating it—contains a provision which is a "generally recognized rule of international law" under Art. 7 of the Constitution, that is, the treaty merely expresses a rule which was previously incorporated into the domestic law by the Constitution, then the constitutional review of this provision will have to take into account all those restrictions which the Constitutional Court in *Dec. 53/1993 (X.13) AB* (MK 1993/147; ABH 1993, 323) also endorsed. Although the generally recognized rules of international law do not stand at the same hierarchical level as the Constitution, the constitutional command of "ensuring their harmony with the domestic law" has to be fulfilled in such a way that the Constitution needs to be interpreted in the light of these specific rules of international law (MK 1993/147 at 8798–99; ABH 1993, 323 at 334).

7. In order to confirm the foregoing, the Constitutional Court refers to the fact that concerning the relationship between domestic and international law, in the development of European law, there is a tendency that the dualist-transformation system is replaced by the monist system. [....] This system is required by European integration, and for this reason even those members of the European Union which still follow the transformation system (*e.g.,* Germany and Italy as founding members and the Scandinavian countries which subsequently joined the European Union) apply the law of the European Union directly, without transformation, and they ensure superiority over national law with the exception of the Constitution. As a result of this, the constitutional courts extend their competences for ex post facto review to international treaties (international law) and the decisions of international organizations which—due to the adoption system—automatically become part of the domestic law.

The examination of international treaties—after they become part of domestic law—fits into the logic of constitutional review. Therefore, in those countries where there is no specific regulation concerning this—due to the universality of the constitutional review—the constitutional courts examine the constitutionality of international treaties in exactly the same way as in the case of domestic law. [....]

VÖRÖS, J., dissenting: [....]

3. In my opinion, without a statutory basis, the Constitutional Court may not exercise a jurisdiction not granted to it by the legislature. As I previously expounded my stand several times [...], the exercise of such a jurisdiction may be challenged from the point of view of legal certainty.

DECISION 39/1997: 1 JULY 1997

ON JUDICIAL REVIEW OF ADMINISTRATIVE DECISIONS

After the system change, legislation reintroduced into Hungarian law several kinds of public bodies—among them commercial and professional chambers and associations—in which administrative competences have also been vested. Obligatory membership and semistate functions were challenged in a series of cases based on the (also newly achieved) freedom of association. While the Constitutional Court laid down criteria that will be apt to brake a development toward a corporate state organization, the medical practitioners' association case presented here is significant for widening the scope of administrative review as well. The decision not only extends the review to administrative discretion but requires that laws regulating the public administration's powers must contain appropriate measures on the basis of which the courts can review the legality of the respective administrative acts.

The petitioners sought ex post facto review of various provisions of Act XXVIII/1994 on the Hungarian Medical Association (HMA).

The Act provided, inter alia, that (a) by s. 2(i), the HMA had the right to agree on the request for exercising the medical profession by entering the name of a foreign practitioner on the Medical Practitioners' National Register; (b) by s. 19(1), the HMA was to accept as a member any Hungarian citizen who applied for membership in accordance with s. 19(2) and fulfilled all the necessary professional and educational requirements; (c) by s. 19(3), the HMA could (at its discretion) consider a request for entry from a foreign practitioner or, if provided for in an international treaty, was required to do so with respect to a non-Hungarian who fulfilled the criteria laid down in s. 19(1) (while the Minister of Health also had to give his assent, any refusal by the HMA effectively vetoed such assent); and (d) by s. 21(5), in respect of a challenge to decisions of the HMA, the claimant had a right to pursue his/her claim before the courts. The Act further provided for a HMA Ethical Committee which could impose certain punishments, *viz.,* reprimand, fine and suspension of HMA membership. The disciplinary procedure was written and the taking of evidence compulsory, as was the practitioner's right to be heard. Appeal against the HMA Ethical Committee led to the National Ethical Committee and thence to the courts.

The petitioners submitted, inter alia, that (a) compulsory membership of the HMA was an unnecessary and disproportionate limit, contrary to Art. 63 of the Constitution, on the free choice of employment and occupation in Art. 70/B; (b) the disciplinary proceedings and punishments of the HMA were contrary to Art. 57 of the Constitution; and (c) the HMA's right to agree under s. 2(i) of the Act and its discretionary power concerning admission of the members of the HMA under s. 19 were contrary to Art. 57(1) as well as to Art. 70/B—such human rights guaranteed by this latter Article were available to all human beings in Hungary and were not limited to enjoyment by Hungarian citizens.

Held, granting the petitions in part:

(1) By a reading of ss. 19(1), (2) and 21(5) of the Act, compulsory membership in the HMA amounted to a necessary and proportional limit on the free choice of employment and occupation in accordance with Art. 70/B of the Constitution. The HMA, like all other professional chambers/associations, possessed the right to regulate itself, to resolve questions which affected the profession's fundamental rights and to determine the essence of the profession and membership of the chamber. This right of chambers, however, was to be regulated by statute and did not permit them to lay down rules affecting human rights. In the present case, except for the fee, HMA membership did not require fulfillment of any condition other than those necessary for the exercise of the medical profession. The free choice of employment and occupation depended on the conditions of becoming a member of the chamber (HMA).

(2) The provisions of the Act on disciplinary proceedings and punishments were constitutional. In the judicial review of the legality of a decision of the public administration, the Constitution, under Art. 57 (as read with Art. 50), required an independent, impartial court established by law which should be fair and open to the public, fulfillment of which requirement permitted a court to decide upon the merits of the case and render a final decision determining rights and duties. Such supervision of legality could not therefore be limited to review of the formal legality of the administrative decision. In these cases, the court was not bound by the facts as determined by the public administrative body in its proceedings nor was it prevented from examining the legality of the exercise of administrative discretion. Moreover deciding on the merits was not contrary to the court instructing the administrative organ, which had made the reviewed decision, to conduct new proceedings. Any legal rule which excluded or restricted the court in such judicial review would be contrary to Art. 57, yet the provisions of the Act on Public Health and the HMA Code of Ethics as well as the practice of the courts clearly indicated that, in the present case, no such exclusions or restrictions in fact existed.

(3) However, while the provision permitting foreign medical practitioners to exercise their profession was constitutional for formal reasons, nevertheless those parts which granted the HMA unlimited discretionary power to refuse membership in the HMA were contrary to Art. 57(1) of the Constitution. The right to free choice of employment and occupation under Art. 70/B was a human right, not one arising only by virtue of citizenship. HMA's right under s. 2(i) of the Act to agree on entry into the National Register and the provision concerning its decision establishing the membership of a non-Hungarian constituted an exercise of public authority, made acccording to the rules of administrative procedure, such decisions normally being susceptible to review by the courts. In essence, this exercise of public authority limited a foreign medical practitioner's right to free choice of employment and occupation by giving the HMA the right to veto the permission of the Minister of Health. Whereas a ministerial refusal could be challenged before the courts, no legal provision regulated the circumstances under which the HMA was to accept or refuse the request of a foreign medical practitioner. Foreign citizenship in such cases was irrelevant—its importance attached merely to the permission and not to the decision itself, which could differentiate foreigners, thereby affecting their human rights under Art. 70/B. Since no legal rule contained any point according to which the courts could review the legality of the

decision, and thus prevented their deciding on the merits of the case, this amounted to a violation of Art. 57 of the Constitution.

IN THE NAME OF THE REPUBLIC OF HUNGARY!

On the basis of a petition seeking an ex post facto review of the unconstitutionality of a legal rule, and concerning a constitutional complaint, the Constitutional Court has made the following

DECISION.

I

1. The Constitutional Court declares: The right of the chambers of professions to regulate and decide a question affecting fundamental rights and determining the essence of a profession, must be regulated by statute, which determines at least the basic content and the limits of that right.

2. In case of regulating the review of the legality of the decisions of the public administration, it is a constitutional requirement that the court shall decide on the merits of the case: the rights and obligations according to the conditions defined by Art. 57(1) of the Constitution. The rule regulating the public administration's competence to decide must contain an appropriate aspect or measure on the basis of which the court reviews the legality of the decision.

II

1. The Constitutional Court declares: ss. 20(2)(b) and 20(3) of the Act XXVIII/1994 on the Hungarian Medical Association (henceforth the Act) are unconstitutional and therefore annuls these sections as of 31 December 1997.

2. That part of s. 2(i) of the Act according to which "to the entry of the foreigner's name on the Medical Practitioners' National Register"; in the first half of s. 19(1) the "Hungarian citizen" part; and also that part of s. 19(3) under which "if an international treaty prescribes, also adopt that non-Hungarian citizen, who fulfills the requirements defined by s. 19(1), and" are unconstitutional.

The "Hungarian citizen" part of para. 2(1), and para. 2(4) of the Minister of Health Decree 11/1972 (VI.30) EüM (henceforth the Decree), are also unconstitutional. The Constitutional Court annuls the unconstitutional regulations as of 31 December 1997.

The provisions concerned will remain in force as follows:

Section 2 of the Act: "The Hungarian Medical Association (henceforth the HMA) [....]

(i) has the right to agree on the request for exercising the medical profession for a definite term without a naturalized diploma."

Section 19 of the Act:

"(1) The member of the HMA can be that person, who" [....]

"(3) The HMA, in case of a request, can admit that applicant as its member who does not fulfill the requirement defined by s. 19(1) (a) regardless of his/her citizenship."

Paragraph 2 of the Decree:

"(1) In their request, that person should be entered into the Medical Practitioners' National Register, who certifies his/her qualification with a diploma issued by one of the Hungarian Medical Universities and concerning whom there exists no ground on which he/she should be removed from the Register."

3. The Constitutional Court rejects the petitions to establish the unconstitutionality of ss. 26, 27, 30(1) (c) and (d) of the Act and the Act as a whole and refuses the petition to establish the unconstitutionality of s. 44(4) of the Act and to annul it.

The Constitutional Court publishes this Decision in the *Hungarian Official Gazette.*

REASONING

SÓLYOM, P., delivering the Opinion of the Court: [....]

III

[....]

2. [....] The Ethical Committee of the HMA can impose the following ethical punishments: reprimand, fine and suspension of the membership. In contrast to the punishment of exclusion, the Ethical Committee has a discretionary power to decide on the imposition of these punishments. The ethical procedure in these cases is not summary; the Act contains the regulations concerning this procedure (ss. 27–29). According to these regulations the disciplinary procedure is written [...] that taking evidence is compulsory [...] and during this procedure the practitioner has to be heard. Against the decision of the Ethical Committee an appeal can be lodged to the National Ethical Committee either by the practitioner affected or by the person who initiated the procedure. In case of appealing against the decision of the National Committee to a court, the rules concerning judicial review of administrative decisions are applicable (Act III/1952 on the Code of Civil Procedure, Chapter XX). [....]

The suspension of membership in the HMA for a definite term (but for not more than six months) means that the medical practitioner is deprived of his/her right to practise the profession. Therefore, the question arises as to whether in the ethical procedure—apart from the presumption of innocence—the general constitutional guarantees [of Art. 57 of the Constitution] can be required, namely that the medical practitioner involved "in legal proceedings" is entitled to a fair and public hearing by an independent and impartial court established by law. These procedural guarantees are also required by art. 6 of the European Convention of Human Rights. Answering the above-mentioned question, the Constitutional Court has taken into account the practice of the European Court of Human Rights, since the judgments on the prohibition from the medical profession played an important role in interpreting art. 6 of the Convention. (See *Le Compte, Van Leuven and De Meyere* (ECtHR, Judgment of 23 June 1981, Series A, No. 43) and *Albert and Le Compte* (ECtHR, Judgment of 10 February 1983, Series A, No. 58).) Reference to these cases of the European Court of Human Rights is well founded because the European Court held that art. 6 was applicable to the interim suspension of the medical practitioner's right to practise, being concerned with a civil law relationship between the patient and the practitioner. In Hungary, the suspension of the practitioner's right to practise also concerns this civil law relationship, since this punishment can be imposed in case of a medical practitioner in the civil service only if he/she was dismissed as a result of a disciplinary procedure or was deprived of office. To prove the "independence" of the HMA's disciplinary boards would be difficult (regardless of the fact that the existence of incompatibility rules [s. 29(2) and (3)] could speak for "impartiality"). Further, the rule which prescribes a written procedure is contrary to the principle of "public hearing." If the procedure of the ethical committees does not fulfill the requirements of Art. 57(1) of the Constitution, the constitutionality of the Act depends on whether the possibility of judicial review concerning the decision at second instance (s. 28(5)) is enough for the constitutionality of the ethical procedure. With this, the Constitutional Court admits that there is no need for courtlike institutions and procedures required by Art. 57 of the Constitution in every instance. On the other hand, the Constitutional Court stresses that the access to a court itself is not enough for the realization of the procedural guarantees; the effective legal protection required by the Constitution depends on what the court can review.

According to the Act, similarly to other decisions of the chamber, there is a possibility for judicial review concerning the decision at second instance in the ethical procedure according to the rules of the judicial review of administrative decisions. Under Art. 50 of the Constitution "the courts shall supervise the legality of the decisions of public administration." Taking into account Art. 57, this provision should be interpreted in such a way that the court shall in fact "determine the civil rights and obligations" of the claimant; all the requirements determined by the Constitution: the court should be independent, impartial and established by law, and the requirements that the court should be fair and open to the public serve this aim. Only by fulfilling this requirement can the court decide constitutionally on the merits of the case, and only in this way can the court render a final decision which determines a right. Supervising the legality of the decisions of public administration therefore cannot be limited constitutionally to reviewing only the formal legality of decisions of this kind. In an action for judicial review of an administrative decision the court is not bound by the facts of the case as determined by the public administrative body; further the court can also review the legality of administrative discretion. Deciding on the merits of the case is not against the fact that the court instructs the administrative organ, which has passed the administrative decision, to conduct a new procedure. Those legal rules which exclude or restrict the court while reviewing the legality of the decision of an administrative organ from deciding on the merits of the case in the above sense are contrary to Art. 57(1) of the Constitution. For this reason, not only that legal rule can be unconstitutional which *expressis verbis* excludes the judicial review going beyond the questions of law, or which leaves such a small area for judicial revision against the discretion of the public administration that we cannot talk about deciding on the merits of a case in the sense of the Constitution, but also that legal rule which by giving an unlimited discretionary power to the public administration does not provide for any legal measure for judicial review.

Ethical misdemeanours adjudicated upon during the ethical procedure are determined by the Act on Public Health (s. 25) and also the Ethical Code of the HMA. To determine and render precisely the content of these general rules concerns the Ethical College's decisions of principle (s. 14) and the practice of the committees proceeding in ethical questions, and it will be binding through the judgments of the courts during the judicial revision of administrative decisions. The judicial practice does not restrict the supervision of the decision of the public administration to the review of the formal legality, but it reviews both the facts of the case and the legality of the evidence and the discretion based upon equity.

Taking into consideration on the one hand the substantive rules of the ethical procedure and on the other hand the constitutional requirement which should be realized during the judicial review of the decisions made in the ethical procedure, and that these are realized in the Hungarian courts, the Constitutional Court rejected the petition seeking to establish the unconstitutionality of the provisions concerning the disciplinary proceedings and punishments (Chapter VI of the Act). [....]

4. [....] Hungarian citizens are entitled to be a member of the HMA, and the membership does not require more than which are otherwise the conditions of exercising the medical profession. The only burden is the membership fee, the other duties being independent of membership in the chamber. The free choice of employment and occupation does not depend on the regulations for exercising the profession, as the petitioners contended, but on the conditions of becoming a member of the chamber (the Constitutional Court has already declared this in detail in its decision on bar associations—*Dec. 22/1994 (IV.6) AB:* MK 1994/40 at 1413–14; ABH 1994, 127 at 132). Under the conditions defined by s. 19(1) of the Act the applicant who applies for membership according to s. 19(2) should be accepted by the HMA, and this is ensured by the right to judicial review regulated by s. 21(5). Based upon the above-mentioned, the compulsory membership is not contrary to Art. 70/B of the Constitution: it does not limit unnecessarily and disproportionately the free choice of employment and occupation. Limiting the exercise of the profession by the punishment regulated by the Act therefor, according to the above-mentioned, is not unconstitutional either. [....]

6. Two petitioners submitted a constitutional complaint concerning ss. 19 and 2(i) of the Act and para. 2(4) of the Decree, which endow the HMA with rights concerning the admission of non-Hungarian-citizen medical practitioners to the HMA, the entry on the Medical Practitioners' National Register and the medical profession, which could be exercized with a foreign diploma. [....]

Section 19(3) does not exclude the possibility that a non-Hungarian-citizen medical practitioner could be a member of the HMA; their entrance into the Register however is not automatic even in that case in which they fulfill the requirement the Hungarian-citizen medical practitioners have to fulfill (s. 19(1)), but it depends on the discretionary decision of the HMA. The HMA does not have a discretionary power if the admission is prescribed by an international treaty. [....]

[T]he Court rejected the petitions to establish the unconstitutionality of the regulation on permitting the exercise of the medical profession for foreign medical practitioners for formal reasons.

6.2. However, the Constitutional Court held the petitions seeking to establish the unconstitutionality of the HMA's right to agree under s. 2(i) and its discretionary power concerning the admission of the members of HMA according to s. 19(3) well founded. The HMA's right to agree under s. 2(i) constitutes exercising public authority. As a result of this right both the ability of the foreigner to exercise the medical profession without a naturalized diploma and the ability of the non-Hungarian-citizen medical practitioner who fulfills the requirements the Hungarian-citizen medical practitioners have to fulfill, inter alia, to have a Hungarian or a naturalized diploma, to exercise the medical profession depends partially on the HMA as well as on the permission of the Minister of Public Health. As a consequence of the HMA's right to agree, it has the right to veto the permission of the Minister of Public Health concerning both the ability of the foreigner to exercise the medical profession without a naturalized diploma and the entry on the Medical Practitioners' National Register. The entry of the medical practitioner's name on the Register is required in order to become a member of the HMA, but the HMA has one further possibility to decide once again, in this case alone, without the Minister, on permitting the foreign medical practitioner to exercise his/her profession when it decides on establishing the membership of a non-Hungarian citizen. This act of the chamber is also an exercise of public authority, made according to the rules of administrative procedure, and the decision refusing HMA membership can be reviewed by the court. [....]

[....] According to the Hungarian Constitution the right to free choice of job and profession is a human right, that is, contrary to some foreign constitutions, not a citizen's right. The HMA's right to agree on the entry on the Medical Practitioners' National Register and the provision concerning its decision on establishing the membership of a non-Hungarian citizen limits the non-Hungarian-citizen medical practitioner's right to free choice of job and profession (Art. 70/B of the Constitution). According to the practice of the Constitutional Court, the right to work (occupation, enterprise) is violated in the most serious way if the person cannot choose a profession; those provisions which exclude the ability to choose because of objective reasons must be examined in the strictest way (*Dec. 21/1994 (IV.16) AB:* MK 1994/40 at 1408; ABH 1994, 117 at 121).

The question under review is primarily not the question as to whether it is possible that, contrary to the fact that whereas the Hungarian medical practitioner is entitled to be a member of the HMA, in the case of a foreigner permission is required for membership, but the constitutionality of the rules on permission. The Act and the Code on Public Health make clear that for the entry of the foreign medical practitioner's name on the Register and for membership of the HMA in the case of a foreign medical practitioner the same requirements should be fulfilled as in the case of a Hungarian medical practitioner. [....] The constitutional problem is that there is no legal provision regulating those points under which the HMA should accept or refuse the request of the foreign medical practitioner. [....] The Constitutional Court recalls that in this question, which affects a human right, the professional chamber cannot lay down rules and could not be given the authority to make such a rule. [....]

Because of the unlimited discretionary power the HMA has, the judicial remedy in case of a refusal of the request for membership is pointless: none of the legal rules contains any aspect or measure according to which the court can review the legality of the decision. In this legal vacuum even that court cannot decide on the merits of the case, like the Hungarian courts, which can supervise the legality of the discretion based upon equity. Therefore, that part of s. 19(3) of the Act according to which the HMA may admit a non-Hungarian citizen who fulfills the requirements defined by s. 19(1) is contrary to Art. 57(1) of the Constitution. Section 2(i) of the Act, under which the HMA has the right to agree on the entry of the foreign medical practitioner's name on the Medical Practitioners' National Register, is also unconstitutional. Section 2(4) of the Code on Public Health, which authorizes the Minister of Public Health to permit the entry on the register with complete discretion and regardless of every aspect, is also unconstitutional. The Constitutional Court remarks that its standpoint is in harmony with the practice of the European Court of Human Rights. (See the above-mentioned judgment in *Albert and Le Compte* (ECtHR, Judgment of 10 February 1983, Series A, No. 43) and also the *Obermeier* case (ECtHR, Judgment of 28 June 1990, Series A, No. 179).)

DECISION 52/1997: 14 OCTOBER 1997

ON REFERENDA AND POPULAR SOVEREIGNTY

Following an amendment to the Constitution that brought detailed rules on referenda into the Constitution and within political turmoils of two competing initiatives for national referenda on the same question (one initiated by voters, which the Government tried to overtake with "its" referendum), the Constitutional Court restated the relationship between direct exercise of power by the people and representative democracy. The Court stated that in the exceptional case when the constitutional requirements of an obligatory referendum had been met this kind of referendum was to be given precedence not only over exercising power through representation but also over other kinds of referenda. The Court laid down, for the Act on Referenda to be passed, procedural rules that would guarantee this precedence and also provide for the possibility of lodging a constitutional complaint with the Constitutional Court in all matters concerning referenda.

The Parliamentary Commissioner for Civil Rights, among other petitioners, requested the interpretation of certain constitutional provisions.

The Constitution (as amended by Act LIX/1997) provided (a) by Art. 28/C(2), that, when at least 200,000 voters petitioned for a national referendum, then the State was obliged to hold one, using for the question the wording already formulated in the petition; and (b) by Art. 28/C(4), that the President, the Government, one-third of MPs or 100,000 voters might initiate a referendum, but it remained within the discretion of Parliament as to whether one should be held as well as the formulation of the question to be put to the people.

This particular field was more closely regulated by Art. XVII/1989 on Referenda and Popular Initiatives, which laid down the procedures, inter alia, for the collection and verification of the requisite number of signatures together with the holding of the referendum itself.

A situation arose whereby, in the course of verification of the signatures collected to initiate a referendum under Art. 28/C(2), the Government sought to initiate a referendum (with parliamentary approval) under Art. 28/C(4) on the same issue but with questions which were contrary to those put in the first proposed referendum.

In accordance with his statutory powers, the Parliamentary Commissioner for Civil Rights sought a ruling from the Court on the interpretation of the relationship between paras. (2) and (4) of Art. 28/C.

Held, giving the interpretation sought:

(1) The obligatory referendum under Art. 28/C(2) took precedence over the discretionary one in Art. 28/C(4). The direct exercise of power by the people enshrined in Art. 2(2) of the Constitution had two essential features: initiation (including the determination of the question to be decided) and enforceability (both as regards the holding of the referendum and the binding force of its result). On the one hand, the obligatory referendum, an

exceptional form of the exercise of the sovereignty of the people, left the people in control of every element of this direct exercise of power. Parliament was obliged not only to ensure that the referendum was held and its result implemented but also to refrain from any act or omission which would influence or frustrate the realization of such exercise, even to the point of preventing other state organs from committing like acts or omissions. On the other hand, the holding of a discretionary referendum, once the 100,000 signatures had been verified, fell within the discretion of Parliament. Thus no guarantee existed as to the continuation of the initiative or to its wording remaining unaltered—Parliament consequently maintained complete control up to the holding of the referendum. As an exercise of power through representation, discretionary referenda therefore ranked below obligatory ones.

(2) The right to a referendum was a fundamental political right according to Art. 70(1) of the Constitution, which right extended to the initiation of the referendum, the signing of sheets and gathering of signatures as well as participation in the vote. Such right was not only to be protected but the State was also obliged to provide the preconditions for its exercise. On the basis of the Constitution, the petition for an obligatory referendum enjoyed protection of an absolute character commencing with the submission (and not with the completion of the verification) of the signatures. While the right to hold a referendum on the question specified in the petition only came into existence with the verification of the requisite number of signatures, this was a declarative not a constitutive act: the existence/absence of support was given at the time of submitting signatures and was merely stated on their verification. Nevertheless, voters had a claim flowing from their right that state organs could not frustrate their right to hold a referendum after the submission of signatures but before verification was completed: this right was also extended to the period of collecting signatures. However, it was for the legislature to decide upon the starting point for the collection and other matters related thereto by amending Act XVII/1989 on Referenda and Popular Initiatives.

IN THE NAME OF THE REPUBLIC OF HUNGARY!

In the matter of petitions seeking an ex post facto review of the unconstitutionality of legal rules, and the establishment of an unconstitutional omission to legislate, as well as in the matter of the request of the Parliamentary Commissioner for Civil Rights for the interpretation of the provisions of the Constitution, the Constitutional Court made the following

DECISION.

I

The Constitutional Court declares: the relation between the different forms of referenda provided for in Art. 28/C(2) and (4) of the Constitution, respectively, is determined by the fact that the direct exercise of power defined in Art. 2(2) of the Constitution as one of the ways of exercising sovereignty by the people is represented in its entirety by the—obligatory—referendum pursuant to Art. 28/C(2). The direct exercise of power is an exceptional form of exercising of the people's sovereign rights, which, however, in the exceptional cases of its realization enjoys supremacy over exercising power through representation. Therefore an obligatory referendum shall be yielded precedence over a referendum enshrining the elements of direct exercise of power and exercising power through representation that can be held discretionary pursuant to Art. 28/C(4).

II

1. The petition of at least 200,000 citizens directed at an obligatory referendum enjoys precedence according to Part I over a discretionary referendum directly on the basis of the Constitution from the submission of the signatures collected to the President of Parliament. From this point in time every decision concerning initiatives in the same subject matter submitted in the course of the collection of signatures and directed at a referendum that can be held discretionary shall be postponed or its implementation shall be suspended until the verification of the signatures is completed. If as a result of the verification of the signatures the referendum must be held, this excludes the referendum that can be held discretionary.

The Act on Referenda shall ensure the precedence of initiatives directed at an obligatory referendum for the course of the collection of signatures in the manner that it also provides for the starting point of the collection of signatures, its duration, the requirements for the content and form of the signature-collecting sheets, as well as appropriate procedural guarantees.

2. The principle of legal certainty as an integral part of the rule of law as enshrined in Art. 2(1) of the Constitution requires that the Act establish an appropriate legal institution for a preventive examination of the constitutionality of the questions proposed to be the basis of the initiative for a referendum.

3. The voters' right to referendum is a fundamental political right granted by the Constitution; therefore the submission of a constitutional complaint to the Constitutional Court against decisions in the matter of the referendum shall be made possible.

4. The Constitutional Court declares that its interpretation of the Constitution is *erga omnes* binding from the day of the pronouncement; it is applicable to cases in progress as well.

5. A procedural violation of the Constitution committed in the course of the legislation process—such as the basing of a law on a referendum held unconstitutionally—may lead to the nullification of the law, even in the absence of the unconstitutionality of its content.

III

The Constitutional Court declares: there exists an unconstitutional omission to legislate as a result of the fact that Parliament, despite the summons of the Constitutional Court to this end, has not harmonized Act XVII/1989 on Referenda and Public Initiatives for Legislation with the Constitution in force. Sections 6(1)(a), (b) and (c); 8(1)(c) and (d); 9(2); 10(1); 11(2); 18(1); 23(6)(a) and (b); 28; and 31(1) of said Act as well as the part of s. 32(1) described below are unconstitutional. The complete elimination of the unconstitutionality necessitates a complete revision of the statutory provisions on referenda and on public initiatives for legislation. Therefore the Constitutional Court calls upon Parliament to fulfill this obligation to legislate—in accordance with the interpretation of the Constitution in this Decision by the Constitutional Court—until 31 December 1997. The Constitutional Court declares null and void the words "based on an unsuccessful verification" in s. 32(1) of Act XVII/1989 with the publication of the present Decision in the *Hungarian Official Gazette,* every remaining provision of said Act in force with effect from 31 December 1997.

As a result of the nullification s. 32(1) of Act XVII/1989 will remain in force with the following content:
Section 32(1): A constitutional complaint may be submitted to the Constitutional Court against decisions rejecting the holding of a referendum or to discuss in the merits public initiatives for legislation, as well as against violations of the statutory provisions concerning the carrying out of the referendum and the establishment of its result.

The Constitutional Court publishes this Decision in the *Hungarian Official Gazette.*

REASONING

KILÉNYI, J., and **SÓLYOM, P.,** delivering the Opinion of the Court: [....]

IV

Paragraphs (2) and (4) of Art. 28/C of the Constitution contain two different types of national referenda. According to the legislative intent to s. 3 of Act LIX/1997 amending the Constitution with inter alia Art. 28/C "the Act defines clearly the different types of referenda on the basis of their title (obligatory—optional) and binding force (decisive—advisory) as well as the persons or organs entitled to initiate them and their permissible subject matter."

The two "types" of referendum to be distinguished on the basis of "title" are on the one hand the obligatory national referendum pursuant to Art. 28/C(2) and the optional national referendum pursuant to Art. 28/C(4) on the other. Art. 28/C(2) stipulates that national referendum shall be held on the petition of at least 200,000 voters. According to Art. 28/C(4) referenda may be initiated by the President, the Government, one-third of the members of Parliament or 100,000 voters, whereupon Parliament may decide that a referendum be held.

The interpretation of Art. 28/C of the Constitution requires the evaluation of both of these "types" of referendum in relation to each other, with special regard for the notion of direct exercise of power and the hierarchy of the "types" of referendum. [....]

According to s. 4(3) of the Act on Referenda, an advisory referendum secures the contribution of the citizens to the decision making of Parliament. In the context, however, of the specific legal institution geared to meet this goal the organs based on representation are not bound by the result of the direct exercise of sovereignty by the people.

If the representative organ is bound by the result of the referendum, then the people become "participants" or "determining factors" in the decision of the representative organ. Nevertheless, the binding force of the result of the referendum is not the sole feature of decisive referenda. What is more, the decisive features of the direct exercise of sovereignty by the people [Art. 2(2) of the Constitution] can be found elsewhere. The substantial difference between the two forms of decisive referendum is what is the (in the words of the legislative intent of the amendment of the Constitution) "title" of the access to the institution of the referendum, that is, to the direct exercise of power: the discretion of Parliament or the fulfillment of the procedural requirement provided for by the Constitution. The new

Art. 28/C of the Constitution distinguishes on the same basis—on the basis of the title of the "decision" to hold a referendum—between the two different types of referendum binding Parliament: the one to be held at the discretion of Parliament [para. (4)] and the one to be held obligatorily [para. (2)].

The Constitutional Court has from the beginning considered the direct exercise of power by the people to have two essential features. In *Dec. 28/1990 (XI.22) AB* (MK 1990/117 at 2313; ABH 1990, 123 at 124) the Court stated that it is only one of the features of direct exercise of power that its result (the decision made by the referendum) is binding on the legislature: "It is an indispensable element of direct democracy that those concerned, *i.e.*, the citizen himself (or a certain number of them) have influence on the institution serving its purposes." The criteria of the direct exercise of power are therefore initiation (including the determination of question to be decided, *i.e.*, the object of the exercise of power) and enforceability (relating not only to the binding force of the result but also to the holding of the referendum). Obligatory and optional referenda differ basically in both respects.

(a) An optional referendum pursuant to Art. 28/C(4) may be initiated by representative organs or organs deriving their power from representation (one-third of the Members of Parliament, Government, President) as well as by 100,000 voters. Every other decision, from the formulation of the question to the actual holding or not holding of the referendum, falls under the discretion of Parliament, upon which the 100,000 petitioners have no influence. There is, therefore, no guarantee of the continuation of the initiative (nor of its remaining unchanged); the representative organ controls completely the situation up to the holding of the referendum. Only the result of the referendum changes power relations and makes the voter a "participant" in the exercise of power. If the initiative was launched by the representative organ or its "descendants," the inclusion of the people serves merely the ex post facto legitimization of the decision of the representative sphere or the preliminary survey of the will of the voters—in the question and then in which and when the possessor of the representative exercise of power in its discretion makes this possible. The expression by the people of their will in this case does not equal the complete, direct exercise of sovereignty by the people.

The optional form of the decisive referendum lacks any form of one of the indispensable elements of the direct exercise of power, enforceability with regard to the holding of the referendum. Rather, this institution serves the co-operation between the exercise of power through representation and directly and can be formed in accordance with the needs of the representative side, in its typical case providing an ex post facto legitimization to decisions made within the institutions of the exercise of power through representation. Its application for the purposes of an ex post facto legitimization lies in the discretion of Parliament with one exception: this exception is at the moment the confirmation of the whole of a new Constitution by referendum.

(b) An obligatory referendum pursuant to Art. 28/C(2) and (3) differs from this on the theoretical level as well. Each element of it is under the "influence" of the voters concerned: the initiation, the formulation of the question as well as the enforceability (provided that the number of signatures necessary has been gathered). The "people" control the situation with regard to every element of the direct exercise of power. In the field of all subject matters of referenda not excluded by the Constitution [Art. 28/C(5)] Parliament has no possibility of influencing either the initiative or the enforceability. On the contrary, it is obliged to carry out every "serving," realizing action with a view to the holding of the referendum and thereafter to abide by its result. Its obligation applies not only to the necessary procedural steps but also entails refraining from every decision or omission that would influence or frustrate the realization of the direct exercise of power. Moreover, it is obliged to prevent other organs from such actions or omissions.

Direct exercise of power as provided for by Art. 2(2) of the Constitution in its entirety is solely the independent and autonomous form of the exercise of power according to Art. 28/C(2) and (3) of the Constitution [as opposed to the co-operative form of the exercise of power according to para. (4)]. The subject of the obligation stemming from Art. 28/C(2) is Parliament, and the obligation contains positive and negative elements, as described above.

(c) The Constitution does not distribute competences between the exercise of power directly and through representation in a manner that certain questions would be reserved for one or the other. The competence of the representative organs is as a rule complete and general. Compared to this, the institutions of direct democracy are exceptional (*Dec. 894/B/1990:* ABH 1990, 247 at 248). Nevertheless, the Constitution contains two provisions on the division of competences. One of these concerns the content: Art. 28/C(5) defines which questions cannot become the subject of a referendum. The other rule on competences is of a procedural nature in that it requires in para. (2) a petition of 200,000 voters in order for an obligatory referendum to be held outside of the scope of subjects excluded from referenda. This non-substantial division of competences has decisive consequences with regard to the hierarchy of the exercise of power directly and through representation as well as to the independence of the former. Should the initiative be supported to the extent required, this places automatically direct exercise of power over the representative organ. Parliament takes an executive role with respect to the question put to a referendum, and it has to ensure that the process of exercising power directly be not jeopardized until the successful referendum, when this obligation changes to one of a substantial nature (*i.e.*, to implement the decision of the people). Since within the scope of "permissible subjects" the provisions of the Constitution on direct exercise of power are predominantly of a procedural character, the protection of this exercise of power has to extend to the whole of the procedure from the initiation of the petition.

(d) Since the amendment of the Constitution by Act LIX/1997 abrogating the previous Art. 19(5), even if direct exercise of power is an exceptional form of exercising sovereignty by the people, in the exceptional cases of its realization it enjoys supremacy over exercising power through representation: Parliament has to implement the people's will. It also follows from this that an obligatory referendum, the sole pure form of direct exercise of power, enjoys precedence over a referendum that can be held at the discretion of Parliament thus enshrining the elements of exercising power through representation. It is unconstitutional if Parliament changes this order of precedence and decides to yield precedence to an optional referendum against an obligatory one.

The Constitutional Court holds that concurring initiatives for referenda of the same binding force—that is, two optional or two obligatory—shall be given precedence in their chronological order. [....]

The rule of chronological order is, however, inapplicable if two initiatives of a different binding force concur, *i.e.*, an obligatory and a discretionary. [....]

Should, therefore, the rule of chronological order apply if initiatives of a different binding force concur, then this would equal the abolition of the legal institution of obligatory referenda. This because in a multiparty parliamentary system opinions are divided on almost every question and there can be a political force interested in frustrating a petition for an obligatory referendum by previously submitting a concurring initiative directed at an optional referendum. [....]

With respect to the "protection period" of petitions for an obligatory referendum and the obligation to refrain of the representative organs—in the absence of a statutory regulation but with regard to the Act to be drafted—a distinction has to be made between the different stages of a petition.

The right to a referendum to be held on the question specified in the petition comes into existence with the verification of the number of signatures necessary. This, however, does not mean that there will be no obligation of state organs to be derived from the right to referenda before the completion of the verification, since the fulfillment of the procedural requirements (the collection of the signatures of 200,000 petitioners) would be impossible without the time period necessary for the exercise of the right, as well as without the protection of this period.

The verification of the signatures is a declarative and not a constitutive act: the existence or absence of the support necessary for a petition for a referenda is given at the time of the submission of the signatures and is merely stated by the verification of the signatures. The voters have no influence on the performance of the verification, especially on its duration. Nevertheless, voters have a claim flowing from the right to referenda that state organs do not frustrate their right to a referendum to be held after the submission of the signatures and until the verification, *i.e.,* until the formal precondition of the right to a referendum to be held is completed. Therefore the petition for a referendum enjoys protection of an absolute character starting with the submission of the signatures (and not with the completion of the verification) directly on the basis of the Constitution.

It shall also be decided whether this protection should extend to the period of collection of signatures as well. If an entitlement flowing from a fundamental right depends on the fulfillment of certain requirements, and the holders of the fundamental right act with a view to fulfilling the requirements, then state organs may not frustrate the acquisition of the entitlement in their discretion.

Consequently, the protection of the exercise of the fundamental right to referenda follows from the Constitution also for the course of the collection of signatures. But there can be no specific rule to be derived from the Constitution that would be appropriate for determining the starting point and the duration of the protection period with regard to the requirements of legal certainty—and especially to the necessity to secure the exercise of the right to initiate a discretionary referendum. Therefore the Constitutional Court calls upon the legislature to regulate in the Act on Referenda the starting point of the collection of signatures, its duration, as well as the requirements for the content and form of signature-collecting sheets. The Act shall also provide for remedies against decisions in these questions. [....]

The right to referenda is a fundamental political right.

According to Art. 70(1) of the Constitution "every adult Hungarian citizen residing on the territory of the Republic of Hungary has the right to [...] participate in national or local referenda or popular initiatives." [....]

The right to referenda as a subjective right extends to the initiation of a referendum, its support (including signing the sheets and gathering the signatures) as well as the participation in the vote. [....]

According to the consistent jurisprudence of the Constitutional Court, however, every fundamental right entails not only an entitlement for a subjective protection but also an objective obligation of the State to provide the preconditions for the exercise of the right. [....]

The constitutional requirement (measure) of the protection of the institution is not necessity and proportionality, but accords to the realization of the constitutional function of the respective institution [*cf.* the requirements for the different forms of the media in *Dec. 37/1992 (VI.10) AB:* MK 1992/59; ABH 1992, 227].

With respect to the obligatory referendum these institutional guarantees shall serve the purpose of ensuring the relevant essential features of the direct exercise of power by the people, the unprejudiced directness, especially the exemption and independence of the referendum and the procedure necessary for it from representative influence, as well as its precedence. Corresponding to the regulation of the obligatory referendum by the Constitution these guarantees are primarily of a procedural character. [....]

A judicial remedy, or a remedy before the Constitutional Court, is a constitutional requirement at every stage of the procedure whereby a decision is made—first of all by the representative organs—capable of disturbing the procedure [concerning the obligatory referendum] or of frustrating its success. [....]

THE CONSTITUTION OF THE REPUBLIC OF HUNGARY [*Act XX of 1949 as revised and restated by Act XXXI of 1989*] as of 1 December 1998

In order to facilitate a peaceful political transition to a state under the rule of law, realizing a multi-party system, a parliamentary democracy and a social market economy, the Parliament hereby establishes the text of the Constitution of the Republic of Hungary—until the adoption of the new Constitution of our country—as follows:

Chapter I.
General Provisions

Article 1.
Hungary shall be a republic.

Article 2.
(1)[1] The Republic of Hungary shall be an independent, democratic state under the rule of law.
(2) In the Republic of Hungary all power is vested in the people, who exercise their sovereignty through elected representatives and directly.
(3) No activity of any organization of society, state organ, or citizen may be directed at the acquisition or exercise by force of public authority, nor at its exclusive possession. Everyone has the right and obligation to resist such activities in a lawful manner.

Article 3.
(1) In the Republic of Hungary political parties may be established and may operate freely, provided they respect the Constitution and legal norms established in accordance with the Constitution.
(2) Political parties shall participate in the formation and expression of the will of the people.

1. Article 2(1) was amended by s. 1 of Act XL/1990 as of 25 June 1990. Between 23 October 1989 and 25 June 1990, Art. 2(1) read as follows: "The Republic of Hungary shall be an independent, democratic state under the rule of law, in which the values of civic democracy and democratic socialism equally prevail."

(3) Political parties may not exercise public power directly. Accordingly, no political party may exercise exclusive control over a state organ. In order to ensure the separation of political parties and public power, the law shall determine those functions and public offices which may not be held by party members or officers.

Article 4.
Trade unions and other representative organizations shall protect and represent the interests of employees, members of co-operatives and entrepreneurs.

Article 5.
The State of the Republic of Hungary shall defend the freedom and power of the people, the independence and territorial integrity of the country, and its borders as established in international treaties.

Article 6.
(1) The Republic of Hungary renounces war as a means of solving disputes between nations and shall refrain from the use of force and the threat thereof against the independence or territorial integrity of other states.
(2) The Republic of Hungary shall endeavour to co-operate with all peoples and countries of the world.
(3) The Republic of Hungary senses its responsibility for the fate of Hungarians living outside its borders and shall promote the fostering of their links with Hungary.

Article 7.
(1) The legal system of the Republic of Hungary accepts the generally recognized rules of international law, and shall further ensure the harmony between domestic law and the obligations assumed under international law.
(2) The procedures for passing legislation shall be regulated by statute, for the passage of which a majority of two-thirds of the votes of the Members of Parliament present is required.

Article 8.
(1) The Republic of Hungary recognizes the inviolable and inalienable fundamental rights of man; to respect and protect these rights is a primary obligation of the State.
(2)[2] In the Republic of Hungary rules pertaining to fundamental rights and duties shall be determined by statute, which, however, may not limit the essential content of any fundamental right.
(3)[3] [Repealed.]

---

2. Article 8(2) was amended by s. 3(1) of Act XL/1990 as of 25 June 1990. Between 23 October 1989 and 25 June 1990, Art. 8(2) read as follows: "Rules pertaining to fundamental rights and duties can only be determined by constitutional Acts."

3. Article 8(3) of the Constitution was repealed by s. 51(1) of Act XL/1990 as of 25 June 1990. Between 23 October 1989 and 25 June 1990, Art. 8(3) read as follows: "The exercise of fundamental rights may only be subjected to such limitations determined in a constitutional Act as are necessary in the interests of national security, internal order, public safety, health and morals or for the protection of the fundamental rights and freedoms of others."

(4) During a state of national crisis, state of emergency or state of danger, the exercise of fundamental rights may be suspended or restricted, with the exception of the fundamental rights enshrined in Articles 54–56, Article 57(2)–(4), Article 60, Articles 66–69 and Article 70/E.

Article 9.
(1) The economy of Hungary is a market economy, in which public and private property shall have equal rights and be granted equal protection.
(2) The Republic of Hungary recognizes and supports the right to enterprise and the freedom of economic competition.

Article 10.
(1) Property of the State of Hungary is considered national wealth.
(2) Fields of exclusive ownership and exclusive economic activity of the State shall be defined by statute.

Article 11.
Enterprises and economic organizations owned by the State shall conduct business independently therefrom in such manner and with such responsibility as defined by statute.

Article 12.
(1) The State supports co-operatives based on voluntary association and recognizes the autonomy of such co-operatives.
(2) The State shall respect the property of local governments.

Article 13.
(1) The Republic of Hungary shall guarantee the right to property.
(2) Expropriation shall only take place in exceptional cases, in the public interest, and only in such cases and in the manner stipulated by statute, with provision of full, unconditional and immediate compensation.

Article 14.
The Constitution guarantees the right of succession.

Article 15.
The Republic of Hungary shall protect the institutions of marriage and the family.

Article 16.
The Republic of Hungary shall make special efforts to ensure a secure subsistence, education and the raising of the young, and shall protect the interests of the young.

Article 17.
The Republic of Hungary shall provide for those in need through a wide range of welfare measures.

Article 18.
The Republic of Hungary recognizes and shall implement everyone's right to a healthy environment.

Chapter II.
The Parliament

Article 19.
(1) The Parliament is the supreme body of state authority and popular representation in the Republic of Hungary.
(2) Exercising its rights flowing from the sovereignty of the people, the Parliament shall ensure the constitutional order of society and define the organization, orientation and conditions of government.
(3) Within this sphere of authority, the Parliament shall:
(a) enact the Constitution of the Republic of Hungary;
(b) pass statutes;
(c) define the country's social and economic plan;
(d) establish the balance of public finances, approve the State Budget and its implementation;
(e) decide on the Government's programme;
(f) conclude international treaties of outstanding importance to the foreign relations of the Republic of Hungary;
(g) decide on the declaration of a state of war and on the conclusion of peace;
(h) declare a state of national crisis and establish the National Defence Council, in the case of war, or imminent danger of armed attack by a foreign power (danger of war);
(i) declare a state of emergency, in the case of armed actions aimed at subverting constitutional order or at the acquisition of exclusive control of power, in the case of grave acts of violence committed by force of arms or by armed groups which endanger the lives and property of citizens on a mass scale, and in the event of natural or industrial disaster (hereafter, "state of necessity");
(j) decide on the deployment of the armed forces, both abroad and within the country;
(k) elect the President of the Republic, the Prime Minister, the members of the Constitutional Court, the Parliamentary Commissioners, the President and Vice-Presidents of the State Audit Office, the President of the Supreme Court and the Chief Public Prosecutor;
(l) upon the recommendation of the Government—submitted to it after the Constitutional Court has been called upon to express its opinion—dissolve representative bodies of local government whose activity is unconstitutional; decide on the territory of counties, their name and seat, as well as on vesting cities with the rights of a county and the establishment of the Districts of the Capital;
(m) exercise general amnesty.
(4) A majority of two-thirds of the votes of the Members of Parliament is required for the decisions specified in points (g), (h), (i) and (j) of Paragraph (3).
(5) [Repealed.]

Article 19/A.
(1) Should the Parliament be obstructed in reaching such decisions, the President of the Republic shall have the power to declare a state of war, a state of national crisis and establish the National Defence Council, or to declare a state of emergency.
(2) The Parliament shall be considered to be obstructed in reaching such decisions, if it is not in session and its convening encounters insurmountable obstacles due to lack of time as well to the events necessitating the declaration of the state of war, state of national crisis or state of emergency.

(3) The Speaker of Parliament, the President of the Constitutional Court and the Prime Minister shall jointly determine whether the Parliament is obstructed, and whether a declaration of a state of war, a state of national crisis or a state of emergency is justified.
(4) At its first meeting following the end of its obstruction, the Parliament shall review whether the declaration of a state of war, state of national crisis or state of emergency was justified, and shall rule on the legality of the measures taken. A majority of two-thirds of the votes of the Members of Parliament is required for this decision.

Article 19/B.
(1) During a state of national crisis the National Defence Council shall decide on the deployment of the armed forces abroad and within the country, and on the introduction of emergency measures as defined in a separate statute.
(2) The National Defence Council is chaired by the President of the Republic, and is composed of the following members: the Speaker of Parliament, the leaders of the parliamentary groups of the political parties represented in Parliament, the Prime Minister, the ministers, and the Commander and the Chief of Staff of the Hungarian Army.
(3) The National Defence Council shall exercise:
(a) the powers transferred to it by the Parliament;
(b) the powers of the President of the Republic;
(c) the powers of the Government.
(4) The National Defence Council may issue decrees, in which it may suspend the application of certain statutes or may deviate from statutory provisions; furthermore, it may take other extraordinary measures, but may not suspend the application of the Constitution.
(5) Decrees of the National Defence Council shall cease to have effect upon cessation of the state of national crisis, unless the Parliament extends the effect of such decrees.
(6) The operation of the Constitutional Court may not be restricted even during a state of national crisis.

Article 19/C.
(1) Should the Parliament be obstructed upon declaration of a state of emergency, the President of the Republic shall decide on the use of the armed forces.
(2) During a state of emergency, the emergency measures defined in a separate statute shall be introduced by decree of the President of the Republic.
(3) The President of the Republic shall immediately inform the Speaker of Parliament of any emergency measures that have been introduced. The Parliament or, should the Parliament be obstructed, the Parliamentary Defence Committee shall remain continuously in session during a state of emergency. The Parliament, or the Parliamentary Defence Committee, shall have the power to suspend the application of emergency measures introduced by the President of the Republic.
(4) Emergency measures introduced by decree shall remain in force for a period of thirty days, unless the Parliament or, should the Parliament be obstructed, the Parliamentary Defence Committee extends its effect.
(5) In other respects the rules governing a state of national crisis shall apply to a state of emergency.

Article 19/D.
A majority of two-thirds of the votes of the Members of Parliament present is required to

pass the statute on the detailed regulations to be applied during a state of national crisis and a state of emergency.

Article 19/E.

(1) In the event that the territory of Hungary is subject to unexpected attack by foreign armed groups, the Government has to take immediate measures to repel such attack and defend the territorial integrity of the country with the anti-aircraft and stand-by air forces of the Hungarian Army, in accordance with the defence plan approved by the President of the Republic—with forces commensurate to the gravity of the attack and prepared for such a role—until the decision on the declaration of a state of emergency or state of national crisis is made, in the interests of protecting the constitutional order, the lives and property of citizens, as well as public order and safety.

(2) In order to take further measures, the Government shall immediately inform the Parliament and the President of the Republic of its measures taken on the basis of Paragraph (1).

(3) A majority of two-thirds of the votes of the Members of Parliament present is required to pass the statute on the rules applicable to immediate measures to be taken by the Government.

Article 20.

(1) The election of Members of Parliament—except for the elections due to the dissolution of Parliament—shall be held in April or May of the fourth year following the election of the previous Parliament.

(2) Members of Parliament shall perform their activities in the public interest.

(3) Members of Parliament are granted immunity, in accordance with the provisions of the statute on the legal status of Members of Parliament.

(4) Members of Parliament are entitled to remuneration adequate to ensure their independence, to specified allowances and to reimbursement of their expenses. A majority of two-thirds of the votes of the Members of Parliament present is required to pass the statute on the amount of remuneration and of reimbursement of expenses as well as on the scope of allowances.

(5) A Member of Parliament may not be the President of the Republic, a member of the Constitutional Court, the Parliamentary Commissioner for Civil Rights, the President, Deputy President or auditor of the State Audit Office, a judge or public prosecutor, an employee of an organ of the public administration—with the exception of the Members of the Government and Parliamentary State Secretaries—nor a professional member of the armed forces, the police or other security organs. Other cases of incompatibility may be established by statute.

(6) A majority of two-thirds of the votes of the Members of Parliament present is required to pass the statute on the legal status of Members of Parliament.

Article 20/A.

(1) The mandate of a Member of Parliament shall cease:

(a) upon completion of the term of Parliament;

(b) upon the death of the Member of Parliament;

(c) upon declaration of an incompatibility;

(d) upon resignation;

(e) upon losing his right to vote.

(2) The Parliament shall decide on a declaration of incompatibility with a majority of two-thirds of the votes of the Members of Parliament present.

(3) Members of Parliament may resign their mandate by making a statement to this effect to the Parliament. A statement of acceptance by the Parliament is not required for the resignation to be effective.

Article 21.
(1) The Parliament shall elect a Speaker of Parliament, Deputy Speakers and Clerks from among its Members.
(2) The Parliament shall establish standing committees from among its Members and may delegate a committee for the investigation of any issue whatsoever.
(3) Everyone is obliged to provide Parliamentary Committees with the information requested by them and to testify before such committees.

Article 22.
(1) The Parliament shall hold two regular sessions annually: every year from 1st February to 15th June and from 1st September to 15th December.
(2) The inaugural sitting of the Parliament shall be convened by the President of the Republic at a date within one month following the elections; in other cases the Speaker of Parliament shall see to the convening of sessions of the Parliament and its individual sittings.
(3) Upon written request by the President of the Republic, the Government or one-fifth of the Members of Parliament, an extraordinary sitting of the Parliament shall be convened. Such request shall contain the grounds for convening the extraordinary sitting, as well as the proposed date and agenda.
(4) The sitting of the Parliament may be adjourned by the President of the Republic no more than once in a parliamentary session and for a period not exceeding thirty days.
(5) During the period of adjournment the Speaker of Parliament has to reconvene the Parliament, upon written request made by one-fifth of the Members of Parliament, at a date no later than eight days following the receipt thereof.

Article 23.
Sittings of the Parliament are open to the public. Upon request by the President of the Republic, the Government or any Member of Parliament and with the assent of two-thirds of its Members, the Parliament may decide to hold a sitting *in camera.*

Article 24.
(1) The Parliament is quorate if more than half of its Members are present.
(2) The Parliament shall pass its decisions with a majority of more than half of the votes of its Members present.
(3) A majority of two-thirds of the votes of the Members of Parliament is required to amend the Constitution and for certain decisions specified therein.
(4) The Parliament shall establish its rules of procedure and order of debate in its Standing Orders, to be adopted with a majority of two-thirds of the votes of the Members of Parliament present.
(5) [Repealed.]

Article 25.
(1) Legislation may be initiated by the President of the Republic, the Government, all Parliamentary Committees, and any Member of Parliament.

(2) The authority to pass legislation is vested in the Parliament.
(3) The Speaker of Parliament shall sign statutes passed by the Parliament and subsequently forward them to the President of the Republic.

Article 26.
(1) The President of the Republic shall see to the promulgation of the statutes within a period of fifteen days following its receipt, or within a period of five days if the Speaker of Parliament requests that the issue be accorded urgency. The President of the Republic shall sign the statutes sent for promulgation. The statutes shall be promulgated in the *Hungarian Official Gazette.*
(2) Should the President of the Republic disagree with a statute or with any provision thereof, prior to signing it, he may return such statute, along with his comments, to the Parliament for reconsideration within the period specified in Paragraph (1).
(3) The Parliament shall debate the statute again and hold another vote on its passage. Following this, the President of the Republic is required to sign the statute forwarded to him by the Speaker of Parliament, and to promulgate it within a period of five days.
(4) Should the President of the Republic consider any provision of a statute to be unconstitutional, he may, prior to signing it, refer it to the Constitutional Court for appraisal within the period specified in Paragraph (1).
(5) Should the Constitutional Court—in extraordinary proceedings—determine the statute to be unconstitutional, the President of the Republic shall return the statute to the Parliament; otherwise he is required to sign the statute and promulgate it within a period of five days.
(6) The President of the Republic shall only sign a statute submitted to referendum if it was confirmed by the referendum.

Article 27.
Members of Parliament may direct a question to the Parliamentary Commissioner for Civil Rights and the Parliamentary Commissioner for the Rights of National and Ethnic Minorities, to the President of the State Audit Office and the Chairman of the National Bank of Hungary, and an interpellation or a question to the Government or any of the Members of the Government, as well as to the Chief Public Prosecutor on any matter which falls within their respective sphere of authority.

Article 28.
(1) The parliamentary term commences with its inaugural sitting.
(2) The Parliament may declare its dissolution prior to the completion of its term.
(3) The President of the Republic may also dissolve the Parliament, simultaneously with the announcement of new elections, if:
(a) the Parliament passes a motion of no confidence in the Government on no less than four occasions in a period of twelve months during the course of one term, or;
(b) in the event that the mandate of the Government ends, a candidate for Prime Minister nominated by the President of the Republic is not elected by the Parliament within a period of forty days from the day upon which the first candidate is nominated.
(4) [Repealed.]
(5) Prior to dissolving the Parliament, the President of the Republic has to request the opinions of the Prime Minister, the Speaker of Parliament and the leaders of the parliamentary groups of the political parties represented in the Parliament.

(6) A new Parliament shall be elected within a period of three months following the declaration of the Parliament's dissolution or the Parliament having been dissolved.
(7) The Parliament shall continue to operate until the inaugural sitting of the new Parliament.

Article 28/A.
(1) During a state of national crisis or a state of emergency the Parliament may neither declare its dissolution nor be dissolved.
(2) Should the term of Parliament expire during a state of national crisis or a state of emergency, its mandate shall be extended until the cessation of the state of national crisis or state of emergency.
(3) During a state of war, or the danger of war or of necessity, the President of the Republic may reconvene a Parliament which has declared its dissolution or which has been dissolved. The Parliament itself shall pass a resolution on the extension of its mandate.

Article 28/B.
(1) Any question falling within the competence of Parliament may be the subject of a national referendum or popular initiative.
(2) A majority of two-thirds of the votes of the Members of Parliament present is required to pass the statute on national referenda and popular initiatives.

Article 28/C.
(1) A national referendum may be held with the objective of taking a decision or of consultation; the holding of a referendum may be obligatory or discretionary.
(2) A national referendum must be held on the petition of at least 200,000 voters.
(3) Should the holding of a national referendum be obligatory, the decision made in the successful referendum shall bind the Parliament.
(4) On the initiative of the President of the Republic, the Government, one-third of the Members of Parliament or 100,000 voters, Parliament may decide in its discretion that a national referendum be held.
(5) A national referendum may not be held:
(a) on the State Budget and its implementation, on central taxes, stamp and customs duties, as well as on the content of the laws concerning uniform requirements on local taxes;
(b) on the obligations arising from international treaties in force and on the content of the laws containing these obligations;
(c) on the provisions of the Constitution on national referenda and popular initiatives;
(d) on such personal questions, and on such questions concerning the establishment (restructuring, dissolution) of organizations that fall within the competence of Parliament;
(e) on the dissolution of Parliament;
(f) on the programme of the Government;
(g) on the declaration of a state of war, state of national crisis or state of emergency;
(h) on the deployment of the armed forces abroad or within the country;
(i) on the dissolution of the representative body of the local government;
(j) on the exercise of general amnesty.
(6) A decisive obligatory referendum is successful if more than half of the voters voting

validly and at least more than one quarter of all persons having the right to vote have given the same answer to the question put.

Article 28/D.
A popular initiative may be submitted by at least 50,000 voters. A popular initiative may be directed at putting onto Parliament's agenda a question falling within its competence. Parliament is obliged to discuss the question contained in the initiative.

Article 28/E.
Signatures may be collected for four months in the case of a petition of the voters directed at a referendum and for two months in the case of a popular initiative.

Chapter III.
The President of the Republic

Article 29.
(1) The Head of State of Hungary is the President of the Republic, who represents the unity of the nation and guards the democratic operation of the State.
(2) The President of the Republic is the Commander in Chief of the armed forces.

Article 29/A.
(1) The Parliament shall elect the President of the Republic for a term of five years.
(2) Any enfranchised citizen who has reached the age of thirty-five prior to the date of election may be elected to the office of President of the Republic.
(3) The President of the Republic may be re-elected to such office no more than once.

Article 29/B.
(1) The election of the President of the Republic shall be preceded by nomination. The written recommendation of no less than fifty Members of Parliament is required for such a nomination to be valid. The nomination must be submitted to the Speaker of Parliament prior to the announcement of the vote. No Member of Parliament may nominate more than one candidate. If a Member of Parliament nominates more than one candidate, all nominations made by this Member shall be invalid.
(2) The Parliament shall elect the President of the Republic by secret ballot. Voting may be repeated should this prove necessary. The candidate who receives a majority of two-thirds of the votes of the Members of Parliament in the first round of voting is elected President of the Republic.
(3) Should no candidate receive such a majority in the first round of voting, a new vote must be held on the basis of a new nomination, in accordance with Paragraph (1). A majority of two-thirds of the votes of the Members of Parliament shall also be required to be elected in the second round of voting.
(4) Should no candidate win the required majority in the second round of voting, a third round of voting must be held. In the third round of voting only those two candidates who received the largest numbers of votes in the second round may stand for election. The candidate receiving a majority of the votes—regardless of the number of votes cast—in the third round of voting is elected President of the Republic.

(5) The election procedure shall be completed within a period of no more than three consecutive days.

Article 29/C.
(1) The President of the Republic must be elected at least thirty days prior to the expiration of the previous President's mandate or, should the President's mandate end prematurely, within thirty days from the date upon which the mandate ends.
(2) The Speaker of Parliament shall announce the elections for the office of President of the Republic.

Article 29/D.
The newly elected President of the Republic shall enter office upon expiration of the previous President's mandate or, should the President's mandate end prematurely, on the eighth day following the announcement of the result of the elections. Prior to entering office, the President of the Republic shall take an oath before Parliament.

Article 29/E.
(1) In the event that the President is temporarily prevented from attending to his duties, or that his mandate should for any reason end prematurely, the Speaker of Parliament shall exercise the powers of the President of the Republic until the newly elected President enters office, with the limitation that the Speaker may not return statutes to the Parliament for consideration, nor to the Constitutional Court for review, may not dissolve the Parliament, and may only grant pardons to individuals upon whom final conviction has been passed.
(2) While acting as the President of the Republic, the Speaker of Parliament may not exercise his powers as a Member of Parliament, and his duties as Speaker of Parliament shall be attended to by the Deputy Speaker of Parliament designated by the Parliament.

Article 30.
(1) The office of President of the Republic is incompatible with all other public, social and political offices or mandates. The President of the Republic shall not otherwise gainfully pursue an occupation and shall not accept remuneration for other activities, with the exception of such activities which fall under the protection of copyright.
(2) A majority of two-thirds of the votes of the Members of Parliament present is required to pass the statute on the amount of remuneration, allowances and reimbursement due to the President of the Republic.

Article 30/A.
(1) The President of the Republic shall:
(a) represent the State of Hungary;
(b) conclude international treaties in the name of the Republic of Hungary; if the subject of the treaty falls within the competence of the legislative, prior approval by the Parliament is necessary for conclusion of the treaty;
(c) accredit and receive ambassadors and envoys;
(d) announce general parliamentary or local government elections, as well as the dates of national referenda;

(e) have the right to participate in and speak at sittings of the Parliament and of its committees;
(f) have the right to propose to the Parliament to take action;
(g) have the right to initiate national referenda;
(h) appoint and dismiss State Secretaries in accordance with rules specified in a separate statute;
(i) appoint and dismiss the Chairman and Vice-Chairmen of the National Bank of Hungary as well as university professors upon the recommendation of persons or organizations specified in a separate statute; appoint and dismiss the university rectors; appoint and promote generals of the armed forces; confirm the President of the Hungarian Academy of Sciences;
(j) confer titles, awards, medals and decorations specified by law and authorize the use thereof;
(k) exercise the right to grant individual pardons;
(l) decide in cases of citizenship;
(m) decide in all issues assigned to his sphere of authority by separate statutes.
(2) The counter signature of the Prime Minister or responsible Minister is required for all of the measures and actions of the President of the Republic listed in Paragraph (1), with the exception of the items specified in Points (a), (d), (e), (f) and (g).

Article 31.
(1) The mandate of the President of the Republic shall cease:
(a) upon completion of the term of office;
(b) upon the death of the President;
(c) upon incapacitation preventing him from attending to his duties for a period of more than ninety days;
(d) upon declaration of an incompatibility;
(e) upon resignation;
(f) upon removal from the office of President of the Republic.
(2) Should grounds for an incompatibility [Article 30(1)] involving the President of the Republic arise during his term of office, upon the motion of any Member of Parliament, the Parliament may resolve to declare the existence of an incompatibility. A majority of two-thirds of the votes of the Members of Parliament is necessary to carry such a resolution. Voting shall be held by secret ballot.
(3) The President of the Republic may resign from office by addressing a statement to this effect to the Parliament. A statement of acceptance by the Parliament is required for the resignation to be valid. Within a period of fifteen days the Parliament may request that the President of the Republic reconsider his decision. Should the President of the Republic stand by the decision, the Parliament may not deny recognition of his resignation.
(4) The President of the Republic may be removed from office on the basis of an intentional violation of the Constitution or any other law committed while exercising his office.

Article 31/A.
(1) The person of the President of the Republic is inviolable; his protection under criminal law shall be provided for in a separate statute.
(2) Should the President of the Republic violate the Constitution or any other law while exercising his office, a motion supported by one-fifth of the Members of Parliament may propose that impeachment proceedings be initiated against him.
(3) A majority of two-thirds of the votes of the Members of Parliament is required to initiate impeachment proceedings. Voting shall be held by secret ballot.

(4) From passage of this resolution by the Parliament until the conclusion of the impeachment proceedings, the President of the Republic may not exercise his powers.
(5) The Constitutional Court shall have jurisdiction to rule upon the case.
(6) Should the Constitutional Court determine that the law was violated, it shall have the authority to remove the President of the Republic from office.
(7)–(8) [Repealed.]

Article 32.
(1) If the impeachment proceedings were initiated against the President of the Republic for an act to be prosecuted under criminal law, committed during his term in office in connection with official activities, then the Constitutional Court shall also apply the basic provisions of criminal procedure in its proceedings. The prosecution shall be represented by a Commissioner for Prosecution elected from among the Members of Parliament.
(2) Criminal proceedings against the President of the Republic for other acts may only be initiated subsequent to the end of his term of office.
(3) Should the Constitutional Court find the President of the Republic guilty of an intentional criminal offence, it may remove the President of the Republic from office and simultaneously apply any punishment and measure prescribed for such offence in the Criminal Code.

Chapter IV.
The Constitutional Court

Article 32/A.
(1) The Constitutional Court shall review the constitutionality of laws and perform the tasks assigned to its jurisdiction by statute.
(2) The Constitutional Court shall annul the statutes and other legal norms that it finds to be unconstitutional.
(3) Everyone has the right to initiate proceedings of the Constitutional Court in the cases specified by statute.
(4) The Constitutional Court shall consist of eleven members who are elected by the Parliament. Members of the Constitutional Court shall be nominated by a Nominating Committee consisting of one Member of the parliamentary group of each political party represented in the Parliament. A majority of two-thirds of the votes of the Members of Parliament is required to elect a member of the Constitutional Court.
(5) Members of the Constitutional Court may not be members of a political party and may not engage in any political activities beyond the duties arising from the competences of the Constitutional Court.
(6) A majority of two-thirds of the votes of the Members of Parliament present is required to pass the statute on the organization and operation of the Constitutional Court.

Chapter V.
The Parliamentary Commissioner for Civil Rights and the Parliamentary Commissioner for the Rights of National and Ethnic Minorities

Article 32/B.
(1) The Parliamentary Commissioner for Civil Rights is responsible for investigating or

having investigated irregularities concerning constitutional rights which have come to his attention and initiating general or specific measures for their remedy.
(2) The Parliamentary Commissioner for the Rights of National and Ethnic Minorities is responsible for investigating or having investigated irregularities concerning the rights of national or ethnic minorities which have come to his attention and initiating general or specific measures for their remedy.
(3) Everyone has the right to initiate proceedings by the Parliamentary Commissioner in the cases specified by statute.
(4) The Parliamentary Commissioners for Civil Rights and for the Rights of National and Ethnic Minorities shall be elected by a majority of two-thirds of the votes of the Members of Parliament, upon the nomination of the President of the Republic. The Parliament may also elect special Commissioners for the protection of certain constitutional rights.
(5) [Repealed.]
(6) The Parliamentary Commissioners shall report annually to Parliament on their activities.
(7) A majority of two-thirds of the votes of the Members of Parliament present is required to pass the statute on Parliamentary Commissioners.

Chapter VI.
The State Audit Office and the National Bank of Hungary

Article 32/C.
(1) The State Audit Office is the organ of Parliament responsible for financial and economic auditing. Within its competence the State Audit Office shall audit the management of public finances, in particular the well-founded nature of the proposed State Budget, the necessity and expediency of expenditures, and countersign contracts pertaining to the assumption of credits for the Budget; it shall review the legality of State Budget expenditures in advance; it shall audit the final accounts of the implementation of the State Budget; it shall audit the management of state assets, the activities of state-owned ventures and enterprises concerning the maintenance in the value or increase of their assets; it shall perform the tasks assigned to its competence by statute.
(2) The State Audit Office shall conduct its audits from the perspective of legality, expediency and efficiency. The State Audit Office shall present the Parliament with a report on the auditing activities it has carried out. Its report shall be made public. The President of the State Audit Office shall present the Parliament with the audit report on the final accounts together with the final accounts themselves.
(3) A majority of two-thirds of the votes of the Members of Parliament is required to elect the President and Vice-Presidents of the State Audit Office.
(4) A majority of two-thirds of the votes of the Members of Parliament present is required to pass the statute on the organization and basic principles of operation of the State Audit Office .

Article 32/D.
(1) The National Bank of Hungary is responsible for issuing legal tender, protecting the stability of the national currency and regulating the circulation of money, in such manner as provided for by a separate statute.

(2) The Chairman of the National Bank of Hungary is appointed by the President of the Republic for a term of six years.
(3) The Chairman of the National Bank of Hungary shall report annually to Parliament on the activities of the National Bank.

Chapter VII.
The Government

Article 33.
(1) The Government shall consist of:
(a) the Prime Minister and
(b) the Ministers.
(2) The Prime Minister shall be substituted by a Minister designated by him.
(3) The Prime Minister shall be elected by a majority of the votes of the Members of Parliament, upon the nomination of the President of the Republic. The Parliament shall decide on the election of the Prime Minister together with the Government's programme.
(4) The Ministers shall be appointed and dismissed by the President of the Republic, based on the nomination of the Prime Minister.
(5) The Government is formed with the appointment of the Ministers. Subsequent to its formation, the Members of the Government shall take an oath before Parliament.

Article 33/A.
The Government's mandate shall end:
(a) upon inauguration of the newly-elected Parliament;
(b) upon resignation of the Prime Minister or the Government;
(c) upon the death of the Prime Minister;
(d) upon the Prime Minister losing his right to vote;
(e) upon the declaration of incompatibility of the Prime Minister; or
(f) if the Parliament passes a motion of no confidence in the Prime Minister and elects a new Prime Minister in accordance with the provisions of Article 39/A(1).

Article 33/B.
The mandate of a Minister shall end:
(a) upon the end of the mandate of the Government;
(b) upon his resignation;
(c) upon his dismissal;
(d) upon his death;
(e) upon his losing his right to vote;
(f) upon the declaration of his incompatibility.

Article 34.
The Ministries of the Republic of Hungary shall be listed in a separate statute.

Article 35.
(1) The Government shall:
(a) protect constitutional order, and protect and guarantee the rights of the citizens;
(b) ensure the implementation of laws;

(c) direct the Ministries and other organs placed under its direct control and co-ordinate their work;
(d) ensure the supervision of the lawful operation of local governments, in co-operation with the Minister of the Interior;
(e) provide for the formulation of social and economic plans and the implementation thereof;
(f) define the tasks of the State in the development of science and culture, and provide for the conditions necessary for the implementation thereof;
(g) define the state system of social welfare and health care services, and provide the coverage for such services;
(h) direct the operation of the armed forces and of the police and other security organs;
(i) take the measures necessary to avert natural disasters and their consequences that endanger the lives and property of citizens (hereafter "state of danger") and to maintain public order and safety;
(j) participate in the determination of foreign policy; conclude international treaties in the name of the Government of the Republic of Hungary;
(k) perform those tasks assigned to its competence by law.
(2) Within its competence, the Government shall issue decrees and pass resolutions. These shall be signed by the Prime Minister. Government decrees and resolutions may not conflict with statutes. Government decrees shall be promulgated in the *Hungarian Official Gazette.*
(3) In a state of danger the Government, if authorized to do so by the Parliament, may issue decrees and take measures which deviate from the provisions of certain statutes. A majority of two-thirds of the votes of the Members of Parliament present is required to pass the statute on the rules applicable in a state of danger.
(4) With the exception of legal norms, the Government shall annul or amend all resolutions or measures of any subordinate organs which conflict with a statute.

Article 36.
In the course of fulfilling its tasks, the Government shall co-operate with the relevant social organizations.

Article 37.
(1) The Prime Minister shall preside at the meetings of the Government and shall ensure the implementation of government decrees and resolutions.
(2) The Ministers shall head the branches of public administration falling within their respective portfolios and direct the public organs subordinate to them in accordance with the provisions of legal norms and government resolutions. Ministers without portfolio shall perform the tasks determined by the Government.
(3) Within the ambit of performing their tasks, Members of the Government may issue decrees. These, however, may not stand in conflict with a statute or with government decrees or resolutions. Such decrees shall be promulgated in the *Hungarian Official Gazette.*

Article 38.
[Repealed.]

Article 39.
(1) The Government is responsible to the Parliament for its operation. It is required to report regularly to the Parliament.

(2) Members of the Government are responsible to the Government and to the Parliament and shall report to the Government and the Parliament on their activities. The legal status, remuneration and method of accountability of Members of the Government and State Secretaries shall be regulated by statute.
(3) Members of the Government may participate and speak at sittings of Parliament.

Article 39/A.
(1) A written motion of no confidence in the Prime Minister may be introduced by no less than one-fifth of the Members of Parliament, indicating the nomination for a candidate for the office of Prime Minister. A motion of no confidence in the Prime Minister is considered a motion of no confidence in the Government as well. Should, on the basis of this motion, the majority of the Members of Parliament express their lack of confidence, then the candidate nominated for the office of Prime Minister in the motion shall be considered to have been elected.
(2) The debate and vote on the motion of no confidence shall be held no earlier than three days and no later than eight days following the submission of the motion.
(3) The Government, via the Prime Minister, may propose a vote of confidence in accordance with the terms specified in Paragraph (2).
(4) The Government, via the Prime Minister, may propose that the vote on the motion it has made simultaneously be considered as a vote of confidence.
(5) Should the Parliament, in the instances set out in Paragraphs (3)–(4), not vote for confidence in the Government, the Government shall resign.

Article 39/B.
Should the mandate of the Government end, the Government shall remain in office until the formation of the new Government and shall continue to exercise the rights accorded to the Government; it may not, however, conclude international treaties and may only issue decrees with the express authorization of a law, in cases when delay is not permissible.

Article 39/C.
(1) If the mandate of the Prime Minister has ended upon the inauguration of the newly elected Parliament or upon the resignation of the Prime Minister or of the Government, the Prime Minister shall exercise his powers as acting Prime Minister, but he shall not have the power to propose the appointment or dismissal of Ministers, and may only issue a decree in urgent cases and on the basis of express authorization provided for by a law.
(2) If the mandate of the Prime Minister has ended as a result of his death, losing his right to vote or the declaration of incompatibility, the Minister who was entrusted by the Prime Minister with his representation shall—with the limitations provided for in Paragraph (1) hereof—exercise the powers of the Prime Minister; should more than one Minister be entrusted with the representation of the Prime Minister, the Minister entrusted in the first place shall exercise such powers.

Article 40.
(1) The Government may form committees for specific responsibilities.
(2) [Repealed.]
(3) The Government has the power to place any branch of public administration under its direct supervision and establish special organs for this purpose.

Chapter VIII.
The Armed Forces and the Police

Article 40/A.
(1) The fundamental duty of the armed forces (Hungarian Army, Border Guard) is the military defence of the country. Within the ambit of its policing activities, the Border Guard shall guard the borders of the country, control border traffic, and maintain order on the borders. A majority of two-thirds of the votes of the Members of Parliament present is required to pass the statute on the tasks of and detailed regulations on the armed forces.
(2) The fundamental task of the police is to maintain public safety and internal order. A majority of two-thirds of the votes of the Members of Parliament present is required to pass the statute on the police and the detailed regulations pertaining to national security activities.

Article 40/B.
(1) With the exception of military manoeuvres carried out according to international treaties and peace-keeping missions upon request of the United Nations, the armed forces may only cross the country's borders with the prior consent of the Parliament.
(2) In the event of armed actions aimed at subverting constitutional order or at the acquisition of exclusive control of public power, or in the case of grave acts of violence committed by force of arms or by armed groups which endanger the lives and property of citizens on a mass scale, during a state of emergency declared in accordance with the provisions of the Constitution, the armed forces may be used if the use of the police proves insufficient.
(3) Within the framework of the Constitution and other separate laws, only the Parliament, the President of the Republic, the National Defence Council, the Government and the responsible Minister shall have the right to direct the armed forces, unless otherwise provided by valid international treaties.
(4) Professional members of the armed forces, the police and the civil national security services may not be members of political parties and may not engage in political activities.
(5) Restrictions on the political activities of nonprofessional members of the armed forces may be established by a statute passed by a majority of two-thirds of the votes of the Members of Parliament present.

Article 40/C.
(1) Unless otherwise provided by valid international treaties, foreign armed forces may not pass through, be used or be stationed in the territory of the Republic of Hungary without the prior consent of the Parliament.
(2) International treaties which affect matters of national defence must be approved by statute and publicly promulgated.

Chapter IX.
Local Governments

Article 41.
(1) The territory of the Republic of Hungary is divided into the capital, the counties, the cities and the municipalities.
(2) The capital is divided into districts. Districts may be formed in cities.

Article 42.
The community of voters of the municipalities, cities, the capital and its districts, as well as the counties have the right to local government. Local government is the independent, democratic management of local affairs affecting the community of voters and the exercise of local public authority in the interests of the population.

Article 43.
(1) The fundamental rights of all local governments (Article 44/A) are equal. The duties of local governments may differ.
(2) The rights and duties of local governments shall be determined by statute. The lawful exercise of the powers of local government is afforded judicial protection; the local government may turn to the Constitutional Court for the protection of its rights.

Article 44.
(1) Voters exercise local government through the representative body [local council] elected by them and by way of local referendum.
(2) With the exception of by-elections, members of local representative bodies and Mayors shall be elected in October of the fourth year following the previous general elections.
(3) The mandate of the representative body shall last until the day of the local government elections. If elections were not held due to the lack of candidates, the mandate of the representative body shall be extended until the day of the by-elections. The mandate of the Mayor shall last until the election of the new Mayor.
(4) A representative body may declare its dissolution prior to the expiration of its mandate and in accordance with the conditions stipulated in the statute on local government. Upon dissolution of the body or its being dissolved [Article 19, Paragraph (3)(l)], the mandate of the Mayor also ends.

Article 44/A.
(1) The local representative body:
(a) shall independently manage and administrate the affairs of local government; its decisions may only be reviewed on the grounds of their legality;
(b) shall exercise the rights of ownership in respect of the property of the local government, independently manage local government revenues, and may undertake entrepreneurial activities at its own liability;
(c) shall be entitled to its own revenues appropriate for performing the duties of local government as prescribed by law, and shall furthermore be entitled to state support commensurate to the scope of such tasks;
(d) shall determine the types and rates of local taxes within the framework established by law;
(e) shall independently establish its own organization and rules of procedure within the framework established by law;
(f) may create symbols and emblems of local government, and establish local honours and titles;
(g) may, in public matters that affect the local population, present initiatives to the decision-making organ responsible;
(h) may freely merge with other local representative bodies, may create local government associations for the representation of their interests, may co-operate with the local govern-

ments of other countries and may be a member of international organizations of local governments.
(2) Local representative bodies may issue decrees, which may not conflict with higher ranking legal norms.

Article 44/B.
(1) The Mayor is the chairman of the local representative body. The representative body may elect committees and create offices.
(2) In exceptional cases, the Mayor may perform duties and exercise powers of the public administration, in addition to his local government responsibilities, in accordance with a law or a government decree authorized by law.
(3) Duties and powers of the public administration may be assigned, by a law or government decree, to the Secretary of the local government and in exceptional cases to the administrators of the Office of Local Government.

Article 44/C.
A majority of two-thirds of the votes of the Members of Parliament present is required to pass the statute on local government. The fundamental rights of local governments may be restricted by a law which also requires the same majority.

Chapter X.
The Judiciary

Article 45.
(1) In the Republic of Hungary justice is administered by the Supreme Court of the Republic of Hungary, the Regional Courts of Appeal, the County Court of the Capital, and the county courts as well as the local courts.
(2) Special courts may be established by law for specific groups of cases.

Article 46.
(1) The courts—unless provided otherwise by statute—shall administer justice as a bench.
(2) In cases and in the manner provided by law, lay judges shall also participate in the administration of justice.
(3) Only professional judges may sit alone or act as president of a bench.

Article 47.
(1) The Supreme Court is the highest judicial organ of the Republic of Hungary.
(2) The Supreme Court shall ensure the uniformity in the application of the law by the courts; its resolutions on the uniformity in the application of the law shall be binding on all courts.

Article 48.
(1) The President of the Supreme Court shall be elected by the Parliament, upon the recommendation of the President of the Republic; the Vice-Presidents of the Supreme Court shall be appointed by the President of the Republic, upon the recommendation of the President of the Supreme Court. A majority of two-thirds of the votes of the Members of Parliament is required to elect the President of the Supreme Court.

(2) Professional judges shall be appointed by the President of the Republic in the manner provided by statute.
(3) Judges may only be removed from office on the grounds and in accordance with the procedure provided by statute.

Article 49.
[Repealed.]

Article 50.
(1) The courts of the Republic of Hungary shall protect and guarantee the constitutional order, as well as the rights and lawful interests of citizens, and shall punish those who commit criminal offences.
(2) The courts shall supervise the legality of the decisions of public administration.
(3) Judges are independent and answer only to the law. Judges may not be members of political parties and may not engage in political activities.
(4) The administration of the courts shall be the task of the National Council of the Judiciary; self-government organs of the judges shall also participate in the administration.
(5) A majority of two-thirds of the votes of the Members of Parliament present is required to pass the statute on the organization and administration of courts, as well as on the legal status and remuneration of judges.

Chapter XI.
The Office of the Public Prosecutor

Article 51.
(1) The Chief Public Prosecutor and the Office of the Public Prosecutor of the Republic of Hungary shall ensure the protection of the rights of the citizens, and shall steadfastly prosecute any act which violates or endangers the constitutional order, and the security and independence of the country.
(2) The Office of the Public Prosecutor shall exercise powers in relation to investigations as provided for by law, represent the prosecution in court proceedings, and supervise the legality of the implementation of punishments.
(3) The Office of the Public Prosecutor shall contribute to ensuring that all organizations of society, government bodies and citizens comply with the law. When the law is violated, the Office of the Public Prosecutor shall act to uphold the law in the cases and manner provided by statute.

Article 52.
(1) The Chief Public Prosecutor shall be elected by the Parliament upon the recommendation of the President of the Republic; the Deputies to the Chief Public Prosecutor shall be elected on the basis of the recommendation made by the Chief Public Prosecutor.
(2) The Chief Public Prosecutor shall be answerable to the Parliament and shall report on his activities.

Article 53.
(1) Public prosecutors shall be appointed by the Chief Public Prosecutor of the Republic of Hungary.

(2) Public prosecutors may not be members of political parties and may not engage in political activities.
(3) The Office of the Public Prosecutor is directed by the Chief Public Prosecutor.
(4) The rules pertaining to the Office of the Public Prosecutor shall be determined by statute.

Chapter XII.
Fundamental Rights and Duties

Article 54.
(1) In the Republic of Hungary every human being has the inherent right to life and to human dignity, of which no one can be arbitrarily deprived.
(2) No one shall be subjected to torture or to cruel, inhuman or degrading treatment or punishment; it is particularly prohibited to conduct medical or scientific experiments on human beings without their consent.

Article 55.
(1) In the Republic of Hungary everyone has the right to freedom and personal security; no one shall be deprived of his freedom except on the grounds and in accordance with the procedure provided for by statute.
(2) Anyone suspected of having committed a criminal offence and having been arrested shall promptly be either released or brought before a judge. The judge is required to hear the person brought before him and shall promptly decide in a ruling provided with a written reasoning on his/her release or arrest.
(3) Everyone who has been the victim of an illegal arrest or detention shall have the right to compensation.

Article 56.
In the Republic of Hungary every human being has legal capacity.

Article 57.
(1) In the Republic of Hungary everyone is equal before the law and, in the determination of any criminal charge against him/her or in the litigation of his/her rights and duties, everyone is entitled to a fair and public hearing by an independent and impartial court established by statute.
(2) In the Republic of Hungary no one shall be considered guilty until his/her criminal responsibility has been established by the final judgment of a court.
(3) Everyone subject to criminal proceedings is entitled to defend himself at all stages of the proceedings. Counsel for the defence shall not be held responsible for opinions expressed in the course of the defence.
(4) No one shall be declared guilty and subjected to punishment for an act which did not constitute a criminal offence under Hungarian law at the time it was committed.
(5) In the Republic of Hungary everyone is entitled to seek a legal remedy, as provided for by the law, against decisions of the courts, the public administration or other authorities which infringe his rights or justified interests. The right to a remedy may be restricted by a statute passed with the majority of two-thirds of the votes of the Members of Parliament present and in the interest of adjudicating disputes in a reasonable time as well as being proportional thereto.

Article 58.
(1) Everyone legally staying in the territory of the Republic of Hungary—with the exception of the cases established by law—has the right to move freely and to choose his place of residence, including the right to leave his domicile or the country.
(2) Foreigners legally staying in the territory of the Republic of Hungary may only be expelled on the basis of a decision made in accordance with the law.
(3) A majority of two-thirds of the votes of the Members of Parliament present is required to pass the statute on the freedom of movement and residence.

Article 59.
(1) In the Republic of Hungary everyone has the right to the good standing of his/her reputation, the inviolability of his/her private home and the protection of his/her personal secrets and data.
(2) A majority of two-thirds of the votes of the Members of Parliament present is required to pass the statute on the protection of personal data.

Article 60.
(1) In the Republic of Hungary everyone has the right to freedom of thought, conscience and religion.
(2) This right shall include the free choice or acceptance of a religion or personal conviction, either alone or in community with others, in public or in private, to manifest his/her religion or personal conviction in religious acts and observances or in other ways, to refrain from its manifestation, to practise and to teach it.
(3) In the Republic of Hungary the church shall operate in separation from the State.
(4) A majority of two-thirds of the votes of the Members of Parliament present is required to pass the statute on the freedom of personal conviction and religion.

Article 61.
(1) In the Republic of Hungary everyone has the right to freedom of expression, and to receive and impart information of public interest.
(2) The Republic of Hungary recognizes and protects the freedom of the press.
(3) A majority of two-thirds of the votes of the Members of Parliament present is required to pass the statute on the public access to information of public interest and the statute on the freedom of the press.
(4) A majority of two-thirds of the votes of the Members of Parliament present is required to pass the statute on the supervision of public radio, television and the public news agency, as well as the appointment of the directors thereof, on the licensing of commercial radio and television, and on the prevention of information monopolies.

Article 62.
(1) The Republic of Hungary recognizes the right to peaceful assembly and shall ensure the free exercise thereof.
(2) A majority of two-thirds of the votes of the Members of Parliament present is required to pass the statute on the right of assembly.

Article 63.
(1) On the basis of the right of association, everyone in the Republic of Hungary has the

right to establish organizations for any purpose not prohibited by law and to join such organizations.
(2) The establishment of armed organizations with political objectives shall not be permitted on the basis of the right of association.
(3) A majority of two-thirds of the votes of the Members of Parliament present is required to pass the statute on the right of association as well as on the financial management and operation of political parties.

Article 64.
In the Republic of Hungary everyone has the right to present, individually or together with others, written petitions or complaints to the relevant public authority.

Article 65.
(1) The Republic of Hungary shall provide, in accordance with the conditions established by statute, asylum to those non-Hungarian citizens who are subject to persecution in their native country or in the country of their habitual residence, on the basis of their race, religion, nationality, belonging to a certain group in society, or religious or political convictions, or whose fear of persecution is well founded, provided that neither the country of their origin nor another country provide them protection.
(2) A majority of two-thirds of the votes of the Members of Parliament present is required to pass the statute on the right to asylum.

Article 66.
(1) The Republic of Hungary shall ensure the equality of men and women in respect of all civil, political, economic, social and cultural rights.
(2) In the Republic of Hungary mothers shall receive support and protection before and after the birth of the child, in accordance with separate regulations.
(3) Separate regulations shall ensure the protection of women and youth in the workplace.

Article 67.
(1) In the Republic of Hungary all children have the right to receive the protection and care of their family, of the State and of the society which is necessary for their proper physical, mental and moral development.
(2) Parents have the right to choose the education to be given to their children.
(3) Separate regulations shall establish the responsibilities of the State with regard to the situation and protection of the family and youth.

Article 68.
(1) The national and ethnic minorities living in the Republic of Hungary participate in the sovereign power of the people: they represent a constituent factor of the State.
(2) The Republic of Hungary shall provide for the protection of national and ethnic minorities. It shall ensure their collective participation in public affairs, the fostering of their cultures, the use of their own languages, education in their own languages and the use of names in their own languages.
(3) The laws of the Republic of Hungary shall ensure representation of the national and ethnic minorities living within the country.
(4) National and ethnic minorities shall have the right to form local and national self-governments.

(5) A majority of two-thirds of the votes of the Members of Parliament present is required to pass the statute on the rights of national and ethnic minorities.

Article 69.

(1) In the Republic of Hungary no one shall be arbitrarily deprived of his Hungarian citizenship and no Hungarian citizen may be expelled from the territory of the Republic of Hungary.

(2) Hungarian citizens may always return to Hungary from abroad.

(3) All Hungarian citizens are entitled to enjoy the protection of the Republic of Hungary while lawfully staying abroad.

(4) A majority of two-thirds of the votes of the Members of Parliament present is required to pass the statute on citizenship.

Article 70.

(1) All adult Hungarian citizens residing in the territory of the Republic of Hungary have the right to be elected and, provided that they are present in the country on the day of the election or referendum, the right to vote in parliamentary elections, local government elections or minority self-government elections, and furthermore to participate in national or local referenda or popular initiatives.

(2) Persons residing in the territory of the Republic of Hungary as immigrants who do not have Hungarian citizenship also have the right to vote in the election of the local government representatives and of the Mayor, as well as the right to participate in local referenda and popular initiatives, in accordance with the regulations of a separate law, provided that they are present in the country on the day of the election or referendum.

(3) The right to vote shall not be granted to persons whose capacity is limited or restricted by being subject to guardianship, or who are subject to the final judgment of a court forbidding them to participate in public affairs, or who are imprisoned on the basis of a final judgment or are under compulsory institutional care on the basis of a final judgment rendered in criminal proceedings.

(4) All Hungarian citizens have the right to participate in public affairs, and furthermore to hold public office in accordance with their suitability, education and professional knowledge.

Article 70/A.

(1) The Republic of Hungary shall ensure the human and civil rights for all persons on its territory without any kind of discrimination, such as on the basis of race, colour, gender, language, religion, political or other opinion, national or social origins, financial situation, birth or on any other grounds whatsoever.

(2) Any kind of discrimination described in Paragraph (1) shall be strictly penalized by the law.

(3) The Republic of Hungary shall promote the equality of rights for everyone through measures aimed at eliminating the inequality in opportunity.

Article 70/B.

(1) In the Republic of Hungary everyone has the right to work and to choose freely his job and profession.

(2) Everyone has the right to equal remuneration for equal work, without any discrimination whatsoever.

(3) All persons who work have the right to an income that corresponds to the amount and quality of work performed.
(4) Everyone has the right to rest time, free time and regular paid vacation.

Article 70/C.
(1) Everyone has the right to establish or join organizations together with others in order to protect his economic or social interests.
(2) The right to strike may be exercised within the framework of the statute regulating such right.
(3) A majority of two-thirds of the votes of the Members of Parliament present is required to pass the statute on the right to strike.

Article 70/D.
(1) Everyone living in the territory of the Republic of Hungary has the right to the highest possible level of physical and mental health.
(2) The Republic of Hungary shall implement this right through the organization of safety at work, health care institutions, medical care, through securing the opportunities for regular physical activity, as well as through the protection of the built and natural environment.

Article 70/E.
(1) Citizens of the Republic of Hungary have the right to social security; in the case of old age, sickness, disability, being widowed or orphaned, and in the case of unemployment through no fault of their own, they are entitled to the assistance necessary for their subsistence.
(2) The Republic of Hungary shall implement the right to social support through the social security system and the system of social institutions.

Article 70/F.
(1) The Republic of Hungary shall ensure the right to education for all its citizens.
(2) The Republic of Hungary shall implement this right through the extension and general access to public education, free compulsory primary schooling, secondary and higher education being available to all persons on the basis of their ability, and furthermore through financial support for training.

Article 70/G.
(1) The Republic of Hungary shall respect and support the freedom of scientific and artistic life, the freedom of learning and of teaching.
(2) Only scientists are entitled to decide on questions of scientific truth and to determine the scientific value of research.

Article 70/H.
(1) All citizens of the Republic of Hungary have the obligation to defend their homeland.
(2) Based on conscription, citizens shall complete armed or unarmed military service, or complete civilian service in accordance with the conditions established by law.
(3) A majority of two-thirds of the votes of the Members of Parliament present is required to pass the statute on conscription.

Article 70/I.
All citizens of the Republic of Hungary have the obligation to contribute to public revenues in accordance with their income and wealth.

Article 70/J.
In the Republic of Hungary parents and guardians have the obligation to ensure the education of their children under the legal age.

Article 70/K.
Claims arising from a violation of fundamental rights, and objections to the decisions of public authorities regarding the fulfillment of duties shall be enforceable in a court of law.

Chapter XIII.
The Basic Principles of Elections

Article 71.
(1) Members of Parliament, members of representative bodies of local governments, Mayors and the Mayor of the Capital are elected by direct, secret ballot, based on the universal and equal right to vote of the citizens.
(2) The members of the local government representative body of counties shall elect the President of the representative body by direct, secret ballot.
(3) Separate statutes shall regulate the election of Members of Parliament, members of representative bodies of local governments and Mayors. A majority of two-thirds of the votes of the Members of Parliament present is required to pass such statutes.

Articles 72–73.
[Repealed.]

Chapter XIV.
The Capital and National Symbols of the Republic of Hungary

Article 74.
The Capital of the Republic of Hungary is Budapest.

Article 75.
The national anthem of the Republic of Hungary is the poem "Himnusz" by Ferenc Kölcsey, set to the music of Ferenc Erkel.

Article 76.
(1) The National Flag of the Republic of Hungary is a tricolour consisting of horizontal red, white and green bands of equal width.
(2) The Coat of Arms of the Republic of Hungary is a vertically divided shield with a rounded base coming to a point. The left field contains eight horizontal bars of red and silver. The right field has a background of red and depicts a base of three green hills with a golden crown resting on the centre hill and a silver patriarchal cross issuing from the middle of the crown. The Holy Crown of St. Stephen rests on the top of the shield.

(3) A majority of two-thirds of the votes of the Members of Parliament is required to pass the statute on the Coat of Arms and National Flag of the Republic of Hungary and the use thereof.

Chapter XV.
Final Provisions

Article 77.
(1) The Constitution is the basic law of the Republic of Hungary.
(2) The Constitution and legal norms established in accordance with this Constitution are equally binding on all organizations of society, state organs and citizens.
(3) [Repealed.]

Article 78.
(1) The Constitution of the Republic of Hungary shall enter into force on the day of its promulgation; the Government shall ensure its implementation.
(2) The Government shall propose the bills necessary to implement this Constitution to the Parliament.

Subject Index